# Shrewd Sanctions

# Shrewd Sanctions

## Statecraft and State Sponsors of Terrorism

### Meghan L. O'Sullivan

BROOKINGS INSTITUTION PRESS
*Washington, D.C.*

*Library of Congress Cataloging-in-Publication data*

O'Sullivan, Meghan L.
   Shrewd sanctions : statecraft and state sponsors of terrorism / Meghan
L. O'Sullivan.
      p.   cm.
Includes bibliographical references (p.   ) and index.
   ISBN 0-8157-0602-2 (cloth)
   ISBN 0-8157-0601-4 (paper)
1. Economic sanctions, American.   2. Terrorism—Prevention—Government
policy—United States.   3. United States—Relations.   4. Persian Gulf
Region—Politics and government—Case studies.   5. Libya—Politics and
government.   6. Sudan—Politics and government.   I. Title.

HF1413.5 .O78 2003
327.1'17—dc21                                                    2002151487

9 8 7 6 5 4 3 2 1

The paper used in this publication meets minimum requirements of the American
National Standard for Information Sciences—Permanence of Paper for Printed Library
Materials: ANSI Z39.48-1992.

Typeset in Minion

Composition by R. Lynn Rivenbark
Macon, Georgia

Printed by R. R. Donnelley
Harrisonburg, Virginia

*Im memory of*
Timothy F. O'Sullivan
*March 5, 1933–September 11, 2001*

# Contents

# Foreword

Economics and diplomacy have too often been treated as not just separate but independent subjects—and professions. In fact, as Meghan O'Sullivan reminds us in the pages that follow, they are closely, often integrally, related. The design and conduct of a wise foreign policy depends in no small measure on the skillful application of economic instruments; and the health of the American economy depends equally on the ability of the United States to use its influence to make the rest of the world as peaceful, prosperous, and democratic as possible.

Meghan's focus is on the practice, sometimes successful and sometimes (to use a favorite Washington word) counterproductive, of the American government using economic measures as carrots or sticks for inducing changes in other governments' behavior. She examines this often misunderstood subject in the context of globalization—that is, the growing interdependence of national economies, cultures, and political systems. She zeroes in on the utility of sanctions as a means of dealing with states also that support terrorism and seek illicitly to acquire weapons of mass destruction.

Meghan's book comes as a timely and sensible contribution to a long-standing debate. In recent years, many commentators have questioned the efficacy of economic tools, especially unilateral measures, to address critical foreign policy challenges. They argue that, with globalization, countries are easily able to avoid the full brunt of unilateral economic sanctions, while those sanctions impose substantial costs on U.S. business and workers.

Others suggest that the growth of U.S. military might makes force a more effective tool. Meghan's work takes into account these sweeping changes that are transforming the world, while addressing the real-world challenges faced by policymakers—the need to address the relative strengths of alternative policy tools, including the costs associated with inaction.

At a time when the challenges abroad demand the careful use and coordination of all foreign policy tools, *Shrewd Sanctions* helps define the proper place for economic instruments in the mix. This book confirms the desirability of multilateral sanctions compared to unilateral measures. But rather than simply rejecting unilateral sanctions across the board, Meghan takes this insight to the next level by exacting under what circumstances unilateral measures can usefully advance U.S. interests and what needs to be done to maximize their utility. She finds, for instance, that although unilateral sanctions may not be well suited to enforce the containment of a regime—particularly as globalization proceeds apace—they could be an essential element in a carefully structured strategy to change dangerous behavior of a government. The result of her approach is a nuanced analysis that exposes the mixed record of sanctions, but attributes it more to how these tools have been employed than to any inherent weakness of sanctions as a foreign policy tool. As the book discusses in detail, sanctions do have a role to play in American foreign policy, but in order for them to realize their potential, U.S. policymakers will need to acknowledge the impact of globalization and American primacy on sanctions and adjust how they use these tools accordingly.

Beyond offering a dispassionate evaluation of sanctions, this book provides new insights into and prescriptions for U.S. policy toward Iran, Iraq, Libya, and Sudan. These states are often grouped as "rogue states" or "state sponsors of terrorism." Some have been designated members of the "axis of evil." Yet, this book reveals the complexities of each case—historically and currently—and the different options open to the United States for addressing them. *Shrewd Sanctions* not only suggests the need for differentiated policies toward these states, but also lays out the contours of such strategies where different approaches are adopted based on whether the United States seeks regime change, containment, or behavior change.

This book is an outgrowth of Meghan's earlier work on economic instruments of foreign policy when she was a fellow in our Foreign Policy Studies program from 1998 to 2000. Under the Brookings Sanctions Project, she co-edited *Honey and Vinegar* with Richard Haass, who was then the director of Foreign Policy Studies. Brookings would like to thank those foundations, companies, and individuals whose generosity allowed *Shrewd Sanctions*—and work on the Sanctions Project more generally—to proceed. The John M. Olin Foundation, the Arca Foundation, the Arthur Ross Foundation, Kuwait Petroleum Corp., the Cantigny Foundation, and Daimler Benz Washington warrant particular mention.

In 2001, Richard and Meghan joined the State Department—he as director of Secretary Powell's Policy Planning Staff and she—after the completion of this book—as a member of his staff. It is a source of pride to all of us at Brookings that two outstanding colleagues have had a chance to put their knowledge and intellects to work in the public service and the national interest.

Strobe Talbott
*President, Brookings Institution*

*Washington, D.C.*
*December 2002*

# Acknowledgments

I incurred many debts in the course of writing this book. To Eric Longnecker, I am especially grateful; without Eric's meticulous work and research assistance, this book would be a very different product.

I also am also deeply appreciative of the encouragement and guidance of Richard Haass, former director of Foreign Policy Studies at Brookings, during the years the book was in progress and beyond. Thanks as well to Jim Steinberg, now serving Brookings in that capacity, whose comments and support also were essential in bringing this book to completion. In addition to Jim, David Baldwin and Robert Litwak read the entire manuscript; Geoffrey Kemp, Suzanne Maloney, Elaine Morton, Gary Sick, Amatzia Baram, Daniel Byman, Andrew Parasiliti, Ray Takeyh, Dirk Vandewelle, Steve Morrison, and John Prendergast read portions of it. I would like to thank them wholeheartedly for sharing their expertise and providing helpful comments.

I am also beholden to the scores of people I interviewed or who participated in Sanctions Project events. Although it is impossible to acknowledge each by name, their insights provided a firm foundation for the writing of this book. To those who provided financial support to the Brookings Sanctions Project, I am truly grateful.

Many others were key in the production of this book and deserve thanks for both their skills and patience. Eileen Hughes and Theresa Walker handled the editing expertly, and Janet Walker ensured a smooth production.

xv

I also appreciate the ongoing efforts of Becky Clark to market the book, the help of Susan Woollen and Beth Schlenoff in preparing the cover, Julia Petrakis's role in creating the index, and Carlotta Ribar's assistance in proof-reading the pages. Tara Miller and Monique Principi also deserve recognition for their assistance in running the Sanctions Project while I was at Brookings.

Finally, I would like to thank my family and close friends for their support during the writing of this book specifically and throughout my career more generally. Although their fingerprints are not directly on this book, their encouragement was vital to its creation.

I wrote this book while I was a fellow in Foreign Policy Studies at the Brookings Institution. Although I did some minimal updating before its publication, the book was written before I joined the Policy Planning Staff at the State Department. As a result, this volume reflects my opinions and assessments as an independent scholar and does not necessarily represent the views of the U.S. government.

# Shrewd Sanctions

# CHAPTER ONE

# Introduction

Scholars and policymakers have long searched for the right combination of policy instruments to tackle the dilemmas of their time. Yet, in the twenty-first century, their quest is arguably more difficult than at any period in the past. Their efforts are complicated by a rapidly changing post–cold war environment, which influences both the challenges faced by the United States and the ways in which every foreign policy tool functions. This book is a piece of this constantly morphing puzzle. It examines an age-old tool, sanctions, to deal with one of the greatest challenges of the post–September 11 environment: states that support terrorism and pursue weapons of mass destruction. Those who expect that this book will either unconditionally applaud or disparage sanctions will be disappointed. Rather than seeking to strengthen either the pro- or anti-sanctions camp, this book highlights how economic tools should and should not be used in a world characterized by the post–cold war markers of globalization and American preeminence.

## Economic Statecraft in American Foreign Policy

The implications of post–cold war economic and political changes for U.S. foreign policy are unfolding every day. We now recognize that globalization—the rapid movement of ideas, people, resources, and goods across boundaries and barriers—has the potential to transform the political landscape as much as the economic environment. It has brought prosperity to many corners of the world and spurred the integration of states and regions. But at the same time, globalization has created new vulnerabilities, particularly for societies as open as that of the United States. In the search for security, globalization is proving to be a cocktail of venom as well as of vitamins.

American preeminence has also brought its own complications. Unrivaled U.S. influence in the military, economic, political, technological, and cultural realms has opened new possibilities for shaping the international environment.[1] Yet it has not freed the United States from making strategic choices or absolved it of the need to take into account the preferences of its allies and friends, particularly when addressing the transnational challenges that are part and parcel of globalization. The September 11, 2001, terrorist attacks and the responses to them—ranging from military action to the tightening of restrictions on global financial flows—were a dramatic demonstration of how post–cold war economic and political changes have shaped the threats facing the United States and its ability to address them.

Although policymakers need to understand how globalization and American preeminence affect all military, diplomatic, informational, and economic types of statecraft, this book focuses most intensely on economic tools.[2] Such instruments will play an important role in the more "activist" U.S. foreign policy agenda that is the result of both a greater perception of threat and a grander sense of U.S. capabilities in the post–September 11 era. Although military force will be a key component in addressing many foreign policy challenges, economic tools will be a frequent accompaniment, in part because their use will be seen as a precondition for securing the support or acquiescence of other countries for U.S. military missions. Economic tools also will be a substitute for military action when the use of force is not appropriate or feasible, either because of the nature of the objectives or simply because the United States cannot undertake an unlimited number of military endeavors simultaneously. Similarly, economic instruments will be both a complement to and a substitute for diplomatic undertakings in protecting and promoting U.S. interests worldwide.

Both positive and negative forms of economic statecraft will be needed to address new foreign policy challenges and maintain other priorities abroad. The centrality and versatility of positive economic tools (better known as inducements or incentives) in advancing U.S. foreign policy interests is demonstrated by their role in one narrow, if important, realm—that of combating terrorism. In the wake of September 11, inducements helped entice countries to join U.S. counterterrorism efforts, both in a broad sense and in the concrete mission of destroying Osama bin Laden's network in Taliban-controlled Afghanistan. Incentives were of particular importance in cases—such as Pakistan—where governments risked political backlash or economic losses because of their cooperation with Washington.[3]

Positive economic tools will be equally important in America's more activist foreign policy quite apart from their role in immediate counterterrorism efforts. They will be used with greater enthusiasm to bring stability to weak and failing states and to find solutions to transnational problems such as the spread of AIDS and other diseases. The United States and other countries also will increase their efforts to use foreign aid and technological transfers to promote equitable development and institution building in some countries, particularly now that poor socioeconomic conditions are seen not just as being of humanitarian concern but also as having security implications that extend beyond a single country's borders. Incentives may also be called upon to serve purposes such as solidifying agreements intended to halt the pursuit of national nuclear programs, as was attempted with North Korea in the 1990s.[4]

Negative economic tools also will be a crucial component of America's more activist foreign policy agenda. They will continue to play a key role in combating terrorism. Financial measures aimed at tracking and freezing the funds of terrorist organizations and individuals related to them are already used to handicap nefarious operations. Coercive economic measures will remain essential in pressuring and isolating countries that continue to lend support to terrorist groups or provide them safe haven in defiance of U.S. demands. Countries that resist cooperating with the United States on other levels—such as in the sharing of information pertaining to terrorism—may also find themselves subject to economic pressure.[5] Outside the counterterrorism agenda, sanctions will maintain their centrality in U.S. efforts to combat the proliferation of weapons of mass destruction, setbacks in democratization, and acts of aggression. They will also be necessary to address the burgeoning agenda of transnational issues, including international crime, trafficking in women and children, and the narcotics trade.

The focus of this book on sanctions opens the door to examining both positive and negative economic tools. Just as the imposition of sanctions is a penalty, their lifting or the prospect of it is—or should be—a real incentive.

Sanctions are a much explored, but still poorly understood, foreign policy instrument. Despite the existing wealth of studies on economic sanctions, the literature, in the words of one scholar, "is among the most contentious and inconclusive in international relations."[6] As discussed in detail in chapter 2, little agreement exists on even the most basic questions surrounding the use of these tools. Much of the existing scholarship is not directed toward policymakers; it is more concerned with how various methodologies and assumptions influence overall assessments of whether sanctions "work." Other studies have made important policy-relevant contributions, but our understanding of how economic sanctions are best employed is still incomplete.[7] For instance, one of the most important conclusions of the sanctions literature to date is the now widely accepted finding that sanctions are most likely to work when they are multilateral. Highlighting this reality to policymakers influenced how many of them think about sanctions and arguably contributed to a more restrained use of unilateral measures. Yet at the same time, this finding left policymakers with a fleet of follow-up questions. Under what circumstances is international cooperation in imposing sanctions most likely to be attained? In the absence of multilateral cooperation, what is the value, if any, of unilateral sanctions?

Sanctions also were deemed to be worthy of further investigation given the sharpening focus of American foreign policy on terrorism and weapons of mass destruction after September 11. Sanctions have played a major role in past U.S. strategies for dealing with both of these global challenges, particularly when the threats have come from states. Policymakers increasingly preoccupied by the need to combat state-sponsored terrorism and the proliferation of weapons of mass destruction are faced with the critical question of whether these issues can be adequately addressed with economic tools.

The conclusions of this study shy away from the simplistic, from the notion that sanctions "work" or "don't work." The reality is that the record of sanctions is mixed; as a result, both successes and failures are examined in this book. Of greater interest than whether the value of sanctions can be summed up in a phrase are the insights revealed from careful analysis of past attempts to use sanctions to deny states resources or to coerce them into changing their behavior. As this book demonstrates, the shrewd use of sanctions in these instances depends on many factors, perhaps the most important being whether the structure of the sanctions regime is appropriate to the task at hand. More often than not, the success or failure of sanctions is not a reflection of the inherent value of sanctions in some abstract sense. Instead, it is a consequence of whether the instruments were well crafted to pursue the objectives of the policymaker. A sanctions strategy designed to change a regime should look very different from one aimed at containment, which in turn should be distinct from a strategy intended to change the behavior of a government. Unfortunately, as revealed in these pages, that has rarely been the case.

## A Map to What Lies Ahead

Chapter 2 sets the scene for this book by addressing broad issues surrounding the use of sanctions in the post–cold war world. It examines how economic and political realities—namely globalization and American preeminence—shaped trends in the use of sanctions throughout the first decade after the collapse of the Soviet Union. Chapter 2 also explores the status of the "sanctions debate," the often animated exchange among policymakers, scholars, and interest groups over the use of economic tools in American foreign policy. In seeking to identify the source of tension between the needs of policymakers and the work of scholars, the chapter examines the various research and political agendas behind the seemingly innocuous question "Do sanctions work?" In doing so, the chapter illuminates a number of ways in which the study of sanctions could be refined to be of greater relevance to policymakers and identifies areas concerning the use of economic tools that deserve further attention. Chapter 2 also offers a multipart methodology to assess sanctions regimes and provides a framework for exploring outstanding questions about the use of sanctions, particularly in the cases that follow.

The next section of the book includes case studies of sanctions-dominated strategies toward Iran, Iraq, Libya, and Sudan. These cases were selected as having the greatest relevance for future efforts to address the nexus of terrorism and weapons of mass destruction. Each of these countries has been officially designated a "state sponsor of terrorism" and placed on the U.S. government's annual terrorism list.[8] Each, to varying degrees, is a suspected proliferator. And each continues in its own right to pose foreign policy concerns and problems for the United States. Collectively, as the four hardest cases in the extended geographic area of North Africa, the Middle East, and the Gulf, they are the ones most likely to shed light on the ability of sanctions to address such fundamental U.S. concerns.

The decision to examine sanctions regimes imposed largely on states rather than on entities within them or transcending them is a deliberate one. Neither terrorism nor weapons of mass destruction nor any of the other problematic behaviors targeted by sanctions can be fully or adequately addressed by limiting U.S. strategies to the state-to-state level. But such policies remain at the core of U.S. efforts. Transnational terrorist networks such as al-Qaida are reliant on sympathetic states to provide them with the support—be it in the form of finances, material or logistical help, or safe haven—necessary to sustain their operations.[9] Similarly, although it is legitimate to worry about the use of weapons of mass destruction by nonstate actors, states are still by far the most likely source of these weapons for such groups.

Not only is this focus on states critical to today's foreign policy agenda, it also provides a fertile ground for solid scholarship and sound prescriptions. In contrast to those analyzing the fledgling, if promising, transnational efforts to block the assets of groups and individuals worldwide, researchers interested in deriving recommendations for dealing with states through economic coercion have decades of experience on which to draw. The United States has long employed sanctions as the main tool for dealing with Iran, Iraq, Libya, and Sudan. In each case, a complex web of sanctions evolved, as both the number and type of sanctions associated with being on the terrorism list expanded and the United States imposed additional restrictions on the country for other egregious behaviors.[10] As a result, the measures in place against Iran, Iraq, Libya, and Sudan are the most comprehensive sanctions regimes that the United States maintains; the economic and, to a lesser extent, political isolation of these countries from the United States is nearly complete.[11] These sanctions regimes therefore provide the best opportunities for investigating many aspects of the use of coercive economic pressure, be it the links between impact and effectiveness, the interaction between sanctions and domestic politics in the target country, or the wrangling over sanctions policy that often occurs in the U.S. domestic realm.

Together, the four cases also provide important contrasts. Each involves a different level of multilateral cooperation, from the most minor to the most comprehensive. In addition to having strict U.S. sanctions imposed on them, Iraq, Libya, and Sudan all endured UN measures of varying intensity; Iran, while never the object of UN sanctions, has been subject to some multilateral restrictions in addition to comprehensive U.S. ones. Collectively, these cases demonstrate how the United States has used sanctions to pursue the full panoply of policy objectives—from regime change to containment to altering relatively small elements of a target country's behavior. Each case also reveals the complexities that arise from pursuing multiple and occasionally competing goals that shift over time; in none of the four cases were terrorism and weapons of mass destruction the only U.S. concerns.

Iran is a country with which the United States has had poor relations since the 1979 revolution unseated the shah and ushered in an Islamic republic. At the top of U.S. concerns in regard to Iran has been its active support for terrorism, particularly the assistance it provides to Palestinian and other groups that use violence to oppose the existence of Israel. Iran's pursuit of weapons of mass destruction and harsh rhetoric against America and Israel also have been sources of anxiety to the United States. Although Washington has failed to gain substantial multilateral support for its efforts to isolate and pressure Tehran with sanctions, the United States has enforced its own nearly comprehensive sanctions regime. This stringent strategy has been largely popular with domestic U.S. constituencies; however, at the end of the last millennium, it was under increasing fire from those who argued for a less confrontational U.S. approach toward Tehran on account of Iranian domestic political changes and the country's status as an important regional power and energy exporter. The U.S. campaign against terrorism energized the debate surrounding U.S. relations with Iran, with some pushing for an even more aggressive approach toward the country and others maintaining that a new convergence of interests could lead to rapprochement between Tehran and Washington. The inclusion of Iran in this study is critical for what it reveals about both the value of unilateral sanctions and the challenges of imposing them on a country experiencing great internal political change.

Iraq has been subject to one of the most extensive sanctions regimes in history. Since sanctions were imposed on Iraq immediately after its 1990 invasion of Kuwait, the country has chafed under multilateral UN sanctions blocking or regulating most of its economic interactions with the outside world. These sanctions were complemented by weapons inspections, military strikes, humanitarian schemes, and U.S. efforts to delegitimize the regime of Saddam Hussein. Although UN resolutions specified that sanctions would remain in place until Iraq cooperated fully with international weapons inspectors, concerns over Iraqi behavior have gone far beyond its pursuit of weapons of mass destruction. The United States and many countries in the region also have worried about Iraq's history of aggression within and outside of its borders, its support for terrorism, and its vehement opposition to Israel. The U.S. domestic debate over Iraq, unlike that over Iran, has been dominated by those supporting a variant of the sanctions-dominated approach and those advocating a more aggressive military strategy against Saddam Hussein. Yet at the international level, growing opposition to sanctions—generated in part by humanitarian concerns and by impatient commercial interests—forced a partial reassessment of the sanctions approach. Examining the Iraqi case is an essential component of any sanctions study, not only because of its uniqueness but because of what more than a decade of multilateral sanctions reveals about the tensions that arise between maintaining economic pressure on a recalcitrant regime and sustaining international consensus for such efforts.

Libya—and the threat that it poses to international security—changed over the last two decades of the twentieth century. During the Reagan administration, the United States viewed Libya's active support for terrorism, its meddling in the affairs of its neighbors, and its opposition to Israel as fundamental challenges to U.S. interests in the region. Although many countries shared U.S. concerns about the radical ways of Libyan leader Muammar Qadhafi, the United States pursued its policies of economic and military coercion against Libya largely on its own throughout the 1980s. Libyan involvement in the bombing of Pan Am 103 in 1988 and a UTA airliner in 1989 ended international apathy toward Tripoli and paved the way for seven years of multilateral sanctions against Libya. Libya's eventual compliance with key UN demands—specifically the surrender of the Pan Am 103 suspects—launched an international debate over the extent of Libya's rehabilitation and the proper pace of the reintegration of Libya into the global economic and political community. Libya's inclusion in this study is critical because this sanctions episode is widely viewed—rightly or wrongly—as the most successful instance of economic penalties moving a regime away from support for terrorism and toward the satisfaction of specific counterterrorism goals.

Sudan is a country that has rarely received the undivided attention of policymakers since the collapse of the Soviet Union lessened its strategic importance. The United States has, nevertheless, sought to juggle a wide range of disparate objectives in Sudan, including curbing state support for terrorism, ending a brutal civil war between Khartoum and the largely southern opposition, providing humanitarian aid for famine-stricken areas of the country, satisfying concerns about the development of chemical weapons, and addressing widespread human right abuses. This varied and complex agenda—and a domestic U.S. debate that has lacked a voice arguing for a more conciliatory approach toward Khartoum—led the United States to rely almost exclusively on a strict economic sanctions regime to pursue its goals in Sudan throughout the 1990s. For a time, U.S. measures were accompanied by UN diplomatic sanctions on Khartoum for its involvement in an assassination attempt on Egyptian president Hosni Mubarak; yet for the most part, U.S. efforts to use coercion to change the behavior of the Sudanese regime have been unilateral. Sudan warrants investigation in this study as an often overlooked case in which Congress was particularly influential in crafting U.S. policy toward the regime. More-over, it demands renewed attention given the efforts of Khartoum to assist the United States in its campaign against terrorism. Whether Washington manages to sustain that cooperation without forgoing the pursuit of other goals in Sudan will shape its future relationship with Khartoum and will have implications for other cases where the United States finds itself facing multiple and competing goals in its war against terrorism.

The cases of Cuba, North Korea, and Syria deserve particular mention, because they are the three other countries designated as state sponsors of terrorism by the United States. Yet, for methodological reasons, they are not subject to the same scrutiny in this book as Iran, Iraq, Libya, and Sudan. Although Syria has many of the attributes of these cases, U.S. policy toward Syria has been driven primarily by the perceived role that Damascus must play in any successful Middle East peace process. As a result, not only is the U.S. sanctions regime in place against Syria far less severe than in the cases examined here, but a reasonable assessment of these tools would require an extensive analysis of the Middle East peace process, which is beyond the scope of this book.[12] North Korea, a state sponsor with clear nuclear ambi-tions, is also outside the purview of this study because past efforts to deal with its nuclear program fall more into the realm of incentives than of sanc-tions. Cuba is omitted from extensive treatment in this study because there are few major concerns about its pursuit of weapons of mass destruction and because its inclusion on the terrorism list reveals more about the U.S. domestic interplay surrounding Cuba than any objective reality concerning Cuba's foment of terrorism. Despite these considerations and qualifications, the cases of Cuba, North Korea, and Syria do provide additional or comple-mentary insights. For this reason, they—and the past use of sanctions against Afghanistan and the Taliban, Burma, China, Pakistan, and Yugoslavia—are discussed in the conclusion of this study.

The final chapter pulls together lessons dispersed throughout the book. Just as chapter 2 contemplates how globalization and American preemi-nence shaped pressures to employ sanctions since 1990, the concluding chapter considers how these two factors influenced *how* sanctions worked— and *whether* they worked—when used to advance U.S. strategic interests over the same period. Synthesizing the findings of cases examined in the book and elsewhere, the conclusion identifies the defining characteristics of a shrewd sanctions approach to state sponsors of terrorism and reveals past impediments to the adoption of such strategies. The final chapter also offers broad guidelines to policymakers wishing to chose more wisely between sanctions and other tools—and between different sorts of sanctions regimes—to ensure a more effective U.S. foreign policy.

# CHAPTER TWO

# Sanctions, Globalization, and American Preeminence

Sanctions became a much-used and much-analyzed foreign policy tool in the first decade after the end of the cold war. This chapter endeavors to put that development in context by building on the argument put forward in the introduction: that globalization and American preeminence have profoundly shaped trends in the use of sanctions. This chapter examines how economic and political changes in the post–cold war world influenced both American willingness to employ sanctions and the actual form that sanctions took; it also launches the exploration of how globalization and American preeminence affected how or *whether* sanctions were effective or useful. This chapter also turns to the sanctions debate to identify the ongoing disagreements in scholarly work on sanctions and to elucidate the differing perspectives of scholars and policymakers concerned with the use of economic tools. After identifying common pitfalls in the analysis of sanctions that continue to obscure a better understanding of these instruments, the chapter presents the methodology that will be used throughout the book. The chapter concludes by highlighting some of the outstanding questions in the study of sanctions that this book seeks to answer.

## Post–Cold War Trends in the Use of Sanctions

Trends in the use of sanctions throughout the 1990s and early 2000s are by no means clear cut. Their mapping is muddled by the lack of a commonly

accepted definition of what constitutes a sanction. Far from being a seman-
tic debate of no consequence, the definition one adopts determines whether
the 1990s are seen as a period of sanctions mayhem or, in the view of Senator Jesse Helms (R-N.C.), one of relative restraint.[1] Counting any restriction
on U.S. economic activity with a country for any purpose—such as limiting
imports of tuna from Mexico for environmental reasons—as a sanction is
likely to lead to the first conclusion; insisting that only nearly comprehensive embargoes imposed for political reasons constitute a sanction lends
itself to the opposite judgment.[2] Similar discrepancies about what percentage of the world's population is "under sanctions" reflect the same lack of
common currency in defining a sanction. Neither definition at either end of
the spectrum is technically wrong, although there is no question that each
has been employed in a calculated manner by groups arguing for either a
rollback of unilateral sanctions or a continuation or extension of their use.
A more sensible and less politicized definition would clearly fall somewhere
in the middle. For the purpose of this book, a sanction will be defined as the
deliberate withdrawal of normal trade or financial relations for foreign policy purposes.[3]

Once a middle-of-the-road definition is agreed upon and applied across
the decades, new patterns in the post–cold war use of U.S. economic sanctions are still evident. Although the popularity of sanctions waxed in the
1990s, the trajectory of their use was neither constant nor linear. The number of times the United States imposed new sanctions against states rose
significantly in the early part of the decade, yet declined as the decade wore
on (figure 2-1).[4] Whereas between 1990 and 1996 the United States imposed
almost fifty sanctions against states, it imposed less than ten new such sanctions in the last four years of the decade (see appendix table 2A-1). Other
developments are less discernible to the casual observer. In addition to the
increase in the number of times sanctions were initiated, the range of goals
pursued with sanctions broadened, just as the types of entities subject to
sanctions expanded. At the same time, congressionally legislated sanctions—once a rarity—became as common as their counterparts mandated
by the executive branch.[5]

How can we best understand these trends? Political and economic circumstances have long influenced American enthusiasm for using economic instruments to pursue security goals. As argued by Michael
Mastanduno, during the cold war, the willingness of the United States to
use its economic power to pursue strategic political goals depended largely
on how it viewed the international system and the position of the U.S.

**Figure 2-1.** *Sanctions Imposed by the United States (Non-UN)*
*on State Actors, 1990–2002*[a]

Number of sanctions

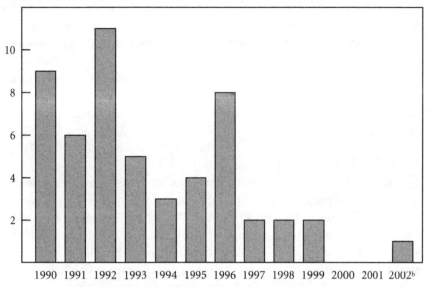

1990 1991 1992 1993 1994 1995 1996 1997 1998 1999 2000 2001 2002[b]

a. This figure includes both U.S. unilateral sanctions and sanctions imposed by the United States
with other states or regional groupings but does not include UN sanctions.
b. As of September 2002.

economy relative to that of the rest of the world.[6] Policymakers were willing to use economic tools to advance U.S. foreign policy goals when the
United States saw the world as threatening and unstable, yet believed its
own economic position was unassailable. During the immediate post–
World War II period—when the United States faced uncertain threats and
weak allies but basked in its economic dominance—policymakers used
financial assistance under the Marshall Plan, transfers of technology, and
differential access to U.S. markets to stabilize Europe and parts of Asia and
cement American influence abroad. CoCom and other efforts to economically isolate the Soviet Union also were critical elements of U.S. foreign
policy during this time. In the 1970s and 1980s, however, American calculations began to change. The international system seemed stable and
orderly, while Americans noted surging economies in other parts of the
world and feared a major U.S. economic decline. The United States then
moved away from using economic instruments primarily for strategic

political purposes; in many arenas, economic instruments were instead preserved for the pursuit of strategic economic goals.[7]

The world has changed dramatically since that time, yet economic and political factors and perceptions continue to shape decisions about America's use of economic tools. At the turn of the millennium, globalization and American preeminence were the realities influencing how vigorously the United States used economic tools to further its strategic aims. As argued below, these two factors stand behind trends in the use of sanctions in the 1990s and early 2000s insofar as they changed U.S. interests abroad, shaped the actors involved in the international arena, and altered the making of foreign policy at home.

### Changing U.S. Interests

Globalization and American preeminence affected the use of economic sanctions by helping to determine the interests and goals embraced by the United States in its foreign policy pursuits. No longer bound by the need to counter Soviet influence in all parts of the world, the United States had the luxury of being more demanding of the countries with which it had cooperative relationships and more selective in choosing which states to befriend. Countries such as Pakistan—whose nuclear pursuits were awkwardly brushed aside throughout the 1980s while the United States required its cooperation to battle Soviet influence in neighboring Afghanistan—found themselves being held to higher standards of conduct or facing economic sanctions and diplomatic démarches in the 1990s. Moreover, as the overriding quest to maintain a bulwark against communism dissolved, global norms that once precluded international scrutiny of domestic practices softened. The United States, and many others in the international community, began to tout the notion that only countries that respected and satisfied the basic human rights and needs of its citizens could expect to be shielded from outside criticism.[8]

Globalization, too, made the internal policies and practices of many countries of more legitimate concern to the United States. As in the preceding decades, an economic or political crisis in a key country could threaten the ability of the United States to protect and pursue its interests in a certain part of the world. But in the 1990s and beyond, the effects of economic turmoil in one country—even if precipitated by domestic factors—were unlikely to be contained within the borders of that one state. The growing integration of economies and the increasing reliance of many states on international capital flows meant that economic strife in one country threatened to trigger widespread regional economic and political instability, as happened during the Asian financial crisis in 1997. Given the potentially close links between political and economic upheaval and the broadening implications of such unrest for U.S. security, objectives that would have been unthinkable or a low priority during the cold war—such as spreading democracy and pushing for transparency or "good governance"—assumed greater prominence on the U.S. foreign policy agenda.[9]

New political and economic realities in the 1990s and the early 2000s changed the menu of goals pursued with sanctions—not only by adding new entrees but also by removing old ones. During the cold war, sanctions often were used as a means of conveying U.S. resolve against communism, both to reassure American allies on the front line with the Soviet Union and to deter countries and factions within them that might contemplate an embrace of communism. U.S. sanctions on Cuba during this period, although unsuccessful in dislodging Fidel Castro, served those purposes. However, in a world devoid of superpower threats to the United States, old sanctions were more difficult to justify solely along these ideological lines, while new sanctions episodes could no longer be advocated for such purposes.

Changing American interests are clearly reflected in the shifting pattern of objectives pursued through U.S. economic sanctions in the post–cold war period and beyond. From 1914 to 1990, the United States most often used sanctions against states to constrain or influence the external behavior of a country or to destabilize a regime.[10] Sanctions were rarely called upon to alter the internal behavior of regimes, with the notable exception of a period in the 1970s when the Carter administration placed improving human rights at the center of its foreign policy and used sanctions to advance this cause.[11] In contrast, since 1990, the majority of non-UN sanctions imposed by the United States against state actors had the aim of changing the domestic conduct of the target. (See figure 2-2.) The use of sanctions was particularly common in U.S. efforts to promote democracy. In fact, the growing use of so-called section 508 sanctions suggests a distinctly post–cold war American preference for fragile democracies to potentially more stable military regimes. Although 508 sanctions—which mandate automatic restrictions on economic and military aid to any country that experiences a coup overthrowing a democratically elected government—were first put into legislation in 1985, they were not invoked until 1990, when elements of the Sudanese military staged a coup against Prime Minister Sadiq al-Mahdi.[12]

**Figure 2-2.** *Sanctions Imposed by the United States (Non-UN) on State Actors, 1990–2002, Internal Compared with External Behavior*[a]

Number of sanctions

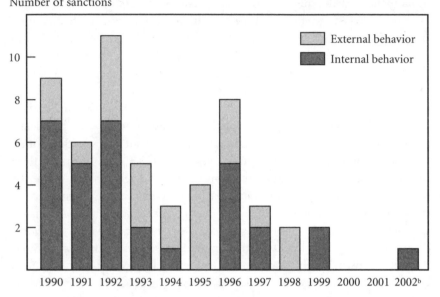

a. This figure includes both U.S. unilateral sanctions and sanctions imposed by the United States with other states or regional groupings but does not include UN sanctions.

b. As of September 2002.

### Bringing New Actors to the Fore

Globalization and the new contours of the international political system also shaped trends in the use of economic sanctions by broadening the range of actors influencing global politics and U.S. strategic concerns. Throughout the cold war, virtually all major initiatives, conflicts, and crises centered around the actions of states. With few exceptions, U.S. adversaries and allies took the form of sovereign countries or alliances comprising them. The machinations of groups within states were generally regarded as being subject to the control of the national authorities under which they resided and, on the whole, beyond the direct influence of the international community. For instance, in 1985, when the United States blamed the Abu Nidal organization for the attacks at the Rome and Vienna airports, it held Libya responsible for the event, imposing unilateral import and export sanctions on Tripoli.[13]

In contrast, post-1990 economic and political changes opened the door for both supranational and substate actors to influence the shape of the world. The collapse of superpower rivalry offered the United Nations new opportunities to exert itself on the global stage. No longer hamstrung by the zero-sum maneuvers of Moscow and Washington, the international body offered a newly effective vehicle to address global concerns. At the other end of the spectrum, the influence of substate actors on international politics also skyrocketed as globalization gave them new tools to create and maintain worldwide networks and new mechanisms with which to influence global events.[14] In some cases, these groups effectively organized themselves to shape global policy and opinion when more conventional representation of their viewpoints was absent, as happened in the campaign to ban landmines.[15] In other situations, nonstate actors exploited new currents of globalization to pose violent challenges to the United States and others. For instance, as more states became unwilling to orchestrate or be directly complicit in terrorist acts, nonstate terrorist groups such as Osama bin Laden's al-Qaida and the Liberation Tigers of Tamil Eelam used global networks to advance their agendas, often placing their organizations beyond the control of any one state structure.[16] In a seemingly less nefarious development, globalization also catapulted companies and businesses into international politics. The growing ability of individual firms to operate outside the purview of the nation-state made their conduct—particularly when it involved the sale of weapons and related technology—of direct concern to the United States.

This changing roster of international actors explains the shifting profile of sanctions episodes involving the United States in the 1990s and early 2000s. During the cold war, U.S. efforts to use economic coercion were mostly unilateral and almost always directed against other sovereign states.[17] In contrast, in the post–cold war world, multilateral sanctions imposed through the United Nations became a much larger component of U.S. sanctions strategies. Whereas the United Nations had resorted to mandatory sanctions only twice between its founding and 1990, in the first decade after the collapse of the Soviet Union the international body imposed multilateral sanctions on eleven different countries and four political movements (some more than once).[18] Particularly in the cases involving more robust sanctions regimes—such as those imposed on Iraq and Yugoslavia—the United States played a significant role in securing and maintaining the multilateral instruments of economic pressure.

Also notable during this post–cold war period was a dramatic increase in the number of nonstate entities sanctioned by the United States and the development of mechanisms to facilitate the sanctioning of these entities.[19] Initially, U.S. sanctions against nonstate actors were largely limited to blacklisting front companies operating in contravention of sanctions or penalizing companies selling military technology useful in the development of weapons of mass destruction.[20] However, in 1995, President William J. Clinton expanded the practice of sanctioning nonstate actors by ordering the freeze of assets of terrorist groups deemed to threaten the Middle East peace process.[21] This practice was codified in 1996 with the passage of legislation creating procedures for the U.S. government to use in identifying foreign terrorist organizations (FTOs), blocking any funds they kept in the United States, and criminalizing transactions with them.[22] The United States also stepped up efforts to name "specially designated nationals"—individuals who were suspected of having a financial relationship with sanctioned states or entities or who themselves engaged in illicit activities—and to prohibit U.S. citizens from entering into transactions with them. Finally, the 1990s saw a revivial in the use of secondary sanctions—tools used to penalize countries or foreign companies for their involvement with third parties.

The proliferation of sanctions on nonstate actors in large part reflects the need to adopt tactics to counter new threats and actors in the post–cold war world and the desire to target the offending actors as directly as possible. But this trend also has its roots in global changes that made new forms of economic pressure possible in the 1990s and beyond. For instance, new technologies allowing for the more precise tracking of funds enabled the United States to freeze the assets of individuals as well as those of governments and countries.[23] Other technologies—such as "electronic tagging"— opened the possibility of tracking dual-use items, thereby limiting certain uses of goods rather than prohibiting their acquisition entirely.[24] Global economic interdependence also created new opportunities for the application of economic pressure. Although secondary sanctions had existed for decades, the integration of economies bolstered their potential by increasing the number and vulnerability of firms that could fall foul of them.[25] Similarly, the desire of foreign companies to raise money in U.S. capital markets presented the opportunity to sanction entities by denying them access to financial markets, an idea embraced by those trying to increase pressure on oil companies doing business in war-torn Sudan. The growing importance of international bodies in fostering economic cooperation also presented new mechanisms of control, making the obstruction of membership in institutions such as the World Trade Organization a penalty of some significance.

*Domestic Dynamics in the Making of Foreign Policy*

Finally, globalization and American preeminence shaped post–cold war trends in the use of economic sanctions by increasing the relative weight of domestic actors in the making of U.S. foreign policy. The demise of the Soviet Union and the rise in American global influence opened the way for Congress to play a more active role in international affairs. This post–cold war congressional independence reflected the belief—at least before September 11—that the stakes in the new international system were far less significant than they had been during the cold war, with its omnipresent, if abstract, threat of nuclear war and destruction. In this environment, Congress felt less compelled to defer to the executive branch on matters of foreign policy and more emboldened to set its own international priorities.

At the same time, the influence of ethnic, religious, and other single-issue lobbies on U.S. foreign policy rose in the decade after the cold war.[26] In part, the ability of such groups to advance their causes also had its roots in the less threatening international environment. In the absence of an overriding Soviet threat, interest groups whose agendas once were subordinated to cold war considerations suddenly had more room to affect the direction of U.S. foreign policy. Post–cold war technological changes also helped magnify the impact that such groups had on policymaking. By speeding up the transfer of information and linking groups with similar concerns across the nation and around the world, globalization fed the creation of powerful nongovernmental networks and increased their ability to wield influence in Washington.[27]

The greater scope for the concerns of interest groups in post–cold war foreign policy dovetailed with the new congressional independence in the global realm and spurred an increase in both the number and type of sanctions legislated by Congress (see figure 2-3).[28] More receptive to the entreaties of interest groups and domestic constituencies advocating economic pressure to pursue their goals, Congress used sanctions to shape U.S. foreign policy on a broad range of issues. For instance, urged on by religious conservatives, Congress passed the 1998 International Religious Freedom Act, a law that both created a mechanism to identify governments that are severe violators of religious rights and mandated modest sanctions to penalize them. Similarly, in 2000, a nongovernmental organization (NGO) campaign against the trafficking in women and girls bore fruit in legislation that withheld certain types of aid from countries whose cooperation in combating such practices was judged to be lacking.[29] The mark of domestic groups

**Figure 2-3.** *Sanctions Imposed by the United States (Non-UN) on State Actors, 1990–2002, Executive Office Compared with Congress*[a]

Number of sanctions

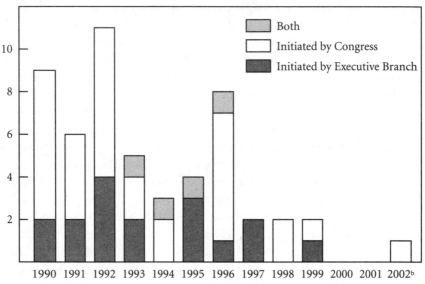

a. This figure includes both U.S. unilateral sanctions and sanctions imposed by the United States with other states or regional groupings but does not include UN sanctions.

b. As of September 2002.

on U.S. policies toward specific countries was even more striking. The American Israel Public Affairs Committee was remarkably successful in shaping the sanctions-dominated approach adopted by the United States toward Iran in the 1990s, while the Families of Pan Am 103 exerted a major influence on U.S. policy toward Libya over the same decade. Other constituencies were able to catalyze support for more limited sanctions, even when the measures sometimes appeared to be against the wider strategic interests of the United States. For instance, the influence of Armenian-American groups ensured that a 1992 ban on most forms of U.S. assistance to Azerbaijan persisted in a modified form throughout the 1990s, even though Azerbaijan remained broadly supportive of U.S. goals in the region and participated in peace talks sponsored by the Organization for Security and Cooperation in Europe (OSCE).

Global political and economic changes not only opened the door to new pressures to apply sanctions, they also galvanized domestic opposition to them. Of the critics of sanctions, American businesses were by far the most prominent and influential. In reaction to the burgeoning use of sanctions by Congress, commercial interests of a wide variety banded together in the latter part of the 1990s, forming organizations such as USA*Engage to advance their interests.[30] In their aggressive efforts to oppose the use of unilateral sanctions in American foreign policy, these business-oriented groups emphasized the sometimes significant economic costs that sanctions can inflict on U.S. commercial interests and highlighted scholarly work that cast doubt on the efficacy of sanctions.

Like other domestic interest groups, U.S. businesses found the post–cold war international atmosphere conducive to promoting their cause. In a world without a Soviet threat, commercial interests not only felt less compelled to muffle their opposition to sanctions but also discovered that their concerns commanded greater attention. Globalization helped propel the antisanctions arguments of the business community to the foreground. U.S. businesses contended that rapid economic changes—including the growing interdependence of economies, the quickness of economic transactions, and the free flow of technologies—increased the costs that U.S. interests bore when the United States employed economic sanctions. According to commercial spokespeople, the unrestrained use of these measures closed off many important markets to U.S. businesses; moreover, the opportunity costs borne by American companies were believed to grow each day as countries under U.S. sanctions developed increasingly sophisticated economic ties with European and Asian firms, limiting the ability of U.S. businesses to resume their previous economic relationships even after sanctions were lifted.[31] Claims by U.S. business representatives that "unilateral sanctions are doing significant damage to U.S. commercial prospects" were commonplace.[32]

In reality, as discussed throughout this book, such costs were both difficult to quantify and often highly concentrated in one or two industries. Yet the power of the arguments made by U.S. commercial interests had less to do with the magnitude of the costs and much more to do with how these costs resonated within a United States being transformed by globalization. In 2000, U.S. exports accounted for roughly 11 percent of the U.S. gross domestic product, up from 5 percent three decades earlier in 1970. In the intervening years, promoting U.S. economic interests abroad had become closely linked to advancing U.S. security considerations and widely acknowledged as essential to maintaining American influence in the world. Moreover, as mentioned earlier, in the past the perceived health of the U.S.

economy had often curbed the reluctance of the United States to bear economic costs in the interest of foreign policy. Globalization, however, diminished the importance of such temporal assessments; even when the U.S. economy was robust, the importance of maintaining the competitive edge of American businesses was seen as critical in a global economy with little tolerance for sluggishness or inefficiency. In this climate, rather than feeling pressure to absorb losses in order to advance U.S. strategic goals abroad, businesses felt justified in pushing for policies that protected their global interests. Policymakers, in turn, were more receptive to their point of view.

The reach and influence of the business lobby was greatly enhanced by the strategic partnerships it made with other domestic groups skeptical about the use of sanctions. Over the 1990s, many humanitarian and religious groups vocally protested sanctions on the basis of their perceived adverse humanitarian effects and on the grounds that they violated international law.[33] In addition, a growing number of scholars and former policymakers voiced concerns that the aggressive use of sanctions irritated American allies and frustrated U.S. diplomatic efforts.[34] This unusual business-humanitarian-diplomatic coalition worked to temper U.S. use of sanctions in the last half of the 1990s.

Together, these interests backed legislative efforts to overhaul how both the congressional and the executive branch employ sanctions.[35] The most notable endeavor was that surrounding Senator Richard Lugar's (R-Ind.) Sanctions Reform Act and its companion bill, the Enhancement of Trade, Security, and Human Rights through Sanctions Reform Act, in the House of Representatives.[36] Had the legislation become law, it would have placed a number of limitations on the presidential use of sanctions and counseled Congress to follow similar guidelines. It would have required the executive branch to make a detailed assessment of the anticipated consequences of sanctions before imposing them as well as demanded ongoing reports on the effects of sanctions that already were in place. Although the legislation had significant bipartisan support,[37] it never became law—in part due to the objections of the Clinton administration, which perceived it as placing both too many constraints on the ability of the executive branch to conduct U.S. foreign policy and too few on Congress.[38]

Nevertheless, the legislation did provide an important focal point and serve as a catalyst for other congressional efforts to reform the use of sanctions. The 106th Congress held seven hearings on the use of sanctions, many of them reflecting the greater awareness of Congress of the variety of costs borne by U.S. interests when sanctions are employed.[39] Whereas a 1984 congressional hearing on sanctions revealed almost no interest in the costs such tools imposed on American businesses, in the late 1990s Congress devoted whole hearings to that very subject.[40] The force of the unusual business-humanitarian-diplomatic coalition arguing for the more restrained use of sanctions—and the heightened sensitivity to the domestic costs of sanctions that its campaign fomented—did produce some tangible results. Most notable was the passage of the Trade Sanctions Reform and Export Enhancement Act of 2000 in October of that year.[41] This law effectively prevents the president from restricting the export of food and medicine as a sanction unless he obtains the prior consent of Congress.[42] Also significant was Congress's October 1998 decision to provide President Clinton with a waiver to ease the U.S. sanctions imposed on India and Pakistan after their May 1998 nuclear tests. The U.S. agricultural lobby, nervous about the markets that it could lose with the termination of U.S. trade credits, was instrumental in this decision. The lifting of restrictions on the sale of U.S. food and medicine to Iran, Libya, and Sudan in April 1999 was yet another demonstration of the power of these odd alliances. Humanitarian concerns provided the backdrop to this move, although the farm crisis occurring in the United States at the time served as the most immediate impetus.

Overall, the nonlinear trend in the use of sanctions in the 1990s and early 2000s is explained in large part by the competing interests of prosanctions and antisanctions constituencies emboldened in their own ways by globalization and America's new role in the world and by the opportunities created for them in the making of post–cold war foreign policy. While the sharp rise in the number of sanctions enacted in the first half of the 1990s reflects the widening of U.S. global interests and the evolution of new actors and additional forms of sanctions, it also reveals the growing salience of ethnic, religious, and other single-issue lobbies and Congress's receptivity to them in the post–cold war world. The tapering off of the number of new sanctions enacted in the mid to late 1990s in part reflects the mobilization of other interest groups—led by American business—to counter the earlier upsurge.

The opposing interests of these constituencies illuminate the nature of the domestic debate over sanctions that occurred throughout much of the first decade of the post–cold war era. Congressional efforts to shape U.S. policy toward Cuba present a microcosm of the tussle of competing interests and how they often played out in the new international environment. In the first half of the 1990s, Congress passed both the Cuban Democracy Act and the Helms-Burton, or LIBERTAD, Act in an effort to increase the pressure on Castro's regime. The impetuses behind these pieces of legislation

and the stricter sanctions they mandated were varied: the influence of segments of the Cuban-American community that were pushing for a tougher
approach toward Castro; a wider belief that Cuba was more susceptible to
U.S. economic pressure in the wake of the collapse of its Soviet benefactor;
and the immediate impact that the downing of a small American plane by
Cuba in 1996 had on U.S. attitudes toward the Cuban government. The new
measures closed existing loopholes in the already stringent sanctions regime
and mandated secondary sanctions—penalties on foreign firms "trafficking" in expropriated American property in Cuba. By the late 1990s, however,
the debate over Cuba was moving in the other direction. New developments
provided a growing counterweight to more traditional Cuban-American
constituencies and pushed for a fresh assessment of the existing sanctions-
dominated Cuba policy. Spearheading opposition to the embargo in its contemporary form were American agricultural interests, which sought to open
Cuban markets in the hope of easing the farm crisis in America's Midwest.
They were joined by some human rights organizations, emerging Cuban-
American groups more in favor of some engagement with the island, and a
loose group of "internationalists" who objected to the earlier secondary
sanctions on the basis of the diplomatic costs they entailed.[43] As Congress
considered slight modifications to the long-standing embargo in 2000 and
2001, these competing visions clashed, exposing the difficulty of revisiting
sanctions policy in the face of active domestic constituencies and vested
interests. Although the congressional debate over Cuba policy did not lead
to dramatic changes in U.S. foreign policy in the year 2000, it testified to the
changing attitudes toward U.S. sanctions in the new global economic and
political environment.[44]

## The Sanctions Debate

The influence of globalization and American preeminence on trends in the
use of sanctions in the post–cold war world is only one of the issues deserving scrutiny in the modern study of economic tools. Of even greater interest is how the same two factors affect the ways in which economic sanctions
work—and, implicitly, *whether* sanctions work—in this post–cold war environment. Conventional wisdom holds that globalization has weakened the
influence of unilateral economic sanctions; as countries integrate themselves into the global economy, they diversify their economic links, frustrating the ability of any one country to compel another through economic
coercion alone.[45] For example, over the course of the 1990s, China not only

increased its exports, imports, and levels of foreign direct investment, but it also lessened its reliance on the U.S. market and expanded its ties to other economies, ultimately diminishing American leverage over Beijing. The same forces, however, increase the influence that multilateral sanctions can exert on a target. While some countries—dating back to the Greek city states of Athens and Sparta—have always been vulnerable to such pressure, what changed dramatically in the post–cold war period was the sheer number of countries that moved from being resistant to multilateral economic sanctions to being relatively susceptible to them.[46] Ten years ago, multilateral sanctions on India—unless they involved oil from Russia—would have had a small impact on the country; in the twenty-first century, even with its uneven opening to the global economy, India would suffer much more under the weight of multilateral economic restrictions.[47]

Although globalization undoubtedly influences the relative impact of unilateral and multilateral sanctions, the bigger picture is much more complex. Not only has the post–cold war environment shaped the *impact* that sanctions have on a target, but it also transformed the ability of such measures to achieve their goals, thereby influencing the *effectiveness* of sanctions. Moreover, globalization and American preeminence influenced how the performance of sanctions compared with that of other instruments at the disposal of policymakers, affecting sanctions' overall *comparative utility*. The complexity of calculating all three factors—and their importance in assessing the ultimate value of sanctions in an era of globalization and U.S. preeminence—makes them and the broader question of how sanctions work a major focus of this book.

Questions of how sanctions work are central to the sanctions debate— the ongoing discussion among scholars, policymakers, and interest groups concerning the use of sanctions. To those on the periphery of the debate, queries such as "Do economic sanctions work?" and "Should we use economic sanctions?" seem virtually synonymous and likely to elicit a straightforward yes or no in response. Yet, far from being easy to answer, those questions capture different realities and expose the various levels at which deliberations about sanctions occur.

Scholars have tended to focus on the issue of whether economic sanctions "work." Do they achieve their objectives? On this matter, there is little agreement.[48] Putting aside important differences over how to define a sanction and demarcate the boundaries of a single sanctions case, one of the most serious areas of contention concerns setting a reasonable standard for success.[49] In the most extensive study of sanctions to date, Hufbauer, Schott, and Elliott measured success in terms of achieving stated policy goals.[50] Others, most notably David Baldwin, have argued that in order to qualify as successful, a sanctions regime does not necessarily have to realize explicit objectives; the mere act of imposing costs on a country can sometimes be all that is required to warrant the classification of sanctions as at least a qualified success.[51] Even where scholars have agreed on what constitutes a successful policy outcome, disputes persist over how to value the contribution of sanctions. Weighing the role of sanctions against those of other tools used in a particular episode, Hufbauer and his colleagues contend that sanctions often deserve some credit for outcomes that were ultimately reached through the use of military force or other means.[52] In contrast, scholars such as Robert Pape insist that resort to military might is tantamount to the failure of sanctions; in his view, only where sanctions themselves bring about the desired result can they be credited with success.[53] These differences in perspective lead some scholars to judge sanctions on Haiti—which did not trigger removal of the military junta but arguably paved the way for military intervention by the United States—as a partial success, while others denounce the use of sanctions in this case as a failure.

Finally, the opinions of scholars continue to diverge over the question of how successful sanctions need to be overall in order to make the claim that sanctions, as a foreign policy tool, "work." After examining 115 cases in which sanctions were used, Hufbauer and his associates concluded that sanctions were successful 34 percent of the time.[54] Some see that success rate as confirming the fecklessness of using sanctions as a foreign policy tool, while others regard a tool that is successful roughly one-third of the time as one of great value.[55]

Policymakers, in contrast, are less preoccupied with such generalizations and more concerned with whether sanctions should be used in a given situation.[56] As a result, they are interested in a number of issues beyond whether sanctions, on the whole, "work." In addition to considering the variety of objectives that sanctions may achieve—be they primary or secondary goals, explicit or unspoken—policymakers want a solid appraisal of the costs required to secure success.[57] Just as a war won at the expense of millions of lives is at best a qualified victory, so too is there a limit to the amount of lost trade or jeopardized influence that it is sensible to accept for a certain change in behavior.

Most important, policymakers want to know how sanctions—in both their prospects for securing various goals and their expected costs—compare with the alternatives available to pursue the same goals, including the option of doing nothing.[58] Military force could very well achieve many of the objectives set out for sanctions, but the costs associated with such action—whether economic, diplomatic, or humanitarian—often are judged to be too high. This calculus underlies what David Baldwin has rightly termed the major paradox in the sanctions debate: policymakers continue to employ economic sanctions, even in the face of scholarship that argues— if not unanimously, then at least overwhelmingly—that sanctions do not "work."[59] In the face of less promising policy options—ones that are more costly to employ or less likely to have the desired effect—rational policymakers will keep reaching for sanctions, regardless of whether the latest journal articles caution them against it.

The sanctions debates among scholars and policymakers should not occur on different tracks that rarely cross. Ideally, scholarship on economic tools should inform policymaking, while the concerns of policymakers should in part shape the questions that scholars pursue. To some extent, this cross-fertilization already occurs. It could, however, be made more productive if discussions and studies of sanctions took care to avoid three common pitfalls in the analysis of sanctions: the equation of impact with effectiveness, a disconnected and incomplete discussion of costs to the sender (the country or entity imposing sanctions), and the tendency to confuse the utility of sanctions with their comparative utility.

Unilateral sanctions are often dismissed as doomed to failure because they are anticipated to have a small economic impact.[60] This logic is widely accepted, even though impact and effectiveness are by no means synonymous. *Impact* is the sheer economic or political damage that sanctions inflict on the target country. *Effectiveness* refers to their ability to achieve the goals established for them. Theoretically, the two are related; it is the impact of sanctions that persuades the target to acquiesce to the sender's goals. This connection also resonates with common sense and is supported by statistical evidence: Hufbauer and his colleagues found in their wide-ranging study that sanctions episodes that had the most profound economic impact on a country were the ones most likely to achieve their goals.[61]

Although there are obvious and important links between impact and effectiveness, their common conflation obscures some important insights into how sanctions function. Equating the two concepts wrongly implies that economic damage will somehow seamlessly translate into political change. In fact, the calculus between economic pressure and political acquiescence is not straightforward. As early as 1967, Johan Galtung argued that in a perverse way UN sanctions strengthened the Rhodesian regime by increasing its domestic support rather than weakening it and forcing it to make difficult political concessions.[62] This "rally around the flag" effect is now commonly accepted as a complicating factor in the equation of economic pain and political gain.[63] As a result, most serious studies of sanctions now are careful to acknowledge that a huge economic impact does not ensure success.

Nevertheless, the failure to distinguish adequately between impact and effectiveness continues to shroud another important possibility: just as economic impact—no matter how devastating—may not be *sufficient* to spur political change in some countries, it also may not be *necessary* for sanctions to have their desired effects. This possibility has thus far been largely overlooked by policymakers and scholars for two reasons. First, few reviews of economic sanctions consider cases in which sanctions were threatened but not imposed on the target country.[64] For instance, most studies would omit the case of Indonesia in 1999, when Jakarta reined in militias opposing the results of the independence referendum in East Timor only after international financial institutions threatened to curtail lending to Indonesia if it failed to curb the violence. Such cases reveal how the threat of sanctions can be effective even when the target suffers no actual economic costs. Second, the assumption that economic impact is necessary for sanctions to be successful stems from the tendency to overemphasize *economic* impact at the expense of the political or psychological impact that sanctions may have on the target. As explored in this book, dismissing a sanctions episode as a complete failure on the basis of its small, even negligible, economic impact could be a mistake without first assessing the broader noneconomic impact that the sanctions may have had.

The second pitfall to be avoided in the analysis of sanctions concerns the costs that the United States and other countries often suffer when they impose sanctions. A great deal already has been done to analyze these costs. In the past, considering the economic costs to the sender was rarely part of the process of evaluating sanctions overall; today, the bizarre practice of assessing sanctions without reference to the economic costs they inflict on those who employ them has become the rare exception rather than the norm.

Despite this progress, the sanctions debate continues to suffer from a variety of ways in which the issue of costs to the sender is treated. The first problem is that the growing attention given to these costs has led some to regard the study of them as an end in itself. Such costs are an inherent part of assessing the *utility* of sanctions—the degree to which goals are achieved at a reasonable sacrifice (effectiveness minus costs). Outside this context,

> *Criteria Used in Evaluating Sanctions*
>
> *Impact:* the sheer economic or political damage sanctions inflict on the target
>
> *Effectiveness:* the extent to which sanctions achieve their goals
>
> *Utility:* the extent to which sanctions achieve their goals, minus the costs incurred in the process
>
> *Comparative utility:* how the utility of sanctions (their effectiveness minus their costs) compares with that of other policy options; whether sanctions were the best choice open to policymakers at the time

costs have little meaning for the study of sanctions; no sanctions episode can be dismissed as a failure on the basis of its costs alone. A second problem is that, despite broad agreement on the need to include these costs in any analysis of sanctions, there is as yet little consensus on how important the costs are or how they should be valued. One estimate that assessed the cost of sanctions to the U.S. economy to be between $15 billion and $19 billion in exports in 1997 has been used to both support and refute arguments that sanctions are costly.[65] Disagreement over how to value the costs is directly related to the growing tendency to consider costs outside the context of effectiveness. How can you discern whether the price you are paying is too high unless you have full knowledge of what you are buying? Finally, considerations of costs borne by the sender—like those suffered by the target—have focused disproportionately on economic costs, sometimes to the near exclusion of political or diplomatic costs. While the nonquantifiable nature of these costs has led some to shy away or overlook their valuation, they are of growing importance in a globalizing, post–cold war world in which the United States can no longer be assured that its allies will acquiesce to many of its policies and priorities abroad.

The third pitfall is perhaps the greatest impediment to having scholarship on sanctions play a more useful role in policymaking: the common tendency to equate the utility of sanctions (whether they achieve their goals at reasonable or proportionate costs) with their *comparative utility* (whether they are the best choice available at the time). Where the benefits of sanctions outweigh their costs, these tools may be judged to be useful or to have utility. However, as repeatedly emphasized by David Baldwin, this assessment says nothing about whether sanctions were the right course to pursue in a given instance;[66] even when the performance of sanctions was itself favorable, another approach—one relying primarily on different tools—might have yielded greater benefits at lower costs, be they humanitarian, political, diplomatic, or economic. Sanctions then would be the comparatively less useful policy choice. Similarly, sanctions that did not achieve many of their goals and involved high costs still could be judged to be the best option in light of the alternatives open at the time. Only by comparing sanctions to other available policy options can a study assess the comparative utility of sanctions—or whether they should be used—both in a particular instance or as a foreign policy instrument overall.

In order to avoid these three pitfalls, this book employs a multipart analysis designed to examine the impact, effectiveness, utility, and comparative utility of sanctions in each of the cases considered. These assessments are woven into the four sections of each chapter. The first section provides the historical *context* of the case in question. Beyond recounting the facts of each case, the discussion seeks to highlight the dynamics that shaped the sanctions policy. It explores tensions between Congress and the executive branch, international concerns and reactions, and shifts in domestic opinions and priorities. The context section weighs the influence of these and other factors throughout the period that sanctions were in place to elucidate how and why objectives changed, tactics shifted, or other developments arose.

The second—and longest—part of each chapter is devoted to making key judgments related to the effectiveness and utility of sanctions in each case. Here, the economic and political impact of sanctions on the target is addressed. The effects of sanctions must be separated from the influence of other factors that would have shaped economic and political conditions in the target even in the absence of sanctions. Although it may be tempting to attribute the economic downturn in Libya in the 1980s to sanctions imposed during that decade, the drop in oil prices over the same period may have much greater explanatory value. Similarly, the weakening of a regime could have its roots in a political backlash created by sanctions, or it could be attributable to domestic factors quite unrelated to external economic pressure. Distinguishing between correlation and causality—the key to evaluating the impact of sanctions—is in itself a tough task. However, it is made more difficult by the poor-to-dismal quality of most statistics available in all the cases studied here; many of the countries in question are closed societies where economic and social data are kept in a haphazard manner and rarely made available to the outside world. Addressing these challenges requires the construction of counterfactuals—scenarios of what might have transpired in the absence of sanctions—based on the economic performance of similar countries not subject to sanctions or on the political and economic trends in the target country before sanctions were imposed. In each case, some effort is made to quantify the economic impact of sanctions in sectors that lend themselves to such calculations.[67] As cautioned in the text, however, these estimates sketch only the roughest outline of economic transactions lost and, for reasons explored in each case, generally result in a considerable overestimation of the economic impact of sanctions.

This second section of each chapter also includes an assessment of whether sanctions achieved the goals laid out for them, a crucial element in evaluating the *effectiveness* of sanctions. Far from being straightforward, this endeavor requires considering the broad range of goals—explicit and implicit, primary and auxiliary, initial and subsequent—embraced by various advocates and crafters of sanctions over time. Each chapter broadly considers the extent to which sanctions changed, weakened, or contained the regime as well as whether sanctions moderated its behavior. When there were notable improvements in a situation, one must gauge to what extent sanctions deserve the credit. In some cases, other policy tools may be responsible for at least part of the observed success; in still others, elements beyond the control of the United States could have been the deciding factor. Again, separating correlation from causality is crucial to making an accurate assessment. In mid 2002, the Iranian political system was unquestionably more open than it was when sanctions were first imposed in 1979 after the revolution.[68] Yet, crediting sanctions for the change would overlook important internal dynamics in Iran that may also be responsible for the shift and that were largely independent of the influence of sanctions.

After determining the extent to which sanctions achieved their goals, the discussion turns to the costs associated with sanctions. One must know the price paid for using sanctions to determine the utility of these tools. In some cases, sanctions might be judged to be useful not because of the great achievements that they can claim but because of the relatively low costs that they entailed in light of more marginal gains. U.S. policy toward Sudan in the 1990s is one such example. In contrast, a sanctions episode that entailed huge costs might still be deemed to have utility if the costs were justified by the attainment of important goals. Sanctions on Iraq might qualify for a judgment along these lines.

Here, every effort is made to highlight the humanitarian consequences of sanctions. However, as with other portions of the analysis, those effects can be difficult to differentiate from a deterioration of the humanitarian situation rooted in other causes.[69] For instance, although the suffering occurring in Iraq under sanctions has been severe, it is no by means certain that most of the distress has been due to sanctions rather than Saddam Hussein's deliberate policies of neglect and mismanagement. Economic, political, and other types of costs borne by the sender also are considered. The use of the word "cost," however, should not suppose that the United States gains no benefits apart from whatever changes in the target country sanctions induce or inspire. In many cases, Congress or the executive branch accrues political benefits from being seen to take the "moral high ground" when imposing sanctions, particularly in the eyes of powerful domestic interest groups.

The third section of each chapter moves beyond assessments to explain the record of sanctions. This broader evaluation explores why sanctions were as effective or had as much utility as the analysis suggests. Why were sanctions able to achieve their goals or why did they fall short? What factors contributed to the utility of sanctions? What factors detracted from it? The coordination between sanctions and other policy tools is highlighted, as are the stakes surrounding the goals pursued, both for the United States or United Nations and for the target country.[70] The performance of sanctions is also contrasted with that of alternative policy instruments to assess the *comparative utility* of sanctions. As stressed earlier, while evaluating the utility of sanctions is of interest, gauging the comparative utility of sanctions is essential to policymakers forced to make difficult choices in the real world. Arriving at such an estimate inevitably involves some awkward post-hoc intellectual gymnastics and the extensive use of counterfactuals. Nevertheless, even though the best efforts are distinctly imprecise, they are worth undertaking given their importance in judging whether sanctions were wisely employed.

Finally, the discussion of each case looks to the future. The fourth and last section of each chapter offers recommendations based on the preceding analysis. It proposes steps to improve U.S. policy toward the country in question, if warranted, with an emphasis on maximizing the utility of the sanctions strategy in place or offering preferable alternatives to it.

## Outstanding Issues to Be Addressed

Examining every case in this fashion allows for a rigorous evaluation of U.S. policy toward Iran, Iraq, Libya, and Sudan. Moreover, by facilitating the comparison of cases, this approach generates greater insight into how U.S. eco

nomic tools function in a post–cold war environment marked by globalization and American preeminence. Equally important, this rigorous case-study
analysis provides material for the closer scrutiny of six issues that deserve
greater attention in the study of sanctions. Each area of inquiry draws on the
findings of earlier sanctions work and offers a new realm for subsequent
studies to add value to the overall understanding of these economic tools.

First, as mentioned in the introductory chapter, a new generation of sanctions scholarship must move beyond the now widely accepted conclusion
that multilateral sanctions are more likely to achieve their goals than unilateral ones. The preference for multilateral measures is easily understood—
given the exponential increase in both the economic and political impacts
associated with multilateral sanctions—and firmly grounded in historical
evidence.[71] But other critical issues remain open to question. Under what
conditions are multilateral sanctions most likely to be secured? How does the
economic and political environment alter the prospects for multilateral
cooperation? And, more specifically, how can the United States craft its unilateral sanctions policies to best serve as a catalyst for multilateral measures
rather than as a substitute for or even an impediment to them? Several cases
in the 1990s and beyond—such as Afghanistan and Libya—demonstrate that
U.S. sanctions can pave the way for multilateral restrictions. A more concerted effort needs to be made to determine what facilitates this process.

A second area demanding more scholarly focus is the relationship
between sanctions regimes and the goals they pursue. Most sanctions studies have counseled policymakers to keep their expectations low. Richard
Haass has advised that sanctions "are unlikely to achieve desired results if
the aims are large or the time is short."[72] Similar words of caution have
emanated from other scholars.[73] Such caution, while clearly warranted
when sanctions are used alone, raises the still-open question of how sanctions can best contribute to a strategy pursuing more ambitious goals. If
sanctions are not well-suited to play a lead role in such efforts, how can they
best complement other tools? Can sanctions regimes be better tailored to
suit the objectives pursued? If so, can benchmarks be drawn to assist policymakers looking for guidance?

Third, sanctions studies should continue to explore when and how impact
translates into effectiveness. Although the latest sanctions scholarship recognizes that "transmission belts" between the two concepts must exist, more
work needs to be done to determine how such mechanisms function.
Existing hypotheses relate mostly to the distribution of power in the society
under sanctions. Bruce Jentleson proposes that sanctions' power to persuade

relates to the structure of elites in a society.[74] T. Clifton Morgan postulates that the more diffuse influence in a country is, the more likely sanctions are to have their intended effects.[75] In related findings, scholars such as Daniel Drezner note that the chances that sanctions will achieve their goals are greatly increased if the sanctioned country is both a democracy and an ally of the country imposing the measures.[76] Building on the work of these scholars requires an in-depth consideration of how sanctions interact with domestic factors in the target country in determining whether economic or political impact is converted into effectiveness.

Fourth, the U.S. domestic dynamics surrounding the use of sanctions are worthy of greater analysis. This chapter already has considered how domestic pressures surrounding the use of sanctions arose as a result of globalization and the end of the cold war political system. Of related and equal interest are the tensions that emerged between Congress and the executive branch around sanctions policy, particularly as Congress assumed a more aggressive foreign policy role and became more active in legislating sanctions. How did this friction influence the shape of individual sanctions policies? What implications, if any, did such discord have for their effectiveness?

A fifth area that warrants more scrutiny is the influence of sanctions on U.S. energy security. Maintaining access to reasonably priced energy resources has long been a major objective of American foreign policy. Yet the most extensive sanctions regimes imposed and enforced by the United States fall on energy exporters: energy commodities are the primary export of the four countries examined in this book. More analysis is needed not only to determine the costs of individual sanctions policy on U.S. energy security—and therefore U.S. economic performance—but also to consider the cumulative effect of maintaining sanctions against several oil exporters.

The sixth and final realm deserving greater attention is how sanctions compare with their alternatives. As discussed at length earlier, even the most thorough examination of sanctions is of limited use if it does not address how the performance of sanctions compares with that of other strategies that might have been employed in their place. Most serious studies of sanctions to date—and not only those advanced by groups with a pro-business agenda—concluded that sanctions should be used with greater discretion.[77] This scholarly work, in conjunction with vigorous advocacy efforts by business and other antisanctions groups, spurred somewhat of a decline of confidence in and enthusiasm for the use of sanctions. Most of these efforts, however, failed to consider the alternatives before concluding that sanctions are overused. If better instruments are in fact available to policymakers, what are they and how should they be wielded? When is the option of doing nothing preferable to employing sanctions? No study of sanctions should be exempt from answering these questions.

In examining a limited number of cases, this book makes no attempt to offer a better estimate of the "success" rate of sanctions or to make a deterimination of whether sanctions in general achieve their goals more or less than the 34 percent of the time postulated by other studies. Even if the small sample size were not problematic, the cases selected are far from representative of an average sanctions episode. Arguably, the goals pursued in these cases are more ambitious and the existing relationships between the United States and the target more hostile than in most other sanctions cases. These factors, in addition to the nondemocratic nature of most of the regimes in question, would lead one to believe that sanctions in these circumstances are likely to be less effective than in others.

This book presents both policymakers and scholars a systematic method for the rigorous evaluation of sanctions policy. Moreover, by examining some of the most controversial sanctions regimes maintained by the United States, it offers a greater understanding of U.S. policies toward Iran, Iraq, Libya, and Sudan, and proposes modifications to these policies where warranted. The thorough evaluation of these cases is, however, not an end in itself. Each chapter sheds light on elements of the six themes delineated above, providing material for the broader discussion of these areas of inquiry in the conclusion and offering insights relevant to the question of whether sanctions can adequately address the threats posed by the nexus of terrorism and weapons of mass destruction. Ultimately, this book is concerned with the fundamental issues of what makes sanctions effective in various political and economic environments, what hinders their judicious application, and how they compare with the alternatives open to policymakers faced with tough choices in 2003 and beyond.

## Appendix 2A

Tables 2A-1 and 2A-2 detail sanctions imposed by the United States or the United Nations on state and nonstate actors since 1990. Note that table 2A-2 includes a wide variety of sanctions, including penalties against companies and firms for export control violations, sanctions on substate actors involved in regional or local conflicts, extraterritorial sanctions against companies for trade or investment in areas that the United States seeks to isolate, and penalties against transnational actors.

Table 2A-1.  *Sanctions Imposed on State Actors by the United States or the United Nations since 1990*

| Date | Target | Primary sender[a] | Reason | Internal or external behavior | Initiated by | Sanction |
|------|--------|-------------------|--------|-------------------------------|--------------|----------|
| 1990 | Iraq | UN | Invasion of Kuwait | External | ... | Trade, finance, aid |
| 1990 | China | U.S. | Proliferation | External | Congress | Military trade, aid, finance |
| 1990 | Pakistan | U.S. | Proliferation | External | Congress | Aid |
| 1990 | Sudan | U.S. | Military coup | Internal | Congress | Aid |
| 1990 | Kenya[b] | U.S. | Human rights | Internal | Executive branch, Congress | Aid |
| 1990 | El Salvador | U.S. | Civil war, human rights | Internal | Congress | Aid |
| 1990 | Liberia | U.S. | Civil war, human rights | Internal | Congress | Aid |
| 1990 | Zaire | U.S., EU, Belgium | Human rights | Internal | Congress | Aid |
| 1990 | Guatemala | U.S. | Human rights | Internal | Executive branch | Aid |
| 1991 | (former) Yugoslavia | UN | Civil war | Internal | ... | Arms embargo |
| 1991 | Kenya | U.S., Western Europe | Democratization | Internal | Executive branch | Aid |
| 1991 | Haiti | U.S., OAS | Military coup | Internal | Executive branch | Trade, finance, aid |
| 1991 | Burma (Myanmar) | U.S. | Narcotics, democratization | Internal | Congress | Trade |
| 1991 | Thailand | U.S. | Military coup | Internal | Congress | Aid |
| 1991 | Yemen | U.S. | Vote against UN resolution approving force against Iraq | External | Congress | Aid |

| Year | Country | Sender | Issue | Type | Actor | Sanction |
|------|---------|--------|-------|------|-------|----------|
| 1991 | Indonesia | U.S., U.K., Netherlands | Human rights | Internal | Congress | Aid |
| 1992 | Iran, Iraq | U.S. | Proliferation | External | Congress | Military trade |
| 1992 | Peru[c] | U.S. | Democratization | Internal | Executive branch, Congress | Aid |
| 1992 | Somalia | UN | Civil war | Internal | … | Arms embargo |
| 1992 | Liberia | UN | Civil war | Internal | … | Arms embargo |
| 1992 | Malawi | U.S., Western Europe | Democratization | Internal | Executive branch | Aid |
| 1992 | Syria[d] | U.S. | Proliferation | External | Congress | Military trade |
| 1992 | Serbia-Montenegro | UN | Civil war | Internal | … | Trade, finance |
| 1992 | Azerbaijan | U.S. | Aggression | External | Congress | Aid |
| 1992 | Cameroon | U.S. | Democratization | Internal | Executive branch | Aid |
| 1992 | Togo | U.S., EU | Democratization | Internal | Executive branch | Aid |
| 1992 | Libya | UN | Terrorism | External | … | Air and arms embargo |
| 1992 | Cuba | U.S. | Democratization | Internal | Congress | Trade |
| 1992 | Nicaragua | U.S. | Civilian control over military, expropriation | Internal | Congress | Aid |
| 1992 | Iran[d] | U.S. | Proliferation | External | Congress | Military trade |
| 1993 | Haiti | UN | Military coup | Internal | … | Trade, finance |
| 1993 | Guatemala | U.S., OAS, Germany | Democratization | Internal | Executive branch | Aid |
| 1993 | Sudan | U.S. | Terrorism | External | Congress/Executive branch | Aid, finance, military trade |

(continued)

Table 2A-1. *Sanctions Imposed on State Actors by the United States or the United Nations since 1990 (Continued)*

| Date | Target | Primary sender | Reason | Internal or external behavior | Initiated by | Sanction |
|---|---|---|---|---|---|---|
| 1993 | Libya | UN | Terrorism | External | … | Finance, trade |
| 1993 | Nigeria | U.S., EU | Human rights, democratization | Internal | Executive branch | Aid |
| 1993 | China[d] | U.S. | Proliferation | External | Congress | Military trade |
| 1993 | Pakistan[d] | U.S. | Proliferation | External | Congress | Military trade |
| 1994 | Nigeria | U.S. | Narcotics trafficking | External | Congress/Executive branch | Aid, finance |
| 1994 | Rwanda | UN | Civil war | Internal | … | Arms embargo |
| 1994 | Gambia | U.S., U.K. | Military coup | Internal | Congress | Aid |
| 1994 | Yemen, Iraq, Iran, Libya, Sudan, Syria | U.S. | Arab boycott of Israel | External | Congress | Military trade |
| 1995 | Iran | U.S. | Terrorism, proliferation, opposition to Middle East peace process | External | Executive branch | Trade, aid, finance |
| 1995 | Afghanistan | U.S. | Narcotics trafficking | External | Congress/Executive branch | Aid |
| 1995 | Peru | U.S. | Border war | External | Executive branch | Arms embargo |
| 1995 | Ecuador | U.S. | Border war | External | Executive branch | Arms embargo |

| Year | Target | Sender | Issue | External/Internal | Congress/Executive branch | Sanction type |
|---|---|---|---|---|---|---|
| 1996 | Colombia | U.S. | Narcotics trafficking | External | Congress/Executive branch | Aid, finance |
| 1996 | Cuba[e] | U.S. | Human rights, democratization | Internal | Congress | Trade, finance, aid |
| 1996 | Sudan | UN | Terrorism | External | … | Diplomatic |
| 1996 | Burma (Myanmar) | U.S. | Human rights | Internal | Congress | Aid |
| 1996 | Niger | U.S., France | Democratization | Internal | Congress | Aid |
| 1996 | State sponsors of terrorism | U.S. | Terrorism | External | Congress | Finance |
| 1996 | Zambia | U.S., Western Europe | Human rights, constitutional reform | Internal | Executive branch | Aid |
| 1996 | Burundi | U.S. | Military coup | Internal | Congress | Aid |
| 1996 | Iran[d] | U.S. | Proliferation | External | Congress | Military trade |
| 1997 | Burma (Myanmar) | U.S. | Democratization | Internal | Executive branch | Finance |
| 1997 | Sierra Leone | UN | Civil war | Internal | … | Arms and oil embargo, travel |
| 1997 | Sudan | U.S. | Terrorism, human rights, destabilizing neighbors | External, internal | Executive branch | Trade, finance |
| 1998 | India | U.S. | Nuclear weapons tests | External | Congress | Aid, military trade, finance |
| 1998 | Pakistan | U.S. | Nuclear weapons tests | External | Congress | Aid, military trade, finance |

(continued)

Table 2A-1. Sanctions Imposed on State Actors by the United States or the United Nations since 1990 (Continued)

| Date | Target | Primary sender | Reason | Internal or external behavior | Initiated by | Sanction |
|---|---|---|---|---|---|---|
| 1998 | Yugoslavia (and Kosovo) | UN | Civil war | Internal | ... | Arms embargo |
| 1999 | Pakistan | U.S. | Military coup | Internal | Congress | Aid |
| 1999 | Indonesia | U.S. | Violence in East Timor | Internal | Executive Office | Aid |
| 2000 | Ethiopia | UN | Border war | External | ... | Arms embargo |
| 2000 | Eritrea | UN | Border war | External | ... | Arms embargo |
| 2001 | Liberia | UN | Support of rebels in Sierra Leone | External | ... | Arms embargo, trade |
| 2002 | Zimbabwe | U.S. | Rule of law | Internal | Congress | Finance |

Sources: The President's Export Council, "Unilateral Economic Sanctions: A Review of Existing Sanctions and Their Impacts on U.S. Economic Interests with Recommendations for Policy and Process Improvement," June 1997 (www.usaengage.org/studies/unilat1.html [August 23, 2002]); Erin Day, "Economic Sanctions Imposed by the United States against Specific Countries: 1979 through 1992" (Congressional Research Service, August 1992); United Nations; U.S. International Trade Commission, "Overview and Analysis of Current U.S. Unilateral Economic Sanctions" (GPO, August 1998); Barry E. Carter, "Study of New U.S. Unilateral Sanctions, 1997–2002," March 2002 (www.usaengage.org/2002sanctions/index.html [September 9, 2002]).

a. U.S. sanctions are implicit where UN ones are listed.

b. There were two sanctions against Kenya in 1990: first, the Bush administration withheld aid already granted to the country; second, Congress withheld new aid for the following year.

c. There were two sanctions against Peru in 1992: first, the Bush administration withheld aid already granted to the country; second, Congress withheld new aid for the following year.

d. Sanctions were imposed on the country's Ministry of Defense.

e. This entry refers to the Helms-Burton Act, which also is listed in table 2A-2. In addition to imposing sanctions on companies, the law codified existing sanctions on Cuba.

Table 2A-2. *Sanctions Imposed on Nonstate Actors by the United States or the United Nations since 1990*[a]

| Date | Target | Primary sender | Reason | Initiated by | Sanction |
|------|--------|----------------|--------|--------------|----------|
| 1991 | Libyan entities (48) | U.S. | Identified as Libyan front companies trying to circumvent existing U.S. sanctions. | Executive branch | Trade, finance |
| 1991 | Chinese firms (2) | U.S. | Proliferation | Congress | Military trade |
| 1991 | Pakistani firm | U.S. | Proliferation | Congress | Military trade |
| 1991 | South African firm | U.S. | Proliferation | Congress | Military trade |
| 1992 | Libyan entities (46) | U.S. | Identified as Libyan front companies trying to circumvent existing U.S. sanctions. | Executive branch | Trade, finance |
| 1992 | North Korean firms (2) | U.S. | Proliferation | Congress | Military trade |
| 1992 | Indian firm | U.S. | Proliferation | Congress | Military trade |
| 1992 | Russian space entity | U.S. | Proliferation | Congress | Military trade |
| 1992 | North Korean firms (2) | U.S. | Proliferation | Congress | Military trade |
| 1992 | Khmer Rouge (Cambodia) | UN | Democratization | . . . | Oil embargo |
| 1993 | UNITA (Angola) | UN | Civil war | . . . | Arms and oil embargo |
| 1994 | Thai firms (3) | U.S. | Proliferation | Congress | Military trade |
| 1994 | Israeli individual and W. European firms (2) | U.S. | Proliferation | Congress | Military trade |

(continued)

Table 2A-2. *Sanctions Imposed on Nonstate Actors by the United States or the United Nations since 1990*[a] *(Continued)*

| Date | Target | Primary sender | Reason | Initiated by | Sanction |
|------|--------|----------------|--------|--------------|----------|
| 1994 | Italian individual | U.S. | Proliferation | Congress | Military trade |
| 1994 | Swiss firms (2) | U.S. | Proliferation | Congress | Military trade |
| 1994 | Austrian, Australian, and German individuals | U.S. | Proliferation | Congress | Military trade |
| 1995 | Hong Kong firms (3) | U.S. | Proliferation | Congress | Military trade |
| 1995 | German and Austrian firms | U.S. | Proliferation | Congress | Military trade |
| 1995 | Russian individual | U.S. | Proliferation | Congress | Military trade |
| 1995 | Cali drug cartel (Colombia) | U.S. | Narcotics | Executive branch | Finance |
| 1995 | Terrorists who threaten the Middle East peace process | U.S. | Terrorism | Executive branch | Finance |
| 1996 | Companies having economic relations with Cuba | U.S. | Trafficking in expropriated property | Congress | Trade, aid, travel |
| 1996 | Companies investing in oil and gas sectors of Iran and Libya | U.S. | Investment as specified | Congress | Trade, aid, finance |
| 1996 | Foreign terrorist organizations | U.S. | Terrorism | Congress | Finance |
| 1996 | Chinese firms | U.S. | Proliferation | Congress | Military trade |

| Year | Entity | U.S./UN | Type | Branch | Sanction |
|---|---|---|---|---|---|
| 1996 | Pakistani firms | U.S. | Proliferation | Congress | Military trade |
| 1996 | North Korean firm | U.S. | Proliferation | Congress | Military trade |
| 1997 | UNITA (Angola) | UN | Civil war | ... | Travel |
| 1997 | Chinese individuals and firms | U.S. | Proliferation | Congress | Military trade |
| 1997 | German individual and firm | U.S. | Proliferation | Congress | Military trade |
| 1998 | UNITA (Angola) | UN | Civil war | ... | Finance, trade |
| 1998 | RUF (Sierra Leone) | UN | Civil war | ... | Arms embargo, travel |
| 1998 | Former German resident | U.S. | Proliferation | Congress | Military trade |
| 1998 | North Korean firm | U.S. | Proliferation | Congress | Military trade |
| 1998 | Pakistani firm | U.S. | Proliferation | Congress | Military trade |
| 1998 | Russian firms (7) | U.S. | Proliferation | Executive branch | Trade |
| 1998 | Individual terrorists | U.S. | Terrorism | Executive branch | Finance Office |
| 1999 | Russian firms (3) | U.S. | Proliferation | Executive branch | Trade Office |
| 1999 | Taliban (Afghanistan) | U.S. | Terrorism | Executive branch | Trade, finance |
| 1999 | Taliban (Afghanistan) | UN | Terrorism | ... | Arms embargo, finance |
| 1999 | Egyptian firms (3) | U.S. | Proliferation | Congress | Military trade |
| 1999 | Foreign narcotics traffickers | U.S. | Narcotics trafficking | Congress | Finance |

(continued)

Table 2A-2. *Sanctions Imposed on Nonstate Actors by the United States or the United Nations since 1990*[a] *(Continued)*

| Date | Target | Primary sender | Reason | Initiated by | Sanction |
|------|--------|----------------|--------|--------------|----------|
| 2000 | North Korean firm | U.S. | Proliferation | Congress | Military trade |
| 2000 | Iranian firms (4) | U.S. | Proliferation | Congress | Military trade |
| 2000 | Iranian firms (2) | U.S. | Proliferation | Congress | Military trade |
| 2000 | RUF (Sierra Leone) | UN | Civil war | ... | Trade |
| 2001 | Taliban (Afghanistan) | UN | Terrorism | ... | Arms embargo, diplomatic |
| 2001 | North Korean firms | U.S. | Proliferation | Congress | Military trade |
| 2001 | North Korean and Chinese firms | U.S. | Proliferation | Congress | Military trade |
| 2001 | Chinese firm | U.S. | Proliferation | Congress | Military trade |
| 2001 | Pakistani firm | U.S. | Proliferation | Congress | Military trade |
| 2001 | Foreign terrorist organizations and individuals | U.S. | Terrorism | Executive branch | Finance Office |
| 2002 | Chinese firms | U.S. | Proliferation | Congress | Military trade |
| 2002 | Armenian, Chinese, and Moldovan firms | U.S. | Proliferation | Congress | Military trade |
| 2002 | Narcotics traffickers | U.S. | Narcotics trafficking | Congress | Financial |
| 2002 | North Korean firms | U.S. | Proliferation | Congress | Military trade |

Sources: *Federal Register*, various years; United Nations.

# CHAPTER THREE

# Influencing
# Iran

Mutual antagonism between the United States and Iran has been an enduring reality in the Gulf region since Iran's 1979 revolution. The United States has repeatedly expressed its concern over Iranian efforts to obstruct peace efforts in the Middle East, particularly through state support of anti-Israel groups espousing violence. U.S. allegations of and objections to Iranian efforts to acquire nuclear and other weapons of mass destruction have also been a continued source of friction. Forming the backdrop to these specific concerns is an American sense of grievance over Iran's postrevolutionary hostility toward the United States and past acts of terrorism believed to be connected to Iran. On the other side, Iran deeply objects to U.S. policies in the wider Middle East and to perceived U.S. meddling in Iranian affairs, including limited American support for Iraq during the Iran-Iraq war as well as U.S. involvement in the 1953 coup in Iran. This resentment is coupled with anger over the shooting down of an Iranian passenger airliner by an American warship in 1988 and with frustration that the United States did not give greater acknowledgment to past Iranian actions—such as Iran's neutrality during the Gulf war and Iran's assistance in creating an interim Afghan government at the Bonn Conference—that were in American interests.

Although U.S. objectives have varied over time, sanctions have been the mainstay of U.S. strategies regarding the Islamic republic. Sanctions were imposed and then lifted by the United States in an effort to secure the

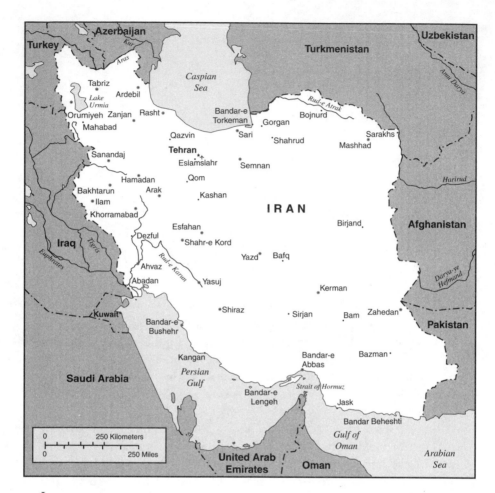

*Iran*

release of Americans held hostage in Tehran in the wake of the revolution. The explicit aim of the subsequent round of sanctions—which are the focus of this chapter—was a sometimes awkward blend of containment and behavior change. Sanctions were viewed as a means of containing Iran's *ability* to procure weapons of mass destruction, support international terrorism, and actively oppose Israel and the Middle East peace process; at the same time, sanctions were perceived as a means of influencing Iran's *desire* to undertake those activities.[1]

Different branches of government also viewed sanctions as serving a variety of implicit and unstated objectives. Most policymakers saw sanctions against Iran as an important part of a broader U.S. strategy to combat terrorism and oppose weapons proliferation. Yet some elements within the government and individual members of Congress also envisioned sanctions as underpinning a strategy to topple the Islamic government of Iran, although regime change was never an explicit goal of the sanctions or U.S. policy. In contrast, as Iranian domestic politics evolved over the years, other U.S. policymakers came to view sanctions as a possible means of influencing the internal debate in Iran in favor of more liberal-leaning factions.

U.S. sanctions have been central not only to American policy toward Iran but also to the failure of both countries to move beyond the stalemate existing between them. According to most Iranian leaders, regardless of their political leanings, as long as sanctions remain in place, Iran will reject any official dialogue with the United States.[2] This inflexible stance has complicated U.S. efforts to revise its own policy toward Iran. An improved relationship, however, would bring clear benefits to each country. For the United States, better relations with Iran would diminish tensions in the region and provide it with a critical ally in the quest to combat or contain the regime of Saddam Hussein, stabilize the Caspian and Central Asian states, and deal with the situation in Afghanistan. Moreover, it would allow the United States to diversify the sources of its energy supplies as well as present American businesses with a growing and increasingly sophisticated market for U.S. products and investment. A more congenial relationship between Washington and Tehran would also demonstrate U.S. support for countries seeking to meld their Islamic identities with democratic processes. For Iran, better relations with the United States could help the government deal with its own security concerns and facilitate Iran's entry into the global economy, which would enable the country to procure the greater volumes of international investment and finance critical to its continued development.

The events of September 11 brought into sharp focus both the common interests and the divergent agendas held by the United States and Iran and spurred many to reconsider the bilateral relationship as well as the U.S. sanctions strategy against Iran. As demonstrated in this chapter, although sanctions have had a greater economic and political impact than is commonly acknowledged, they have been ineffective; they have achieved strikingly few of the goals set out for them, particularly given that they cannot take much credit for what positive developments did occur in Iran over the period they have been in place. Sanctions against Iran have also lacked utility, as they entailed significant costs to a variety of U.S. interests. Given this assessment, U.S. policymakers should be open to an alternative approach to the current sanctions-dominated strategy in place toward Iran. Devising and adopting such a policy—one that better promotes U.S. interests in the short and medium term, while not precluding the emergence of a more fully democratic regime in the long term—is overdue.

## The Historical Context of Sanctions

The history of U.S. sanctions against Iran dates back to the February 1979 Iranian revolution, the subsequent seizure of the U.S. embassy in Tehran, and the capture and detention of scores of American diplomats.[3] The United States responded to these developments by suspending military relations. It froze the sale of hundreds of millions of dollars' worth of military items ordered under the shah's regime, embargoing the equipment and impounding the financing for the sales. These immediate steps were followed by a series of economic measures against Iran, including a freeze of $12 billion in Iranian assets and a ban on imports from Iran to America that soon evolved into a prohibition on all commerce and travel between the two countries. The United States subsequently severed diplomatic relations with Tehran. Although U.S. efforts to get UN sanctions imposed on Iran failed, some countries joined the United States in applying economic pressure on the new Islamic republic. Both the European Community and Japan banned the export of arms, placed holds on the extension of new credit to Iran, and curtailed imports of Iranian oil.

The multilateral nature of some of these sanctions and the large amount of assets impounded by the United States created significant leverage for American diplomats negotiating with Iran. On January 19, 1981, the Algiers Accord was signed, committing Iran to release the American hostages who had been in captivity for more than 400 days and paving the way for the normalization of economic relations between Iran and the United States.[4] Bilateral trade resumed and most Iranian assets were unfrozen, although disputes over the return of some Iranian assets persist, even as they remain under the jurisdiction of the United States–Iran Claims Tribunal at the Hague.[5]

Despite the resumption of economic ties, political relations between the two countries remained strained even though the United States and Iran shared some important cold war interests. In January 1984, the U.S. government placed Iran on the U.S. Department of State's terrorism list, partially in response to allegations of Iranian involvement in the 1983 suicide attack by Hizbullah on U.S. Marine barracks in Lebanon that left 241 dead. At the time, being designated a state sponsor of terrorism barred Iran from receiving various types of U.S. assistance, obligated the United States to oppose lending by international financial institutions to Iran, and subjected Iran to more stringent export controls.[6] Over time, more and more sanctions became associated with the terrorism list; by the late 1980s, the transfer of any item on the munitions list and the provision of any bilateral assistance to Iran were prohibited.[7]

Although all state sponsors of terrorism—the countries on the terrorism list—were subject to these sanctions, such restrictions on Iran also were a key component of a wider U.S. strategy in the Gulf that sought to balance the power of Iran and Iraq against one another. Concerned about the dominance of an aggressive, expansionist Islamic power in the region, the United States "tilted" toward supporting Iraq in the ongoing Iran-Iraq war.[8] In conjunction with its own sanctions, the United States tried to stem the flow of weapons to Iran through Operation Staunch—an effort by the Reagan administration to orchestrate an international arms embargo against Iran.[9] President Reagan further intensified pressure on the Iranian regime in 1987 by designating Iran a major narcotic-trafficking country and prohibiting nearly all imports into America from Iran.[10] This import ban, although justified by the president as a measure to increase pressure on Iran to cease its support for terrorism, exempted Iranian crude oil refined in a third country and allowed American oil companies to continue purchasing Iranian oil and selling it in non-U.S. markets.

At least initially, the years following Iran's reluctant acceptance of a 1988 UN-brokered ceasefire with Iraq appeared to mark a new era of relative moderation for Iran. The death of Supreme Leader Ayatollah Ruhollah Khomeini in June 1989 removed the most prominent face of the revolution from the picture. Just over one month later, in July 1989, Ali Akbar Hashemi

## U.S. Sanctions against Iran

**November 14, 1979**    President Jimmy Carter issues executive order 12170, freezing $12 billion in Iranian assets and imposing an import ban, in response to the seizure of the U.S. Embassy in Tehran.

**April 1980**    President Carter bans all commerce and travel between Iran and the United States, except for humanitarian aid, due to the continuing hostage crisis.

**January 19, 1981**    Sanctions are lifted as a result of the Algiers Accord, which leads to the unblocking of most Iranian assets in U.S. banks and their foreign subsidiaries and the lifting of the trade embargo.

**January 1984**    The United States designates Iran a supporter of terrorism, leading to a prohibition on arms-related exports and sales (from 1986), controls on the export of dual-use items, a ban on most forms of economic assistance, and U.S. opposition to loans and aid from international financial institutions (IFIs).

**1987**    President Ronald Reagan names Iran a major narcotics-trafficking country. Sanctions imposed duplicate those already in place.

**October 29, 1987**    President Reagan prohibits nearly all imports from Iran in response to its support for terrorism.

**1992**    *Iran-Iraq Non-Proliferation Act*    This act tightens exports to Iran by banning the sale of items on the U.S. Munitions List (redundant), suspends dual-use technical exchange agreements, and ends any economic aid (redundant). It also provides for sanctions against firms or people assisting Iran's conventional weapons programs. In 1996, it is amended to require mandatory sanctions against any government helping Iran to acquire weapons of mass destruction.

**March 15, 1995**    President Bill Clinton issues executive order 12957, prohibiting any U.S. involvement in the development of the Iranian petroleum industry. He cites Iran's sponsorship of terrorism, opposition to the Middle East peace process, and pursuit of weapons of mass destruction as justification.

**May 6, 1995**    President Clinton bans virtually all economic transactions with Iran.

**April 1996**    *Antiterrorism and Effective Death Penalty Act*    This act prohibits financial dealings with Iran and prohibits aid to countries providing Iran with military assistance.

**August 5, 1996**    *Iran-Libya Sanctions Act*    ILSA stipulates penalties against foreign firms making substantial investments (more than $20 million) in Iranian oil and gas development.

**August 19, 1997**    President Clinton issues executive order 13059, further restricting U.S. exports to third countries when the goods are destined for reexport to Iran. This order confirms that virtually all trade and investment activities with Iran are banned.

**May 18, 1998**    Clinton administration issues a waiver to the company Total and its minority partners for investment in Iran's South Pars field.

**June 23, 1998**    President Clinton vetoes the Iran Missile Proliferation Sanctions Act.

**July 1998 and January 1999**    President Clinton imposes sanctions on ten Russian entities for their alleged involvement in Iran's missile development.

**December 1998**    Iran is removed from the U.S. government's list of major narcotic-producing countries.

**April 1999**    President Clinton issues an executive order that allows the export of food and medicine to Iran, Libya, and Sudan.

**September 1999**    U.S. State Department's *Report on International Religious Freedom* cites Iran as a serious violator of religious freedom. No new sanctions are imposed.

**November 1999**    President Clinton issues a waiver to Boeing to provide spare parts for airplanes that were purchased by Iran before sanctions were in place and that were still under warranty.

**March 14, 2000**    *Iran Nonproliferation Act*    This act seeks to tighten controls on Iran's ability to acquire weapons technology by prohibiting the export of goods on the banned list to any foreign entity found to have provided Iran with weapons technology. It specifically bars "extraordinary" U.S. payments to Russia for the International Space Station unless the president determines that Russia is not aiding Iran's weapons program.

**March 17, 2000**    Secretary of State Albright announces the lifting of U.S. sanctions on some non-oil exports, including carpets, caviar, and pistachios.

**October 28, 2000**    The FY2001 Agriculture Appropriations bill becomes law. It contains a provision banning U.S. government export guarantees for countries on the terrorism list. However, it contains a presidential waiver.

**January 2001**    Sanctions are imposed on a North Korean company under the Iran Nonproliferation Act for providing Iran with missile parts.

**June 2001**    Sanctions are imposed on a North Korean company and two Chinese companies under the Iran Nonproliferation Act for providing Iran with missile parts and chemical weapons components.

**August 3, 2001**    Congress reauthorizes the Iran-Libya Sanctions Act for another five years.

**January 29, 2002**    President Bush delivers a State of the Union address in which he brands Iran, Iraq, and North Korea as the "axis of evil."

**May 9, 2002**    Sanctions are imposed on Moldovan, Armenian, and Chinese firms for selling weapons-related goods to Iran.

Rafsanjani, the speaker of the Iranian parliament and a perceived pragmatist at the time, was elected president. Soon after coming to office, Rafsanjani embarked on a quest to remodernize and rehabilitate Iran after years of war and revolution. In that quest he sought to exploit Iran's long-standing ties with European countries to secure trade credits, aid, and markets for Iranian goods. Believing Iran to be settling into a period of moderation and enticed by the potential of economic cooperation, Europe crafted its "critical dialogue" policy toward Iran. This approach sought to influence the regime in Tehran on issues of European concern—such as human rights and weapons proliferation—through the expansion of economic and diplomatic ties.[11]

The United States was much less quick to embrace Iran's supposed moderation, although a "détente" between the two countries seemed more plausible at the beginning of the 1990s than at any time since the revolution. The end of the Iran-Iraq war, the Iranian-negotiated release of Western hostages from Lebanon, and Iran's tacit support of the U.S.-led Desert Storm coalition suggested a possible basis for greater cooperation. The administration of George H. W. Bush reportedly probed prospects of improving relations with Tehran, beginning with the president's intimation that "goodwill begets goodwill" in his inaugural speech.[12] Indirect talks between the Bush administration and Iran during the Gulf war eased some tensions. At about the same time, the Hague Tribunal ruled that the United States had to compensate Iran for the advance payments it made for arms purchases under the shah's regime, leading the United States to return $278 million to Iran in November 1991.

Such gestures, however, did not spark a significant thawing of U.S.-Iranian relations. In fact, in the following year, Congress passed further sanctions directed against Iran. The Iran-Iraq Arms Nonproliferation Act of 1992 tightened restraints on trade with Iran by requiring the denial of all sales of military items, dual-use items, and products on the commerce control list to Iran as well as Iraq.[13] This legislation also stipulated sanctions against foreign entities—whether individuals, firms, or countries—that transferred conventional arms to Iran. Later, Congress amended this law so that it applied to entities providing Iran or Iraq with technology aiding their acquisition of weapons of mass destruction.[14]

The Iran-Iraq Arms Nonproliferation Act of 1992 was the first step in moving away from the traditional balance of power strategies practiced by United States in the Gulf for decades toward treating Iran and Iraq as equal threats. The Clinton administration solidified this departure from past policy with the 1993 articulation of its "dual containment" policy, which sought to curb and contain the two Gulf powers simultaneously. First put forward by Martin Indyk, then the senior director for Near East and South Asian Affairs at the National Security Council, the dual containment policy was intended to reflect changing realities in the Gulf and the Middle East more broadly.[15] American influence in the region was arguably at its peak, with the recent defeat of Iraq and a promising Middle East peace process under-way. No longer feeling the need to play Iran and Iraq off against one another, the Clinton administration sought to isolate the positive develop-ments occurring elsewhere in the region from the influence of the two countries. Although Iraq had been vilified since its invasion of Kuwait years earlier, an article by Anthony Lake, then the national security adviser, and subsequent testimony by U.S. officials escalated the negative rhetoric used in relation to Iran.[16] This hardened verbal stance became an important com-plement to sanctions in U.S. policy toward Iran for the rest of the decade.

With Iraq already struggling under comprehensive multilateral sanctions and weapons inspection regimes, the Clinton administration attempted to persuade its allies to adopt more restrictive policies toward Iran through a dialogue held between the United States and the European Union Troika.[17] The United States did not campaign for a multinational severance of eco-nomic relations with Iran, but it did press for multinational restrictions on arms exports to Iran and a moratorium on the extension or rescheduling of new export credits and new lending by international institutions. Europe's extensive economic ties with Iran—and its critical dialogue policy—impeded U.S.-European cooperation on Iran policy. Yet a perceived hypocrisy also hin-dered the growth of a more coordinated policy. Washington's allies viewed with suspicion U.S. efforts to press others to isolate Iran while America reaped large financial rewards from its remaining economic links with the country. During a visit to the United States in February 1995, German Chancellor Helmut Kohl publicly made reference to a press report indicating that U.S. oil companies were among the largest consumers of Iranian oil.[18]

This imbalance between U.S. actions and rhetoric was only one of several factors fueling the fire for a more punitive U.S. approach toward Tehran in the mid-1990s. Concerns over Iran's nuclear ambitions were also growing. Successful U.S. efforts to convince France and Germany to prohibit their companies from selling Iran light-water reactors had encouraged Iran to turn to Russia, with which Iran completed a deal in February 1995 for the completion of a nuclear reactor at Bushehr.[19] Of even greater significance were the accelerated efforts of the American Israel Political Affairs

Committee (AIPAC) to build support for a tougher U.S. approach toward Iran.[20] In part, AIPAC took on this new role in the wake of the election of Yitzhak Rabin as prime minister of Israel and Rabin's subsequent decision to deal more directly with the White House, rather than use American organizations as conduits, on matters of foreign policy. Also instrumental in explaining AIPAC's new direction was the increasing violence in Israel and growing alarm over the actions of anti-Israel groups that had close links with Iran, such as Hizbullah and Hamas.[21] Topmost among AIPAC's allies was Senator Alphonse D'Amato (R–N.Y.), who introduced legislation into the newly Republican-controlled Congress to ban all trade with Iran in early 1995.[22]

The Clinton administration, subject to vigorous lobbying by AIPAC and individual members of Congress, was amenable to taking further steps against Iran. However, it preferred that the executive branch, rather than Congress, initiate any action in order to allow the president maximum flexibility. In fact, President Clinton's March 1995 executive order prohibiting all American involvement in the development of the Iranian petroleum industry was issued one day before the Senate was to hold a hearing on the D'Amato legislation. Domestic political factors, however, were not the only impetus for the president's move. Also important was Iran's recent decision to award the U.S. firm Conoco a contract to develop the Sirri offshore oil and gas fields in Iran.[23] The offering of this contract to an American company—the first such contract to be awarded to a foreign entity since the revolution—was later understood to be an Iranian gesture of goodwill; yet, at the time, the Clinton administration did not recognize it as such. Instead, the contract—although completely within the bounds of legality—was viewed as highly inappropriate by administration officials and drew sharp criticism from members of Congress.[24] Two months after the March executive order was issued, the president banned virtually all economic transactions with Iran. As articulated in the executive order, the goal of terminating economic links with Iran was to "curb" Iran's pursuit of weapons of mass destruction, its support of international terrorism, and its opposition to the Middle East peace process.[25]

Although these two executive orders were successful in preempting legislated sanctions on U.S. economic interaction with Iran, they did not completely undercut congressional efforts to find further ways of increasing pressure on Iran. In 1995, Newt Gingrich(R-Ga.), then Speaker of the House, recommended that the United States actively work to overthrow the Iranian regime and later advanced a proposal to allocate $20 million for that purpose.[26] Moreover, Congress enacted a number of secondary sanctions in 1996 to compel U.S. allies to join American efforts to contain Iran. The first, but less publicized, secondary sanctions came into effect under the Antiterrorism and Effective Death Penalty Act of 1996; in addition to prohibiting virtually all financial transactions with countries deemed to be supporters of terrorism, this law required that the president withhold foreign assistance to any country that provided aid or military assistance to a country on the U.S. terrorism list.[27] It also stripped Iran and other state sponsors of terrorism of their sovereign immunity in cases in which U.S. plaintiffs sue them for damages.[28]

More notable and more controversial were the secondary sanctions laid out in the Iran-Libya Sanctions Act (ILSA). D'Amato, the author of the legislation, sought to supplement the existing executive orders with measures that would force foreign companies to end their involvement in Iran. The first version of ILSA advocated a secondary boycott of any foreign firm trading with Iran.[29] The extreme nature of this legislation—and the démarches delivered to the administration by European countries as various forms of it were being considered—spurred the Clinton administration to negotiate with Congress for a softening of the terms of the bill. In its final form, the ILSA legislation mandated that the president impose at least two of six possible sanctions on any foreign entity investing more than $20 million a year in the Iranian or Libyan energy industry.[30] With regard to Iran, the law provided two sorts of presidential waivers. The first, a national interest waiver, can be used if the president decides that it is in the national interest of the United States to waive the stipulated sanctions on a specific company. The second, a country waiver, can be used when a parent country of the company making the investment agrees to impose economic sanctions on Iran; in this case, all nationals of that country would be exempt from ILSA sanctions.[31] Passed in August 1996, the bill included a "sunset" provision demanding that the law be explicitly renewed after five years or allowed to lapse.

As predicted, after sailing through both houses of Congress unopposed, ILSA brought a nearly universal torrent of protests from abroad. The European Union quickly issued a regulation forbidding its companies from complying with ILSA and assuring them that they would be eligible to recover any damages suffered as a result of its application.[32] Moreover, claiming that ILSA violated international trade agreements against the extraterritorial application of national laws, Europe threatened to bring the matter before the World Trade Organization.[33]

Separate but related to these efforts to intensify pressure on Iran through sanctions was the development of the Clinton administration's policy toward the Caspian region.[34] In the wake of the collapse of the Soviet Union, the administration of George H. W. Bush was quick to establish relations with the countries of the Caspian and Central Asia and to create an American presence in the area. At the time, both the U.S. government and many American companies believed that the region held massive oil reserves and could eventually offer the United States an opportunity to significantly diversify its oil suppliers. The contours of a specific policy toward this region began to emerge during the latter part of the first Clinton administration. In 1995, the United States formally embraced a "multiple" pipeline policy intended to advance broad U.S. geopolitical and economic interests.[35] While in theory the policy was meant to support numerous pipelines, in practice support for a pipeline running from Baku, Azerbaijan, to Ceyhan, Turkey, became the centerpiece of U.S. policy. Although this pipeline was not necessarily viewed as the most commercially viable, it was considered crucial, not only to boost Turkey's economy but to prevent Iran from assuming a critical role in future energy projects in the region. Beyond support for the Baku-Ceyhan pipeline, the Clinton administration sought to isolate Iran from developments in the Caspian by emphasizing that foreign firms involved in the construction of energy transit routes through Iran could be subject to sanctions under ILSA.[36]

Perhaps ironically, as the United States was constructing one of the most stringent unilateral sanctions regimes it had imposed on any country, Iran was in the agonizing process of moving away from its revolutionary ideology and notions of pan-Islamism to a more tempered pragmatic nationalism. While this transition had been underway at least since the end of the Iran-Iraq war in 1988, at no time was it more evident than when Mohammed Khatami was elected president in 1997. Khatami, previously a low-profile, mid-level cleric who had resigned from his post of minister of culture and Islamic guidance and later headed the National Library, swept the polls dramatically by claiming 69 percent of the popular vote.[37] His talk of increased democracy and promises of social moderation and respect for freedom of opinion, human rights, and pluralism had special appeal for Iranian women and the country's burgeoning youth population.[38]

Khatami's election was greeted with optimism from Iranians who had voiced their preference for a freer society in casting their votes for him. Although the Iranian parliament was still dominated by more conservative elements, many believed that the balance of power—long held by state clerics wanting to perpetuate the dominance of religious institutions in politics—had finally shifted to other clerics or lay people who desired a more central place for elected bodies. This optimism was manifested in a flourish of new publications touting a greater role for democracy and religious tolerance in Iranian society in the initial post-election period.[39] These changes were hoped to reflect positively on Iran's relations with the outside world and emboldened President Khatami, in an unprecedented interview with CNN in January 1998, to call for a "dialogue of civilizations" between the United States and Iran.[40]

In contrast to other countries in the region and around the world, the United States did not warm quickly to the new face of Iran. Although congressional attitudes fluctuated over this period, every action taken by Congress sought to apply greater pressure on Tehran and any entity aiding Iran. For instance, Congress agreed not to override President Clinton's veto of the Iran Missile Proliferation Sanctions Act of 1998 only after the president pledged that he would sanction Russian companies aiding Iran's missile program through an executive order.[41] Despite the fulfillment of this promise in July 1998 and January 1999,[42] Congress passed even broader legislation in March 2000 authorizing sanctions against any country, group, or individual the United States believed to be transferring technology or information that could help Iran develop weapons of mass destruction.[43] This increased scrutiny of Iran's weapons programs was matched by greater congressional attention to the country's treatment of religious minorities. Congress pressed for the application of additional sanctions on Iran as a result of its continued identification as one of the worst violators of religious freedom in the world since the practice of ranking such countries began in 1998.[44]

Unlike the actions taken by Congress, the approach adopted by the Clinton administration in the late 1990s was more conciliatory and signaled a greater flexibility in thinking about Iran.[45] Initial gestures—such as the designation of the Iranian opposition group Mujahedin-e Khalq as a foreign terrorist organization in October 1997 and the removal of Iran from the list of major narcotics-producing countries a year later—were small.[46] Other actions that slightly eased barriers between Iran and the United States were actually taken more in response to domestic or international pressures, not as overtures to Iran. For instance, in order to avoid a major confrontation with Europe over the first substantial European investment in Iran's energy sector since ILSA became law, the Clinton administration issued a waiver in May 1998 that exempted the French company Total from ILSA-mandated sanctions.[47] Similarly, President Clinton's April 1999 decision to remove restrictions on the export of food, medicine, and medical equipment to Iran (as well as Libya and Sudan) was widely perceived in both the United States and Iran as a reaction to intense lobbying by the American agricultural lobby and growing humanitarian concern about the effects of sanctions more broadly rather than as an opening to Iran.[48]

U.S. gestures made toward the end of the Clinton administration specifically in the hope of launching a process of engagement with Tehran were of greater significance. In a June 1998 speech to the Asia Society, Secretary of State Madeleine Albright called for a climate of mutual understanding between the United States and Iran and the construction of a road map to better relations.[49] The Iranian response to this offer disappointed administration officials, yet did not deter them from making additional overtures.[50] In March 2000, in a speech designed to coincide with the Iranian new year, Albright announced several small, unilateral changes in U.S. policy toward Iran.[51] In addition to acknowledging past U.S. involvement in Iranian internal affairs and expressing regret over U.S. support for Iraq during the Iran-Iraq war, Albright declared the lifting of sanctions on a variety of non-oil Iranian imports, including carpets, caviar, and pistachios. Equally significant, she underscored the American commitment to resolving U.S.-Iranian disputes over outstanding claims and assets.[52]

Over the time that U.S. policy was slowly evolving, Iran was consumed with its own internal political conflicts. Although frequently represented as a clash between reformist and conservative camps, the realities behind Iranian domestic political struggles were much more complex. President Khatami was supported by a centrist-leftist coalition known as the Second Khordad Front—a loose grouping of parties embracing a range of liberal-leaning positions on both the shape of reform and the pace at which it should occur. Similarly, the more conservative forces in Iran came together in another diverse coalition of well-entrenched groups interested in blocking the introduction of greater democracy and accountability into Iranian politics and society. These two loosely configured groups continuously clashed over differing interpretations of how society should be run and where ultimate authority rests in the Islamic republic. The Iranian constitution, rather than being a mechanism for resolution of these disputes, prolonged them by providing for multiple and overlapping bases of power in society. Visible clashes between political factions were rooted in these differing visions of the Iranian state and competing foundations of influence. Despite commanding broad popular backing, President Khatami and his supporters were continuously challenged by conservative elements controlling the judiciary and other key institutions such as the security services. From the first days of his presidency, Khatami's government faced a continuing wave of arrests and demotions of key allies in the government and its bureaucracy.[53]

Even in the face of these serious and real challenges to Khatami, in February 1999 reformist parties swept the first local and municipal elections held in Iran since the revolution, winning 60 to 70 percent of the vote.[54] Even more dramatic were the results of Iran's February 2000 parliamentary election, which significantly changed the composition of Iran's parliament, the Majlis. Against the expectations of most analysts within and outside Iran, reform-minded candidates won 189 of the 290 seats in the Majlis, decisively wrenching parliament away from conservatives and delivering another popularly elected institution to reformist control.[55] Together, these elections signaled to both advocates and opponents of reform in Iran the widespread desire of the Iranian population for change and moderation.

But rather than ushering in a new period of relative freedom for Khatami and his supporters, the landslide election in 2000 triggered a conservative backlash against many of Iran's pro-reform institutions and individuals. Given that a relatively freewheeling press had come to symbolize the more open political environment established in the first years of Khatami's presidency, the continuous arrests of journalists and the forced closure of scores of liberal-leaning newspapers since early 2000 have been a tremendous setback for Khatami and his supporters. Similarly, the jailing of intellectuals for fraudulent or greatly exaggerated crimes—such as participating in an April 2000 conference in Berlin that was disrupted by anti-regime demonstrations—stripped the reformist camp of many of its most effective leaders.[56]

Perhaps not surprisingly, Iranian leaders focused more on these intensifying internal battles of survival than they did on responding to U.S. gestures. Although some Iranian politicians—including Khatami—made mixed comments in response to Albright's gestures, subsequent months saw an overall increase in hostile rhetoric from many factions in Iran.[57] Supreme Leader Ali Khamenei dashed any immediate hopes for a more conciliatory relationship between the United States and Iran by declaring that any discussions of rapprochement with the United States would qualify as "an insult and treason to the Iranian people."[58]

Iran's cold response to tentative American initiatives, as well as its continued refusal to talk with the United States, undercut the arguments of prominent former U.S. policymakers and scholars for a more nuanced U.S.

policy toward Iran.[59] Continued turmoil in Iran's domestic politics dampened U.S. enthusiasm for further American gestures to Iran, notwithstanding the huge margins by which Khatami was elected for his second term in
office in June 2001.[60] Persistent allegations of official Iranian involvement in
the bombing of Khobar Towers also helped arrest any forward movement.[61]
In this climate, AIPAC and others easily persuaded Congress to renew ILSA
for a full five-year term in the summer of 2001, despite lukewarm arguments by the Bush administration for a modified ILSA.[62]

The events of September 11, 2001, jolted the usual hostility between Iran
and the United States. Thousands of Iranians held candlelight vigils to
express their sympathy for the victims of the terrorist attacks. And subsequent U.S. efforts to eliminate the Taliban and al-Qaida changed the prospects for U.S.-Iranian relations. Shiite Iran had long opposed the Taliban,
not only as a radical Sunni movement on its borders that was fiercely repressive of Shiite ethnic minorities, but as a regime whose rule fueled a major
narcotics problem within Iran.[63] Through international forums, the United
States sought Iran's assistance as a supporter of the Afghan opposition, a
large neighbor of Afghanistan's, a leader of the Shiite Islamic world, and as
a country whose help was key in managing Afghanistan's humanitarian crisis. Beyond lending limited support for the military campaign through such
acts as offering to rescue American military personnel in distress, Iran
largely cooperated with U.S. and international efforts to forge a new government for Afghanistan through its participation in Six Plus Two talks and
the Bonn Conference.

Although such developments suggested opportunities for greater dialogue and even rapprochement, the path to broader U.S.-Iranian cooperation and better bilateral relations remained complicated by many factors.
Despite the overt support of Iran for the new government in Afghanistan,
certain elements of the Iranian regime worked at cross-purposes to the
United States and the new Afghan government. Of even greater concern was
that the Iranian regime also escalated its support for terrorism, particularly
to groups committed to opposing Israel through violence. In an international climate more polarized against such acts, a hardening of U.S. attitudes—epitomized by President George W. Bush's categorization of Iran as
part of an "axis of evil"—heightened U.S.-Iranian differences rather than
minimized them. Fractious domestic Iranian politics created further hur-
dles for those wanting greater dialogue on both sides. In particular, the continued unpopularity of Khamenei—and the growing frustration of the

population with Khatami and his counterparts—created questions about who in Iran could be a legitimate partner to the United States.[64]

## Judging the Effectiveness and Utility of Sanctions on Iran

Assessing the sanctions-dominated strategy toward Iran is a multilayered process, as suggested by the methodological discussion in chapter 2. It requires making judgments about the impact of sanctions—the damage sanctions inflict on the target country—as well as assessing the extent to which sanctions achieved the objectives set out for them. Such findings lie behind the *effectiveness* of sanctions. The costs associated with the use of sanctions must also be gauged, so that the *utility* of sanctions—that is, whether sanctions achieved their goals at a reasonable price—can be determined.

### Economic Impact

The Iranian economy has been in varying states of disarray since 1979. In the decades after the revolution, the country's growth was volatile and ultimately insufficient to translate into a rise in per capita income for Iran's growing population. High inflation and unemployment plagued the economy, forcing a decline in the standard of living for those with jobs and frustrating those without. Iranian efforts to modernize the economy moved at a disappointing pace, and the country continued to be in urgent need of large volumes of foreign and domestic investment to rejuvenate key sectors and spur growth in new ones. Compounding these problems was the sizable debt burden that Iran struggled under for most of the 1990s as a result of overzealous borrowing in the first years of the decade. Only at the turn of the millennium, with the strengthening of international oil prices, did Iran's economy look any brighter.

Iran's economic problems grew roughly in tandem with the intensification of U.S. economic pressure, yet one cannot assume that U.S. sanctions caused them. The challenge—complicated by the incomplete and unreliable nature of Iranian data—is to separate the effects of sanctions from those of other elements that shaped the Iranian economy over the same time.[65] Quite apart from U.S. economic pressure, a number of other factors—war, reconstruction efforts, the price of oil, and political obstacles to reform—determined trends in the Iranian economy since the revolution.

For instance, the war with Iraq was a major factor shaping the economic climate of the 1980s. During that time, Iran set aside its postrevolution economic plans and functioned as a highly centralized, war-driven economy, where state managers with little experience—and a rhetorical and philosophical commitment to "social justice" dating back to the revolution—ran the economy. Despite the declining price of oil—the commodity that today still generates 80 percent of Iran's foreign exchange—Iran managed to grow sporadically over the eight years of the conflict.[66] Nevertheless, the war damage sustained by Iran in terms of lost population and destroyed infrastructure deeply hurt the country's future economic prospects.[67]

The postwar period was ostensibly a period of rebuilding and reform. However, efforts to restructure the economy laid out under the First Five-Year Plan (1989–94) were only partially realized, in part because Iran's Majlis hindered the implementation of many of President Rafsanjani's reforms. Although Iran achieved impressive growth rates for the first part of the decade, fundamental structural economic imbalances persisted. The government continued to print money to finance the government deficit, to provide large subsidies on food and fuel to the population, to maintain multiple and unrealistic exchange rates, and to support inefficient public sector enterprises.[68]

This postwar period not only was a time of lost opportunities to correct old problems, it also marked the creation of new economic imbalances. In the wake of the Iran-Iraq war, Tehran placed a high priority on repairing damaged infrastructure and industries and embarked on an arms procurement drive to replace its severely depleted stock of weapons. Initially, Iran sought to rebuild the economy by itself, seeking external assistance only in the form of foreign finance and credit.[69] Over the span of 1989–93, Iran more than quadrupled its level of foreign debt; by the end of that period, it had amassed more than $23 billion in debt, much of it in short-term borrowing.[70] By mid-1993, Iran had fallen $3 billion in arrears on its debts due to lower-than-anticipated oil prices, poor economic management, and an unrealistic exchange rate system. Against the wishes of the United States, Iran's creditors, led by Germany, allowed for a piecemeal rescheduling of Iran's debts on a bilateral basis.[71]

The ambitious debt repayment timetable that Iran negotiated with its creditors influenced the economy in two major ways. First, it helped convince the Rafsanjani government, as well as subsequent governments, of the need to open Iran to foreign investment if the country was to achieve much of its desired modernization. Second, the need to meet payments to its creditors dominated the country's economic policy for the rest of the

1990s, forcing Iran to virtually halve its imports between 1992 and 1995.[72] Although Iran's ability to maintain this discipline and make its payments was impressive, import compression extracted heavy economic costs by adding to inflationary pressures and dampening economic activity more broadly.[73] The non-oil export sector, a key component in Iranian efforts to diversify the heavily oil-dominated economy, was particularly badly affected, as productive inputs became more costly and scarce.[74] Despite these efforts, Iran was again unable to make its debt repayments later in the decade. After careful adherence to its payback scheme, the low oil prices of late 1998 and early 1999 drove the country once more to the edge of default, although the goodwill it had accrued with its bilateral creditors enabled it yet again to restructure its debt.[75]

Domestic political struggles also frustrated the efforts of President Khatami to undertake needed economic reforms, such as privatizing unprofitable state industries, balancing the budget, and reforming the exchange rate.[76] In the first few years of his presidency, Khatami faced the opposition of the largely conservative Majlis; after the February 2000 elections, economic reforms were on occasion stalled by an unexpected alliance of conservatives and those on the Islamic left who opposed the opening of the economy to outside influences.[77] Even more significant in slowing down economic restructuring was Khatami's reluctance to push for painful economic changes in the face of the already volatile political situation.[78]

Despite the slowness of economic reform in Iran, the economy was buoyed by the unusually high oil prices of 2000 and 2001. For every dollar increase in the price of oil, Iran gained more than $2.5 million a day—almost $1 billion a year.[79] These economic windfalls allowed Iran to make it through the most demanding phase in its debt repayment schedule and began to bolster the economy more broadly as foreign reserves increased and restrictions on imports were eased.[80] Nevertheless, despite this good fortune and the establishment of a "stabilization fund" to spread Iran's oil profits over periods of high and low oil prices, the economy remained unsteady due to a lack of serious reform.[81]

The profound influence that factors besides sanctions had on Iran's economic performance since the revolution is shown in figures 3-1 and 3-2. The rate of growth of Iran's gross domestic product reflects not only that of the Middle East region but also the price of Iranian crude oil over the past decade.[82] The importance of regional and international factors—as well as domestic economic policy—in explaining Iran's economic performance

### Figure 3-1. *Iran's Real GDP Growth Compared with Price of Iranian Oil, 1988–2001*

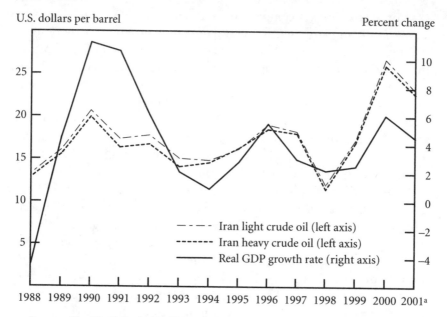

U.S. dollars per barrel

Percent change

Sources: The World Bank, *World Development Indicators 2001*, CD-ROM, and Economist Intelligence Unit, *Country Report: Iran*, June 2002, for GDP growth rates. Organization of Petroleum Exporting Countries, *OPEC Annual Statistical Bulletin 1997; OPEC Annual Statistical Bulletin 2000*; and U.S. Energy Information Administration for oil prices.
a. Economist Intelligence Unit estimate.

does not suggest that sanctions had no impact; it only indicates that sanctions were far from a dominant influence on Iran's economy during this period. Therefore, rather than looking for evidence of massive dislocations in the economy caused by sanctions, a more subtle approach is needed— one that examines the extent to which sanctions exacerbated the weaknesses in the Iranian economy and presented additional economic difficulties to Iranian policymakers.

TRADE. U.S. trade sanctions on Iran did not deal a devastating blow to the country in the sense of depriving it for long of goods essential to its well-being or broader development. For the most part, sanctions inflicted lesser costs, particularly in the first years after their imposition. The overall cost to Iran of trade sanctions was somewhat mitigated by the weakening of the trade relationship between the United States and Iran that already had occurred following the 1979 revolution.[83] Other factors, particularly Iran's

**Figure 3-2.** *Real GDP Growth: Iran Compared with Middle East Region, 1985–2001*

Percentage

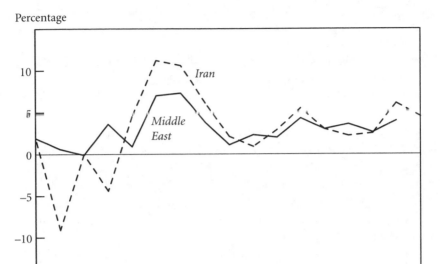

Sources: The World Bank, *World Development Indicators 2002*, CD ROM, for Middle East averages and Iran's growth rates to 1995. From 1995 onward, Iran's growth rates were taken from Economist Intelligence Unit, *Country Report: Iran*, March 2001 and June 2002.
    a. Economist Intelligence Unit estimate.

ability to reconfigure its trade patterns over time, also played a role in diminishing the costs.

The 1987 U.S. ban on *imports* from Iran did have short-term negative repercussions on the Iranian economy, although they diminished considerably as Iran diversified its trade. For instance, the ban terminated American purchases of Iranian products such as carpets and pistachios—trade that had accounted for almost one-fifth of Iran's non-oil exports. Eventually, however, Iran adjusted its trade patterns, selling more non-oil products to other countries and even finding ways to meet the demands of U.S. consumers through third markets.[84] As a result, the actual costs borne by Iran as a result of the import ban were far less than the $8 billion in non-oil imports that Iran could have been expected to sell to the United States from 1987–2000 in the absence of sanctions (see appendix table 3A-1).[85] The fact that the March 2000 lifting of restrictions on the import of Iranian carpets, caviar, and pistachios into the United States did not provide a boost for the

Iranian economy in part indicates the extent to which markets already had adjusted to sanctions.[86]

Similarly, the impact of the U.S. import ban on Iranian oil was confined to a short period. Even after it was imposed in 1987, U.S. companies were allowed to continue lifting Iranian crude oil as long as they directed it to non-U.S. destinations; this loophole virtually eliminated the costs suffered by Iran. In fact, by 1994, American companies had become the largest consumers of Iranian oil, reselling $4 billion of it each year to third markets.[87] When the 1995 executive orders closed this loophole, Iran did experience some short-term costs as it struggled to find companies to take control of the 20 to 25 percent of Iranian crude oil that American firms had been responsible for marketing.[88] Iran reportedly was forced to sell this crude at a discount of 30 to 80 cents per barrel, incurring a loss of several million dollars over a three-month period.[89] However, after this initial discomfiture, other countries—Japan and other Asian countries in particular—took up the slack created by the departure of U.S. companies.[90] As a result, although Iran's oil exports dipped slightly in 1995, the year sanctions were imposed, they recovered fully the following year.[91]

The provision of the May 1995 executive order that banned U.S. companies from *exporting* virtually any item to Iran also imposed only modest direct costs on Iran, which were concentrated in the initial years of the ban.[92] Costs were limited by the small volume of U.S. goods being purchased by Iran at the time that sanctions were imposed; in 1994, only 3 percent of Iran's imports came from the United States.[93] Nevertheless, immediately after the new restrictions went into effect, Iran had to scramble to find alternative methods of securing the goods it once imported from the United States. Iran often was easily able to replace American items with comparable products, given that none of America's allies followed suit in curtailing their trade with Iran. Australia and New Zealand, for instance, quickly replaced American wheat exports with their own commodities.[94] In other cases, over time Iran developed alternative ways of obtaining American products, either on the black market or through third countries such as the United Arab Emirates.

Although Iran was able to satisfy its import needs regardless of American sanctions, it paid a cost—albeit a declining one—to do so. In the initial period after the sanctions were imposed and before Iran had established alternative suppliers, Iran was forced to salvage spare parts to meet many of its needs for more sophisticated items once supplied by the United States.[95] Moreover, even after Iran found new trade partners, it often had to pay a premium    a difference in quality or price between U.S. products and their substitutes—to satisfy its needs.[96] The costs of securing substitutes for American food and consumer items, which constituted 86 percent of U.S. exports to Iran before the embargo, were marginal or almost inconsequential.[97] Goods considered to be high-tech by the U.S. government, however, were more costly to replace.[98] All in all, although nearly $2 billion in U.S. exports might have been expected to be sold to Iran from 1995 to 2001 in the absence of sanctions, the actual costs to Iran are likely to be less than one-tenth of that total (see appendix note, page 98). Although the April 1999 change in U.S. regulations to allow the sale of food and medicine to Iran had the potential to further mitigate that loss, political tensions and the continued prohibition on U.S. export credits for sales to Iran ensured that trade in these items stayed well below pre-sanctions levels.[99]

A broad look at Iranian trade patterns over the 1990s and beyond suggests that Iran reacted to U.S. sanctions by diversifying its trade partners, not only away from the United States but from western countries in general. As seen in figure 3-3, before the U.S. ban on the sales to Iran in 1995, a clear majority (67 percent) of Iranian imports came from the United States, Europe, Japan, and other industrialized countries;[100] however, just five years later in 2001, this number had diminished significantly (53 percent), with Asian countries such as China becoming much more significant markets.[101] Comparable shifts in the destinations of Iranian exports also are notable, with European countries becoming less significant markets for Iranian goods between 1987 and 2000.[102] Here again, Iranian ties to Asian markets and other developing countries grew (figure 3-4).

EXTERNAL AID, FINANCE, AND INVESTMENT.  The effect of U.S. sanctions on financial flows to Iran was significant, although not crippling to the economy. In ways far subtler than choking Iran off from external sources of funds, sanctions shaped the finance and investment flowing to Iran, sometimes with surprising secondary effects on the economy and economic management.[103]

For instance, the impact of U.S. opposition to lending by international financial institutions (IFIs) to Iran influenced the economy in both direct and indirect ways. Most obviously, American pressure caused the World Bank to suspend lending to Iran shortly after the bank had decided in 1991 to resume its program in Iran and approve $847 million in support of six development projects for the country.[104] This freeze on lending, which began in 1994, continued at some cost to Iran until the World Bank voted,

## Figure 3-3. *Iran's Imports by Country or Region of Origin, Various Years*

### Iran's Imports by Country or Region, 1978[a]

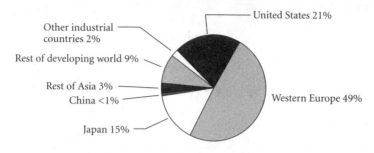

Other industrial countries 2%

Rest of developing world 9%

Rest of Asia 3%

China <1%

Japan 15%

United States 21%

Western Europe 49%

### Iran's Imports by Country or Region, 1994[b]

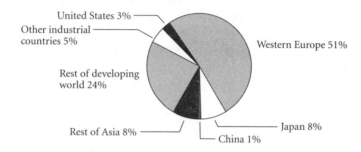

United States 3%

Other industrial countries 5%

Rest of developing world 24%

Rest of Asia 8%

Western Europe 51%

Japan 8%

China 1%

### Iran's Imports by Country or Region, 2001[c]

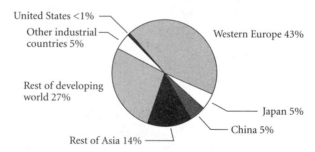

United States <1%

Other industrial countries 5%

Rest of developing world 27%

Western Europe 43%

Japan 5%

China 5%

Rest of Asia 14%

Source: International Monetary Fund, *Direction of Trade Statistics Yearbook,* 1984 and 1998, and *Direction of Trade Statistics Quarterly,* June 2002.

a. U.S. and other country exports. Total Iranian imports = $19.533 billion, 1978 dollars.

b. U.S. and other country exports, the year before the U.S. export ban. Total Iranian imports = $11.795 billion, 1994 dollars.

c. U.S. and other country exports. Total Iranian imports = $17.662 billion, 2001 dollars.

**Figure 3-4.** *Iran's Exports by Country or Region of Destination, Various Years*

### Iran's Exports by Country or Region, 1978[a]

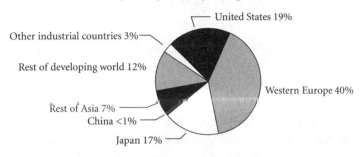

United States 19%

Other industrial countries 3%

Rest of developing world 12%

Rest of Asia 7%

China <1%

Japan 17%

Western Europe 40%

### Iran's Exports by Country or Region, 1986[b]

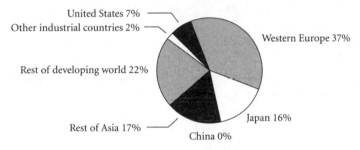

United States 7%

Other industrial countries 2%

Rest of developing world 22%

Rest of Asia 17%

China 0%

Western Europe 37%

Japan 16%

### Iran's Exports by Country or Region, 2001[c]

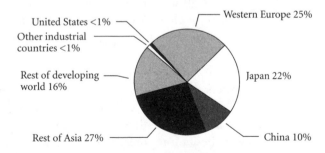

United States <1%

Other industrial countries <1%

Rest of developing world 16%

Rest of Asia 27%

Western Europe 25%

Japan 22%

China 10%

Source: International Monetary Fund, *Direction of Trade Statistics Yearbook,* 1984 and 1993, and *Direction of Trade Statistics Quarterly,* June 2002.

a. U.S. and other country imports. Total exports = $22.358 billion, 1978 dollars.

b. U.S. and other country imports, the year before the U.S. import ban. Total exports = $8.019 billion, 1986 dollars.

c. U.S. and other country imports. Total exports = $25.796 billion, 2001 dollars.

over the objections of the United States, to resume lending to Iran in May 2000.[105]

Of greater significance than the dollar amounts directly lost by Iran was the influence of sanctions and U.S. pressure in limiting Iran's options when the country was faced with debt crises at two junctures in the 1990s. Most countries would have sought assistance from international institutions when confronted with an external shock such as the debt crisis triggered by Iran's short-term borrowing; other oil-producing countries in similar situations have secured Contingency and Compensatory Financing Facility (CCFF) assistance from the International Monetary Fund (IMF).[106] However, sanctions and U.S. pressure precluded that option for Iran.[107] Instead, Iran was forced to implement acute austerity measures in order to meet the new terms of its debt agreements, even with the bilateral assistance it was able to cobble together from its individual county creditors.

How the "success" of sanctions in forcing this adjustment is evaluated over the longer term is still to be seen.[108] Unquestionably, the measures taken by Iran resulted in serious short- and medium-term economic costs. As described earlier, Iran paid a price in growth as a result of the import compression policies it was forced to implement for much of the 1990s. Yet, in an unexpected way, bearing these costs was to Iran's benefit. Had Iran been able to secure additional financing to ease its debt crisis until oil prices improved, it is possible—even likely—that Iran would have continued to amass debt well beyond the level that its economy could responsibly service. Removing that option—and forcing the country to engage in painful financial restructuring—greatly improved Iran's long-term economic prospects. In 2001, after years of austerity, Iran boasted the lowest debt/GNP ratio of any country in the region and of all but two other states in the developing world, making it well-situated to embark on a program of further economic reform.[109] Perhaps ironically, sanctions and American pressure could well deserve credit for forcing Iran to adopt much-needed fiscal prudence.

The impact of sanctions and American pressure on the extension of bilateral trade credits to Iran was smaller and more difficult to gauge than the impact on multilateral lending. Over the course of the 1990s, European export credit agencies were hesitant to offer Iran much credit for the purpose of providing insurance cover for exports to Iran. This reluctance cannot be directly attributed to U.S. sanctions, although some of these institutions do take the existence of U.S. sanctions into account in their risk assessments. On the whole, decisions to extend bilateral trade credits to Iran were more a response to Iran's overall economic prospects and its broader relations with western European and Asian countries than a reaction to certain U.S. policies. This hypothesis is supported by the fact that new trade credits to Iran expanded from a trickle to a stream once Iran's financial situation improved in 2000.[110]

Sanctions also influenced investment in Iran. Although sanctions were plainly unable to stop the flow of investment into Iran, they were an effective bar on U.S. investment in Iran in general and American involvement in the Iranian energy industry in particular. Since Conoco relinquished its contract to develop Iran's Sirri fields in 1995, no American company has been able to bid on any tender of the National Iranian Oil Company (NIOC). This bar on U.S. involvement played a modest role in forcing NIOC to offer increasingly attractive contracts to foreign firms in the late 1990s.[111] By reducing the number of large companies vying for Iranian contracts, sanctions reduced the leverage that NIOC had with other foreign firms interested in investing in Iran.[112]

Although sanctions unquestionably shaped the *composition* of foreign investment in Iran, the more critical issue is whether they influenced the overall *volume* of foreign investment.[113] Iran's oil industry continued to chafe under domestic production constraints throughout the 1990s and beyond, as suggested by the country's constant position as a price hawk in OPEC meetings and its inability to meet OPEC quota hikes in 2000.[114] Projections made in the mid-1990s of how much production capacity Iran would have at the turn of the millennium remained unfulfilled; in 2000, Iran produced approximately 300,000 barrels a day *less* oil than it had anticipated. What is open to question is to what extent U.S. sanctions played a role in stymieing the industry. Did sanctions keep non-U.S. foreign firms from investing in Iran's energy sector and developing its production capabilities? If so, what was the consequence for Iran's revenue flows?

Attributing the entirety of Iran's shortfall in production to any one factor would be too simplistic. The neglect suffered by Iran's oil fields in the wake of the revolution and during the Iran-Iraq war still affects the industry today.[115] Of equal importance in explaining the shortfall is Iran's investment climate. Iran only gradually opened itself to foreign investment in its energy industry. In a slow and tortured process, Iran progressively reinterpreted its constitution to permit greater foreign participation in its economy, including the extension of "buy-back" deals in which foreign companies investing in Iran would be repaid for their work in crude oil.[116] Over time, NIOC sweetened the initially unattractive deals it offered to foreign investors as it became more sophisticated and comfortable in dealing with them. Nevertheless, despite numerous tenders and drawn-out bidding con-sultations, the pace at which deals were closed between Iran and its foreign investors was surprisingly slow.[117] Those delays, however, cannot be attrib-uted to external factors either; they are instead largely the result of Iranian obstacles and deterrents. Not only were the buy-back contracts that Iran offered less commercially appealing than other forms of investment, they also became increasingly politicized, making foreign investors even more wary of them.[118] The uncertain standing of foreign investment in Iran's legal system and ambiguities in legislation governing foreign investment also hindered the closing of deals.[119]

Despite the importance of these internal factors, sanctions did have some influence on the development of Iran's production capabilities; however, sanctions delayed development more than they prevented it. Unilateral U.S. sanctions had little influence on the behavior of foreign firms eager to gain access to Iran's oil fields, as was demonstrated by Total's quick embrace of the deal that Conoco was forced to relinquish. In contrast, ILSA and the secondary sanctions it mandated did initially have a chilling effect on flows of foreign investment into Iran. From mid-1995 through 1996—the period that ILSA was being crafted in the U.S. Congress, amid much fanfare and international publicity—NIOC offered eleven projects to potential foreign investors in an opening of the Iranian oil industry unprecedented since the revolution.[120] Not one of those deals had been signed by the time ILSA became law in August 1996, despite Iran's reported willingness to improve the terms of its initial offerings.[121] Foreign enthusiasm for investment in Iran remained at lower-than-expected levels for the rest of 1996 and 1997. Iran's investment climate certainly accounted for some of the hesitance of foreign firms to close deals, thereby substantially reducing their costs of complying with ILSA.[122] But companies—particularly those with large busi-ness interests in the United States—also were reluctant to expose themselves to American penalties once the passage of ILSA became imminent.[123]

The deterrent value of ILSA virtually collapsed after May 1998, when—prodded by Congress to reach a decision about whether ILSA should be invoked for recent foreign investments—the Clinton administration issued the first waiver to a company violating the terms of the American law and promised additional waivers for similar investments by European compa-nies.[124] No longer frightened by the threat of sanctions and more and more enticed by the increasingly attractive deals offered by NIOC, foreign firms signed contracts worth billions of dollars to develop various Iranian oil fields after the 1998 waiver.[125] As Iran secures more foreign investment in its energy sector, it will gradually close the gap between its actual production and its anticipated or desired production, thereby diminishing and eventually annulling the effect of ILSA over time.[126]

However, even if only by delaying the development of Iranian oil fields, ILSA did impose a real, if finite, cost on Iran. Had Iran offered more attractive deals and foreign firms signed more contracts during the 1995–98 period, Iran's production would have been higher in the late 1990s and early 2000s. The country then would have been in a better position to benefit from the rebounding price of oil in the late 1990s. Instead, ILSA helped slow the already sluggish process of dealmaking and contributed to the handcuffing of Iran's production capability over this period, ultimately keeping Iran from fully benefiting from surging oil prices at the end of the decade.[127]

Finally, sanctions and U.S. pressure more generally also harmed Iran's economic interests in the Caspian region. Due to its geographic location, Iran stands to be a major player in the development and transport of the substantial energy resources in the Caspian and Central Asia.[128] Yet together, the two prongs of U.S. policy—support for the Baku-Ceyhan pipeline and the continued threat of sanctions against foreign companies developing Iran's pipelines—slowed the development of Caspian resources and stifled Iranian economic influence in the region.[129] In contrast to the fecklessness of ILSA in stopping foreign investment in offshore Gulf and onshore Iranian oil fields after 1998, the threat of secondary sanctions continued to provide a deterrent to firms that might have otherwise been willing to help Iran expand its Caspian ports, link its domestic transport system to the rest of the region, and complete construction of a pipeline from Iran to Turkey. Moreover, by inhibiting oil swaps by U.S. firms, U.S. policy curbed the integration of Iran into the region to its north and prevented Iran from establishing itself as a primary transport corridor for regional energy supplies.[130]

### Political Impact

The political impact of sanctions on Iran has been varied, but on the whole it has been more detrimental than conducive to the pursuit of U.S. interests in Iran. U.S. sanctions did not formalize Iran's status as an international pariah; in contrast, during the late 1990s Iran mended many relationships with its neighbors and the broader international community.[131] Yet despite failing to halt Iran's rapprochement with many countries, U.S. sanctions did frustrate Iran's efforts to operate as a normal member of the international community. Repeated U.S. moves to exclude Iran from global institutions such as the World Trade Organization angered and humiliated Iran, a country that believes that it has a global leadership role to play.

Even more than influencing Iran's external environment, sanctions—as the most visible sign of American antagonism—played into domestic political conflicts within Iran. For decades, relations with the United States have been the "third rail" of domestic Iranian politics.[132] No individual or faction can advocate compromise or even dialogue with the United States without opening itself to fierce criticism from its political competitors and thereby creating a real risk to its own domestic viability. Although relations with the United States may have taken on this domestic importance even in the absence of sanctions, these measures exacerbated the situation by providing a strong nationalist rationale for opposing dialogue and unifying an otherwise fractious political elite. Some Iranian politicians and clerics—fearful that improved relations with America could undermine their power—have used sanctions as a barricade behind which they can fend off openings from the United States. "No official dialogue until sanctions are lifted" has become a convenient rhetorical mantra from which almost no Iranian leader—including Khatami—has been willing or able to separate himself.[133] As a result, the concrete nature of sanctions dampened the prospects of a gradual rapprochement with the United States that could have served U.S. interests, a rapprochement that might have been less visible, less controversial, and less subject to appropriation by one side of the political debate in Iran.

In this domestic struggle, sanctions strengthened the hand of conservative elements of society relative to that of those more in favor of reform. Sanctions provided an excuse for the failures of the Iranian economy, deflecting the need for serious economic changes, which would threaten the interests of conservative institutions and elements of society such as the powerful *bonyads* and *bazaaris*.[134] Moreover, sanctions weakened Iranian moderates and pragmatists in the 1990s by discrediting their tentative efforts to bridge the distance between Iran and the United States. From the Iranian perspective, gestures made by both President Rafsanjani and President Khatami were rebuffed with sanctions. The United States responded to Rafsanjani's landmark offer of Iran's first major foreign oil contract to an American firm with the imposition of sanctions; similarly, in the eyes of many Iranians, Khatami's call for a dialogue of civilizations in his 1998 CNN interview was met with continued economic penalties.[135] Although, overall, the weaknesses of the reform movement in Iran are much more attributable to domestic factors, sanctions added to the challenges faced by reformers rather than eased them.

### Goals Achieved

Evaluating the achievements of U.S. sanctions on Iran is complicated by the numerous goals pursued through their use. Analyzing the extent to which each goal was realized is critical. Given that positive developments in Iran cannot automatically be attributed to the influence of U.S. sanctions, it is equally important to assess whether and to what extent sanctions contributed to bringing about any desired change.

CHANGING, WEAKENING, OR CONTAINING THE REGIME. The extent and intensity of American opposition to the regime in Iran is not simple to characterize. Certainly, at any time since the revolution, the U.S. government would have been pleased to see the end of the Islamic regime in Tehran. Some members of Congress even proposed advancing funds to destabilize or overthrow the government.[136] Nevertheless, regime change was never an explicit goal of sanctions throughout the 1980s, 1990s, and the early 2000s. Neither the executive orders imposing sanctions on Iran—nor the statements of U.S. officials defending them—discuss overthrowing the regime in Tehran or the hope for its downfall. Even the earliest pronouncements of the dual containment policy to isolate and pressure Iran and Iraq simultaneously declared that "normal relations with Iran are conceivable" and that "the Clinton administration is not opposed to Islamic government in Iran."[137]

Both the executive branch and Congress did hold a firm and explicit commitment to the aggressive isolation and containment of the Islamic regime. Throughout much of the 1990s, senior U.S. officials emphasized the importance of containing Iran through unilateral policies and vigorous efforts to convince other countries to curtail their economic and military contacts with Iran.[138] The U.S. goal was clearly to weaken the regime, perhaps not with the explicit intention of facilitating its overthrow but certainly with the firm goal of hindering its development and rendering it less capable of pursuing objectionable behavior and jeopardizing peace pursuits in the Middle East.

Over this period, striking developments did occur in Iran's domestic politics. The regime did not change in the sense of revolution or by shedding its Islamic nature. But—reflecting Iranians' desire for change—new, more moderate elements emerged in the power structure and took control of certain institutions, such as the presidency and the Majlis. Broadly speaking, these developments boded well for U.S. interests. Nevertheless, claiming them to be a victory for sanctions would be premature, for two reasons. First, continued instability in domestic Iranian politics calls into question the real significance of these changes for curbing the extremes of the regime.[139] Second, if American sanctions, or U.S. pressure more generally, did play any role in spurring this course of events, it was extremely small. Rather than being a reaction to sanctions, domestic political changes in Iran reflected internal dissatisfaction with the evolution of the Iranian revolution and a growing desire for modernization, although perhaps not along western lines.

The record of sanctions in achieving the narrower goal of depriving the regime of resources to pursue its agenda is more mixed. As discussed in detail in the preceding section, sanctions clearly had some impact on Iran's economy, particularly in the early years before Iran adjusted to the sanctions and while its economy was struggling due to factors independent of sanctions. During those initial years, sanctions reinforced negative economic trends, creating additional problems for Iran when it faced mounting debt or had difficulty attracting foreign investors because of the poor investment terms it offered to them. Moreover, sanctions did effectively curtail the flow of U.S. investment to and trade with Iran and forced Iran to pay some limited costs in the process. Those achievements, however, affected Iran's economic fortunes only on the margins. The economic impact of sanctions overall fell far short of that necessary to effect any sort of economic containment of Iran and amounted to no more than a mere ripple in the tidal wave of other influences, particularly fluctuations in the price of oil.

The military containment of Iran, in contrast, was much more notable, although not entirely—or even largely—due to U.S. sanctions. Trends in Iran's purchases of weapons from foreign sources over the 1990s suggest the influence of both sanctions and other factors. The severance of the military relationship between Iran and the United States did terminate military sales and assistance to Iran, which had been worth billions of dollars over the last half of the 1970s (figure 3-5). Several factors, however, make it difficult to attribute those losses directly to sanctions. First, even in the absence of formal sanctions, the military relationship between the two countries would have deteriorated greatly in the wake of the revolution and the emergence of an anti-American government in Tehran. In fact, no statutory ban on sales of military equipment to Iran formally existed until 1986, although a prohibition on sales was adhered to as a matter of broad U.S. policy.[140] Second, even if the United States had remained willing to sell arms to Iran in the

**Figure 3-5.** *U.S. Military Sales and Assistance to Iran, 1950–2000*

Billions of U.S. dollars

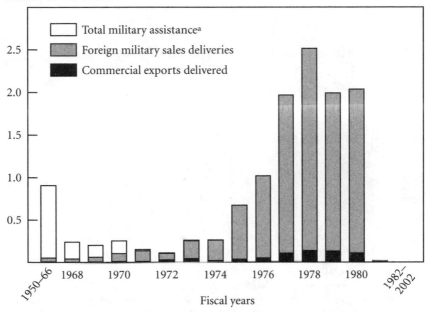

Fiscal years

Source: Defense Security and Cooperation Agency, *Facts Book*, various years.

a. The total military assistance category consists of the Foreign Military Finance Program, Military Assistance Program agreements, IMET, and excess defense articles. Excess defense articles are pieces of military equipment that the U.S. military no longer needs and offers for sale to foreign countries at reduced or no cost. The receiving country is responsible for the costs of shipping and restoring equipment if necessary.

1990s, the country's policy of cutting imports would have nonetheless led to some decline in its purchases of military items.

Similarly, the reduction in Iran's procurement of weapons from non-U.S. sources over the 1990s has its roots in several factors (figure 3-6). The steady decline in new arms agreements between Iran and countries subject to U.S. pressure over the decade suggests the success of U.S. diplomacy and the sanctions that underpinned it. Certainly, the U.S.-EU dialogues on this issue deserve some credit for limiting Iranian conventional weapons capabilities over that period. At the same time, it is feasible that the Antiterrorism and Effective Death Penalty Act, by threatening to cut off aid to countries selling arms to states on the U.S. terrorism list, also prevented some major weapons sales to Iran.[141] The waning Russian military sales to Iran through the second

**Figure 3-6.** *Iranian Arms Buys by Supplier, 1987–99*

Billions of U.S. dollars

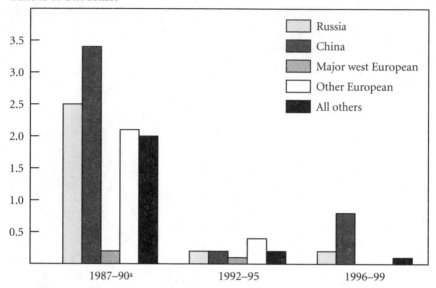

Source:  Richard Grimmett, *Conventional Arms Transfers to Developing Nations, 1987–95* (Congressional Research Service, August 4, 1995, p. 57), for 1987–90 numbers; and Anthony H. Cordesman, *The Gulf in Transition: U.S. Policy Ten Years after the Gulf War, The Challenge of Iran* (CSIS, October 30, 2000, p. 37), for all others.

a. Iranian arms procurements during this period were inflated, because of Iranian ambitions to rearm after the Iran-Iraq war ended in 1988.

half of the decade—as well as Moscow's 2001 announcement that Russia would begin selling conventional arms to Iran—suggest that the Gore-Chernomyrdin agreement did limit Russian military sales while it was in effect from 1995 to 2000.[142]

Other factors also played a role in shaping Iran's procurement patterns, as is suggested by the fact that countries more resistant (but not immune) to U.S. pressure, such as China and North Korea, did not fully assume the weapons contracts with Iran that other countries forwent. Iran tempered its ambitions to acquire conventional weapons in light of the taming of Iraq's military capabilities under UN sanctions. Moreover, Iran may have decided to focus its procurement efforts on weapons of mass destruction, rather than conventional items, in the wake of Iraq's use of chemical weapons during the Iran-Iraq war.[143] Also of consequence were Iran's domestic financial

**Figure 3-7. *Iranian Defense Expenditures***

Billions of current U.S. dollars

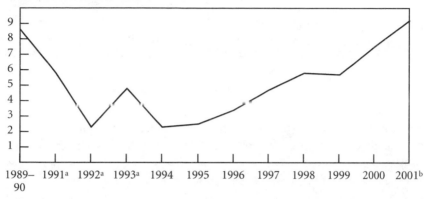

1989–   1991[a]   1992[a]   1993[a]   1994   1995   1996   1997   1998   1999   2000   2001[b]
90

Source: International Institute for Strategic Studies, *The Military Balance,* various years.
a. International Institute for Strategic Studies estimate.
b. Budgeted.

problems and its need to service its debt throughout most of the 1990s. The upsurge in Iranian military spending and military imports at the turn of the millennium—as Iran's debt diminished and its external balances improved—supports the hypothesis that domestic economic factors played a large role in shaping Iranian procurement patterns (figure 3-7).

MODERATING THE BEHAVIOR OF THE REGIME. Moderating specific egregious Iranian behaviors has long been the explicit focus of U.S. policy and the rationale for sanctions. U.S. officials have continually criticized Iran for its efforts to acquire weapons of mass destruction, its support for international terrorism, and its opposition to Israel and efforts to make peace in the Middle East. Congress and the sizable Iranian-American community have also repeatedly voiced concern over human rights in Iran. In the past, this list of grievances also included attempts by Iran to dominate the Gulf and subvert Arab governments in the region.[144]

Originally, Clinton administration officials pointed to these actions largely to justify their efforts to curb resources flowing to Iran but voiced little hope for real behavior changes from Tehran. For instance, a 1994 article by Anthony Lake called for Iran to demonstrate "its willingness to abide by international norms and abandon policies and actions inimical to regional peace and stability"; at the same time, Lake grouped Iran into the category of countries he described as "exhibit[ing] a chronic inability to engage constructively with the outside world."[145] Later in the decade, particularly after Khatami became president in 1997, the United States began to place a greater emphasis on tangible changes in Iranian behavior as a prerequisite not for dialogue but for the lifting of sanctions.[146] Yet despite this shift toward a more earnest pursuit of Iranian behavior changes, Iran has made few significant modifications to its problematic behavior.

Iranian attitudes toward Israel and the Middle East peace process have not changed substantially. To the extent that they have fluctuated, it has been more in relation to the status of the Middle East peace process than any other factor. While the peace process appeared to be bearing fruit and commanded the support of most countries in the region, segments of the Iranian regime tempered their rhetoric against Israel.[147] Although denouncing the entire peace process as being fundamentally flawed, then-President Rafsanjani declared in 1995 that Iran would not stand in the way of peace between Syria and Israel or even the Palestinians and Israel.[148] Similarly, in his much-heralded CNN interview in January 1998, President Khatami distanced himself from the use of terrorism as a tool of international politics when he declared, "Any form of killing of innocent men and women who are not involved in confrontations is terrorism. It must be condemned, and we, in our turn, condemn every form of it in the world."[149] Although this more moderate rhetoric was welcome, there was little evidence that it was matched by a significant withdrawal of funding and material support for radical groups opposing Israel or promoting the use of international terrorism more broadly.[150]

Even these largely cosmetic signs of moderation disappeared once the peace process collapsed in 2000 and a new uprising began in Palestinian areas of the West Bank and Gaza. Iran then sharpened its statements and reenergized its actions against Israel. At least at the rhetorical level, these efforts encompassed all elements of the Iranian government, not just perceived hard-liners. President Khatami himself met with groups targeting Israeli citizens and called for an economic boycott of Israel and full support for the Palestinian uprising.[151] In April 2001, Tehran sponsored an international conference to support the intifada, bringing together representatives of Arab and Muslim countries with the leaders of violent anti-Israel groups in the hopes of forming a more coordinated campaign against Israel.[152] Iran's Revolutionary Guard Corps and the Ministry of Intelligence and Security reportedly increased their support to groups such as Hizbullah, Hamas, the Palestinian Islamic Jihad, and Ahmad Jabril's Popular Front for the Liberation of Palestine–General Command (PFLP-GC).[153] The January

2002 Karine A incident, which involved the shipment of fifty tons of arms from Iran to the Palestinian Authority, further alarmed U.S. officials. These ongoing links and activities—as well as continued suspicions of Iranian involvement in the bombing of the Khobar Towers—spurred the U.S. government to rank Iran as the most active state sponsor of terrorism in the world.[154]

In contrast to its persistent and intensifying support for anti-Israel groups, Iran did reduce its state-sponsored violent activities in Europe and in the southern Gulf states over the 1990s. Its curtailment of assassinations of dissidents in Europe and its decline in support for radical groups in neighboring countries occurred in the context of the greatly improved relations between Iran and much of the rest of the world.[155] Since Khatami took office, Iran hosted the Organization of the Islamic Conference in Tehran, mended relations with the Gulf states of Kuwait, Qatar, and Bahrain, and even established a security pact with its longtime adversary, Saudi Arabia.[156] In Europe, Iran's rehabilitation was no less significant, with even Britain restoring full diplomatic relations with Iran in September 1998 after the resolution of the Rushdie affair.[157]

This selected departure from support for terrorism and regional extremism cannot, however, be attributed to U.S. sanctions; it is much more an outgrowth of internal changes in Iran.[158] In part, this moderation is a manifestation of the mellowing of the regime, a gradual shift away from promoting Islamic extremism to a more pragmatic nationalism emphasizing domestic development over revolution abroad. Although this evolution accelerated under Khatami, it was under way before he came into office. The labored opening of certain sectors of the Iranian economy to foreign investment that occurred under Rafsanjani was an admission that Iran needed outside help to develop; the gradual and partial moderation of Iran's external behavior that followed suggested Iran's realization of the need to curtail its actions in Europe if it expected investment to continue, debt restructuring to be granted when needed, and trade to flourish. In particular, the Mykonos trial—which found Iranian officials guilty of orchestrating assassinations in Berlin and caused Europe to recall its ambassadors in protest—heightened the Iranian perception that continued engagement with Europe was contingent on improved international behavior.[159] Similarly, Iran recognized that the promotion of radical groups in neighboring countries further destabilized the region, dampening Iran's own economic prospects and appeal and diverting attention from its own internal challenges.

Regarding weapons proliferation, U.S. sanctions were part of a larger international framework addressing Iran's pursuit of weapons of mass destruction. This framework was unable to curb Iranian *ambitions*. Iran claims that its nuclear efforts are geared toward the legitimate development of a civilian nuclear program and are necessary because of Iran's growing energy needs and diminishing oil reserves. Yet Iran's long and continuous record of seeking nuclear-related equipment and technical expertise and its clandestine efforts to acquire fissile material and other items unnecessary for the peaceful use of nuclear energy point to an active program to acquire nuclear weapons.[160] Sanctions and the larger framework in which they were situated also did not sway Iran from its endeavors regarding non-nuclear weapons of mass destruction (WMD). Iran reportedly maintains one of the largest active chemical weapons programs in the developing world, despite being one of the original signatories to the Chemical Weapons Convention.[161] Iran has also continued its vigorous efforts to build a strategic ballistic missile force and to become self-sufficient in missile production.[162] Although the exact state of Iran's WMD capability is uncertain, the trend over the period during which U.S. sanctions were in place was toward expansion and consolidation of these programs, not their elimination.[163]

Sanctions—in conjunction with international export controls and U.S. diplomacy—can, however, claim some success in frustrating the *realization* of Iran's WMD aspirations by limiting the range of suppliers willing to provide needed material and technology to Iran. Associations enforcing broad export controls—such as the London Suppliers Group—kept many western nuclear technologies away from Iran. The influence of such organizations was complemented by U.S. efforts to convince and cajole Germany, France, and to a lesser extent China to terminate or curtail their transfer of nuclear technology to Iran. The threat of U.S. secondary sanctions against firms transferring any WMD material or technology—made real when the United States sanctioned Russian and Chinese entities providing controlled technologies to Iran—reinforced U.S. diplomatic efforts to frustrate Iran's pursuits.

Success in narrowing the roster of countries and companies selling sensitive material and technology to Iran is, however, not the same as stopping such sales. Iran was able to continue its WMD endeavors with the help of a few key partners. On the nuclear front, Russia remains involved in the construction of Iran's Bushehr reactors, which the United States is concerned provides a cover for Russian nuclear scientists to work in Iran and supply the country with technology and expertise needed to develop nuclear weapons.[164] Similarly, Russian, Chinese, and North Korean assistance continues to be vital in Iran's non-nuclear WMD programs, particularly in the ballistic missile realm.[165]

Finally, sanctions appear to have had little effect on widespread human rights abuses in Iran.[166] Iran's volatile domestic politics make it difficult to point to a singular trend in the human rights situation within Iran. Under Khatami, Iranians enjoy more personal freedom, relatively greater opportunities for public expression and debate, and a society that more closely adheres to the rule of law. The culture of impunity that once existed in Iran has been challenged, as suggested by the trial of individuals held responsible for orchestrating assassinations of political liberals and dissident writers.[167] Yet, as discussed elsewhere, Iran's intensifying internal power struggle has resulted in sporadic crackdowns on the press and the repression of political dissent by conservative elements of the regime.[168] Human rights issues that touch less directly on the domestic political struggle in Iran—such as religious persecution, torture, and unlawful imprisonment—also were subject to both improvements and setbacks over the past decade.[169]

### Costs Borne

HUMANITARIAN COSTS. Iran has made significant improvements in the conditions under which its citizens live since the end of the Iran-Iraq war. Changes in human indicators over the 1990s reveal upward trends in education, health, and basic services. Infant and maternal mortality declined significantly, immunizations and access to sanitation and health services improved, and more young Iranians, particularly girls, gained access to education. These overall positive trends disguise the drain caused by economic turbulence, economic mismanagement, and the emigration of many educated Iranians—all exacerbated by sanctions, but not entirely or even largely caused by them—on Iran's efforts to promote human development and sustain public services. But they do confirm that the overall humanitarian picture in Iran is a relatively positive one.

Looking beyond basic health and human indicators to economic well-being reveals a deteriorating picture. Low economic growth and a rapidly increasing population over the 1980s and 1990s ensured that unemployment and underemployment are persistent features of Iran's economy.[170] Rapid inflation and efforts by the government to reduce the level of subsidization it provides to the population also have taken a large toll on the Iranian standard of living. A survey conducted by Iran's Central Statistics Organization concluded that, for the average Iranian, annual expenses in the late 1990s rose tenfold higher than increases in yearly income.[171]

The hardships borne by Iranians are a reflection of Iran's overall economic problems of the past decades, which have been only in the most minor sense due to U.S. sanctions. To the extent that it is possible to make a connection between rising inflation and sanctions, some causality between sanctions and the humanitarian situation can be claimed. For instance, in April 1995, the widely held belief that the United States would impose sanctions on Iran in the near future seriously undermined Iran's currency, the rial, causing its free market value to plummet dramatically from around 900 rials to the dollar to 7,000 rials to the dollar by the end of the month.[172] The Iranian government responded to this crisis by imposing harsh restrictions on foreign exchange and reinforcing artificial exchange rates. Both these measures only perpetuated the crisis by locking Iran into a costly spiral fueled by foreign exchange shortages, further pushing up inflation (figure 3-8). Although genuine, the impact of sanctions on the exchange rate and levels of inflation was relatively short-lived, soon being overpowered by the influence of other economic variables.[173] Variation in the rate of inflation since mid-1995 suggests that the connection among sanctions, inflation, and declining living standards is only partial at best.

COSTS TO THE UNITED STATES. U.S. sanctions affected a variety of American interests, quite apart from their influence on Iran's economy and society. For instance, sanctions had a small negative impact on the U.S. energy situation.[174] Sanctions on Iran did hinder the United States from diversifying the foreign sources of its oil and, by preventing U.S. firms from operating in Iran, deprived the United States of more complete knowledge of the state of Iran's energy industry and the global energy market. Moreover, as discussed earlier in the chapter, ILSA did delay the development of Iran's production capability for a short period, with some negative repercussions for the worldwide supply of oil. Although Iran will develop its lost capacity over time, thereby annulling the effect of ILSA, the extra capacity that Iran could have brought to the global oil market in 1999 and 2000 in the absence of ILSA might have had a dampening effect on oil prices during those years, all else being equal. This extra capacity would have reduced the vulnerability that the United States and other countries experienced during that time (given the very limited spare capacity then available in oil-producing countries) and thereby bolstered their ability to withstand other shocks and supply disruptions.[175] Apart from these few short-term effects, there is little evidence that sanctions have greatly hampered the development of Iranian oil and gas fields and therefore significantly damaged global oil markets and the U.S. economy.

**Figure 3-8.** *Inflation in Iran, 1992–2001*

Percentage

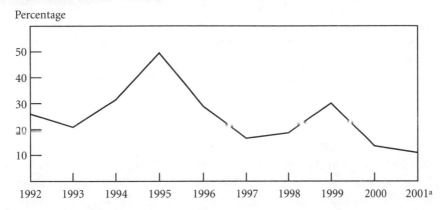

Source: Economist Intelligence Unit, *Country Profile: Iran,* 1998–99; *Country Report: Iran* (First Quarter 1999), p. 9; and *Country Report: Iran,* June 2002.
a. Economist Intelligence Unit estimate.

Broader U.S. economic interests also suffered as a result of the sanctions on Iran.[176] Of those losses, the costs of lost trade are the least consequential. Not only did the small levels of trade between the United States and Iran minimize the costs of the embargo, but U.S. exporters and importers, like those in Iran, adjusted to the imposition of trade sanctions by finding new markets for their goods. For the most part, these adjustments occurred without great cost, except in a few cases where large contracts held by American companies were terminated due to U.S. concerns over the potential military application of some civilian goods.[177] Once these adjustments are taken into account, direct losses to U.S. firms are only a fraction of the nearly $2 billion of sales that U.S. companies would have made to Iran from mid-1995 to 2001 in the absence of sanctions (appendix table 3A-2).[178]

In contrast to the minor costs of trade sanctions, the 1995 executive orders barring the involvement of any U.S. firm in Iran entailed more substantial economic losses for American firms. Although U.S. oil companies operating in Iran did not hold any fixed assets in the country at the time sanctions were imposed, the investment ban involved some less tangible losses.[179] Companies responsible for lifting and marketing nearly one-fifth of Iranian crude oil in 1995 suffered short-term costs of adjustment and lost a stream of profits that could have amounted to approximately $2 billion from 1995 to 2000 (appendix table 3A-3).[180] Of even greater significance were the investment opportunities lost to American firms as Iran began to open its energy industry and other sectors to foreign investment. As discussed elsewhere, over the last half of the 1990s Iran tendered approximately $50 billion in contracts, signing contracts with non-U.S. firms valued at $12 billion in the oil and gas industry alone.[181] What proportion of these deals would have gone to U.S. firms had they been permitted to compete with their foreign counterparts is impossible to know.[182] However, one can surmise that the costs of excluding U.S. oil companies from Iran was substantial and stands to rise even further if non-U.S. foreign firms begin to develop Iranian resources in the Caspian.

Sanctions also affected U.S. political interests in a variety of ways, most of them negative. On the whole, the sanctions-dominated approach adopted by the United States was detrimental to regional stability. Although sanctions played a role in slowing Iranian efforts to acquire weapons of mass destruction and build greater conventional capabilities, they also helped ensure a continuously hostile relationship between Iran and the United States and essentially forced the United States to forfeit the opportunity to manage the possible emergence of Iran as a nuclear power. Moreover, the U.S. policy of dual containment—by perpetuating confrontation with two major powers in the region—helped preclude the emergence of a more peaceful and stable arrangement that could have served America's regional strategic interests at lower financial and diplomatic costs.[183] Looking northward, U.S. efforts to isolate Iran also endangered the stability of Caspian and Central Asia states.[184] These countries would have benefited from the development and use of alternative energy routes out of the region that would have been explored in the absence of both sanctions and U.S. support for the Baku-Ceyhan pipeline.[185] Instead of nurturing the growth that was critical for political stability in this region, U.S. policy inadvertently increased the reliance of these countries on Russia for the export of their resources and helped shore up their authoritarian leaders.[186]

A further political cost associated with U.S. sanctions on Iran was the tension these measures created in U.S. relations with other countries. For much of the 1980s and 1990s, the United States relentlessly lobbied its friends and allies to adopt stricter measures against the Iranian regime. As discussed earlier, although these efforts met only with limited success, they were generally regarded as an American prerogative, particularly once Washington demonstrated that it was willing to bear economic costs to promote its political agenda. Europe, however, reacted to the 1996 passage of ILSA with indignation and outrage, seeing it as an unacceptable recourse to economic coercion to achieve what diplomatic pressure failed to produce.

In the eyes of many countries, ILSA and the secondary sanctions it mandates violate international law and contravene the membership rules the United States agreed to when joining the World Trade Organization. By issuing and promising waivers to companies violating the terms of ILSA, the United States was able to sidestep a trade war with Europe. But the renewal of ILSA and continued large-scale European investments in Iran's energy sector suggest that ILSA could pose an ongoing threat to U.S.-European relations. Even if the United States and Europe are able to avoid further confrontations over ILSA, this episode will not have been free of cost. ILSA, and its efforts to force U.S. allies to comply with laws against their judgment and their will, at least temporarily, estranged America from countries whose cooperation was essential to preserving U.S. interests not only in Iran, but in the world more broadly.

Standing in contrast to these political costs are the real and alleged political benefits that sanctions delivered to the United States. Some argue that the threat of sanctions under ILSA catalyzed further European cooperation on proliferation issues.[187] In fact, when issuing the first "national security" ILSA waiver for Total, the Clinton administration made such claims.[188] Yet, it is likely that Secretary Albright noted a vague standard of increased European cooperation more to justify the waiver than as testimony to the power of ILSA. U.S. diplomats deeply involved in discussions with Europeans over Iran report not only that their progress was well established *before* ILSA was enacted, but also that the bill actually complicated their conversations with Europeans about Iran instead of providing additional leverage.[189] ILSA could have catalyzed greater European cooperation had it extended more reasonable prospects for securing a "country waiver" that would exempt all firms from a given country from sanctions on the basis of that nation's improved cooperation with the United States. However, the ILSA legislation specified that such a waiver could be granted only if the country in question imposed economic sanctions on Iran, making it unlikely that any European country would meet the standard.

Although the political benefits of sanctions did not outweigh their costs, sanctions did deliver some real political benefits to policymakers and politicians who supported their use. Because the legislative agenda toward Iran was largely driven by groups interested in marginalizing and punishing the country, members of Congress saw little reason not to support punitive measures. In the words of one congressional staffer, a vote for sanctions against Iran was a "no-brainer"—a decision viewed as having political benefits and little, if any, downside.[190] Such thinking explains the unanimous passage of ILSA in 1996, as well as the overwhelming support for its renewal in 2001, despite widespread skepticism about its value. For the most part, the sanctions-dominated approach was popular with the American public, whose perception of Iran remained heavily influenced by the hostage crisis of more than two decades earlier.[191]

## Explaining the Record of Sanctions on Iran

As explored in detail above, sanctions on Iran did have a notable impact—more through restrictions on external finance and investment than through limitations on trade—but were neither effective nor useful. They achieved some goals, such as helping slow Iran's weapons procurement and development and prevented Iran from pursuing objectionable behavior with the proceeds of commercial interaction with the United States. But overall, the accomplishments of sanctions were slim, particularly when matched against the ambitious objectives sought by policymakers. Sanctions did not significantly weaken or contain the regime and were almost entirely unsuccessful in changing the behavior of the Iranian government in regard to the pursuit of weapons of mass destruction, opposition to efforts to bring peace to the Middle East, support for international terrorism, or violations of human rights. Although some political developments in Iran in the 1990s bode well for U.S. interests, there is little evidence that U.S. sanctions had any real role in spurring those changes. Worse yet, despite their ineffectiveness, the price tag sanctions carried was not insignificant; sanctions harmed U.S. interests in the energy, economic, and political realms.

### *Accounting for the Achievements and Disappointments of Sanctions*

The ineffectiveness of U.S. sanctions on Iran and their lack of utility are attributable both to their poor record in achieving results and to the significant costs associated with their use. Some analysts attribute the inability of sanctions to attain greater goals in Iran to their small economic influence. Other more sophisticated analyses ascribe it to the complex nature of Iranian domestic politics. Certainly, both elements were important parts of the full story. However, the role of other factors—including U.S. domestic politics, the largely unilateral nature of sanctions, and the failure of policymakers to sufficiently supplement sanctions with other policy tools—must also be acknowledged.

The sanctions regime, while intending to serve many objectives simulta-neously and over time, was not particularly well suited to pursue any of them. Sanctions had little hope of successfully containing Iran, mostly because of their unilateral nature. American efforts proved most successful in the military arena, where U.S. policymakers were able to attain some measure of multilateral cooperation. In this realm, sanctions took on an important function in underpinning the American position in U.S.-EU dis-cussions on topics of common concern, such as Iran's nuclear ambitions. Sanctions of a different sort helped secure an agreement to limit Russian sales of conventional weaponry to Iran in the later part of the 1990s. In this instance, a congressionally inspired law mandating secondary sanctions on Russian entities transferring weaponry to Iran provided the Clinton admin-istration with some leverage in its negotiations with Moscow.[192] Never-theless, because these multilateral measures encompassed only selected countries, they failed to fully choke off the flow of potentially dangerous military items to Iran.

More effective military containment of Iran might have been achieved had the United States been able to secure a UN arms embargo on the coun-try. A UN resolution to this effect would have given greater credibility and force to U.S. labors to crimp resources to Iran. Efforts to secure such a meas-ure, however, were never vigorously pursued, in large part because China and Russia—two of Iran's most important suppliers and permanent mem-bers of the UN Security Council—would not have agreed to an arms em-bargo in the absence of a clear threat to international security comparable with the one posed by Iraq in 1990. The United States might have also been more successful in the military containment of Iran had it convinced other countries to limit their commercial interaction with Iran, thereby truly impinging on the resources at Iran's disposal. As explored elsewhere in this chapter, the United States met with little success in such efforts, failing to get even its European allies on board given the robust economic links and strong historical ties between Europe and Iran.[193]

These realities surely complicated U.S. attempts to win European support for multilateral economic pressure on Iran, but they do not fully explain the failure of those efforts. As French willingness to support punitive measures against Iraq in the 1990s demonstrates, strong historical and economic ties between Europe and the Gulf need not automatically preclude Europe from backing more confrontational policies. Instead, the greatest hurdle to American efforts was the fact that Europe and much of the rest of the world did not perceive Iran to constitute the threat that the United States did. The United States was unable to alter the European view, at least in part because of its limited willingness to share intelligence with other countries. In the absence of a "smoking gun," Europe saw no reason to jeopardize its relationship with Iran and continued to pursue a conciliatory policy it viewed as more conducive to influencing Iranian behavior and more satisfying to its own interests. Not believing that Iran posed a real danger and delighting in signs of Iran's moderation under Khatami, Europe was perplexed by an American policy that seemed to harden as Iran appeared to liberalize. This paradox, in the eyes of many Europeans, was best explained by the powerful role of American domestic groups—AIPAC in particular—in influencing U.S. policy toward Iran.

Only the most optimistic observer could have hoped that U.S. efforts would persuade Europe to match American sanctions against Iran. U.S. sanctions, however, could have continued to complement American diplomatic attempts to work with Europe to apply pressure on Iran in selected areas of common concern. Yet rather than underpinning those efforts, U.S. sanctions policy frustrated them. The passage of ILSA and its threat to sanction European companies investing in Iran backfired. Instead of forging another path to multilateral pressure on Iran—albeit a confrontational one rather than one paved by consensus—ILSA made multilateral cooperation in regard to Iran more difficult to achieve because it incensed U.S. allies.

Another reason for the poor performance of the U.S. sanctions regime on Iran was that it was poorly suited to the goal of convincing Tehran to change its behavior on any of the fronts that the United States found objectionable. Most important, sanctions were not coupled with the use of other policy tools appropriate to the goal of behavior modification. For example, the dialogue necessary to guide even the most straightforward behavior change strategy was lacking. Not only was there no direct and frequent diplomatic contact through embassies, but Iran's unwillingness to speak with the United States precluded even the most occasional and low-level direct official contacts between the two countries. Without such routine channels of communication, any U.S. or Iranian effort to lay even the most tenuous groundwork for resolving outstanding issues was complicated and often misconstrued. The failure of U.S. officials to recognize the 1995 deal offered to Conoco as an officially sanctioned olive branch is only the most obvious example of such miscommunication.

Had there been a sustained dialogue between Iranian and U.S. officials, the complicated interplay between the executive branch and Congress over sanctioning Iran might have translated into some U.S. leverage with the Iranian regime. In the case of the renewal of most-favored-nation status for China under President George H. W. Bush in 1992, the combination of congressional pressure to suspend China's trade preferences and executive reluctance to do so led China to make some limited changes in its behavior before Congress voted.[194] A similar interplay might have occurred with Iran. Although both Congress and the Clinton administration were interested in imposing some sanctions on Iran, the administration was much less enthusiastic about the passage of ILSA when it was in the negotiating phases.[195] Although internal fissures in Iranian politics certainly would have complicated Iran's ability to deflate the impetus behind the U.S. legislation, a behind-the-scenes dialogue with the Clinton administration might have persuaded Iran to take certain steps that would have given the president a reason either for discouraging passage of the bill or for pushing harder to weaken it.[196]

Further exacerbating the inability of sanctions to function as a catalyst for Iranian behavior changes was the American rhetoric that accompanied sanctions' use. Rather than coupling sanctions with statements of how Iran could best meet the conditions for lifting the measures, the rhetoric employed by U.S. officials was almost uniformly hostile. Not only had Iran—along with other "backlash states"—been deemed "incapable of engaging with the outside world," but, in the lexicon of the Clinton administration, it was a "rogue state."[197] As a "rogue," Iran was presumed to be beyond rehabilitation; by definition, it was a country that violated international norms and contravened commonly accepted standards of international behavior. Not surprisingly, this rhetoric helped fuel American distrust of Iran and justified the pursuit of a missile defense, but it did nothing to encourage Iran to change its behavior.[198] Faced with comprehensive sanctions and acerbic rhetoric (and selected calls by members of Congress for its overthrow), the Iranian regime had little reason to assume that any modifications it made in its actions would be recognized by the United States or would result in any improvement in relations. The Iranian perception that the United States was unwilling to acknowledge Iran's past efforts to act in accord with U.S. desires—as during the Gulf war—further reinforced Iranian skepticism.

Perhaps the most important reason why sanctions failed to elicit any change in Iran's actions was that the stakes associated with the behavior in question were high and the costs of Iranian noncompliance with U.S. demands were low. Iranian pursuit of weapons of mass destruction, for instance, is rooted in an authentic sense of vulnerability and a history that includes Iraqi use of chemical weapons against Iran. Iran believes that its WMD programs are vital to its security, not only as a counterbalance to nuclear-armed Israel, but also in light of concerns over the ambitions of its neighbor to the west, Iraq, and the nuclear demonstrations of its neighbors to the east, Pakistan and India. Given the region in which Iran resides, the stakes in renouncing its pursuit of weapons of mass destruction are extremely high, unless other security arrangements are made to ensure its survival. Similarly, Iran's perception that being a leader of the Islamic world required it to support anti-Israel groups meant that the stakes in forgoing this activity also were considerable; the regime did not consider its opposition to the Middle East peace process to be extraneous to its existence. Because of the importance of these activities to Iran, the choice between ending them or enduring the comparatively small costs associated with U.S. sanctions has been an easy one.

Iran's domestic politics vastly complicated and further raised the stakes associated with any change of behavior. As discussed earlier, domestic politics made it extremely risky for any Iranian faction to be seen as responding to U.S. entreaties or demands.[199] The fear of Iranian politicians that their precarious domestic positions could be upset or endangered by contact with—or even by an insufficiently distant attitude toward—the United States made it particularly difficult for sanctions to achieve their goal of moderating Iranian behavior. Quite simply, Iran's domestic politics were too contentious to expect Khatami or other leaders to reevaluate Iranian actions in response to whatever incentive the lifting of sanctions provided. The Clinton administration may have inadvertently reinforced the paralysis of reform-minded politicians by crafting its overtures as a direct response to their political victories. Rather than strengthening them as hoped, in all likelihood such moves made Khatami's followers more vulnerable to attack by Iranian conservatives and therefore less prone to respond in the manner hoped.

### Comparing the Utility of Sanctions to Alternatives

Although the sanctions-dominated policy pursued by the United States toward Iran was ineffective and lacked utility, as emphasized throughout this book, it can be regarded as a poor choice only if other strategies existed that could have delivered better results at more reasonable costs. For this reason, it is worth briefly considering three alternative approaches and assessing whether they might have been preferable to the U.S. strategy that evolved over the 1990s.

One theoretical alternative was a more aggressive strategy coupling sanctions with military measures. In practice, such an approach would have been problematic for many reasons. First, selected military strikes by the United States against Iran at any point in time in the 1990s would have been unlikely to achieve any American goal. Rather than toppling the regime, limited strikes would have strengthened it; instead of causing Iran to abandon its pursuit of weapons of mass destruction, strikes would have intensified it.[200] Such strikes also would have surely incurred greater costs, whether measured in terms of lost lives, international condemnation, rising anti-Americanism in Iran, or increasing support for terrorism against U.S. targets. More sustained military intervention geared toward regime change would have posed even further problems. The regional and international costs associated with direct U.S. military involvement for this purpose would have been tremendous, without even taking into account the problems that even a successful strategy would have created in Iran.[201]

Similarly, military support for an Iranian opposition group was, in practice, an unrealistic alternative. Quite simply, no opposition group offered a viable vehicle to challenge the regime. The Mujahedin-e Khalq Organization (MKO), while a persistent thorn in the side of Tehran, was discredited as both a terrorist organization and an ally of Saddam Hussein.[202] While the former crown prince and a constellation of liberal, secular Iranian activists in exile oppose the Islamic regime in Iran, they lack popular support and any capacity to pose a threat to the Iranian government.[203] Even had a group existed that offered the United States the chance to pursue a more aggressive policy, the benefits of such an approach are by no means clear cut. If unsuccessful, U.S. support for a group seeking to overthrow the regime would have ensured continued U.S.-Iranian hostility, created additional barriers to dialogue, and further belied any notion that the United States was seeking to change the behavior of the regime rather than the regime itself. A successful strategy might have installed a weak government in Tehran; it would certainly have incurred the long-term resentment of the Iranian people toward the United States, just as U.S. involvement in the 1953 coup against Mohammed Mossadeq did.

Another possible alternative to the sanctions-dominated approach pursued by Washington was a strategy of conditional engagement. The United States and Iran might have embarked on a gradual process of reconciliation, perhaps guided by a road map demarcating the issues of concern to both sides and charting a course toward better relations. Ample evidence exists that in the final years of the Clinton administration U.S. officials sought such an approach with Iran. Yet their attempts bore no more fruit than the ineffective sanctions-driven policy. Actual U.S. offers to craft a road map—such as that extended by Secretary Albright in June 1998—were rebuffed categorically by Iran. Subsequent U.S. efforts in March 2000 to launch a pattern of cooperation with modest unilateral gestures met with no greater success.[204] In the absence of an Iranian partner both willing and able to engage with the United States, a conditional engagement strategy with Iran was a nonstarter. Moreover, because such an approach never truly got off the ground, it had no opportunity to demonstrate that its execution could substantially lessen the costs associated with the sanctions status quo.[205]

A final alternative to consider is the option of doing nothing. The United States might have decided to let economic ties between Iran and the United States flourish in the hope that commercial contact would translate into political influence in Tehran. The European Union essentially pursued such an approach. As mentioned, under its strategy of critical dialogue in the 1990s, the EU promoted both commercial relations and strategic discussions with Iran. Trade and investment between Europe and Iran thrived, but the EU could point to only very selected achievements in influencing the behavior of the Iranian regime. Except on the margins, Iranian actions continued to be shaped by internal factors, not external actors.[206]

Gauging whether a similar U.S. strategy would have had comparable results is, of course, difficult. It is, however, likely that the United States would have fared no better than the EU had it chosen to do nothing or to adopt a business-as-usual approach.[207] Yet even if this strategy did not advance U.S. objectives significantly better than a sanctions-dominated one, it might have been judged to have greater utility on the basis of its lower costs. Such an approach would have clearly reduced the economic costs to the United States as trade and investment flowed, while better serving U.S. energy interests by allowing American oil companies to operate in Iran. In the absence of ILSA, the international political costs associated with the sanctions-dominated approach also would have been far less. Nevertheless, doing nothing or embracing a business-as-usual approach toward Iran in the face of continued Iranian support for terrorism and opposition to Israel would have been intolerable to U.S. citizens and vigorously protested by influential groups such as AIPAC. As a result, the domestic political costs of such an approach could be severe, possibly transforming an otherwise poor results/low-cost strategy into a poor results/high-cost one.

## Looking Ahead

In the immediate wake of the events of September 11, the prospects for an improved U.S.-Iranian relationship looked good. The heightened U.S. focus on counterterrorism—and obvious American readiness to use military force in the face of terrorism    created new pressures on Iran to reconsider the extent and nature of support it provided to groups such as Hizbullah and Hamas. At the same time, two factors influenced the willingness and ability of U.S. leaders to ease sanctions on Iran in return for sincere and substantial changes in Iranian behavior: the growing sense that the United States could benefit more from cooperation than from confrontation with Iran and the decreasing ability of domestic groups to shape U.S. foreign policy when fundamental U.S. security interests are at stake. The initial post–September 11 window for better bilateral relations appears to have shut. But even so, U.S. policymakers may still have good cause to reconsider their sanctions-dominated strategy against Iran.

Many of the arguments made in favor of revising U.S. policy toward Iran are based on a straightforward cost-benefit analysis. Advocates of a new strategy often contend that the United States should embrace a policy that allows it to better advance its economic, energy, and broader geopolitical interests in the region rather than maintain the sanctions-dominated one that has proven so feckless at promoting its narrower strategic goals. Although this line of reasoning is a compelling one, it overlooks the weight that these Iran-specific strategic issues—particularly Iran's support for violent anti-Israel groups and pursuit of weapons of mass destruction—carry in American domestic politics and the centrality of these issues to U.S. security considerations. It is no coincidence or mere oversight that these specific strategic goals have almost entirely eclipsed the pursuit or protection of the other American interests affected by U.S. policy toward Iran.

As a result, the much-needed new approach cannot be justified simply because it lowers the costs of U.S. policy. Rather, it must offer an improved means of advancing the same specific strategic interests in Iran *as well as* more general economic, commercial, and geopolitical interests in the region. Barring a major shift in Iran's long-standing posture against dialogue with the United States, it is unlikely that any change in U.S. policy, no matter how dramatic, will lead to significant immediate improvements in U.S.-Iranian relations. Yet given the rising dissatisfaction and frustration of the Iranian population with all elements of the regime—including Khatami—a new U.S. strategy should not be narrowly tied to the fortunes of reformers or the president himself. It should recognize that change in Iran could come gradually, through the moderation of the current regime or the gradual empowerment of democratically elected leaders at the expense of the clergy. Or it could come suddenly, the result of mass demonstrations that challenge the regime and bring its downfall overnight. In short, a new approach must offer an improved path for pursuing and securing short- and medium-term U.S. interests, while at the same time leaving the door open for a fundamental change in the nature of the regime, however it evolves in the future. In practice, such an approach would have several broad elements.

First, the United States should maintain and broaden all avenues of engagement and cooperation with Iran that serve the two countries' mutual interests.[208] Iran's problematic behavior in western Afghanistan notwithstanding, official contacts conducted through the Six Plus Two talks in 2001 and early 2002—and Iranian participation at the 2001 Bonn conference to form an interim government in Afghanistan—demonstrated that Iran and the United States can work together to promote common agendas. This cooperation not only helped secure a better future for Afghanistan, but it suggests the value of expanding U.S.-Iranian talks and ties in areas such as counternarcotics, refugees, the environment, and, most important, the future of Iraq. Unofficial contacts between Iranians and Americans also can and should be expanded, such as by further liberalizing laws regulating the operation of U.S. nongovernmental organizations (NGOs) in Iran, promoting nongovernmental seminars and conferences between academics and private citizens, and finding ways to ensure a steady flow of people and information between Iran and the United States, new security arrangements notwithstanding.[209]

Second, the United States should eliminate restrictions that only entrench the interests of the most conservative elements of the regime and work against those interested in promoting greater transparency and accountability within Iran. Lifting the remaining restrictions on civilian trade between the United States and Iran would fall into this category. Taking this step makes sense for a number of reasons. As seen from the earlier analysis in this chapter, the impact of trade sanctions on Iran diminished dramatically over time. Allowing civilian trade to resume therefore would not substantially increase resources flowing to the regime. In fact, it could have the opposite net effect; Iran's purchase of American nonmilitary items would actually reduce the amount of foreign exchange available to Tehran to support behavior that the United States finds objectionable. Moreover, such trade in civilian items would help Iran's fledgling private sector and possibly challenge the current stranglehold that more conservative elements of Iranian society have on the import-export trade. The exchange of goods and business people between the United States and Iran would also widen the exposure of Iranians to the United States, complementing efforts to expand unofficial contacts between the two countries. The United States also should end its opposition to Iran's accession to the WTO and instead facilitate it. Allowing Iran to accede to the WTO would not amount to granting the regime a favor; although accession is desired by Tehran, it could have major repercussions for the regime. By demanding greater transparency and accountability, WTO accession could well undermine the basis of support for more conservative elements of the regime, such as those who run the *bonyads*.

Finally, the United States should seek an official dialogue with the Iranian regime as the best way to address the issues of greatest concern to the United States and its allies in the region: Iran's support for terrorism and its pursuit of weapons of mass destruction. Tehran may be more willing to engage in such a dialogue in the post–September 11 international environment, just as the United States may need to consider new ways to expand current levels of exchange to induce a broader dialogue. With the goal of a more substantive dialogue in mind, the president may wish to lift some restrictions on U.S. investment in Iran, while keeping in place the sanctions related to Iran's designation as a state sponsor of terrorism. Allowing U.S. companies to operate in Iran as long as their activities fall under ILSA's $20 million limit will not amount to a significant windfall to Iran; as explained earlier, current restrictions on U.S. involvement in Iran's energy sector have had only a minor impact on Iran's ability to modernize its energy industry. Yet such a move would not only advance U.S. energy and economic interests but also serve U.S. strategic interests if it helped catalyze a serious and authoritative dialogue with Iran. The continuation of ILSA by Congress and the relaxation of some executive order sanctions by the president could conceivably create an ideal dynamic for the start of a U.S.-Iran dialogue. As was the case with China and extension of its most-favored-nation status in 1991, the tensions and competing approaches of the executive branch and Congress could provide a face-saving opportunity for Iran to enter into a dialogue with the executive branch. At the same time, such a situation would allow the president to begin discussions with Iran while still wielding leverage; not only would the sanctions associated with the terrorism list still be in place, but significant U.S. involvement in Iran's energy sector would still be effectively barred by ILSA.[210]

Such developments—while not impossible to envision—are a long way off. The pace at which this distance will be covered depends largely on Iran's willingness to make serious and substantive changes in its behavior. Yet however slowly U.S. policymakers travel down this road, they should recognize the need to cultivate domestic constituencies that would welcome better relations with Iran once it abandons support for terrorism. Given congressional interest in Iran and the web of legislative restrictions related to Iran, any rapprochement—whenever it occurs—will require the support of Congress. Yet congressional opposition to Iran remains strong, as demonstrated by the overwhelming backing for the renewal of ILSA in 2001.[211] The administration should not whitewash Iran's behavior in areas of concern to the United States and its allies. But it should present a more nuanced portrait of Iran to the American public—one that does not paint the country with a broad brush and instead underscores the aspirations of the Iranian people and highlights how Iran can be a positive player in the international community as well as a troublesome one. True rapprochement between Iran and the United States ultimately depends on serious changes in the behavior of the regime in Tehran today or a fundamental change in the nature of the regime. The United States should be prepared to welcome either eventuality.

## Appendix 3A

Tables 3A-1 and 3A-2 present estimates of the costs to Iran and the United States of lost trade with one another. Table 3A-3 reports Iran's export earnings from crude oil since the imposition of U.S. sanctions in mid-1995. The note below presents a rough calculation of the cost to Iran of lost imports from the United States.

Note to Appendix 3A: *Estimates of the Costs to Iran of Lost Imports from the United States.* As shown in table 3A-2, the direct loss of Iran as an export market cost U.S. businesses $1.93 billion (not accounting for the fact that some of these exports inevitably found other markets). This also represents the initial cost to Iran of lost imports from the United States. Assuming that Iran was able to replace the imports that it formerly secured from the United States, the cost to Iran would be the price differential between what it would have paid to get the products directly from the United States and what it had to pay to obtain the products from other sources or third-party suppliers. According to information calculated by the Foreign Trade Division of the U.S. Bureau of the Census, 14 percent of U.S. exports sold to Iran in 1994 were classified as high-tech; the remaining 86 percent did not warrant this classification. One can therefore estimate that 14 percent of the imports were difficult to replace, possibly requiring a mark-up of 20 percent over what Iran would have paid to the United States directly. Iran probably was required to pay little more to replace the remaining 86 percent, perhaps on the order of 5 percent. Therefore, the cost of obtaining or replacing the imports normally secured from the United States between 1995 and 2001 (the latest available data) is [($1.93 billion)*.14]*.20 + [($1.93 billion)* .86]*.05 = $137 million.

Table 3A-1. *Estimated Costs to Iran of Lost Exports to the United States, 1987–2001*[a]
Millions of 2001 dollars

| Year | Total Iranian non-oil exports (A) | Hypothetical non-oil exports to the U.S.[b] (A × 0.183 = B) | Actual total exports to the U.S. (C) | Estimated actual non-oil exports to the U.S.[c] (D) | Estimated non-oil exports lost due to sanctions (B − D = E) | Chain-weighted price deflator for GDP, 1996 = 100 (F) | Estimated lost non-oil exports to U.S., real dollars (E × [117.9/F] = G) |
|---|---|---|---|---|---|---|---|
| 1987–88[d] | 1,161 | 212 | 0 | 0 | 35[d] | 78.2 | 53 |
| 1988–89 | 1,036 | 190 | 9 | 0 | 190 | 81.5 | 275 |
| 1989–90 | 1,044 | 191 | 9 | 0 | 191 | 84.4 | 267 |
| 1990–91 | 1,312 | 240 | 2 | 0 | 240 | 85.9 | 329 |
| 1991–92 | 2,649 | 485 | 260 | 0 | 485 | 85.5 | 669 |
| 1992–93 | 2,988 | 547 | 1 | 0 | 547 | 88.0 | 733 |
| 1993–94 | 3,747 | 686 | 0 | 0 | 686 | 90.4 | 895 |
| 1994–95 | 4,825 | 883 | 1 | 0 | 883 | 94.0 | 1,108 |

| Year | | | | | | | |
|---|---|---|---|---|---|---|---|
| 1995–96 | 3,251 | 595 | 0 | 0 | 595 | 96.6 | 726 |
| 1996–97 | 3,106 | 568 | 0 | 0 | 568 | 00.0 | 670 |
| 1997–98 | 2,876 | 526 | 0 | 0 | 526 | 04.4 | 594 |
| 1998–99 | 3,013 | 551 | 0 | 0 | 551 | 08.9 | 597 |
| 1999–00 | 3,362 | 615 | 2 | 2 | 613 | 13.4 | 637 |
| 2000–01[e] | 4,000 | 732 | 159 | 159 | 573 | 17.6 | 574 |
| 2001–02 | 4,181 | 765 | 135 | 135 | 630 | 17.9 | 630 |
| **Total** | | | | | | | **8,756** |

Sources: Economist Intelligence Unit, Country Profile: Iran, various years; International Monetary Fund, Direction of Trade Statistics, various years.

a. The breakdown between oil and non-oil exports is assumed to be critical, as oil exports formerly going to the United States were largely absorbed by other countries, with little cost to Iran. Non-oil exports are likely to be more market specific and therefore to represent a greater loss to Iran.

b. Non-oil exports are multiplied by 0.183, the percentage of Iranian non-oil exports that went to the United States in 1985.

c. From 1988 to 1992 exports from Iran to the United States were primarily oil related; from 1999 to 2000, they were non-oil exports. Column D is necessary to distinguish between all actual exports to the United States and non-oil exports to it.

d. The estimate for lost Iranian non-oil exports to the United States in 1987 is 1/6 of the estimate for the entire year, since the embargo was in effect for only two months of the year.

e. The number reported for Iran's non-oil exports for 2000–01 is extrapolated from data that cover only the first three quarters of the year.

**Table 3A-2. Estimated Direct Costs to the United States of Lost Exports to Iran, 1995–2001[a]**

Millions of 2001 dollars

| Year | U.S. exports to Iran (A) | Industrial country exports to Iran (B) | Non-U.S. industrial country exports to Iran[b] (B − A = C) | Hypothetical U.S. exports to Iran[c] (C × 0.0470 = D) | Estimated annual impact of trade sanctions, nominal dollars (D − A = E) | Chain-weighted price deflator for GDP, 1996 = 100 (F) | Estimated annual impact of trade sanctions, real dollars (E × [117.9/F] = G) |
|---|---|---|---|---|---|---|---|
| 1995–96 | 476 | 7,846 | 7,370 | 346 | −130 | 96.6 | −159 |
| 1996–97 | 83 | 8,851 | 8,768 | 412 | 329 | 100.0 | 388 |
| 1997–98 | 38 | 8,289 | 8,251 | 387 | 349 | 104.4 | 395 |
| 1998–99 | 0 | 7,026 | 7,026 | 330 | 330 | 108.9 | 357 |
| 1999–00 | 53 | 6,175 | 6,122 | 287 | 234 | 113.4 | 244 |
| 2000–01 | 18 | 7,178 | 7,160 | 336 | 318 | 117.6 | 319 |
| 2001–02 | 9 | 8,401 | 8,392 | 394 | 385 | 117.9 | 385 |
| **Total** | | | | | | | **1,928** |

Sources: See table 3A-1.

a. These estimates account only for lost trade outside the military sector. Military sales are not included in the trading statistics available.

b. Using non-U.S. industrial country exports to Iran as the basis of the counterfactual allows the calculation to indirectly take a number of important elements into consideration—Iranian domestic policies that led to both the influx of imports in the early 1990s and the severe restrictions on imports beginning in 1994, fluctuations in the price of oil, and trends in the industrial economies—all of which influenced Iran's import patterns and would have affected U.S. trade in the absence of sanctions.

c. Non-U.S. industrial country exports to Iran from 1989 through the first half of 1995 are multiplied by 0.0470, the average relationship between U.S. exports to Iran and non-U.S. industrial country exports to Iran from 1989 through the first half of 1995. This end date was chosen because the ban on all exports to Iran began in mid-1995. The year 1989 was chosen as the starting date because it marks several important changes that affect the trading patterns of the following years: the end of the Iran-Iraq war and the beginning of reconstruction, the election of President Rafsanjani, the beginning of the First Five-Year Plan, and the first efforts at economic liberalization.

Table 3A-3. *Iran's Export Earnings from Crude Oil since the Imposition of U.S. Sanctions*[a]

Millions of 2000 dollars

| Year | Crude oil export revenue (A) | Chain-weighted deflator for GDP, 1996 = 100 (B) | Crude oil and gas exports, real dollars (A × [117.6/B] = C) |
|---|---|---|---|
| 1995–96 | 14,973 | 96.6 | 18,278 |
| 1996–97 | 19,441 | 100.0 | 22,863 |
| 1997–98 | 15,553 | 104.4 | 17,519 |
| 1998–99 | 10,048 | 108.9 | 10,851 |
| 1999–00 | 16,098 | 113.4 | 16,694 |
| 2000–01 | 25,443 | 117.6 | |
| **Total** | | | **111,598** |

Source: Organization of Petroleum Exporting Countries, *Annual Statistical Bulletin*, 2000, p. 5.

a. Since the Iranian fiscal year ends on March 21, the number for exports from 1995 to 1996 actually signifies earnings from March 1995 to March 1996. This conveniently coincides with the issuance of the executive order banning U.S. investment in the oil industry (March 1995), although firms could still market their liftings to third countries until the May 1995 trade ban.

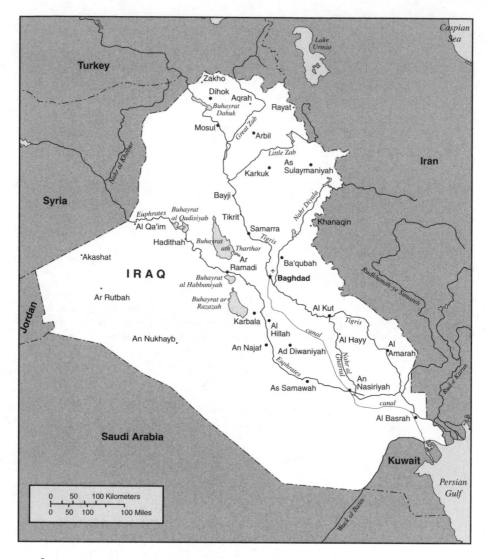

*Iraq*

# CHAPTER FOUR

# Inhibiting
# Iraq

When sanctions were imposed on Iraq in 1990, few policymakers or observers expected them to be in place a decade later. Most observers predicted that Iraqi president Saddam Hussein would not survive his defeat in Kuwait. They anticipated that Iraq would grudgingly, but quickly, comply with United Nations resolutions, paving the way for the lifting of sanctions and the resumption of more normal, if guarded, relations with the international community. None of those expectations materialized. The history of sanctions on Iraq has been one of deception, frustration, and conflict at many levels. Sanctions neither ushered in a victory for a new post–cold war order nor facilitated the international rehabilitation of Iraq. Instead, more than a decade of sanctions strained the multilateral coalition that first opposed the Iraqi invasion of Kuwait, contributed to a humanitarian crisis in Iraq, and led many to call into question the credibility of sanctions as a tool of foreign policy.

Sanctions on Iraq were criticized from both ends of the political spectrum. Those on the right contended that sanctions failed to achieve what they considered to be the ultimate goal, the ejection of Saddam Hussein from power. These critics held sanctions to unrealistic standards, ignoring not only that sanctions achieved many important goals but also that sanctions were never intended to force a regime change. At best, sanctions were hoped to increase the chances of Saddam's ouster by contributing to internal Iraqi discontent. From the left, critics alleged that sanctions were responsible for the humanitarian crisis in Iraq. Without question, the impact of sanctions on Iraq was tremendous, evident not only in Iraq's economic indicators, but also in every economic and political decision made by the regime since 1990. Yet one must also recognize that the economic and humanitarian conditions in Iraq are attributable not only to the sanctions, but also to a variety of other factors, including the policies and practices of Saddam Hussein and the destruction and neglect caused by two devastating wars. Confusing correlation with causality has been the mistake of these detractors.

A more balanced assessment finds that sanctions on Iraq, while falling short of some expectations, deserve a great deal of credit for the imperfect yet considerable containment of Saddam Hussein's regime. As explored in this chapter, their success in this department helps explain their shortcomings in other areas, whether in achieving more ambitious goals related to regime change or in shaping a framework for exacting behavior changes from Iraq. Nevertheless, the importance of containing Iraq and sanctions' crucial role in that endeavor are key factors in the overall assessment of sanctions: sanctions on Iraq not only were effective and had utility, but also compared favorably with many of the other options open to policymakers at the time.

## The Historical Context of Sanctions

In the decades since Saddam Hussein came to power in 1979, relations between Iraq and the United States have ranged from cooperative to hostile. Over this period, U.S. sanctions played an intermittent role in pursuing American goals. Economic penalties were first imposed in 1979 when the Carter administration compiled a list of "state sponsors of terrorism." Iraq, which had provided funding, training, and safe haven to the Palestine Liberation Organization and other terrorist groups of the time, was a prime candidate for the state sponsor designation and became subject to the limitations on aid and the sale of dual-use items and military equipment that accompanied it.[1] Three years later, Iraq was removed from the terrorism list, ostensibly to reward it for progress it had made in combating terrorism.[2] In all likelihood, Iraq's "rehabilitation" was more a reflection of the dual U.S. goals of limiting Soviet influence on Iraq—which once was significant—and keeping vehemently anti-American Iran from gaining regional dominance by defeating Iraq in the ongoing Iran-Iraq war.[3]

Whatever the motives, that step toward rapprochement paved the way for more expansive U.S.-Iraqi relations over the course of the Iran-Iraq war.

Throughout the 1980s, American contacts with Iraq expanded gradually. An initial tilt toward Iraq in the war against neighboring Iran increasingly gave way to a U.S.-Iraqi relationship that involved full diplomatic relations and a significant volume of trade.[4]

When President George H. W. Bush took office in 1989, the two Gulf powers had just signed a UN armistice in 1988 ending the war between them.[5] After a review of U.S. policy toward Iraq, the new American administration embarked on a strategy of limited engagement with Saddam Hussein.[6] This decision was widely supported by Iraq's Arab neighbors, who believed that despite Saddam's past reprehensible acts (including the use of chemical weapons against Iraqi Kurds in 1988), Iraq was moving into a period of moderation. The new American approach was intended to encourage this Iraqi temperance through limited interactions facilitated by the extension of U.S. agricultural and trade credits. Although the policy was roundly criticized in retrospect for its failures, at the time, President Bush and his advisers saw it as a calculated risk that might pay off in the form of a more stable Gulf region.[7]

Iraq's invasion of Kuwait on August 2, 1990, surprised the world and ended any American hopes of moderating the behavior of Saddam Hussein. U.S. policy quickly shifted from one of engagement to one of confrontation.[8] President Bush issued executive orders imposing unilateral sanctions, including an immediate freeze on Iraqi and Kuwaiti assets and the suspension of all U.S.-Iraqi economic interactions.[9] Within four days, the United States had successfully catalyzed the United Nations to pass UN resolution 661, which put in place full multilateral economic, financial, and military sanctions on Iraq and Kuwait.[10] A previous resolution (660) condemned Iraq's invasion of Kuwait and called for Iraq's immediate withdrawal. In the following month, the United States returned Iraq to its list of countries supporting terrorism, a move that had symbolic importance even if the sanctions that the designation invoked were redundant at the time.

Although some observers hoped that the stringent multilateral sanctions against Iraq would in themselves force Iraq's retreat, few were so optimistic.[11] As sanctions squeezed Iraq's economy during the final months of 1990, the United States was busy constructing a military option. American forces sent to the Gulf—originally to defend Saudi Arabia from further Iraqi aggression—later formed the basis of an international coalition intent on evicting Iraq from Kuwait if Saddam Hussein did not withdraw his troops from Kuwaiti territory by the deadline of January 15, 1991. To many, this military coalition of more than forty countries signaled both the American leadership and new commitment to international norms that would mark the post–cold war world.[12] The coalition, through Operation Desert Storm, forced Iraq to withdraw from Kuwait on February 27, 1991, after six weeks of military action.[13]

The terms of the armistice signed by Iraq and the allied coalition in the wake of the withdrawal were embedded in two UN resolutions. The first, UN resolution 686, was concerned primarily with Iraq's position regarding Kuwait. The second, UN resolution 687, was aimed at disabling the Iraqi threat in the region and clearly stipulated the steps that Iraq had to take before international sanctions would be rescinded (see accompanying box). The resolution specifically links lifting sanctions on imports from Iraq, including oil, with the elimination of Iraq's weapons of mass destruction (WMD) programs and its missile delivery systems; lifting sanctions on non-humanitarian exports to Iraq depends on the Security Council's periodic review of Iraq's compliance with all relevant UN resolutions.[14] UN resolution 687 formed the backdrop to the protracted struggle between Iraq and the international community over Iraq's WMD program, its support for terrorism, Iraqi-Kuwaiti relations, and the provision of compensation to entities and people harmed by Iraq's invasion of Kuwait.

Since the end of the Gulf war, the United States and the United Nations have used a number of tools to pursue the objectives embodied in UN resolution 687. During the time that multilateral sanctions have been in place, UN weapons inspection teams traversed Iraq, no-fly zones prevented Iraqi planes from flying over much of Iraqi territory, military strikes hit a variety of Iraqi targets, and various elements of the Iraqi opposition received U.S. support. Although each of these instruments has been controversial, economic sanctions have been the most visible and most contested tool of all.

### 1991–1993

Two features marked the years immediately following the imposition of sanctions and the stipulation of the conditions for their removal: UN Security Council cohesion around the goal of disarming Iraq and Iraqi unwillingness to accept UN resolutions and its responsibilities under them. In defiance of UN resolution 687, Iraq initially refused to recognize Kuwait's sovereignty and the inviolability of the UN-demarcated border.[15] At the same time, although allowing the United Nations Special Commission (UNSCOM) on Iraqi soil, Iraq continued to thwart its mission and deny that Iraq had an obligation to cooperate with the disarmament body.[16]

> *UN Security Council Resolution 687*
> *April 8, 1991*
> —Required Iraq to recognize the UN-demarcated border with Kuwait.
> —Demanded Iraq destroy, remove, or render harmless all its chemical and biological weapons and ballistic missiles with a range greater than 150 kilometers.
> —Created the UN Special Commission to supervise and document Iraqi WMD disarmament.
> —Required Iraq not to acquire or develop nuclear weapons or nuclear weapons–usable material.
> —Requested the International Atomic Energy Agency to inspect Iraq's nuclear capabilities.
> —Required Iraq to return all Kuwaiti property seized in the Gulf war.
> —Reaffirmed that Iraq is liable under international law for losses and damages incurred during the Gulf war. Created a fund to pay claims made against Iraq and created the UN Compensation Committee to administer the fund.
> —Reaffirmed the import and export sanctions on Iraq.
> —Required Iraq to assert that it will not support acts of international terrorism.

Saddam also rejected UN resolutions designed to ease the hardships on the Iraqi population during this period. The UN sanctions regime, as delineated in UN resolution 661, contained humanitarian provisions for the sale of medicine and food supplies to Iraq from the outset.[17] Yet the realization that the embargo was contributing to suffering on the ground prompted the United Nations to propose a program under which Iraq could sell its oil and use the proceeds to purchase food and medicine, all under UN supervision.[18] Iraq rejected this proposal and cut off negotiations concerning it in October 1993, arguing that UN control of the funds and distribution of the goods violated its sovereignty. Additional efforts by the United Nations to make the scheme more attractive to Iraq did not receive a positive response from Baghdad until years later.

# U.S. and UN Sanctions against Iraq

**December 29, 1979**    Iraq is put on the State Department's original list of state sponsors of terrorism, leadings to controls on exports of dual-use items, a ban on most forms of economic assistance, and opposition to loans and aid from international financial institutions (IFIs).

**December 29, 1981**    Congress prohibits *direct* aid to Iraq in the Foreign Assistance Appropriations Act; the prohibition is continued in subsequent appropriations.

**March 1, 1982**    Iraq is taken off the list of state sponsors of terrorism.

**March 30, 1984**    The Commerce Department embargoes sales to Iraq of five chemicals with potential weapons applications. Three more chemicals are added to the list in October 1984, which is expanded again in July 1987 and February 1989, bringing the total number of chemicals banned to fifty. Bans on biological agents and precursors are added in February 1989.

**October 30, 1986**    Congress prohibits *indirect* aid to Iraq in the Foreign Assistance and Related Programs Appropriations Act; the prohibition is continued in subsequent appropriations.

**January 29, 1988**    President Reagan waives the ban on indirect aid to Iraq on the grounds of national interest.

**January 17, 1990**    President Bush waives the prohibition on direct aid in the form of Export-Import Bank credits, guarantees, and insurance on the grounds of national interest.

**August 2, 1990**    Iraq invades Kuwait. President Bush declares a national emergency and bans all exports and imports to and from Iraq, except for humanitarian donations. The Department of State revokes all licenses and approvals authorizing the export or transfer of defense articles to Iraq.

**August 6, 1990**    The UN Security Council passes UNSC resolution 661, imposing a multilateral trade embargo on Iraq, except for humanitarian goods, and a freeze on Iraqi and Kuwaiti assets abroad.

**September 1, 1990**    Iraq is placed back on the list of state sponsors of terrorism, leading to a ban on arms-related exports and sales, controls on exports of dual-use items, a ban on most forms of economic assistance, and opposition to loans and aid from IFIs.

**November 5, 1990**    In the Foreign Operations Appropriations Act, Congress bans all military sales to Iraq; the licensing of items on the munitions list; the export of all nuclear equipment, materials and technology; U.S. support for assistance from IFIs, Export-Import Bank credits and guarantees; and assistance or credit from the Commodity Credit Corporation. This legislation codifies the sanctions in effect under executive order.

**January 15, 1991**    Operation Desert Storm begins as the United States and its allies launch the air war against Iraq.

**February 27, 1991**    After 100 hours of ground war, Iraq is ejected from Kuwait and the allied coalition halts the fighting.

**March 3, 1991**    Cease-fire talks begin between Iraq and the United Nations.

**April 3, 1991**    The UN Security Council passes UNSC resolution 687. See the box on page 109 for provisions.

**April 1991**    A no-fly zone over northern Iraq is established after Saddam brutally puts down a Kurdish rebellion. Iraqi aircraft are prohibited from flying north of the 36th parallel.

**August 15, 1991**    The UN Security Council passes UNSC resolution 705, allowing Iraq to export a limited amount of oil in exchange for food and other humanitarian supplies. On September 19, 1991, the Security Council passes UNSC resolution 712, also to establish an oil for food program. Both are rejected by Iraq.

**August 1992**    A no-fly zone over southern Iraq is established. Iraqi planes are prohibited from flying south of the 33rd parallel; the restricted area is expanded to the 32nd parallel in 1996.

**October 23, 1992**    The Iran-Iraq Arms Non-Proliferation Act requires the denial of all license applications for the export of dual-use items to Iraq and Iran and mandates sanctions against firms or people assisting Iraqi or Iranian conventional weapons programs. Congress amends the act in 1996 to include penalties for the transfer of technology or material necessary for building weapons of mass destruction.

**November 26, 1993**    Iraq formally accepts its obligations under UNSC resolution 715 to cooperate with UNSCOM and accept long-term monitoring of its weapons programs.

**October 1994**    Iraq masses troops along the Kuwaiti border. The United States sends 50,000 troops to the region and Iraq withdraws its troops.

**November 1994**    Iraq formally recognizes Kuwait's border as called for by UNSC resolution 687.

**April 14, 1995**    The Security Council passes UNSC resolution 986, allowing Iraq to export $2 billion of oil every 180 days for food and humanitarian supplies.

**August 1995**    Saddam's son-in-law, Hussein Kamel, who is in charge of Iraq's weapons programs, defects to Jordan and gives the United Nations information regarding Iraq's WMD programs. In response, Iraq turns over thousands of documents to UNSCOM, claiming Hussein Kamel had hidden them.

**January 1996**    Iraq agrees to the terms of UNSC resolution 986 to establish the Oil for Food program.

**April 1996**    The Antiterrorism and Effective Death Penalty Act prohibits aid to countries providing Iraq with military assistance and aid and prohibits financial dealings with Iraq.

**May 1996**    Iraq and the United Nations sign a memorandum of understanding outlining how the Oil for Food program will be implemented.

*(continued)*

## U.S. and UN Sanctions against Iraq (continued)

**August 1996**   At the invitation of the Kurdistan Democratic Party, Iraqi troops enter the city of Irbil and crush the forces of the Patriotic Union of Kurdistan. In response, the United States launches Operation Desert Strike and launches forty-four cruise missiles at targets south of Baghdad.

**December 1996**   The first oil under the Oil for Food program is exported from Iraq.

**March 1997**   The first humanitarian supplies under the Oil for Food program arrive in Iraq.

**January–February 1998**   Iraq continues to restrict access of UNSCOM to sites it says are presidential palaces. The crisis is defused with the help of UN Secretary General Kofi Annan.

**August 5, 1998**   Iraq announces that it will no longer cooperate with UNSCOM and IAEA inspectors.

**October 31, 1998**   Iraq terminates its cooperation with UNSCOM and IAEA. The Iraq Liberation Act is signed by President Clinton. It calls for $97 million in U.S. aid to help groups seeking the overthrow of Saddam Hussein.

**November–December 1998**   The crisis over the UNSCOM inspectors intensifies. In November, just before the United States and Britain plan to launch air strikes, Kofi Annan works out a last-minute settlement.

**December 16, 1998**   In an action known as Operation Desert Fox, the United States and Britain launch four days of air strikes against Iraq in response to Iraq's refusal to allow inspectors access to sites.

**December 17, 1999**   The Security Council passes UNSC resolution 1284, which replaces UNSCOM with a new monitoring body, the UN Monitoring, Verification, and Inspection Committee (UNMOVIC). The resolution states that if Iraq cooperates with the new body for 120 days, sanctions will be suspended for a period of 120 days, renewable by the Security Council if Iraq continues its cooperation. It also lifts the ceiling on the amount of oil Iraq can export under the Oil for Food program and calls for the creation of a fast-track procedure to allow for the quicker approval of contacts under the program.

**March 1, 2000**   The United Nations begins implementation of the new fast-track procedure for approving contracts.

Saddam Hussein's unwillingness to engage seriously with the United Nations in the initial years of sanctions reflected several factors. Saddam, paradoxically, enjoyed a period of relative stability between late 1991 and mid-1993. He had pulverized Kurdish and Shiite rebellions without evoking intervention from the international community beyond the establishment of a "safe haven" in the north of Iraq and no-fly zones in the north and south of the country.[19] And he had convinced the Sunnis that in his absence,

**October 31, 2000**    In response to a demand by Iraq, the United Nations authorizes the Oil for Food program to be denominated in euros rather than dollars.

**December 1, 2000**    Iraq announces its intention to place a fifty-cent-per-barrel surcharge on all oil exported under the Oil for Food program, to be deposited in Iraqi banks outside UN control. The United Nations objects to the surcharge.

**February 2001**    New U.S. Secretary of State Colin Powell announces his plan for "smart sanctions" on Iraq, which would lift sanctions on most consumer goods, tighten controls on military items, and clamp down on Iraqi oil smuggling in an attempt to reduce the suffering of ordinary Iraqi citizens while containing Saddam's ability to reconstitute his weapons capability.

**June 1, 2001**    The Security Council extends the ninth phase of the Oil for Food program for thirty days in an effort to reach an agreement on the U.S. sanctions plan. Iraq suspends oil exports from June 4 through July 10 in protest.

**November 29, 2001**    The United Nations passes UNSC resolution 1382, which renews the Oil for Food program and commits Security Council members to reviewing and agreeing upon a Goods Review List of items to be prohibited for sale to Iraq.

**January 29, 2002**    President George W. Bush delivers a State of the Union address in which he labels Iraq, Iran, and North Korea the "axis of evil."

**May 14, 2002**    The United Nations passes UNSC resolution 1409, which cements sanctions reform for Iraq. The new procedures expedite the sale of civilian goods to Iraq by transferring the process of approving pending sales for any product not on the Goods Review List (a compilation of mainly dual-use items) from the sanctions committee to UNMOVIC/IAEA experts. Items on the Goods Review List are referred to the sanctions committee.

**October 16, 2002**    The U.S. Congress passes a resolution, signed into law on October 16, authorizing the president to use force against Iraq if necessary to compel Iraq to get rid of its WMD programs.

**November 8, 2002**    The United Nations unanimously adopts resolution 1441, which guides the return of weapons inspectors to Iraq. The resolution warns of "serious consequences" if Iraq does not comply with its terms and agree to its complete disarmament of weapons of mass destruction.

they would be victims of Iraq's Shiite majority. Economic hardship had not yet fundamentally challenged Saddam's rule; although shortages and inflation existed, the Iraqi president still had sufficient resources to distribute rations to the population and to protect the interests of the elite upon which his regime depended. Under these circumstances, Saddam had little impetus to cooperate with the United Nations, particularly given that he believed that the quickest route to sanctions relief was through resistance.

*1994–1998*

When defiance of the United Nations brought Iraq no closer to freeing itself from sanctions, Baghdad gradually shifted to a more subtle strategy involving partial compliance—or at least the veneer of cooperation—with UNSCOM and concerted efforts to provoke discord among the members of the UN Security Council. On November 26, 1993, Iraq formally acknowledged its obligations under UN resolutions to cooperate with UNSCOM and accept a long-term weapons monitoring regime.[20] Following this declaration, a period of greater cooperation between UNSCOM and Iraq ensued, although Iraqi foot-dragging and deception continued.[21] In addition to this increased, if still limited, cooperation on the weapons inspection front, in November 1994 Iraq finally recognized the sovereignty of Kuwait, fulfilling one of the terms of the original cease-fire resolutions.

These steps, while still leaving Iraq far short of complying with the original UN resolutions, were sufficient to lead some members of the international community to call for the modification of the sanctions regime. In the summer of 1994, Russia began to insist that the United Nations set a definite timetable for lifting the sanctions on Iraq.[22] France was originally more circumspect in its demands for easing the sanctions, but began Baghdad's rehabilitation by hosting Iraqi deputy prime minister Tariq Aziz in Paris in January 1995.[23] Pressure for change was building, undoubtedly augmented by the numerous discussions Iraq had held with various countries and foreign companies hoping to invest in the Iraqi oil industry once sanctions were lifted.[24]

This pressure, however, bore no fruit, due largely to continued U.S. opposition to any easing of the embargo on Iraq.[25] Two developments, moreover, tempered foreign enthusiasm for lifting the sanctions during this period. First, in October 1994, Iraq threatened to discontinue cooperation with UNSCOM and proceeded to amass a large number of Iraqi troops on the Kuwaiti border. Only in the face of a united Security Council and a show of force by the United States did Iraq disperse its forces.[26] Second, and of greater consequence, were the events following the August 1995 defection to Jordan of Hussein Kamel, Saddam's son-in-law. The former head of the Iraqi Military Industrial Organization and the founder of the Special Security Organization (Iraq's most important internal security body), Hussein Kamel had intimate knowledge of Iraq's weapons development programs and brought new information to western authorities on issues such as Iraq's biological weaponization. In an apparent effort to discredit Hussein Kamel, Iraqi officials suddenly revealed large amounts of information and documents concerning Iraq's weapons programs to UNSCOM and the International Atomic Energy Agency (IAEA), claiming that the information had been hidden by Hussein Kamel.[27] Together, these disclosures revealed that Iraq had falsified and withheld evidence relevant to UNSCOM's mission. Iraq had dramatically misrepresented the state of its WMD programs and had a long way to go before being effectively disarmed of them.[28]

Although this series of events stymied Iraq's campaign to have the sanctions removed, Saddam continued his pattern of selective cooperation against an overall background of intransigence. The most notable instance was Iraq's acceptance, after years of pressure from the UN Security Council, of the Oil for Food program in 1996.[29] Under the terms of the agreement struck between Iraq and the UN Security Council—enshrined in UN resolution 986 and a May 1996 memorandum of understanding between Iraq and the United Nations—Iraq was permitted to purchase food and medicine from the proceeds of its oil sales to meet the civilian needs of its population.[30] Iraqi oil began to flow to international markets in December 1996, and the first humanitarian supplies reached Iraq in March 1997.

As discussed later in the chapter, Saddam was forced to accept UN resolution 986 to save his regime from economic collapse and political turmoil. He had resisted the UN Oil for Food program for so long partly because he perceived it to be a tool to prolong the sanctions and partly because he found the deteriorating humanitarian situation in Iraq to be a valuable asset in his propaganda war to lift the sanctions. In reality, his acceptance of the program hardly amounted to relinquishing the humanitarian card. In the years following the start of the program, the humanitarian situation received even greater attention from the international community and increasingly served as the primary argument for lifting the sanctions on Iraq.[31] At the same time, the Iraqi regime was able to use the Oil for Food program to promote its political agenda through economic ties.[32]

Saddam Hussein's strategy to get sanctions lifted went beyond commercial intrigues. Over the course of 1996 and beyond, he became progressively emboldened, provoking crisis after crisis in the realization that each one strained the increasingly fractious UN Security Council and the consensus for sanctions. In the last days of August 1996, Iraqi tanks and artillery entered the northern Kurdish safe haven at the invitation of the Kurdish Democratic Party (KDP) to help it take control of the city of Irbil from its rival, the Patriotic Union of Kurdistan (PUK). With British logistical help, the United States responded with Operation Desert Strike, which entailed the launch of forty-four cruise missiles against Iraqi antiaircraft sites in southern Iraq.[33] Such force triggered a mixed reaction from the increasingly divided international community, with some countries—such as Russia, France, and many Arab states—maintaining that Saddam's military moves within Iraq's borders were legitimate.[34]

Subsequent efforts by Iraq to strain the coalition revolved around the actions of UNSCOM.[35] In late 1997, while demanding a timetable for the lifting of sanctions, Iraq refused entry to two American members of UNSCOM and placed limits on UNSCOM's access to certain locations. This crisis was diffused by Russian foreign minister Yevgeny Primakov, who by this point had become an ardent advocate of ending the sanctions on Iraq.[36] The deal brokered with the Iraqis eased the immediate tensions, yet Iraq continued to restrict UNSCOM inspectors and threaten to evict them from Iraq if their work was not completed within six months. Such behavior spurred another crisis in January 1998, which was resolved through the intervention of UN secretary general Kofi Annan one month later. In a controversial memorandum of understanding, Annan and Iraqi deputy prime minister Tariq Aziz agreed that Iraq would confirm its acceptance of UN resolutions and grant UNSCOM members full access to inspections sites. In return, Iraq secured the right to have special "senior diplomats" accompany UNSCOM members when they inspected eight presidential palaces.[37] The UN Security Council commended Annan's efforts with the unanimous passage of UN resolution 1154, which also warned that continued Iraqi intransigence "would have the severest consequences for Iraq."[38]

Again, the life span of renewed Iraqi cooperation was short. Iraq triggered another crisis on August 5, 1998, when it curtailed the ongoing monitoring efforts of UNSCOM and the IAEA. Iraqi-UN relations deteriorated even further shortly after this action, when, in the wake of the resignation of Scott Ritter (the chief of UNSCOM's Concealment Investigations Unit), accusations arose that UNSCOM had provided intelligence to the United States and Israel.[39] The United Nations declared its decision to postpone any consideration of lifting sanctions until Iraq resumed full cooperation with UNSCOM and the IAEA. Iraq defied calls for its compliance and ceased all efforts to work with these organizations on the last day of October in 1998.[40]

Unlike in earlier standoffs between Iraq and the United Nations, opposition to Iraq's position in August 1998 was widespread. France and Russia, which had backed Iraq in its standoff with UNSCOM in February, and Kofi Annan, who had negotiated the settlement to that dispute, were reluctant to once again extend their support to Iraq in the face of its most recent betrayal of earlier agreements. Rather than immediately threatening to use force to end the crisis, the United States and Britain mobilized support for military efforts to confront Iraq.[41] Although these labors did not garner the vocal support of many European countries, they also were not publicly rejected.[42] Some Arab countries were more outspoken in condoning force if Iraq did not back down, with eight states issuing a statement to that effect.[43] In mid-November, just as military strikes by the United States and the United Kingdom looked unstoppable, Kofi Annan brokered a last-minute agreement in which Iraq reversed its stance and air strikes were halted at the last moment.[44]

The UNSCOM team and its chief, Richard Butler, reported one month later that Iraqi cooperation was insufficient, rendering the group unable to continue its work in Iraq.[45] One day later, on December 16, 1998, the United States launched a four-night bombing campaign called Operation Desert Fox. Although the United Kingdom participated in the strikes and the action drew some support from U.S. allies, many key countries vehemently criticized the use of force. Russia, China, and France voiced varying degrees of indignation, taking particular offense that they were not consulted prior to the strikes, as had been customary in the past.[46] Meanwhile, the citizens of many Arab countries expressed their outrage in public demonstrations, some of which became violent.[47] In addition to this backlash from abroad, the limited nature of Desert Fox led many U.S. commentators to question the utility of the strike.[48] Although U.S. officials declared the operation a success because it retarded Saddam's development of weapons of mass destruction, such gains came at high costs.[49] Not only did the episode damage the already seriously fractured international coalition to contain Iraq, but it firmly closed off the option of returning weapons inspection teams to Iraq for the foreseeable future.

The crises of 1994–98 exposed an underlying difference of opinion in the Security Council between those who believed that compromise and negotiation were necessary and worthwhile to ensure Iraq's eventual compliance with UN resolutions and those (the United States most prominently) who believed that the appropriate way of dealing with Iraq's intransigence was through steady pressure and occasional military force. But increasingly, disputes between Security Council members concerned not only the means that the United Nations used to advance its goals but also the objectives that it should pursue.

Over this period, differences between U.S. and UN objectives concerning Iraq moved from muted tension to sporadic but open conflict as the United States publicly oscillated between the goal of containing Saddam Hussein and of overthrowing him.[50] Despite an apparent desire to see the demise of the Iraqi regime and early proclamations linking the removal of sanctions to Saddam's departure, the administration of George H. W. Bush sought to keep American desires for regime change largely separate from UN sanctions.[51] Shortly after President Clinton took office, the United States moved to an even less provocative stance, explicitly linking U.S. objectives to UN resolutions.[52] Clinton administration officials justified this less confrontational position as being more consistent with international opinion, but at the same time not straying far from the essence of the American desire to depose Saddam; in the eyes of the Clinton administration, Iraq would be unable to comply with all UN resolutions as long as Saddam stayed in power.[53] Nevertheless, U.S. and UN policy remained at odds in a more subtle way: the United States insisted that Iraq must comply with *all* UN resolutions, not just the ones concerning disarmament, before it would be free from sanctions.[54] This approach was later abandoned in favor of a more robust one when in a March 1997 speech at Georgetown University, Secretary of State Madeleine Albright stated that UN sanctions would remain in place as long as Saddam Hussein was in power.[55] Despite her unequivocal statement, the Clinton administration gradually backed away from this hard-line position, opting once again to focus on the less ambitious goal of containing Saddam.[56]

These fluctuations in U.S. goals were the product of friction in the American domestic sphere. During the 1990s the Clinton administration sought to reshape American policy in the Gulf and the Middle East more broadly. In the wake of Iraq's defeat and the 1993 Oslo Accords, the Clinton administration perceived a new climate to be emerging in the region. Arab opposition to Saddam Hussein and budding peace efforts between Israel and its neighbors suggested a new era. In the view of Clinton administration officials, if the negative influences of Iraq and Iran could be cordoned off, peace might take root in the Middle East. This thinking generated a new strategy in the Gulf, one that departed from past efforts to balance Iran and Iraq against one another. Termed "dual containment," the new U.S. policy sought to weaken both powers and keep them on the sidelines of international affairs.[57] Rather than conforming to an aggressive, internationally unpopular strategy to topple Saddam Hussein, the logic of dual containment argued for a more careful approach that emphasized maintaining international sanctions on Iraq and sought to garner global support for isolating Iran.

Congressional acts initially complemented the dual containment approach. In 1992, Congress passed the Iran-Iraq Arms Non-Proliferation Act, which demanded the denial of all license applications for the export of dual-use items to Iraq and Iran and mandated sanctions against foreign entities that transferred conventional weaponry to these countries.[58] In 1996, Congress modified this legislation to include penalties for the transfer of technology and materials for weapons of mass destruction. The 1996 passage of the Antiterrorism and Effective Death Penalty Act—a law that, among other things, required the president to withhold foreign assistance to any country that provided aid or military assistance to a country on the U.S. terrorism list—solidified the trend toward secondary sanctions. The comprehensive nature of UN sanctions made most of these measures redundant, yet they provided reinforcement of the military sanctions in place and helped define the parameters of the American dual containment policy.

As the 1990s progressed, congressional attitudes favoring a more aggressive strategy toward Iraq were increasingly at odds with the approach of the Clinton administration. Over the course of the 1997 and 1998 crises between Iraq and UNSCOM, Congress voiced its support for tougher actions by passing resolutions highlighting Iraq's breach of the UN cease-fire and endorsing unilateral U.S. military action to deal with Iraqi obstreperousness.[59] Frustrated with the oscillating commitment of the Clinton administration to the Iraqi opposition, Congress passed the 1998 Iraq Liberation Act. This legislation, which President Clinton reluctantly signed into law on October 31, 1998, endorsed a more aggressive rollback strategy toward Iraq and authorized up to $97 million to pursue Saddam's ouster. In addition to providing funds for the Iraqi opposition, the law reiterated past congressional support for the creation of a war crimes tribunal for Saddam Hussein.

### 1998–2002

The ejection of UNSCOM from Iraq in 1998 removed a flashpoint for confrontation between Iraq and the international community and froze efforts to advance the disarmament of Iraq. Yet, far from ushering in a period during which the status quo was quietly maintained, the years from 1998 to 2002 were marked by intensifying discord over Iraq, both in the international and the U.S. domestic spheres.

At the international level, the cleavages of conflict changed. Whereas disputes in the early to mid-1990s were largely between Iraq and the United

Nations, those in later years were notable for the diverging interests of members of the international community over Iraq and the laborious efforts made to strike compromises among them. As the 1990s came to a close, the growing isolation of the United States and its efforts to maintain pressure and sanctions on Iraq stood in contrast to the interests of other countries in easing sanctions and gaining greater access to Iraq.

The United Nations struggled to redefine its sanctions policy toward Iraq after UNSCOM's departure. Two broad perspectives emerged over the course of 1999. France, China, and Russia pressed for a more forgiving approach toward Iraq, citing the failure of past punitive approaches and the dire humanitarian situation in Iraq.[60] These arguments often only thinly disguised the strong desire of these countries to resume normal commercial relations with Iraq. With the exception of Saudi Arabia and Kuwait, the countries of the Gulf Cooperation Council (GCC) also lobbied for the easing of sanctions, largely on humanitarian grounds. Countering these calls for leniency was the United States, backed by Britain, which insisted on maintaining a hard line on sanctions in the face of Saddam's defiance of UN demands. Over the course of 1999, the UN Security Council debated two competing proposals for modifying Iraqi sanctions, each reflecting these competing perspectives and offering a different approach to weapons inspections.[61]

Efforts to reconcile the proposals and the viewpoints they represented came together on December 17, 1999, when the United Nations passed UN resolution 1284. This resolution replaced UNSCOM with the UN Monitoring, Verification, and Inspection Commission (UNMOVIC), a new body tasked with furthering the work of its predecessor.[62] Under the terms of the resolution, once Iraq fully cooperated with UNMOVIC for 120 days, trade sanctions on nonmilitary and dual-use items would be suspended, subject to a review by the Security Council every 120 days. No explicit mechanism was offered for the permanent lifting of sanctions. Other provisions of UN resolution 1284 required less cooperation from Iraq to come into effect. The resolution lifted the ceiling on the amount of oil that Iraq could sell under the Oil for Food program. It also streamlined approval procedures and other routine duties of the UN Sanctions Committee, which was entrusted with implementing Iraq's Oil for Food scheme.[63] Although the passage of UN resolution 1284 signaled continued international concern regarding the WMD disarmament of Iraq, the abstention of China, France, and Russia from the vote approving the resolution indicated ongoing divisions on the council and foreshadowed the events of the following year.[64]

Iraq rejected the terms of UN resolution 1284 and the resumption of weapons inspections, closing the door on a cooperative resolution and promoting new nodes of international tension. In June 1999, the United States revised the terms of engagement governing the U.S. and British planes patrolling the no-fly zones in Iraq in response to increasingly aggressive Iraqi efforts to shoot them down. Whereas before Operation Desert Fox, pilots on patrol responded to Iraqi provocations by attacking only their source, the new rules authorized pilots to broaden the scope of targets if they were attacked. This shift in policy intensified the confrontation between Washington and Baghdad, leading to the almost daily bombing of Iraq. These escalations rankled Arab countries and fueled Iraqi accusations that the United States deliberately targeted and killed Iraqi civilians.[65]

The fragile international consensus concerning Iraq came under even greater strain in 2000. Unusually high international oil prices fueled demand for Iraqi oil, which Iraqi smugglers strove to satisfy. The November 2000 reopening of the long-closed Iraq-Syria pipeline enabled Syria to receive tens of thousands of barrels of Iraqi oil outside of the UN Oil for Food mechanism.[66] With each barrel of oil that crossed the border out of Iraq, Iraq became more firmly integrated into the regional economy. Moreover, the breakdown of the Middle East peace process and the resumption of violence between Israel and the Palestinians posed further problems. Saddam's adept positioning of himself as the champion of martyred Palestinians strengthened the link between Arab support for the Palestinians and what was increasingly perceived by the Arab street as U.S. persecution of Iraqi civilians.[67] Together, these economic and political factors stoked more efforts to rehabilitate Iraq into the region and the international community. The fraying of international support for sanctions became evident in the autumn of 2000 when—after a decade of an effective flight ban on Iraq—airliners from Russia, France, Egypt, Turkey, Jordan, and other countries began landing at the newly opened Baghdad International Airport.[68] Emboldened by these developments, Iraq imposed a "surcharge"—a fee to be paid into Iraqi coffers outside of the UN Oil for Food program—on each barrel of oil it exported.[69]

The administration of George W. Bush inherited this rapidly deteriorating situation in January 2001 and was quick to make it a top priority in its foreign policy agenda. Shortly after the new administration took office, Secretary of State Colin Powell sought support for a modified sanctions regime that would further liberalize civilian trade with Iraq while tightening restrictions on Iraqi smuggling of oil.[70] Rather than advocating these changes in the hopes of enticing further Iraqi cooperation on WMD disarmament, Powell justified them on humanitarian grounds and on the need to shore up the flagging international commitment to maintaining key elements of the sanctions regime. A new sanctions approach was presented as one of "three baskets" being reconsidered in molding a revised Iraq policy under the Bush administration; the other two were U.S. support for the Iraqi opposition and patrol of the no-fly zones.

After battling significant domestic and international resistance to Powell's efforts, the United States was successful in further streamlining sanctions on Iraq.[71] Early attempts to introduce a "smart sanctions" regime were rejected by Iraq's neighbors, who were loath to take a more active role in monitoring trade with Iraq, and Russia, which extracted significant economic benefits from its relationship with Iraq and Iraqi appreciation for the role Moscow played in obstructing a new sanctions regime. Nevertheless, persistent negotiations—and the changed international environment in the wake of the September 11, 2001, terrorist attacks—produced UN resolution 1409 on May 14, 2002. The new resolution expedited the sale of civilian goods to Iraq by transferring the power to approve most contracts under the Oil for Food program from the sanctions committee (composed of Security Council members) to UNMOVIC/IAEA technical experts. Only items found on the Goods Review List, a 332-page document cataloguing dual-use items, still need the approval of the sanctions committee.

The impact of the events of September 11 on Iraq policy went far beyond a push for sanctions reform. They dramatically altered the context of the debate about U.S. policy toward Iraq. The World Trade Center and Pentagon attacks reframed the Bush presidency and America's role in the world. In this revised environment, U.S. tolerance for the regime of Saddam Hussein greatly diminished and expectations that even the most successful strategy of containment would be sufficient to protect U.S. interests were called into question. Heightened concerns about the nexus between weapons of mass destruction and support for terrorism catapulted Iraq up on the Bush administration's list of priorities and strengthened the hand of those arguing for an active, robust regime change strategy.

## Judging the Effectiveness and Utility of Sanctions on Iraq

A solid analysis of sanctions on Iraq requires a systematic appraisal of the economic and political impact of sanctions on the country, the goals achieved by the imposition of sanctions, and the costs incurred by the use of these tools. Careful consideration of each factor is the key to determining the effectiveness of sanctions (whether they advanced policy objectives) and the utility of these tools (whether they achieved goals at reasonable costs).

### Economic Impact

By nearly every measure, the economy of Iraq has been in dire straits since 1990, when sanctions were imposed. According to the best estimates available, Iraq's economy shrank by five-sixths between 1990 and 1991. Ten years after the Gulf war, Iraq's economy was only half the size that it had been before the invasion of Kuwait.[72] For virtually the entire decade of the 1990s, Iraq straggled far behind most of its neighbors in terms of GDP and per capita GDP. By other standards, such as the rate of inflation and the size of overall debt burdens, Iraq was in a far worse position than almost every country in the Gulf, the Middle East, and North Africa through 1999 (table 4-1).[73] Positive trends became apparent only after 1997 and the start of the Oil for Food program.

This grim picture is not the product of sanctions alone. Iraq's economic plight in the 1990s and beyond is also attributable to the rule of Saddam Hussein and the economic choices that his regime made since the end of the Gulf war. The condition of the Iraqi economy is also a reflection of the poor economic situation in Iraq *before* sanctions were imposed in August 1990. The eight-year war with Iran, concluded just two years earlier in 1988, inflicted an estimated $130 billion in damage on the economy and left Iraq heavily indebted to some Gulf states and western financial institutions.[74] Hostilities between the two Gulf powers had completely stalled development of Iraqi oil fields and reduced Iraq's existing oil production.[75] By the end of the Iran-Iraq war, Iraqi per capita income had dropped dramatically to $1,500 from $4,000 just eight years earlier.[76] In the two years following the cease-fire with Iran before the invasion of Kuwait, Iraq struggled with inflation rates of nearly 40 percent, a falling standard of living, sporadic shortages of goods and foreign exchange, and large-scale underemployment.[77] In short, Iraq's economic prospects were hardly bright before the sanctions were imposed.[78]

The economic breakdown so evident in Iraq in the 1990s was also the legacy of the 1991 Gulf war. The six-week air campaign seriously damaged Iraq's power sector, manufacturing industry, and other critical infrastructure.[79] In an effort to disrupt the supply of fuel to the Iraqi military, coalition bombing aggressively targeted Iraq's oil industry. According to a UN team sent to examine the oil situation in Iraq in July 1991, damage from the

Table 4-1. *Comparative Economic Indicators, 1998–2001*

| Country | GDP ($ billions) | GDP per head ($) | Average consumer price inflation (percent) |
|---|---|---|---|
| *Iraq*[a] | | | |
| 1998 | 4.6 | 203 | 140.0 |
| 1999 | 22.0 | 976 | 135.0 |
| 2000 | 31.8 | 1,376 | 70.0 |
| 2001 | 27.9 | 1,184 | 60.0 |
| *Jordan* | | | |
| 1998 | 7.3 | 1,223 | 4.4 |
| 1999 | 7.5 | 1,225 | 0.6 |
| 2000 | 7.8 | 1,172 | 0.7 |
| 2001 | 9.0 | 1,730 | 1.8 |
| *Syria* | | | |
| 1998 | 14.4 | 926 | 1.1 |
| 1999 | 16.5 | 1,038 | −0.5 |
| 2000 | 16.6 | 998 | 0.0 |
| 2001 | 19.8 | 1,154 | 0.4 |
| *Iran*[b] | | | |
| 1998 | 59.5 | 959 | 19.3 |
| 1999 | 51.6 | 816 | 21.0 |
| 2000 | 64.4 | 1,011 | 14.5 |
| 2001 | 82.3 | 1,270 | 11.3 |
| *Saudi Arabia* | | | |
| 1998 | 143.8 | 7,138 | −0.3 |
| 1999 | 139.4 | 6,990 | −1.4 |
| 2000 | 164.9 | 8,059 | −0.8 |
| 2001 | 183.3 | 8,730 | −0.4 |

Source: Economist Intelligence Unit, *Country Profile: Iraq*, 2000, various years.
a. Estimates.
b. Year beginning March 21.

war had reduced productive capacity by more than half and crippled refin-ing capabilities.[80] Later estimates suggest an even greater decline in oil pro-duction from 1990 to 1991, perhaps in the realm of 85 percent.[81] Water purification systems were also devastated by the war, leaving Iraq capable of purifying only a quarter of the volume of water the country had consumed before the war.[82] The Gulf war air attacks and the brief ground war also in-flicted major human casualties on Iraq.[83]

Yet, even acknowledging the importance of these factors, it is difficult to understate the role of sanctions in shaping Iraq's economy throughout the 1990s and into the 2000s. The multilateral, comprehensive sanctions regime put in place terminated virtually all legal, nonhumanitarian trade—both military and civilian—between Iraq and the rest of the world. Until the Oil for Food program got under way in 1997, hardly any goods crossed Iraq's borders in either direction. Over time, this forgone trade amounted to huge losses to Iraq and inhibited recovery from the war. In the absence of sanctions, Iraq could have been expected to export more than $250 billion in oil and other goods from 1990 to 2000—approximately $200 billion more than it actually did even when the exports under the Oil for Food program are taken into account (see appendix tables 4A-1 and 4A-2). Similarly, calculations based on Iraqi imports of nonmilitary goods before sanctions were imposed suggest that Iraq might have imported more than $185 billion in such items from 1990 to 2000, again, a good $165 billion more than it actually did import over that time (see appendix tables 4A-3 and 4A-4). In addition to having lost access to these civilian imports, Iraq was forced to discontinue its efforts—at least its overt and legal ones—to rebuild its military after the Iran-Iraq war (figure 4-1).

On the financial side, the sanctions had a dramatic impact on Iraq both immediately and over time. The imposition of sanctions led to a prompt freeze of nearly $4.5 billion in assets belonging to the Iraqi government worldwide, causing Iraq's credit rating to plummet as Iraq defaulted on all foreign financial commitments in the wake of the freeze.[84] Loans and credits that Iraq had been receiving ground to a halt once UN sanctions came into effect. Foreign assistance slowed to a trickle.[85]

Other costs, particularly the impact of sanctions on the Iraqi oil industry, are more difficult to gauge. As of 2002, Iraq's oil fields were by all accounts in dire condition. Iraq had been able to make some repairs to its heavily damaged oil industry after the Gulf war, first by using spare parts secured through smuggling and stripping older machines and later through the use of some oil equipment legally secured through the UN Oil for Food program.[86] These measures enabled Iraq to produce oil at pre–Gulf war levels in 1999. Energy experts agree, however, that Iraq did so only by employing techniques that were damaging the long-term prospects of its fields.[87]

Iraq's ability to further increase its production and fulfill Iraqi oil ministry ambitions to expand existing capacity to 6 million barrels a day depends heavily on foreign investment. Even while under sanctions, Iraq concluded or negotiated many contracts with European and Asian companies to develop

**Figure 4-1.** *Iraq's Arms Imports, 1987–99*[a]

Billions of U.S. dollars

Percentage

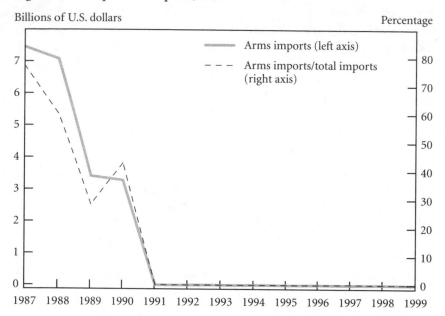

Source: U.S. Department of State, Bureau of Arms Control, *World Military Expenditures and Arms Transfers*, 1998, 1999–2000.
  a. Constant 1999 dollars.

its oil fields in the future; in the estimation of some experts, the execution of such contracts could enable Iraq to more than double its production capacity within a few years.[88] Although the continuation of sanctions precludes implementation of these contracts, their existence aids speculation about what the state of Iraq's oil industry might have been at the turn of the millennium in the absence of sanctions. Assuming that Iraq had welcomed foreign investors in its oil industry in the post–Gulf war era (after decades of excluding them) and given these investors attractive terms, it is conceivable that Iraq would have had the capacity to produce 6 million barrels a day by the late 1990s.[89] What that extra capacity would have meant for Iraq in monetary terms is open to question, given that Iraq's additional production or mere spare capacity—as well as its inclusion in OPEC—might have significantly reduced international oil prices over the last half of the 1990s and early 2000s.[90] However, it is almost certain that the cumulative losses suffered as a result of lost investment and lost oil exports far exceed the already

Figure 4-2. *Real GDP Growth: Iraq Compared with Middle East Region, 1977–2000*

Percent change

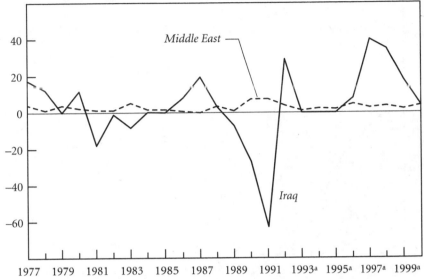

Sources: International Monetary Fund, *International Financial Statistics Yearbook 1998* for Iraqi growth rates to 1989. From 1990 onward, Iraqi growth rates were taken from Economist Intelligence Unit, *Country Profile: Iraq,* 1996, 1999, and *Country Report: Iraq,* June 2002. The World Bank, *World Development Indicators,* CD-ROM 2002, for Middle East averages.

a. Economist Intelligence Unit estimate.

substantial $176 billion that Iraq would have earned had it continued to export at 1990 levels at actual prices between 1990 and 2000 and would be closer to the $250 billion that Iraq would have earned if it had expanded along with other oil-producing countries (see appendix 4A-1). Iraq will reach that production level at some point in the future, making its losses largely temporal rather than permanent.[91]

Unlike other sanctions episodes examined in this book, the comprehensive, multilateral nature of the sanctions regime against Iraq largely eliminates the need to determine to what extent the curtailment of transactions with the outside world is the result of sanctions. Comparisons of Iraq's growth rates with regional averages or the price of oil also reveal little correlation, suggesting the enormous effect of sanctions (figures 4-2 and 4-3). Rather than cataloguing the economic links severed, it is of greater interest

**Figure 4-3.** *Iraq's Real GDP Growth Compared with Price of Iraqi Oil, 1988–2000*

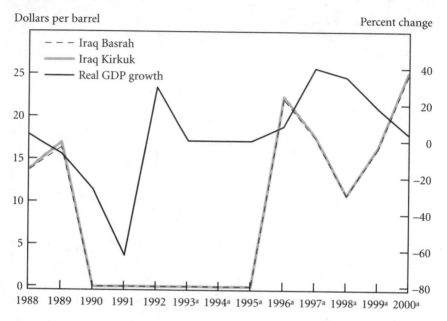

Sources: International Monetary Fund, *International Financial Statistics Yearbook,* 1998, and Economist Intelligence Unit, *Country Profile: Iraq,* 1996, 1999, and *Country Report,* June 2002, for GDP growth rates. Organization of Petroleum Exporting Countries, *OPEC Annual Statistical Bulletin 2000,* for oil prices.

a. Economist Intelligence Unit estimate for GDP growth rate.

to examine how the economic isolation and pressure created by sanctions reverberated through the Iraqi economy as a whole and affected government policymaking and economic strategies. In economic terms, the period from 1990 to 2002 is best analyzed in two segments. For the first half of this period, Iraq was virtually isolated from the outside world and left alone to cope with its economic collapse. In the later years, Iraq had much greater global interaction through the Oil for Food program, allowing it not only to better address its economic woes, but also to pursue its political agenda through economic activities.

1990–1996. The first half of the 1990s in Iraq can be roughly characterized as a time when both the government and the population at large were drawing down their available resources in an effort to manage the economic consequences of the UN sanctions. The government developed mechanisms to deal with its economic isolation, as did the average Iraqi family. In the very short term, Iraq was able to fend off the worst economic effects of sanctions thanks to the bumper agricultural crop of 1990 and the substantial resources—in food, spare parts, and other goods—that Iraq plundered from Kuwait.[92] Moreover, Iraq's inability to legally purchase large quantities of military items eased immediate pressure on the country's foreign exchange reserves.

Coping with sanctions over the longer term required more than good fortune and opportunity. The Iraqi regime spent its first five or six years under sanctions preoccupied with two major tasks: maintaining and rationing food supplies to the population at large and protecting the elites who were the key to Saddam's survival from the effects of sanctions.[93] By giving farmers priority access to fuel and machinery and keeping agricultural prices high, the regime hoped to encourage and increase Iraq's domestic agricultural production.[94] Although this approach reaped modest benefits, the agricultural sector continued to be inhibited by the loss of expatriate farm workers and shortages of fertilizer, seeds, spare parts, and farm equipment. After disappointing harvests in 1991 and 1992, the government employed more coercive tactics toward farmers, but without noticeably better results.[95]

As a result, the government also adopted a strategy to ensure that sufficient resources existed to import necessary food items, as was allowed under the UN sanctions regime.[96] Iraqis were banned from importing all luxury items and a wide range of consumer goods.[97] In addition, the government smuggled oil, sold its once substantial gold reserves, and printed money to buy foreign exchange on the black market in an effort to amass adequate resources to purchase food and other items abroad.[98] A U.S. initiative adopted by the United Nations in September 1992 that authorized countries to release frozen Iraqi assets for humanitarian purposes also helped Iraq in these endeavors.[99]

Efforts to maintain food supplies and to accumulate foreign exchange from any source were crucial to Saddam's efforts to protect his inner circle. With those resources, the regime acquired spare parts on the black market to reconstitute its military and to execute huge investment projects such as the draining of the southern marshes, which was seen as important in eliminating resistance to the regime.[100] Saddam also sought to placate his supporters by granting members of the military and those in important civil posts repeated salary increases, a practice made possible only by the unrestrained printing of currency.[101]

These coping strategies were short-term measures that had some notable drawbacks and often were at odds with one another. In particular, the continuous government-induced price rises for agricultural goods and the printing of currency dramatically fueled inflation, which already was high due to the shortage of food and other items. Fluctuations in the value of Iraq's currency, the dinar, also spurred rampant inflation. Such oscillations were closely connected to the continuation of sanctions: the dinar would strengthen temporarily before the UN Security Council met to discuss Iraqi sanctions and would plunge after the council announced that sanctions would remain in place. This pattern was particularly pronounced in the mid-1990s, when Iraq and the United Nations were negotiating the Oil for Food program.

All these factors—sanctions, government policies, and the economic imbalances that both created—triggered a major economic crisis in the middle of the decade. Rapidly rising food prices prompted the government to initiate an emergency austerity program in late 1995.[102] The government stopped printing money, clamped down on the black market, announced higher taxes, and frantically began to sell off state-owned property.[103] But rather than easing the crisis, these measures only exacerbated it by further weakening the dinar and driving prices even higher. Faced with inflation estimated by the governor of the Iraqi Central Bank to be as high as 65,000 percent in late 1995, the regime cut back on food rations and announced a freeze on salaries.[104]

These moves posed a serious threat to the regime by jeopardizing its ability to keep key elements of Iraqi society content. Unable to see any other way of reversing economic trends, Saddam restarted negotiations with the United Nations over a possible Oil for Food program.[105] Talks were reinitiated in February 1996, the details of a deal were finally struck in November, and oil began to flow for export under the scheme in December 1996.

1997–2001.  The Oil for Food program marked a new phase for the Iraqi economy under sanctions. As explored in greater detail later in the chapter, the scheme increased the overall supply of food and medicine, although it was no substitute for a normally functioning economy. The program also had broader beneficial effects on the economy as a whole. The year 1997 marked the first time that Iraq's GDP expanded since the imposition of the sanctions, although the dramatic growth rates of 40 percent (for 1997) and 35 percent (for 1998) represented little real positive gains, given the extremely low base from which they were measured. Substantial drops in inflation also occurred over time as the food situation gradually stabi-

**Figure 4-4.** *Iraq's Oil Production Exports and Earnings, 1976–2001*

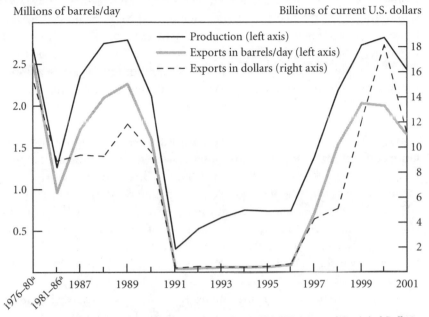

Millions of barrels/day — Billions of current U.S. dollars

Sources: Organization of Petroleum Exporting Countries, *OPEC Annual Statistical Bulletin,* various years; United Nations Office of the Iraq Program; U.S. Department of Energy, Energy Information Administration, for 2001 production; and Economist Intelligence Unit, *Country Profile: Iraq,* 1999–2000, p. 25.

Notes: 1999 and 2000 exports in barrels are from OPEC estimates, and 2001 exports in barrels and dollars are estimates based upon data from the United Nations Office of the Iraq Program.

a. Average annual numbers.

lized.[106] Although the Oil for Food program did not rejuvenate domestic production in most sectors, it played a large role in the partial revitalization of the oil industry.[107] Estimates suggest that oil production nearly tripled and export levels increased more than seventeen-fold in just the two years from 1996 to 1998.[108] As mentioned, by 1999 Iraq was producing almost as much oil as it had in 1989 and was earning more (at least in current dollars) from its oil exports than it had in the year before the invasion of Kuwait (figure 4-4).[109]

The start of the Oil for Food program also marked a new chapter for Iraq's economic policy. No longer preoccupied with supplying monthly food rations, Saddam Hussein could focus on other economic priorities. In addition to restoring and boosting Iraqi oil production, the regime had two main economic preoccupations. First, the regime sought to maximize the resources available to it outside the UN-controlled Oil for Food program. Doing so was essential to its efforts to consolidate and maintain its power within Iraq. As in the first years under sanctions, the regime needed sizable funds in order to placate important constituencies, such as the military and the security apparatus, through a range of expensive undertakings. Securing a steady supply of luxury consumer items and building lavish state accommodations for Saddam's inner circle were part of this effort. Continued military expenditures—despite international sanctions and a real dearth of finances—also were essential to keeping important groups content. The foreign exchange that the regime saved each month after the Oil for Food program eliminated the need to import food, however, was insufficient to meet those expenses.[110] Instead, Saddam financed his endeavors primarily through his extensive and ever-growing smuggling networks.

From the very beginning, the smuggling of Iraqi oil occurred in contravention of sanctions. In addition to the export of Iraqi oil to Jordan, which the United Nations "noted," illicit oil transactions occurred across the border between Jordan and Iraq. The border with Turkey also was a primary crossing point for goods smuggled in and out of Iraq.[111] Smuggling with the collusion of Iraq's longtime enemy, Iran, also rose steadily.[112] Either through its long porous border, or, more popularly, through its waterways in the Gulf, Iran was one of the most important and fastest-growing channels for the illicit export of Iraqi oil in the 1990s.[113]

Although the volume of oil being smuggled out of Iraq in the 1990s was difficult to gauge, an upward trend was clear.[114] In the early part of the decade, Iraq continued to produce oil in excess of its domestic needs, suggesting that smuggling was occurring from the outset.[115] Illicit sales rose as oil production increased and the legal export of oil under the Oil for Food program made smuggling more difficult to detect. Iraq's growing ability to refine crude oil at home and the "sanctions fatigue" felt by Iraq's neighbors further facilitated smuggling efforts. Estimates of the number of barrels of oil smuggled out of Iraq each day rose from 50,000 in 1998 to more than 600,000 by the end of 2000.[116] Such large volumes and the rising price of oil made illicit sales of oil hugely profitable for the regime in Iraq, which reportedly had a monopoly on smuggling apart from that occurring through Kurdish territory in northern Iraq.[117] Although the regime received only a portion of profits from the sale of each barrel of oil, some estimates suggested that by 2002, Saddam was earning between $2 billion and $3 billion a year from smuggling.[118]

Iraq's second economic preoccupation in the late 1990s was to negotiate economic contracts with foreign firms in ways that sought to increase international pressure to rescind the sanctions. Over time, Iraq intensified its efforts to strike executory-type deals (deals pending the lifting of sanctions) with foreign companies to develop the Iraqi oil industry.[119] Iraq engaged in discussions toward this end in the early part of the 1990s; negotiations over the second half of the decade and beyond produced actual signed contracts.[120] Not coincidentally, Iraq signed or negotiated the most prominent of the deals with companies based in countries holding permanent seats on the UN Security Council: Russia and China concluded deals to develop already discovered oil fields in Iraq while French companies came to provisional understandings with Iraq to develop other areas.[121] Given the poor state of the oil industries in China and Russia in particular, those contracts clearly gave priority to politics and the hope of intensifying Chinese and Russian pressure to lift sanctions rather than to sound investment.

The strategy of using executory-type oil contracts to create political pressure for lifting sanctions was one part of Iraq's commercial-cum-political agenda. The Oil for Food program also provided useful opportunities to cultivate commercial contacts with countries sympathetic to Iraq's quest to be free of sanctions.[122] Instead of negotiating these deals on a purely economic basis, Iraq transformed the process into a highly political one. At first glance, it appears that Iraq sought to cultivate stronger economic links with the United States, given the robust trade in Iraqi oil that quickly developed with the United States after the Oil for Food program got under way. Whereas in 1997 the United States consumed only 12 percent of Iraqi oil exports, in 1999 the United States imported more than 600,000 barrels a day from Iraq, accounting for 44 percent of the dollar value of Iraq's exports. These figures, however, do not provide insight into Iraq's political agenda, given that they only capture the flow of oil from Iraq to other countries *after* the oil was marketed by foreign companies.

Of greater interest is the award of contracts by the Iraqi government to foreign companies seeking to market Iraqi oil. Iraq's original approach to the disbursement of these contracts was to favor companies domiciled in countries on the Security Council, spreading contracts relatively evenly among them. In the first phase of the Oil for Food program, companies in France, Russia, the United States, and the United Kingdom absorbed contracts to market more than half of the barrels of oil to be exported.[123] The Iraqi government pursued this initial strategy presumably in the hope that

**Figure 4-5.** *Contracts Awarded by the Iraqi Government to Market Oil*[a]

Millions of barrels

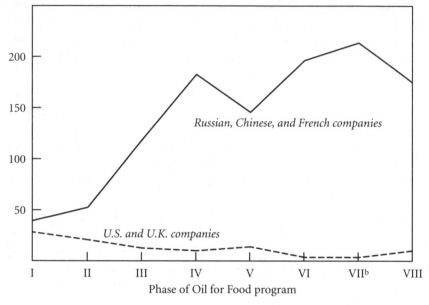

Phase of Oil for Food program

Sources: United Nations Office of the Iraq Program, weekly updates; and *Middle East Economic Survey,* various issues.

a. Each phase of the Oil for Food Program is approximately six months long; phase I began in December 1996.

b. Total exports in phase VII and their distribution between companies are estimates extrapolated from hard data available through January 5, 2002.

commercial contact with each country would strengthen political pressure to lift the sanctions on Iraq. However, within the first year of the Oil for Food program, Iraq's oil minister announced that Iraq would give priority to contracts with companies based in "friendly" countries.[124] Russia, France, and to a lesser extent China became the major beneficiaries of this shift (see figure 4-5). By phase III of the Oil for Food program, companies from these three countries had been awarded contracts to market almost 65 percent of Iraqi oil, while American and British companies claimed the right to market less than 7 percent.[125]

Iraq's creation of a surcharge on oil sales enabled it to meld its pursuit of resources outside the Oil for Food program with its quest to use economic influence for political gain. Starting in December 2000, Iraq required firms marketing Iraqi oil to pay it directly 50 cents per barrel. This practice largely backfired, as the United States, the United Kingdom, and the United Nations combated the surcharge by establishing a policy of pricing Iraq's oil retrospectively. Under this scheme, Iraqi exports of oil declined notably, as the uncertainty of purchasing oil without knowing its exact price diminished demand (see figure 4-4). Whatever the monetary benefit to Iraq, the surcharge episode did alter the profile of firms dealing directly with Iraq. Iraq signed many more contracts with unknown oil companies—many of them apparently based in countries more sympathetic to Iraq. Less subject to international scrutiny than major oil companies, these firms allowed Iraq to continue exporting oil through favored middlemen with less oversight from the United Nations or western governments.

The agreements Iraq established with foreign companies for the purchase of civilian goods under the Oil for Food program reflect similar patterns to those governing the export of oil. Although initial contracts were fairly evenly distributed among Security Council members, the share going to U.S. companies declined dramatically after Iraq declared its intention to impose trade sanctions on "hostile" countries after the Desert Fox bombings in December 1998 (figure 4-6).[126] Iraq further politicized the Oil for Food program to its advantage by announcing in 1999 that it would refuse to trade with any company filing claims with the UN Compensation Commission for damages sustained as a result of the Iraqi invasion of Kuwait. This statement reportedly led to the withdrawal of hundreds of millions of dollars' worth of compensatory claims.[127]

By early 2001, Iraqi efforts to use economic links to political advantage were no longer limited to executory oil agreements and the manipulation of contracts through the Oil for Food program. Pressures for Iraq's rehabilitation—fueled in part by political factors and in part by Iraq's growing economic role in the region due to its smuggling and legitimate Oil for Food trade—led to the signing of bilateral trade deals between Iraq and other Middle Eastern countries. The free trade agreement signed between Iraq and Egypt in January 2001 established a joint trade zone and abolished all tariffs between Baghdad and Cairo; an Iraq-Syria trade deal signed at the same time and an Iraqi-UAE deal clinched later in the year included similar provisions.[128] Although the agreements have little real economic significance as long as sanctions are in place and all legal trade is regulated by the Oil for Food program, their closing had important political implications for Iraq. Trade ties between Iraq and Saudi Arabia and Lebanon also

**Figure 4-6.** *Iraqi Imports under the Oil for Food Program by Origin,*
*1996–2001*

Millions of U.S. dollars

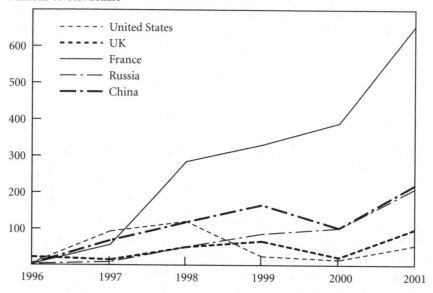

Source: International Monetary Fund, *Direction of Trade Statistics,* various years.

strengthened in 2001, demonstrating the breadth of Saddam's economic
and political convalescence.[129]

### Political Impact

Sanctions had a significant negative impact on both the Iraqi regime's
international standing and its domestic strength. In the absence of sanctions, Iraq would be more integrated into the regional and global community. Particularly during the 1990s, sanctions were fairly effective in isolating Baghdad politically. Although the sanctions regime did not explicitly
forbid the flight of passenger planes to Iraq or the establishment of diplomatic relations with Baghdad, for virtually all of the 1990s, most countries
refrained from making such overtures.[130] In 2000 the political force of sanctions began to erode more rapidly, in part due to sanctions fatigue and in
part to Arab disappointment and anger over the failing Middle East peace

process. The single most important factor chipping away at the political impact of sanctions was Saddam Hussein's success in convincing much of the world that the human suffering in Iraq was the result of an American-led, sanctions-backed conspiracy against the Iraqi people, rather than largely a product of his own making. From Qatar to France to Venezuela, alleviating the suffering in Iraq became equated with lifting the sanctions, even though, as argued later in this chapter, that link is far from certain given the priorities of the Iraqi regime. Sanctions allowed Iraq to present itself to the world as a victim, patching over global memories of its past aggression and thereby aiding it immeasurably in its rehabilitation efforts in the region and beyond. Yet, even despite this significant erosion of support for sanctions, Iraq remained far more isolated in the world in 2002 than it would have been in the absence of sanctions.

Saddam did find a number of ways to turn sanctions to his domestic advantage in the short term. Sanctions created an external enemy in the form of the United States (more so than the United Nations) and perpetuated a "siege mentality" in Iraq, both of which the regime exploited to deflect criticism from its rule and to justify its own repressive behavior. Saddam also used sanctions to solidify his domestic political position by selectively provoking crises with the international community in ways that exposed the fractiousness of the Security Council and allowed Saddam to portray himself as more powerful than his international opponents.[131] Finally, sanctions increased the dependence of virtually all Iraqis on Saddam for their physical well-being. Through his vast smuggling networks, Saddam provided the Iraqi elite with access to luxuries and essential commodities; through the Oil for Food program, Saddam controlled the distribution of free food rations in all but the Kurdish north, enabling him to pose as the provider for his people in the face of international economic aggression.

Despite the variety of ways in which Saddam sought to turn sanctions on Iraq to his advantage, there is no question that over the long term sanctions made the regime far weaker than it would have been in their absence. The discontent and hardship that sanctions caused—and were perceived to cause—seriously eroded the domestic legitimacy of the regime. In the past, Saddam justified his rule by pointing to the prosperity of the country and its formidable military establishment and by relying on his extended family and Sunni clans. More than a decade of sanctions narrowed his base of support considerably, as multiple coup attempts and tribal rebellions over the period suggest. Saddam stayed in power in spite of sanctions, not because of them. The longevity of his rule was made possible by the repressive nature of the regime, the fractiousness of Iraqi society, and Saddam's mastery of the Iraqi power structure.[132]

### Goals Achieved

The success or failure of UN sanctions on Iraq in achieving the goals set out for them was mixed from the outset. In the pre–Gulf war period, sanctions alone did not force Saddam Hussein to withdraw Iraqi troops from Kuwait; however, they did play a critical role in keeping Kuwaiti wealth out of Iraqi hands and in buying sufficient time for the United States to organize a broad-based international coalition.[133] Even more important, the imposition and maintenance of sanctions in the period between the invasion and the start of the Gulf war was an essential "box-checking" exercise; the failure of sanctions to compel Iraq to withdraw from Kuwait convinced many actors initially averse to the use of military force of the need for stronger actions, thereby building support for eventual military action against Iraq.[134]

In assessing the performance of sanctions beyond this pre-war period, two complicating factors must be kept in mind. First, U.S. and UN policy toward Iraq involved a variety of tools besides sanctions. The use and threat of military force, intensive diplomacy, the maintenance of safe havens and no-fly zones, covert action, and support for the Iraqi opposition all played into Saddam Hussein's calculus to act as he did. Although neatly separating out the effects of each tool is a futile task, acknowledging where a combination of instruments affected a particular course of action is critical. Second, UN sanctions were used to pursue multiple objectives. UN resolutions passed after the Gulf war demanded that Iraq destroy or cease pursuit of all nuclear, chemical, and biological weapons as well as missiles having a range beyond 150 kilometers. At the same time, Iraq was called on to recognize the UN-demarcated border between Iraq and Kuwait, return all Kuwaiti property it held in its possession, repatriate all Kuwaiti and other POWs and missing persons, and compensate those who suffered for its invasion of Kuwait. Finally, the United Nations expected Iraq to renounce all forms of terrorism. In addition to these explicit UN objectives, now and again the United States articulated its own additional demands, stating on occasion that sanctions on Iraq would remain in place until a new regime took power in Baghdad. Although the record of sanctions in achieving each of these goals must be considered, any final assessment of sanctions must acknowledge that the UN sanctions regime was crafted and implemented with a particular set of goals in mind.

CHANGING OR CONTAINING THE IRAQI REGIME. Sanctions failed to provoke a change of regime in Baghdad, whether by forcing Saddam to step aside, instigating a successful coup from within his own ranks, or inciting outside opposition to overthrow him. As discussed in the previous section, sanctions did weaken the legitimacy of Saddam's rule, although not sufficiently to bring about his downfall. Even acknowledging these limitations, sanctions—and the policy that they underpinned throughout the 1990s and beyond—can claim credit for other significant accomplishments in the realm of containing the Iraqi regime.

Although it is always difficult to claim success based on what did *not* occur, UN and U.S. efforts were critical in containing Iraqi external aggression. In the time between Saddam's ascension to power in 1979 and the Gulf war, Iraq was almost constantly engaged in bloody conflicts with its neighbors, all of which it provoked. Yet after 1992, Iraq's regional bellicosity was limited mostly to the rhetorical realm.[135] A more subdued Saddam Hussein was essential to regional stability and the unfolding of the Middle East peace process over the course of the 1990s.

Although the use of military force deserves some credit for the more tamed Saddam of the 1990s, sanctions also advanced the military containment of Iraq in important and varied ways. First, sanctions were successful in keeping resources out of the hands of the regime, thereby limiting Iraq's military expenditures. As mentioned before, sanctions were responsible for depriving Saddam of control of between $175 billion and $250 billion in oil revenue from 1990 to 2000, depending on the calculations employed. That loss of revenue seriously hampered his pursuit of conventional arms. Although the UN sanctions regime did not entirely prevent him from acquiring military goods, spare parts, and technology through smuggling and illegal contracts, it did make his quest much more difficult, haphazard, and expensive.[136] No reliable indicators exist concerning Iraqi defense expenditures since the Gulf war, but available estimates suggest that they were down to anywhere between one-tenth and one-thirtieth of what they were after the Iran-Iraq war.[137] According to one analyst, although Iraq has continued to spend between 33 and 45 percent of its much-reduced, post–Gulf war GDP on military expenses, it would have spent at least an additional $21 to $25 billion on military imports alone between 1991 and 2000 if it had had access to greater resources.[138] Although growing smuggling and increasingly porous borders gradually eroded the effectiveness of sanctions, international control of the proceeds of the vast majority of Iraqi oil sales through the UN escrow account remained a key factor in Iraq's containment.

In addition, sanctions were instrumental in the effort to diminish Iraq's weapons capability through the use of another tool, UN weapons inspections. Because sanctions were a key element in coercing Iraq to initially accept weapons inspectors and in extracting Iraqi cooperation with UNSCOM throughout much of the 1990s, they deserve some of the credit for what weapons inspections achieved while they operated in Iraq.[139] Although limited and erratic, Iraq's cooperation with UNSCOM did result in significant progress toward curbing Iraq's weapons of mass destruction programs and its missile arsenal and prevented the research and progress that would have occurred in their absence. Iraq's disarmament was most complete in the nuclear realm due to the joint efforts of UNSCOM and the IAEA, which reported that Iraq had completed the disclosure of its nuclear program in April 1998.[140] UNSCOM made substantial progress in eradicating Iraq's chemical weapons and ballistic missile capability, destroying hundreds of missiles and missile warheads, tens of thousands of chemical munitions, and hundreds of tons of chemical weapons agents.[141] In contrast, Iraqi biological weapons programs were more difficult to pursue, due not only to continued Iraqi misrepresentation of its efforts in this area, but also to the relatively simple materials and technology needed to create biological weapons. As a result, the threat posed by Iraq's biological weapons remained a cause of substantial concern throughout the tenure of UNSCOM and beyond.

Finally, sanctions and strict export controls helped constrain Iraqi weapons capability by curbing the sale of WMD components and technology to Iraq. The restrictions were at first an important complement to UNSCOM as it worked in Iraq from 1991 to 1998. Once inspections were halted, those controls became the only means to restrain what could be assumed to be a continued and persistent effort by Iraq to acquire weapons of mass destruction.[142] How successful the restrictions on their own were in forestalling Iraqi weapons acquisition is open to question; reports of Iraqi efforts to procure dual-use items and to reconstruct missile production complexes and former dual-use chemical production facilities suggest the inability of sanctions and export controls to fully stem Iraqi access.[143] Nevertheless, the effect of sanctions in containing Iraqi WMD capability is best appreciated if one considers what Iraq's WMD status would be in their absence. In the view of some experts, had Iraq not been under sanctions, in all likelihood it would have possessed several nuclear weapons and much more advanced chemical and biological programs by 2000.[144]

CHANGING THE BEHAVIOR OF THE REGIME. In contrast to the generally impressive, if not perfect, record of sanctions in containing Iraq economically, militarily, and, for a time, politically, the ability of sanctions to coerce the regime to change its behavior has been extremely poor. The clearest success in this department—Baghdad's 1994 recognition of the UN-demarcated Iraqi-Kuwaiti border—is attributable both to the threat of military force as well as to the pressure of sanctions.[145] Beyond this achievement, successes in convincing the regime to alter its conduct were scarce. Although sanctions aided UNSCOM and the IAEA in achieving measurable progress toward eliminating Iraq's weapons threat, at least for the period they were able to operate in Iraq, they had seemingly no impact in compelling Saddam to genuinely accept Iraq's disarmament or in altering his unwavering commitment to Iraq's WMD programs. Saddam demonstrated the high priority he placed on maintaining and eventually reconstituting these programs through his extensive efforts to deceive UN inspectors about Iraq's WMD pursuits and his continued refusal to comply fully with UN resolutions concerning Iraqi disarmament, even at extremely high costs to Iraq. As chronicled in UNSCOM reports and independent accounts of those involved with the disarmament efforts, Iraq consistently misrepresented the extent of its weapons programs, concealed information necessary to the efforts of the inspectors, and actively obstructed UNSCOM from carrying out its mandate.[146] Iraq also revealed its commitment to its WMD program by using its very scarce resources to advance its ongoing missile program and by pursuing the purchase of items such as the gyroscopes needed for missile navigation and dual-use matter needed to create chemical or biological weapons.[147]

Sanctions also seem to have had no impact on Iraqi support for terrorism. They did not compel Baghdad to eliminate its ties to terrorist organizations, cease its efforts to assassinate its opponents overseas, or end its support for the Mujahedin-e Khalq, the Iranian dissident group and designated foreign terrorist organization.[148] At the same time, there is little evidence that sanctions spurred Iraq to greater levels of involvement in terrorism, either by actively sponsoring groups such as al-Qaida or directly instigating terrorist acts of its own.

Finally, although the no-fly zones played an important role in deterring Saddam from wide-scale persecution or elimination of the Iraqi Kurds in the north or Iraqi Shia in the south, sanctions themselves had no obvious positive effect in altering how Saddam treated his population. Despite UN resolution 688, which called on the regime to show a greater respect for human rights, personal freedoms in Iraq declined from an already extremely low base over this period, with human rights organizations and western governments decrying Iraq as one of the most repressive societies in the world.[149] In addition to the persecution of many segments of its own population, whether Kurds, Shia, Turkomans, or other non-Arab minorities, Iraq refused to release or account for the approximately 600 Kuwaitis taken during the Gulf war.[150]

### Costs Borne

HUMANITARIAN AND SOCIAL COSTS.    An assessment of the humanitarian impact of sanctions demands stripping away the rhetoric so prevalent in many of the discussions concerning the sanctions on Iraq. It involves first making a responsible evaluation of the humanitarian situation on the ground, a task complicated by the limited statistics in existence and the questionable credibility of many of those that are available. It then requires assessing to what extent this situation is attributable to sanctions and to what extent other factors—such the long-term effects of the Iran-Iraq war, the damage inflicted during the Gulf war to Iraqi infrastructure, decisions made by Saddam about allocating resources, and the drought that decimated much of the region in 1999 and 2000—bear responsibility for it.

Comparing basic indicators of the humanitarian situation in Iraq with those of other countries reveals the extent to which Iraqi human development fell behind regional averages over the 1990s. Once boasting one of the most comprehensive welfare states in the region, throughout much of the 1990s Iraq ranked behind most Gulf Cooperation Council (GCC) countries in the areas of life expectancy, percentage of low-birthweight babies, and immunization rates.[151] Similarly, if the situation in Iraq in the 1990s as measured by these indicators is compared with the conditions in Iraq before the Gulf war, a steep decline in most conditions is evident. Yet although living conditions in Iraq in 2001 remained significantly worse than those in other countries in the region and even in comparison to those in Iraq in the past, the Iraqi humanitarian situation was not static over the last decade of the twentieth century. After deteriorating substantially in the first half of the 1990s, living conditions in Iraq did show some improvements in the final years of the decade.[152]

The first few years after the Gulf war were a period of abrupt adjustment, not simply for the state and its policymakers, but for the population in general. Although the regime was able to hold off the most severe effects of the embargo in the immediate days and weeks following its imposition, the isolation of the economy soon began to take a toll on the Iraqi people. Before long, Iraq's heavy dependence on agricultural imports translated into food shortages. Unemployment rates rose steeply as the economy contracted due to both Iraq's largely severed trade relations with the rest of the world and destruction from the war. Inflation—pushed upward as goods became more and more scarce—rapidly eroded the purchasing power of Iraqis, leaving them struggling to supplement government food rations with purchases on the open market. The vast majority of Iraqis sought to cope with the situation by systematically selling off family assets, although that strategy provided no long-term solution and eventually forced many even once well-off families into penury.

As the sources and value of Iraqi income dwindled, the standard of living of most Iraqis also eroded due to the deterioration of Iraqi social infrastructure. Under stress long before the Gulf war, the Iraqi education system continued its decline. Not only were facilities and supplies limited, but more and more families began to withdraw their children from school so that they could work and supplement household incomes.[153] Shortages of medicines, medical equipment, and medical specialists affected both the quality of Iraqi health services and civilian access to them. Facilities for the purification of water and treatment of waste, destroyed in the Gulf war and largely kept in disrepair by ongoing sanctions, further exacerbated conditions.

Increased poverty, food insecurity, eroded social services, and deteriorating infrastructure contributed to sharp increases in malnutrition, disease, and mortality rates in Iraq.[154] Although those trends are easy to establish, less certain are the numbers bandied about to quantify them.[155] A great deal of attention was given to estimates offered by the Iraqi Ministry of Health, which claimed in 2000 that sanctions resulted in the needless deaths of 1.35 million Iraqis, mostly children.[156] In many cases, the media, international nongovernmental organizations (NGOs), and even various UN agencies commandeered these government statistics, giving them more credibility than they warranted.[157] Almost certainly, the Iraqi government seriously exaggerated the statistics in a deliberate effort to win international support for lifting sanctions.[158] More realistic are numbers provided by an epidemiologist who constructed estimates for Iraqi child mortality rates based on more dependable statistics on malnutrition, infrastructure, immunization rates, food prices, and other data at his disposal. Under the scenario considered to be "most likely," this study calculated that in the period from August 1990 to March 1998, approximately 227,000 more Iraqi children under five years of age died than would have been predicted for the same span of time in pre-Gulf war Iraq.[159] This total—substantially lower than the numbers submitted by the Iraqi government but still of huge consequence—can be attributed to the Gulf war and the additional hardships borne by Iraqis since its end. The results of a UNICEF study conducted in Iraq in 1999 are consistent with these findings and reveal more than a doubling of infant and child mortality rates over the 1990s.[160]

The aggregate nature of these statistics obscures the reality that the intensity of human suffering in Iraq varied across different segments of society.[161] The urban poor reportedly fared the worst in absolute terms, having little cushion to stave off the effects of economic collapse. Iraqis with few sources of income and the greatest need for social services—such as the elderly, the sickly, and the many female-headed households that existed after the Iran-Iraq and Gulf wars—suffered the most. Changes in Iraq's middle class also were dramatic. Rather than having been eliminated by the combined effects of emigration and impoverishment, the Iraqi middle class is likely to have changed its composition and character. To some extent, this "new" class earns its living from smuggling opportunities; other members of a mid-level or professional stratum survive by working for the regime to maintain the structures of the Iraqi state. Although little is known about this stratum of society, given members' dependence on the regime and illegal transactions for their living, they almost certainly do not have the sympathy for democracy and accountability or the pro-western attitudes commonly associated with the middle class in much of the developing world.

The region in which individuals live and the ethnic group or religious sect to which they belong also have had considerable influence on their prospects for survival and overall well-being in Iraq in the 1990s and beyond.[162] For instance, the three Kurdish northern provinces have fared very differently from the rest of Iraq. Initially subject to an internal embargo by Baghdad after the 1991 uprising, this area did poorly, suffering from high unemployment, food and housing shortages, and large numbers of refugees living in tent cities because of fear of Iraqi military attacks. However, the establishment of Operation Provide Comfort in 1991, the Oil for Food program (which allowed the United Nations, not the Iraqi regime, to distribute food and medicine in the north), and a thriving trade in smuggled goods changed the situation. By the mid-1990s, the Kurdish north boasted the most normally functioning economy and the highest standard of living in all of Iraq. A widely cited report suggests that infant and child mortality rates in northern Iraq declined since the implementation of the Oil for Food Program, as opposed to the rest of Iraq, where levels rose throughout most of the 1990s.[163]

The situation in Baghdad-controlled parts of Iraq was more variable. The largely Shiite south of the country suffered the most, with the highest rates of malnutrition and the worst problems with medical facilities and inadequate infrastructure concentrated in areas such as Amara and the southern city of Basra. In the central part of the country, inhabited mostly by Sunni Muslims, the picture was more uneven. Although areas of extreme deprivation existed, Saddam ensured that localities key to his power base, such as the city of Tikrit, were relatively buffered from economic collapse.[164] Even within Baghdad, a tour through different neighborhoods suggested that not all Iraqis have suffered in the same way. Villas, designer shops, and art galleries stud the area of Mansour, where many of the Ba'ath party elite reside, while the conditions in Saddam City, a satellite area where migrant Shia from the south reside, are grim by any standard.[165]

The humanitarian situation overall has improved somewhat since the Oil for Food program began in 1996–97. Although the scheme did not reverse the decline in human development in Iraq, it arrested some of the worst trends of the first half of the 1990s and led to some substantial improvements over time. Perhaps most notable, the Oil for Food program stabilized worsening malnutrition rates by increasing the availability of food and stabilizing its price.[166] Despite these significant successes, the relatively poor performance of the Oil for Food program in other sectors compromised its ability to reverse the negative trends in mortality. Translating the greater availability of food into improvements in infant and child mortality and malnutrition rates would have demanded advances in water, sanitation, health services, and even education.[167] Yet, little progress was made in any of those sectors throughout the 1990s. According to a report from the UN Secretary General in early 2000, Iraq's water and sanitation facilities remained in poor condition.[168] Although the situation continued to improve into the 2000s, essential drugs remained difficult to secure and many routine medical treatments continued to be unavailable; as publicized frequently in the western media, many health care facilities struggled to function without electricity or sufficient supplies for sanitation. Education facilities also continued to deteriorate.[169]

Attributing all the human suffering in Iraq to the UN sanctions regime risks confusing correlation with causality. While the sanctions cannot be fully disentangled from the human suffering that occurred in Iraq, they did not bear even the lion's share of the responsibility for it. Multilateral sanctions precipitated the humanitarian crisis in Iraq by forcing a severe contraction of

Iraq's economy; however, it was the Iraqi regime that perpetuated this crisis. Most fundamentally, Saddam refused to comply with UN resolutions, which charted the way for Iraq to free itself from sanctions. Had the regime cooperated with UNSCOM and fully disarmed, as it agreed to do in the UN armistice, sanctions on Iraq would have been in place only a short time. Instead, Saddam chose to place his WMD programs above the well-being of Iraqis. Early on, he recognized how the suffering of the Iraqi people could be a potent tool in his quest to have sanctions lifted before Iraq fully disarmed. As a result, instead of taking the numerous opportunities presented to him to alleviate the suffering of his own people, Saddam consistently chose courses of action that ensured continued civilian hardship.

For example, for five years Saddam rejected UN efforts to launch a humanitarian program that would allow Iraq to sell its oil in return for food and medical supplies, despite repeated efforts by the United Nations to make the program more palatable to him.[170] As discussed earlier, Saddam relented and accepted the Oil for Food scheme only when a domestic economic crisis threatened his regime. The positive impact that this program had on the well-being of Iraqis demonstrated the huge human costs paid by average Iraqis for Saddam's refusal to adopt the program five years earlier than he did.

Also fallacious is the argument that the regime cannot provide for its citizens because a significant share of its oil revenues are used to support UN efforts in Iraq. The United Nations does direct 28 percent of Iraq's export earnings to administer its Iraq programs and to compensate victims of the Gulf war. Yet Iraq had access to more resources in 2000 for the purchase of food, medicine, and other humanitarian goods than it had to cover all of its expenditures in almost any year in the 1980s—a time when Iraq not only was providing services to its citizens but also waging a war with Iran and purchasing vast quantities of weaponry from abroad. The problem in the late 1990s was less the volume of resources available to the regime for humanitarian purposes than its own disinterest in using them. In the final months of 2000, billions of dollars of uncommitted funds languished in the UN escrow account, awaiting Iraqi action to allocate them to the purchase of food, medicine, and other essentials.

In addition to failing to use all the funds at its disposal for humanitarian purposes, the Iraqi regime repeatedly resisted taking full advantage of the Oil for Food scheme in other ways, doing so only when it came under intense international pressure. For instance, whether intentionally or through carelessness, Iraq submitted countless incomplete contracts to the UN Sanctions Committee, presumably with the knowledge that the contracts would be frozen or seriously delayed. The UN Secretary General also documented how the Iraqi government continuously failed to order the full amounts of nutritional supplements available for the most needy in Iraq, even in the face of UN urging.[171] Instead, the regime gave priority to ordering commodities and equipment having value to the military and security apparatus—such as communications devices and electricity—at the expense of purely humanitarian procurements such as food, health, and educational resources.[172] The regime also showed its disregard for average Iraqis by resisting the efforts of the United Nations to link the Oil for Food program to local agricultural production, a move that would contribute to the much-needed rejuvenation of Iraq's local economy.[173]

The regime also contributed to Iraqi suffering by failing to deliver vast quantities of humanitarian goods to the Iraqi people for their benefit. Although the delivery of some items improved over time in response to international pressure, vast quantities of medicine and medical equipment languished in warehouses.[174] According to UN observers, only 15 percent of the medical equipment delivered to Iraq since the Oil for Food program began had been distributed by early 1999.[175] The United Nations blamed logistics and Iraqi institutional weaknesses for these shortcomings.[176] While those bottlenecks were surely part of the problem, reports that the regime smuggled medicine out of Iraq and sold it on the black market suggest less benign reasons behind government failures to deliver goods to the population.[177] Inadequate distribution was also a problem in the education and water and sanitation sectors.[178]

Saddam also demonstrated his questionable commitment, if not virtual indifference, to abating the humanitarian situation in Iraq through his use of the resources at his disposal over much of the 1990s and beyond. Although the United Nations controls all proceeds from legal Iraqi oil sales, as explored earlier, the Iraqi government acquired considerable resources through its illicit trade. Saddam channeled his smuggling profits and other sources of income not into improving living conditions in Iraq but into securing and legitimizing his regime.[179] Military expenditure remained a top priority of the government, with the June 2000 missile test demonstrating the regime's willingness to channel scarce resources into upgrading its military if sanctions or covert sales permit it. Saddam also spent approximately $2 billion on Iraq's Third River Project between 1992 and 1997, during the period of the most acute deprivation.[180] Ostensibly intended to improve farming conditions in southern Iraq by draining swamps in the region, this massive undertaking appeared to have been a security measure aimed at destroying terrain in which many Iraqi Shia fighting Saddam's regime took refuge. Had Saddam dedicated a portion of those resources to improving Iraqi hospitals or sewage systems or countless other humanitarian endeavors, the suffering in Iraq would have been substantially reduced.[181]

Finally, Saddam sought to block even the smallest measures by the international community to aid Iraqis outside the Oil for Food program. He repeatedly refused to allow a team of specialists appointed by the United Nations into Iraq to investigate humanitarian conditions.[182] Similarly, efforts made by international NGOs to operate in Iraq for humanitarian purposes were frustrated specifically by the regime's failure to grant visas and internal travel permits and more generally by its interference with NGO operations.[183]

While recognizing Saddam's large role in prolonging and exacerbating the suffering of average Iraqis, one must acknowledge that shortcomings in the Oil for Food program added to their hardships. At the most general level, the program (in conjunction with sanctions) distorted the economy and made normal, profit-seeking economic behavior difficult or meaningless, helping to discourage entrepreneurs and private producers, particularly farmers, by robbing them of incentives to produce. More specifically, several shortcomings in the program frustrated international efforts to mitigate hardships. For instance, members of the Security Council—the United States in particular—often placed holds on large numbers of contracts, a practice that impeded the smooth implementation of the scheme (figure 4-7).[184] Some members opposed the sale of large amounts of equipment critical for the repair of sanitation systems, water purification facilities, and other civilian infrastructure in Iraq on the grounds that dual-use items such as water chlorinators and pesticides would be used for military rather than humanitarian purposes. Although Iraq accused U.S. and U.K. members of the Sanctions Committee of holding up contracts for political reasons, the United Nations confirmed that incomplete or vague applications caused most of the delays.[185] Whatever the reason for the bottlenecks, they compromised the UN program and limited its ability to address the humanitarian situation in Iraq. The new "smarter sanctions" procedures introduced as a result of the passage of UN resolution 1409 in May 2002 should simplify and expedite the process significantly.[186]

Figure 4-7. *Iraq's Humanitarian Contracts on Hold, by Sector*

Millions of U.S. dollars

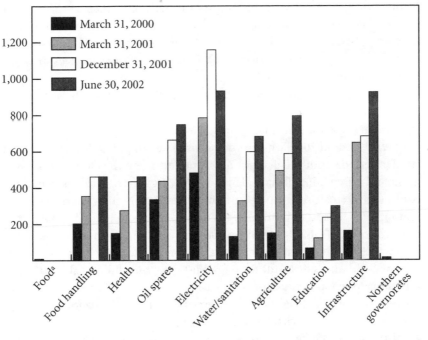

Source: United Nations Office of the Iraq Program, "Basic Figures," various dates (www.un.org/ Depts/oip/latest/basicfigures.html).

a. Includes food and health-sector supplies bulk-purchased by the government of Iraq for the three northern governorates.

COSTS TO UN AND U.S. INTERESTS. More than ten years of sanctions on Iraq have resulted in numerous and widespread costs, even beyond the ones borne by Iraq. Although funds from the sale of Iraqi oil allowed the United Nations to avoid most of the economic costs associated with its extensive involvement in Iraq over the years, the episode entailed serious political costs for the international organization. The common perception that UN sanctions—not to mention UN weapons inspections teams— failed in Iraq carries heavy political baggage. The fierce criticism of the United Nations concerning the morality of its involvement in Iraq damaged its reputation. Moreover, the overly simplistic but widespread belief that sanctions were solely responsible for the human suffering in Iraq weakened international interest in using economic penalties for foreign policy objectives.[187] Given the few instruments available to the United Nations to address external aggression or other unacceptable violations of international law, the growing reluctance to employ sanctions—particularly when based on an incomplete assessment of sanctions on Iraq—could harm the ability of the international body to react to challenges to peace and security in the post–cold war era.

Iraq's neighbors and others in the region also endured substantial economic losses despite efforts to alleviate the effects of sanctions on third parties.[188] Turkey estimated that it lost $35 billion abiding by the embargo between 1990 and 2000, while Jordan claimed $5 billion in lost trade over a similar period.[189] Although expanding trade through the Oil for Food program and burgeoning illicit trade gradually eased those burdens, sanctions continued to create substantial economic pressure on many countries in the region.[190] In contrast to the declining economic costs to Iraq's neighbors, the political costs of upholding the sanctions mounted as time passed. Arab governments found it increasingly unpopular to defend the sanctions in the face of Saddam's successful propaganda campaign linking the lifting of sanctions to the alleviation of Iraqi suffering. Once the Middle East peace process ground to a near halt, many governments in the region found the isolation of Iraq to be virtually untenable.

Although this chapter cannot offer a complete examination of the losses suffered by all countries, it does consider the costs endured by the United States. The multilateral nature of sanctions influenced the shape and magnitude of economic costs. Unlike in Iran and Libya, in Iraq U.S. companies did not bear one-sided opportunity costs associated with unilateral prohibitions on investment. Given that the sanctions prohibited foreign investment in Iraq by any source, American companies were not standing on the sidelines as non-U.S. companies signed and executed lucrative deals in the energy sector.[191] U.S. firms nevertheless could ultimately find themselves at a disadvantage: the American interpretation of the sanctions regime prevented U.S. companies from negotiating executory-type contracts with Iraq pending the lifting of sanctions, while Russian, Chinese, and other firms signed such deals.[192] If Iraq honors these provisional contracts once sanctions are removed, U.S. firms could be sidelined from major exploration opportunities in Iraq.[193]

While U.S. losses associated with forgone investment opportunities under multilateral sanctions are less than under unilateral regimes, the opposite holds true for damages incurred as a result of abrogated trade. As seen in other cases examined in this book, the effects of unilateral trade sanctions often gradually diminish as global trade patterns reconfigure. Multilateral sanctions—by effectively removing a market from the world trading community—inhibit readjustment. The resulting global surplus in certain products would have made it harder to find markets for them or forced down their price. As a result, U.S. exporters might have had marginally more trouble in redirecting their trade to other destinations and therefore have been more sensitive to the crunch of Iraqi sanctions. Given the considerable volume of trade occurring between the United States and Iraq before the Gulf war, costs borne by U.S. exporters accumulated over time.[194] These losses—which nevertheless represent an extremely small proportion of overall U.S. exports during that period—were compounded by the $5 billion that U.S. firms lost when contracts with Iraq and Kuwait were abrogated in the immediate wake of the invasion.[195] Although the Oil for Food program had the potential to mitigate many of the losses to U.S. exporters by offering the United States an opportunity to resume legal exports to Iraq, the volume of U.S. sales to Iraq through this program remained low.[196]

The potential of sanctions to seriously damage U.S. energy interests remained largely unfulfilled. When the embargo was imposed in 1990, petroleum and petroleum products constituted the bulk of U.S. imports from Iraq. Sanctions forced the United States, as well as other countries depending on Iraqi oil, to look to other sources to satisfy their energy needs. While the withdrawal of 4 million barrels a day of Iraqi and Kuwaiti oil could have caused substantial turmoil in the international oil market, the willingness of OPEC countries to increase their oil production immediately blunted its impact.[197] Without great difficulty, the United States replaced Iraqi oil imports by increasing its own domestic production and by turning primarily to Saudi Arabia—and to a lesser extent to Venezuela, Gabon, and Iran—to satisfy its outstanding energy needs.[198] Oil prices, which were rising even before August 1990, rose more sharply after the invasion and peaked in late 1990 at more than $35 per barrel. Nonetheless, this spike in prices was short-lived; the price of OPEC's reference basket fell to less than $20 per barrel by the end of the short war.[199]

With the commencement of Iraqi oil exports under the Oil for Food program, the United States once again became a significant importer of Iraqi oil, and by 2000 was importing more Iraqi oil than before the Gulf war (figure 4-8). That year, U.S. oil companies, either directly or through foreign middlemen, bought approximately 613,000 barrels of Iraqi oil a

**Figure 4-8.** *Iraqi Oil Exports to the United States, 1989–2001*

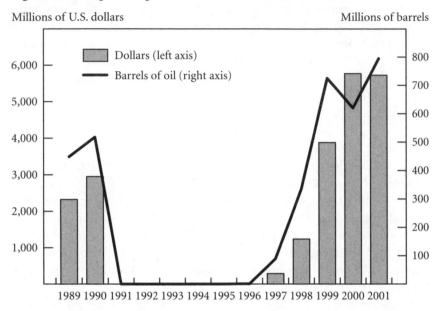

Source: Energy Information Administration, "Petroleum Imports by Country of Origin, 1960–2000" (www.eia.doe.gov/pub/pdf/multi.fuel/aer2000/sec5_11.pdf [August 9, 2001]), and "Petroleum Imports from Bahrain, Iran, Iraq, and Kuwait" (www.eia.doe.gov/emeu/mer/txt/mer3-3a [August 30, 2002]); International Monetary Fund, *Direction of Trade Statistics,* various years.

day, constituting 5.5 percent of U.S. oil imports.[200] Only Canada, Saudi Arabia, Venezuela, Nigeria, and Mexico supplied more oil to the United States that year.

Despite such relatively smooth sailing, sanctions on Iraq did harm U.S. energy interests in more subtle ways. First, as discussed, in the absence of sanctions Iraq would likely have produced significantly more oil than it did in 2000, with a corresponding dampening effect on international oil prices, all other things being equal.[201] Second, sanctions on Iraq heightened uncertainty in the global energy markets, with adverse implications for the United States and other oil-importing countries. Speculation over the removal of sanctions, as well as Saddam's occasional politically inspired hold-up of Iraqi exports, fueled sometimes dramatic fluctuations in the price of oil over the 1990s and beyond.[202] Although OPEC producers consistently calibrated their production to ensure that price increases caused by Iraqi actions were fleeting, the uncertainty created by price volatility hampered planning and budgeting by oil producers and consumers alike.[203] Iraq's "oil weapon" was not nearly as significant as some analysts and pundits warned, but it was real nonetheless.[204]

Finally, maintaining UN sanctions on Iraq affected U.S. political interests in a variety of ways. Without recounting the success of sanctions in containing Iraq for such a long period, it can be said that sanctions brought many political benefits to the United States in terms of advancing U.S. goals in regard to both Iraq and the region more broadly. Yet, although the United States did benefit from sanctions, it also bore some substantial political costs as a result of them.

Domestically, the issue of sanctions on Iraq—and U.S. policy toward Iraq overall—was a divisive one. Any policy that commits U.S. resources abroad is likely to become the subject of debate. The domestic discord over Iraqi sanctions—although not close to the rancor that categorized U.S. policy toward South Africa in the 1980s—pitted a wide range of American actors against one another. At one end of the spectrum, human rights organizations, religious groups, and other segments of civil society railed against the sanctions, drawing attention to the suffering in Iraq through protests, unauthorized visits to Iraq, and publications.[205] A small group of elected representatives notwithstanding, Congress as a whole pushed in the other direction, arguing for a more aggressive strategy focused on aiding the Iraqi opposition and getting rid of Saddam Hussein.[206] The acrimony between Congress and the Clinton administration over the appropriate shape of U.S. policy toward Iraq—and the role of sanctions in it—contributed to the fluctuation of American goals and to sporadic declarations that sanctions would continue until a new regime was in place in Baghdad.

Such domestic divisiveness was connected to the international political costs borne by the United States in the 1990s and early 2000s as a result of the sanctions. The proclamations of "regime change" goals not shared by the vast majority of the UN member states not only hastened the dissolving consensus of the Security Council, but also encouraged the belief that the United States hijacked the United Nations for its own foreign policy purposes. The strain that these perceptions created between the United States and other countries was nevertheless outweighed by the tension that arose between America and many European and Middle Eastern countries over the U.S. use of force in Iraq and American inflexibility in modifying or lifting sanctions. The widespread perception of U.S. indifference to the suffering of the Iraqi people, fueled by Saddam's propaganda efforts, exacerbated this discord.

The resentment that arose toward the United States over its position on Iraqi sanctions and its growing isolation on this issue before September 11 were problematic in themselves. They contributed to the relative weakening of U.S. power in the region since its peak in 1990 and arguably compromised the ability of the United States to influence events in the region beyond Iraq.[207] It is unlikely that the U.S. position on Iraqi sanctions had much of an adverse impact on American efforts to facilitate a Middle East peace while negotiations between Israel and the Palestinians were proving fruitful. Yet once the tide shifted away from reconciliation to confrontation in the Middle East, U.S. policy toward Iraq became an important source of Arab resentment of the United States and its presence in the region. Saddam's successful portrayal of himself as the vanguard of Palestinian interests only complicated U.S. efforts to mediate disputes in the region.

## Explaining the Record of Sanctions on Iraq

The sanctions in place against Iraq since 1990 deserve more credit than they are often given. Despite not achieving all the goals set out for them, sanctions played an essential role in realizing crucial objectives. Saddam remains in power in Baghdad and questions about Iraq's WMD programs persist, yet thanks in large part to sanctions, the Iraqi regime was contained with a fair degree of success. While tolerance for Saddam's capabilities has diminished dramatically in the post–September 11 environment, there is no question that these capabilities are far less than they would have been in the absence of sanctions. This achievement, however, came at considerable cost, in part because sanctions contributed to—although they were not wholly or even primarily responsible for—wide-scale human suffering in Iraq. Multilateral sanctions also involved other costs, such as the economic losses suffered by Iraq's neighbors and damage done to U.S. economic, energy, and political interests. Yet even in the face of these costs and the mixed record of sanctions in meeting all their goals, sanctions on Iraq still warrant the judgment of both being effective and having utility, given the importance of what they *did* achieve in containing Saddam Hussein and, thus far, preventing the nuclearization of a country led by an aggressive, antiwestern leader who has demonstrated his willingness to employ weapons of mass destruction in the past.

*Accounting for the Achievements and Disappointments of Sanctions*

Although the sanctions on Iraq were effective, they were not uncondi-tionally so nor as effective as they might have been in other circumstances. Sanctions were a key factor in achieving a successful measure of contain-ment, but they failed to bring about the fall of the regime or to exact any notable change in its behavior. The most basic reason for this selective effec-tiveness is that sanctions were used to pursue too many conflicting objec-tives simultaneously. Pursuing each goal in the most effective fashion would have demanded a range of sanctions strategies—a particular sanctions re-gime accompanied by different policy tools for each purpose. Attempting to advance the goals of regime change, containment, and behavior change all at once inevitably meant that some elements of the strategy used to advance one goal occasionally undercut efforts to achieve the other goals. Not sur-prisingly, on all three fronts, the results of this almost haphazard use of sanctions and their companion tools fell short of what might have been achieved with a more focused strategy.

Although the mix of sanctions and other instruments over time was far from static, overall, the sanctions regime in place and the tools used in con-junction with it were best suited to the goal of containing the regime. It is therefore not surprising that the greatest achievement of sanctions and U.S. policy over this period fall into the realm of containment. Here, the multi-lateral nature of sanctions was critical to the military, economic, and polit-ical containment of Iraq. Without the cooperation of other members of the Security Council and Iraq's neighbors, sanctions—and the United States—would have been entirely unable to keep the volume of resources, whether measured in foreign currency or weapons and WMD technology, away from Saddam that they did.

In this endeavor, the *universal*, multilateral structure of sanctions also was important. Had a regional body, rather than the United Nations, man-dated multilateral sanctions on Iraq, its oil wealth would have enticed other countries not bound by the regional sanctions to trade with Iraq. Less obvi-ous but of equal importance is that the UN nature of sanctions helped stave off some of the greatest potential challenges to sanctions. Although Russia, France, and China all had strong domestic interests pushing for their uni-lateral abrogation of the sanctions, they refrained from seriously and openly violating them. Such action would have undermined the United Nations, which would have in turn undercut their own international influence as permanent members of the Security Council. In this way, the UN nature of sanctions on Iraq served as a brake to what might have been a much more rapid collapse of the sanctions regime.

Nevertheless, the use of other policy tools did undercut the international consensus to maintain sanctions and thereby strained efforts to contain the regime through their use. In some cases, these added measures were taken—somewhat paradoxically—to advance containment efforts. For instance, the creation and implementation of the Oil for Food program was essential not only from a moral and humanitarian point of view, but also because the human suffering in Iraq posed the greatest challenge to international support for sanctions. Yet, however critical, this program clearly provided Saddam with the ability to manipulate members of the international community and to test their cohesion on the goal of containing his regime. As examined earlier in the chapter, Saddam artfully advanced his political agenda through the economic links made possible through the Oil for Food scheme.

In addition, weapons inspections both advanced and hindered containment efforts. To the extent that they served as an instrument for the forceful, if incomplete, disarmament of Iraq, they were a key complement to sanctions in the pursuit of containment. But, because UNSCOM required some level of cooperation from Iraq in order to function, it provided Saddam with opportunities to instigate crises and aggravate tensions within the Security Council. UNSCOM and the provocations surrounding it became the backdrop to the emergence of a fundamental disagreement between Council members about the overall character of UN policy toward Iraq. Certain members believed that Iraqi compliance would best be induced through a policy that engaged the regime and therefore preferred to depend heavily on diplomacy and compromise. Others, the United States in particular, believed that Iraq could only be compelled to comply with UN demands and therefore sought to rely more on punitive measures. This gap proved more difficult to bridge as the challenges of containment grew over the 1990s.

Similarly, some military aspects of the U.S. strategy to contain Saddam chafed against international efforts to maintain sanctions for the same purpose. The U.S. military presence in the Gulf and in neighboring states was a key element in the containment of Saddam. So too were the sporadic, small-scale, punitive bombings of Iraqi military installations and air defense stations carried out by forces patrolling the no-fly zones over Iraq. Although important components of the overall U.S. strategy to contain Saddam, these measures fueled resentment in the region. Not only did the government of Saudi Arabia become increasingly agitated by the U.S. Air

Force squadrons stationed in its country to enforce the southern no-fly zone over Iraq, but U.S. military forces in the Gulf became a more general point of grievance for some countries and groups. While Iran had long called for the United States to pull its military out of the region, even countries whose security is guaranteed by U.S. military forces advocated a toned-down U.S. military presence.[208]

The tensions arising between maintaining international and regional consensus for sanctions and supplementing sanctions-backed containment efforts with humanitarian and military measures were somewhat unavoidable and generally manageable, at least while the Middle East peace process was on track. There was, however, no excuse for the failure of both the United States and the United Nations to better employ another tool that could have dramatically strengthened efforts to contain Saddam through sanctions: the tool of information. The United States made only feeble efforts to counter Saddam's well-orchestrated propaganda campaign to convince the world that sanctions—not his own indifference—were responsible for the suffering of Iraqis. While messengers paid by Iraq paraded the streets of the Arab world with grim photographs of the "sanctions-induced" suffering in Iraq, the U.S. government released policy reports rarely read or even seen by people outside the U.S. foreign policy community. Perhaps nothing could have shored up international support for sanctions better than a more effective, continuous, and concerted effort to educate both Americans and the world about Saddam's disregard for the well-being of Iraqis by highlighting his actions to frustrate international humanitarian relief efforts and his preference for spending Iraqi resources on nefarious rather than charitable purposes.

Even more detrimental to international agreement on the importance of maintaining sanctions to contain Saddam was the use of other policy tools aimed at advancing entirely separate objectives. In particular, U.S. support for the Iraqi opposition undercut broader containment efforts. Modifying U.S. declaratory policy to state that sanctions would remain in place until Saddam was removed from power might have bolstered the Iraqi opposition, but it also undermined UN resolutions that declared otherwise, and therefore weakened the overall basis for the international containment of Iraq. Material support for the opposition reinforced this corrosion.

Regime change was not an objective well-served by UN sanctions on Iraq. In part, this is hardly surprisingly, given that provoking the ouster of Saddam was never a goal espoused by the United Nations or even openly advocated by any U.S. allies. The inability of sanctions to achieve this ambitious goal is more an example of the United States asking too much from sanctions than it is a testimony to the weakness of these economic instruments. Sanctions conceivably might have advanced the goal of regime change had they been part of an overall strategy to do so, but alone they were unlikely to have any hope of succeeding. For sanctions to truly serve the purpose of regime change, they should have been coupled with other instruments—such as robust support for an effective opposition backed by regional actors—to form a coherent strategy to achieve that end. Instead, U.S. support for the opposition was weak and sporadic. In 1996, a limited U.S. commitment to covert action contributed to a situation in which thousands of CIA-backed Iraqi agents were killed in Irbil. Similarly, rather than rounding out a strategic vision, assistance given to the Iraqi National Congress in the late 1990s amounted to little more than a gesture intended to placate U.S. domestic constituencies. This support was not only an inadequate companion to sanctions if the goal of regime change was a serious one, but, as mentioned, it adversely affected efforts to achieve other goals. Moreover, as was the case with containment, other tools employed alongside sanctions to advance other goals undercut the objective of regime change. Arguably, had the world been more dedicated to regime change than it was interested in other objectives—including minimizing harm to Iraqi civilians and the pressure their suffering placed on the international coalition—it would not have advanced the Oil for Food program. The 1995 domestic economic crisis that forced Saddam to adopt the UN scheme suggested that sanctions—if ruthlessly applied—could have seriously challenged the regime.

Finally, the sanctions regime also was not particularly well-crafted to advance the goal of modifying the behavior of the regime; the power of sanctions to compel such a change was hampered by the pursuit of other goals and the use of companion tools to pursue them. First, the U.S. embrace of regime change and the U.S. declaration that sanctions would stay in place until Saddam was ousted undercut any Iraqi incentive to comply with UN resolutions that supposedly mapped out the road to the lifting of sanctions. UN resolution 1284, which many hoped would encourage further Iraqi cooperation with the United Nations, exacerbated Iraqi suspicion over what actions were needed before sanctions would be removed by referencing only conditions for the "suspension" of sanctions, not for "lifting" them.

In addition, the structure of the sanctions regime did not encourage Saddam's regime to cooperate with the demands of the United Nations and its weapons inspectors. Although UN resolution 687 demarcated the steps that Iraq must take before any sanctions were rescinded, the sanctions regime did not encourage Iraqi compliance by offering any rewards, even verbal ones, for Iraqi moves in the direction of meeting disarmament requirements.[209] The unwillingness to acknowledge partial Iraqi fulfillment of UN demands reflected U.S. concerns that to do so would encourage the erosion of containment.[210] But at the same time, the reluctance to even verbally commend Iraq for positive moves undercut the chances of extracting behavior changes; holding all the incentives for nothing short of full compliance, while morally appealing, would not have been effective in inducing long-term cooperation even had the regime been predisposed to cooperate.[211]

Moreover, had the sanctions regime really served as a bargaining mechanism to induce Iraqi behavior change, it would not only have offered greater and graduated incentives for movement in the direction desired by the international community, but it also would have incorporated further penalties for noncompliance. Instead, because of fundamental differences of opinion within the Security Council on how to deal with Iraq, Iraqi defiance of UNSCOM only occasionally provoked a firm response from the international community. The United States failed to make sterner and more systematic responses to Iraqi obstreperousness because to do so would have threatened the international consensus buttressing the sanctions regime and containing Iraq, even though such measures would have been more conducive to getting Iraq to change its behavior. Instead, more often than not, Iraqi intransigence elicited diplomatic dispatches and intensive efforts to strike a compromise; in short, Iraq was rewarded rather than penalized for its obstinacy, a strategy definitely not well-suited to securing positive, long-term changes in behavior.

Besides the structure of sanctions and the other tools used to promote the goals of regime change and containment, other factors also inhibited the ability of sanctions to generate changes in Iraqi behavior. Two in particular made it likely that, even if U.S. and UN strategies toward Iraq had been entirely designed to evoke changes in Iraqi behavior, Iraq would have remained resistant. First and most important was the nature of the regime of Saddam Hussein. Because Saddam was able to protect his inner circle from the worst effects of economic collapse, the economic dislocations partially caused by sanctions created little leverage over him; his ever-expanding black market links and his indifference to the suffering of Iraqis as a whole removed a major impetus for the regime to comply with UN resolutions. In a less authoritarian system, Saddam may have been forced to relieve human-itarian conditions (ideally, by complying with UN resolutions), either to gar-ner support at elections or to ease the demands of civil society. However, given the lack of alternative bases of power and influence in Iraq at the turn of the millennium, Saddam was at almost complete liberty to ignore the eco-nomic collapse of his country and the dire conditions under which the vast majority of his citizens lived.

The second brake on Iraqi compliance was the high stakes of the demands made by the United Nations. In the eyes of the Iraqi regime—and presum-ably in the view of many average Iraqis—the complete disarmament of Iraq of weapons of mass destruction not only would leave the country extraordi-narily vulnerable, but it would deprive Iraq of an important instrument of coercion. Iraq has claimed on numerous occasions that it would accept mon-itoring of its weapons if similar mechanisms were imposed on all the coun-tries in the region, including Israel.[212] While one can debate the sincerity of these pledges, they do point to the fact that Iraq sees itself to be living in a dangerous region, where Israeli nuclear capabilities and Iranian nuclear pur-suits are viewed as highly threatening. It is plausible—even probable—that Iraq also perceives its WMD capabilities as having offensive and coercive value.[213] The willingness of the regime to suffer immense costs rather than comply with UN resolutions suggests that it equated its survival with the maintenance of its WMD programs. If that is the case, no matter how well-suited the sanctions were to the goal of behavior change and regardless of whether all policy instruments were coordinated to achieve that end, the international community would not have been able to persuade Saddam Hussein to relinquish his WMD pursuits fully, completely, and voluntarily.

## Comparing the Utility of Sanctions to Alternatives

The value of the sanctions-led strategy pursued by the United Nations and the United States can only truly be assessed when it is compared with other policy alternatives open to policymakers at the time. Questioning the effectiveness and utility of the sanctions-dominated approach is sensible only if another strategy might have realized more goals at lower costs. Were any such strategies available to policymakers over the 1990s and into the 2000s?

One possible alternative was to apply sustained military pressure or pro-vide robust military support for the opposition in Iraq. Over the course of the 1990s, many critics lamented the failure to adopt these methods, either at the end of the Gulf war when uprisings in Iraq challenged Saddam's rule or in the years that followed. In retrospect it is tempting to view the decision not to continue the Gulf war until Saddam was ousted from power as short-sighted; however, at the time, policymakers carefully considered the value and risks of a military-dominated strategy. It was by no means viewed as a clear path to a friendlier government in Baghdad. Removing or eliminating Saddam was one challenge; establishing a palatable new regime was another. Real concerns existed about the nature of a post-Saddam regime, as there were no assurances that it would even resemble the moderate, secular, pro-western regime sought by the United States. Some considered installing a government an attractive option, but at the time most viewed the prospect of a long-standing U.S. entanglement in Iraq as distinctly undesirable. In the absence of a continued strong U.S. or international presence in Iraq, which few wanted, many in the region and beyond feared Iraq's disintegration.

In addition to concerns about the prospects for the success of a military-led approach in the 1990s, policymakers estimated that the costs of such a strategy would be unacceptably high. Quite apart from the expense of waging a modern military war, thousands of American lives could be lost, a sum that would be just a fraction of anticipated Iraqi deaths. Policymakers also anticipated that such military action would seriously damage the international coalition opposing Saddam. Most governments in the region did not support military moves of this nature, being both wary of the precedent it would set and concerned that the possible fracturing of Iraq would exacerbate their own internal problems.[214] The early crumbling of the coalition would have all but ensured that if the United States failed to bring about anything short of a democratic, pro-western government in Baghdad, it would have little support for the continued containment of Iraq through sanctions or other means. The cost and benefit calculations may have changed in the wake of September 11. But at the time, when weighed against the expectation that continued sanctions and the humiliation of the Gulf war defeat would dislodge Saddam from power before long, policymakers anticipated that the military alternative—with its uncertain chances of success and potentially high costs—would be less effective or have less utility than the sanctions-led approach adopted.[215]

A second alternative to the sanctions-led strategy actually employed was a more conventional deterrence policy in which the United States or the international community specified severe consequences for Iraqi actions that crossed "red lines"—such as the development of WMD capabilities or military incursions into neighboring countries. This approach would have required the maintenance of sanctions on military and some dual-use items but would have otherwise allowed Iraq to engage in normal trade and diplomatic relations with the rest of the world. If pursued immediately in the wake of the Gulf war, in the short and possibly medium term, this strategy would have avoided many of the humanitarian and economic costs that came to be associated with the sanctions-dominated approach actually employed. However, in the long run, the price of such a strategy could have been huge. In control of Iraqi resources and amassing wealth from its oil exports, Saddam Hussein would have continued his vigorous pursuit of weapons of mass destruction; in time, his programs almost certainly would have reached fruition. Even if the weapons remained unused, their existence would have dramatically altered the security landscape of the Middle East, leaving Israel and Iraq's Arab neighbors more vulnerable to blackmail and conventional Iraqi aggression. If the weapons were employed, the costs—in terms of lost lives and physical destruction—could be massive.

Adopting this more conventional military deterrence strategy *after* several years of more complete sanctions makes even less sense than it would have immediately after the Gulf war. The policy would still have had potentially catastrophic consequences if it led to a nuclear-equipped Saddam Hussein, no matter how far down the road. But it also is by no means clear that, if adopted in 2001, this approach would have improved the living conditions of the average Iraqi. Under such a plan, the United Nations would relinquish control over the proceeds of Iraqi oil sales, handing them over to the Iraqi regime. But once in command of these resources, Saddam would contemplate how to allocate them among many competing priorities. He would be forced to continue to pay war reparations and would need to begin to service Iraq's now-staggering foreign debt. At the same time, he would wish to continue with the rehabilitation and further development of the Iraqi oil industry, and he would almost certainly seek to escalate Iraq's militarization and pursuit of weapons of mass destruction. Under these circumstances and in light of Saddam's manifest indifference to the suffering of Iraqis, it is almost impossible to imagine that Saddam would allocate more than the 72 percent of Iraq's annual oil revenue to meeting the needs of his people, which is the amount devoted to them under the Oil for Food program.

A final alternative to consider is an engagement-oriented approach whereby the United Nations and the United States would transform sanctions into a bargaining mechanism as explored in the previous section. Through the use of incentives and penalties, all efforts would be designed to entice Iraq to disarm. However, as discussed earlier, the nature of the Iraqi regime and the stakes associated with the UN demands make it unlikely that such an approach would be the most effective or have the greatest utility. Particularly after more than a decade of confrontation, Saddam would almost certainly be unwilling to engage in a sincere and verifiable process of disarmament even if the sanctions regime were structured differently. Moreover, the costs of such an approach would grow as containment of the regime became difficult to achieve as an engagement strategy was pursued.

## Looking Ahead

In comparison to the stylized alternatives explored above, the broad sanctions-led approach pursued by the international community throughout the 1990s into the 2000s was the one with the greatest utility. The terrorist attacks of September 11, 2001, and the campaign against terrorism that followed, however, changed the international environment in ways that suggest that a radically different approach toward Iraq may now be feasible and desirable. Although the assessments of Saddam's activities remain much the same as they were before September 11, the United States views the consequences of his behavior with greater alarm. The costs of continuing an imperfect (even if largely successful) containment of Iraq are valued differently in a new environment in which support for terrorism and weapons of mass destruction are seen as the greatest threats to U.S. and global security. Moreover, after September 11, diminished U.S. domestic opposition to the use of force to achieve foreign policy goals has opened new possibilities for addressing the Iraqi threat—ones that were inconceivable in the first half of 2001.

Whether the United States chooses to challenge the regime of Saddam Hussein more directly in the future remains open to question, as does the form that such a challenge might take. What is certain, however, is that sanctions will play a role in the run-up to that decision and in any one of three scenarios that may emerge as a result of it.

The sanctions regime—and its connections to weapons inspections—should play a central role in U.S. efforts to make a case for regime change and to secure support from other countries in this endeavor. Rather than focusing on Iraq's less compelling links with terrorism, the United States should make Iraq's WMD capability the centerpiece of its campaign to win international approval for ousting Saddam. In so doing, Washington should make every effort to introduce a robust weapons inspection regime into Iraq. This quest will demand that the United States reaffirm the goals embraced in UN resolutions. Too often over the 1990s, U.S. intentions regarding the lifting of sanctions on Iraq were ambiguous or openly in conflict with UN resolutions, giving Saddam one reason to avoid complying with them. Although the United States should resist all efforts to weaken the terms of the UN inspection teams, it should reiterate support for resolutions that promise Iraq sanctions relief in return for its total disarmament of weapons of mass destruction. Moreover, any new resolution on inspections should go beyond resolution 1284—which stipulated only the conditions for the suspension of sanctions—to specify the terms necessary for lifting sanctions. Such clarifications are not likely to change Saddam's behavior; however, that is not their objective. Rather, by stating clearly the path that Iraq must follow—and demonstrating that the United States is willing to take "yes" for an answer—Washington can once again draw attention to Saddam's obstreperousness and his role in prolonging the stalemate.

Sanctions also can play an important role in the vigorous public diplomacy campaign that must accompany any U.S. efforts to convince others of the need to remove Saddam from power. In addition to verbally highlighting the threat posed by Iraqi WMD pursuits and pushing for further weapons inspections, the United States should seek more concrete measures to underscore Saddam's recalcitrance. The establishment of time limits on Iraq's ability to determine how money in the UN escrow account is spent is one measure that could draw international attention to the ways in which Saddam evades his responsibilities and harms the well-being of Iraqis. The United Nations could assume the responsibility of apportioning the money for Iraqi needs if Iraq does not allocate the funds in a timely manner, as has often been the case.

The longer-term function of sanctions will depend on which of three scenarios materializes after the United States commits itself to a particular course of action. In the first scenario, the United States could decide to settle for the containment of Saddam through existing measures. Greater cooperation from Iraq's neighbors and an international consensus to punish violators of the sanctions regime will be essential if this option is to be a viable response to the Iraqi threat in the post-September 11 environment. In order to achieve this, the United States will need to spearhead an effort to reframe sanctions much along the more ambitious lines pursued in 2001 and early 2002. More robust "smart sanctions" should be part and parcel of consultations about the fate of the Iraqi regime; countries reluctant to support a U.S.-led military attack on Iraq should see their only alternative as being one in which they are held as fully accountable for their interaction with Iraq.

Over time, maintaining international consensus behind continued credible sanctions could require making additional reforms to alleviate concern about the humanitarian effects of sanctions and to deflate the criticisms of those suffering economic losses. Several reforms may be appropriate in these instances. First, the United Nations could explore the possibility of allowing foreign investment in the civilian economy, as long as it is subject to constraints—perhaps enshrined in a mandatory investment code—that ensure that investments do not result in cash inflows to the regime. In addition, the United Nations and the United States could continue to push Iraq to allow Iraqi farmers to sell their produce directly to the UN program for distribution as rations; this change would be an important step toward breathing some life back into the crushed local economy without shoring up the regime. An oil-for-debt mechanism that would allow countries such as Russia and France to begin collecting on the significant debts Iraq owes them could also ease commercial pressures in these countries to cast aside the sanctions.

In the event that the United States opts for the long-term containment of Saddam's regime, allowing highly structured and strictly accountable foreign investment in the Iraqi oil industry could eventually be justified. Such an adjustment would alleviate inevitable economic pressures in France, Russia, China, and other countries to lift sanctions. At the same time, by increasing the amount of oil Iraq could export, foreign investment would allow Iraq to boost imports of food and other commodities through the Oil for Food program. Structured foreign involvement in the Iraqi oil industry would also put an end to the dangerous extraction procedures currently being employed, which endanger the long-term viability of some of Iraq's oil fields. This change may not only be in the interest of future generations of Iraqis, but also be to the advantage of countries such as the United States that depend on foreign sources of oil. These benefits could be realized with no additional gain to the regime if foreign involvement was limited to technical foreign service contracts (which already are permitted under UN resolutions) or to buy-back deals, which allow foreign firms to develop fields and receive payment in cash or oil through the Oil for Food program.

A second option is that the United States chooses to openly pursue its goal of regime change in Iraq, but does not espouse an invasion or large-scale military action to achieve it. In this scenario, Iraq policy will be hampered by the tension that exists between the stated American goal of regime change and the one of containment pursued by the rest of the world. Although the United States can still pursue more robust measures to isolate Saddam, its efforts are likely to be undercut by the resentment generated by some who object to America using UN tools to pursue distinctly U.S. goals. To outweigh the drawbacks created by this tension, the United States must complement sanctions with other tools, such as robust support for the opposition and public diplomacy efforts in which the United States lays out clearly and persistently the benefits that will accrue to the Iraqi people and the next Iraqi regime. Washington should also focus on chipping away at various obstacles to other countries' acceptance of regime change as a goal in Iraq. For instance, an oil-for-debt mechanism created today could diminish the desires of creditor countries to keep Saddam in power tomorrow; similarly, any assurance that the oil contracts negotiated with Saddam's regime will have some value in a post-Saddam environment could dilute Russian and Chinese aversion to regime change. Articulating an American desire for a representative, territorially intact Iraq with an autonomous Kurdish zone would also ease fears in the region that regime change would mean Iraq's disintegration and assure the Kurds that they would not be worse off once Saddam is gone.[216]

Sanctions will play a very different role if the United States pushes ahead with a military operation to force regime change in Iraq. The importance of sanctions in this instance will be their ability to help shape the character of the post-Saddam Iraqi government. Once a military campaign is under way, it is sensible to agree to a cease-fire only after a new regime in Iraq has agreed to forsake its WMD pursuits and submit to robust inspections. Sanctions will be critical in ensuring Iraqi compliance with inspectors. Although some sanctions should be removed and others suspended at the outset to demonstrate good faith, the full and official lifting of sanctions should be tied to the verified elimination of Iraqi capabilities. Sanctions also will have a legitimate role in shaping the outward orientation of the regime as well as its domestic behavior. While sanctions on imports from Iraq are explicitly tied to weapons of mass destruction, sanctions on exports to Iraq are linked more broadly to the satisfaction of UN resolutions, which include the decent treatment of Iraq's population and peaceful coexistence with its neighbors.[217] The United States will also wish to calibrate the lifting of its own unilateral sanctions to strike the right balance between welcoming the new regime into the international community and ensuring that its behavior meets minimum international and domestic standards.

# Appendix 4A

Tables 4A-1 through 4A-4 present estimates of the effects of sanctions on Iraqi exports and nonmilitary imports. Note that the methodology used in tables 4A-1 and 4A-2 assumes that Iraq would have maintained the same dollar share of oil-producing country export revenues over the decade. An alternative method—calculating what Iraq would have earned had it sold the same volume of oil as it exported in 1989 throughout the 1990s at actual prices over that decade—yields somewhat smaller estimates of Iraqi exports in the absence of sanctions ($176 billion) than are reported in table 4A-1.

**Table 4A-1.** *Estimated Total Iraqi Exports in the Absence of Sanctions*
Millions of 2000 dollars

| Year | Global oil-producing-country exports (A) | Hypothetical Iraqi exports absent sanctions[a] (A × 0.088 = B) | Chain-weighted price deflator for GDP, 1996 = 100 (C) | Estimated Iraqi exports absent sanctions, real dollars (B × [117.6/C] = D) |
|---|---|---|---|---|
| 1990 | 192,900 | 16,975 | 85.9 | 23,240 |
| 1991 | 175,800 | 15,470 | 85.5 | 21,279 |
| 1992 | 188,000 | 16,544 | 88.0 | 22,109 |
| 1993 | 180,500 | 15,884 | 90.4 | 20,663 |
| 1994 | 186,800 | 16,438 | 94.0 | 20,565 |
| 1995 | 209,800 | 18,462 | 96.6 | 22,476 |
| 1996 | 249,900 | 21,991 | 100.0 | 25,862 |
| 1997 | 259,400 | 22,827 | 104.4 | 25,713 |
| 1998 | 198,400 | 17,459 | 109.0 | 18,837 |
| 1999 | 232,100 | 20,425 | 113.4 | 21,181 |
| 2000 | 347,900 | 30,615 | 117.6 | 30,615 |
| **Total** | | | | **252,540** |

Source: International Monetary Fund, *Direction of Trade Statistics*, various years.

a. Total oil-producing-country exports are multiplied by 0.088, the ratio of Iraqi exports to total oil-producing-country exports in 1989 and the first half of 1990.

**Table 4A-2.** *Estimated Iraqi Exports Lost due to Sanctions*

Millions of 2000 dollars

| Year | Global oil-producing-country exports (A) | Hypothetical Iraqi exports absent sanctions[a] (A × 0.088 = B) | Actual Iraqi exports (C) | Estimated Iraqi exports lost due to sanctions (B − C = D) | Chain-weighted price deflator for GDP, 1996 = 100 (E) | Estimated Iraqi exports lost due to sanctions, real dollars (D × [117.6/E] = F) |
|---|---|---|---|---|---|---|
| 1990 | 192,900 | 16,975 | 10,314 | 6,661 | 85.9 | 9,119 |
| 1991 | 175,800 | 15,470 | 487 | 14,983 | 85.5 | 20,609 |
| 1992 | 188,000 | 16,544 | 609 | 15,935 | 88.0 | 21,295 |
| 1993 | 180,500 | 15,884 | 471 | 15,413 | 90.4 | 20,051 |
| 1994 | 186,800 | 16,438 | 382 | 16,056 | 94.0 | 20,088 |
| 1995 | 209,800 | 18,462 | 424 | 18,038 | 96.5 | 21,960 |
| 1996 | 249,900 | 21,991 | 503 | 21,488 | 100.0 | 25,270 |
| 1997 | 259,400 | 22,827 | 2,819 | 20,008 | 104.4 | 22,538 |
| 1998 | 198,400 | 17,459 | 4,951 | 12,508 | 109.0 | 13,495 |
| 1999 | 232,100 | 20,425 | 9,564 | 10,861 | 113.4 | 11,243 |
| 2000 | 347,900 | 30,615 | 12,846 | 17,769 | 117.6 | 17,769 |
| **Total** | | | | | | **203,437** |

Source: See table 4A-1.

a. See table 4A-1, note a.

**Table 4A-3. Estimated Total Iraqi Nonmilitary Imports in the Absence of Sanctions**
Millions of 2000 dollars

| Year | Global oil-producing-country imports (A) | Hypothetical Iraqi imports absent sanctions[a] (A × 0.095 = B) | Chain-weighted price deflator for GDP, 1996 = 100 (C) | Estimated Iraqi imports absent sanctions, real dollars (B × [117.6/C] = D) |
|------|------|------|------|------|
| 1990 | 114,900 | 10,916 | 85.9 | 14,944 |
| 1991 | 136,700 | 12,987 | 85.5 | 17,862 |
| 1992 | 158,200 | 15,029 | 88.0 | 20,084 |
| 1993 | 144,200 | 13,699 | 90.4 | 17,821 |
| 1994 | 128,400 | 12,198 | 94.0 | 15,260 |
| 1995 | 148,100 | 14,070 | 96.6 | 17,128 |
| 1996 | 156,700 | 14,887 | 100.0 | 17,507 |
| 1997 | 162,100 | 15,400 | 104.4 | 17,347 |
| 1998 | 154,700 | 14,697 | 109.0 | 15,856 |
| 1999 | 150,200 | 14,269 | 113.4 | 14,797 |
| 2000 | 181,600 | 17,252 | 117.6 | 17,252 |
| **Total** | | | | **185,858** |

Source: See table 4A-1.

a. Total oil-producing-country imports are multiplied by 0.095, the ratio of Iraqi nonmilitary imports to total oil-producing-country imports in 1989 and the first half of 1990.

**Table 4A-4.** *Estimated Iraqi Nonmilitary Imports Lost due to Sanctions*

Millions of 2000 dollars

| Year | Global oil-producing-country imports (A) | Hypothetical Iraqi imports absent sanctions[a] (A × 0.095 = B) | Actual Iraqi imports (C) | Estimated Iraqi imports lost due to sanctions (B − C = D) | Chain-weighted price deflator for GDP, 1996 = 100 (E) | Estimated Iraqi imports lost due to sanctions, real dollars (D × [117.6/E] = F) |
|---|---|---|---|---|---|---|
| 1990 | 114,900 | 10,916 | 6,526 | 4,390 | 85.9 | 6,009 |
| 1991 | 136,700 | 12,987 | 423 | 12,564 | 85.5 | 17,280 |
| 1992 | 158,200 | 15,029 | 603 | 14,426 | 88.0 | 19,278 |
| 1993 | 144,200 | 13,699 | 533 | 13,166 | 90.4 | 17,127 |
| 1994 | 128,400 | 12,198 | 499 | 11,699 | 94.0 | 14,636 |
| 1995 | 148,100 | 14,070 | 665 | 13,405 | 96.6 | 16,319 |
| 1996 | 156,700 | 14,887 | 567 | 14,320 | 100.0 | 16,840 |
| 1997 | 162,100 | 15,400 | 1,137 | 14,263 | 104.4 | 16,066 |
| 1998 | 154,700 | 14,697 | 1,808 | 12,889 | 109.0 | 13,905 |
| 1999 | 150,200 | 14,269 | 1,830 | 12,439 | 113.4 | 12,900 |
| 2000 | 181,600 | 17,252 | 2,212 | 15,040 | 117.6 | 15,040 |
| **Total** | | | | | | **165,401** |

Source: See table 4A-1.

a. See table 4A-3, note a.

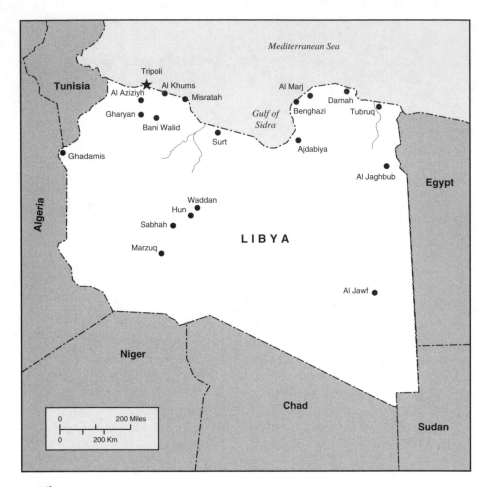

*Libya*

# CHAPTER FIVE

# Limiting
# Libya

Minor fluctuations in intensity notwithstanding, U.S.-Libyan relations were hostile throughout the 1980s and 1990s. The United States repeatedly voiced its opposition to Libyan radicalism—be it in the form of support for terrorism, foreign policy adventurism, pursuit of weapons of mass destruction, or opposition to the Middle East peace process. Libyan objections to the United States were no less enduring, with Libya's leader, Colonel Muammar Qadhafi, decrying U.S. support for Israel and perceived American imperialism.[1] This already bitter relationship was sharply poisoned by Libyan responsibility for the 1988 Pan Am 103 bombing and U.S. military action against Libya in 1986.

The antagonism between the United States and Libya continued into the 2000s, even in the face of altered circumstances that might have been expected to ease relations between the two countries. Certainly, the collapse of Tripoli's former patron, the Soviet Union, removed one barrier to more constructive relations. Even more recent improvements in Libyan behavior—which have in the view of many U.S. allies warranted a recalibration of policy toward Libya—have not made the rocky road between Washington and Tripoli less difficult to travel. The frigidity of U.S.-Libyan relations can in part be understood by the unattractiveness of the Libyan regime, the centrality of the unpredictable and erratic Qadhafi to it, and the ongoing perception that Libya still has the potential to threaten U.S. interests, even if its interests in doing so are diminished. Faced with these realities, and highly

mobilized domestic constituencies pushing for the continued marginalization and punishment of Libya, U.S. policymakers have seen little urgency—
and considerable risk—in rushing to improve relations with Tripoli.

Both U.S. and UN sanctions have been at the core of American policy to
oppose Libyan practices, keep the regime on the margins of international
respectability, and compel Libya to change its behavior. Perhaps ironically,
the partial effectiveness of sanctions themselves—which, as explored in this
chapter, owes as much to circumstances as it does to the sanctions—created
a dilemma for the United States. Once Libya turned over the Lockerbie suspects and UN sanctions were suspended, the United States could no longer
pursue its broad implicit goal of containing Libya by enlisting multilateral
cooperation for the much more narrow explicit goal of seeking justice for
the Lockerbie bombing. The United States maintained all of its unilateral
sanctions against Libya in the wake of the Lockerbie verdict, calling for
Libya to meet all UN demands before multilateral sanctions could be formally lifted (as opposed to their suspension). One need not question the
obvious importance of holding Libya to UN resolutions to ask whether a re-
evaluation of U.S. policy toward Libya is warranted. What can policymakers expect to achieve with a unilateral sanctions-dominated strategy when
much of the international community is eagerly welcoming Libya back into
the fold? Even if a sanctions-led policy was sensible in the 1990s when multilateral cooperation was forthcoming and Libyan threats were tangible,
does the approach suit 2003 and beyond? What is the best way to consolidate recent positive changes in Libyan behavior and entice Libya to satisfac-
torily address remaining concerns around Lockerbie and any of its residual
passive support for terrorist groups? If Libya's response is satisfactory in the
realm of terrorism, how should the United States shape its strategy to contend with Libya's pursuit of weapons of mass destruction?

These questions gained new urgency in the wake of the September 11,
2001, terrorist attacks on the United States. Libya has been a useful partner
to the United States in its rejuvenated campaign to eradicate terrorism; it
could prove to be a serious obstacle or irritant in the future if it chose to be.
How the United States modifies or maintains its current policy toward Libya
is part of the equation that will determine whether Libya and the United
States work together against terrorism or work against one another as they
have for the last decades. Libyan behavior, of course, is the other, more central, determinant. How the United States meets the as-yet unencountered
challenge of rehabilitating a once-rogue regime will have repercussions

beyond U.S.-Libyan relations. Other countries and regimes penalized by the United States will look to the Libyan case to see whether rehabilitation is possible. A complete understanding of how sanctions shaped the past years of confrontation between the United States, Libya, and the United Nations can help policymakers navigate the challenges and, possibly, the opportunities presented by Libya in 2003 and beyond.

## The Historical Context of Sanctions

Warm relations between Libya and the United States served the interests of both sides for the first decades after Libyan independence in 1951. The United States maintained an air base just outside Tripoli, providing King Idris of Libya with much-needed revenue in the post–World War II era. After the discovery of Libyan oil in 1959, U.S. companies assumed a leading role in developing the country's oil industry, helping it become the fifth largest producer of oil among OPEC states by 1967. These close, mutually beneficial ties encouraged the United States to reserve immediate judgment when young Captain Muammar Qadhafi and an unknown Revolutionary Command Council (RCC) took control of the country in a coup in 1969.[2] The new Libyan leadership refrained from antagonizing the United States in the first years after it assumed power, although it demanded that the United States relinquish Wheelus Air Force Base and the Alwitia gunnery range in 1970 as had been planned. Although Libya nationalized some American and other foreign oil interests in 1973, U.S. officials reacted in a muted manner, initially hoping that the young regime would continue to shun the Soviet influence that many of its Arab counterparts welcomed.

This uncertain concord gave way to hostility as Libyan activities were increasingly seen to be at odds with U.S. interests as the 1970s wore on. Allegations of Libyan involvement in both the killing of Israeli athletes at the 1972 Munich Olympics and the 1973 assassination of the U.S. ambassador to Sudan raised concerns about Libyan support for terrorism. This alarm grew as Libya reached out to support radical Palestinian groups and the Irish Republican Army with its oil largess. Qadhafi grew more vocal in his opposition to any accommodation with Israel, pitting his voice and resources against U.S. efforts to facilitate an Arab-Israeli peace in general and the Camp David Accord in particular.

Libya's growing radicalism and strengthening relationship with Moscow made Libya an immediate target of the Reagan administration when it took office in January 1981. Eager to project a new era of American strength in the wake of the Soviet invasion of Afghanistan and the Iranian revolution and its aftermath, the Reagan administration viewed a more confrontational approach toward Libya as an important way of demonstrating American power and protecting U.S. interests in the region.[3] The new U.S. administration set the stage for the subsequent escalation of policy by closing the Libyan People's Bureau in Washington, D.C., in May 1981, on the grounds that Libya was promoting global terrorism and destabilizing regional governments. This severance of official ties was followed by the curtailment of unofficial contacts; in response to allegations that Libya had sent agents abroad to assassinate high-level U.S. officials, the Reagan administration imposed a ban on the travel of U.S. passport holders to Libya and called on Americans living in Libya to leave the country.[4]

From the outset, U.S. efforts to weaken Qadhafi under President Ronald Reagan included covert action and limited military confrontations.[5] Within the first six months of taking office, the Reagan administration began a covert program to assist Libyan political exiles in their quest to oppose Qadhafi. Through this intensified pressure, the United States sought to limit Libyan meddling in Chad and to support the Chadian government of Hissen Habre against Libyan military incursions. U.S. covert activities reportedly gained greater momentum after the release of a June 1984 CIA assessment that concluded that only by unseating Qadhafi could the United States hope to curtail Libyan aggression and the threat it posed to American interests.[6] During this time, the United States and Libya clashed—figuratively and militarily—over Libyan claims that the Gulf of Sidra was within Libyan territorial waters, whereas the United States insisted that it constituted an international waterway.

Economic pressure was gradually introduced into the mix. Since 1979, Libya had been classified by the United States as a state sponsor of terrorism, a designation that mandated a number of automatic penalties, including controls on the sale of military and dual-use items, U.S. opposition to loans from international financial institutions to Libya, and a prohibition on most forms of U.S. bilateral assistance.[7] These penalties compounded other restrictions on the sale of military goods and aircraft that had been in place well before the United States designated Libya a state sponsor and placed it on the terrorism list.[8] Citing Libyan support for terrorism, President Reagan added another layer of sanctions on Libya in March 1982 when he imposed a ban on imports of Libyan crude oil. This move accompanied a tightening of restrictions on U.S. exports to Libya to prohibit the sale of sophisticated oil and gas technologies and equipment that could not easily be purchased from alternative sources abroad.[9] Congress—which had rejected a legislated oil embargo on Libya proposed by Senator Gary Hart (D-Colo.) just a few months earlier—was broadly supportive of these moves.[10]

Libya met these U.S. steps to isolate and pressure it with increased support for radical organizations that used violent tactics to pursue their goals and with greater zeal in opposing Arab and African governments friendly with the United States.[11] Terrorist attacks at the Rome and Vienna airports in the final days of 1985 prompted a further escalation of U.S. measures against Libya. In January 1986, linking these deadly assaults to Libya, President Reagan invoked the International Emergency Economic Powers Act to terminate most remaining economic activity between the United States and Libya. The new executive orders froze Libyan foreign assets in the United States, halted virtually all exports and imports between the two countries, forbade all loans and credits to the Libyan government, and prohibited all other financial transactions between U.S. citizens and Libya.[12] The severity of these measures was soon softened by provisions that exempted the economic transactions of the foreign subsidiaries of U.S. firms.[13] In subsequent months, in response to protests by U.S. oil companies operating in Libya and the realization that their immediate withdrawal would constitute a windfall to the Libyan government, the United States negotiated an agreement that essentially froze for three years the assets of the five American oil companies operating in Libya at the time.[14]

In part, the Reagan administration chose to respond to the Rome and Vienna airport attacks with economic sanctions rather than military force because of its inability to ensure that military strikes would hit the proper targets in Libya.[15] Yet, more important, the administration did not see these sanctions as a substitute for military action but rather viewed them as a vehicle to more forceful measures. On one hand, the administration saw sanctions as a launching point for subsequent efforts to gain multilateral cooperation for economic restrictions against Libya. On the other, steps curtailing economic interaction—and ordering the withdrawal of U.S. citizens from Libya—were viewed as important prerequisites to the use of military force. President Reagan stated, "If these steps do not end Qadhafi's terrorism, I promise you that further steps will be taken."[16]

Much to the dismay of the U.S. administration, the countries of Europe largely resisted U.S. entreaties to follow the American lead and impose sanctions on Libya.[17] Although many countries in western Europe were alarmed by Libya's radical behavior, they refrained from adopting collective measures

## U.S. Sanctions against Libya

**September 1, 1969**    Muammar Qadhafi seizes power in a coup against King Idris.

**1978**    The United States bans military equipment sales to Libya.

**December 29, 1979**    Libya is one of the countries put on the first list of state sponsors of terrorism, which leads to controls on exports of dual-use items, a ban on most economic assistance, and opposition to loans and aid from international financial institutions.

**February 15, 1980**    U.S. embassy in Tripoli is closed.

**May 6, 1981**    The United States closes Libya's embassy, or "People's Bureau," in Washington.

**August 1981**    U.S. warplanes are fired upon and shoot down two Libyan planes in the Gulf of Sidra.

**December 11, 1981**    The Reagan administration declares U.S. passports invalid for travel to Libya.

**March 10, 1982**    President Reagan embargoes crude oil imports from Libya and restricts exports of sophisticated oil and gas equipment to Libya.

**November 15, 1985**    President Reagan bans the import of refined petroleum products from Libya.

**December 27, 1985**    Terrorist attacks occur at the Rome and Vienna airports, killing 19 people and wounding 110. The United States links the attacks to the Abu Nidal Organization, which has close ties to Libya.

**January 7, 1986**    President Reagan imposes a comprehensive trade embargo on Libya; all exports and imports are banned. The United States also freezes Libyan government assets in the United States.

**April 5, 1986**    A bomb explodes at a West Berlin discotheque frequented by U.S. servicemen, killing three people and wounding more than 150.

**April 15, 1986**    European ministers agree to reduce the number of Libyan diplomats in Europe and limit their mobility. They also agree to impose stricter visa requirements and procedures for Libyans.

**April 15, 1986**    U.S. bombers attack targets in Libya around Tripoli and Benghazi in retaliation for the Berlin bombing, only hours after European countries make their decisions regarding Libya.

**May 5, 1986**    The leaders of the G7 industrial countries issue a declaration at their Tokyo meeting that vows to fight terrorism and singles out Libya specifically. The declaration states that G7 countries will refuse to export arms to countries involved in terrorism, improve extradition procedures for bringing suspected terrorists to trial, make more restrictive rules for entry for persons suspected of terrorism, and place limits on terrorist countries' diplomatic missions and personnel.

**June 30, 1986**    U.S. Treasury Department forces U.S. oil companies in Libya to leave but authorizes them to sign standstill agreements with Libya. These agreements allow the Libyan National Oil Company to operate the fields while the U.S. companies are absent. U.S. companies to maintain ownership rights for three years.

**December 21, 1988**   Pan Am flight 103 explodes over Lockerbie, Scotland, killing 270.

**September 19, 1989**   French airliner UTA 772 explodes over Niger, killing 171.

**October 1991**   A French judge calls for the arrest of four Libyan intelligence officers suspected in the UTA bombing.

**November 15, 1991**   Two Libyans, Abdel Basset Ali Mohamed al-Megrahi and Al-Amin Khalifa Fhimah, are indicted by a U.S. court for the bombing of Pan Am 103.

**March 31, 1992**   The UN Security Council passes resolution 748, which calls on Libya to turn over the suspects in the Lockerbie and UTA cases. The resolution threatens an air and arms embargo and a reduction in the number of diplomatic personnel at Libyan embassies around the world if Libya does not comply.

**April 15, 1992**   The UN sanctions go into effect.

**November 11, 1993**   The Security Council passes resolution 883, strengthening existing sanctions by further tightening the air restrictions, banning exports to Libya of selected equipment for downstream oil and gas sectors, and freezing existing Libyan funds and financial resources abroad.

**April 1996**   The Antiterrorism and Effective Death Penalty Act prohibits financial dealings with Libya and U.S. aid to countries providing Libya with military assistance and aid.

**August 5, 1996**   The Iran-Libya Sanctions Act penalizes firms making a substantial (more than $40 million) investment in the Libyan energy sector.

**August 24, 1998**   The United States and Britain propose holding the Lockerbie trial in the Netherlands under Scottish law.

**August 27, 1998**   The Security Council passes resolution 1192, which promises to suspend the sanctions on Libya if the two suspects are turned over.

**April 5, 1999**   Libya turns over the two suspects to the Hague. UN sanctions are suspended.

**June 11, 1999**   Libyan and U.S. officials meet for the first time in eighteen years to discuss the UN sanctions.

**March 25, 2000**   U.S. State Department officials visit Libya to assess whether or not it is safe to lift the ban on travel to Libya.

**April 27, 2000**   A Sense of the Senate resolution advises the president not to lift the travel ban on Libya and requests that the president consult with Congress on U.S. Libya policy.

**May 3, 2000**   Lockerbie trial opens.

**November 24, 2000**   U.S. State Department renews the travel ban on Libya.

**January 31, 2001**   The verdict is issued in the Lockerbie trial. Megrahi is found guilty; Khalifa Fhimah is acquitted.

**August 3, 2001**   The Iran-Libya Sanctions Act is reauthorized for another five years.

**November 2001**   A German court rules that Libya's intelligence service was at least partly responsible for the 1986 bombing of a Berlin disco.

**March 14, 2002**   The conviction against Megrahi is upheld in an appeal.

that went beyond an arms embargo. Even Britain, which had severed diplomatic relations with Libya in 1984 after an English policewoman was killed outside the Libyan diplomatic mission in London, was reluctant to curtail economic transactions with Libya.[18] Falling far short of its goal of coordinated multilateral sanctions, the Reagan administration was forced to settle for "gentlemen's agreements"—the pledges of European governments to try to keep their companies from taking advantage of the departure of U.S. firms from Libya.

The United States met the next terrorist attack linked to Libya—a bombing of a disco in West Berlin popular with American servicemen—with military force. Heightened tension and limited confrontations between U.S. and Libyan forces in the waters of the Gulf of Sidra throughout the spring of 1986 gave way to air raids on Tripoli and the area around Benghazi in April 1986.[19] These strikes—which targeted military airfields, barracks, and suspected terrorist training camps—could have been an attempt to assassinate the Libyan leader; at the very least, they were geared to do physical and psychological damage to Libya. The action, although signaling the seriousness with which the United States intended to deal with Qadhafi and other sponsors of terrorism, failed to injure Qadhafi physically or dislodge him from power.[20] Although the military action drew condemnation from many quarters, Europe as a whole did impose the diplomatic sanctions against Tripoli it had agreed to the day of the attacks, while some individual countries promised to review their trade policies with Libya. A G7 summit held a few weeks later elicited another antiterrorism declaration, along with private commitments from some countries to take additional steps against terrorist networks.[21]

The April 1986 bombing of Libya marked the height of U.S.-Libyan confrontation during the Reagan years. By the late 1980s, Libya's radicalism appeared to be waning. At the domestic level, Qadhafi called for greater respect for human rights and endorsed more private economic initiatives, although these appeals did not result in fundamental reforms to the Libyan system. On the international scene, mending relations with Egypt set the tone for more productive interactions with the rest of the Arab world. At the same time, the Libyan withdrawal from Chad in 1987 paved the way for more cooperative relations with Libya's North African neighbors and Libyan participation in the founding of the Arab Maghreb Union in 1989. Qadhafi coupled these actions with a pronouncement that Libya would no longer sponsor radical groups and causes, leading many to believe that

Libya would soon resume a more respected place in the international community. These changes, although not leading to a rapprochement with the United States, helped spur a re-evaluation of U.S policy toward Libya. The weakening of the Soviet Union—and the growing perception that Qadhafi was more an irritant than a threat—encouraged the Reagan team to move away from a policy intended to oust Qadhafi toward one with the objective of isolating him.[22] The administration of George H.W. Bush continued this less confrontational approach, maintaining pressure on Libya through rhetoric intended to discredit Qadhafi and blacklisting Libyan businesses believed to be connected with his regime.[23]

Evidence linking Libya with the 1988 explosion of Pan Am 103 over Lockerbie, Scotland, and the 1989 explosion of the French airliner UTA Flight 722 over Niger abruptly halted Libya's budding efforts to rehabilitate its international standing. In October 1991, a French judged called for the arrest of four Libyan intelligence officers suspected of involvement in the UTA bombing; several weeks later, the United States and Britain indicted two Libyan security officials, Abdel Basset Ali Mohamed al-Megrahi and Al-Amin Khalifa Fhimah, for their alleged involvement in the Lockerbie attack. The United States, France, and the United Kingdom jointly called on Libya to surrender all those charged with the crime for trial and to cooperate with all pending investigations.[24]

In January 1992, under the chairmanship of the United Kingdom, the United Nations Security Council unanimously passed resolution 731, calling on Libya to comply with the requests made by Britain, the United States, and France. Two months later, the Security Council passed resolution 748, reaffirming its earlier resolution and threatening U.N.-mandated sanctions if Libya failed to relinquish the accused subjects within two weeks.[25] The prospect of sanctions prompted Libya—which had rejected the UN demands as a violation of Libyan sovereignty—to suggest compromise scenarios involving the trial of the two Lockerbie suspects in a third country.[26] Although the Arab League considered Libya's offers to be worthy of further exploration, the Security Council rejected them as inadequate. As a result, a ban on all air links with Libya, an embargo on all arms sales, and the reduction in personnel at Libyan embassies came into effect on April 15, 1992. As stated in the UN resolution, the sanctions would be lifted once Libya satisfied several conditions, including the surrender of the two Lockerbie suspects and the cessation of all forms of and support for terrorism. The resolutions also called on Libya to take responsibility for the actions of its officials and pay compensation to the families of the victims if guilt was established. These objectives united the international community in their imposition of sanctions, causing U.S. policymakers to suppress any desires they might have had for a more aggressive strategy.

Despite widespread compliance, at least on the air ban and embargo on military sales, Qadhafi remained adamantly opposed to turning over the suspects. With Qadhafi's refusal to yield, the UN sanctions were renewed every three months, while the United States, the United Kingdom, and France worked to build a consensus for the strengthening of sanctions in the face of Libyan noncompliance. In the United States, the Families of Pan Am 103 in particular and Congress in general pushed the Clinton administration to secure tighter UN sanctions on Libya.[27] Finally, in November 1993, the Security Council passed resolution 883, mandating additional measures against Libya.[28] Although the new restrictions did not include the oil embargo that the United States had sought over German and Italian objections, they did include a ban on certain oil technology and equipment and a freeze on the overseas assets of the Libyan government.[29]

Although the UN sanctions remained in place in this form for nearly seven years, the period from 1993–99 was hardly a static one. During this time, both sides of the dispute invested much energy in trying to alter the status quo. Libya, for its part, continued to search for a way to end the UN sanctions without fully meeting demands to hand the suspects over to the United States or Britain.[30] In this quest, Libya declared its willingness to surrender the two men to a third party or the International Court of Justice (ICJ) at the Hague and asked the ICJ to rule on whether it had the jurisdiction to hear the Libyan claim. At the same time, Libya actively courted the opinion of Arab and African countries, drawing on past Libyan support for African liberation movements that had since come to power and distributing its petrodollars to countries willing to push for a lifting of the sanctions. This campaign bore fruit; both the Council of the Arab League and the Organization of African Unity (OAU) supported Libya's ICJ compromise and petitioned the UN Security Council to consider it more seriously.[31]

While international attitudes toward the sanctions were softening, domestic pressures were building in the United States for a tougher approach toward Libya. Under pressure from Congress and the Families of Pan Am 103, the Clinton administration sought unsuccessfully to garner an international coalition in favor of stronger UN measures.[32] In the meantime, the newly Republican-controlled Congress contemplated how it might create further pressure on countries it saw as acting against U.S. interests, particularly through the support of terrorism. When, in December 1995, Senator Alphonse D'Amato (R-N.Y.) introduced legislation to impose secondary sanctions on foreign companies investing in Iran's energy industry, Senator Edward Kennedy (D-Mass.) —who represented many of the families that lost members in the Pan Am bombing—added Libya to the bill in a last minute amendment.

This legislation—named the Iran-Libya Sanctions Act (ILSA)—became law in August 1996, after the Clinton administration had worked with Congress to soften some of its original provisions. In its final form, the new law mandated that the president impose at least two of six possible sanctions on any foreign company violating UN sanctions or investing more than $40 million a year in Libya's petroleum sector.[33] ILSA did include a provision that allowed the president to waive the sanctions for any particular company on the grounds that doing so served the national interest of the United States.[34] As anticipated, Europeans strongly opposed ILSA, seeing it as an affront to their vital economic interests as well as a violation of international agreements to which the United States was a party.[35] Soon after ILSA became law, the European Union passed a statute barring compliance with extraterritorial sanctions and threatened to take the issue to the World Trade Organization if the United States imposed sanctions under ILSA.

The passage of ILSA was the most notable congressional initiative against Libya in the 1990s, but hardly the only one. In August 1996, Congress passed the Antiterrorism and Effective Death Penalty Act, a law that increased pressure on Libya and other state sponsors of terrorism by both prohibiting all financial transactions with them and mandating the imposition of sanctions on third countries that sell weapons to them.[36] This legislation also revoked the sovereign immunity of these countries in the face of U.S. courts, paving the way for civil suits against Libya and other countries believed to be behind particular acts of terrorism.

Despite continuous domestic pressure for a more aggressive approach toward Libya, the Clinton administration took two actions that made it the subject of criticism from hard-line advocates. First, in May 1998, it granted a "national interest" waiver to French, Russian, and Malaysian companies investing close to $2 billion in the Iranian energy sector in violation of ILSA.[37] This waiver, in combination with assurances from Secretary of State Madeleine Albright that further waivers could be expected for similar investments in Iran, dampened a looming flashpoint between the United

States and Europe.[38] Even though the Clinton administration was noticeably opaque about its intentions to enforce ILSA with respect to Libya, the waiver appeared to allay the fears of foreign firms that they would be sanctioned for future investments in Libya.

Second, in August 1998, the United States and Britain put forward a compromise proposal under which the Lockerbie suspects would be tried by an all-Scottish court in the Netherlands, instead of in Scotland or America as the earlier Security Council resolutions stipulated. Rapid erosion of multilateral support for UN sanctions against Libya had spurred the two countries to offer this compromise.[39] The international isolation of Libya was crumbling, as foreign dignitaries visited Tripoli and African leaders welcomed airplanes carrying Qadhafi to their capitals.[40] Even more alarming still was the growing intolerance of regional bodies for the continued sanctions. In September 1997, the Arab League approved a resolution calling on Arab countries to "take measures to alleviate the sanctions on Libya";[41] the OAU went beyond this intent, declaring in June 1998 that members would cease complying with all sanctions against Libya as of September, unless the United States and Britain agreed to try the suspects in a neutral country. U.S. and British officials feared that international pressure to lift the sanctions would soar if the ICJ—which had decided in early 1998 that it had jurisdiction to hear Libya's claim—were to rule that Libya was not bound to surrender the two suspects.[42]

Although Libya quickly accepted the British-U.S. proposal in principle, Tripoli demanded numerous clarifications and assurances before it would surrender the Pan Am suspects. Several months of negotiations ensued, where UN Secretary General Kofi Annan, assisted by Nelson Mandela and representatives from Saudi Arabia and elsewhere, sought to allay Libyan concerns.[43] Acting as intermediaries, these men consulted with Britain—which was more interested in resolving the impasse than the United States—and Libya to reach acceptable compromises.[44] As part of this effort, the UN Security Council passed UN resolution 1192, which explicitly stated that UN sanctions would be suspended once Libya handed over the suspects, although a complete lifting of the sanctions would only follow once Libya had satisfied all the demands of the original resolutions. Moreover, in a move that was to be the source of much scrutiny and criticism, Annan provided Libya with a letter assuring Qadhafi that the trial would not be a vehicle for undermining the Libyan regime.[45]

Libya's surrender of the two Lockerbie suspects to the Netherlands on April 5, 1999, and the conclusion of the trial—which found Abdel Basset al-

Megrahi guilty and acquitted Al-Amin Khalifa Fhimah—on January 31, 2001, left the international community divided over how to treat Libya. In the wake of the trial, some countries were eager to close the chapter on the Lockerbie era. Motivated by economic ambitions and the belief that the best way to consolidate the positive changes in Libya's behavior was to engage it, they argued for Libya's rapid reintegration into the global polity and economy. Libya sought to take advantage of these leanings and to ease its rehabilitation with Europe by providing compensation to the families of those killed in the UTA bombing and the relatives of the British policewoman killed in 1984.[46] Libya's efforts to expedite its reintegration also included the offer of new opportunities to international investors.[47]

The United States stood in contrast to countries and leaders taking this position.[48] Supported by the United Kingdom, the United States reacted to both the surrender of the suspects and the verdict of the trial by calling on Libya to meet the other demands of the UN resolutions, including taking responsibility for the actions of its officials and providing appropriate compensation.[49] Although acquiescing to the suspension of sanctions once the suspects were delivered to trial, the United States lobbied fiercely to prevent the UN Security Council from holding a vote on whether to formally lift the sanctions on Libya.[50] Both the Clinton and subsequent Bush administrations declared they would oppose the lifting of UN sanctions and remained committed to continuing pressure on Libya until it met the full demands of the UN resolutions.[51] The U.S. Congress also demonstrated no inclination to soften its stance on Libya in the wake of the Lockerbie trial and related developments, as was demonstrated by the renewal of ILSA legislation before its expiration in August 2001.[52] Libyan refusal to accept any responsibility for the bombing and the absence of a commitment to compensate the victims' families had further hardened American constituencies and, at least previous to September 11, 2001, rendered any debate over how to improve U.S. relations with Libya irrelevant.[53]

The events of September 11 helped changed the context in which the United States and Libya grappled with their disagreements. Libya quickly condemned the attacks and extended sympathy to the American people. Calling the Taliban "Godless promoters of political Islam," Qadhafi described U.S. military actions in Afghanistan as justified as acts of self-defense.[54] Libya reportedly backed up this rhetorical stance with actions to assist the United States in its campaign against terrorism.[55] These shifts did not produce any tangible adjustments in U.S. policy as the American government stood by its calls for Libya to fulfill UN resolutions and focused more intensely on Libya's WMD pursuits. But they—and the upholding of the conviction of al-Megrahi in an appeal—did set the stage for sporadic trilateral talks between the British, U.S., and Libyan governments and for promising negotiations between Libyan and American lawyers on the issue of compensation for the families of those who died in Pan Am 103.

## Judging the Effectiveness and Utility of Sanctions on Libya

A comprehensive analysis of sanctions on Libya has several components. One must determine the damage inflicted on Libya, or the economic and political impact of sanctions. Also important is the extent to which sanctions advanced the goals sought by policymakers (effectiveness) and the costs endured by the United States and others, including Libya's population, as a result of the use of these tools. These assessments provide the basis for judgments about the effectiveness of sanctions (what objectives these tools achieved) as well as the utility of sanctions (their usefulness when costs as well as goals achieved are considered).

### Economic Impact

Over the decades that U.S. and UN sanctions were in place, the economic performance of Libya grew progressively worse. After showing great promise in the 1970s when its oil wealth boosted growth and per capita incomes, Libya's economy began to falter in the 1980s. Libya's economic prospects steadily declined throughout the 1990s, at least until the very end of the millennium. Sanctions—both multilateral and unilateral ones—contributed to this overall decline. Yet the more interesting question is the *extent* to which sanctions are responsible for Libya's deteriorating economic circumstances. To investigate this question more closely, three periods in Libya's economic history—corresponding to the various phases of economic sanctions—are examined.

1980S TO 1992: U.S. UNILATERAL SANCTIONS. The Libyan economy weakened at about the same time that the Reagan administration first imposed U.S. unilateral sanctions on it. Growth rates, which averaged over 10 percent a year during 1975–79, suddenly turned negative, signaling a contraction in the economy. Revenue from exports dropped dramatically, placing pressure on foreign exchange reserves and necessitating a cutback on imports. These curbs on imports forced a retrenchment of important development projects geared toward the diversification of the economy.[56] Meanwhile, pressure on the balance of payments forced Libya to draw down its reserves and kept it from making payments on its trade debts. Having contracted large numbers of development projects to foreign companies, Libya began to struggle to pay for them and increasingly sought barter deals in the place of cash transactions.[57]

Although this economic distress coincided with the imposition of U.S. sanctions, many factors contributed to the economic problems that Libya experienced during this time. First, the state of the international oil market was a huge determinant of Libyan economic fortunes. After a decade of high oil prices, which burnished Libya's economic prospects and led some to claim Libya "cannot fail to prosper,"[58] the price of oil dropped precipitously in the 1980s largely as a result of economic downturn in the OECD countries and disputes within OPEC.[59] Prices took a huge plunge in 1986, the year that the Reagan administration imposed comprehensive sanctions on Libya. The tumbling price of oil reverberated throughout Libya's economy. Libya's broader plans for development were closely linked to the performance of the oil industry as oil revenues were responsible for generating more than 95 percent of Libya's foreign exchange; the country relied on the foreign exchange brought in by energy-related exports to purchase food, technology, and capital equipment needed for daily survival and the modernization and diversification of the economy.

Internal Libyan practices and policies were also responsible for the economic downturn of the 1980s, as is suggested by the fact that Libya's economic performance dragged behind other oil-exporting countries subject to similar external shocks (figures 5-1 and 5-2). The greater part of Qadhafi's second decade in power was a period of accelerated radicalism. As mentioned earlier, Qadhafi intensified his foreign policy adventurism and support for radical groups during the 1980s and began the construction of a chemical weapons plant at Rabta. Qadhafi's radicalism extended to the economy, with the Libyan leader propagating a quixotic ideology and an agenda best described as an awkward mix of socialism, Arab nationalism, and populism.[60] In his efforts to translate these principles into practice, Qadhafi banned the ownership of private property and called for the elimination of private savings. Such "reforms" had disastrous effects on productivity, explaining much of Libya's economic downturn in the 1980s. By 1987 Qadhafi recognized the need to reverse some of these edicts—leading him to allow greater economic freedom and limited private enterprise in the later part of the decade—but not before the toll on the Libyan economy had mounted.

In comparison to the influence of international oil prices and Qadhafi's radical policies, the impact of U.S. economic sanctions on the Libyan

**Figure 5-1.** *Real GDP Growth, Libya Compared with the Middle East and North Africa, 1975–2001*

Percentage

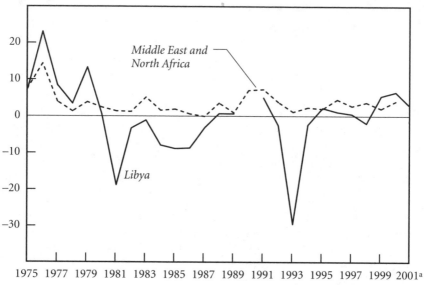

Sources: International Monetary Fund, *World Development Indicators 2002*, CD-ROM, for Middle East and North Africa numbers and Libya numbers to 1990. After 1990, Libya GDP numbers from Economist Intelligence Unit, *Country Profile: Libya*, 1998–99, 2000–01, and 2001, and *Country Report: Libya*, July 2002.
    a. Economist Intelligence Unit estimate.

economy in the 1980s was small.[61] However, as examined below, sanctions did influence some important Libyan economic decisions and increased the vulnerability of the country to the UN economic measures that were to follow in the 1990s.

TRADE AND INVESTMENT PATTERNS. U.S. trade sanctions did not inflict significant monetary costs on Libya but did shape the country's economic partners and influence its economic strategies. Although the United States was the largest consumer of Libyan exports in 1981, subsequent constraints on the U.S. purchase of Libyan products barely affected the Libyan economy.[62] Initially, the impact of the 1982 ban on imports of Libyan crude into the United States was mitigated by the continued entry of Libyan oil

**Figure 5-2.  *GDP Growth Rates, Libya Compared with Oil Exporting Countries, 1975–2000***

Percentage

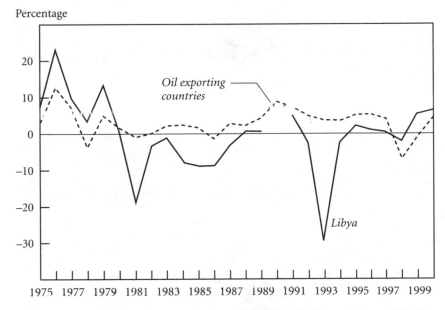

Sources: IMF, *World Development Indicators 2001*, CD-ROM, for Libya numbers to 1990. After 1990, Libya GDP numbers from Economist Intelligence Unit, *Country Profile: Libya*, 1998–99, 2000–01, and 2001, and *Country Report: Libya*, July 2001. Oil exporting numbers from IMF, *International Financial Statistics*, 2001.

into the American market through purchases on the spot oil market or as a refined product.[63] In the medium and longer term, Libya limited the damage of sanctions by diversifying its trade partners (figure 5-3). Given the appeal of Libyan oil as a high-quality crude located close to Europe, other industrial countries such as Germany and Italy gladly assumed the Libyan exports that the United States forwent. Global trading patterns were merely reconfigured. The United States turned to North Sea oil to make up for sources lost under the embargo; in turn, the United Kingdom increased its imports from Libya by 350 percent over the first thirteen months of the American import ban.[64] Over time, countries such as Brazil and Turkey also became more dependent on Libyan oil. When the U.S. ban on crude imports was extended to cover all Libyan goods in 1986, Libya's coping

## Figure 5-3. *Libyan Exports, 1980, 1987, 1994*

### Libyan Exports, by Country and Region, 1980[a]

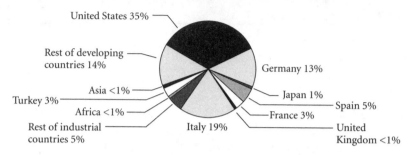

### Libyan Exports, by Country and Region, 1987[b]

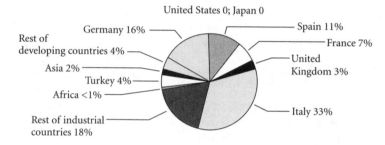

### Libyan Exports, by Country and Region, 1994[c]

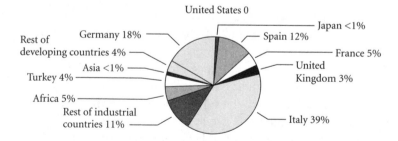

Source: IMF, *Direction of Trade Statistics Yearbook,* 1987, 1994, and 1999.
a. U.S. and other country imports; total exports are $21.919 billion, 1980 dollars.
b. U.S. and other country imports; total exports are $8.047 billion, 1987 dollars.
c. U.S. and other country imports; total exports are $7.849 billion, 1994 dollars.

strategy was similar; it redirected a substantial portion of the small volume of non-oil exports it had sold to America to other destinations. As a result of this reconfiguration of trade patterns, the costs to Libya of U.S restrictions on the purchase of its products were minimal, amounting to no more than a fraction of the approximately $180 million in non-oil exports that Libya would have sold to the United States from 1986 to 2001 in the absence of sanctions (see table 5A-1 in the appendix to this chapter).[65]

Of greater significance than the small sums of trade lost to Libya as a result of the import ban was the unexpected influence that this prohibition had on Libyan investment patterns. In 1983 Libya began investing its petrodollars in refining and marketing assets in Europe. During the next decade and beyond, Libya acquired refineries and petrol stations across western and eastern Europe, as well as in Malta and Egypt. These investments gave Libya guaranteed outlets for its crude oil and granted it more flexibility in the marketing of its output. In part, the decisions to develop Libyan interests in downstream operations abroad was based in sound commercial logic.[66] Yet the loss of the U.S. market to Libyan oil exports in 1982 also figured in these calculations.[67] Although the American ban only inflicted minor short-term costs on Libya when it was forced to market nearly one-third of its oil to other destinations, this episode—and ongoing U.S. efforts to convince other countries to restrict their commercial relations with Libya—persuaded Tripoli of the need to secure additional markets for its oil. Over time, Libya's procurement of refining and distribution outlets fortified Libya's economic integration with Europe, thereby strengthening the political links Tripoli had with countries across the Mediterranean.

Export controls and, ultimately, a complete ban on U.S. exports to Libya did involve some costs to Libya, although they were concentrated and, for the most part, diminished over time.[68] As was the case with the import ban, Libya was able to readjust its trade patterns to substitute European or Asian products for those it formerly secured from the United States. Replacing U.S. goods required little effort or cost, except in two sectors of the economy that were disproportionately affected by sanctions. The Libyan aviation industry suffered under U.S. export regulations, as the United States withheld airplanes and other types of technology from Libya beginning in the 1970s.[69] Similarly, as discussed subsequently, the restrictions on U.S. oil technology and equipment created frustrations and obstacles for Libya. In some instances, Libya was able to acquire comparable technology and equipment from other sources or to secure U.S. goods and spare parts on the black market, although it often had to pay substantial premiums for such items. Nevertheless, Libya's overall ability to find substitutes for American products greatly diminished the overall costs of sanctions on U.S. exports to Libya, reducing them to a roughly estimated $850 million.

EXTERNAL FLOWS. U.S. sanctions on financial flows also imposed minimal costs on the Libyan economy. Restrictions on bilateral aid from the United States had no practical impact, as no such monies had flowed to Libya even before sanctions formally prohibited them. The 1986 freeze of Libyan foreign assets in the United States also caused relatively little disruption, given that Libya had long avoided holding substantial assets in U.S institutions. In any case, legislation mandating stricter sanctions on Libya had been percolating in the U.S. Congress for most of the previous year, allowing Libya ample opportunity to withdraw any liquid assets from the United States before the freeze was imposed. According to the Economist Intelligence Unit, the U.S. freeze affected only about $100 million of all Libyan overseas assets of more than $5 billion, less than 2 percent of the total.[70]

Other American financial restrictions—which included U.S. opposition to lending from the World Bank and International Monetary Fund to Libya—were also of minor consequence given Libyan independence from these institutions. Libya was already not eligible to borrow from the World Bank, as its oil wealth made it too affluent to qualify for such assistance.[71] Although Libya could have borrowed from the IMF, it had never done so, preferring instead to finance fluctuations in its balance of payments by running down its foreign reserves and paring back its imports. According to the OECD, Libya only claimed $3.6 billion of foreign debt in 1986, compared with Algeria's $25.4 billion and Egypt's $45.7 billion.[72]

U.S. sanctions, however, did have a modest hand in diminishing the enthusiasm of non-U.S. lenders and creditors for Libya throughout the 1980s.[73] By solidifying and formalizing the already growing tendency of the international community to equate Libya with radicalism, terrorism, and a high degree of unpredictability, U.S. sanctions—along with U.S. military maneuvers, caustic rhetoric, and diplomatic wrangling—magnified international wariness of Libya and contributed to the decisions of international banks, shipping companies, airlines, and credit agencies to re-evaluate the risks associated with doing business in Libya.[74] The effect of sanctions on this outcome, however, should not be overestimated. As mentioned earlier, Libya's domestic circumstances and economic policies were major deterrents to the greater involvement of international export agencies and other creditors in Libya in the 1980s.[75] In this situation, U.S. sanctions played no more than a minor supporting role.

THE ENERGY SECTOR, 1980S–92. Two factors would be apparent in any snapshot of the Libyan energy sector in the early 1990s, years after U.S. sanctions were imposed but before UN measures came into effect. First, Libya had maintained its oil production and energy exports during the 1980s and into the 1990s at levels in line with its OPEC quota. Second, the Libyan oil sector was in serious need of modernization.[76] Both observations, however, belie the true impact of U.S. sanctions on the Libyan energy sector.

Although Libya maintained constant levels in its production and export of oil, sanctions did affect Libya's production capabilities. This impact was gradual, rather than immediate, given that the Libyan National Oil Corporation assumed the operation of oil fields run by U.S. oil companies as soon as sanctions were imposed. This rapid action allowed Libya to avoid the substantial decline in crude output or exports that might have occurred when, in 1986, U.S. firms were forced to freeze their involvement in the production and marketing of approximately one-third of Libya's oil to Europe and other regions.[77] Sanctions were instead responsible for a steady — although not dramatic—downturn in production at the fields once operated by American companies. Despite its best efforts, Libya was unable to stem the natural decline in production of these fields as the 1980s wore on. Not only did difficulties in securing spare parts create uncertainties, but Libyan oil workers did not possess the needed technological knowledge or managerial expertise to boost production when it began to decline.[78] A combination of factors prevented Libya from utilizing the skills of foreigners to address these problems. In large part, Libya desired to operate these fields independent of outside assistance. However, "gentlemen's agreements" negotiated between European governments and the United States added to the wariness of foreign companies to step in where American firms had claims.[79] The declining output from these major fields, however, was masked by Libya's success in attracting new investment to explore and develop other fields in the country, enabling Libya to maintain constant overall production levels in the face of sanctions (figure 5-4).

Attributing the dilapidated state of Libya's overall industry in the early 1990s to U.S. sanctions would be as erroneous as claiming that sanctions did not affect Libyan production capabilities. Instead, the decline in Libya's

**Figure 5-4.** *Libyan Oil Production, Exports, and OPEC Quotas, 1978–2001*

Thousands of barrels per day

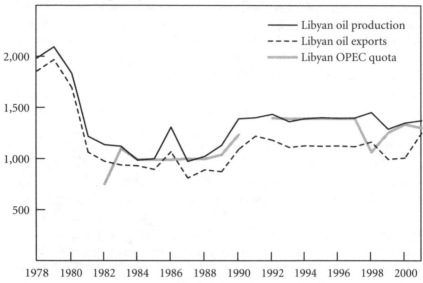

Sources: *OPEC Annual Statistical Bulletin,* various years; Judith Gurney, *Libya: The Political Economy of Oil* (Oxford University Press, p. 96); U.S. Department of Energy, Energy Information Administration, *Country Analysis Brief: Libya,* July 2002.

Note: OPEC production quotas began in March 1982; they were temporarily suspended in 1991 in the wake of the Gulf war.

oil industry had its roots in several places, most of which had no relation to sanctions. First, overall levels of investment in the energy sector were inadequate to counter the deterioration of Libya's older oil fields, some of which had been producing since the 1950s. In large part, this shortfall was the fault of the Libyan regime, which had made insufficient investments in this sector since the Libyan state took over most international oil operations in 1973.[80] Insufficient investment levels were also the result of lukewarm international interest in the Libyan oil industry. In part, the tepid enthusiasm of foreign oil companies was due to the poor terms of the agreements offered by the Libyan regime to foreign firms. Yet it was also a reflection of the state of global oil markets in the 1980s. Many companies decreased their worldwide exploration activities over that period, given the large amount of spare capacity that existed in OPEC countries at that time.[81] As discussed earlier, Libya's revolutionary reputation was also a deterrent to investors, even to those in the oil industry; a 1991 article contemplating the discrepancy between Libya's reputation as a country possessing vast untapped oil sources and the relatively low investment made by large companies in Libyan oil exploration quoted an oil industry official as saying, "As soon as the word Libya is mentioned, thoughts turn to Lockerbie, the IRA, Rabta and scandal, and that's often it."[82] Although Qadhafi's radical agenda left the oil industry largely untouched, it served as a disincentive to investors who might otherwise have been drawn to Libya's economy. The importance of unilateral U.S. sanctions in this picture was limited to reinforcing Libya's negative image, a real but not necessarily decisive factor.

Overall, the monetary consequences of the constraints created by U.S. sanctions on the energy sector during the 1980s were relatively small. Although, in the absence of U.S. sanctions, Libya would have had the capability to produce more oil, it is unlikely that Libya would have exported vastly higher quantities throughout the decade had sanctions not been in place. In part, Libya had made a political decision in the 1970s to scale back production in favor of conserving its resources. Moreover, Libya was at least technically constrained by its OPEC quota, which it nearly met or exceeded every year throughout the 1980s. In better circumstances and with fewer constraints, Libya might have been able to keep down the costs of its production or have lobbied more vigorously for a raise in OPEC quotas, rather than being a consistent advocate of restraining OPEC production.[83] Libya might have also profited more handsomely when OPEC rescinded its production quotas during the Gulf war. Apart from these scenarios, U.S. sanctions did not impose serious losses on Libya's oil industry. However, they did leave the oil industry vulnerable and dampened its long-term prospects, thereby affecting the viability of the economy as a whole as Libya moved into a period during which it experienced greater international pressure.[84]

1992–2000: MULTILATERAL UN SANCTIONS ON LIBYA. After a brief respite from the economic doldrums in the early 1990s, Libya underwent a period of even greater economic distress. From 1992 and 1999, the Libyan economy grew on average only 0.8 percent a year, while per capita income fell in real terms and high rates of inflation persisted.[85] As in the previous period, many factors account for Libya's plunging economic fortunes throughout most of the 1990s. The fate of Libya's economy continued to be closely tied to the international oil market and the price of oil, which

**Figure 5-5.** *Value of Libya's Oil Exports Compared with Price of Libyan Oil, 1975–2001*

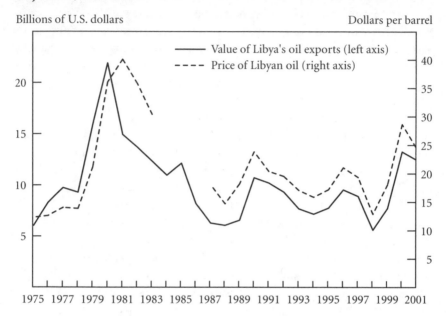

Billions of U.S. dollars                                    Dollars per barrel

Legend:
——— Value of Libya's oil exports (left axis)
- - - Price of Libyan oil (right axis)

Sources: *OPEC Annual Statistical Bulletin,* various years; U.S. Department of Energy, Energy Information Administration, *Country Analysis Brief: Libya,* July 2002.

dropped to new lows during this decade. Fluctuating prices caused Libya's export earnings to vary tremendously during these years, a development that had repercussions throughout the entire economy (figure 5-5).[86] But, as once again suggested by Libya's dramatic departure from regional trends, country-specific dynamics also underpinned Libya's weak economic prospects. Certainly, domestic economic management continued to be a problem. Although the economic reforms Qadhafi introduced in the late 1980s did rejuvenate some elements of the economy, they still left the state in charge of large swaths of the economy and poorly poised to manage the intervals of low oil prices. And much more so than in the previous decade, both U.S. and UN economic sanctions posed an overall drag on the Libyan economy in the 1990s.

The effects of UN financial measures were largely indirect. The immediate pain of the UN freeze on Libyan overseas assets was mitigated by Libyan efforts to preempt it by relocating liquid assets from vulnerable locations to areas less likely to comply with UN financial sanctions.[87] The Libyans were given ample time to execute this transfer, partially because the UN Security Council resolution mandating the freeze was passed three weeks before it came into effect but also because Libyans had long expected a tightening of the sanctions in light of U.S. rhetoric. While not placing huge volumes of Libyan assets beyond Tripoli's grasp, the freeze did force Libya to curtail its refining and distribution interests abroad and to take measures to reduce its standing in existing ventures to minority levels. In this way, the international freeze on Libyan assets limited the income Libya earned abroad and hampered the country's ability to make payments to foreign companies. In more prosperous times, these constraints might have been a mere irritant; yet throughout the 1990s, when Libyan foreign exchange reserves were dwindling because of the plummeting price of oil, such restrictions were more burdensome, placing further limits on Libya's trade and adding to Libya's difficulties in securing short-term credit.

Trade restrictions mandated by the UN resolution had more pointed effects. Although the UN sanctions only proscribed small categories of exports to Libya, these direct losses were more likely to be borne by Libya in full, as the multilateral nature of the UN sanctions hindered the adjustment of trade patterns that occurred under unilateral sanctions. Libya's inability to replace many of the banned items had serious implications for two sectors of the country's economy. First, the prohibition on spare parts for airplane maintenance squeezed the aviation industry, already hurting from U.S. unilateral sanctions. Libya was able to keep some of its airplanes operable, as demonstrated by Qadhafi's 1997 visits to African countries in violation of the UN air ban and Libya's maintenance of some internal flights.[88] However, the dramatic drop in air traffic, the shortage of spare parts, and the lack of qualified technical staff contributed to a sharp decline in the value of the industry.[89] Second, UN sanctions crippled Libya's downstream oil sector. The UN ban on the export of equipment needed for the maintenance of refineries and other downstream operations forced Libya into a costly and inefficient search for substitute parts. Moreover, such restrictions prevented Libya from upgrading its refineries to produce more gasoline for domestic consumption. As a result, Libya was compelled to set aside foreign reserves for the import of lighter fuels and to use some of its best quality crude to make gasoline rather than jet fuels or the like.[90] In some cases, Libya acquired needed parts on the black market, although estimates suggest that Libya was forced to pay close to four times the market price for such equipment.[91]

Table 5-1. *Value of the Libyan Dinar (LD) against the U.S. Dollar*

| Exchange rate | January 1993 | July 1994 | January 1995[a] | December 1995 | October 1996 | November 1998[a] |
|---|---|---|---|---|---|---|
| Official | 0.28 | 0.30 | 1.02 | 1.02 | 0.36 | 0.45 |
| Black market | 1.8 | 3.5 | 4.0 | 3.6 | 3.6 | 3.5 |

Source: Various Economist Intelligence Unit reports.

a. Libya devalued its currency twice in the 1990s, once in January 1995 and once in November 1998. It also devalued the dinar in January 2002.

Besides creating tangible new constraints on specific sectors of the economy, UN measures had more diffuse effects on the Libyan economy. Perhaps most detrimental was the uncertainty perpetuated by the sanctions. Particularly in the early years, foreigners and Libyans alike watched the workings of the Security Council closely, wondering if sanctions would be lifted or if they would be intensified with each 120-day review that the United Nations conducted.[92] Persistent Libyan efforts to craft a compromise over the Lockerbie suspects, waning international support for the UN measures, and ongoing U.S. efforts to build a consensus for harsher sanctions all intensified the uncertainty. As long as sanctions remained in place, those living and working in Libya were forced to deal with an erratic supply of imports and, at least initially, an untested "parallel" account system that allowed Libya to continue trading oil internationally, even while its overseas assets were frozen.[93] These qualms were amplified by fears that, in the absence of greater multilateral action, the United States would resort to more unilateralist policies, an option deemed possible in light of the 1986 U.S. bombing of Libya.

The climate of uncertainty damaged Libya's economy in several ways throughout the 1990s. Most tangibly, it weakened the Libyan currency, driving down the value of the Libyan dinar (table 5-1). As a result, inflation in Libya soared, particularly given that the country relied heavily on imported goods for daily survival. Inflationary pressures were exacerbated by mark-ups imposed on food and other consumer products that had to be transported to Libya by sea or overland routes owing to the ban on flights into the country. The growing importance of black markets—sometimes encouraged, sometimes aggressively suppressed by Qadhafi—pushed prices even higher.

The uncertainty created by economic sanctions also created direct and indirect financial problems for the Libyan regime. Not knowing whether or when UN sanctions would be intensified, Tripoli devoted inordinate resources to creating a cushion of reserves and assets that it could rely on if an oil embargo or other additional sanctions were imposed on Libya.[94] This stockpiling limited the availability of funds that the government could devote to satisfying daily needs and investing in capital-intensive projects. Fluctuating oil export earnings—in conjunction with the pressures created by the inflation and depressed currency—aggravated this shortage of resources and forced the government to curtail development projects. Although work on the Great Man-Made River prestige irrigation project continued, albeit at a slow pace, many other forms of domestic investment halted.[95] Although the UN arms embargo on Libya inadvertently freed up Libyan resources for civilian purposes, shortages of foreign exchange remained acute throughout the 1990s.

Sanctions—through the inconveniences they caused, the uncertainty they spawned, and the domestic investment they constrained—also quelled a sector that could have been an economic engine for Libya in the 1990s: tourism. Easily accessible to Europe, possessing vast archeological ruins, and having a Mediterranean coastline, Libya might have earned billions from tourism over at least part of the period that UN sanctions were in place. Libya's neighbor, Tunisia, amassed between $1.5 billion and $2.0 billion a year from tourism in the later part of the 1990s;[96] such figures represent 10 to 24 percent of Libya's total export earnings over the same years.[97] Admittedly, Libya's poor tourist infrastructure and the earlier reluctance of the Libyan regime to encourage foreign visitors held back visitors in the 1990s. Yet, the extent to which sanctions helped suppress these numbers is evident when the volume of travelers to Libya in 1995 (85,000) is compared with that in 2001 (190,000), the first full year after the suspension of sanctions.[98]

Although UN measures placed no restrictions on the involvement of international firms in Libya, the uncertainty created by sanctions also formed an adverse climate for investors and business people, even beyond the practical difficulties they faced because of the UN flight ban. The virtual lack of international interest in investing in the Libyan economy outside the energy sector cannot be solely attributed to sanctions, given Libyan restrictions on such investment and the absence of international interest even before sanctions were in place. However, the growing reluctance of international firms to do business in Libya while it was under UN sanctions was apparent by the higher rates charged by international firms working there.

UN and U.S. sanctions also intersected with domestic and global developments to dampen, but not entirely curb, international interest in Libya's energy sector in the 1990s. During the decade, Libya was able to maintain a steady stream of largely European investment in its oil sector and, to a much lesser extent, its gas industry.[99] While not seriously affecting the volume of investment in Libya's energy sector, sanctions did influence the nature of foreign involvement in it.

First, UN and U.S. sanctions shaped the profile of international oil companies doing business in Libya. Although large firms long involved in Libya maintained their presence there throughout the period sanctions were in place, most of the new investors showing interest in Libya during this time were small-to-medium enterprises with more limited capabilities and services. This profile is in part explained by domestic and international factors unrelated to sanctions; although Libya offered increasingly attractive production sharing agreements to international firms as the 1990s progressed, the terms of these agreements still compared poorly with those that the same firms could expect elsewhere. Moreover, outstanding regulatory and fiscal issues downgraded the appeal of investments in Libya, particularly when low oil prices were sapping the enthusiasm of many firms to sign new deals worldwide. In this environment, both U.S. and UN sanctions had a "magnifying effect"; the multilateral sanctions reinforced the disincentives provided to foreign firms by other international and domestic factors. UN and U.S. sanctions compounded the already lackluster attitudes of large firms that might have considered investing in Libya in more propitious times.

Sanctions also influenced the nature of investments that international companies working in Libya were able and willing to make. Although many of these firms were enthusiastic about developing fields where the oil was easy to extract, few were keen to make more complex and far-reaching investments. In the uncertain political climate that UN sanctions created, most firms were wary about undertaking investments that would require many years to recoup. Similarly, ambitious exploration projects lacked great appeal. As a result, Libya's energy industry operated largely on second-rate technologies and equipment, with few firms bringing in enhanced oil recovery techniques and other measures that were critical to bolstering the production of Libya's older fields and expanding Libya's energy industry.

Against the more pervasive effects of UN sanctions, U.S. sanctions continued to constrain the daily operation and the much-needed refurbishment of the fields once run by American firms. Although the Libyan National Oil Corporation (NOC) and associated Libyan firms kept these fields in production, their declining output betrayed Libya's ongoing struggle to keep them operational with increasingly decrepit U.S. equipment. These difficulties frustrated Libyan efforts to maintain and increase the production capabilities of its oil industry overall; in 1998, one industry source estimated that production from NOC-operated fields was declining by 8 percent a year, largely because the corporation lacked the technology and equipment necessary to stabilize output.[100]

In contrast to the effects of UN sanctions and the original U.S. measures, the impact of America's ILSA legislation was very small. Until the Clinton administration issued the May 1998 waiver to Total for investments in Iran, ILSA had some "magnifying" effect; it presented yet another reason for large firms to be wary of investments in Libya. However, even at its peak, ILSA's marginal value in deterring investment once all the other factors are accounted for remained small, as indicated by investment patterns in Libya that did not change markedly after ILSA's passage in 1996.[101] Unlike the situation in Iran, where the National Iranian Oil Company was opening its industry to foreign investment for the first time, outside involvement in Libya's energy sector was long-standing. It was therefore less in need of large investments that grossly superseded ILSA's original $40 million threshold. Moreover, most firms found ways to evade ILSA regulations by amending old contracts to incorporate new investments, rather than signing new contracts that would make them vulnerable to U.S. secondary sanctions.[102]

How serious was the cumulative impact of the many ways in which sanctions affected the energy industry on Libya's overall production capabilities? At one level, it is undeniable that sanctions—by influencing the nature of foreign involvement in Libya and by hindering the refurbishment of certain fields—provided an impediment to greater oil production. In the absence of sanctions, at the turn of the millennium, Libya would have been closer to realizing its avowed goal of producing 2 million barrels a day (from its actual 1.287 million barrels a day in 1999).[103] Nevertheless, given the international and domestic situation, production levels would have still fallen short of this benchmark had sanctions not been in place. Some of the constraints that sanctions posed were not of great significance in the Libyan context; for instance, smaller companies may not have not been able to offer Libya the most sophisticated technology, but the relative ease with which Libyan oil can be extracted lessened the significance of these technological shortfalls. Even more important in weighing the ultimate impact of sanctions on the oil industry is the reality that, in many respects, sanctions were a redundant constraint on the further development of Libya's industry outside the downstream sector throughout much of the 1990s. Without significant changes in domestic practices or shifts in the international environment, Libya would have still struggled to attract the sort of investment it desired even if sanctions were not in place. Nevertheless, sanctions provided real leverage. Although they were just one factor responsible for the state of Libya's upstream industry over the 1990s, without their removal, Libya could not expect any real improvements in its main industry and therefore in its overall economic situation. Sanctions did not drag Libya's economic performance down markedly, but they were a real impediment to Libya's ability to catapult itself to greater economic heights.

2000–02: POST-UN SANCTIONS AND CONTINUED U.S. UNILATERAL SANCTIONS. Beginning in 1999, the state of Libya's economy improved dramatically. After years of virtual stagnation, growth turned robust and inflation subsided. Libya's foreign reserves swelled, as did the interest of international investors in Libya.[104] The suspension of sanctions in April 1999 helped fuel this economic revival, not only by removing tangible constraints on economic activity and interaction with Libya but by dulling the opprobrium surrounding the country and the uncertainty that had long pervaded it.

Although it is tempting to conclude that Libya's economic rejuvenation was the result of the suspension of UN sanctions alone, several other factors also contributed to the brightening of Libya's economic prospects at the outset of the new millennium. The upswing in international oil prices—which began shortly after UN sanctions were suspended—was a major element in explaining the state of Libya's economy in 2001. In part, the surging international oil market was an important element in renewed international interest in developing Libya's energy resources; the small amounts of spare capacity in OPEC countries in 2001, in combination with persistent high oil prices, explains a great deal of the renewed impetus to invest not only in Libya but other countries as well. Moreover, the sudden enthusiasm of foreign investors for Libya reflected international expectations that Libya was about to overhaul its domestic practices in the oil industry to make them more amenable to international companies. Although these hopes were yet to be realized by mid-2002, Libya stoked anticipations by convening large conferences for oil and gas investors and by claiming that the introduction of a new petroleum law governing foreign investment was imminent.

Even in the face of these powerful influences, sanctions might be expected to have a dampening effect on Libya's economy as long as UN sanctions are not officially lifted but only suspended. At the margins, this is true. Yet the "magnifying" effect that UN sanctions have had on the Libyan economy when international and domestic factors were grim cannot be expected to carry the same weight in times of economic good fortune and perceived Libyan political moderation. Perhaps most realistically, the suspended—not lifted—UN sanctions will continue to hamper Libya's ability to attract tourists and to lure investors into the less lucrative non-oil segments of its economy. Similarly, the ability of U.S. unilateral sanctions to play a magnifying role is greatly diminished, not only by improving global and domestic circumstances, but also by the growing international impression that U.S. policy is governed by domestic interests and is therefore not a reasonable measure of the risks associated with doing business with Libya. In contrast, ongoing U.S. restrictions on the activity of American companies in Libya will pinch as long as Libya continues to honor the agreements it forged with U.S. oil companies in the 1980s.

### Political Impact

The political impact of sanctions on Libya was considerable, particularly over the course of the 1990s once UN sanctions reinforced U.S. ones. Like the economic effects of these measures, their political impact was amplified by other circumstances to cumulatively place significant pressure on the regime. Most directly, U.S. and later UN sanctions reinforced international wariness of the regime and helped circumscribe Qadhafi's political influence on the global stage. Other factors, including the use of other policy tools and Qadhafi's own behavior, also contributed to Libya's overall political isolation. As a result, Qadhafi—a leader who, by his own admission, was bored by the task of day-to-day governance and yearned for a more pronounced role in international politics—found himself politically sidelined by western countries (even those dependent on Libya's economic resources) and Arab states. The political marginalization that sanctions imposed on the regime seemed all the greater, as it complemented what would have in itself been a gulf between Libya and much of the Arab world in the 1990s given Qadhafi's fierce opposition to the Middle East peace process for much of the decade and growing Arab support for it. Libya's global political estrangement was compounded by the physical isolation of the country, which resulted from the severance of air links between Libya and the rest of the world.

Sanctions shaped Libya's political environment in even more subtle ways. For instance, the political reorientation of Libya away from the Arab world toward Africa over the 1990s is in part attributable to the influence of UN sanctions. Qadhafi, who long perceived himself to be a great Arab leader and an inheritor of Nasser's vision, was hugely disappointed by the unwillingness of the Arab League or individual Arab countries to contravene the UN sanctions against Libya.[105] At the same time, African leaders and countries gave Libya a warm reception and were sympathetic to its cause, a contrast that helped move Qadhafi away from his long-term cause of Arab unity toward the promotion of the "United States of Africa" and, eventually, support for the establishment of the African Union in July 2002.[106] Sanctions also molded the domestic environment in which the Qadhafi regime operated. Interestingly, sanctions did not result in a persistent "rally around the flag" phenomenon in Libya. Although Qadhafi had some limited success in portraying Libya as a victim of international aggression and in blaming sanctions for the domestic troubles of the country, these efforts bore diminishing fruit over time. Never having commanded the popular support of Libya's citizens or successfully mobilized them to back his radical policies and visions, Qadhafi lacked the political legitimacy that might have inspired a groundswell of support when he was perceived to be under attack.

Instead, sanctions helped weaken an important pillar on which Qadhafi's regime rested: economic well-being. The Libyan regime and its citizens had gradually formed a compact over the years since Qadhafi came to power in 1969. While Qadhafi was largely free from domestic political constraints to pursue his extremist agendas, most Libyans expected the means to live relatively comfortable and prosperous lives.[107] The economic impact of sanctions—in combination with other factors such as Libya's burgeoning population and the weakness of the oil market—strained the regime's ability to meet the long-standing expectations of the Libyan population for economic security. The standard of living of Libyans began to decline with the imposition of UN sanctions. Although economic frustrations were paramount in the minds of most Libyans, many were also dismayed by the physical isolation they felt from the United States and Europe—once the grounds for the vacations, shopping trips, and education of the Libyan elite.[108]

As Libya's economic problems intensified, political challenges to Qadhafi's regime increased. Discontent within Libya's army mounted as a result of economic malaise, unpaid salaries, poor capabilities, and the humiliation of the poorly executed venture in Chad.[109] In 1993 an army uprising seriously imperiled Qadhafi's rule and required harsh measures to quell, including the execution of six senior army officers. Threats to Qadhafi's regime also emanated from a mushrooming Islamic opposition that was not only influenced by neighboring Islamic movements in Egypt and Algeria but also was fueled by economic stagnation.[110]

## Goals Achieved

The various sanctions in place against Libya were intended to pursue a wide range of goals, some of them espoused openly by the United Nations, others held more quietly by the United States. On many levels, progress toward achieving these varied goals is notable. Yet the influence of sanctions in realizing these objectives must be weighed against the impact of other factors. In most cases, sanctions in themselves cannot claim full credit for the goals achieved; rather, the impact of sanctions combined with the effects of other domestic and international influences to cumulatively have the results sought by the United States and the international community.

CHANGING OR WEAKENING THE REGIME. Although U.S. and UN goals concerning Libya never visibly clashed, they were often at odds with one another. The objectives pursued by the United Nations were narrowly focused around securing Libyan cooperation in the UTA and Lockerbie investigations and ending Libyan support for terrorism; U.S. goals, in contrast, were much broader in scope, ranging from a desire during much of the Reagan administration for a change in the regime in Tripoli to a firm and bipartisan ambition to contain the Qadhafi regime to the fullest extent possible throughout the late 1980s and 1990s.

Unilateral U.S. sanctions proved unable to achieve in any serious way the far-reaching objectives pursued by the United States to change or weaken the regime during the 1980s. As noted, U.S. sanctions did have a "magnifying" effect, exacerbating the political marginalization that Qadhafi experienced during Libya's most radical years and compounding the economic problems that Libya suffered during the same time. This influence, however real, hardly constituted the economic or political containment of Libya. At best, U.S. sanctions can claim to have imposed some limited economic costs on Libya, most of them temporary in nature, which diminished the volume of resources flowing to the regime at the margins.

U.S. efforts—through sanctions and diplomacy—also failed to secure any significant military containment of Libya in the 1980s and early 1990s. Although the American prohibition on arms sales to Libya was complemented by selected efforts of other countries to impede Libyan access to weaponry, the collective effect of these measures fell far short of containment, particularly given the well-developed military relationship between Libya and the Soviet Union. In fact, throughout the 1980s, Libya devoted huge sums of money to building its military arsenal, its growing economic troubles notwithstanding. Libya increased the proportion of its gross domestic product devoted to military expenditure in 1980–89 and expanded the size of its armed forces in 1980–91.[111] Military imports also soared during this time, with one report estimating that between 1979 and 1983, Libya purchased more than $12 billion of military equipment, the highest per capita military expenditure of any North African country.[112] In 1984 Libya was reportedly spending more than $2 billon dollars annually on the acquisition of arms.[113] Moreover, Libyan military pursuits were apparently not limited to the conventional realm during this period, with suspicious activity at Rabta believed to signal the construction of a chemical weapons plant.

Perhaps ironically, the broad U.S. goals of containing or weakening the regime were best served in the 1990s, when UN and U.S. sanctions were both in place and the formal goals behind the UN measures were much more modest. Although Qadhafi was not dislodged from power, his base of support narrowed and he became subject to greater internal challenges during this time. As already discussed, sanctions played an important if indirect role in weakening Qadhafi's regime by undermining his support within segments of the military and the wider population insofar as sanctions hastened their rejection of Qadhafi's unsustainable political and economic experiments. Even more concretely, UN and U.S. sanctions—though not isolating Libya economically by any real measure—did contribute to the genuine political and military containment of Libya during the 1990s.

Libya's military emasculation throughout the 1990s is readily apparent to even the most casual observer. Although Qadhafi preserved the size of Libya's armed forces throughout this decade, procurement of weapons and other military items fell to negligible levels.[114] According to a 1997 CIA report, Libyan efforts to acquire unconventional weapons—including ballistic missiles and chemical weapons—also stalled during this decade.[115] These trends—and their severity—were attributable to several factors. First, arms sales to Libya were waning even before the UN arms embargo was put in place in 1992. U.S. and European restrictions on sales of military equipment dated back to 1978 and 1986 respectively, but the collapse of the Soviet Union in the early 1990s had removed Libya's main supplier of arms from the international scene. Other countries, such as Czechoslovakia, had earlier been cajoled by diplomatic pressure from the United States to scale back their military sales to Libya. These developments—when coupled with Libya's economic problems and record of nonpayment for earlier arms shipments—would have dampened military sales to Libya even had the UN weapons embargo not been imposed.[116]

**Figure 5-6.** *Libya: Arms Imports as a Percentage of Total Imports,*
*1979–99*

Percentage

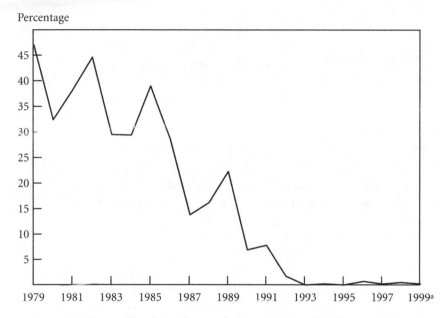

Source: U.S. Department of State, Bureau of Arms Control, *World Military Expenditures and Arms Transfers*, various years.
a. Department of State estimate.

Nevertheless, sanctions were important in ensuring that military sales to Libya did not simply decline but virtually ended (figure 5-6). Once the UN ban was in place, Libya's recorded imports of military items plummeted. Although Libya was able to purchase some weaponry on the black market, the structure of the "parallel" account system made it more difficult to siphon money away to purchase illegal arms without attracting international attention. Recorded military imports, which had already dropped from their peak of $3.2 billion a year in the early 1980s to $410 million in 1991, fell to zero in 1993, the year after sanctions were imposed.[117] The influence of sanctions in curbing Libyan military expenditure is also evident by the vigor with which Libya pursued new arms purchases in the wake of the suspension of sanctions in 1999.[118]

MODERATING THE BEHAVIOR OF THE REGIME.  Sanctions were also employed in the hopes of bringing about a number of changes in the actions of the Libyan government. In this realm, as well as that of changing or weakening the regime, U.S. demands went well beyond UN ones to encompass a wide variety of Libyan behaviors. The U.S. executive orders first imposing unilateral sanctions on Libya failed to cite any objectives beyond dealing with the "extraordinary threat" that Libya posed to U.S. national security and foreign policy.[119] Yet in less formal pronouncements, administration officials explained that the purpose of American sanctions was to coerce the Qadhafi regime to change its behavior in three specific areas: its support for international terrorism and extremist movements, its attitude toward the state of Israel, and its desire to attain and stockpile weapons of mass destruction.[120] Ending Libya's foreign policy adventurism was seen as a less pressing goal in the 1990s, although in the previous decade, it had also been an American priority. The domestic behavior of Qadhafi's regime was seen as the least urgent issue surrounding Libya, although Congress occasionally voiced distress over human rights issues in Libya.[121]

By 2002, in most (but not all) of these areas of concern, Libya had taken notable strides in the desired direction, even if further actions were still sought by the United States. Most notably, Libya's support for terrorism and extremist groups declined significantly in the 1990s. The most tangible evidence of Libya's changing attitude toward terrorism was its 1999 surrender of the Lockerbie suspects and its purported willingness to pay compensation to the victims' families in 2002. Beyond these steps, Libya appeared to end its direct involvement in terrorist acts and took additional actions to dissociate itself from terrorism.[122] Whereas in 1989 the U.S. government reported that Libya supported more than thirty terrorist networks and revolutionary regimes worldwide, a decade later U.S. officials acknowledged credible Libyan moves to distance itself from terrorism, including the expulsion of the Abu Nidal organization from Libya and the severance of ties with groups such as the Popular Front for Liberation of Palestine-General Command and Palestinian Islamic Jihad.[123] In its 2001 report, the U.S. State Department stated that "Libya appears to have curtailed its support for international terrorism, although it may maintain residual contacts with a few groups."[124]

Related to this declining support for terrorism is the more moderate posture Libya has taken toward Israel since the latter part of the 1990s.[125] Qadhafi's vocal protests of the 1993 Israeli-PLO Oslo Accords and his statements of support for groups that opposed it through the use of violence was no surprise.[126] For decades, opposition to Israel and to those who supported it formed the cornerstone of Libyan foreign policy. However, as the 1990s progressed, Libya not only withdrew its support for rejectionist Palestinian groups but pledged its backing for the Palestinian Authority and Chairman Yasser Arafat.[127] Qadhafi even counseled moderation by discouraging Arafat from unilaterally declaring Palestinian statehood as he had threatened to do in September 2000.[128] Although Qadhafi's speeches and condemnations of Israeli incursions into Palestinian areas are still strident, Libya's cautious support for the Saudi two-state peace initiative at the Beirut 2002 Arab League Summit suggests a new Libyan willingness to accept the Israeli state under certain circumstances.

Qadhafi's retreat from his destabilizing and meddling ventures in African states from Chad to Uganda to Tunisia is even more clear-cut. Libya brought its overt involvement in Chad to a close in 1987 and wound down indirect participation in most regional insurgencies in the years that followed.[129] Notably, over the span of the decade, Libya's relations with Egypt went from hostile to cordial to collaborative as Libya stopped aggressive actions along the border between the two countries and began to work with its eastern neighbor on regional initiatives.[130] At the turn of the millennium, much of Qadhafi's involvement in Africa was of a different nature than his past belligerent adventurism.[131] Rather than disrupting the domestic politics of other countries or aggravating their disputes with neighbors, Qadhafi sought to mediate some of them. In countries such as Sudan, Uganda, and the Congo, Qadhafi's efforts appeared largely geared toward encouraging reconciliation of hostile parties.[132]

Despite these significant positive developments, serious concerns remain about Libya's pursuit of weapons of mass destruction, particularly chemical weapons and ballistic missiles to deliver them.[133] These anxieties mostly relate to Libya's desire to acquire these capabilities and develop indigenous production of them, rather than to concrete evidence that Tripoli has made significant progress in this direction. Over the 1980s and 1990s, Libya halted activity at two suspected chemical weapons sites in response to international scrutiny.[134] Yet, the suspension of UN sanctions eased the constraints on Libya's pursuit of necessary components and technology, possibly opening the way for Libya to resume WMD-related activities. The discovery of Chinese Scud missile parts being smuggled to Libya through Britain in January 2000 provided clear evidence of Libya's ongoing ambitions.[135] Moreover, the CIA reported in 2001 that Libya had re-established contact with suppliers of goods and expertise needed for WMD development and warned that renewed talks between Tripoli and Moscow on reviving Libya's allegedly civilian nuclear program could provide Libya with an opening to conduct weapons-related research and development.[136] Nongovernmental sources also warned of Libya's ongoing pursuits but noted that the very low scientific and technological base of the country will hamper such advances.[137]

Finally, in contrast to other positive developments, the human rights situation in Libya saw only sporadic improvements since the 1980s, with the overall trend in the downward direction.[138] During the 1980s, Qadhafi's approach toward internal security—and political and economic liberalism more broadly defined—was as erratic as his foreign policy. For much of that decade, Qadhafi pursued his opponents ruthlessly, openly promoting a policy of eliminating "stray dogs" or opponents of the regime. For a brief time in the late 1980s, Qadhafi publicly condemned capital punishment, sought to curb the powers of the revolutionary committees, freed more than 400 political prisoners, and promised legal reforms to protect human rights.[139] However, these movements toward political liberalization were short-lived, as Libya's Islamic opposition gained strength and became the target of searing crackdowns by the regime well into the 1990s.[140]

Overall, the record of positive changes in Libya's behavior when sanctions were in place—while not complete or uniform—is significant. Yet it would be hasty to declare a victory for U.S. policy or UN sanctions on this basis before more closely assessing the role of sanctions in bringing about these shifts. Many factors beyond sanctions shaped Libyan actions and proclivities. Particularly during the 1980s, when sanctions were unilateral, other policy tools including U.S. military force also weighed on Libya. Even UN sanctions were accompanied by vigorous diplomacy at different points in the 1990s. Moreover, Libyan attitudes and actions were influenced by the tumultuous international political and economic changes that occurred while sanctions were in place. The Soviet Union collapsed, depriving Libya of an important source of largess and support. Libya's anti-imperialism mantra became outdated, as the nonaligned movement lost momentum and countries around the globe moved out of a postcolonial mentality and toward an era of globalization. Revolutionary zeal gave way to statesmanship, as many of Qadhafi's old allies found themselves, if not in power, then in positions of political influence.

What is clear is that although sanctions—UN ones in particular—deserve much credit for the positive changes occurring in Libya, they cannot on their own claim all the success. Rather, sanctions complemented domestic challenges and international changes to inspire a significant reorientation of Libya's external behavior. Sanctions contributed to and hastened a domestic crisis—that would have likely eventually occurred in the absence of sanctions—which forced the regime to reorder its priorities and change its course of action. To some extent, other tools—including the use or threat of military action—also deserve credit for forcing the regime to realize that it would be costly to continue its extremist behavior.[141] As explored earlier, sanctions contributed to—but did not entirely cause—an economic crunch that had political ramifications for the regime. This crisis forced the regime to turn inward, compelling it to disengage from entanglements beyond Libya's borders, such as its involvement with terrorist groups espousing agendas unrelated to Libya's domestic situation. More specifically, the urgency to resolve the domestic crisis prompted the regime to search for ways to relieve the pressure of sanctions—either by proposing compromise scenarios for the trial of the Lockerbie suspects or using Libyan influence to chip away at various countries' compliance with the sanctions. Ultimately, when presented with a face-saving proposal to turn the suspects over to the Netherlands—and a guarantee from the United Nations that such action would lead to the suspension of sanctions—Qadhafi took it, seeing it as his most immediate and direct route to a measure of relief from his domestic economic and political woes.

Also important in explaining changes in Libyan external behavior is Qadhafi's reorientation of his country away from the Arab world toward Africa.[142] Here, again, sanctions had a modest influence on this transformation. Qadhafi came to view Africa not only as a source of support for the lifting of sanctions but as a realm where he could escape the political isolation of sanctions and assume the prominent place in international politics that he sought. The increased attention Qadhafi expended on Africa, in turn, allowed and demanded a moderation in Libya's foreign policy. It no longer made sense for radical opposition to Israel to be the centerpiece of the country's foreign policy. Moreover, Qadhafi's quest to enlist the support of African states and organizations such as the OAU required a shift away from nonstate actors that challenged these institutions, bringing Libya more firmly into the political mainstream.

### Costs Borne

HUMANITARIAN COSTS. Sanctions on Libya did not precipitate a humanitarian crisis by any standard, although they did significantly diminish the standard of living of most Libyans. These effects are largely traceable to the UN restrictions, whereas the humanitarian impact of U.S. unilateral sanctions is on the whole too small to measure.[143]

As most available humanitarian indicators suggest, Libya was able to meet the basic needs of its citizens throughout the period that UN sanctions were in place. In fact, Libya's infant mortality rate declined over this period, while the number of children vaccinated remained very high, even above the coverage extended in neighboring Egypt.[144] Libyan life expectancy rose and both adult and youth illiteracy rates declined in the 1990s.[145] The constancy of these basic human indicators was in part attributable to coping mechanisms developed by Libyans in the face of economic adversity, but it also reflected continued state subsidies on food and the provision of health and education services, even at diminished quality.

The main influence of UN sanctions on the humanitarian situation in Libya was through the inflation that sanctions encouraged (figure 5-7). Although Libya's economic woes had many sources, as discussed earlier, a solid link existed between UN sanctions and high rates of inflation.[146] The Libyan government claimed that sanctions increased the price of goods by more than 200 percent, although it offered no basis for this estimate.[147] Regardless of the exact levels of inflation weathered by Libyans, constantly rising prices chipped away at the purchasing power of the average citizen.[148] This erosion was particularly acute, given that the Libyan government employed nearly 70 percent of the population and public sector wages did not increase, even nominally, over the 1980s and 1990s.[149] In this situation, even the Libyan regime's most extreme efforts to dampen inflation proved insufficient to keep rises in the cost of living from far outstripping the economic resources of average families by as much as one-third a year.[150]

Libyan claims that sanctions were responsible for the evident deterioration of the public services were greatly exaggerated and part of a larger political effort to erode support for sanctions by overstating their humanitarian impact.[151] Sanctions can only be viewed as contributing to the overall decline in the quality of state-provided services—especially in the health sector—in very limited ways; severed air links frustrated the efforts of Libyans to receive medical attention abroad, while the deteriorating living standards of public servants forced many of them to seek second and third jobs, with negative implications for the quality of care they provided. Libya's worsening relationship with western countries, the United States in particular, also led to a sharp decline in the number of Libyan students pursuing their education abroad, placing added strain on the domestic education system. Even recognizing these sanctions-related constraints, the deterioration in the Libyan public sector over the time that sanctions were in place was

**Figure 5-7.** *Inflation in Libya, 1992–2000*

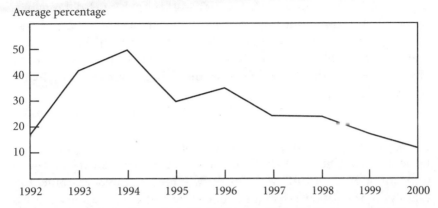

Source: Economist Intelligence Unit, *Worldwide Cost of Living Survey;* Economist Intelligence Unit, *Country Profile: Libya,* 2001, p. 45.

much more a function of domestic factors unrelated to external economic pressure. Escalating economic mismanagement and corruption, as well as the burgeoning Libyan population, were the greatest burdens on the public sector throughout the 1990s.[152]

COSTS TO THE SENDERS.  A careful consideration of all the costs borne by countries who upheld UN sanctions against Libya is beyond the scope of this chapter. However, a cursory assessment suggests that, on the whole, these economic and political costs were extremely small and generally outweighed by the benefits of sanctions. Although restrictions on the sale of specific oil-related equipment did adversely affect some European suppliers, the overall maintenance of economic interaction between Europe and Libya meant these costs were minor in the face of otherwise healthy economic relations. Apart from the United States, Russia suffered the greatest burden of those imposing UN sanctions, not only because the measures terminated its (albeit waning) military relationship with Tripoli, but because the freeze on Libyan assets inhibited Libya from servicing its large debt to Russia.[153] Outside of Europe, some countries in the region actually benefited from the sanctions on Tripoli; Libya's neighbors became the conduits of goods and people in and out of Libya given that the UN sanctions regime allowed most trade with and travel to Libya to continue, yet prohibited the air links to facilitate them. Tunisia, in particular, boomed as much of the economic interaction between Libya and the outside world was channeled through its borders.[154] In terms of the impact of sanctions on the political interests of non-U.S., non-Libyan actors, the costs were few while the benefits were many. Most notably, the United Nations—sorely in need of a boost in the face of increasing criticism over its sanctions on Iraq—was able to claim important successes in the Libyan episode.[155]

Calculations of the costs of sanctions to U.S. interests are more complicated, given the comprehensive U.S. sanctions regime that existed independently of UN sanctions. The costs of sanctions on U.S. energy interests, however, are attributable to both sets of sanctions—not only the unilateral imposition of American measures.[156] By impeding the development of Libya's oil production capabilities, both U.S. and UN sanctions affected global energy supplies. However, throughout most of the 1990s when Libya would have realized more production had sanctions not been in place, the economic impact of more oil on the global market would have been slim. In the face of weakening demand and sagging oil prices, additional Libyan oil—or even the simple existence of additional spare capacity in Libya—would have been of little consequence to consumers. In contrast, at the end of the decade, when prices were peaking and OPEC production was more limited than before, additional Libyan production capabilities could have dampened high international energy prices. Greater production by Libya would have added stability to the market and lessened the vulnerability of the United States and other countries to fluctuations and external shocks at a time of great sensitivity. With the suspension of UN sanctions, Libya will make strides toward reaching its production goals, greatly diminishing any costs to global energy interests. Yet as long as U.S. sanctions remain in place and fields formerly run by the American companies are not refurbished, a residual dampening on Libya's production capabilities will remain; its influence on global energy markets and interests will, however, depend on the state of the international oil market in the years ahead.

Other damage done to U.S. energy interests is more directly attributable to the U.S. sanctions regime and is unrelated to UN measures. Although the fungibility of oil enabled the United States to ban Libyan oil imports with no serious consequences for the satisfaction of its energy needs, such measures narrowed U.S. energy sources and kept the United States from its goal of minimizing dependence on any one supplier. Moreover, in curtailing economic interaction between the United States and Libya, U.S. sanctions forced the United States to relinquish any influence or knowledge that it might have wielded or gained had its firms stayed involved in one of OPEC's primary oil producers.

Besides affecting U.S. energy interests in these ways, the prohibition on U.S. involvement in Libya's energy sector created more specific losses for American firms that could not invest in Libya while their international competitors did. The extent of these opportunity costs is difficult to assess because it is uncertain how involved U.S. firms would be in Libya's energy industry had sanctions not been imposed. The difficulties of working in Libya, as well as international circumstances discussed earlier, would have acted as a constraint on greater U.S. involvement in Libya.[157] Nevertheless, in the absence of sanctions, U.S. companies would have maintained a substantial presence in the country, yielding them regular benefits and positioning them for the time when Libya revamped its energy industry to offer even more lucrative contracts.

Even more specifically, sanctions imposed costs on American oil companies operating in Libya before the 1986 sanctions were put in place. Together, these companies—Occidental, Marathon, Amerada Hess, Conoco, and W. R. Grace—controlled close to 400,000 barrels of oil a day and claimed substantial assets in Libya.[158] Each year that sanctions were in place, these firms lost an estimated $100 to $200 million in profits that would have accrued from marketing this oil.[159] Other related losses are more difficult to estimate, given the uncertainty surrounding the fate of U.S. assets and their titles to Libyan oil fields.[160] These firms no longer claim Libyan assets on their books. Yet, if Libya continues to honor the old standby agreements negotiated in the 1980s, and U.S. law eventually allows these firms to reclaim their assets and some rights to reserves, these companies could recoup significant losses.[161]

These economic costs of sanctions, though highly concentrated in the U.S. oil industry, did not represent major losses for the American economy as a whole. Economic costs not related to the energy industry borne by the United States as a result of sanctions were even more marginal. Losses from curtailed trade, for instance, were minor. As already mentioned, through a reconfiguration of its trade patterns, the United States replaced Libyan imports—which were almost entirely oil or petroleum products—with relative ease. Similarly, of the nearly $12 billion in exports that the United States would have sold to Libya in 1981–2002 in the absence of sanctions (see appendix 5A-2), American exporters suffered only a fraction of these losses.[162] These exports were redirected to other destinations, although the process was somewhat less seamless when it came to products from the aviation and oil sectors. The net losses borne by these two industries as a result of these lost contracts and trade was below their face value. But the high-tech nature of the sales and the relatively few global consumers of commercial jets meant that sanctions did strike a blow to this sector of the U.S. economy.[163] Similarly, the U.S. oil industry assumed a significant portion of the losses borne by the United States as a result of severed trade relations with Libya over the 1980s and 1990s.[164]

Finally, U.S. sanctions on Libya influenced U.S. political interests in a number of sometimes conflicting ways. The sanctions-dominated policy toward Libya did serve most domestic American interests well; sanctions were a vehicle for addressing the needs of an influential constituency, the families of the victims of the Pan Am 103 bombing. Although not an end in themselves, U.S. sanctions against Libya also allowed U.S. administrations over time—as well as members of the American Congress—to be seen as taking a firm stand against terrorism, an extremely popular position at home. Embracing a hard-line policy against Libya came at little domestic political cost for government figures as Libya had no real friends advocating political engagement with Libya or Qadhafi.[165] Libya's lack of political weight in the American political spectrum meant that efforts to escalate measures against Libya—such the original passage of ILSA and its subsequent renewal—were extremely difficult to resist once they were put in motion.

The U.S. sanctions-dominated policy advanced more than domestic political interests. In helping to delegitimize Qadhafi and in expressing a firm U.S. commitment to combat terrorism, sanctions advanced U.S. goals in the region, particularly at a time of precarious Arab-Israeli rapprochement. Moreover, U.S. sanctions—at least those imposed in the 1980s—were a tangible demonstration that the United States was willing to bear costs to advance its goals; as a result, unilateral sanctions provided a basis for the limited, yet still significant, American success in galvanizing other countries to impose multilateral sanctions on Libya.

In contrast, secondary sanctions mandated through ILSA had the opposite effect, damaging U.S. political interests and suggesting that Libya's standing in U.S. foreign policy had grown out of proportion to the threat that Tripoli posed. Unlike the unilateral sanctions imposed a decade earlier, ILSA did not help catalyze international support for measures against Libya, but rather impeded them. The passage of ILSA infuriated Europe and other countries, which viewed the new law as a brazen effort to impose American laws and ideals on the conduct of other nations. By seeking to use American economic influence where U.S. diplomacy had failed, ILSA virtually ensured that the United States would not secure sufficient political support for the expansion of UN sanctions against Libya that Washington sought. More-over, the secondary sanctions mandated by ILSA threatened to instigate a trade war and jeopardize U.S.-European cooperation on other issues. The issuance of an ILSA waiver to France's Total for its investment in Iran, and the signal that more waivers would follow in similar circumstances, man-aged to avert an immediate clash with Europe. However, while emasculating ILSA, the waiver was unable to annul the global perception that America would resort to coercive economic tactics, even against its allies, when diplomatic coercion failed.

In the wake of the suspension of UN sanctions, U.S. policy toward Libya is in danger of incurring even greater political costs. The United States is right to press Libya to fulfill the demands of UN resolutions in full. How-ever, the credibility of U.S. policy and sanctions as a tool more generally is dependent on U.S. ability and willingness to take "yes" for an answer. By maintaining the same unyielding policy in the face of significant changes by Libya, the United States risks undermining the ability of sanctions to entice other countries and leaders to modify their ways. Such a result would rep-resent a large political cost to the United States, as it would essentially nar-row the already limited range of tools that America has to deal with coun-tries it considers adversaries.

## Explaining the Record of Sanctions on Libya

The coexistence of U.S. and UN sanctions precludes an easy assessment of their individual effects and an accurate evaluation of how effective each set of sanctions was independent of the other. Together, it is clear that sanc-tions—UN ones more so than U.S. measures—had a moderate economic and significant political impact on Libya. More important, this impact translated into effectiveness and utility. Many of the goals sought by the United States and the international community were realized, at costs that—while highly concentrated—did not come close to outweighing the benefits of the approach. Impact translated into effectiveness in part be-cause sanctions reinforced international and domestic circumstances, ulti-mately creating a diverse and compelling set of motivations leading Qadhafi to move away from some of his most problematic actions. The importance of external factors does not annul the achievements of sanctions, but it does compel a more nuanced view of how they worked successfully.

### Accounting for the Achievements and Disappointments of Sanctions

Two factors greatly contributed to the ability of sanctions to somewhat weaken the regime—although not leading to its overthrow—and, more successfully, to the more modest goal of containing it. First, the impact of sanctions, both economic and political, reinforced independent domestic and international trends. As a result, sanctions—instead of working against external trends and influences—magnified pre-existing difficulties. For instance, U.S. sanctions reinforced independent international perceptions that Libya was a poor credit risk or presented a highly volatile investment climate, amplifying the reluctance of international creditors to lend to Libya or international businesses to invest there. This "magnifying effect" was considerably greater under UN sanctions. On top of opaque domestic practices, uncertain legal protections, and a weak international oil market, UN measures provided yet another deterrent to firms that were weighing their global options. In a more positive external environment, the dampening effects of sanctions could have been easily overridden by investors' enthusiasm. Yet in the climate of the late 1980s and 1990s and in the context of Libya, they confirmed the instincts of many to limit their exposure there. Similarly, in an already precarious domestic political environment, the pressure of sanctions proved threatening to the regime, whereas a government of greater legitimacy could have more easily weathered the effects of sanctions or even parlayed them into support for it.

Second, the multilateral nature of UN sanctions was key to the effective containment of Libya for many years, if not at an economic level, then at a military and political one. This multilateral success was hardly achieved overnight. The United States exerted great effort throughout the 1980s to secure the cooperation of other countries in pressuring Libya through economic sanctions. Some limited measures taken by Europe and Japan notwithstanding, America met with little success in galvanizing multilateral support for its sanctions policy during that decade. In contrast, in the 1990s, efforts to craft international support for measures against Libya proved fruitful, culminating in targeted UN sanctions against Libya. What accounts for this failure in the 1980s and the success of the 1990s?

The bombings of Pan Am 103 and the 1989 UTA flight were the most obvious impetuses for multilateral action. Unlike other terrorist attacks attributed to Libya, these acts killed hundreds of people—the majority of them citizens of three of the five permanent members of the UN Security Council. While the significance of these explosions cannot be underplayed, these bombings contributed to a wider international awakening, in Europe in particular, that Qadhafi's Libya was less of a nuisance and more of a systematic threat to international order. Smaller but consistent terrorist acts had mapped an increasingly clear pattern of Libyan-sponsored terror.[166] Other concerns over Libyan behavior were also coming into focus. For instance, although Europe had long dismissed American allegations about the construction of a chemical weapons plant at Rabta as a U.S. attempt to build support for its hard-line policy, European disquiet mounted once German investigations undertaken in 1990 revealed that the plant had in fact been intended for such uses.[167]

In addition to the broadening perception of the Libyan threat, the decline of the Soviet Union opened new possibilities for an international response to Libya's behavior. Much of Europe had shied away from aggressive action against Libya in the 1980s, fearing that a confrontation could trigger a larger problem by unsettling Tripoli's long-term ally, the Soviet Union; in 1990 and beyond, this brake on action had vanished. Moreover, as the cold war ended, new patterns of cooperation emerged. The recent Gulf war had highlighted how the United Nations—no longer hostage to zero-sum games between Washington and Moscow—could be an effective instrument for collective action.

The road to multilateral action in the 1990s was also paved by the moderate and consensual approach taken by the administration of George H. W. Bush, which contrasted with the more aggressive and unilateralist tactics pursued under President Reagan. With few exceptions, Europeans and others resisted the entreaties of the Reagan administration in part because they perceived U.S. policy toward Libya in the 1980s to be largely driven by domestic factors. At the time, U.S. sanctions were viewed as a manifestation of American desires to project U.S. power and influence in the world in the wake of a series of defeats, including the Soviet invasion of Afghanistan, the Islamic revolution in Iran, and the still recent American losses in Vietnam. This perception was created not only by the overall posture of the Reagan administration, but also by the American pursuit of regime change—a goal that was viewed by many outside of the United States as being far out of proportion to the threat posed by Qadhafi. The sequencing of Reagan administration actions was also not conducive to forging a broad-based coalition against Libya. In 1986, Europe in particular was peeved that the United States bombed Libya only hours after European countries had agreed to take some limited measures against Tripoli in response to U.S. pressure. The timing of such events diminished the impression that recently imposed U.S. sanctions were intended to serve as a basis for gaining international support for a multilateral strategy toward Libya; instead, it suggested to many that the real purpose of U.S. sanctions was to serve as a backdrop for unilateral military force, regardless of the opinions or efforts of U.S. allies abroad.

In comparison, the approach adopted by the United States after Libyan officials were indicted for the Lockerbie bombing was viewed more positively by U.S. allies. Instead of responding with military force, the George H.W. Bush administration, and later, the Clinton one, pursued multilateral action through the United Nations. Although the pursuit of the Lockerbie case on legalistic lines entailed notable drawbacks, it did facilitate the attainment and maintenance of a broad international coalition.[168] Bringing U.S. goals—at least explicit ones—into line with international ones to focus narrowly on the resolution of the Lockerbie and UTA bombings and the termination of Libyan support for terrorism was essential in the quest to build a coalition for UN sanctions. Another factor facilitating UN action was the anti-terrorism nature of the resolutions. Some countries—particularly those in the nonaligned movement—overcame their objections to the use of sanctions specifically because they were intended to combat terrorism.[169] Finally, the leading role taken by Britain in crafting the UN measures against Libya was critical in signaling to other countries that these efforts represented an international desire to impose sanctions, rather than solely a U.S. one.

Lastly, the targeted nature of the UN sanctions eventually agreed on—although short of the actions desired by the United States—helped ensure international support for them. They were seen by many countries as more commensurate with the goals being pursued. Their narrow scope also curbed the economic costs that most countries were forced to suffer as a result of implementing them, thereby increasing the likelihood of compliance. Moreover, targeted sanctions limited the humanitarian impact of UN measures, a factor that was key in maintaining support for UN sanctions over many years.[170]

Beyond imposing a certain political and military containment on Libya for much of the 1990s, sanctions were also a key factor in coercing and cajoling the regime into changing some elements of its behavior. Much of sanctions' success in this department depended on the nature of the Libyan regime, which allowed the impact of sanctions to be translated into political action. Qadhafi—much more so than Saddam Hussein or Fidel

Castro—was susceptible to pressure.[171] In particular, Qadhafi's pursuit of prominence in global politics gave the international community some leverage over the Libyan leader. Domestically, Qadhafi was sensitive to discontent within his military. Sanctions, by targeting the Libyan military and Qadhafi's mobility and political image, were well calibrated to exploit these points of pressure. In addition, Qadhafi possessed adequate power to make potentially divisive and controversial decisions and carry them out.[172] The Libyan regime—while not as monolithic as often portrayed—was dominated by a small group of elite Libyan actors, including Qadhafi.[173] Although Qadhafi insisted that the authority to hand over the Lockerbie suspects resided with the General People's Congress, the decision to relinquish the two men was essentially his to make.[174] The suppression of Libya's Islamic movement through a major offensive in 1998 allowed Qadhafi to consolidate his rule and, therefore, to take politically sensitive steps such as handing over the Lockerbie suspects to the Netherlands without fearing a major domestic backlash.[175]

While these Libyan-specific factors were important in understanding the success of sanctions, the structure of the UN sanctions regime also helps explain why these instruments were effective in inducing some behavior changes, although, thus far, not all of those desired. Instead of merely outlining the framework for Libya's capitulation to international demands, the sanctions regime was the foundation of a larger bargaining structure between Libya and the United Nations, one that led to a compromise on the handover of the Lockerbie suspects. Several factors enabled the sanctions to be instrumental in achieving this objective. First, the goal of surrendering the two men to a court in either Scotland or the United States was well defined and easily verifiable. Moreover, it was not an objective that inherently or directly threatened the survival of the regime. When combined with the willingness of both sides to compromise at the margins, the clarity and nature of this goal provided a solid basis for negotiation. The concrete nature of the action sought also enabled the United Nations to pledge definitively and unanimously that the sanctions would be suspended once this goal was met, thereby giving Libya an important incentive to meet the UN demands.[176] Perhaps surprisingly, the dynamic surrounding the sanctions created pressure on the United States and Britain to be more flexible. The compromise proposals Libya offered when first threatened with UN sanctions in 1992 were deemed insufficient to forestall sanctions at the time; however, the erosion of international support for the sanctions by the end of the decade, and the growing sentiment of even some Security Council members that Libya's proposals should be considered more seriously, created a new international atmosphere.[177] The final necessary ingredient to close the gap between the two sides was sustained dialogue and the engagement of mediating figures such as Kofi Annan and Nelson Mandela.

No single one of these factors would have ensured success. Rather, their simultaneous occurrence enabled sanctions to induce some of the desired changes in Libyan behavior. But it is also clear that sanctions and the strategies that accompanied them were not perfect; major issues remained unresolved at the time sanctions were suspended in 1999. Conceivably, the prospect of the official lifting of UN sanctions, now contingent on Libya's full satisfaction of demands ensconced in UN resolutions, could spur Libya to go the final mile in addressing international concerns. Yet the possibility exists that these concerns will go unresolved, as Libya's rapid reintegration into the global political and economic scene progresses. Given these realities, it is worthwhile to ask whether sanctions might have been even more effective had they been structured differently.

Although sanctions provided the basis of a bargaining mechanism between Libya and the United Nations, this process was haphazard and inadvertent. Sanctions would have been more effective had they been explicitly structured to calibrate their suspension or removal with various stages of Libyan compliance. For instance, rather than suspending all UN sanctions upon the surrender of the suspects, UN resolutions could have specified that such action would trigger the suspension of the air embargo and diplomatic constraints. This move would have provided an incentive to Libya to release the two men but also would have allowed the international community to maintain leverage to cajole Libya into further compliance. Suspension of restrictions on the sale of oil equipment to Libya could have been guaranteed to follow Libya's acceptance of responsibility for the acts of its officials and the payment of compensation to the families of the victims. Finally, an official lifting of the sanctions could have been contingent on Libya discontinuing all support for terrorism and groups that espouse it.

Because UN sanctions were not calibrated in this fashion, U.S. unilateral sanctions are being called on to serve the purpose of extracting the last elements of Libyan compliance. This strategy, however unintentional, could prove effective. However, several factors seriously limit the power of U.S. sanctions to achieve these ends. First, U.S. sanctions were never structured in a way to evoke behavior changes but were geared much more narrowly toward their original objective of regime change and, later, containment. Recognizing its inability to galvanize an international coalition to pursue its more ambitious goals, the United States settled for a UN effort aimed at the more modest goal of changing Libyan behavior regarding terrorism. This temperance was critical in solidifying international support for limited UN sanctions on Libya. Yet the tensions between the U.S. and UN approaches are evident now that UN sanctions have been suspended. The structure of U.S. sanctions would need to be altered to make them more effective in further modifying Libya's behavior

## Comparing the Utility of Sanctions to Alternatives

Even though the sanctions-led approach toward Libya was largely effective and useful (in the sense of achieving goals at reasonable costs), other policy options might have brought about similar—or even better—results at lower costs. One alternative strategy that might have been pursued throughout the 1990s was an approach in which military force, not sanctions, was the main component.[178] A military-led strategy, however, would have in all likelihood been less effective. Seeking to unseat Qadhafi from power through backing the Libyan opposition offered little promise. The formal opposition to the regime—in exile and weak from factional divisions—never provided a viable alternative to Qadhafi, nor did it have the capabilities to pose a military challenge to his rule.[179] Direct U.S. military force, if applied persistently and at sufficient levels, could have conceivably led to Qadhafi's demise, either physically or through his overthrow. Yet such an approach would not solve the dilemma of what sort of regime could replace Qadhafi's. In the 1990s, the beneficiaries of Qadhafi's downfall would have been elements of the army or members of Libya's Islamic opposition, neither of which could be expected to pursue policies more to the liking of Washington.

A military approach also might have involved additional costs if Libya responded to American-led military aggression with further acts of terrorism similar to the Pan Am 103 bombing. Vigorous military action would also have eroded the international consensus for continued UN sanctions on Libya as well as fueled anger in the Arab world. In the 1990s, when the United States was struggling to maintain the fragile coalition against Saddam Hussein and trying to facilitate peacemaking in the Middle East, the costs of military force against Libya would have been far out of proportion to what such action could have hoped to achieve.

Another alternative to the sanctions-dominated strategy in the 1990s was for the United States simply to "do nothing" or maintain a "business-as-usual" approach. Similar to its European allies, the United States could have begun the 1990s seeking to influence Tripoli through the force of its words and diplomatic condemnations, leaving aside economic pressure. Yet, again, this alternative had little appeal or promise to be more effective. Given the economic and political turbulence of the time, Qadhafi might have mellowed somewhat even in the absence of formal economic sanctions. Yet, without such tools and the leverage they created, critical, specific goals—such as the surrender of the Lockerbie suspects—would have not been achieved. Moreover, although a "business-as-usual" approach would have reduced damages to U.S. economic or energy interests that resulted from the sanctions-dominated policy employed, the domestic political costs of conducting relations in this way would have been enormous.

Other alternative approaches essentially amount to variations of the strategy pursued by the United States and the United Nations. A full multilateral embargo on Libyan oil would have had a devastating effect on the economy, possibly leading to its collapse within a year by one study's estimation.[180] Given the nature of the Libyan regime, and its susceptibility to pressure, it is reasonable to surmise that such a blockade would have triggered Qadhafi's rapid capitulation had the United States convinced other countries to support such an effort.[181] However, had the domestic political situation in Libya made the stakes associated with meeting international demands extraordinarily high, Qadhafi might have continued to resist UN demands, even at great costs. In another scenario, the United States might have adopted only targeted sanctions against Libya, thereby easing the economic costs associated with its unilateral measures. This more economically temperate approach is the most attractive of the alternatives, although it would have drawn domestic fire and possibly handicapped U.S. efforts to build an international consensus for multilateral measures. Ultimately, this brief analysis suggests that the broad outlines of the sanctions-based approach advanced and undertaken by the United States were not only an effective and useful policy, but it had the greatest comparative utility of the options available to policymakers at the time.

## Looking Ahead

Before September 11, 2001, the stalemate between the United States and Libya seemed likely to fester for a long time. A powerful U.S. constituency led by the Families of Pan Am 103, balanced only by a weak contingent of forces arguing for more expansive commercial relations with Libya, ensured fierce domestic political opposition to any rapprochement. At the same time, Qadhafi's uncooperative and rhetorically belligerent behavior in the wake of the Lockerbie verdict diminished hopes for a breakthrough initiated by Tripoli. Together, these realities seemed to be a recipe for continued antagonism.

The terrorist attacks on the United States changed this environment and added to the urgency of both sides to address the U.S.-Libyan relationship. The United States has an interest not only in working with Libya in a common cause against terrorism if it can, but in ensuring that Libya's departure from terrorism is authentic, complete, and irreversible. September 11 gave Libya an added impetus to prove that it has fundamentally altered its behavior in order to avoid a much more ardent U.S. campaign to isolate and punish it.

Although the basis for a new relationship exists, the issues remain much the same. The United States will continue to demand that Libya meets the four demands delineated in UN resolutions, including taking responsibility for the actions of Abdel Basset al-Megrahi and paying compensation to the families of the victims of Pan Am 103. While justified in sticking to these demands, the United States must acquiesce to the formal lifting of UN sanctions once Libya has fulfilled them. It would be a serious mistake for the United States to instead "move the goalposts" in the hopes of using UN sanctions to address other concerns not related to Pan Am 103. Doing so would dash hopes of a more cooperative relationship with Libya and frustrate U.S. allies, including Britain, seeking to put Pan Am 103 behind them in a just way. Such action would have grave consequences apart from Libya, as it would fuel the global perception of American unilateralism and diminish the likelihood that the United Nations would employ sanctions in the future. Equally important, moving the goalposts would signal to other state sponsors of terrorism that rehabilitation is not possible. This message would undermine U.S. and international efforts to get countries to move away from support for terrorism.

Even once UN sanctions are lifted, the United States will have a full panoply of unilateral sanctions to address other legitimate concerns it has about Libyan behavior. Two goals will loom large on the U.S. agenda. First, the United States will seek to consolidate the improvements that Libya has already made in its behavior regarding terrorism and terminate any residual links with terrorist organizations. Second, the United States will wish to address Libyan WMD pursuits, most likely by forging an international consensus on the need to keep sensitive weapons and technologies away from

Libya. In addition, U.S. policymakers could aim to reduce the costs borne by the United States in pursuit of these added objectives, although securing Libyan behavior consistent with international norms outweighs the importance of diminishing the costs of U.S. policy toward Libya.

Much of the trajectory of U.S.-Libyan relations will be determined by Libya. The United States will have little tolerance for half-measures taken to address terrorism or qualified offers of cooperation from Tripoli. If Libya chooses the path of confrontation—or even noncooperation—with the United States, it can expect greater penalties and pressure.

Nevertheless, the centrality of Libyan actions to the future of bilateral relations does not diminish the fact that whether Libya chooses to work with or against America has profound implications for the United States. Libya's cooperation could offer Washington important insights into the operation of terrorist networks and valuable intelligence about them. More important, though, is eliminating Libya's role as a state sponsor of terrorism. If the estrangement between Libya and the United States grows wider and Tripoli reverts to an active role in sponsoring terrorist groups, Libya could be a thorn in U.S. efforts to eradicate terrorism worldwide.

Because the consequences of a failed relationship are potentially as serious for the United States as they are for Libya, U.S. policymakers should seize the moment to ask whether the sanctions strategy pursued by the United States in 2002 is conducive to a mutually beneficial U.S.-Libya rapprochement and whether it is well suited to achieve the goals outlined above. Several factors suggest it is not. The U.S. sanctions regime was originally intended to propel a change in regime and then subsequently seen as an instrument of containing the Qadhafi regime. As a result, the structure of U.S. sanctions is poorly suited to enticing Libya to change its behavior. In order for sanctions to serve this function, several modifications must be made to reorient them toward the goal of moderating Libya's behavior. A failure to do leaves sanctions doomed to the pursuit of containment, a feckless quest for unilateral measures.

First, care must be taken to ensure that U.S. rhetoric matches the goal of behavior change and is not geared toward regime change or perpetual containment. The Clinton administration began this process, not only by discontinuing the parlance of "rogue regimes" but by explicitly stating "Libya is not Iraq."[182] These rhetorical gestures pared back the perception that the United States would never accept Libya's rehabilitation under any circumstances, a view that diminished Libya's incentive to mend its ways and undermined the leverage of sanctions.

Second, the sanctions regime needs to be accompanied by greater dia-logue between Libya and the United States if sanctions are to be a vehicle for behavior change. For more than eighteen years, no direct discussions occurred between Washington and Tripoli. Only once the Lockerbie suspects were in the Netherlands did the two countries meet face-to-face.[183] Although this meeting—and sporadic ones that followed it—are positive develop-ments, more systematic dialogue should be established. The opening of diplomatic posts in each country is unlikely to be feasible for some time; however, placing Libyan staff at the Libyan interest section at the United Arab Emirates' embassy in Washington and American personnel at the U.S. interest section in the Belgian embassy in Tripoli would be a useful step.

Third, the United States should acknowledge the changes in behavior that Libya has made and indicate that it will continue to recognize similar progress. Already some U.S. officials have verbally taken note of Libya's efforts. But more concrete gestures are warranted and will be essential to securing and maintaining ongoing Libyan cooperation. Again, allowing UN sanctions to be lifted once Libya meets UN requirements is key. Once that occurs, the president could certify that Libya has met the requirements of UN resolutions, which opens the door to the termination of ILSA sanctions on Libya. Although this move is not required by law, it would be one way for the U.S. government to demonstrate that it is willing to respond to Libyan progress without suffering undue political costs. In fact, given that the ILSA legislation essentially ties secondary sanctions on firms doing business in Libya to Libya's compliance with UN resolutions, a U.S. decision not to cer-tify would be construed negatively, both by Libya and U.S. allies.

A menu of other possible appropriate measures includes removing the twenty-five-mile travel ban on Libyan diplomats in New York, encouraging people-to-people exchanges, or lifting current restrictions on American nonprofit and nongovernmental organization projects in Libya. These steps are minor, yet they could create a more constructive dynamic between the United States and Libya as the two countries try to forge a path to better relations. Travel restrictions on U.S. citizens visiting Libya should be eased and then lifted once such limitations are no longer warranted on security grounds; this move, however, should not be construed as a gesture to Libya, but would rather be the termination of a restriction of U.S. constitutional rights once the security situation no longer demands it. As demonstrated by U.S. moves to freeze the assets of the Libyan Fighting Group—one of Tripoli's enduring challengers—the United States may be able to make ges-tures to Libya in unexpected ways at no cost—or even a net gain—to itself.[184] Allowing Libya to pursue its application to join the World Trade Organization would be one such example. It would be a signal of U.S. flexibility but would commit Libya to making many domestic changes that would promote transparency and accountability in the country, which could only bring Libya closer to international standards of behavior, not further away.

U.S. policymakers should work to construct a detailed road map to improved relations once Libya fully complies with UN resolutions. By outlining U.S. concerns, as well as the sanctions that the United States pledged to remove once each issue was adequately addressed, this road map would chart the course to better bilateral relations and provide further incentives to the Libyan regime to comply with U.S. demands. Divided into phases, the road map could address issues related not only to terrorism but also to weapons of mass destruction and regional peace initiatives. If and when Libya takes actions in accordance with this plan, the United States must be willing to gradually disassemble its sanctions regime.

Efforts to move down this path will be complicated by domestic U.S. politics and the strength of groups in Congress and elsewhere firmly opposed to any efforts to ease the hard-line policy in place against Libya, regardless of the changes it makes. Both Washington and Tripoli should keep these U.S. domestic issues in mind as they move forward. Libya, aware of its dire image in the United States, should seek to improve its standing, not only by restraining its anti-American rhetoric but also by undertaking initiatives that underline a new commitment to international norms and regional stability. With the recent surges in oil revenues, Libya could launch humanitarian programs to complement Qadhafi's efforts to create a role for himself in peacemaking. At the same time, U.S. policymakers must keep Congress apprised of their moves with Libya and of developments in the North African country that signal opportunities or setbacks to U.S. interests. Ideally, with sustained attention and continued improvements in Libyan behavior, the conversations in Congress about U.S. interests in regard to Libya will become more nuanced, gradually creating an opening for improved relations when the circumstances warrant it.

None of these recommendations would entail completely forfeiting what leverage the United States has through its unilateral sanctions. Any one of them or more would, however, signal an important shift in the tone of U.S. policy away from a punitive approach toward one cajoling Libya to keep moving down the path of reform and moderation. Although it is unlikely to be popular with the U.S. domestic audience, this reorientation is warranted at a number of levels. First, these steps, without renouncing economic lever-age at the outset, transform the U.S. sanctions regime from one that can never hope to contain Qadhafi unilaterally to one that stands the best chance of reforming his behavior. Although U.S. sanctions will never have the force of multilateral ones, sanctions structured in this way are most likely to entice Libya to fully comply with UN resolutions and address American concerns. Second, the risks of *not* restructuring sanctions in this manner are considerable. The argument for lifting UN sanctions when Libya has complied also holds true when discussing unilateral sanctions. By maintaining virtually the same monolithic, punitive sanctions regime that has been in place since 1986, the United States is telling Qadhafi that his behavior has little or no impact on the shape of U.S. policy. There can be no better way of dissuading Qadhafi from moderation than sending him this message. By not adjusting U.S. policy in the slightest way to new realities, the United States risks undermining its own sanctions as well as its efforts to encourage other "rogue" regimes to reform their behavior. If tangible changes are not met with tangible responses—even if they are largely sym-bolic—few regimes holding difficult relations with Washington will see the benefit of modifying their ways.

Some will argue against tweaking the U.S. approach toward Libya by claiming that a sanctions-dominated strategy can once again serve as a cat-alyst for multilateral pressure against Libya. Barring new evidence linking Libya to terrorism or renewed actions by Libya to support terrorism, U.S. sanctions are unlikely to play this role; in the view of many countries, Libya satisfied UN requirements by turning over the Lockerbie suspects and coop-erating with the trial. In addition, the credibility of U.S. policy toward Libya is waning, as the United States appears to many as unwilling to acknowledge Libyan reform.[185] The passage and subsequent renewal of ILSA, rather than serving as the basis for multilateral actions as intended, had just the oppo-site effect.[186] Not only did it damage U.S. efforts to secure international sup-port for tougher sanctions against Libya in the second half of the 1990s, but it was interpreted by American allies as a signal that U.S. policy toward Libya is increasingly hostage to domestic groups and interests.

If new evidence does arise connecting Libya with more egregious behav-ior, multilateral sanctions are a real possibility that should be pursued with vigor. In this instance, the United States will find that having pursued a modified approach will have actually been in its favor. By revealing a mod-icum of flexibility, the United States will have undercut the perception that American policy is driven by domestic interests. It will have demonstrated its ability to gauge its policy to reflect realities in Libya, not just pressures at home. This restored credibility will give the United States a better footing to advance new sanctions if Libya is found to renew its support for terrorism or provide safe haven to terrorists. Moreover, it will aid the United States in its pursuit of international restrictions on the sale of weapons and related technology to Libya until it complies with all international conventions and satisfies concerns about its pursuit of weapons of mass destruction. In short, shaping U.S. policy to promote behavior changes—rather than the isolation and containment of Libya now—will serve U.S. interests no matter what the future holds.

## Appendix 5A

Tables 5A-1 and 5A-2 present estimates of the costs to Libya and the United States of lost trade with one another.

Note to Appendix 5A:  *Estimates of the Costs to Libya of Lost Imports from the United States.*  As shown in table 5A-2, the direct loss of Libya as an export market cost U.S. businesses approximately $11.7 billion over the period 1981–2001 (not accounting for the fact that some of these exports inevitably found other markets). This would also represent the initial cost to Libya of lost imports from the United States. In the absence of information concerning the breakdown of U.S. exports to Libya, the assumption is made that 15 percent of these exports were difficult to replace, possibly requiring a mark-up of 20 percent over what Libya would have paid to the United States directly. Libya probably was required to pay little more to replace the remaining 85 percent, perhaps on the order of 5 percent. So, the cost of obtaining or replacing the imports normally secured from the United States between 1981 and 1999 (the latest available data) is [($11.7bn)*.15]*.20 + [($11.7bn)*.85]*.05 = $848 million.

**Table 5A-1. Estimated Direct Costs to Libya of Lost Exports to the United States, 1986–2001.**

Millions of 2001 dollars

| Year | Total Libyan exports (A) | Non-oil exports[a] (A × 0.05 = B) | Hypothetical non-oil exports to the U.S.[b] (B × 0.02 = C) | Actual exports to the U.S. (D) | Estimated non-oil exports lost due to sanctions (C − D = E) | Chain-weighted price deflator for GDP, 1996 = 100 (F) | Estimated lost non-oil exports to U.S., real dollars (E × [117.9/F] = G) |
|---|---|---|---|---|---|---|---|
| 1986 | 6,729 | 336 | 6.7 | 2 | 4.7 | 75 | 7.4 |
| 1987 | 8,047 | 402 | 8.0 | 0 | 8.0 | 78.2 | 12.1 |
| 1988 | 6,908 | 345 | 6.9 | 0 | 6.9 | 81.5 | 10.0 |
| 1989 | 8,617 | 431 | 8.6 | 0 | 8.6 | 84.4 | 12.0 |
| 1990 | 13,878 | 694 | 13.9 | 0 | 13.9 | 85.9 | 19.0 |
| 1991 | 11,212 | 561 | 11.2 | 0 | 11.2 | 85.5 | 15.5 |
| 1992 | 9,942 | 497 | 9.9 | 0 | 9.9 | 88.0 | 13.3 |
| 1993 | 7,542 | 377 | 7.5 | 0 | 7.5 | 90.4 | 9.8 |
| 1994 | 7,860 | 393 | 7.9 | 0 | 7.9 | 94.0 | 9.9 |
| 1995 | 8,497 | 425 | 8.5 | 0 | 8.5 | 96.6 | 10.4 |
| 1996 | 10,118 | 506 | 10.1 | 0 | 10.1 | 100.0 | 11.9 |
| 1997 | 9,560 | 478 | 9.6 | 0 | 9.6 | 104.4 | 10.8 |
| 1998 | 6,032 | 302 | 6.0 | 0 | 6.0 | 108.9 | 6.5 |
| 1999 | 6,824 | 341 | 6.8 | 0 | 6.8 | 113.4 | 7.1 |
| 2000 | 11,190 | 560 | 11.2 | 0 | 11.2 | 117.6 | 11.2 |
| 2001 | 11,260 | 563 | 11.3 | 0 | 11.3 | 117.9 | 11.3 |
| **Total** | | | | | | | **178.3** |

Source: Economist Intelligence Unit, *Country Profile: Libya*, various years; IMF, *Direction of Trade Statistics*, various years

a. Total exports are multiplied by 0.05, the percentage of exports that were non-oil. It is assumed that Libya was able to redirect its oil exports at almost no cost.

b. Non-oil exports are multiplied by 0.02, the estimated percentage of Libyan non-oil exports going to the United States in 1984. This year is used as the baseline because in 1984 there were no sanctions on Libya's exports of non-oil goods and U.S. imports of refined oil from the Ras Lanuf refinery were still minimal.

Table 5A-2. *Estimated Direct Costs to the United States of Lost Non-Military Exports to Libya, 1982–2001*

Millions of 2001 dollars

| Year | Actual U.S. exports to Libya (A) | Actual U.S. exports to oil-exporting countries (B) | Actual U.S. exports to oil-exporting countries minus Libya (B − A = C) | Hypothetical U.S. exports to Libya[a] (C × 0.029 = D) | Estimated annual impact of sanctions (D − A = E) | Chain-weighted price deflator for GDP, 1996 = 100 (F) | Estimated annual impact of sanctions, real dollars (E × [117.9/F] = G) |
|---|---|---|---|---|---|---|---|
| 1981 | 524 | 20,732 | 20,208 | 586 | 62 | 64.3 | 114 |
| 1982 | 331 | 22,097 | 21,766 | 631 | 300 | 63.0 | 562 |
| 1983 | 210 | 16,419 | 16,209 | 470 | 260 | 65.7 | 467 |
| 1984 | 220 | 13,864 | 13,644 | 396 | 176 | 70.5 | 294 |
| 1985 | 342 | 11,958 | 11,616 | 337 | −5 | 73.2 | −8 |
| 1986 | 51 | 10,377 | 10,326 | 299 | 248 | 75.7 | 387 |
| 1987 | 0 | 10,558 | 10,558 | 306 | 306 | 78.2 | 462 |
| 1988 | 0 | 13,347 | 13,347 | 387 | 387 | 81.5 | 560 |
| 1989 | 0 | 12,717 | 12,717 | 369 | 369 | 84.4 | 515 |
| 1990 | 0 | 12,981 | 12,981 | 376 | 376 | 85.9 | 517 |
| 1991 | 0 | 18,254 | 18,254 | 529 | 529 | 85.5 | 730 |
| 1992 | 0 | 21,131 | 21,131 | 613 | 613 | 88.0 | 821 |
| 1993 | 0 | 19,832 | 19,832 | 575 | 575 | 90.4 | 750 |
| 1994 | 0 | 18,042 | 18,042 | 523 | 523 | 94.0 | 656 |
| 1995 | 0 | 19,589 | 19,589 | 568 | 568 | 96.6 | 694 |
| 1996 | 0 | 22,380 | 22,380 | 649 | 649 | 100.0 | 765 |
| 1997 | 0 | 25,884 | 25,884 | 751 | 751 | 104.4 | 848 |
| 1998 | 0 | 25,417 | 25,417 | 737 | 737 | 108.9 | 798 |
| 1999 | 0 | 21,031 | 21,031 | 610 | 610 | 113.4 | 634 |
| 2000 | 18 | 20,137 | 20,119 | 584 | 566 | 117.6 | 567 |
| 2001 | 10 | 20,410 | 20,400 | 592 | 582 | 117.9 | 582 |
| **Total** | | | | | | | **11,713** |

Source: See table 5A-1.

a. Actual U.S. exports to oil-exporting countries minus Libya are multiplied by 0.029, the average ratio of U.S. exports to Libya to U.S. exports to oil-exporting countries minus Libya in 1979–80.

# Sanctioning
# Sudan

Although never strong, U.S. strategic concerns in Sudan weakened considerably after the collapse of the Soviet Union and the decline of Moscow's influence in Africa. As these global developments reshaped relationships around the world, Sudan's 1989 coup—which brought then-brigadier general Omar al-Bashir and his National Islamic Front (NIF) supporters to power—pushed Washington and Khartoum further apart.[1] From that time, American dealings with Sudan have been dominated by concerns about Sudanese support for terrorism, the civil war between the government and primarily southern rebels, countrywide violations of human rights including infringements of religious freedom, concern over the development of chemical and biological weapons, and the authoritarian practices of the government. Quite apart from these concerns has been an enduring U.S. commitment to humanitarian relief in Sudan and extensive American involvement in Operation Lifeline Sudan, a consortium of UN agencies and nongovernmental organizations (NGOs) working to alleviate the widespread famine in southern Sudan.[2] Although the post–cold war agenda between Washington and Khartoum has been complex, rarely was it seen to be of any great strategic importance to a United States recently liberated from combating Soviet influence in the developing world.

Dwindling strategic interests, however, did not result in a progressive marginalization of Sudan in U.S. foreign policy. Instead, the situation

*Sudan*

merely shaped the sources and nature of American attention given to Sudan and conditioned the policies adopted in its regard. Given the absence of strong strategic interests, the influence of the executive branch in U.S. policy toward Sudan was eclipsed by congressional action and the force of nongovernmental groups that tended to be aligned with the southern armed insurgents. Many special interest groups—from religious conservatives to African American constituencies—were decisive in crafting U.S. policy toward Sudan over the 1990s, although they failed to prompt Washington to devote major political, military, or economic resources to solving the problems in Sudan. The result was a U.S. strategy toward Sudan marked by proliferating layers of sanctions and a domestic discourse heavily weighted toward punishment and penalty. Arguably, in this context, sanctions were viewed as much or more of a means of highlighting America's moral standing toward the war in Sudan than they were seen as tools to strategically advance the panoply of American foreign policy objectives in Sudan.

The major influence of domestic groups in crafting U.S. policy—and the wide variety of U.S. concerns in Sudan—complicated efforts to formulate an effective and useful American strategy. What emerged in the 1990s was a policy whose ultimate political objectives were unclear and whose tactics were often at cross purposes. At an official level, U.S. policy throughout the 1990s and beyond purported to be geared toward changing the behavior of Khartoum on several fronts.[3] Nevertheless, the goal of regime change lurked close to the surface of official White House rhetoric and was clearly evident in the statements of some members of Congress.[4] Moreover, military support for neighboring states—justified as necessary to help them resist "destabilization" from Khartoum—was interpreted by many as support for the overthrow of the Sudanese government. As explored in this chapter, the sanctions-dominated strategy toward Sudan was neither well structured to achieve its goals nor well coordinated with other policy tools in a way that enhanced the ability of sanctions to serve U.S. interests more successfully. Both comprehensive U.S. sanctions and very limited UN ones had only a negligible direct impact on Sudan, one that fell far short of that necessary to effectively contain the regime at any level. However, given Sudan's growing desire to modernize its economy and integrate itself into the global market, certain U.S. restrictions threatened to pose real obstacles for Sudan as it gradually removed domestic constraints on its ascension to the international financial system. This implicit leverage on Sudan's future, however, was not used to create a bargaining framework between Washington and Khartoum through which the United States could compel and coerce Sudan to change its behavior in areas of concern. Instead, the United States sought to change Khartoum's behavior with a rigid, unilateral sanctions regime that held little hope of containing the government of Sudan and was coupled with policy tools more suited to a regime change strategy. Not surprisingly, this overall approach yielded only a few real benefits in the 1990s and 2000. Ultimately, sanctions on Sudan during this period can only be judged as being effective and having utility in a very modest sense: the small gains made were achieved at extremely low costs.

The terrorist attacks of 2001 changed the landscape of U.S.-Sudanese relations. The intensified emphasis on counterterrorism and Sudan's apparent willingness to aid the United States in its campaign against terrorism raised the strategic importance of Sudan to the United States. This reality and the new sense of international threat to the United States subdued the influence of narrowly focused interest groups on U.S. foreign policy overall and on U.S. policy toward Sudan in particular. These developments spurred a renewed urgency to have a policy toward Sudan that is effective in achieving specific goals, not just one that is morally appealing. The post–September 11 environment offered an opportunity to re-evaluate the past sanctions-dominated approach taken toward Sudan and provided a context for greater U.S. engagement with Sudan.

## The Historical Context of Sanctions

Tensions between the United States and Sudan predate the rule of President al-Bashir. Serious strains were evident in the late 1960s, when Sudan terminated diplomatic relations on account of U.S. support for Israel in the 1967 war, and throughout the early 1970s, when members of the Black September group assassinated the U.S. ambassador and deputy chief of mission to Sudan in Khartoum.[5] Relations began to improve in the second half of the 1970s, as the United States grew increasingly concerned about Soviet influence in the Horn of Africa. In the early 1980s, U.S. aid to Sudan rose steadily, partially to ensure continued Sudanese support for the Camp David Accord and partially because Washington saw Sudan as a rampart against Menguistu Haile Mariam's Soviet-supported Ethiopia.[6]

Large amounts of U.S. military assistance to Sudan continued despite the resumption of the civil war between the government and southern rebels in 1983—shortly after President Gafar Nimeiri modified national law to be compatible with sharia Islamic law and effectively abrogated the 1972 Addis Ababa peace agreement by redividing the south into three provinces.[7] Perhaps ironically, among the first sanctions to be imposed on

Sudan were those enacted against the democratically elected government of Sadiq al-Mahdi, which had moved into office one year after a bloodless military coup had unseated Nimeiri in April 1985.[8] In December 1988, the United States was forced to suspend all new economic and military aid to Sudan under the Brooke amendment, legislation that mandates a termination of aid to all countries more than one year in arrears in their payments on past U.S. aid.[9]

Relations between the United States and Sudan gradually deteriorated after June 30, 1989, when al Bashir seized power in a coup, promptly dissolved the National Assembly, suspended the constitution, and banned all political parties.[10] Although the coup added a further layer of justification for the sanctions already in place, al-Bashir's outward political independence led Washington to suspend immediate judgment on the new regime. However, as 1990 progressed, al-Bashir's close ties to and involvement with the National Islamic Front (NIF), the political party of the Muslim Brotherhood led by Hassan al-Turabi, became apparent. Relations between the United States and Sudan soured over the repressive nature of the new regime and its Islamic fundamentalist bent. Khartoum's support for Iraq during the Gulf war further widened the gap between Sudan and the United States— as well as alienated other western and most Arab nations from Sudan.[11] It also led Congress to prohibit any military cooperation or assistance to Sudan in November 1990.[12] Several months later, in April 1991, the United States suspended Sudan's trade preferences under the Generalized System of Preferences to protest the country's failure to protect workers' rights.[13]

Although the administration of George H. W. Bush imposed no further sanctions on Sudan during its time in office, it became increasingly concerned about Khartoum's behavior. Particularly after the visit of Iranian president Hashemi Rafsanjani to Khartoum in December 1991, unease grew in Washington over Sudan's developing links with radical groups and wayward regimes.[14] Actions by the Sudanese government that obstructed humanitarian relief efforts also drew blunt criticism from Washington, while Congress and the executive branch repeatedly called on both parties to the Sudanese conflict to end human rights abuses.[15] Over time, the administration became less optimistic about Khartoum's willingness to seek a negotiated settlement, at least in part because splits in the Sudan People's Liberation Army (SPLA) in 1991 encouraged the government of Sudan to believe that a military solution was possible.[16] Although the Bush administration reportedly considered providing support to southern forces battling Khartoum shortly before it left office, the deep internal divisions within the SPLA made the United States wary of backing it with direct aid.[17]

## U.S. and UN Sanctions against Sudan

**December 1984**   The United States suspends bilateral economic aid to Sudan pending an agreement between Sudan and the IMF on economic reforms in Sudan. Aid resumes in 1985 after an agreement is signed.

**December 1988**   The Brooke amendment of the Foreign Operations Appropriations Act mandates that all new bilateral economic and military aid to Sudan is suspended, given that Sudan is more than one year in arrears on its past U.S. aid and military loans.

**February 28, 1990**   Section 513 of the Foreign Operations Appropriations Act reinforces existing sanctions under the Brooke amendment in response to the June 1989 coup, which ousts the democratically elected Sadiq al-Mahdi.

**November 5, 1990**   Congress specifically bans IMET and Foreign Military Financing for Sudan in the Foreign Operations Appropriations Act. This reinforces sanctions imposed through the Brooke amendment and section 513.

**April 25, 1991**   President George H. W. Bush suspends Sudan's trade preferences under the Generalized System of Preferences, citing Sudan's failure to promote and protect workers' rights.

**August 1993**   Sudan is designated a state sponsor of terrorism by the secretary of state, which leads to a ban on arms-related exports and sales, controls on exports of dual-use items, and a ban on most forms of economic assistance, and requires opposition to loans and aid from international financial institutions to Sudan.

**April 26, 1996**   UNSC Resolution 1054 imposes diplomatic sanctions on Sudan for its failure to account for three suspects in a 1995 assassination attempt on Egyptian president Hosni Mubarak. The resolution calls on all members to reduce the number and level of Sudanese diplomats within their countries, restricts the movements of remaining diplomats, deny travel visas for members of the Sudanese government and military, and asks international organizations not to hold conferences in Sudan.

**August 16, 1996**   The UN Security Council passes resolution 1070, which calls for an air embargo on Sudan. The resolution, however, is never enforced.

**August 24, 1996**   The Antiterrorism and Effective Death Penalty Act becomes law, prohibiting financial transactions to countries on the U.S. terrorism list. A loophole was left that allowed transactions with Sudan and Syria unless such deals were known to be linked to terrorist activities.

**November 22, 1996**   President Clinton announces a decision to ban the entry of Sudanese officials into the United States, citing compliance with UNSCR 1054.

**November 3, 1997**    President Clinton issues Executive Order 13067, which bans all imports from and exports to Sudan, freezes all assets of the Sudanese government inside the United States, and ends financial transactions with Sudan by closing the loophole in the Antiterrorism and Effective Death Penalty Act.

**July 1, 1998**    The Office of Foreign Assets Control publishes its regulations enforcing Executive Order 13067, which allows U.S. companies to apply for licenses to import Sudanese gum arabic.

**April 28, 1999**    President Clinton announces the lifting of prohibitions on U.S. commercial sales of most agricultural commodities and medicine and medical equipment to Sudan, Libya, and Iran. The regulations are finalized in July 1999.

**February 2000**    The Office of Foreign Assets Control clarifies its sanctions on companies involved in the Greater Nile Petroleum Operating Company in Sudan, including Canada's Talisman Energy, saying that U.S. citizens or companies and their foreign branches cannot engage in trade or financial transactions with GNPOC or the Sudan state oil company. The sanctions only apply to the activities of the GNPOC and do not prevent other business with the companies involved.

**May 8, 2001**    The U.S. Securities and Exchange Commission decides to press companies operating in countries under U.S. sanctions to provide a full disclosure of their activities before they can be listed on the New York Stock Exchange.

**September 6, 2001**    President Bush appoints former senator John Danforth as special envoy to Sudan.

**September 28, 2001**    UN sanctions are lifted after a 14-0 vote by the Security Council. The United States abstains.

**January 19, 2002**    U.S. efforts secure a partial cease-fire in the Nuba Mountains.

**April 26, 2002**    The Danforth report is released. It downplays the possibility of secession for the south and proposes sharing of oil revenue between the north and south as a prelude to a larger settlement. It advocates cautious, continued U.S. engagement.

**July 20, 2002**    The Machakos Protocol is signed between the government of Sudan and the SPLM. It provides for a six-month preinterim period to be followed by a six-year interim period, at the end of which a referendum will be held in the south to determine whether it remains unified with the north or secedes.

**October 21, 2002**    President Bush signs Congress's Sudan Peace Act into law, which requires him to certify every six months that the Sudanese government and the SPLA/M are negotiating in good faith. Capital market sanctions are not included in the law, although other sanctions are threatened if Khartoum is found to be interfering in aid efforts or not negotiating with honest intentions.

The Clinton administration adopted a more aggressive posture toward Sudan soon after coming into office. At the time, the NIF government was actively seeking to export radicalism through the vigorous support of insurgencies in neighboring countries, raising serious concerns about regional stability. In this environment, Clinton administration officials formulated a strategy intended to simultaneously pressure Khartoum through U.S. diplomacy and regional military efforts. The United States began this new campaign to increase pressure on Khartoum by placing Sudan on the U.S. terrorism list in August 1993. In doing so, the new administration cited the growing presence of Islamist movements and terrorist groups—including the Abu Nidal organization, Hizbullah, and Palestinian Islamic Jihad—in Sudan.[18] Also important in the designation of Sudan as a state sponsor of terrorism was what officials referred to as credible "reports of training in Sudan of militant extremists that commit acts of terrorism in neighboring countries."[19] As a result of this categorization, several sanctions went into effect immediately. Besides reaffirming the prohibitions on military aid and nonhumanitarian assistance that were already in place, the terrorist designation also obliged the United States to oppose lending from international financial institutions to Sudan and entailed a number of other sundry trade and financial restrictions.[20]

International concern over Sudanese support for terrorism was borne out in June 1995, when an unsuccessful assassination attempt was made on Egyptian president Hosni Mubarak while he was attending a summit of the Organization of African Unity in Addis Ababa. Subsequent Ethiopian investigations implicated Khartoum in the scheme and identified three of those involved in the plot as seeking refuge in Sudan.[21] On the basis of these findings, Egypt and Ethiopia, firmly backed by the United States, pushed for a series of resolutions against Sudan in the United Nations. The first, UN resolution 1044, called on Sudan to extradite the three suspects to Ethiopia for trial immediately and to terminate its support for terrorism.[22]

In the absence of any real progress in this direction, the United Nations passed resolution 1054 on April 26, 1996, imposing diplomatic sanctions on Sudan for its continued refusal to comply with UN demands. The resolution called on all member states to reduce the size and mobility of the staff at Sudanese diplomatic missions, limit the travel of members of the Sudanese regime, and ban the convening of international or regional conferences in Sudan.[23] Despite the mild terms of the sanctions, few states implemented them. Several countries expelled one or two Sudanese diplomats from their capitals; the United States only sent one official back to Khartoum.[24] Russia and China—which had both abstained in the vote for the sanctions—took no action to comply. The prohibition on international conferences was also not adhered to, as was evident by meetings of the World Bank's Nile Basin Initiative in Khartoum in July–August 2000 and March 2001 and the Libyan-sponsored Sahel and Sahara regional group in Khartoum in October 2001.[25] Sudan's intransigence catalyzed the adoption of another round of UN sanctions several months later in August 1996.[26] Although devised to have greater impact by instituting an air embargo, the sanctions laid out in UN resolution 1070 were never implemented.[27]

This failure to bring multilateral economic pressure on Sudan, even in the face of ample evidence of its complicity in the attack on President Mubarak, deeply disappointed the United States, which had been pushing Egypt to craft a more robust sanctions regime to place before the Security Council. Egypt, however, had resisted, as it was reluctant to create pressures it feared would undermine the territorial integrity of Sudan and thereby potentially threaten Egyptian access to the Nile waters.[28] Cairo's perception that it could better influence events in Sudan through its own bilateral relationship, rather than the international sanctions desired by the United States, also played into its calculation not to push for tougher measures. Egypt had also reportedly opposed efforts to impose a weapons embargo on Khartoum, believing that such a restriction could ensure the south's victory and possible secession in the ongoing civil war.[29] Such protests, as well as an international climate inhospitable to UN sanctions on account of the situation in Iraq, dampened U.S. optimism for securing further multilateral measures against Sudan.

Meanwhile, pressure was building in the United States for a tougher bilateral approach toward Sudan for a number of reasons beyond the poor prospects for multilateral action. First, there was a growing perception that the fortunes of the opposition were shifting. The National Democratic Alliance—a loose arrangement of mostly religiously oriented political parties based in Eritrea and united primarily in their opposition to the Khartoum regime—began coordinated military action for the first time in the mid-1990s, opening a new front to the conflict in the northeast and further stretching government troops formerly concentrated in the south.[30] In addition, the SPLA was gaining strength after several difficult years in the early 1990s when internal discord and the loss of support from Menguistu's regime had seriously weakened the organization. Finally, angry over Khartoum's interference in their own affairs, the frontline states of Ethiopia, Eritrea, and Uganda began to support the SPLA in earnest.[31] Emboldened by these factors, the SPLA launched its first major offensive in five years in late 1996, capturing large swaths of the south and bringing to a boil the conflict that had been simmering since government forces began recapturing many southern towns in 1991.

U.S. domestic constituencies, who were outraged by the behavior of the Sudanese government toward the south, fueled the sense of urgency to take stronger action against Khartoum. Humanitarian organizations condemned the continued interference of the regime in the workings of Operation Lifeline Sudan; African Americans and other human rights groups abhorred reports of abductions and enslavement by government-backed militias; the Christian right and an assortment of NGOs were infuriated by government aerial bombings of civilian areas, including churches and hospitals.[32] Congress, responsive to these groups and appalled by the atrocities in Sudan, began to go beyond its earlier statements, which had merely expressed disapproval of the situation in Sudan, to introduce legislation calling for the establishment of an office to monitor religious persecution and advocating the use of sanctions to pursue the elimination of slavery in Sudan.[33]

Together, these factors invigorated the campaign of nongovernmental groups to impose on Khartoum, in the words of one activist, "the most stringent unilateral sanctions regime conceivable."[34] As support for such a move was building in Congress, President Clinton issued executive order 13067, which prohibited all trade with Sudan, froze all the assets of the Sudanese government in the United States, and closed any remaining loopholes that had allowed companies to conduct financial transactions with Sudan or invest there even after legislation prohibited this activity with all states on the terrorism list the previous year.[35] As spelled out in the executive order, the termination of all economic relations with Sudan was done in reaction to Khartoum's continued support for terrorism, its efforts to destabilize its neighbors, and its dismal human rights record.[36] Some speculate that the executive branch took this action in the hopes of deflating legislation percolating in Congress at the time. It was feared that legislation under consideration to address religious persecution would have not only mandated sanctions on Sudan, but also would possibly require that sanctions be placed on Syria, Egypt, and Saudi Arabia—countries that the United States was eager to stay on good terms with to further its pursuit of Middle East peace, the containment of Iraq, and the continuous supply of oil.[37]

Regardless of the motives behind the executive order, the 1997 sanctions set the stage for a further hardening of U.S. policy toward Sudan over the next years. The only slackening of pressure during this time—the April 1999 decision to allow U.S. companies to sell food and medicine to Iran, Libya, and Sudan—could hardly be construed as a gesture to Khartoum. Instead, it was a reflection of broader developments: the mounting agriculture crisis in the United States, a gradual reassessment of sanctions by Congress and the executive branch, and rising concern over the humanitarian costs of sanctions in general.[38] This move was one exception to the overall trend toward increasing pressure on Sudan.

In October 1998, Congress passed the International Religious Freedom Act in an effort to elevate the issue of religious freedom in U.S. foreign policy. In addition to creating a body to monitor these violations and requiring the State Department to make an annual report of them, this law authorized the president to place sanctions on the worst offenders.[39] In every year that has since passed, Sudan has been identified as an egregious violator of religious rights due to its restriction of the religious practices of non-Muslims.[40] Although no new sanctions were imposed as a result of this designation, this legislation gave the existing sanctions regime extra justification.[41]

The harder-line approach taken toward Sudan in the second term of the Clinton administration involved more than just added sanctions. Although the United States refrained from providing direct military aid to the southern rebels, President Clinton did authorize $20 million in nonlethal military aid to the "frontline" states of Ethiopia, Eritrea, and Uganda in 1997 in an explicit effort to help them combat insurgencies fueled by the government of Sudan.[42] Moreover, on August 20, 1998, in the wake of the lethal bombing of U.S. embassies in Kenya and Tanzania, the United States struck the Al-Shifa pharmaceutical plant in downtown Khartoum with cruise missiles, believing it to be a chemical weapons plant owned by a member of Osama bin Laden's terrorist network. The decision to take this action was only known to a few of the top officials in the Clinton administration at the time and turned out to be a highly controversial move, even within the administration's own ranks. "Al-Shifa" —as the episode came to be known—marked a turning point in U.S. policy toward Sudan, not only because the use of military force signaled an escalation in the confrontation but because subsequent revelations called into question the soundness of the intelligence on which the strike was based.[43]

Diplomatic maneuvers to marginalize Sudan were another key element of the U.S. sanctions-based strategy. The rhetoric of policymakers at the highest level was acerbic and prominent administration officials on occasion traveled to the region and publicly denounced Khartoum.[44] On a trip to Uganda in 1997, Secretary of State Madeleine Albright met with southern rebel leader John Garang and strongly condemned the regime in Sudan.[45] In a bolder move in November 2000, Assistant Secretary of State Susan Rice visited southern Sudan without Khartoum's permission and condemned the government of Sudan for its bombing of civilians and support for militias involved in the slave trade.[46] The government of Sudan vehemently protested this series of events as a violation of Sudanese sovereignty and a confirmation that the United States is "committed to policies of hypocrisy and to action to impose its imperialist blood-sucking agenda to the detriment of the world's people."[47] A less confrontational diplomatic endeavor involved the appointment of Harry Johnston, former Democratic congressman from Florida, to be special envoy for Sudan in August 1999.[48]

In contrast to the ever-hardening U.S. position, European and Asian countries sought greater contact with Sudan in the 1990s, particularly as the country's oil industry blossomed. Sudan's potential as an oil producer had been known since the U.S. company Chevron discovered significant quantities of oil in Unity state and Blue Nile in August 1980.[49] But it was only in the early 1990s, when a Canadian oil company named Arakis purchased part of the Chevron concession, that Sudan's oil resources began to be developed in earnest. In December 1996, Arakis (whose interests were later to be purchased by Canada's Talisman) formed a consortium with the China National Petroleum Corporation (CNPC), the Malaysian state oil company Petronas, and the Sudanese government.[50] Called the Greater Nile Petroleum Operating Company (GNPOC), this group began the rapid development of oil fields in central southern Sudan and completed a pipeline from there to the Red Sea town of Port Sudan.[51] The involvement of these and other foreign oil companies in Sudan allowed Khartoum to begin exporting more than 138,000 barrels per day of its "Nile Blend" crude in 1999. A domestic refinery, financed by the Chinese National Petroleum Company and completed in June 2000, enabled Sudan to virtually eliminate its import of oil. Sudan's rapid emergence as an exporter of light, sweet crude fueled international interest in Sudan's energy sector in the late 1990s and early 2000s.

Khartoum's international political position also improved considerably during this period. At the regional level, the resumption of conflict between Ethiopia and Eritrea in May 1998 and Uganda's preoccupation with both its intervention in Congo and coming national elections helped remove tensions at Sudan's borders. At the same time, Khartoum took measures to restore its standing in the region, including decreasing or ending support for regional opposition movements, apologizing for its stance during the Gulf war, and acknowledging Egyptian concerns over Nile waters.[52] Domestic events also allowed Khartoum to project a more moderate countenance to the world. In a surprise move in December 1999, President al-Bashir unseated Hassan al-Turabi from his position as speaker of parliament, a turn of events widely welcomed by Sudan's neighbors and the broader international community who saw the ideological Turabi as representing Sudan's more radical elements. Sudan parlayed these developments into greater international political acceptance; perceiving the regime to be moving toward moderation, Europe opened a dialogue with Khartoum similar to the critical dialogue it had attempted with Iran.[53] Khartoum also convinced many countries—including Egypt and Ethiopia and some Security Council members—to press for the lifting of UN sanctions on Sudan. Although the United States blocked this move and Sudan's campaign to gain a seat on the UN Security Council in October 2000, significant support for these motions signaled the gradual international rehabilitation of Khartoum.

These international trends notwithstanding, an unusual but powerful array of U.S. domestic groups had elevated Sudan's place in America's foreign policy agenda by the time that President George W. Bush entered office in January 2001. Khartoum's growing oil wealth sparked fears that in a few years Khartoum would have the financial resources to subdue the south through force alone, leading many to believe that the window for exerting pressure on Khartoum to end the civil war was rapidly closing. These qualms—and growing evidence that the drive for oil extraction had worsened human rights abuses in southern areas—compounded the pre-existing list of concerns over Khartoum's other egregious behaviors. The new American president discovered that Sudan had become a rallying point for influential Republican interests in both Congress and the executive branch. In a notable exception to the Bush administration's original reluctance to involve itself in conflicts abroad, President Bush pledged that his administration would "continue to speak and act for as long as the persecution and atrocities in Sudan last" and appointed Andrew Natsios, chief of the U.S. Agency for International Development, as U.S. special humanitarian coordinator for Sudan in May 2001; four months later, following the announcement of an expansion of U.S. humanitarian aid to Sudan, the president announced former senator John Danforth as special envoy to Sudan. For its part, Congress—after authorizing the president to provide non-lethal aid to the opposition in November 2000—was poised to renew efforts to legislate further sanctions against Sudan.[54] Momentum on Capitol Hill was building for "capital markets sanctions" or measures that would effectively prevent companies investing in Sudan from being listed on the New York Stock Exchange or the NASDAQ.[55]

The events of September 11 slowed momentum for an even more punitive U.S. policy and created an opening for increased cooperation between

Washington and Sudan. In the days immediately following the terrorist attacks in the United States, Khartoum responded quickly to U.S. calls for international assistance to track and target the networks of al-Qaida. As a former host to Osama bin Laden in the early 1990s, Sudan maintained extensive files on the terrorist leader and had valuable knowledge of the funding and inner working of his organization. Khartoum promptly shared this information and other intelligence with U.S. officials and reportedly arrested numerous individuals suspected of having links to bin Laden's networks.[56] In appreciation of this newfound cooperation—tainted, but not destroyed by hardening rhetoric and angry street protests opposing U.S. and British bombing of Afghanistan—the United States acquiesced to the lifting of UN sanctions against Sudan on September 28, 2001, and quietly quelled pending legislation for imposition of capital market sanctions. Much to the alarm of many activists, these developments signaled the possibility that rapprochement between Khartoum and Washington had been given a jump start.

The new standard of bilateral counterterrorism cooperation between the United States and Sudan did not lead Washington to disregard other important outstanding issues between the two countries. The less confrontational relationship did, however, pave the way for more active U.S. involvement in the civil war. Senator Danforth proposed that he would evaluate the desire of both sides to find a peaceful resolution to the conflict by their commitment to four confidence-building measures: a limited cease-fire in the Nuba mountain area, an agreement not to target or attack civilians, the appointment of an international commission to investigate the problem of slavery and forced abductions in Sudan, and respect for "zones of tranquility," which would allow humanitarian organizations to carry out vaccinations. In his report released on April 26, 2002, Danforth claimed that the actions of both sides—while not perfect—were sufficient evidence of their willingness and interest in pursuing further steps toward peace.

Subsequent diplomatic initiatives spearheaded by the rejuvenated Inter-Governmental Authority on Development (IGAD) produced the Machakos Protocol, signed by the Government of Sudan and the Sudan People's Liberation Movement on July 20, 2002. This protocol was a significant breakthrough, even though it leaves open a number of important issues, including the relationship between the state and religion and the borders of the southern region. The agreement launches a six-month "pre-interim" period during which both parties will end hostilities, formulate mechanisms to monitor the cessation of hostilities, and establish a new constitutional framework. An "interim" period of six years will then follow, ending with an internationally monitored referendum for the people of southern Sudan to decide whether to remain united with the north or to secede. Much work on all sides must be done before these developments translate into lasting peace in Sudan. But, as discussed toward the end of this chapter, this progress does alter the framework of U.S. policy, highlighting an important challenge to the United States: how to ensure existing sanctions not only advance U.S. counterterrorism goals but also provide the most useful complement to ongoing diplomatic initiatives geared toward peace

## Judging the Effectiveness and Utility of Sanctions on Sudan

As with Iran, Iraq, and Libya, a thorough assessment of sanctions on Sudan involves looking at the impact of sanctions—the damage that sanctions did to Sudan economically and politically. It also involves discerning the goals that sanctions achieved and the costs that were incurred as a result of this process. These evaluations are necessary to determine whether sanctions were effective and whether they had utility in the sense of achieving their goals at a reasonable cost.

### Economic Impact

The Sudanese economy improved substantially over the first four years that sanctions were in place. After a series of major economic crises in the early and mid-1990s, Sudan successfully reversed many negative economic trends in the later part of the decade. Estimates suggest that the economy grew by nearly a quarter from 1996 to 1999 and place growth for the year 2000 in the range of 7–8 percent (figure 6-1).[57] Inflation, once the scourge of the Sudanese economy, leveled out to 10 percent in 2000, down from more than 130 percent just four years earlier.[58] Similarly, the new millennium was a major turning point for the Sudanese external account, as the country claimed its first trade surplus ever.[59] The accuracy of these statistics must be viewed with some skepticism given the difficulty of collecting statistics in a war-torn, developing country such as Sudan and the low priority these efforts command. One must also view these achievements as occurring in a country that remains mired in conflict and poverty. Nevertheless, these figures do point to overall real improvements in the Sudanese economy from 1997 onward and signal accomplishments that have been acknowledged and even commended by international financial institutions.[60]

**Figure 6-1.** *Sudan, Real GDP Growth Rate Compared with Regional Growth Rates, 1985–2001*

Growth rate

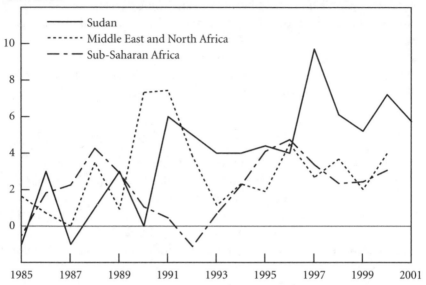

Sources: World Bank, *World Development Indicators 2002*, CD-ROM, for all numbers except Sudan growth 1997–2001, which came from Economist Intelligence Unit, *Country Report: Sudan,* June 2002.

Sudan's relative economic upturn began in 1997, shortly after the imposition of UN sanctions and during the same year that comprehensive U.S. sanctions were put in place. Sudan's improving economic climate over this period, however, should not automatically be construed as evidence that sanctions had no economic impact; rather, it points to the necessity of identifying the driving forces behind Sudan's economic performance, if not sanctions, and of distinguishing whether the Sudanese economy might have improved more substantially in the absence of sanctions.

Sudan's improving economic situation during the late 1990s is largely a result of two related factors: the government's new commitment to putting its economic house in order and the influence of oil. In February 1997, after years of estrangement, Sudan signed an adjustment program with the International Monetary Fund (IMF) with the purpose of stabilizing the economy and gradually mending its relationship with the institution.[61] Since that time, Sudan has defied the expectations of many by keeping to a modest schedule of IMF payments and instituting reform programs outlined by the organization. Khartoum's discipline in adhering to these agreements bore fruit in the form of growing confidence in the Sudanese currency, dramatic reductions in the rate of inflation, and robust growth rates. Fiscal deficits declined substantially, although the war—and the difficulty the Ministry of Finance had in resisting demands from the military government for increased defense spending—continued to put pressure on the economy.

The rapid development of Sudan's oil industry at the end of the 1990s and in the early 2000s substantially enhanced Khartoum's ability to adhere to IMF-set targets. Poised to become a medium-scale oil producer, Sudan suddenly had far greater resources at its disposal than ever before. Beyond dramatically bolstering export revenues, Sudan's oil production and domestic refining capabilities relieved it of the need to devote substantial foreign exchange to the import of oil. In 1996, Sudan spent $350 million, or 26 percent of its total import bill, on purchasing oil from foreign sources.[62] In contrast, in 2000, Sudan earned more than $1 billion from its own oil exports (figure 6-2).[63] According to Finance Minister Mohammed Khair al-Zubair, the oil sector boosted industrial growth by almost half in 2000, lifting its percentage of Sudan's overall growth by 5 percent in the same year.[64] Although agriculture remains the engine of the Sudanese economy, the importance of the oil sector will rise as oil flows increase and the government reaps greater profits from investments in the years ahead.[65]

The economic impact of sanctions on the Sudanese economy paled in comparison to the weight of these domestic factors. Economic sanctions did, however, extract some costs of their own.

TRADE. U.S. trade sanctions imposed on Sudan in 1997 had a negligible impact on the Sudanese economy. In part, the minimal impact of these measures was due to the nature of trade relations between the United States and Sudan. For years previous to the sanctions, the share of Sudan's exports going to the United States remained stable, despite the coup in Sudan in 1989, Sudan's allegiance to Iraq during the Gulf war, and the U.S. designation of Sudan as a state sponsor of terrorism in 1993. While resilient, the volume of exports was very small, minimizing the disruption caused by the ban (figure 6-4). On average, Sudan sold only 3.8 percent of its total exports to the United States between 1990 and the onset of sanctions in 1997.[66] The composition of bilateral trade was even more important in limiting the

**Figure 6-2.** *Sudan, Net Oil Exports, 1998–2003*

Millions of U.S. dollars

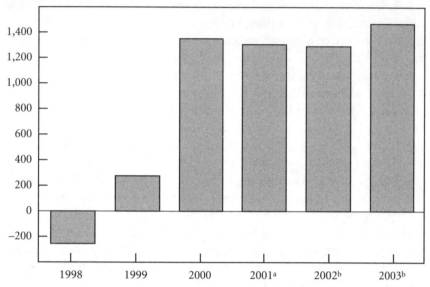

Sources: For 1998, Economist Intelligence Unit, *Country Profile: Sudan,* 2000, p. 52; for 1999–2003, Economist Intelligence Unit, *Country Report: Sudan,* June 2002.

a. Estimate.

b. Economist Intelligence Unit forecast.

costs that Sudan bore as a result of the U.S. ban on its exports. Shipments of gum arabic—a substance used for stamps, cosmetics, and soft drinks produced naturally by only a few countries in the world—accounted for the majority of Sudanese exports to the United States.[67] The difficulty of finding alternative suppliers for this import triggered a fierce debate in the United States between domestic political and business interests and African policy specialists over the wisdom of banning the purchase of Sudanese gum arabic.

The result of this debate was a licensing procedure that enabled U.S. firms to buy gum arabic from Sudan despite the sanctions.[68] Although one might expect Sudan to suffer some export losses as a result of the uncertainty surrounding the durability of this exemption and the cumbersomeness of the licensing procedures, any such losses were minimized by the willingness of other countries to absorb the slack in U.S. purchases.[69] As

**Figure 6-3.** *Total Gum Arabic Exports from Sudan,*
*by Primary Destination*

Metric tons

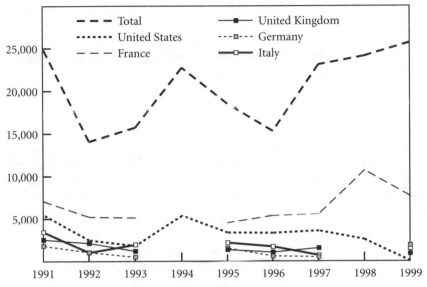

Sources: For 1991–93, "Exudate Gums: Gum Arabic, Gum Talha and Other Gums," Food and Agriculture Organization, www.fao.org/docrep/v9236e05.htm (April 23, 2001); for 1994–95 exports to U.S., "Imports Commodity Report," U.S. Customs Service, http://govinfo.kerr.orst.edu (May 10, 2001); for 1996–99 exports to the U.S., "Report IM 145," U.S. Department of Commerce, Bureau of the Census; for 1994–99 exports to Europe, *Eurostat*.

figure 6-3 shows, the volume of total Sudanese exports of gum arabic actually rose during the last years of the 1990s, aided by increased purchases from European countries.[70] As a result, Sudan was nearly fully compensated for the roughly $190 million worth of additional exports that it would have sold to the United States in 1997–2001 in the absence of U.S. sanctions (table 6A-1 in the appendix to this chapter).

Similarly, Sudan only bore very small costs as a result of no longer being able to buy U.S. products. Unlike exports to the United States, Sudan's purchases of American goods had been declining slowly since the 1980s, reflecting an overall Sudanese shift away from industrial suppliers toward imports from developing countries, particularly those in the Middle East.[71] U.S. products had accounted for over a tenth of all foreign products purchased by Sudan in 1990, yet this number was down to 4 percent in 1996, the year before the sanctions were imposed (figure 6-5). Total losses, however, were far less than even this small percentage would indicate, as Sudan replaced abrogated American contracts with relative ease, causing Sudan to bear only the price differential between securing American goods and foreign ones.[72] The 1998 U.S. decision to allow American firms to export food and medicine to Sudan further diminished the impact of lost imports from the United States. As a result, the total costs to Sudan as a result of the ban on U.S. exports to it were less than one-tenth of the nearly $400 million in additional trade that would have occurred in the absence of sanctions in 1997–2001,or less than one half of 1 percent of the value of Sudan's imports over that same period (table 6A-2).

EXTERNAL FINANCIAL FLOWS. U.S. and UN sanctions influenced external financial flows to Sudan in three ways: through their direct impact, their "magnifying" impact, and their ability to constrict Sudan's economic options in the present or future. The direct impact of sanctions on financial flows was extremely small. Being solely political and diplomatic in nature, the UN sanctions on Sudan necessarily had no direct economic impact. The 1997 U.S. sanctions, however, did entail some direct costs, the most obvious being the freezing of some $33 million in Sudanese assets in the United States at the time.[73] The prohibition on U.S. investment in Sudan was of greater consequence, although the limited involvement of U.S. firms in Sudan minimized its effects. American oil companies had approached Sudan with caution since Chevron's departure in 1984; as a result, no U.S. oil company was forced to disentangle itself from major operations in Sudan when sanctions were imposed.[74] As intended, the sanctions effectively precluded future American involvement in Sudan's budding oil industry. Yet, as discussed below, the medium- and long-term significance of this ban for Sudan was minimal, given the willingness of other foreign oil firms to invest.

Although international financial institutions did terminate their lending to Sudan in the early 1990s, U.S. sanctions cannot take credit for this development. The World Bank suspended disbursements to Sudan in April 1993, while the IMF imposed a "declaration of noncooperation" against Sudan in 1990 and three years later suspended its voting and related rights.[75] These moves were not precipitated by American pressure. Facing a country with a debt load nearly equal to 200 percent of its GDP, an ongoing civil war, a deteriorating agricultural sector, the constant need to import oil and foodstuffs, high inflation, and general economic mismanagement, the IMF declared Khartoum in default on its IMF loans in February 1986 when

Sudan was more than $200 million in arrears on its payments. It was this dire economic situation that the IMF and World Bank cited when freezing their relationships with Sudan in the early 1990s.[76]

Despite the small direct effects of sanctions on financial flows, in limited instances, U.S. and UN measures worked together to create a "magnifying effect"; without directly prohibiting non-U.S. companies from investing or involving themselves in Sudan, sanctions reinforced the independent concerns of markets and financial actors that any sort of economic partnership with Sudan was a high-risk endeavor.

Creditors did curtail or terminate their involvement in Sudan throughout the 1990s. Official aid and loans to Sudan dropped substantially; in the second half of the decade, apart from aid to the World Food Program, such flows were virtually nonexistent.[77] Private creditors, once actively involved in Sudan in the 1970s, showed little sign of re-engaging throughout most of the 1990s.[78]

In most cases, the additional deterrent provided by sanctions was not needed to keep foreign companies, banks, and other institutions out of Sudan. Factors apart from sanctions provide more than sufficient explanation for the steep declines in official flows and the virtual absence of private flows to Sudan during this time. Certainly, Sudan's support for Iraq during the Gulf war, and its subsequent backing for regional Islamist groups, was behind the decline in aid and finance from many Middle Eastern countries in the early to mid-1990s.[79] More important, Sudan's dismal economic performance and unstable economic policies convinced international lenders to steer clear of Sudan. Even in the absence of sanctions, multilateral and bilateral donors and private financial actors would have passed over Sudan for most of the decade. Sanctions and their influence on the confidence of markets and governments in Sudan reinforced these trends and decisions; however, given the dire situation in Sudan at the time, their influence probably had an extremely limited net impact on the final composition of external flows over this period.

Although this assessment holds true for most sectors of the Sudanese economy, the oil industry is an important exception. Given the large profits associated with this sector, most firms are willing and accustomed to working in high-risk environments. As discussed earlier, many foreign oil companies were not deterred by the economic or security environment in Sudan and made significant investments there. Although neither U.S. nor UN sanctions stopped investment in the oil sector, they did have some influence on the profile of companies doing business there. U.S. and UN sanctions

Figure 6-4. *Sudan's Exports, 1990, 1998, 2001*

### Sudan's Exports, by Country and Region, 1990[a]

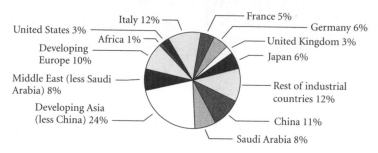

United States 3%
Italy 12%
France 5%
Germany 6%
Africa 1%
United Kingdom 3%
Developing Europe 10%
Japan 6%
Middle East (less Saudi Arabia) 8%
Rest of industrial countries 12%
Developing Asia (less China) 24%
China 11%
Saudi Arabia 8%

### Sudan's Exports, by Country and Region, 1998[b]

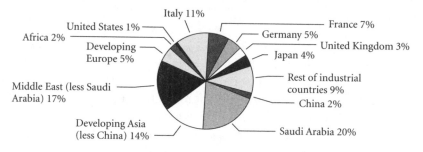

Italy 11%
United States 1%
France 7%
Africa 2%
Germany 5%
Developing Europe 5%
United Kingdom 3%
Japan 4%
Middle East (less Saudi Arabia) 17%
Rest of industrial countries 9%
China 2%
Developing Asia (less China) 14%
Saudi Arabia 20%

### Sudan's Exports, by Country and Region, 2001[c]

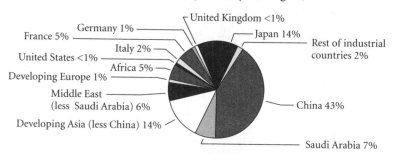

United Kingdom <1%
Germany 1%
Japan 14%
France 5%
Rest of industrial countries 2%
Italy 2%
United States <1%
Africa 5%
Developing Europe 1%
Middle East (less Saudi Arabia) 6%
China 43%
Developing Asia (less China) 14%
Saudi Arabia 7%

Source: International Monetary Fund, *Direction of Trade Statistics Yearbook, 1996*, and *Direction of Trade Statistics Quarterly*, December 1999 and June 2002.
a. U.S. and other country imports; total exports are $517.7 million, 1990 dollars.
b. U.S. and other country imports; total exports are $539 million, 1998 dollars.
c. U.S. and other country imports; total exports are $2.08 billion, 2001 dollars.

*Figure 6-5.  Sudan's Imports, 1990, 1998, 2001*

### Sudan's Imports, by Country and Region, 1990[a]

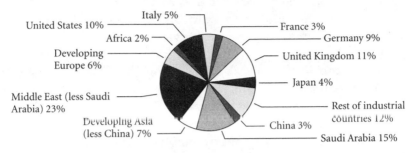

United States 10%
Italy 5%
France 3%
Germany 9%
Africa 2%
United Kingdom 11%
Developing Europe 6%
Japan 4%
Middle East (less Saudi Arabia) 23%
Rest of industrial countries 12%
Developing Asia (less China) 7%
China 3%
Saudi Arabia 15%

### Sudan's Imports, by Country and Region, 1998[b]

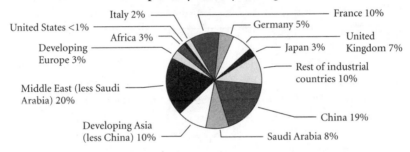

Italy 2%
France 10%
United States <1%
Germany 5%
Africa 3%
United Kingdom 7%
Japan 3%
Developing Europe 3%
Rest of industrial countries 10%
Middle East (less Saudi Arabia) 20%
China 19%
Developing Asia (less China) 10%
Saudi Arabia 8%

### Sudan's Imports, by Country and Region, 2001[c]

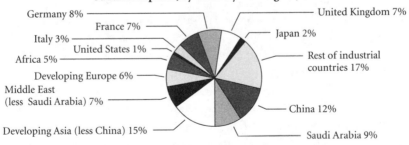

Germany 8%
United Kingdom 7%
France 7%
Japan 2%
Italy 3%
United States 1%
Rest of industrial countries 17%
Africa 5%
Developing Europe 6%
Middle East (less Saudi Arabia) 7%
China 12%
Developing Asia (less China) 15%
Saudi Arabia 9%

Source: IMF, *Direction of Trade Statistics Yearbook, 1996,* and *Direction of Trade Statistics Quarterly,* December 1999 and June 2002.
    a. U.S. and other country exports; total imports are $1.185 billion, 1990 dollars.
    b. U.S. and other country exports; total imports are $1.9917 billion, 1998 dollars.
    c. U.S. and other country exports; total imports are $1.7504 billion, 2000 dollars.

magnified the pre-existing disincentives to invest in Sudan, helping to keep larger oil companies away from Sudanese oil fields. The broad significance of this, however, should not be overestimated given Sudan's extremely limited capacity to absorb foreign investment in the 1990s and the large deterrents already in existence independent of sanctions. But if Sudan does not adequately address other deterrents to investment (be they security considerations or economic problems), U.S. sanctions—as a factor that pushes potential investors over the "tipping point" in their decision to stay away from Sudan—could have a greater impact as Sudan looks to expand its oil production to areas demanding expertise only provided by western firms. If the overall investment environment improves in Sudan, sanctions may wield little influence on the decisions of non-U.S. investors.

Although the direct and indirect effects of sanctions on financial flows to date have been small, some U.S. restrictions could wield even greater leverage over Sudan in the future. As Sudan continues to get its economic house in order and becomes more desirous of integrating itself into the global economy, U.S. sanctions could prove important in limiting economic options open to Sudan and in delaying (if not ultimately impeding) Sudan's full rehabilitation into the international economic arena. Although some governments and multilateral organizations have begun to extend small credits and project loans to Sudan, as of mid-2002 the country had not yet been able to secure any large-scale Paris-Club bilateral aid.[80] Sudan's difficulties in finding countries willing to reschedule its debt have been even more significant. Sudan, as one of the most heavily indebted countries in the world, has no serious prospects of ever fully repaying its debt. In order to secure large-scale finance from global creditors at any point in the future, it will need to be included in the Heavily Indebted Poor Countries (HIPC) initiatives from which it is currently excluded on political grounds. Moreover, if Sudan is to secure additional IMF lending further down the road, it will first need to find creditors willing to restructure its debt before the IMF will accept the country as a member in good standing. So far, the efforts of Sudan to find allies in these quests have been largely in vain.[81] The reluctance of international creditors to play these roles is not only a product of sanctions but other economic and political factors as well.[82] However, it is possible that—even in the face of the country's continued economic convalescence—U.S. sanctions and the diplomatic efforts they underpin will keep Sudan from finding sympathetic large-scale creditors. Further down the road, the United States could also limit economic options open to Sudan by blocking its accession to the World Trade Organization, something in which Khartoum has already indicated interest.

ECONOMIC MANAGEMENT. The imposition of sanctions—particularly UN ones—did in a very small way frustrate the prudent management of Sudan's economy. Speculation about the imposition of UN sanctions in 1996 added to the weakness of the Sudanese pound and contributed to its downward spiral that year.[83] Sanctions, however, were only one of many factors placing strain on the currency and therefore can claim only the smallest responsibility for the plunging pound and the economic chaos that resulted from it.[84] The ongoing war and the resulting massive economic imbalances were far more important factors leading to the serious devaluation of the pound in 1996. The stabilization of the Sudanese currency during the next several years—despite the imposition of additional sanctions—supports the conclusion that domestic economic factors (in this case, Sudanese adherence to IMF programs), rather than sanctions, had much greater influence on the currency.

### Political Impact

Sanctions affected Khartoum's political environment in several important ways. First, U.S. sanctions had a major influence on the development of the policy debate on Sudan in Washington. Unlike discussions surrounding policy toward other oil-producing countries under sanctions, those concerning U.S. policy toward Sudan have been virtually devoid of forceful advocates of engagement or normalization of relations.[85] This dynamic is in large part due to the egregious behavior of the government in the civil war. But it also reflects how sanctions stunted the development of actors on the other side of the debate. Because sanctions were imposed before any U.S. oil company became seriously involved in Sudan's petroleum sector, commercial voices have been relatively silent on U.S. policy toward Sudan. This quiet is in contrast to the more vocal positions taken by some oil companies concerning U.S. relations with Iran, Libya, or even Iraq—countries with which American oil companies were deeply involved before the onset of sanctions. Moreover, the sanctions have effectively frustrated efforts of the Sudanese government to hire lobbyists who might have been able not only to better explain the vagaries of the American political system to Khartoum, but also to help it influence the policy debate on Capitol Hill, even if only in a small way.

In addition, U.S. and UN sanctions, while not entirely responsible for Khartoum's international isolation over the 1990s, formalized it. The tepid nature of the UN sanctions, and the international perception that U.S. sanctions were domestically motivated, tempered the isolating effects of the sanctions, but did not eliminate them. Although cosmetic reforms and a few authentic changes in the regime's behavior helped Khartoum's international rehabilitation, sanctions continued to hamper Sudan's full acceptance into the international community. Perhaps most important, UN sanctions gave the United States an effective tool to keep Sudan from securing a seat on the UN Security Council in October 2000. Arguing that no country subject to UN sanctions should sit on the council, the United States delivered a serious blow to Sudan's efforts to reintegrate itself into the international community. Sanctions also proved an important—although not the only—impediment to Sudan's failed efforts to join the World Trade Organization, secure observer status with the International Francophony Organization (OIF), and reactivate its membership with the Cotonou Agreement, at least until 2002.[86]

Finally, sanctions had some influence on the domestic environment in which the Sudanese regime operated. Sanctions augmented the paranoia of the regime by reinforcing its belief that the United States firmly backed the SPLA. In doing so, sanctions inadvertently allowed the regime to justify repressive measures. Nevertheless, although Khartoum was mildly successful in translating sanctions into pockets of support among international actors generally opposed to the United States, it was not able to parlay sanctions into a domestic propaganda point. Neither UN nor U.S. sanctions triggered the "rally around the flag" effect seen in many other countries subject to such measures. The failure of sanctions to elicit this response among the population of Sudan can be explained by the overall unpopularity and lack of legitimacy of the regime in Khartoum, as well as the exceedingly small economic impact of the measures. If the sanctions benefited any political grouping in Khartoum, it was the opposition, who saw sanctions as vindication of their struggle.[87]

### Goals Achieved

Assessing how well sanctions on Sudan achieved their goals requires evaluating whether a variety of U.S. and UN objectives were met, be they implicit or explicit, primary or secondary. It also demands gauging the role of sanctions in bringing about these changes. One cannot automatically assume the success of sanctions simply because it is possible to point to positive developments; the influence of sanctions must be untangled from that of other factors to the best extent possible.

CONTAINING OR WEAKENING THE REGIME. Regime change was never an explicit goal behind the U.S. sanctions, although during the

Clinton administration many American actors in Congress and the executive branch did hope that sanctions would contribute to the downfall of the government in Khartoum. Not only did sanctions not achieve this implicit goal, but they did not appear to significantly weaken the regime by creating serious domestic strife. Neither did they challenge the regime by preventing it from carrying out major portions of its agenda.[88]

U.S. sanctions—mostly because of their unilateral nature—also did little to enforce the containment of the regime in Khartoum at any level. As described earlier, although precluding U.S. economic involvement in Sudan, sanctions did not inflict significant economic costs on the country. U.S. sanctions also cannot truly take credit for the military containment of Sudan. Figure 6-6 shows how prohibitions on military sales and assistance to Sudan terminated considerable military flows.[89] However, even in the absence of sanctions, the military relationship between Washington and Khartoum would have tapered off in the early 1990s. The civil war, which intensified after the NIF government came to power, would have dampened American enthusiasm for military sales to and contacts with Sudan. The end of the cold war and Haile Menguistu's fall from power removed the urgent need to indirectly counter Soviet influence through military support for Sudan. Perhaps most important, the rise of a fundamentalist, Islamist regime hostile to the United States, coupled with Khartoum's support for Saddam Hussein during the invasion of Kuwait, would have cemented the end of the U.S.-Sudanese military relationship.

The ability of sanctions to contain or weaken the regime militarily was overwhelmed by domestic and international developments that made it easier for Khartoum to secure weaponry over the period that sanctions were in place. The resources the government of Sudan obtained from oil exports were a huge boon to Khartoum's war efforts. According to the IMF figures provided by the government of Sudan, Khartoum anticipated its defense expenditures would rise by 50 percent between 1999 and 2001, the year when Sudan began to run a trade surplus because of its oil exports.[90] Newly flush with foreign exchange, Khartoum was well poised to benefit from the excess of inexpensive, highly lethal weapons easily available for purchase in the wake of the cold war. Broad U.S. sanctions may have even inadvertently helped Khartoum *increase* its access to weaponry. As a clear manifestation of American animosity toward Sudan, sanctions strengthened Khartoum's appeals for assistance from countries and private Islamic sources opposed to the United States. Although unclassified data on official arms sales to Sudan in the 1990s do not reveal procurement surges from any particular source,[91]

**Figure 6-6.** *Total U.S. Military Sales and Assistance to Sudan, 1950–2000*

Millions of U.S. dollars

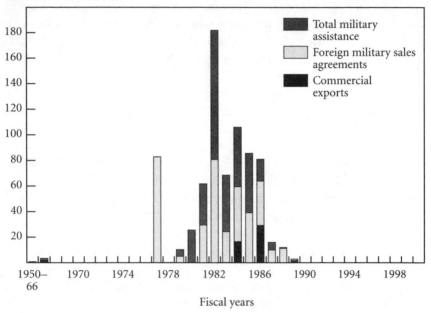

Fiscal years

Source: Defense Security and Cooperation Agency, *Facts Book,* various years.
Note: The total military assistance category consists of Foreign Military Finance Program, Military Assistance Program, MAP Merger Funds, and IMET.

reports of military cooperation between Khartoum and Iran, Libya, Russia, and even Iraq were common.[92]

MODERATING THE BEHAVIOR OF THE REGIME.   U.S. and UN officials stressed that sanctions were intended to change the behavior of the regime in Khartoum. UN measures focused narrowly on ending Khartoum's support for terrorism; comprehensive U.S. restrictions were geared toward addressing a much broader slate of behaviors. As laid out in the 1997 executive order and reiterated in a number of statements by Clinton administration officials, U.S. sanctions sought to modify the behavior of the Sudanese regime concerning its support for terrorism, efforts to destabilize neighboring countries, repression of political and human rights, and prosecution of Sudan's civil war.[93]

Over the second half of the 1990s and beyond, Sudan appreciably scaled back its support for terrorism. Once an active pivot of international terrorism, Sudan took measures—including the extradition of Carlos the Jackal to France, the expulsion of Osama bin Laden, the closure of the Popular Arab and Islamic Conference forum, and the signing of all international conventions for combating terrorism—suggesting its seriousness about addressing terrorism even before the events of September 11.[94] In the wake of the attacks on the World Trade Center and the Pentagon, Sudan significantly increased its cooperation with the United States on counterterrorism issues. Yet, although it acknowledged Sudan's progress as of 2002, the U.S. government still sought additional steps from Sudan to address more wide-ranging terrorism-related concerns.[95] Before the United States will consider removing Sudan from its terrorism list, Sudan must expel terrorist groups that continue to use Sudan as a safe haven and as a base for supporting other organizations and operations outside Sudan.[96] Accelerated discussions between Washington and Khartoum would provide the government of Sudan with an opportunity to tackle these issues and shed its classification as a state sponsor of terrorism.[97]

Khartoum's decision to distance itself from terrorism (partially if not completely) is the result of a complex web of factors, which cumulatively led the regime to conclude that active support for terrorism was no longer in its interest. Both changes in the Sudanese domestic arena and sanctions deserve much of the credit for moving Sudan down this road. In the early 1990s, when the NIF was solidifying its power and seeking to create a fundamentalist state, the Sudanese regime saw itself as the vanguard of an Islamic revolution. In this environment, support for and links to Islamic militants were a key component of its ideology. U.S. disapproval was most likely immaterial. However, as the regime consolidated power, lost the financial backing of many Arab states that once supported it, and began to look to the future development of the country, its support for terrorism and the international exclusion it resulted in became more of a hindrance to Khartoum's ambitions. UN and U.S. sanctions, which formalized Sudan's status as an international pariah, remained an obstacle to Sudan's eventual integration into the world economy. Besides the "blacklisting" signified by sanctions, Sudan came under frequent attack—verbally and even literally—by its neighbors for its support for Islamist groups within their own borders.

Two factors were critical in explaining why the pressure Khartoum felt from sanctions and other sources successfully translated into tangible progress on the terrorism front. First, domestic changes within Sudan, most notably the marginalization of al-Turabi and his radical Islamist leanings, created space for al-Bashir's government to engage with the Americans on the issue of terrorism and scale back its support for it on certain fronts. Second, the use of other tools helped transform the pressure of sanctions into progress. Cooperation on matters of terrorism accelerated at the very end of the 1990s when the United States supplemented its sanctions with a "counterterrorism dialogue" between Washington and Khartoum. This limited engagement between the two countries provided a formal mechanism for the United States to communicate to Sudan the specific steps it needed to take to be removed from the terrorism list and for Sudan to present evidence of the progress that it was making in this direction. Moreover, although the U.S. sanctions regime was too rigid to allow American negotiators to encourage progress by offering the gradual lifting of sanctions, they were able to pledge that the United States would allow the lifting of UN sanctions in return for Sudan's increased cooperation.

A decline in Sudan's meddling outside its borders, most evident by Sudan's improved relations with its neighbors, was related to Khartoum's declining support for terrorism. The shift to more responsible international conduct is most dramatic with Egypt, the country that led the charge to impose UN sanctions on Sudan after the 1995 assassination attempt on President Mubarak. The amelioration of ties between Khartoum and Cairo has been most marked since al-Turabi—believed to be an ardent supporter of Egyptian Islamic groups—was ousted from his position as speaker of parliament. In response to Khartoum's scaled-back support for Egyptian fundamentalist groups, Egypt accelerated its dealings with Sudan, seeking a posture that helps preserve the unity of Sudan while discouraging the more fundamentalist tendencies of the regime. In 2000, Egypt re-established diplomatic relations with Sudan and deepened joint efforts with Libya to find a settlement to the conflict in Sudan.

Most of Sudan's relationships with its southern and eastern neighbors also improved around the turn of the millennium. Diminished Sudanese support for rebel groups such as the Eritrean Islamic Jihad helped pave the way for the reestablishment of diplomatic relations between Sudan and Eritrea in January 2000. Similarly, Sudan's relationship with Ethiopia improved in the late 1990s, leading to the resumption of flights between the two countries and the expansion of contacts between governments. In contrast, Sudan's relationship with Uganda has been slower to mend, due to alleged

Sudanese support for the Lord's Resistance Army in northern Uganda and supposed Ugandan aid to the SPLA in southern Sudan. [98]

The changing nature of Sudan's relations with its neighbors—as well as with Middle Eastern countries further afield such as Kuwait and Saudi Arabia—is not directly attributable to sanctions. Sudan's relative rapprochement with the countries on its borders was made possible by a number of factors, including the gradual moderation of the regime domestically and its move to distance itself from active support for terrorism. As discussed, sanctions did facilitate some of these gains, but the military pressure placed on the government of Sudan by the southern insurgents was of equal if not greater importance in altering Khartoum's behavior because it forced the government to seek ways of minimizing external assistance provided by neighboring states to the SPLA. Khartoum's diminished support for violent Islamic groups seeking to overthrow neighboring regimes, as well as its pursuit of better relationships with governments in the region, is best seen in this light, rather than as a direct outgrowth of economic pressure from the United States.

In contrast to some notable improvements in Khartoum's external behavior, the internal behavior of the regime has been generally poor over the period sanctions have been in place. Mixed trends are evident in the sphere of political liberalization. During the final years of the 1990s, the government of Sudan took some steps intended to signal a more liberal political atmosphere in the country. A new constitution was introduced in 1998 that, although confirming sharia as the basis for all legislation, allowed the formation of political organizations after a decade-long ban on their activity and promised a referendum on southern self-determination. [99]

These steps appear largely cosmetic in nature and seem, in themselves, to be of limited significance beyond allowing al-Bashir to claim a measure of domestic and international legitimacy. In practice, the freedom of political "associations" remains very limited. The regime's commitment to democratic elections is almost entirely rhetorical, as demonstrated by the heavy rigging that occurred during the December 2000 presidential and parliamentary elections and President al-Bashir's moves in 2002 to grant himself extraordinary powers even in the absence of a state of emergency.

Khartoum's earlier successes in luring an important opposition party out of the NDA and the return of key leaders from exile at first seemed to indicate a gradual authentic political mellowing of the regime. [100] Yet the refusal of these figures to join the government and their opposition to al-Bashir's "refoms" suggest that Khartoum's negotiations with the northern opposition are part of the regime's efforts to weaken the opposition by fragmenting it. They are, however, also motivated by Khartoum's desire to end its international isolation, of which sanctions are an element. Until these reforms and the adoption of rhetoric acceptable to the international community translate into political changes with real substance, it would be premature to claim these developments as any sort of victory for sanctions. From the time sanctions were imposed, at least until 2001, little or no progress was evident in Sudan's human rights practices or in Khartoum's conduct of the war.[101]

Khartoum's human rights record has been dismal over the period sanctions have been in place. Reports of extrajudicial killings, unlawful and arbitrary detainment, and harassment of opposition figures by government security forces were fairly common as were limitations on the right of individuals to worship freely.[102] Government security forces and government-sponsored militias were also reported to be heavily involved in abducting women and children into conditions of slavery.[103]

In the conduct of the war Khartoum has also acted grimly, its conduct worsening in the late 1990s and early 2000s, as government forces employed increasingly aggressive and deadly tactics to exploit the country's oil reserves. Widespread reports suggest that the government cleared swaths of oil-rich areas in the central and southern parts of the country through violence and intimidation.[104] The government's conduct of the war violated other international protocols, as government forces targeted noncombatants on the ground and bombed civilian centers such as churches, hospitals, and schools from the air.[105] Moreover, the government used its power to approve Operation Lifeline Sudan flights to deny humanitarian relief operations access to areas where some of the greatest suffering occurred.[106]

It would be confusing correlation with causality to assume that the sanctions-dominated approach of the United States was largely responsible for the positive—if still tentative and incomplete—steps taken by the regime toward peace in 2002. For the bulk of the period during which sanctions were in place, there was virtually no progress made in the direction of resolving the conflict. The IGAD continued to serve as an occasional forum for the government and the southern rebels to conduct peace negotiations, although its ability to play a constructive role was frequently hampered by the stresses and strains in the relationships between its members (Djibouti, Eritrea, Ethiopia, Kenya, Somalia and Uganda), Khartoum, and the southern forces. Neither Khartoum nor the SPLM had approached the talks with a deep commitment to resolving the conflict.[107] The seriousness with which each side regarded the negotiations largely depended on its military position on the battlefield. Rather than pushing the conflict to "ripeness," the ongoing stalemate between the two sides led each to believe that it could secure victory through military measures. The slow progress of IGAD, and its exclusion of key players within and without Sudan, inspired the launch of another peace initiative, this one orchestrated by Egypt and Libya and encompassing the northern opposition in Sudan as well as the southern groups. As discussed later in this chapter, it was only when the nature of U.S. policy shifted from one that was sanctions dominated to one characterized by both pressure and engagement that progress was made toward calming the civil war.

### Costs Borne

HUMANITARIAN COSTS. Neither U.S. nor UN sanctions resulted in notable humanitarian costs. This is not to deny that at various times, the situation in parts of the south has resembled a "humanitarian catastrophe" after nineteen years of civil war, multiple famines, recurrent drought, and wide-scale displacement.[108] This humanitarian situation in the south, as dire as it has been and continues to be in some places, has no relation to the impact of sanctions.[109] Neither U.S. nor UN sanctions precluded the United States (or other countries) from making substantial contributions to the extensive humanitarian relief efforts conducted in southern Sudan. The United States has been by far the largest donor to these humanitarian operations, contributing almost $600 million in humanitarian assistance between 1998 and 2001.[110]

Humanitarian conditions in the north are subject to different factors. The opening of a northeastern front to the war in 1996 created conflict-related humanitarian problems, while a drought displaced nearly 200,000 from the north in 2001. These conditions helped spur a 2001 decision by the U.S. government to begin providing humanitarian aid to the north, in a departure from past U.S. policy that almost exclusively focused on aid to the south and the victims of the war.[111] Overall, the population in the north suffers less from the direct ravages of war than it does from underdeveloped, or nonexistent, government services in health and education.[112] Khartoum has shifted resources away from public services to its military quests, contributing to a decline in living standards throughout the past decade.[113] Government efforts to comply with IMF prescriptions had a mixed impact on the standard of living; privatization measures and the removal of subsidies exacerbated downward trends, although the end of rampant inflation had the benefit of arresting the rapid erosion of salaries.

As in the south, sanctions cannot be blamed for poor conditions in the north. To the extent that UN sanctions were responsible for further weakening the already imperiled currency in 1996, it could be argued that sanctions aggravated declining living standards by contributing to inflation and the rising cost of living. However, as discussed, the contribution of sanctions to the downward spiral of the Sudanese pound was minor in comparison to greater and more direct pulls on its value. Had sanctions interfered with the flow of remittances to Sudan, their effect on the population at large would have been greater given Sudan's dependence on these external flows. Yet most remittances to Sudan stem from expatriate workers in the Middle East and did not experience any substantial interruption owing to UN or U.S. sanctions.[114]

Interestingly, the Sudanese government strongly argued against the implementation of the second round of UN sanctions on the grounds that it would adversely affect the humanitarian situation in the country.[115] Once the United Nations passed UN resolution 1070, it delayed its implementation to allow for the investigation of the potential humanitarian consequences of aviation sanctions. The UN Department of Humanitarian Affairs presented its findings to the UN Security Council in February 1997. Its report dismissed concerns that the aviation ban would affect the humanitarian operation in the south on the grounds that most food aid arrived by land or by planes registered outside of Sudan. Yet, it argued that the air embargo could harm food production, medical evacuations, and the distribution of medications.[116] Although this report became the formal rationale for why no additional measures were put in place, in reality, the reluctance of some of the members of the Security Council to impose additional, open-ended sanctions in light of the UN experience in Iraq was more influential in this decision.

COSTS TO THE UNITED STATES. Although sanctions on Sudan inflicted some costs on the United States, these costs have overall been extremely small. Given the very modest economic links between the United States and Sudan at the time sanctions were imposed, the economic costs borne by U.S. commercial interests as a whole have been minor. In terms of lost trade, the vast majority of the additional $400 million in exports U.S. companies would have sold to Sudan in 1997–2001 in the absence of sanctions are likely to have gone to other export markets, bringing total losses to

**Figure 6-7.** *Total Imports of Gum Arabic into the United States,*
*1991–2000*

Metric tons

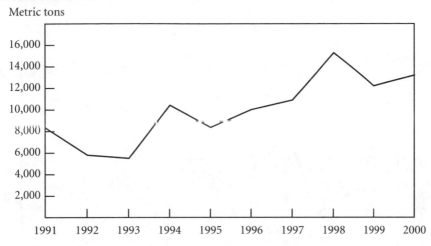

Sources: For 1991–94, "Exudate Gums: Gum Arabic, Gum Talha and Other Gums," Food and Agriculture Organization, www.fao.org/docrep/v9236/V9236e05.htm (April 23, 2001); for 1995, "Imports Commodity Report," U.S. Customs Service, http://govinfo.kerr.orst.edu (May 10, 2001); for 1996–2000, "Report IM 145," U.S. Department of Commerce, Bureau of the Census, Foreign Trade Division.

only a fraction of that total (table 6A-2 in the appendix to this chapter).[117] Lifting the ban on the sale of food and medicine to Sudan and other countries on the terrorism list in 1998 further eased the costs borne by U.S. farmers, who had exported $14 million of agricultural goods to Sudan in 1996.[118] As discussed earlier, procedures allowing for the continued purchase of gum arabic mitigated the highly concentrated costs that a full ban on Sudanese imports would have entailed for a few U.S. businesses. As shown in figures 6-7 and 6-8, U.S. importers of gum arabic enjoyed an uninterrupted supply over the period in question, either from Sudan or alternative producers. Other U.S. imports once secured from Sudan—mostly sesame products—were easily replaced with purchases from other suppliers.

Finally, sanctions on American investment in Sudan imposed hardly any direct costs on U.S. firms, although they did involve more notable indirect ones. Few U.S. firms were forced to terminate lucrative investments within

**Figure 6-8.** *Gum Arabic Exports to the United States, by Source, 1991–2000*

Metric tons

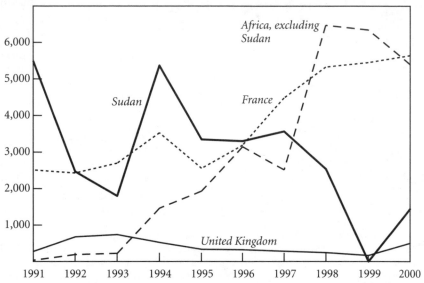

Sources: For 1991–94, "Exudate Gums: Gum Arabic, Gum Talha and Other Gums," Food and Agriculture Organization, www.fao.org/docrep/v9236/V9236e05.htm (April 23, 2001); for 1995, "Imports Commodity Report," U.S. Customs Service, http://govinfo.kerr.orst.edu (May 10, 2001); for 1996–2000, "Report IM 145," U.S. Department of Commerce, Bureau of the Census, Foreign Trade Division.

Sudan once sanctions were imposed. Yet their mandatory exclusion from Sudan did present opportunity costs to companies that might have otherwise invested in Sudan. Discussions between General Motors and U.S. telecommunications companies before the onset of sanctions—as well as statements from Sudanese government officials—suggest that Sudan would have been amenable to U.S. private investment.[119] In all reality, these opportunity costs are likely to have been fairly small outside the oil industry, where foreign firms not constrained by U.S. sanctions have only just become interested in greater involvement. Lost opportunities to invest in Sudan's oil industry will only be of real consequence once the conflict is resolved and Sudan's projections of ample reserves prove true.[120] The difficulties faced by

Talisman from its own shareholders reveal the many extra costs of being involved in Sudan's oil industry.[121]

The United States has borne few political costs for the imposition and maintenance of sanctions on Sudan. The positive developments in the civil war in 2002—reflecting to a large extent increased U.S. interest and involvement—seem to demonstrate that the hard-line policy of the United States did not greatly jeopardize its ability to play the role of peace broker, at least in the initial phases of the peace effort. Yet, the perception that Sudan was the innocent victim of U.S. aggression was instrumental in garnering Khartoum's support from radical states. But this view was much more the result of other elements of U.S. policy toward Sudan, including U.S. humanitarian aid for the opposition, nonlethal military support to neighboring states, and the 1998 military strikes against the Al-Shifa factory. Certainly, Al-Shifa, much more so than the imposition of U.S. sanctions, undermined the credibility of U.S. policy in the region and hindered the ability of the Clinton administration to take the lead in addressing problems in Sudan.

Sanctions against Sudan have had tremendous popular domestic political value. With virtually no constituency to oppose them except a small pocket of American firms importing gum arabic, a vote for sanctions against Sudan has been an undisputed political winner. Congressional resolutions calling for more sanctions on—and a tougher approach to—the regime in Khartoum sailed through the Senate and the House of Representatives.[122] Particularly as domestic constituencies embraced the issue of Sudan and raised public awareness of the civil war and human rights situation, members of Congress and the executive branch saw the domestic political benefits of a policy that was tough on Sudan. Only in the face of tangible progress made at Machakos has Congress been willing, at least temporarily, to cease pushing for a more punitive approach toward Khartoum.

## Explaining the Record of Sanctions on Sudan

The effectiveness and the utility of sanctions on Sudan were very modest. Although sanctions might prove to exert more economic influence on Sudan if the country continues its program of economic reform and tries to gain greater access to the global economy, they had an extremely small impact on Sudan in the 1990s and early 2000s; this limited impact seriously undercut efforts to weaken the regime or keep economic or military resources away from it. The ability of sanctions to keep Khartoum on the margins of political respectability and to influence Khartoum to change certain elements of its behavior was somewhat better. Sanctions—in conjunction with other elements—were one of several factors explaining some of the real, if incomplete, improvements in the external behavior of the regime, especially concerning its support for terrorism and efforts to destabilize Sudan's neighbors. For most of the period in question, sanctions proved unable to sway Khartoum in any noticeable way to change its internal behavior concerning human rights and the conduct of the war; only when sanctions were combined with other tools of engagement did they become part of a successful equation to move Khartoum in a promising direction regarding the war. The overall judgment that sanctions on Sudan had modest utility is based as least as much on their low costs as on their slim record of achieving their goals; although sanctions achieved few of their goals, their poor performance was somewhat diminished by the minimal costs borne in employing them.

### Accounting for the Achievements and Disappointments of Sanctions

Sanctions fell short of their potential in Sudan because they—and the strategies that they supposedly underpinned—were poorly coordinated and poorly formulated to suit the goals at hand. The failure of sanctions to contain or weaken the government in power, for instance, is largely the result of the structure of the sanctions regime. The sanctions on Sudan that were multilateral were merely diplomatic and not enforced, while the sanctions that were robust and executed were unilateral. As a result, the economic impact of sanctions was minuscule; the political impact, while more significant than the economic, was immensely watered down. In the end, there was little hope of keeping significant economic or military resources away from the regime with these tools as they were employed.

The unilateral nature of economic measures against Sudan is only the starting point of a critical evaluation of sanctions. In explaining why multilateral economic sanctions were not put into place, one might turn to cultural differences between the United States and its European and Asian allies who tend to prefer dialogue to coercion. Or one could take note of the oil reserves to be developed in Sudan and deduce that the lure of profit and the imperative of countries such as China to feed their growing energy needs virtually ensured that multilateral sanctions against Sudan were a nonstarter.

Although these factors certainly played into the failure to secure multilateral economic measures against Sudan, U.S. sanctions also did not serve as a sound basis for achieving multilateral cooperation against Sudan. First, in the eyes of many foreign countries, sanctions did not claim the credibility and moral legitimacy that U.S. policymakers had hoped would underpin their diplomatic efforts. These qualities were undercut by the perception abroad that sanctions against Sudan were domestically driven, imposed or urged on the executive branch by a Congress catering to influential domestic interest groups such as the Christian right.[123] In these circumstances, many saw long-standing U.S. resistance to lifting UN sanctions on Sudan—even after Egypt declared its willingness to see them lapse—as demonstrative of the power of these lobbies in Washington.[124] Efforts to shield American businesses from the costs of U.S. sanctions further damaged their credibility and morality. The effective exemption of gum arabic imports from the sanctions struck foreigners as particularly hypocritical, although some diplomats also point to the 1998 decision to let U.S. farmers sell produce to Sudan as another instance in which the United States was not willing bear the economic consequences of taking the moral high ground.[125]

Finally, the ability of U.S. sanctions to serve as a solid foundation for efforts to secure multilateral measures against Sudan was undercut by the use of other instruments by the United States in its overall Sudan policy. To some foreign countries, U.S. support for the SPLA robbed U.S. sanctions of a potentially legitimate role in bringing about an end to the war in Sudan. Despite U.S. protests, many countries—even U.S. allies—believed that the United States provided military support to the opposition.[126] Even more damaging to the quest to use unilateral sanctions as a springboard to multilateral ones was the bombing of Al-Shifa and the controversies that followed it. Many saw Al-Shifa as "totally knocking the moral argument out of U.S. policy toward Sudan," and thereby extinguishing what little prospect there had been for getting multilateral cooperation to pressure Sudan.[127]

Putting aside the issue of multilateralism, there is still ample ground to criticize the effectiveness of U.S. sanctions in 1997–2001. Although one reasonably expects multilateral sanctions to be superior to unilateral ones, it does not necessarily follow that unilateral ones must always do poorly in achieving their objectives. There are grounds for questioning whether U.S. sanctions—even given their unilateral nature—might have been expected to deliver more. Assuming the answer is yes, why did unilateral sanctions fall so short of many of their goals?

The failure to incorporate U.S. sanctions on Sudan into a larger, coherent foreign policy strategy for most of the period during which sanctions were in place impaired the effectiveness of these tools. Although a number of other foreign policy tools did accompany the use of sanctions, these instruments lacked coordination in pursuit of an agreed-upon goal. As a result, sanctions became a tool, but not one serving any particular objective.

If the desired goal really had been regime change in Khartoum, sanctions did not form the basis of an effective strategy toward this end. Had the United States been serious about overthrowing the NIF government, it should have not relied on sanctions as the basis of that policy. Given their weak economic and political impact and the high stakes involved, sanctions—to be an effective part of a regime change strategy—should have been coupled with robust support for the opposition. Despite the forceful rhetoric and occasional military gestures in that direction, the United States chose not to provide the insurgents with the support that could have enabled them to win the war or topple the regime. As a result, it is not surprising that sanctions were of little use in ushering in a new government in Khartoum.

Despite being ostensibly geared toward moderating the regime in Khartoum, the overall U.S. policy toward Sudan also did not support sanctions as a tool of behavior change during the Clinton administration. The harsh rhetoric of administration officials and members of Congress, the use of military force in 1998, the provision of military support to east African countries hostile to Sudan in 1997, and the vocal moral support given to the southern forces all created the distinct impression—on the part of Khartoum and others—that the real goal of U.S. policy was to bring down the NIF regime. Although inaccurate, the widespread belief that the United States provided the SPLA with extensive military assistance reinforced this outlook. Convinced that the United States sought the downfall of the NIF government, Khartoum had little to no incentive to comply with lesser demands made of it to change its behavior.

Insufficient formal channels of dialogue between Khartoum and the United States for most of the time that sanctions were in place also thwarted the ability of sanctions to modify the behavior of the regime during this period. Without a formalized mechanism for articulating expectations and presenting progress, sanctions were seen as monolithic, rather than an element in a bargaining process urging Khartoum down a path of better behavior. Not coincidentally, where these formal dialogues existed—for counterterrorism purposes—sanctions had the most impact. Although less formal avenues were present, the lack of a functioning U.S. embassy in Khartoum from 1996 to 2001 hindered communication that would have been an essential part of any bargaining procedure involving sanctions. Equally important, the dearth of diplomatic presence hampered the ability of the United States to execute such a strategy, by hindering the gathering of U.S. intelligence necessary to craft a bargaining process and to verify gradual changes in behavior.

The importance of sanctions being properly supplemented by other tools to form a larger foreign policy strategy geared toward behavior change is forcefully underscored by the tentative successes secured in 2002 and beyond. A new U.S. approach was instrumental in securing the Machakos Protocol and producing rough if imperfect adherence to the four confidence-building measures laid out by Senator Danforth. Diplomatic engagement —through Danforth's mission and the U.S. observer role at the IGAD talks— was an important element in the modified U.S. strategy. But diplomacy itself did not make a more effective policy. Rather, the introduction of serious diplomatic initiatives infused the other tools of U.S. foreign policy with new influence. In particular, the introduction of dialogue greatly enhanced the leverage of sanctions. Of even greater importance was the new perception created by the U.S. response to heightened Sudanese counterterrorism cooperation after September 11, 2001; U.S. acquiescence to the lifting of UN sanctions, as well as the quelling of the capital market sanctions in the Sudan Peace Act, suggested that the United States was willing to recognize improved behavior by recalibrating its policies to suit new realities. In this context, U.S. sanctions served as an appropriate complement to dialogue, their lifting being an incentive for further progress and their imposition a disincentive for backtracking. The implicit threat of military force after September 11 also almost certainly encouraged the government of Sudan to engage constructively both with Danforth and IGAD.

## Comparing the Utility of Sanctions to Alternatives

As stressed throughout this book, concluding that a sanctions-led strategy was largely ineffective or lacked utility is only of interest to policymakers if there were no alternative approaches that would have been more successful. Only if other strategies existed that would have achieved better results at reasonable costs can policymakers be faulted for their poor choices. Even without the detailed construction of alternative scenarios, it is worth considering whether three different sorts of strategies might have been more effective in achieving the behavior changes that were supposedly the focus of U.S. policy toward Sudan over the late 1990s.

First, it is not clear that a military-led strategy would have better achieved U.S. objectives at an acceptable cost. A military approach that involved direct U.S. intervention could easily be imagined to attain U.S. goals—conceivably by forcing regime change—but would have been costly in economic terms and domestic political ones, not to mention the strife that might have resulted in Sudan had the United States pursued such a policy. Particularly in the wake of U.S. intervention in Somalia, these costs would have been viewed as unacceptable to policymakers and the American public, notwithstanding the high possibility of achieving the desired results.

Robust military support for the opposition, while more politically feasible, was also uncertain to wield better results at acceptable costs. This strategy may have ended the civil war by leading to a victory for the southern insurgents. However, especially if this victory translated into a messy separation for the south, this outcome may not have stopped the bloodshed or violence in Sudan. Unquestionably, this support—and the possible secession of the south—would have created serious tensions with Egypt that could have had repercussions for U.S. interests elsewhere, particularly in the Middle East peace process. Moreover, Khartoum's support for international terrorism could have increased, if the government of Sudan viewed terrorism as a legitimate tool to counter U.S. influence in Sudan. An end to the civil war might also have continued to be elusive, even despite forceful American support for the opposition. The seriously fragmented ranks of the south could have prevented U.S. support from translating into effective military prowess, yet bolstered the confidence of the southern forces so much that it undermined their incentive to make concessions when negotiating for peace. Although other military-led scenarios are conceivable given the complex situation, it is highly questionable whether a military-led strategy would have been more effective than a sanctions-dominated approach.

Second, the United States might have chosen to "do nothing" or adopt a "business-as-usual" approach. Some argue that commercial interaction and continued dialogue would have afforded more influence over Khartoum. Although it is difficult to assess the validity of this assertion over the long term, such a policy would be difficult to sustain toward a country where as many as 2 million people have died since 1983 because of war or related hardship.[128] The lack of real progress secured by the European Union in its dialogue with Khartoum, as well as Talisman's inability to influence the behavior of the government in the oil-rich areas in the south, suggests that engagement with no sticks would not convince Khartoum to undertake steps it believes are against its interests. Moreover, while there would be some economic benefits to such an approach, they would in all likelihood be modest and would be outweighed by the significant political costs that a strategy of unconditional engagement would have generated.

Finally, rather than a sanctions-dominated approach, the United States could have attempted a strategy of conditional engagement. This would have entailed crafting a credible road map—one that did not simply demand Khartoum's capitulation on all issues but which detailed the concerns of both sides and how the relationship had to progress in order for tangible improvements to be realized, including the lifting of sanctions. Given the power struggle taking place between al-Turabi and al-Bashir, effective conditional engagement with Khartoum in the late 1990s may have been difficult or even impossible if the fractured leadership prevented the regime from delivering on promised commitments. However, Khartoum might have changed more elements of its behavior than it did under the sanctions-led strategy if it had been offered a clearly delineated path to international rehabilitation (through the eventual—if distant—normalization of relations with the United States), incentives in the form of the lifting of sanctions to move along that path, and a complement of other appropriate tools. As just considered, the events of 2002 support this hypothesis. While a conditional engagement approach would have required more diplomatic resources, its costs would not have differed substantially from the sanctions-dominated approach actually pursued. As progress was made and sanctions were gradually lifted, minor costs currently borne today would be eliminated. This approach would have one large additional benefit; if it failed, the flexibility that the United States had demonstrated in its conditional engagement with Khartoum would help the United States build support for a more punitive approach.

## Looking Ahead

In many respects, the events of September 11 increased the chances of establishing a more constructive relationship between Khartoum and Washington. In the span of just a few weeks after the attacks in America, bilateral relations advanced substantially as Sudan responded to U.S. calls for greater cooperation on the issue of terrorism. Khartoum's alacrity in assisting the United States in the initial months was fueled in part by the fear of U.S. military strikes against those whose cooperation was not forth-coming, as well as by the realization that the U.S. campaign on terrorism provided an unforeseen opportunity to establish better relations with America.

Robust cooperation on counterterrorism issues will be an important part of the U.S.-Sudanese relationship for the foreseeable future. Maintaining this cooperation—which began, if with less vigor, before the events of September 11—will be a priority of the Bush administration and, conceivably, subsequent administrations. The United States can best ensure ongoing Sudanese assistance if it makes clear to Sudan that continued cooperation will lead to better U.S relations in general, and Sudan's eventual removal from the U.S. terrorism list more specifically. Ideally, the terrorism list would be reformed to give policymakers added flexibility in cementing the cooperation of states that are interested in definitively moving away from their past support of terrorism; being able to use the list as a tool in this way would demand the ability to incrementally suspend sanctions associated with the terrorist designation. In the absence of such changes, verbal pledges and gestures to Sudan outside the U.S. sanctions regime could suffice. Already, the removal of UN sanctions was one such signal. U.S. policymak-ers should resist pressures to link the removal of Khartoum's place on the terrorism list to the internal behavior of the regime, as such a linkage would seriously undermine the incentive Khartoum has to engage with the United States on issues of terrorism and undercut the credibility of sanctions more generally.[129] Sudan's removal from this list will not immediately translate into economic benefit for Khartoum, given the complex web of sanctions currently in place against the country, but it would lift the opprobrium asso-ciated with being designated a state sponsor of terrorism.[130] A continued and accelerated U.S.-Sudanese counterterrorism dialogue is essential to ensure that incentives translate into further action from Khartoum in removing itself fully from the terrorism business.

The real challenge in U.S.-Sudanese relations will not be maintaining cooperation on counterterrorism, but ensuring that other concerns in the bilateral relationship do not become casualties in the broader U.S. quest to combat terrorism. The United States must find ways of working with Khar-toum, while maintaining pressure on it to change its internal behavior and find a peaceful resolution to the civil war. Washington will not be able to do this with a rigid, unilateral sanctions regime coupled with tools best suited to regime change pursuits. Instead, success will demand a more sophisticated strategy employing a range of tools in concert. As discussed in the previous section, adjustments made to the U.S. strategy in late 2001 and 2002 have already begun to move American policy in the right direction; the maintenance of sanctions—coupled with diplomatic initiatives, the implicit threat of force or increased support to the opposition, and gestures demonstrating that the United States is willing and able to respond positively when the government of Sudan improves its behavior—has already produced some promising results. The primary difficulty for the United States will be to maintain pressure on Khartoum in the areas in which it is most vulnerable, while signaling to the government of Sudan that authentic, verifiable changes in its behavior will be recognized by the United States and lead to improvements in its international standing.

Ideally, the United States would coordinate with other countries to formulate a package of penalties and incentives. This toolkit would not only be of use in efforts to move Khartoum away from support of groups that engage in terrorism but could also empower IGAD negotiators as they work to clinch a comprehensive peace agreement. A key element of this package should be increased pressure on Sudan's oil industry.[131] The United States cannot achieve this alone. As U.S. policy toward Iran has demonstrated, while the United States can greatly frustrate the economic integration of a country into the world, it cannot single-handedly prevent it. Past U.S. efforts suggest that pushing for UN sanctions on the oil industry is all but certain to lead to a dead end, particularly given recent positive developments in Sudan; instead, policymakers must search for ways of securing multilateralism that are more nuanced and have greater prospects of being realized.

The creation and promotion of a rigorous, universal investment code is one feasible way of creating more pressure on Sudan. Similar measures undertaken in South Africa and Northern Ireland, while not in themselves delivering huge benefits, were positive influences in larger efforts to resolve conflicts. The United States could take the lead in formulating the investment code, or it could work with the United Nations or the Organization of African Unity to craft the initiative.[132] For this code to be a vehicle for greater pressure on the regime, it must be more than a mechanism that simply provides foreign oil companies investing in Sudan a veneer of legitimacy for their controversial operations. Rather, it needs to go beyond providing guidelines of responsible investment and seeking commitments from companies investing in Sudan to maintain pressure on Khartoum in the area of human rights and the waging of the war; it must demand that companies take tangible actions in order to claim that they are adhering to the investment code. In the six month pre-interim period envisioned by the Machakos Protocol, appropriate steps would involve finance and material support for mechanisms to monitor the cease-fire. In the six-year interim period before the referendum on the status of the south, the investment code could demand that companies investing in Sudan support programs to advance governance and economic development in southern Sudan. Such programs do not need to be seen as counter to Khartoum's interests; only through the creation of a stable, less economically deprived environment in the south is there any possibility that southern Sudanese will vote for unity when given the chance.

An investment code for Sudan would be best if it were mandatory.[133] However, even if adherence to the code were voluntary, it could have significant benefits. It would serve as an important tool in the already quite successful nongovernmental campaign to place pressure on oil companies investing in Sudan through "capital market activism."[134] Having a widely accepted benchmark against which to judge the operations of foreign oil firms would assist activists seeking to diminish the funds that such firms can raise on the New York Stock Exchange; knowing that a firm is violating or not adhering to a UN-formulated investment code will have greater influence on individuals and corporations thinking of investing in these companies than the more subjective assessments of NGOs.

Some will argue that multilateralism can be achieved through the legislation of capital market sanctions against companies investing in Sudan's oil sector. In reality, these measures are likely to be detrimental to the cause of peace in Sudan, rather than instrumental to it. If capital market sanctions are enforced, they will create tensions with American allies already resentful of U.S. efforts to use secondary economic pressure to achieve what they have failed to secure through diplomacy.[135] This situation would undermine the ability of the United States to introduce its concerns over Sudan into its bilateral dialogues with the Chinese and others, stunting perhaps the most sensible path to multilateral cooperation and one not yet fully explored. These tensions could also create larger bilateral problems between the United States and foreign countries, which perhaps outweigh the utility of secondary sanctions on Sudan. Moreover, the enforcement of capital market sanctions would by no means ensure the termination of oil investment in Sudan; foreign companies can turn to capital markets in London and elsewhere in order to inoculate themselves against possible U.S. capital market reprisals, as Talisman has done.[136] If capital market sanctions legislation is written to include a presidential waiver, the waiver is likely to be employed in an effort to minimize tensions with countries more central to U.S. foreign policy, such as France, China, and Canada. Such action would avoid diplomatic rows, but would further undermine the credibility of sanctions and of U.S. policy toward Sudan overall.

Nevertheless, eschewing capital market sanctions at the official level should not mean opposing nongovernmental efforts to put pressure on foreign investors in Sudan through capital market activism. The U.S. government could support NGO activism against Sudan in more subtle ways, such as by supporting the investment code initiative described above or facilitating dialogues between American NGOs and their increasingly active counterparts in Europe.[137]

Regardless of the particular focus that U.S. efforts to secure multilateralism take, it is essential that sanctions are made a more credible complement to diplomacy. Ending exemptions currently offered to U.S. businesses wishing to evade the impact of sanctions, particularly those associated with the importation of gum arabic could help restore sanctions' credibility. This step could be achieved in one of two ways: by closing the loopholes to make the trade ban comprehensive or by lifting the trade ban altogether. Either action would be an improvement on the current situation, which above all communicates a moral desire to curtail all economic transactions with Sudan, but an inability or unwillingness to adhere to it in the face of adverse economic consequences. U.S. policy also needs to underscore how positive changes in Khartoum's behavior will result in improvements in its relationship with the United States. Restoring this bargaining element to the sanctions regime will require maintaining open channels of engagement with the regime in the counterterrorism realm as well as in efforts to reach a comprehensive peace agreement.

A road map charting the path toward better relations between the United States and Sudan would be a useful element in reorienting the current U.S. strategy toward behavior change. The Danforth mission already set out the initial phases of a road map by challenging Khartoum—and to a lesser extent the SPLM—to adhere to confidence-building measures. The United States should go one step further and map out the additional steps that Khartoum needs to take (in counterterrorism efforts and in negotiations with IGAD) for U.S. sanctions to be incrementally lifted. It should also coordinate with other international actors to lay out incentives—such as debt restructuring, lending by international financial institutions, and investment in oil and infrastructure—to be given to the government of Sudan once a complete peace deal is clinched and its implementation is under way.

Refashioning sanctions—to support a fuller U.S. strategy where multiple tools reinforce one another—stands a much greater chance of securing U.S. goals in Sudan at a reasonable price. Sanctions remain a critical part of such a careful strategy because their lifting can constitute an important incentive and because their re-imposition can be done in the face of resistance or duplicity. Pursuing a U.S. approach along these lines will require presidential leadership, as interested domestic constituencies need to be apprised of the strategy and its rationale, even if some will not be won over by it. While this strategy will be less attractive to domestic audiences demanding further punitive action against Khartoum, it is more likely to bring about the results that most claim to desire. Moreover, it is the best insurance policy against Sudanese backtracking on the painstaking progress already secured. A flexible and responsive U.S. policy today is the one most likely to serve as a foundation for international action against Khartoum if it reverses course or reneges on its commitments tomorrow.

## Appendix 6A

Tables 6A-1 and 6A-2 present estimates of the costs to Sudan and the United States of lost trade with one another.

Note to Appendix 6A:  *Estimates of the Costs to Sudan of Lost Imports from the United States.*  As shown in table 6A-2, the direct loss of Sudan as an export market cost U.S. businesses $392 million (not accounting for the fact that some of these exports inevitably found other markets). This figure also represents the initial cost to Sudan of lost imports from the United States. Assuming that Sudan was able to replace the imports that it formerly secured from the United States, the cost to Sudan would be the price differential between what it would have paid to get the products directly from the United States and what it had to pay to obtain the products from other sources or third-party suppliers. According to information calculated by the Foreign Trade Division of the U.S. Bureau of the Census, 11 percent of U.S. exports sold to Sudan in 1996 and 1997 were classified as "high-tech"; the remaining 89 percent did not warrant this classification. One can therefore estimate that 11 percent of the imports were difficult to replace, possibly requiring a mark-up of 20 percent over what Sudan would have paid to the United States directly. Sudan probably was required to pay little more to replace the remaining 89 percent, perhaps on the order of 5 percent. So, the cost of obtaining or replacing the imports normally secured from the United States between 1995 and 2001 (the latest available data) is [($392 million)*.11]*.20 + [($392 million)*.89]*.05 = $26.1 million.

Table 6A-1. *Estimated Direct Costs to Sudan of Lost Exports to the United States, 1997–2001*

Millions of 2001 dollars

| Year | Total Sudanese exports (A) | Hypothetical exports to U.S.[a] (A × 0.0405 = B) | Actual exports to U.S. (C) | Estimated exports lost due to sanctions (B − C = D) | Chain-weighted price deflator for GDP, 1996 = 100 (E) | Estimated lost exports to U.S., real dollars (D × [117.9/E] = F) |
|------|------|------|------|------|------|------|
| 1997 | 478 | 19 | 12.0 | 7 | 104.4 | 8 |
| 1998 | 538 | 22 | 3.0 | 19 | 108.9 | 20 |
| 1999 | 700 | 28 | 0.0 | 28 | 113.4 | 30 |
| 2000 | 1,368 | 55 | 1.7 | 54 | 117.6 | 54 |
| 2001 | 2,080 | 84 | 3.3 | 81 | 117.9 | 81 |
| **Total** | | | | | | **193** |

Source: IMF, *Direction of Trade Statistics*, various years.

a. Total exports are multiplied by 0.0405, the average percentage of Sudanese exports going to the United States during 1990–96.

**Table 6A-2.** *Estimated Direct Costs to the United States of Lost Exports to Sudan, 1997–2001*
Millions of 2001 dollars

| Year | U.S. exports to Sudan (A) | Industrial country exports to Sudan (B) | Non-U.S. industrial country exports to Sudan (B − A = C) | Hypothetical U.S. exports to Sudan[a] (C × 0.1420 = D) | Estimated annual exports lost due to sanctions, nominal dollars (D − A = E) | Chain-weighted price deflator for GDP, 1996 = 100 (F) | Estimated annual impact of trade sanctions, real dollars (E × [117.9/F] = G) |
|------|------|------|------|------|------|------|------|
| 1997 | 41.0 | 562.0 | 521.0 | 74 | 33 | 104.4 | 37 |
| 1998 | 7.0 | 720.0 | 713.0 | 101 | 94 | 108.9 | 102 |
| 1999 | 8.0 | 674.0 | 666.0 | 95 | 87 | 113.4 | 90 |
| 2000 | 18.3 | 651.6 | 633.3 | 90 | 72 | 117.6 | 72 |
| 2001 | 19.1 | 792.4 | 773.3 | 110 | 91 | 117.9 | 91 |
| **Total** | | | | | | | **392** |

Source: See table 6A-1.

a. Non-U.S industrial country exports to Sudan are multiplied by 0.1420, the average ratio of U.S. exports to Sudan to non-U.S. industrial country exports to Sudan over 1990–96.

# CHAPTER SEVEN

# Shrewd Sanctions: Economic Tools and U.S. Foreign Policy

This book reveals that sanctions—particularly when used to confront states that sponsor terrorism and pursue weapons of mass destruction—are neither a panacea nor a placebo. While they can be useful in limiting the resources available to countries to undertake certain activities in one case, they can fall woefully short of this goal in others. While sanctions may successfully dissuade one state from its problematic behavior, they may prove feckless in influencing the actions of another country. This mixed record should not be viewed with frustration. Instead, it provides fertile ground to draw lessons across cases and determine how and when sanctions can best be used. This chapter demonstrates how the failures and shortcomings of sanctions are generally not because these tools are intrinsically weak, but are more the result of the flawed ways in which sanctions are commonly employed. It then identifies a number of ways to strengthen the performance of sanctions in an age of American preeminence and globalization.

## Economic Tools in an Age of Global Terrorism

The United States will employ economic tools with even greater vigor in the first decades of the new millennium than it did in the immediate post–cold war period. During the decade between the collapse of the Soviet Union and the 2001 terrorist attacks, America was uncertain of its enemies and focused on imprecise and as-yet unrealized threats. The lines between U.S. allies and rivals were not always distinct; although the ends of the spectrum—marked by NATO members and so-called rogue states—were clearly demarcated, the predilections of many other countries toward the United States were often more difficult to judge. These vague threats and the uncertain landscape of America's friends and enemies contributed to the erratic and selective use of American economic power for foreign policy purposes in the 1990s, as discussed in chapter 2. The attacks on the World Trade Center and the Pentagon clarified the dangers facing the United States and its allies. President George W. Bush's challenge to countries to join the United States in the fight against terrorism, while not eliminating the middle ground, firmed up the divide between friend and foe, sometimes in surprising ways.[1] The greater urgency and increased clarity in foreign policy following the events of September 11 encouraged the United States to marshal its economic power for foreign policy pursuits. In this endeavor, the use of economic sanctions has been and will continue to be key.

The changing international environment will do more than increase the enthusiasm for using economic tools; it will shape the patterns and trends behind their use in specific ways. Chapter 2 examines how two dominant factors in the immediate post–cold war world—globalization and American preeminence—fashioned pressures to use sanctions by affecting U.S. interests, international actors, and the domestic process of making foreign policy. Elements of the post–September 11 environment will have similar influence. The defining factors of this new environment may take time to coalesce and identify; after all, analysts and pundits struggled throughout the entire 1990s to coin a phrase to capture the contours of the post–cold war world. What is already clear is that globalization and American power will continue to be important characteristics of this new era. These two phenomena will sculpt U.S. interests, international actors, and the making of American foreign policy in a variety of ways—ultimately affecting trends in the use of sanctions in the new millennium.

September 11 sharpened American foreign policy priorities. In the week following the World Trade Center and Pentagon attacks, Secretary of State Colin Powell forcefully declared that cooperation in the fight against terrorism "will be a means by which we measure our relationship with them [other countries] in the future."[2] Although the United States remains concerned with promoting democracy and human rights, combating terrorism and the proliferation of WMD have catapulted to the top of the foreign policy agenda. Whereas in the long run, these two sets of goals are complementary, in the short and medium term, they frequently clash. Where this is the case, the United States is likely to tackle terrorism at the expense of advancing other concerns, just as opposing communism trumped the advancement of other U.S. interests and values during the cold war. One of the primary challenges for the United States will be striking the right balance between protecting its people and shores and promoting its values—although advancing democracy abroad may ultimately be one of the best ways to protect Americans at home.

Shifts in U.S. priorities may not necessarily force an absolute decline or rise in the number of times the United States employs sanctions over the next decade, but it will influence the ends to which sanctions are used. Sanctions enacted against Pakistan for its October 1999 military coup were waived in the autumn of 2001 to help secure Islamabad's cooperation against al-Qaida and the Taliban, demonstrating how the use of economic pressure for democratization will sometimes be curtailed in the face of other pursuits. Similarly, long-standing concerns over human rights abuses by the Indonesian military, which have been the basis for an embargo on U.S. military sales to the archipelago since 1999, have been largely overtaken by the need to solidify the support of the government in Jakarta, particularly as it comes under pressure from extremist Indonesian groups. Post–September 11 American foreign policy is also likely to have a greater focus on failed states; now that their consequences are viewed as strategic as well as humanitarian, the United States will be more hesitant to use sanctions to address the shortcomings of weak states, lest such efforts push the state to collapse. Instead, they will turn to incentives.

At the same time the United States pares back economic sanctions for some purposes, it will ramp up efforts to use them to pursue counterterrorism goals, such as blocking the assets of foreign terrorist organizations and placing pressure on countries that harbor or support terrorist groups. Secondary sanctions may also find new impetus as the United States and even the United Nations take firmer measures to punish those violating multilateral embargoes.

The international environment after September 11, like the immediate post–cold war one that preceded it, will also shape the range of actors subject to sanctions. As in the past, some countries—mostly those deemed state sponsors of terrorism—will fall foul to wide-ranging restrictions. However, earlier trends toward sanctioning nonstate actors will intensify as the United States devotes greater energy to targeting terrorist organizations and their associates, as well as companies or institutions affiliated with them. Several factors will bolster this trend in the years ahead. Technological advances will offer greater possibilities for targeting sanctions below the state level. The United States will employ sanctions against sub-state actors in cases where America needs to maintain overall cooperation with the government, but wishes to curtail its activities. Episodes, such as the one when the United States imposed sanctions on Chinese firms in September 2001 for selling missile technology to Pakistan, will become more common. Finally, the United States may resort to sanctioning certain entities not simply because of the threat they pose to America, but also as a means of securing the support of the governments which they threaten. Measures imposed against the Islamic Movement of Uzbekistan, the Libyan Islamic Fighting Group, or Jaish-I-Mohammed could be seen at least partially in this light.[3]

Finally, the domestic process of making foreign policy will be different in the post–September 11 world than it was in the post–cold war period preceding it. As noted in chapter 2, the end of the cold war political system created greater space for the influence of interest groups and opened the door for more congressional activism in the crafting of foreign policy. Both these trends will be checked by U.S. efforts to focus more concertedly on the threats posed by terrorism and the strategies available to combat it. In such an atmosphere, Congress is less likely to chart its own waters and complicate the efforts of the executive branch to execute U.S. foreign policy. Congressional-executive tension in the international realm will persist, but Congress will be less prone to force the hand of the president through legislated sanctions. Similarly, activists, ethnic lobbies, and American business people will continue their efforts to shape U.S. foreign policy according to their interests, but their voices will be more muted and their successes less pronounced.

## The Shrewd Use of Sanctions

This book demonstrates that the shrewd use of sanctions, in the past and in the future, depends on two factors. First, the structure of the sanctions regime—what type of sanctions are employed, whom they target, and what mechanisms are required to lift them—must be crafted to suit the circumstances of the case in a way that best advances the objectives at hand. In short, the sanctions regime must be "well-suited" to the goals pursued. A sanctions regime intended to advance the goal of regime change should look different from one expected to accomplish containment. Both should differ substantially from a sanctions regime proposed to bring about changes in the behavior of an existing regime. Second, the use of sanctions must be appropriately coupled with that of other policy tools. Sanctions on their own will result in little more than raised expectations, ones that are almost certain to be disappointed. Imposing sanctions in itself does not constitute a foreign policy strategy; sanctions are policy *instruments* that need to be combined with other tools in order to form coherent and effective *strategies*. This of course is also true of other policy instruments, although the tendency to employ sanctions on their own is more conspicuous than with other tools.

Although each sanctions regime would need to be carefully crafted to fit the country in question and the situation at hand, it is useful to briefly consider what stylized sanctions regimes would look like if they were shrewdly crafted to advance three categories of goals: behavior change, containment, and regime change. Sanctions whose primary aim is to change certain behaviors of a leadership are in some respects the most difficult to fashion. Policymakers need not be only—or even primarily—concerned that sanctions have an impact; they also must focus on whether the impact of sanctions is translated into effectiveness—whether the pain sanctions inflict succeeds in compelling the targeted government to make political changes. Sanctions regimes that form the basis for a bargaining framework between the sanctioned country and the United States or the United Nations are most conducive to this sort of success.[4] The structure of sanctions must be flexible enough to accommodate and encourage gradual changes in the behavior of the target, ideally by allowing restrictions to be lifted or letting them lapse incrementally as the country takes actions desired by the United States. Although not essential to success, this process works best if there is a reciprocal element to it, even if it is not nearly an equal one. Sanctions used for this purpose must be accompanied by dialogue between the two countries, preferably in a regular and institutionalized way that allows each side to articulate its expectations and demonstrate the reforms it has undertaken; in an ideal situation, a road map—a document that charts out carefully calibrated steps along the path to better relations—would anchor these discussions.[5] Finally, the shrewd use of sanctions for behavior change will often demand the use of additional penalties and incentives apart from those offered by imposition and lifting of sanctions to coerce and entice a country down the road of rehabilitation.

Although the successful use of sanctions in this fashion is relatively rare, policymakers do have some guidance from history. The case of Vietnam offers an excellent example of how a sanctions regime that is both suitably structured and accompanied by other policy tools can provide a useful framework to much improved bilateral relations with a former adversary.[6] After many years of little contact and mutual hostility between the United States and Vietnam, the collapse of Hanoi's Soviet benefactor opened up new possibilities for U.S.-Vietnamese rapprochement. This transformation of the relationship did not happen overnight but rather was the product of a painstaking four-stage process in which Hanoi cooperated with the Cambodian peace process and gradually provided Washington with the information it sought concerning prisoners of war and soldiers missing in action. In return, the United States incrementally lifted sanctions, provided humanitarian aid, stopped vetoing lending to Vietnam from international financial institutions, and generally eased Vietnam's entry into the global economy. Frequent contact between U.S. and Vietnamese officials helped keep this process moving, as did occasional American threats to arrest progress and maintain sanctions if greater cooperation from Hanoi were not forthcoming. By July 1995, the United States and Vietnam had treated the open sores in their relationship and resumed normal economic and diplomatic ties, which culminated in the signing of a bilateral trade agreement in July 2000. Although far less dramatic an example, much of the success of U.S. officials in securing the compliance of Chinese firms with international property rights agreements also stemmed from the shrewd use of sanctions. Rather than imposing sanctions immediately when such agreements were violated, sanctions became an integral part of a behavior change strategy. In extensive dialogues with their Chinese counterparts, U.S. officials both threatened sanctions for noncompliance and offered technical assistance to Chinese entities willing to make changes in their operations— a strategy that proved successful.[7]

A sanctions regime whose aim is the containment of a government or country need not have all the bells and whistles of a behavior change approach. At least in the short and medium term, policymakers using sanctions to isolate a regime need be less concerned about ensuring that the pressure of sanctions induces political change in the target society; instead, their more immediate focus is on maximizing the economic, political, or military impact of sanctions. Keeping resources away from a regime or distinguishing it from countries abiding by international norms is in itself a legitimate goal of sanctions. Such a goal is not inconsistent with the long-term desire of having a country change its behavior, but it is distinct from it. Given the importance of maximizing the impact of sanctions if containment is to be achieved, sanctions must be multilateral if they are to be shrewdly employed for containment purposes. Mandatory sanctions imposed by the United Nations will be the most effective, not only because they will be the most universal but because the backing of the United Nations serves as a deterrent to the violation of sanctions. Regional sanctions, however, can further the political isolation of a regime, whereas the more sophisticated the economy of the target, the greater the impact of a coalition of OECD countries that severs links with it. The shrewd use of sanctions for containment also demands the simultaneous use of a variety of other tools. Incentives employed in these instances are less likely to be directed at the sanctioned regime; instead, they should be aimed at shoring up the enthusiasm of other countries for the continued isolation of the target, either by compensating them for economic losses borne as a result of enforcing sanctions or by minimizing the humanitarian impact of sanctions within the target. Public diplomacy campaigns and the use of military force can also be important companion instruments to sanctions in a containment strategy.

The recent history of Yugoslavia demonstrates how the shrewd use of sanctions can lead to effective containment. A wide range of opinion exists about how effective UN sanctions in place against Yugoslavia from 1992 to 1995 were in forcing the Bosnian Serbs to end the war.[8] Much less disputed, however, is the success of sanctions in diminishing the economic resources available to Belgrade and, therefore, limiting the support it could extend to the Bosnian Serbs in the ongoing war in Bosnia.[9] To a large extent, the formidable impact of UN sanctions in the 1990s was due to their universal nature and their comprehensive character. Virtually all countries severed trade, travel, financial, and cultural relations with Yugoslavia from 1992 to 1995. Nevertheless, the imposition of sanctions alone would not have been sufficient to contain Yugoslavia; also important were the networks of sanctions assistance missions that provided technical assistance to countries bordering Yugoslavia and tasked with enforcing and monitoring the sanctions.[10] The containment of Belgrade was further enhanced by the threat of force implicit in the NATO bombing of Bosnian Serbs and an international presence in Kosovo and Macedonia.[11]

Shrewd sanctions geared toward the goal of regime change demand yet another type of sanctions regime. When the United States desires a new government to assume power in a country and has the commitment to shape its policy accordingly, sanctions should be crafted to squeeze the leadership and state structures, while also nurturing any potential points of opposition in the society.[12] In countries with a substantial private sector, an appropriate sanctions regime will target restrictions on the travel and assets of the leadership as well as the sectors of the economy and companies through which rulers enrich themselves. When the state is more dominant or the divide between private and public is more difficult to discern, sanctions for regime change may be nearly comprehensive, with exemptions only for humanitarian purposes. Multilateral support for these measures, while hugely desirable, is not as critical as when sanctions are used for containment. Rather, what is of greatest concern is that sanctions are supplemented with other policy instruments; sanctions alone should never be expected to achieve a change in regime. Through the use of supplementary tools, especially public diplomacy, the United States and its partners should create and widely publicize a positive vision of an alternative future for the target country under a new regime. In doing so, it should articulate the benefits that will accrue to a regime that meets specified standards in terms of being representative, respectful of human rights, and willing to adopt a program of economic reform if needed. These "incentives" may be pledges of debt relief, international recognition, or reconstruction aid that, ideally, could be underwritten by a commitment of funds or the creation of an appropriate institution to administer them. Moreover, if a reasonably credible opposition exists, the United States should work with it to bolster its capabilities and prepare for the challenges of governing. In some situations, this support will amount to aid and technical support to civil society; in others, it may involve a variety of military support.

Sanctions were used shrewdly to promote what essentially amounted to a regime change strategy toward South Africa in the 1980s and early 1990s.[13] After years of international pressure and domestic upheaval, the apartheid government of the National Party relinquished power, paving the transition to majority rule in 1994. Notably, the vast majority of sanctions imposed against South Africa were not multilateral in a universal sense; an arms embargo on South Africa was the only measure embraced by the United Nations.[14] Nor were most of the sanctions regimes adopted against Pretoria comprehensive; instead, they were as diverse as the countries applying them.[15] Even the United States was selective in the sanctions it imposed, maintaining diplomatic contact with Pretoria and allowing some economic links to continue.[16] More important, sanctions were only part of the equation of U.S. policy. The United States provided nearly $100 million of economic assistance to black civil society in South Africa, supporting nongovernmental groups and overt political organizations in the first U.S. development assistance program openly embracing political objectives. The impact of sanctions, in conjunction with engagement with forces opposing apartheid, made international involvement one important factor leading to the change of regime in South Africa.[17]

### Assessing the Past Record

The success or, in most cases, the failure to use sanctions shrewdly—in the sense of structuring sanctions regimes to suit their goals and complementing sanctions with other policy tools—to a large degree explains the outcomes of the cases examined in this book.[18] Sanctions against Libya, for instance, helped contain the Qadhafi regime for a time and were an important tool in getting it to change key elements of its behavior. UN sanctions—more so than the unilateral American sanctions that existed independent of them—deserve much of the credit for these accomplishments. Their multilateral, universal nature was a crucial element in ensuring the political isolation and military marginalization of Libya throughout much of the 1990s. The role of sanctions in inducing Libya to move away from its support for terrorism and to meet key goals demanded by the international community, such as the handover of the Lockerbie suspects, was more complex. As discussed in chapter 5, by exacerbating an already weak economy, sanctions contributed to an economic and political crisis of the Qadhafi regime. Meanwhile, a number of factors made the UN sanctions regime more conducive to encouraging behavior change; sanctions became the basis for a bargaining framework for the resolution of the disputes between the UN and Libya, rather than a charter for Libya's capitulation. A series of developments shaped this metamorphosis. Pressure from the Organization of African Unity to lift the sanctions on Libya compelled the United States and Britain to offer a compromise to Libya concerning the trial of the Lockerbie suspects. This proposal spurred a serious diplomatic initiative to bridge remaining divides between the parties, one that involved the mediation efforts of UN Secretary General Kofi Annan, South African president Nelson Mandela, Saudi Arabia's ambassador to the United States Prince Bandar bin Sultan, and others. Moreover, the United Nations extended a major incentive to Libya in 1998 when, in an effort to encourage Libyan compliance with UN demands, it passed a resolution explicitly declaring that UN sanctions would be suspended once Libya handed over the Lockerbie suspects. This bargaining dynamic created around sanctions, and the use of other tools to cement it, were essential in gaining Libya's compliance with key elements of UN resolutions.

Similarly, the success of sanctions in containing Iraq for more than a decade—and their failure to effect regime change or significant behavior changes such as Iraq's voluntary disarmament—reflect the structure of the sanctions regime and the use of other tools by the United States and the United Nations. Again, the multilateral nature of the sanctions regime in place against Iraq was essential in achieving the long-term containment of Iraq. Also important, however, were supplementary efforts to bolster this containment with other tools. U.S. and British patrols of the no-fly zones directly enhanced containment efforts, while the large-scale humanitarian relief program undertaken by the United Nations helped maintain multilateral support for the sanctions regime and, as a result, was vital to the containment of Iraq. In contrast, the sanctions regime was hardly poised to deliver results in the realms of regime change or behavior modification. Accompanying efforts to support the opposition against the regime of Saddam Hussein were weak and piecemeal. Similarly, not only was no attempt made to create a bargaining framework around the sanctions regime to entice Iraq to disarm, but great efforts were made by the United States to ensure that no relief from international pressure—even in a rhetorical sense—would be granted to Iraq short of its full compliance with UN demands.

Much of the ineffectiveness of U.S. sanctions against Iran can also be explained by the fundamental mismatch between the goals pursued and the sanctions strategy employed. The United States relied on sanctions both as a means of containing the Islamic republic and in an effort to sway the regime to stop its support for terrorism, opposition to Israel, and pursuit of weapons of mass destruction. In pursuing these goals, the United States put in place one of the most rigid sanctions regimes possible but failed to get multilateral support for most elements of it. As a result, the sanctions regime was neither suited to the containment of Iran (given that it was unilateral), nor flexible enough to serve as a basis for a more gradual rapprochement between the two countries. Moreover, with the exception of the final year of the Clinton administration when efforts were made to launch a bilateral dialogue, sanctions were virtually the entirety of the U.S. strategy toward Iran. With the exception of biting rhetoric—which was more suited to complement the goals of regime change or containment than behavior change—the United States employed no other major policy tools to effect change in Iran in the 1990s, in part because Tehran rejected official dialogue.

Finally, the United States also failed to use sanctions shrewdly to deal with Sudan throughout the 1990s. Although ostensibly pursuing changes in the behavior of the Khartoum regime regarding terrorism, human rights, and its civil war with the largely southern opposition, sanctions were not obviously linked to progress in any of these realms. Instead, the sanctions regime put in place was monolithic, inflexible, and not coupled with dialogue or other tools suggesting that rehabilitation was possible if Khartoum were to modify its actions.[19] Moreover, although the United States did employ other instruments in its policy toward Sudan, these tools were poorly coordinated with sanctions, if at all.[20] Fierce rhetoric, military support to neighboring countries, military strikes on Sudan in 1998, and moral—if not material— backing for the opposition cumulatively smacked much more of a regime change strategy than one geared to entice Khartoum to change its behavior through the gradual easing of sanctions. The use of these companion tools, and the impression they created that the United States sought a new regime in Sudan, undermined Khartoum's incentive to comply with lesser, explicit U.S. demands relating to its behavior. UN sanctions, in contrast, did correspond more closely to Sudan's support for terrorism, yet the fact that they were largely diplomatic sanctions and barely enforced undercut their leverage considerably.

In contrast, changes made to U.S. policy toward Sudan in 2001 and early 2002 underscore the possibility of using sanctions as part of a behavior change strategy. The announcement of Senator Danforth as special envoy to Sudan added an element of engagement into U.S. policy for the first time in years. Small U.S. moves—such as the acquiescence to the lifting of UN sanctions and the quelling of the capital market sanctions in the Sudan Peace Act—made in response to increased Sudanese counterterrorism cooperation signaled to Khartoum that there was some benefit to altering its behavior to bring it in line with U.S. demands and desires. The combination of this new awareness and the opening of a new channel of dialogue in the form of the Danforth mission transformed U.S. sanctions from minor economic irritants into points of leverage in a broader framework of negotiation. This recasting of U.S. policy helped pave the way for the promising (if far from complete) accomplishments in mid-2002, including the Nuba Mountain cease-fire and the Machakos Protocol.

Other cases apart from those analyzed in this section also demonstrate the payoffs of using sanctions shrewdly and the drawbacks of failing to do so. Cuba has been subject to an American sanctions regime geared toward its containment, but poorly suited to achieve its goals given its unilateral nature and the failure to couple sanctions in any significant way with other policy tools. Not surprisingly, the U.S. embargo on Havana has borne little fruit. In Burma or Myanmar, U.S. sanctions have also been largely ineffective in achieving the implicit goal of getting the military junta to cede to the democratically elected leadership of Aung Sang Suu Kyi and her National League for Democracy party.[21] In part, the irrelevance of U.S. policy can be explained by the fact that the United States has pursued an objective tantamount to regime change, with limited, largely unilateral sanctions not supplemented with other policy instruments.[22]

### Explaining Past Failures

Why has the shrewd use of sanctions been so rare in the past? The haphazard use of sanctions is in part due to a lack of strategic thinking. The notion that sanctions regimes can and should be structured in different ways depending on their goals is not widely recognized. Instead, the actions of politicians and policymakers often suggest a perceived linear relationship between sanctions and their objectives: the more goals pursued, the greater number of restrictions warranted. When new goals are adopted toward a regime or country, additional sanctions are simply added to the existing body of restrictions. If all the relevant contacts are already severed, lawmakers have shown no reluctance to "double" or "triple" sanctions against a country, that is, to impose redundant measures on it. At one point, the United States had three unrelated measures in place against Pakistan, all of them banning most forms of aid to it; the United States also simultaneously maintained three separate prohibitions on U.S. nonhumanitarian aid to Sudan at one time.[23] Rarely, if ever, has the embrace of new objectives been used as opportunity to re-evaluate the existing sanctions regime and readjust it to ensure that it is well-suited to the goals that the United States hopes most to achieve. Another impediment to the shrewd use of sanctions is the near political impossibility of scaling back restrictions as bilateral relations worsen; although it is counterintuitive, moving from a strategy of containment to regime change may sometimes demand lifting certain sanctions to bolster nonstate elements of an economy or society. Finally, strategic thinking about sanctions has also been impaired by a tendency to see sanctions as a substitute for other action, not a complement. This propensity increased in the first decade of the post–cold war era, when American reluctance to use military force and sustain casualties in combat grew with the impression that the United States faced few serious threats abroad.

To be fair, the absence of strategic thinking is not the only—nor perhaps the greatest—reason for the sorry abuse of sanctions in the past. Three other factors also explain this outcome, and, in doing so, elucidate why it has been so difficult to translate what strategic thinking has occurred into practice. First, the diffuse process of making sanctions policy has inhibited the shrewd use of sanctions. In each case examined in this book, and in many apart from them, the sanctions regime in place owes its existence to numerous designers. Sanctions against Iran are the product of various executive orders and several congressional initiatives, not to mention a loose smattering of restrictions on weapons and dangerous technologies adopted by third countries. Iraq, Libya, and Sudan are all subject to sanctions regimes crafted by Congress, the executive branch, and the United Nations. Adding to this quagmire is the fact that sanctions regimes are generally built up over time; the swift and comprehensive sanctions imposed on Iraq in 1990 after its invasion of Kuwait were the exception, rather than the norm. Generally, a sanctions strategy takes shape gradually, with different congresses and various administrations—holding their own views and variations of the same objectives— each contributing a piece to the puzzle. For instance, the United States first began to restrict commerce with Libya in the late 1970s through executive orders prohibiting the sale of certain aircraft and military equipment to Tripoli; in 2001, Congress was still adding to the sanctions regime when it renewed the Iran-Libya Sanctions Act (ILSA) and revised the threshold over which foreign investments in Libya's energy sector would elicit secondary sanctions on the companies making them.[24] Too many architects—building a sanctions regime over a long period of time—usually result in a flawed structure not well-suited to the pursuit of regime change, containment, *or* behavior modification. Having too many cooks in the kitchen has also hampered efforts to supplement sanctions with the right companion tools.

An overabundance of chefs is particularly detrimental to crafting sanctions regimes geared toward the goal of inducing behavior changes in a country. As explored earlier, sanctions used toward this purpose must be flexible, enabling the United States to quickly respond to positive developments in a bilateral relationship. This process always demands close coordination between Congress and the executive branch, given the sharp interest of Congress and many of its constituents in U.S. policies toward sanctioned countries. But when some of the sanctions in place are imposed by Congress, some by the executive branch, and some at the behest of the United Nations, using the gradual lifting of sanctions to frame a bargaining process can become extremely complicated or downright impossible. For instance, U.S. efforts throughout the 1990s to cajole and coerce North Korea to abandon its nuclear pursuits were at times hampered by congressional reluctance to support the efforts of the Clinton administration to lubricate the process with aid and the easing of sanctions.[25] Similarly, congressional threats to legislatively impose a travel ban on Americans visiting Libya if the executive branch were to lift the one in place hampers the ability of the president to make gestures to encourage Libya's further compliance with UN and U.S. demands.[26]

Although the number of actors making sanctions policy has often complicated and frustrated the shrewd use of these tools, in rare instances, it has created a dynamic that increased their effectiveness. For example, congressional-executive discord surrounding Beijing's human rights record and the granting of most favored nation (MFN) to China in 1992 helped induce the Chinese government to release some dissidents from jail, hand out more lenient sentences to those convicted, and sign prison labor agreements with the United States.[27] Unlike previous episodes, China calculated that such concessions were necessary in late 1991 and 1992, given the political climate in the United States at the time. With a Democratic Congress pushing for the denial of MFN for China, and the popularity of President George H.W. Bush (a supporter of the renewal of MFN) seriously in decline, the threat of revoking MFN was much more real than it had been in the past.[28] Perhaps even more unexpectedly, in extraordinary circumstances, friction between UN and U.S. sanctions has had similar positive benefits.[29] In both the case of Libya and Sudan, decisions by the United Nations to suspend UN sanctions—made possible by the acquiescence of Washington—provided the United States with an opportunity to signal to Tripoli and Khartoum its willingness to recognize positive, if incomplete, changes in their behavior when the U.S. sanctions regimes were too inflexible to provide such indications.

A second obstacle to the shrewd use of sanctions has been the complex agendas that the United States holds with many of the countries that it has sanctioned. The necessity or desire to pursue many goals at the same time has undermined the effectiveness of sanctions in several ways. In some cases, the existence of multiple and competing interests has diminished the credibility of the threat of American sanctions. For instance, in 1985 Congress passed the Pressler amendment, legislation that required the United States to impose sanctions on Pakistan if the president was unable to certify annually that Islamabad was not in possession of a nuclear device. Even though the United States had a record of severing aid to Pakistan for its nuclear activities in the late 1970s, U.S. reliance on Pakistan to counter Soviet influence in neighboring Afghanistan greatly diluted the threat to do so a decade later.[30] Similarly, the force of U.S. threats to use broad sanctions to compel China to change its behavior lessened as the United States became more reliant on Chinese markets to absorb its products.[31]

Even when the United States has a uniformly antagonistic relationship with the country in question, efforts to advance multiple goals can still diminish the effectiveness and utility of sanctions. In these instances, the simultaneous pursuit of many objectives can lead to a situation in which some elements of one strategy undercut elements of the other, compromising the shrewd use of sanctions for any purpose. Nowhere has this tangle of strategies been more evident than in the case of Iraq. In one capacity or the other, the United States saw sanctions against Iraq as a central element of strategies aimed at changing the regime of Saddam Hussein, containing Iraq militarily, economically, and politically, and altering the behavior of Baghdad, particularly regarding its efforts to acquire and stockpile weapons of mass destruction. The United Nations, while never embracing the first goals, acquiesced to the second, and endorsed the third.

Rather than neatly complementing each other, these numerous objectives—and the use of sanctions and other tools to pursue them—were often at cross purposes. In its tepid efforts to challenge the Iraqi regime in the 1990s, the United States allocated small portions of money to the Iraqi National Congress and, at times, declared that it would not allow UN sanctions to be lifted until Saddam Hussein was evicted from power. By calling into question whether Iraqi compliance with UN resolutions would lead to the lifting of sanctions, such gestures removed the greatest incentive Iraq had to change its behavior and meet international demands. More important, while having little effect on the balance of power in Baghdad, this support for the opposition and the shifts in U.S. declaratory policy irritated American allies in the region and the United Nations and complicated efforts to maintain the international coalition so essential to the containment of Iraq. Ensuring ongoing international support for the containment of Iraq not only demanded minimizing tensions surrounding the question of Saddam's ouster; it also required alleviating the humanitarian situation in Iraq and exercising a certain restraint in the use of military force against Baghdad. As a result, UN and U.S. efforts to change the behavior of the Iraqi regime were also compromised by the overriding ambition to contain Iraq and the use of sanctions and other tools to advance that goal. On the one hand, desires to maximize the pressure on Iraq kept the United States from allowing the lifting of sanctions to be calibrated to encourage positive, if far from complete, changes in Iraq's behavior. On the other hand, efforts to minimize international tensions and maintain the international consensus for Iraq's containment prevented the more forceful use of military strikes to penalize Iraq for its continued unwillingness to disarm. Efforts to balance these multiple goals and the strategies best suited to advance them resulted in weak initiatives such as Operation Desert Fox. This four-day bombing campaign did not extract Iraqi compliance with weapons inspectors and did little to advance the containment of Iraq over the medium or long term, yet angered U.S. allies and threatened the fragile coalition opposing Saddam.

The final constraint on the shrewd use of sanctions has been that the goals pursued by the United States have often changed—sometimes dramatically—over the period that sanctions have been in place. As a result, policymakers have frequently found themselves pursuing one type of goal with a sanctions regime suited to a different sort of objective altogether, much to the detriment of their efforts. U.S. sanctions on Iran, for instance, were imposed in the mid-1990s when the leadership in Tehran was viewed as almost wholly hostile toward the United States. Since that time, the rise to power of more moderate elements in Iran caused the United States in the late 1990s to shift its focus away from regime change and toward the pursuit of particular behavior changes by Iran.[32] Despite this significant revision in goals, the structure of the sanctions regime remained extremely rigid, frustrating the efforts of policymakers to use it to entice Tehran into dialogue with the United States. U.S. sanctions on Libya provide an even more stark example of the same phenomenon. Economic measures were first imposed on Tripoli as part of the Reagan administration's strategy to unseat Colonel Muammar Qadhafi from power. As U.S. officials gradually abandoned efforts to expel Qadhafi from power and moved to embrace the goal of containing Libya, the sanctions stayed in place. When the United Nations imposed sanctions on Libya in the wake of the Lockerbie and UTA bombings, the United States submerged its larger goal of containing Libya in favor of a multilateral strategy ostensibly geared to change the behavior of Tripoli, although the United States made no changes to its own sanctions policy. When UN sanctions were suspended in 1999, U.S. diplomats struggled to encourage and consolidate positive changes in Libya's behavior with a sanctions regime first constructed to facilitate Qadhafi's overthrow.

## Toward the Better Use of Sanctions

Using sanctions shrewdly is no easy task. As seen in this chapter and throughout this book, the numerous obstacles to the wise use of these tools are not easily overcome. This section harkens back to the areas identified in chapter 2 as deserving more attention and draws on the findings of this chapter and the entire book to explore areas relevant to the shrewd use of sanctions. The discussion of each lesson below takes the context of global-ization and American primacy into account as specific recommendations are offered to guide the expectations and actions of policymakers.

### Securing Multilateral Sanctions

The cases in this book not only confirm the much-heralded conclusion that multilateral sanctions are the most effective form of economic pressure, but also suggest that even targeted or limited multilateral measures are preferable to comprehensive, unilateral ones. What successes sanctions claimed in Iraq and Libya owe a great deal to the multilateral nature of the pressure applied on these states. Without international support, sanctions would never have kept the more than $250 billion in oil revenues Iraq might have earned in the absence of sanctions out of Saddam's reach over the 1990s (see chapter 4 appendixes). Similarly, putting aside the economic pressure of multilateral sanctions on Libya, the universal character of sanc-tions cemented Qadhafi's political isolation in a way that unilateral or even regional sanctions would have not done and, in doing so, contributed—if indirectly—to Qadhafi's movement away from his most objectionable behavior. Even UN sanctions on Sudan—mere diplomatic measures that were only partially adhered to—magnified international wariness over Sudan's internal problems and therefore helped curbed its economic prospects at the margins. These same sanctions also provided the United States with an important tool in its successful quest to deny Khartoum a seat on the UN Security Council in 2000, a development that added to the mar-ginalization of the regime.

One of the areas chapter 2 identified as deserving further attention is how policymakers can secure multilateral sanctions. The superiority of multilateral sanctions need not imply that unilateral sanctions are useless, but does strongly suggest that the best unilateral sanctions are those that catalyze multilateral action. Certainly, some of the most effective sanctions regimes—such as those against Iraq or Libya—began with unilateral Ameri-can initiatives.[33] These cases are often cited to support the argument that unilateral sanctions are needed to demonstrate American leadership before multilateral action can be attained.[34] However compelling this line of think-ing, other cases—where unilateral sanctions have not galvanized interna-tional support for U.S. goals—suggest that demonstrating leadership through sanctions is more than about just imposing the restrictions. And leadership is more than about being the first to impose an arms embargo or a travel ban on a country peripheral to the national interest. Under what circumstances and through what strategies are U.S. policymakers most likely to be able to parlay unilateral sanctions into multilateral ones, particularly multilateral measures that involve sacrifice for those imposing them? This study reveals that a range of factors determine whether unilateral sanctions serve as a springboard or concrete shoes in the pursuit of such multilateral restrictions.

"Springboard" sanctions almost always require a shared perception that a regime or entity poses a threat to international security. Most often, this threat goes beyond creating a sense of insecurity, but has clear, concrete manifestations. In the post–cold war world, acts of terrorism have been an effective platform for springboard sanctions—partially because of their violent, tangible nature—but also because each permanent member of the UN Security Council holds its own concerns about terrorism. After years of resisting U.S. entreaties to impose sanctions on Libya, the United Nations was moved to action against Tripoli in the wake of the Lockerbie and UTA bombings; similarly, the involvement of Osama bin Laden in the 1998 embassy bombings in Africa and his refuge in Taliban-controlled Afghanistan greatly lubricated U.S. efforts to secure multilateral sanctions against the Taliban. Certain characteristics of the U.S. sanctions regime can also determine whether sanctions are of the springboard variety. Sanctions imposed by the executive branch are far more likely to provide a sound basis for multilateral action than their congressional counterparts, which are often viewed abroad as the products of domestic politics rather than reactions to external threats.[35] Of equal importance is whether the U.S. sanctions regime conveys credibility to potential U.S. partners overseas. Sanctions—such as those on Sudan—that are imposed with moralistic rhetoric but are riddled with exemptions and exceptions to limit the costs borne by U.S. companies, often ring hollow to those whose support Washington seeks for wider measures. This is particularly true when such steps would entail greater losses for other countries than they do for the United States. The weak enforcement of penalties against American firms violating U.S. sanctions—and scandals such as the Iran-Contra one—also undermine U.S. efforts to gain international support by calling into question American commitment to address the very problems Washington is urging others to tackle with sanctions.

Faced with an external threat, and armed with a credible, unilateral sanctions regime (ideally) crafted by the executive branch, policymakers stand the best chance of transforming unilateral measures into more broadly supported ones. To maximize the chances of success in these situations, U.S.

policymakers should enlist the assistance of a key ally in pushing for UN or regional measures. European leadership was key in securing multilateral measures against the former Yugoslavia, as was Egypt's place at the helm of efforts to impose UN sanctions against Sudan.[36] Having the support of a strong and vocal partner can allay concerns that the United States is hijacking international institutions for its own purposes and therefore neutralize a point of potential resistance to joint cooperation. Moreover, U.S. policymakers should commit themselves to gaining international cooperation through intense diplomatic efforts and, when the situation is important enough to warrant it, the extension of inducements to allies who are reluctant to come on board.

Policymakers should not delude themselves by thinking that secondary sanctions offer a potential vehicle to multilateral cooperation. The increased interest in secondary sanctions in the 1990s is in part a reaction to post–cold war political and economic realities. In the wake of the collapse of the cold war system, the United States was less able to compel others through political force to follow its foreign policy preferences and prescriptions. As a result, it searched for new ways to use its economic strength—and the international tangle of economic linkages fostered by globalization—to coerce other nations to adopt policies to its liking. As the cases examined in this book demonstrate, secondary sanctions have rarely catalyzed the desired cooperation. Secondary sanctions are, in fact, a distinguishing marker of a "concrete shoe" sanctions regime—one that impedes, rather than assists, the pursuit of multilateral measures. Instead of helping shape a multilateral approach toward Iran or Libya, efforts to use economic coercion to attain international cooperation irked U.S. allies and complicated American efforts to find common areas of interest and methods of action.

Policymakers intent on using secondary sanctions to compensate for the diffusion of global economic power should modify their use of these tools. At the very least, secondary sanctions regimes should always offer "country waivers"—mechanisms that exempt all the firms in a country from the effects of sanctions if the targeted government cooperates with the United States. Rather than prescribing the exact sort of cooperation desired, the U.S. government should have some leeway to judge whether a government meets this standard. Offering governments such waivers only if they impose sanctions equivalent to U.S. measures—as was done under ILSA with the case of Iran—does not constitute a reasonable or workable compromise. Offering them such relief for more private, behind-the-scenes cooperation or for tightening their dual-use item licensing process may be more realistic and in the end produce better results.

### Making the Most of Unilateral Sanctions

Not all—or even most—U.S. unilateral sanctions will be springboards to multilateral action. Many unilateral sanctions will remain solo restrictions imposed by the United States. What is the value, if any, of these measures? Can unilateral sanctions serve a useful function in achieving U.S. foreign policy goals even if they fail to spur multilateral cooperation? Those who have dismissed unilateral sanctions as "chicken soup diplomacy"—just a palliative to soothe the American desire to take action—would argue that they cannot.[37] However, this book reveals two important points about the place of unilateral sanctions in American foreign policy. First, as critics contend, they have been disappointing in the leading role that they have often played in post–cold war American foreign policy. Second, there *is* an appropriate role, though more of a supporting one, for unilateral sanctions in U.S. foreign policy, even if sanctions are not of the springboard variety.

Both of these judgments relate to the impact of unilateral sanctions in a globalized world. This book reveals that unilateral measures can do economic and political damage to the target, even if the magnitude of it falls greatly short of that exacted by multilateral measures. This finding goes against the popular conviction that rapid globalization has nearly annulled the impact that unilateral sanctions have on the target country. In fact, as exposed by the analysis in this book, the influence of globalization has not been one dimensional. While diminishing the effects of some restrictions, globalization has also enhanced the impact that other measures can exert in certain situations.

The integration of economies worldwide and the rapid spread of technology have nearly squelched the *direct* effects of unilateral trade and investment sanctions. The initial shock of U.S. trade sanctions fades quickly, as countries diversify their trade partners. The pace and ease of this adjustment is related to the type and nature of the products traded, more than it is a reflection of the volume of trade once occurring between the United States and the sanctioned country. Where the target country sells a fungible commodity in high global demand, the realignment of trade patterns can be almost seamless. Neither oil-exporting Iran nor Libya had more than fleeting difficulty in finding new consumers for their goods. Similarly, countries exporting high-demand goods that few others produce need not be overly concerned about trade sanctions; even had the United States not exempted imports of Sudanese gum arabic from the U.S. sanctions regime, Sudan could have easily found alternative buyers for this product.[38] Countries that relied on the United States for the purchase of more sophisticated items faced a greater struggle to find substitutes for these products, yet the spread of technological knowledge has gradually eased their battle. Many items once only available from U.S. manufacturers can now easily be purchased from other sources. Globalization has also diminished the pain countries suffer when the United States prohibits American investment in their economies; many states still desire U.S. investment, yet international businesses from France to China have for the most part filled the gap created by the absence of American firms and offered largely comparable services and expertise.

Globalization, on the other hand, has also opened opportunities for U.S. unilateral sanctions to inflict substantial *indirect* costs on countries. As the world has grown more economically integrated, the appeal of and benefits to membership in international organizations and institutions have grown dramatically. Yet entrance into these forums is often a political battle in which the United States still has disproportionate influence over the outcome. To the extent that the United States can block or frustrate a state's accession to these forums, it can impose serious opportunity costs on a country. These losses are not tangible and are extremely difficult to quantify. But, by narrowing the economic options a country can pursue, U.S. actions can help shape the course of a country's economic future. Consider Iran. Successful U.S. efforts to keep international financial institutions from lending to Iran in the 1990s prevented Tehran from securing assistance from the International Monetary Fund to address a serious crisis spurred by plunging oil prices. Unable to follow the course of action open to most countries experiencing major external shocks, Iran was forced to embark on a severe austerity program in order to maintain its debt payments. Although over the long run this program was to Iran's benefit, it also inflicted short-term costs on the country as major reductions in imports dampened growth and fueled inflation. In time, Sudan will feel a similar crunch on its economic choices if the United States continues to oppose its inclusion in the Highly Indebted Poor Countries (HIPC) initiative, thereby effectively blocking Sudan's long-term ambitions to secure assistance from the IMF and the World Bank.[39] U.S. desires to block countries' WTO accession—while being against U.S. interests in the long run given the power of WTO membership to make societies more transparent and accountable—does provide leverage to the United States in the short run.

When the fundamentals of a country's economy are weak, U.S. sanctions will have additional indirect repercussions. By creating uncertainty, they can complicate economic planning and hinder economic reform.[40] More important, when export prices are low, domestic policies are unsound, or local politics are unstable, U.S. sanctions can have a "magnifying" effect— one that deters non-U.S. investors, banks, or credit agencies already uncertain about the value of getting involved in a country. For instance, in the 1980s, during some of Qadhafi's most radical years, U.S. unilateral sanctions served as an additional indicator of the instability of Libya, thereby playing a small role in curtailing the interest of international firms in Libya at a time when factors independent of sanctions were already counseling the restraint of foreign companies. Although the magnifying effect of U.S. sanctions is often very small, it is of greatest consequence to countries integrating themselves into the global marketplace and desirous of foreign involvement in their economy.

Establishing that unilateral sanctions can have an impact—perhaps even a significant one in specific instances—is not in itself sufficient to redeem them from their second-class citizenship. Such redemption would require demonstrating that this impact can be effective in achieving foreign policy goals. Even the maximum impact of unilateral sanctions will most likely be too small to achieve any effective measure of containment in today's world. For this reason, only rarely should policymakers rely on unilateral sanctions to contain a regime either politically or economically. At a political level, the United States can seek to ostracize a country in the post–cold war world, but it is by no means assured of generating a global perception that the country in question is an international pariah. The efforts of the Clinton administration to brand Cuba, Iran, Iraq, Libya, North Korea, and Sudan as "rogue" states helped shore up popular U.S. support for isolating these regimes. Yet such rhetoric did not create an international reality. Many countries, in fact, viewed American talk of rogue states as more of an indicator of U.S. domestic politics and an American penchant for punitive policies than a reflection of the character of these countries.[41] When many nations share concerns about the behavior of a country, U.S. efforts to politically isolate that country might have greater resonance; this "magnifying" effect, however, will fall greatly short of achieving political containment. Similarly, while unilateral sanctions may inflict some losses on a country's economy and its military, such costs are likely to be a mere fraction of what effective economic or military containment would demand.

Although the pursuit of containment through unilateral sanctions will almost always be fruitless in a globalized world, the same unilateral measures—if used properly—can be useful in changing the behavior of a regime. In some instances, the modest impact of unilateral sanctions can provide sufficient leverage to anchor a larger bargaining process geared toward altering specific actions of a government.[42] As already noted, adequate leverage is least likely to be secured when the target economy is relatively unsophisticated and the country does not have ambitions to be integrated into global political and economic networks; in contrast, unilateral sanctions are likely to have enough impact—and therefore provide sufficient leverage to frame a process of behavior change—when the target country wishes to assume a more prominent place in the international economic and political arena.[43] In these cases, policymakers will need to structure sanctions, as well as the other policy tools that accompany their use, to suit behavior change goals. As described earlier, whether sanctions can help induce behavior changes depends a great deal on whether the sanctions regime is flexible enough to respond to advances and reverses in the relationship between the United States and the targeted country. Moreover, such success depends on whether sanctions are complemented by vigorous diplomatic discussions and, ideally, the extension of additional incentives and penalties outside the sanctions regime.

Policymakers can make the most of unilateral sanctions if they steer clear of trying to contain regimes through their use and instead gear these measures to undeprin more flexible strategies for behavior change. The bad reputation of unilateral sanctions is arguably more because policymakers have ignored this lesson than it is a reflection of the inherent fecklessness of these tools. Particularly when used to address "rogue states," unilateral sanctions have been employed as measures of containment, not behavior change. Although the goals touted have often called for the target to abandon certain actions, the rigid comprehensive sanctions regimes usually employed and the instruments that accompany them (or, in more cases than not, the lack of instruments used alongside sanctions) have been more suited toward containment. As a result, sanctions regimes such as those in place against Cuba and Iran have neither contained regimes nor induced them to change their behavior.

### Gauging the Political Response of the Target

When regime change or behavior modification is the objective of U.S. policy, the impact of sanctions must be translated into political change before success can be declared. In these situations, the political response of the target to external pressure is far more important than the nature or extent of the impact of sanctions. In many cases, the two will not appear commensurate. For instance, more than in any other instance, sanctions on Iraq demonstrated the substantial gap that can exist between impact and effectiveness.[44] Other cases, too, revealed this point in less dramatic ways. For instance, U.S. sanctions on Iran were in fact *not* devoid of impact as is often alleged, yet the effectiveness of these measures was extremely poor. Sanctions on Sudan also laid bare this disconnect, if in a different manner; their effectiveness, while still minor, was far greater than their negligible economic impact would have suggested was possible. Together, these cases confirm the variable link between impact and effectiveness. In doing so, they underline the pleas made in chapter 2 for greater consideration of both how and when impact translates into effectiveness and how sanctions interact with domestic factors in the target country.

Policymakers looking to use sanctions effectively should be aware of several factors that determine how a leadership responds to pressure and, therefore, influence whether the economic or political impact of sanctions will lead to political change. Most important in determining the political response of the target is the nature of the relationship between the United States and the sanctioned country. Sanctions are much more likely to be effective when threatened or imposed in the context of a cordial or friendly relationship.[45] In these circumstances, the influence of sanctions is magnified because their use risks jeopardizing a connection whose benefits extend far beyond the area in dispute. Moreover, the channels of communication that exist in such relationships provide ready mechanisms for dialogue, clarification, and compromise, while trust facilitates success by making the target confident its compliance will be met with the removal of restrictions.[46] In short, in warm or even simply respectful bilateral relations, the proper framework for using sanctions as a tool of behavior change is often already in place.[47] In contrast, when sanctions rear their head in hostile relationships—such as the four examined in detail in this book—they are less likely to evoke the desired political response. In these cases, the imposition or threat of sanctions is a manifestation of an overall sour relationship, one that has fewer mechanisms in place to strike a mutually acceptable resolution to the crisis. The antagonistic context also leads the targeted country to question whether compliance with demands made will actually result in the easing of sanctions.

When considering the use of sanctions in the context of already hostile bilateral relations, policymakers should keep in mind three rules of thumb about gauging the reaction of the targeted regime. First, the political response of the target is less likely to be favorable to the United States when sanctions result in a "rally around the flag" effect that strengthens the targeted regime. This reaction depends less on the actual impact of sanctions and more on whether the citizens of the targeted country are suffering economic hardship or political humiliation, even if it is not attributable to sanctions. The modest success of the Taliban in uniting portions of the devastated Afghan population against extremely limited sanctions and those who imposed them can be explained in this light.[48] A nationalist reaction of this sort will also be most pronounced when the regime in question has some legitimacy over the people it governs, either through religious roots, democratic credentials, tribal connections, or the like. In contrast, regimes that have little independent domestic legitimacy—such as Qadhafi's regime in Libya or the National Islamic Front in Khartoum—will struggle to translate the imposition of sanctions into political support for their rule. Also important in gauging the intensity and longevity of the "rally around the flag" effect is the level of interaction between the target and the sender after the sanctions are imposed. The virtual absence of contact between the United States and Libya throughout the 1990s limited the resonance of Qadhafi's regular harangues against America, thereby frustrating his efforts to get political mileage out of the sanctions. In contrast, the proximity of Cuba to America and the large number of Cuban Americans living in the United States has ensured frequent—if minor—confrontations between Havana and Washington. These constant irritations and provocations have provided a fertile context for Fidel Castro's efforts to blame the U.S. embargo for Cuba's ills, allowing Castro to capitalize on U.S. sanctions on the island.[49]

Second, fractious domestic politics in the target will often determine its response to sanctions. Although in some cases sanctions can exploit cleavages in society to the advantage of those who impose them, more often, such fissures in the target inhibit the quick or predictable response of the sanctioned country.[50] When major divides exist within the ruling elite, the imposition of sanctions often compounds domestic power struggles, complicating the response of the government to them. U.S. sanctions against Iran did not elicit a significant response from Tehran in large part because the complicated political dynamics within Iran paralyzed the ability of Iranian leaders to react to U.S. pressure. Given the ever-shifting balance of power between those subscribing to President Mohammed Khatami's more moderate vision of Islam and society and those adhering to the more conservative notions of the Supreme Leader Ali Khamenei, no political leader or faction would risk making a controversial overture to the United States.[51] While Iran's power struggles played out visibly on the streets, in the courts, and in the media, domestic tensions in other countries may be less discernible to the outside observer but are equally important in determining how a country reacts to sanctions. In Sudan, for example, the brewing tensions between President Omar al-Bashir and Speaker of Parliament Hassan al-Turabi complicated the Sudanese response to sanctions. Only once al-Bashir evicted the more fundamentalist al-Turabi from government in 1999 did Khartoum embark on a more earnest effort to untangle itself from terrorism. Even in countries where no fissures in the leadership are evident to outsiders, sanctions can influence or even exacerbate existing cleavages. Although one can only speculate about the inner workings of the Taliban, the compromises it suggested to deal with Osama bin Laden when faced with the threat of UN sanctions in November 1999 may have been the product of an intense internal debate.[52] If so, the rejection of this offer by the United Nations could have discredited more moderate elements in the Taliban, contributing to the hardening of attitudes and actions within the movement noted by experts in 2000 and 2001.[53]

Finally, although the nature of demands made on the target influence its reaction to sanctions, evaluating whether sanctions are likely to evoke the desired political response involves more than a cursory assessment or categorization of these goals. As acknowledged by many scholars and practitioners, a government is more likely to comply when the demands made of it are "modest," rather than when they are "ambitious."[54] Although ambitious and modest goals may often correspond with "high" and "low" politics, a more careful approach would recognize two relative dimensions to the classification of goals. First, the domestic politics and international circumstances of a country—not the views of the international community—determine whether a demand is ambitious or modest. For South Korea, relinquishing its nuclear program did not threaten the regime or the viability of the country; for Iran, a country wedged between nuclear Pakistan and aspiring Iraq, the same demand may seem tantamount to suicide in the absence of new security arrangements. Second, there is almost always a temporal aspect to classifying a goal as modest or ambitious; a changing domestic or international environment can alter whether a regime views a demand as threatening to its survival or relatively benign. For instance, in 1992, Qadhafi may have believed that handing over Abdel Basset al-Megrahi—a member of a powerful tribe on which Qadhafi depended for domestic support—to the United

States or Britain would have jeopardized his rule. However, in 1999, in the wake of a military crackdown on Libya's Islamic opposition and the subsequent consolidation of his power, Qadhafi felt sufficiently empowered to deliver the Lockerbie suspects to the Netherlands.[55] Similarly, the widespread famine and the threat of state collapse in North Korea may have influenced Kim Il Sung's and Kim Jong Il's assessment of whether Pyongyang's nuclear program was vital to the regime's survival.

Paying more attention to domestic realities can help policymakers use sanctions more effectively. At the very least, greater awareness of these factors can help condition expectations of what sanctions can achieve in any given situation. Because sanctions, even at their best, are awkward and blunt tools, U.S. policymakers should be wary of trying to use them to affect particular outcomes in domestic political battles. However, armed with better information about the internal political dynamics of a country, American policymakers can be more confident that the sanctions they put in place will not turn into weapons of those factions fighting against U.S. interests as was done in Iran—where the sanctions-dominated U.S. strategy gave Iranian politicians and clerics opposed to warmer relations with the United States a justification for their enduring hostility. Moreover, better knowledge of domestic realities can help policymakers best present their demands and may encourage policymakers to couple their demands with incentives for compliance when such an approach could affect the calculations of a regime.

### Putting Costs in Perspective

Assessing the costs associated with sanctions—be they humanitarian, economic, or political—is an essential part of determining the utility of sanctions.[56] Equally important, however, is putting those costs in an appropriate context. Without a sense of what constitutes a reasonable cost, sanctions policy will be more easily held hostage to the arguments of special interest groups. In fact, although holding down the costs of sanctions is often beneficial, in most cases, it is neither necessary nor desirable to eliminate costs altogether.

More than any other one issue, sanctions imposed on Iraq in 1990 recast thinking about the link between humanitarian costs and economic sanctions. The Iraqi experience squashed the once-common belief that sanctions could induce political change by simply applying adequate pressure on the population. Moreover, the suffering of Iraqis galvanized the United Nations to find ways to address the human needs of a population in a sanctioned country, ultimately demonstrating that the international community—through creativity and perseverance—can address humanitarian costs sometimes associated with sanctions when necessary.[57] While these are positive contributions to the understanding of sanctions and the implementation of sanctions policy, the heightened sensitivity to the humanitarian effects of sanctions has had unwelcome side effects. In particular, the failure to adequately distinguish the effects of sanctions from the influence of other factors has led many to overestimate the suffering caused by sanctions. In Iraq, critics have been quick to blame sanctions for the misery of the Iraqi people, when their condition is much more attributable to decisions made by Saddam Hussein. As a result, international reluctance to use sanctions has grown far beyond whatever hesitance might be warranted on humanitarian grounds. This sensitivity has also encouraged countries or organizations to mask their political or economic agendas through humanitarian objections as was done in Sudan when humanitarian concerns became a front for political reservations over enforcing the second round of UN sanctions.

Sanctions should almost never be allowed to cause any form of extreme deprivation. Nor should policymakers expect sanctions to work solely through pressure exerted on the average citizen. Nevertheless, some discomfort (not despair) of the population at large is often conducive to sanctions' success. In regimes that are—even in minor ways—vulnerable to societal pressure, a palpable sense among citizens that their economic fortunes are stagnating or that their standard of living is deteriorating can ratchet up pressure on a regime. This was the case in Serbia, where the civilian economy limped along while the country was under sanctions. People were able to maintain a semblance of normalcy but were denied prosperity. This balance was critical to the success of sanctions; Serbs remained focused on freeing themselves from sanctions, but their suffering under them did not constitute a humanitarian crisis that undermined support for sanctions abroad or jeopardized the ability of Serbs to reconstruct their country once Milosevic was no longer in power. Similarly, the moderate, yet not excessive, curb that sanctions placed on the Libyan standard of living contributed to a growing sense of dissatisfaction with Qadhafi's regime. This disquiet was one of several factors slowly pressuring Tripoli to surrender the Lockerbie suspects.

Similarly, keeping down the costs borne by the United States as a result of sanctions is key to the utility of these tools, but eliminating them could be counterproductive. Sanctions on Sudan were judged to have utility only in the most modest way; only when viewed in light of the negligible costs associated with imposing and enforcing sanctions could the small progress made toward realizing U.S. goals be deemed acceptable. In this case, however, exemptions made to minimize U.S. business losses due to sanctions may have actually diminished the overall utility of these tools; by leading some countries to question the credibility of U.S. policy toward Sudan, they frustrated U.S. efforts to gain multilateral cooperation to pressure Khartoum.

The findings of this book clearly support the view that sanctions can entail a variety of costs to the parties that impose them. Yet, on the whole, the economic costs borne by the United States for the sanctions regimes it has in place are not unreasonable or even substantial, particularly when seen in the context of the whole U.S. economy. The influence of sanctions on specific industries or sectors, however, can be sizable.[58] Sanctions can also entail notable political costs. For example, the passage of laws mandating secondary sanctions against Cuba, Iran, and Libya in the 1990s—although not seriously jeopardizing any bilateral relations with allies—did create unnecessary friction between the United States and Europe. Other political or diplomatic costs of sanctions may be less pronounced at official levels—such as the irritations that developed between the United States and countries in the Middle East over U.S. policy toward Iraq—but are equally important.

Even while acknowledging these costs, the evidence does not support the conventional wisdom that sanctions are costly or "expensive" tools—in the sense of inflicting a high price for what is gained. For the most part, this judgment is best made on a case-by-case basis. In some instances the United States is getting a bargain when it or the United Nations uses sanctions. Sanctions on Iraq involved sizable economic and political costs, but they were on the whole a small price to pay for more than a decade of containment of an aggressive regime bent on attaining and stockpiling weapons of mass destruction. In other cases, sanctions are wildly overpriced for the benefits they are securing. Take the case of U.S. sanctions on Iran. The costs borne by the United States for its sanctions-dominated policy toward Iran, while notable, were not huge in the sense of crippling American industries or seriously fracturing relations with allies. However, given the paltry achievements of this particular sanctions policy, sanctions on Iran look more like a swindle. One hundred dollars may be a reasonable price for a bicycle, but it is certainly a great deal to pay for a lollipop.

It is important to see sanctions and the costs associated with them in a broad context, especially when the sanctions may affect U.S. energy security. Although sanctions had an impact on impeding the development of the sanctioned country's capacity to produce oil, only in the case of Iraq could this effect be construed as significant. In Iran, Libya, and Sudan, internal factors and domestic policies were larger obstacles to the development of their energy resources than were sanctions. The *collective* impact of these policies on energy security is, however, greater. Certainly, sanctions simultaneously in place against four oil producers have frustrated the U.S. goal of diversifying its energy supplies. Moreover, although difficult to quantify, the joint effects of sanctions are likely to have dampened global oil production enough to affect energy prices over time. Higher oil prices not only represent a cost to the United States and other industrialized countries in themselves, but they translate into even higher costs in terms of lost growth. At the same time, if sanctions collectively force up the price of oil, they inadvertently offer an economic boon to the very oil-exporting economies that America has sought to contain.

Policymakers should be careful not only to assess the costs of sanctions but to view them in a variety of contexts, particularly when faced with the arguments of special interest groups seeking to portray sanctions as either costly or inexpensive. Some value will always be derived from seeing the costs of sanctions in relation to the U.S. economy as a whole, in regard to a certain industry or region, or with respect to a particular American goal such as diversifying energy suppliers. The policymaker, however, should acknowledge that none of these assessments in themselves can be sufficient to reject or endorse the use of sanctions overall or in a particular instance. Instead, policymakers should consider economic and political costs in the context of what the United States is gaining from the use of sanctions. Only then can they determine whether the price paid by the United States and others is justified.

### Prioritizing Goals

Sanctions regimes imposed on state sponsors of terrorism have almost always embraced the goals of containment and behavior change simultaneously. UN sanctions on Iraq were expected to deliver on both fronts concurrently, as were U.S. measures put in place against Iran, Libya, and Sudan. Yet in practice, it may be impossible to adequately pursue both types of goals at the same time. As discussed earlier, doing so can lead to conflicting strategies, compromising what might have been achieved had the goals of policymakers been more narrowly defined to one set of objectives or the other. Moreover, the pursuit of containment and behavior modification at the same time has had the unfortunate side effect of warping popular perceptions of the success of sanctions. Too often, sanctions regimes that advance both causes are evaluated solely on their ability to change the behavior of a country. Achievements in the realm of containment are overlooked or dismissed as less important. For instance, many view sanctions on Iraq as a failure because they were unable to get Saddam Hussein to agree to the full disarmament of Iraq, even though the same measures have an impressive record of largely containing the regime over a long period. Similarly, sanctions on Libya are often seen as a success, not primarily because they contained Qadhafi's regime at a political and military level for many years, but because they contributed to Libya's decision to surrender the Lockerbie suspects and to move away from supporting terrorism.

The conflation of containment with behavior change is understandable. The two concepts are related. Successful containment can be a goal in itself, to the extent that keeping military items, economic resources, or political legitimacy from a regime is seen as a worthy achievement on its own. Yet it can also alter the calculation of a regime over the long term in favor of abandoning certain behaviors. Yet, even while possibly providing the impetus for reform, sanctions well suited to containment are unlikely to consolidate behavior shifts or effectively govern the process of behavior change—which is not instantaneous, but gradual, painstaking, and often subject to reverses.

The challenge to policymakers, of course, is confronting the reality of multiple objectives. Although there is no "solution" to this problem, highlighting it can have two beneficial effects. First, it forces policymakers to recognize that there is a cost to piling goals on top of one another. This realization will encourage them to prioritize goals when possible, knowing that the pursuit of multiple goals can diminish the chances of achieving any of them. Second, exposing this reality may encourage policymakers to focus on goals for which the tools they have at their disposal are most appropriate. A gardener with only hedge clippers is better off focusing on trimming bushes than he is at devoting his limited energy to uprooting a tree. Policymakers may prioritize behavior change because it is preferable to containment or because the unilateral sanctions at their disposal are most appropriate to such a pursuit. When some measure of multilateral cooperation is available, policymakers may opt for a containment strategy, one that will be most successful if it is uncomplicated by simultaneous efforts to change key areas of the regime's behavior.

Given the link between containment and behavior change, policymakers need to be prepared for a time when they should shift their strategy. The case of Libya suggests the importance and difficulty of adapting polley in this way. Since UN sanctions—which had inadvertently created a framework for encouraging behavior change—were suspended, the United States has struggled to modify its policy in a way that continues to encourage Libyan reform, rather than vainly pursue the containment of Libya with unilateral sanctions. Failure to do so risks squandering what leverage U.S. sanctions do provide and hinders the effectiveness of U.S. policy toward Libya overall.

Although no magic recipe for this transition exists, several factors increase the likelihood of it proceeding more smoothly when the time is ripe. First, an administration that has maintained regular consultations with Congress on relations with the country in question is best poised to successfully convert one strategy to another. Such efforts will pay off, ideally in the form of greater support for policy modifications but at least in diminished criticism of such changes. Second, when policymakers begin to move away from a containment strategy toward one aimed at behavior change, they must resist the urge to only recalibrate one tool at a time. Although they can move slowly, the recasting of approaches demands rethinking of all the tools in place simultaneously. For instance, adjusting rhetoric and public diplomacy efforts to the goals at hand is essential. As officials in the Clinton administration learned in the 1990s, it was counterproductive to lambaste countries as rogues at the same time efforts were under way to entice these countries back into the family of nations. Finally, maintaining some channels of communication with the target country—even while its containment is sought—is critical in ensuring a smooth transition.[59] The decision to close an embassy or impose a ban on the travel of U.S. citizens to a country should be strictly related to security considerations, not made as a political gesture or statement. When security concerns do preclude an official U.S. presence in the country, efforts should be made to maintain contact at some other level on a regular basis. Not only will these connections provide useful information to the United States in an ongoing fashion, but they will enable Washington to better time its efforts to move toward a more engaged relationship if and when circumstances warrant.

### Making Sanctions Regimes More Flexible

Flexibility is the key to a successful sanctions regime in a behavior change strategy. When trying to coerce and cajole a country to take steps to modify its actions, U.S. policymakers need to be able to respond to new developments with speed and certitude. As discussed elsewhere, they must be able to calibrate U.S. policy—and the sanctions regime in particular—to gradual improvements in the target's behavior and to credibly offer further induce-ments if greater cooperation is forthcoming.

Although eliminating some of these rigidities would be impossible—as it would entail removing the politics from policymaking—policymakers and analysts have proposed several mechanisms geared toward increasing the flexibility of sanctions. Most of them are welcome improvements on how sanctions policy has been made in the past. As noted by many analysts and policymakers, presidential waivers, for instance, should always be included in legislation imposing or mandating sanctions. Not only do they enable the president to react to sudden developments or crises, but their existence can help transform tension between the executive branch and Congress over sanctions into a bargaining dynamic with the target country. As discussed in chapter 3, conceivably congressional-executive disputes over sanctions on Iran could provide U.S. officials with some leverage in a future dialogue between Washington and Tehran. Exit strategies or road maps—which pro-vide clear understandings of what must be achieved for sanctions to be lifted and the benefits that will gradually accrue as the country traverses this path—will also make sanctions regimes more flexible by diminishing battles surrounding their removal.

The terrorism list—a mechanism through which many countries are sanctioned—could also be reformed to allow for greater flexibility. Cur-rently, once a country is designated a state supporter of terrorism, an exten-sive array of sanctions takes effect immediately and remains in place until the country is taken off the terrorism list.[60] A more useful process would allow for some separation of the actual designation from the penalties asso-ciated with it, either in a two-tiered process or through the provision of presidential waivers that would give the executive the authority to remove sanctions gradually. Abolition of the existing "all or nothing" approach would have important advantages. First, it would diminish the discrepancies between the countries placed on the terrorism list and those actually sup-porting terrorism. The current system encourages the State Department to shy away from naming countries to the list that are at least as deserving of the designation as Cuba and North Korea (two countries currently consid-ered state sponsors) when sanctioning them could exacerbate their terror-ism problem rather than mitigate it. Ending this double standard would increase the credibility of the terrorism list, and therefore, the opprobrium associated with being placed on it and its utility as a policy tool. More im-portant, allowing policymakers and counterterrorism officials to calibrate penalties to reflect the specifics of each situation would make for better policy. On one hand, it would allow policymakers to dangle more tangible inducements (in the form of lifting sanctions) in front of countries seriously seeking to shed the terrorist designation. On the other hand, it would provide the flexibility that policymakers need to address many of the complicated scenarios that will arise as the United States continues its efforts to combat global terrorism; if the number of countries that are viewed to provide some support for terrorism grows beyond the small circle of so-called rogue states, the United States will need a mechanism that allows it to apply pressure to countries that are struggling to address their terrorist problems, without entirely cutting off contact with them. At the very least, U.S. policymakers should use the already available designation of "not fully cooperating with U.S. antiterrorism efforts" more aggressively.[61] The only mandatory sanctions associated with this designation are restrictions on military sales and assistance, although other sanctions may be added at the discretion of the president. If employed more regularly, this added category could provide a much-needed way station for countries either moving toward or away from a full-fledged state sponsor of terrorism designation.

Sunset provisions—although garnering much support in recent years—should be avoided rather than embraced. Many see these mechanisms—which limit the life of sanctions to a particular period unless they are specifically renewed—as a sensible way of combating the tendency of sanctions to stay in place long after they are useful and, therefore, a vehicle for making sanctions more flexible. Yet, despite the best of intentions, sunset provisions create new hazards without solving old problems. Laws or resolutions declaring that sanctions will lapse unless specific action is taken undermine the impetus of the target to comply with the demands of sanctions. The advantage shifts to the sanctioned entity, which is encouraged to wait patiently until the designated time has passed in the hopes that sanctions will be lifted without the need for it to make difficult choices or sacrifices. Moreover, there is little evidence that sunset provisions encourage thoughtful re-evaluation of the sanctions tool at timely intervals. Instead, extensions of sanctions scheduled to lapse can simply force contentious debates at awkward times. Consider the renewal of ILSA legislation just before its five-year time limit expired in 2001. Although widely considered a seriously flawed law, virtually all members of Congress voted for its extension, concerned that doing otherwise would send the wrong signal to Libya and Iran. Unwilling to send the positive message that letting ILSA expire would communicate, Congress opted to renew ILSA, sending a hostile message to both Iran and Libya when a more subtle, nuanced signal might have been appropriate. Because letting sanctions lapse will never be considered a judgment-neutral action, sunset provisions will always be ensconced in political debates, limiting their ability to function as a mechanism to clear ineffective or antiquated measures. Past efforts to modify Iraqi sanctions—be it to incorporate the Oil for Food program, to compel Iraq to accept a new weapons inspection team, or to rejuvenate international support for the sanctions in 2001 and 2002—demonstrate how slow and painful the process of re-evaluating sanctions can be. But they also reveal that such reassessments are possible and need not be prompted by an artificial external mechanism that brings its own costs with it.

In the end, restoring greater flexibility to sanctions regimes may be less about reforming old or designing new mechanisms than it is about establishing better coordination between branches of government. As discussed throughout the book, sanctions—particularly those intended to change the behavior of a regime—work best when they create a bargaining dynamic. Tension between Congress and the executive branch over the use of sanctions can provide leverage in diplomatic negotiations. When Congress is debating restrictions, the efforts of the president or the secretary of state to extract certain reforms or changes from a government are more credible when the threat of congressionally mandated sanctions looms. Yet such leverage is greatest before Congress imposes sanctions. For this reason, Congress should consider adopting a graduated approach to the imposition of sanctions. Congress, as a matter of policy, could first use its resolutions and deliberations to provide continuous guidance and recommendations on sanctions policy to the executive branch.[62] Only after it judges that the president has disregarded its advice, or has been unable to achieve certain objectives diplomatically, should Congress move to legislate its own sanctions. Such a multitiered approach often occurs inadvertently; institutionalizing it, or adopting guidelines that make it more likely, could heighten the effectiveness of U.S. sanctions policy by prolonging the period during which the executive branch can extract behavior changes from the target.

## The Wise Policymaker

In the decades ahead, policymakers will struggle to find the proper tools to address the broad challenges faced by the United States. Sanctions can and should play an important role in these efforts, but only if they are used to greater effect than in the past. The necessary recalibration of these tools holds particular importance for how the United States deals with the threat posed by states that both support terrorism and pursue weapons of mass destruction. As the United States continues its efforts to combat terrorism, maintaining sanctions that are ineffective will carry increasing costs: either they will be insufficient to stem the threat posed by states that continue to sponsor terrorism or they will be obstacles to striking more cooperative relationships with countries that are ready and able to put terrorism in their past. As discussed in this chapter, making sanctions more effective—in either circumstance—will require rethinking both how the structure of sanctions matches the goals pursued and how sanctions are coupled with other foreign policy tools to form coherent strategies.

Even if policymakers do all that they can to make sanctions more effective and to use these tools more wisely, a successful foreign policy will sometimes depend on *not* using sanctions. As stressed throughout this book, sanctions may be more or less effective, but whether they have comparative utility—whether they should be used in any given circumstance—depends on how the alternatives compare to sanctions. In some cases, a sanctions-dominated strategy may seem to be an unsatisfying option, but it is the best one available to policymakers at the time. Sanctions on Iraq throughout the 1990s, for instance, are a good example of how a sanctions approach can be the wisest selection of a poor set of choices.

In other instances, a sanctions regime—even one that may have some benefits—should be discarded or revised if a more useful option is at hand. U.S. sanctions on Iran or Cuba are prime candidates for such an assessment. To advocate an alternative to a sanctions-dominated strategy in place is not to say that the sanctions regime has produced no benefits; in the case of Iran, U.S. sanctions have kept some resources away from Tehran, whereas sanctions on Cuba have created some pressure on Castro's regime. Nor does advancing an alternative to sanctions in these instances mean renouncing U.S. goals to further democracy in Cuba or end Iranian support for terrorism, pursuit of weapons of mass destruction, or opposition to Israel. Rather, discarding or reforming sanctions in favor of another approach in these cases would be a pragmatic shift, one that acknowledges that there are more useful ways of pursuing, and achieving, the same objectives. A more open economic and political relationship between the United States and Cuba—perhaps one that employs investment codes rather than sanctions—would almost certainly be a better way to bolster stability and prospects for a smooth democratic transition on the island. With Iran, a more nuanced approach toward Tehran might remove the United States from the "third rail" of Iranian domestic politics, thereby increasing the chances of a bilateral dialogue in which the United States could address its strategic concerns. It could also allow the United States to achieve many goals—regarding Iraq, Afghanistan, and counternarcotics—that are in the natural interests of the United States and Iran.

Performing this assessment—whether sanctions-dominated strategies have more utility than the other approaches available—is truly the greatest challenge to the wise policymaker. It involves gauging not only how globalization and American preeminence have affected the use of sanctions but also how these same factors have influenced the use of other policy tools. Only when various strategies have been subjected to the same rigorous analysis can policymakers choose intelligently among sanctions and their alternatives. Making sanctions more effective is an important task, but making foreign policy more successful—through greater or lesser use of sanctions—is the ultimate mission.

# Notes

## Chapter One

1. The question of how the United States should exploit or utilize its current dominance has fed a burgeoning literature. See, for instance, Stephen G. Brooks and William C. Wohlforth, "American Primacy in Perspective," *Foreign Affairs* (July/August 2002), pp. 20–33; Stephen M. Walt, "American Primacy: Its Prospects and Pitfalls," *Naval War College Review*, vol. 55, no. 2, pp. 9–28; Richard N. Haass, "What to Do with American Primacy?" *Foreign Affairs* (September/October 1999); Zbigniew Brzezinski, *The Grand Chessboard: American Primacy and Its Geostrategic Imperatives* (New York: Harper Collins, 1997).

2. This typology of the four sorts of statecraft (military, informational, diplomatic, and economic) was first devised by Harold Lasswell. See Harold Lasswell, *Who Gets What, When, How* (New York: McGraw-Hill, 1936), and Harold Lasswell, *World Politics Faces Economics* (New York: McGraw-Hill, 1945). For more on the various distinctions within each area of statecraft, see David A. Baldwin, *Economic Statecraft* (Princeton University Press, 1985), especially pp. 8–28.

3. The United States was quick to facilitate debt relief for and waive long-standing sanctions against Pakistan in the hope that those actions would provide President Pervez Musharraf political cover for his controversial decision to support U.S. efforts to root out Osama bin Laden. Humanitarian aid also was a critical part of these initial efforts; not only was it needed to relieve the suffering of Afghans, but it was important to illustrate that the United States was not at war with Islam or the people of Afghanistan.

4. In contrast to the vast literature on the use of foreign aid or incentives for development purposes, the strategic use of incentives to deal with countries with which the United States has adversarial relations is only beginning to be explored. See Richard N. Haass and Meghan L. O'Sullivan, eds., *Honey and Vinegar: Incentives, Sanctions, and Foreign Policy* (Brookings, 2000); Jean-Marc F. Blanchard, Edward D. Mansfield, and

Norrin M. Ripsman, eds., *Power and the Purse: Economic Statecraft, Interdependence, and National Security* (London: Frank Cass, 2000); and David Cortright, ed., *The Price of Peace: Incentives and International Conflict Prevention* (New York: Rowman & Littlefield Publishers, Inc., 1997).

5. Secondary sanctions, which penalize a third country for assistance given to another nation, could also regain popularity in the ongoing campaign against terrorism if national security issues are seen to triumph over broader economic and diplomatic interests.

6. See Bruce W. Jentleson, "Economic Sanctions and Post–Cold War Conflicts: Challenges for Theory and Policy," in Paul C. Stern and Daniel Druckman, eds., *International Conflict Resolution after the Cold War* (Washington: National Academy Press, 2000), p. 123.

7. The list of studies that have made serious contributions to the understanding of sanctions is long, and a good deal of the literature is discussed or noted in chapter 2.

8. The U.S. government compiles an annual "terrorism list" which identifies countries deemed to support terrorism as a matter of policy—either through active involvement or acquiescence to the operation of terrorist groups on their soil.

9. In the past, state sponsors often provided direct support to terrorist organizations with which they shared animosities or agendas. As the 1990s progressed, the enthusiasm of many (but not all) state sponsors for supporting terrorist groups in this fashion waned; many states moved toward a more passive support for terrorism, through which they provided the terrorist groups a physical base of operation. See Paul Pillar, *Terrorism and U.S. Foreign Policy* (Brookings, 2001), pp. 157–75.

10. The terrorism list was created by Section 6(j) of the Export Administration Act of 1979. At the time, designation as a state sponsor of terrorism not only carried symbolic weight, but it also entailed a variety of economic penalties to pressure and isolate the country. The associated sanctions were initially limited to prohibitions on aid and controls on the sale of military items, yet, over time, more restrictions became associated with being placed on the terrorism list. In 1996, Congress passed the Antiterrorism and Effective Death Penalty Act, a law which prohibited virtually all financial transactions with state sponsors of terrorism as well as called for secondary sanctions against countries that provided them with military support. This law also revoked the sovereign immunity of state sponsors in American courts of law, opening the way for civil suits against these countries.

11. These four sanctions regimes are among the most comprehensive ever maintained by the United States during peacetime. In fact, even economic and political contacts with the Soviet Union during the cold war were less restricted than are contacts between the United States and Iran, Iraq, Libya, and Sudan.

12. Not only does the United States maintain full diplomatic relations with Syria, but it allows financial transactions with the country, as long as they are not known to support terrorist activity.

# Chapter Two

1. For two varying perspectives, see Jesse Helms, "What Sanctions Epidemic? U.S. Business' Curious Crusade," *Foreign Affairs*, vol. 78 (January/February 1999), pp. 2–8,

and Richard N. Haass, "Sanctioning Madness," *Foreign Affairs*, vol. 76 (November/December 1997), pp. 74–85.

2. There is also debate about whether economic warfare (in the sense of using economic instruments to affect the military position of a country) should be included under the rubric of economic sanctions or whether it represents another category of statecraft. This study considers such efforts to qualify as sanctions. For a discussion about this debate, see David Baldwin, *Economic Statecraft* (Princeton University Press, 1985), pp. 36–38. For a sensible discussion of defining a sanction and other methodological challenges in the study of sanctions, see Bruce Jentleson, "Economic Sanctions and Post-Cold War Conflicts: Challenges for Theory and Policy," in Paul C. Stern and Daniel Druckman, ed., *International Conflict Resolution after the Cold War* (Washington: National Academy Press, 2000), especially pp. 123–31.

3. This definition excludes restrictions such as those mandated by the Brooke amendment (which calls for severance of aid to any country that is more than one year in arrears on past U.S. loans) or those resulting from labor or trade disputes. While such restrictions are not included in the appendixes to this chapter, they are discussed where relevant in the case chapters.

4. It should be noted that efforts to quantify sanctions episodes from 1990 to 2001 are limited to sanctions that are imposed on states or countries (appendix table 2A-1). However, appendix table 2A-2 also tracks sanctions imposed during this time against nonstate actors; these sanctions are separated from sanctions against states, given the greater difficulty in listing each sanction imposed on a company, political movement, or one of hundreds of individuals and the methodological problems that would arise from equating each such sanction with a sanction imposed on a country. Trends in sanctioning nonstate actors are considered later in this chapter.

5. If one limits the study to U.S. unilateral sanctions (opposed to ones imposed with some cooperation from other states or international or regional institutions) against state actors, the ratio of congressionally legislated measures to those imposed by the executive branch is almost 2 to 1. See appendix table 2A-2.

6. Michael Mastanduno, "Economics and Security in Scholarship and Statecraft," *International Organization*, vol. 52 (Autumn 1998), pp. 825–54.

7. This statement is, of course, a general one. Notable instances in which the United States used economic tools to promote its security interests—such as in its encouragement of the Middle East peace process—existed.

8. See Francis Deng, *Sovereignty and Responsibility: Conflict Management in Africa* (Brookings, 1996). UN Secretary General Kofi Annan has also repeatedly spoken out about how states cannot hide behind their sovereignty to persecute their own populations. See for instance Kofi A. Annan, *The Question of Intervention: Statements by the Secretary-General* (New York: United Nations Publications, 1999).

9. It is important to note that this broadened agenda is not exclusively an American one; almost every industrial country donor has a democracy component to its overseas programs. Moreover, international financial institutions first embraced good governance in 1989 after a World Bank report blamed much of Africa's economic failure on political weaknesses and institutions. See Thomas Carothers, *Aiding Democracy Abroad: The Learning Curve* (Washington: Carnegie Endowment for International Peace, 1999).

10. Included in this characterization are sanctions imposed to discourage nuclear proliferation (such as those put in place against Pakistan, South Africa, Brazil, Argentina, and India in the late 1970s and early 1980s).

11. It is interesting to note that in the majority of the cases in which the United States imposed sanctions to address specific behaviors, the target country was an ally or a friendly nation. See Gary Clyde Hufbauer, Jeffrey J. Schott, and Kimberly Ann Elliott, *Economic Sanctions Reconsidered*, 2d ed. (Washington: Institute for International Economics, 1990), pp. 16–27.

12. The 508 (then called section 513) sanctions were first passed in December 19, 1985, as part of P.L. 99-190, which was a resolution to continue appropriations for the rest of FY1986.

13. See the chapter on Libya for more information on this episode. The decision to sanction Libya for Abu Nidal's action also reflected the nature of the relationship between Tripoli and the organization.

14. Although some terrorist organizations spanned these decades, many of their relationships with state actors changed significantly over this time as these groups shifted from being agents of the state to being supporters of the state (al-Qaida and the Taliban being the most extreme example).

15. In 1992, a group of NGOs and individuals sharing the goal of banning the use of land mines throughout the world founded the International Campaign to Ban Landmines. In large part due to the work of this organization, 121 countries negotiated a treaty on banning land mines in September 1997. The campaign and its coordinator were awarded the Nobel Peace Prize for their efforts in the same year. See www.icbl.org (June 13, 2002).

16. In the wake of the September 11 attacks, funding sources of transnational networks such as Osama bin Laden's al-Qaida were closely examined. Although eliciting less attention, national liberation groups—particularly ones with large diasporas—also have benefited greatly from globalization. The Liberation Tigers of Tamil Eelam, for example, used vast shipping networks and the resources of expatriate Tamils to support and assist their struggle against the Sri Lankan state. See Rohan Gunaratne, "Internationalization of the Tamil Conflict (and Its Implications)," in Siri Gamage and I. B. Watson, eds., *Conflict and Community in Contemporary Sri Lanka: "Pearl of the East" or the "Island of Tears"?* (London: Sage Publications, 1999), pp. 121–22.

17. Of the 115 episodes of sanctions examined by Hufbauer, Schott, and Elliott, almost none deal with sanctions against a nonstate actor.

18. The four political movements were the Khmer Rouge in Cambodia, UNITA in Angola, the Revolutionary United Front in Sierra Leone, and the Taliban in Afghanistan. For an analysis of these episodes and the trends behind the more frequent use of UN sanctions, see David Cortright and George Lopez, *The Sanctions Decade: Assessing UN Strategies in the 1990s* (Boulder, Colo.: Lynne Rienner Publishers, 2000).

19. See appendix table 2A-2.

20. The Arms Export Control Act was amended in November 1990 to include sanctions on nonstate actors for proliferation in missile technology and was again amended in December 1991 to include sanctions on nonstate actors for proliferation in chemical and biological weapons technology. See Section 73(a)(2)(A) of the Arms Export Control Act (22 U.S.C. 2797b(a)(2)(A)); and Sections 81(a) and 81(b) of the Arms Export

Control Act (22 U.S.C. 2798(a), 2798(b)). Scores of Libyan companies were blacklisted in 1991 and 1992; the United States blacklisted 300 Pakistani and Indian companies after Islamabad and Delhi conducted nuclear tests in 1998.

21. William J. Clinton, *Executive Order 12947*, January 23, 1995. The number of groups and individuals targeted in this fashion increased in August 1998 with executive order 13099, which added Osama bin Laden, al-Qaida, and two other individuals to the list.

22. Antiterrorism and Effective Death Penalty Act of 1996, P.L. 104-132, August 24, 1996. This legislation and the Foreign Terrorist Organization (FTO) list it created complemented the practice of identifying and sanctioning state sponsors of terrorism, which began in 1979. In reality, this new law did not catalyze much action in the late 1990s; at the time of the September 11 terrorist attacks, only $301,000 worth of FTO assets had been frozen in the United States. See Office of Foreign Assets Control, *Terrorist Assets Report: 2000 Annual Report to the Congress on Assets in the United States Belonging to Terrorist Countries or International Terrorist Organizations* (Department of the Treasury, January 2001), p. 12.

23. For example, name recognition software—which has existed in the United States in some form since the 1980s—allows banks to identify and interdict transactions by targeted individuals. See David Cortright, George Lopez, and Elizabeth S. Rogers, "Targeted Financial Sanctions: Smart Sanctions That Do Work," in David Cortright and George Lopez, eds., *Smart Sanctions: Targeting Economic Statecraft* (Lanham, Md.: Rowman & Littlefield Publishers, 2002), and David Cortright and George Lopez, *Sanctions and the Search for Security* (Boulder, Colo.: Lynne Rienner, 2002).

24. Such technology is still in its early phases. See David Cortright, George Lopez, and Alistair Millar, "Smart Sanctions: Restructuring UN Policy In Iraq" (Fourth Freedom Forum, March 2001), pp. 13–14 (www.fourthfreedom.org/pdf/smartreport.pdf [October 15, 2001]).

25. See George E. Shambaugh, *States, Firms, and Power: Successful Sanctions in United States Foreign Policy* (Albany, N.Y.: State University of New York Press, 1999), pp. 161–212.

26. See Tony Smith, *Foreign Attachments: The Power of Ethnic Groups in the Making of American Foreign Policy* (Harvard University Press, 2000).

27. See L. David Brown and others, "Globalization, NGOs, and Multisectoral Relations," in Joseph S. Nye and John D. Donahue, eds., *Governance in a Globalizing World* (Brookings, 2000), pp. 275–78, and Wolfgang H. Reincke, "The Other World Wide Web: Global Public Policy Networks," *Foreign Policy* (Winter 1999/2000), pp. 44–57.

28. Not only did the number of legislated sanctions rise, but Congress moved from primarily advancing sanctions that cut off aid to countries during the cold war to more ambitious legislated measures that terminated trade, prohibited investment, or imposed secondary measures on countries or companies maintaining economic or military relations with state sponsors of terrorism.

29. The Victims of Trafficking and Violence Protection Act of 2000 calls for the president to submit an annual report to Congress on trafficking in persons around the world. The report must also include a list of countries that are not meeting "minimum standards for the elimination of trafficking." The United States will then withhold nonhumanitarian and non-trade assistance from countries so designated and vote against lending from international financial institutions to those countries. See Section 110 of *Victims of Trafficking and Violence Protection Act of 2000*, P.L. 106-386 (GPO, 2000).

30. USA*Engage is a consortium of more than 600 American businesses united to oppose the use of unilateral sanctions. See www.usaengage.org (June 13, 2002).

31. See Donald L. Losman, "Economic Sanctions: An Emerging Business Menace," *Business Economics*, vol. 33 (April 1998), pp. 37–42, and Don Deline, chairman, USA*Engage, *Letter to President George W. Bush*, August 2, 2001 (www.fourthfreedom. org/pdf/smartreport.pdf [October 15, 2001]).

32. William A. Reinsch, president of USA*Engage, testimony at Iran-Libya Sanctions Extension Act of 2001: Hearing before the Subcommittee on the Middle East and South Asia of the House International Relations Committee, 107 Cong. 1 sess., May 9, 2001; also see, Frank Kittredge, testimony at Sanctions Revisited: Hearing before the Subcommittee on International Economic Policy and Trade of the House Committee on International Relations, 105 Cong. 2 sess., September 10, 1998.

33. See, for example, Voices in the Wilderness (www.nonviolence.org/vitw/ [June 13, 2002]); Campaign against Sanctions on Iraq (www.cam.ac.uk/ societies/casi/ [June 13, 2002]); and Christian Aid (www.christian-aid.org.uk/ [June 13, 2002]). Also see Karine Morin and Steven H. Miles, M.D., for the Ethics and Human Rights Committee, "The Health Effects of Economic Sanctions and Embargoes: The Role for Health Professionals," *Annals of Internal Medicine* (2000), vol. 132, pp. 158–161, and the American Association for World Health, *Denial of Food and Medicine: The Impact of the U. S. Embargo on Health and Nutrition in Cuba* (Washington: American Association for World Health, 1997).

34. See, for example, Richard N. Haass, testimony at The Use and Effect of Unilateral Trade Sanctions: Hearing before the Subcommittee on Trade of the House Committee on Ways and Means, 106 Cong. 1 sess., May 27, 1999.

35. For more details on legislative initiatives to reform sanctions, see Dianne Rennack, "Economic Sanctions: Legislation in the 106th Congress" (Congressional Research Service, December 15, 2000), especially pp. 3–16.

36. The Senate bill, S. 757, was introduced on March 25, 1999, but never got out of the Foreign Relations Committee. The House bill, H.R. 1244, was introduced on March 24, 1999. It also never left the committee stage, but the Subcommittee on Trade of the House Ways and Means Committee did hold hearings on the bill on May 27, 1999.

37. The Senate version of the bill introduced in the 106th Congress (S. 757) had 38 sponsors and cosponsors (22 Republicans and 16 Democrats); the House version (H.R. 1244) was supported by 112 sponsors and cosponsors (76 Republicans and 36 Democrats).

38. Clinton administration officials objected to how the legislation would constrain the executive branch but only set forth guidelines for Congress (given that legislation could not bind future sessions of Congress). They also protested a loss of executive flexibility in imposing or lifting sanctions as circumstances required. See Stuart E. Eizenstat, testimony at The Use and Effect of Unilateral Trade Sanctions: Hearing before the Subcommittee on Trade of the House Committee on Ways and Means, 106 Cong. 1 sess., May 27, 1999.

39. The same consciousness was also manifest in the changing presentation of U.S. costs by the executive branch. Virtually every statement made by a member of the executive branch regarding sanctions in the late 1990s at least acknowledged the commercial costs to the United States. See, for instance, Stuart Eizenstat, testimony given to the Bipartisan Senate Task Force on Sanctions, 105 Cong. 2 sess., September 8, 1998; Dan

Glickman, testimony given at Sanctions Reform: Hearing before the Senate Committee on Foreign Relations, 106 Cong. 1 sess., May 11, 1999; and Stuart Eizenstat, testimony given at Sanctions Reform, July 1, 1999. Earlier State Department reports often did note the domestic costs that can be associated with sanctions. However, the costs were generally downplayed as the unavoidable price of U.S. leadership. See, for example, "Economic Sanctions to Combat International Terrorism," *Department of State Bulletin*, October 1986, p. 27.

40. Compare East-West Economic Issues, Sanctions Policy, and the Formulation of International Economic Policy: Hearing before the Subcommittee on Europe and the Middle East and on International Economic Policy and Trade of the House Committee on Foreign Affairs, 98 Cong. 2 sess., March 29, 1984, with Use and Effect of Unilateral Trade Sanctions: Hearing before the House Committee on Agriculture, 105 Cong. 1 sess., October 23, 1997; Economic Sanctions and U.S. Policy Interests: Hearing before the Subcommittee on Trade of the House Committee on Ways and Means, 105 Cong. 2 sess., June 3, 1998; Sanctions Revisited: Hearing before the Subcommittee on International Economic Policy and Trade of the House Committee on International Relations, 105 Cong. 2 sess., September 10, 1998; Sanctions Reform: Hearing before the Senate Committee on Foreign Relations, 106 Cong. 1 sess., May 11, July 1, and July 31, 1999; and Do Unilateral Economic Trade Sanctions Unfairly Penalize Small Business?Hearing before the Subcommittee on Tax, Finance and Exports of the House Committee on Small Business, 106 Cong. 1 sess., June 24, 1999.

41. See Trade Sanctions Reform and Export Enhancement Act of 2000, which was Subtitle C of Title I of the Technical Assistance, Trade Promotion, and Anti-Corruption Act of 2000.

42. There are, however, four circumstances in which the president is permitted to use restrictions without prior approval from Congress. See Rennack, "Economic Sanctions: Legislation in the 106th Congress," p. 8.

43. See *U.S.-Cuban Relations in the 21st Century: A Follow-on Chairman's Report of an Independent Task Force Sponsored by the Council on Foreign Relations* (Council on Foreign Relations, 2001); Irving Louis Horowitz, "The Cuba Lobby Then and Now," *Orbis*, vol. 42 (Fall 1998), pp. 553–63; Tom Carter, "GOP-Led Group to Oppose Embargo," *Washington Times*, April 5, 2001; and Frank Davies, "Group Focused on Cuba Policy Forms in D.C.," *Miami Herald*, March 29, 2001.

44. At the turn of the millennium, neither side of the Cuban debate had emerged victorious in its vision of what shape U.S. Cuba policy should take. Instead, the debate looked certain to be both heated and protracted. In 2000, the Republican leadership in the House and Senate squelched a popular vote in both houses of Congress to lift restrictions on travel and the unconditional sale of food and medicine to the island, settling on a much watered-down compromise. See Mark P. Sullivan and Maureen Taft-Morales, *Cuba: Issues for Congress* (Congressional Research Service, updated September 27, 2001), pp. 14–15, and Mark P. Sullivan, *Cuba: U.S. Restrictions on Travel and Legislative Initiatives in the 107th Congress* (Congressional Research Service, updated October 10, 2001), pp. 7–10.

45. This is true except in increasingly rare circumstances in which the economy of a country remains heavily (or exclusively) integrated with that of the United States. Comprehensive U.S. sanctions on Canada or Mexico, for instance, could result in huge

pressure on these countries given their dependence on the United States for 87 percent and 88 percent of their exports, respectively. IMF, *Direction of Trade Statistics Yearbook*, 2000.

46. See "Measuring Globalization," *Foreign Policy*, January/February 2001, pp. 56–65. Based on their examination of international travel, international telephone communications, Internet access, and foreign direct investment, *Foreign Policy* magazine and the A.T. Kearney Global Business Policy Council concluded that countries are becoming more and more globalized.

47. See Eileen M. Crumm, "The Value of Economic Incentives in International Politics," *Journal of Peace Research*, vol. 32 (August 1995), pp. 313–30.

48. For a taste of the debate in the 1990s see Elizabeth Rogers, "Economic Sanctions and Internal Conflict," in Michael E. Brown, ed., *The International Dimensions of Internal Conflict* (MIT Press, 1996), pp. 411–34; Robert Pape, "Why Economic Sanctions Do Not Work," *International Security*, vol. 22 (Fall 1997), pp. 90–136; and Elliott, "The Sanctions Glass: Half Full or Completely Empty?" *International Security*, vol. 23 (summer 1998), pp. 50–65. Disagreements about whether sanctions "work," however, predate this decade. For earlier detractors of the value of sanctions, see M. Doxey, *Economic Sanctions and International Enforcement* (Oxford University Press, 1971); M. Doxey, "International Sanctions: A Framework for Analysis with Special Reference to the UN and Southern Africa," *International Organization*, vol. 26 (Summer 1972), pp. 527–50; A. P. Shreiber, "Economic Coercion as an Instrument of Policy: U.S. Measures against Cuba and the Dominican Republic," *World Politics*, vol. 25 (April 1973), pp. 387–413; K. Knoor, "International Economic Leverage and Its Uses," in K. Knorr and F. Trager, eds., *Economic Issues and National Security* (Lawrence, Kansas: Allen Press, 1977), pp. 99–126; R. Renwick, *Economic Sanctions* (Harvard University, 1981). For those arguing that sanctions can play a positive, if limited role, see M. S. Daoudi and M. S. Dajnai, *Economic Sanctions: Ideas and Experience* (London: Routledge and Kegan Paul, 1983); Lisa L. Martin, *Coercive Cooperation: Explaining Multilateral Economic Sanctions* (Princeton University Press, 1992); Jonathan Kirshner, *Currency and Coercion: The Political Economy of International Monetary Power* (Princeton University Press, 1995); and Kim Richard Nossal, "International Sanctions as International Punishment," *International Organization*, vol. 43 (Spring 1989), pp. 301–22.

49. Scholars also hold a variety of opinions regarding what constitutes a sanctions "case." As Baldwin notes, the U.S. embargo on Cuba could be seen as a single case or many, broken down into periods demarcated by the involvement of other countries, the nature of the goods blocked or goals achieved, or the passage of time. Hufbauer, Schott, and Elliott define a sanctions case as starting with the first recorded sanctions threat or first official sanctions event and ending when either the sender or target changes behavior or the sanctions "just wither away." See Baldwin, *Economic Statecraft*, p. 146; and Hufbauer, Schott, and Elliott, *Economic Sanctions Reconsidered*, p. 43.

50. See Hufbauer, Schott, and Elliot, *Economic Sanctions Reconsidered*, pp. 41–42. This Institute for International Economics study examines 115 cases in which sanctions were used by international bodies, the United States, or other countries. Considering each case on a variety of levels, including the nature of the goals pursued, the extent of economic damage inflicted, and the other policy tools that accompanied the sanctions, the study seeks to assess the overall effectiveness of sanctions as a policy tool.

51. See Baldwin, *Economic Statecraft,* pp. 130–144, and Patrick Clawson, testimony at The Iran-Libya Sanctions Act: Hearing before the Senate Banking, Housing, and Urban Affairs Committee, 107 Cong. 1 sess., June 28, 2001.

52. See Hufbauer, Schott, and Elliot, *Economic Sanctions Reconsidered,* pp. 92–93, and Elliott, "The Sanctions Glass: Half Full or Completely Empty?" pp. 54–57.

53. See Pape, "Why Economic Sanctions Do Not Work," and Robert Pape, "Why Economic Sanctions Still Do Not Work," *International Security,* vol. 23 (Summer 1998), pp. 66–77.

54. See Hufbauer, Schott, and Elliot, *Economic Sanctions Reconsidered,* p. 93.

55. See Rogers, "Economic Sanctions and Internal Conflict."

56. See David Baldwin, "The Sanctions Debate and the Logic of Choice," *International Security,* vol. 24 (Winter 1999/2000), pp. 80–107, especially pp. 85–86.

57. Ibid.

58. See Baldwin, *Economic Statecraft,* pp. 118–130.

59. See Baldwin, "The Sanctions Debate and the Logic of Choice," pp. 80–81.

60. See, for example, Ernest Preeg, *Feeling Good or Doing Good with Sanctions: Unilateral Economic Sanctions and the U.S. National Interest* (Washington: Center for Strategic and International Studies, 1999), p. 193.

61. Hufbauer, Schott, and Elliott found that sanctions episodes that qualified as "successes" by the standards of their study cost the target country an average of 2.4 percent of its GDP; in contrast, "failed" sanctions attempts cost the target country only 1 percent of GDP. This finding led them and others to conclude that comprehensive sanctions were much more likely to achieve their goals than more limited measures. See Hufbauer, Schott, and Elliott, *Economic Sanctions Reconsidered,* pp. 101–02.

62. Johan Galtung, "On the Effects of International Economic Sanctions with Examples from the Case of Rhodesia," *World Politics,* vol. 19 (1967), pp. 378–416.

63. See, for instance, Thomas G. Weiss and others, "Toward a Framework for Analysis," in Thomas G. Weiss and others, *Political Gain and Civilian Pain: Humanitarian Impacts of Economic Sanctions* (Lanham, Md.: Rowman & Littlefield, 1997).

64. Richard Parker notes the practical obstacles to including the threat of sanctions in large studies, including difficulties in identifying the many times in which sanctions were threatened over the course of history. However, he points out that the exclusion of threat cases diminishes assessments of the effectiveness of sanctions; in many instances, if the sender's goals were achieved without resorting to trade restrictions or confrontation, threats that were not carried out represent the greatest successes. Richard W. Parker, "The Problem with Scorecards: How (and How Not) to Measure the Cost-Effectiveness of Economic Sanctions," *Michigan Journal of International Law,* vol. 21 (Winter 2000), pp. 261–62.

65. See Gary Clyde Hufbauer and others, "U.S. Economic Sanctions: Their Impact on Trade, Jobs, and Wages" (Institute for International Economics, April 1997). Business groups have cited this figure as overwhelming evidence that sanctions are a costly foreign policy tool, wreaking serious damage on specific domestic interests and the health of the U.S. economy as a whole. In contrast, others point out that the $15 to $19 billion figure is only a small fraction of American exports in 1997 (1.6 to 2 percent), leading them to dismiss the complaints of U.S. commercial interests. In the minds of these critics, economic

sanctions are a bargain foreign policy tool. For an example of the business argument, see European-American Business Council, *Is the Price Too High? The Cost of U.S. Sanctions Policies*, Washington, D.C., October 1997, especially pp. 7–8; for an example of the opposing argument, see Helms, "What Sanctions Epidemic?" p. 7.

66. Baldwin rightly points out that the most complete assessment not only would compare the costs and benefits of employing sanctions with their alternatives, but also would consider what could be achieved with the money or political capital saved by pursuing a less costly approach. See Baldwin, *Economic Statecraft*, pp. 123–28.

67. These calculations are made through the creation of counterfactuals; the poor and incomplete quality of data available for these countries precluded the use of economic regressions.

68. As detailed in the chapter on Iran, while U.S. sanctions were first imposed in 1979, most restrictions were lifted in the early 1980s and imposed again in the 1990s.

69. For a discussion of the difficulties in measuring the impact of sanctions on living conditions, see Richard Garfield, "The Impact of Economic Sanctions on Health and Well-Being" (London: Overseas Development Institute, November 1999).

70. For the development of a model that considers both the stakes to the sender as well as the distribution of power in the target society, see T. Clifton Morgan and Valerie L. Schwebach, "Fools Suffer Gladly: The Use of Economic Sanctions in International Crises," *International Studies Quarterly*, vol. 41 (March 1997), pp. 27–50, and T. Clifton Morgan, Dina Al-Sowayal, and Carl Rhodes, "United States Policy toward Iran: Can Sanctions Work?" (James A. Baker Institute for Public Policy, Rice University, 1998) (www.rice.edu/projects/baker/pubs/studies/caspain/uspti/uspti.html [June 19, 2002]).

71. Many of the sanctions episodes regarded as successful during the cold war and after were multilateral in nature. Although it is overly simplistic to attribute the positive outcomes in South Africa and Yugoslavia only to sanctions, the influence of these measures was magnified by the fact that many countries supported them.

72. See Richard N. Haass, "Conclusion: Lessons and Recommendations," in Richard N. Haass, *Economic Sanctions and American Diplomacy* (Council on Foreign Relations, 1998), p. 197.

73. See Hufbauer, Schott, and Elliott, *Economic Sanctions Reconsidered*, pp. 94–95, and Kimberly Ann Elliott, "Factors Affecting the Success of Sanctions," in David Cortright and George A. Lopez, eds., *Economic Sanctions: Panacea or Peacebuilding in a Post–Cold War World?*" (Boulder, Colo.: Westview Press, 1995), p. 53.

74. See Bruce Jentleson, "Economic Sanctions and Post–Cold War Conflicts: Challenges for Theory and Policy," in Paul C. Stern and Daniel Druckman, eds., *International Conflict Resolution after the Cold War* (Washington: National Academy Press, 2000), pp. 135–36.

75. See T. Clifton Morgan, Dina Al-Sowayal, and Carl Rhodes, "United States Policy toward Iran: Can Sanctions Work?"

76. See Daniel W. Drezner, *The Sanctions Paradox: Economic Statecraft and International Relations* (Cambridge University Press, 1999), p. 308.

77. See Haass, *Economic Sanctions and American Diplomacy*; Preeg, *Feeling Good or Doing Good with Sanctions*; Jentleson, "Economic Sanctions and Post–Cold War Conflicts," and Hufbauer, Schott, and Elliott, *Economic Sanctions Reconsidered*.

# Chapter Three

1. See Robert H. Pelletreau, assistant secretary of state for Near Eastern affairs, "Ban on Trade and Investment with Iran," testimony given at U.S. Sanctions on Iran before the Subcommittee on International Economic Policy and Trade of the House International Relations Committee, 104 Cong. 1 sess., May 2, 1995 (www.state.gov/www/regions/nea/950502.html [May 24, 2002]).

2. See Fataneh Enferadi, "The Issue of Relations with America and Iran's National Interests," *Khorasan*, April 12, 2000; Commentary by Mahmud Shahidi, republished in *Entekhab*, March 7, 2001.

3. Initially, as many as sixty-six hostages were taken, although only fifty-two were held for the full 444 days. An oil embargo also was imposed by western countries in the early 1950s in response to the growing concern over the actions of the Iranian government, which had just nationalized the Anglo-Iranian Oil Company.

4. See Hossein Alikani, *Sanctioning Iran: Anatomy of a Failed Policy* (New York: I.B. Taurus Publishers, 2000), pp. 66–153, and Robert Carswell, "Economic Sanctions against Iran," *Foreign Affairs*, vol. 60 (Winter 1981–82), p. 253.

5. Iran maintains that the United States still needs to compensate it for 1,200 military sales that Iran paid for, but that the United States never allowed to be completed. Iran claims that the United States owes it as much as $6.4 billion. In addition, the United States and Iran are still working on a number of other assets disputes, mostly dating from 1981. See the Atlantic Council of the United States, *Thinking beyond the Stalemate in U.S.-Iranian Relations*, vol. 1, *Policy Review*, policy paper, May 2001, p. 17.

6. At the time, assistance associated with the Foreign Assistance Act was prohibited. In August and December 1985, the section of the Foreign Assistance Act that prohibits aid to state sponsors of terrorism was amended to specifically prohibit assistance under the Agricultural Trade and Development Act, the Peace Corps Act, and the Export-Import Bank.

7. Additional restrictions associated with Iran's designation as an international sponsor of terrorism include: the denial of contracts worth $100,000 or more to Iranian firms, the withholding of U.S. funding to international institutions by the amount that they spend on Iran, and the denial of foreign tax credits to U.S. companies doing business in Iran. Further restrictions that were tied to the terrorist designation in the 1990s are discussed subsequently.

8. The Iran-Iraq war began in September 1980, when Iraq invaded Iran in an attempt to seize the southwestern oil area, or "Arabistan." For an discussion of American policy during the Iran-Iraq war, see Shahram Chubin and Charles Tripp, *Iran and Iraq at War* (Boulder, Colo.: Westview Press, 1988) pp. 188–240.

9. This campaign was undertaken notwithstanding the weapons delivered to Iran during the 1985–86 Iran-Contra Affair. See Thomas L. McNaugher, "Walking Tightropes in the Gulf," in Efraim Karsh, ed., *The Iran-Iraq War: Impact and Implications* (St. Martin's Press, 1989), p. 186.

10. This designation triggers a number of sanctions; however, the sanctions were merely duplications of restrictions already in place on Iran. The import ban was justified as a measure to counter unprovoked assaults on Gulf shipping specifically and to curtail

Iranian sponsorship of terrorism more generally. See Ronald Reagan, *Executive Order No. 12613*, October 30, 1987.

11. The EU endorsed critical dialogue as its official policy toward Iran in December 1992. For an evaluation of the EU's critical dialogue policy, see Johannes Reissner, "Europe and Iran: Critical Dialogue," in Richard N. Haass and Meghan L. O'Sullivan, eds., *Honey and Vinegar: Incentives, Sanctions, and Foreign Policy* (Brookings, 2000), pp. 33–50.

12. See George H. W. Bush, "Inauguration Address," *Public Papers of the Presidents: George Bush, 1989*, vol. 1 (GPO, 1990), pp. 1–4.

13. The Iran-Iraq Non-Proliferation Act of 1992 was passed as part of the National Defense Authorization Act of that year. See Title XVI of *National Defense Authorization Act for Fiscal Year 1993*, P.L. 102-484 (GPO, 1992).

14. The amendment was passed as part of the *National Defense Authorization Act for Fiscal Year 1996*, P.L. 104-106 (GPO, 1996). The law stipulates the imposition of mandatory sanctions (the barring of U.S. government procurement and U.S. export sanctions) as well as provides for additional discretionary sanctions where appropriate (the suspension of U.S. aid, military sales, other military and dual use exchanges, and the voicing of U.S. opposition to international loans).

15. See Martin S. Indyk, "The Clinton Administration's Approach to the Middle East," speech to the Washington Institute for Near East Policy, May 18, 1993 (www.washingtoninstitute.org/pubs/indyk.htm [May 24, 2002]).

16. Anthony Lake, "Confronting Backlash States," *Foreign Affairs*, vol. 73 (March/April 1994), pp. 45–55. Also see Pelletreau, "Ban on Trade and Investment with Iran," and Peter Tarnoff, under secretary of state for political affairs, "Containing Iran," testimony given at U.S. Policy on Iran before the House International Relations Committee, 104 Cong. 1 sess., November 9, 1995 (www.state.gov/www/regions/nea/951109.html [May 24, 2002]).

17. The EU Troika consists of representatives of the previous, current, and next holder of the six-month rotating EU presidency.

18. "The President's News Conference with Chancellor Kohl," *Weekly Compilation of Presidential Documents*, February 13, 1995. In 1994, the United States was Iran's largest overseas customer, with American companies handling $4 billion in Iranian crude oil. See "A Convenient Marriage," *Economist*, February 25, 1995, p. 42.

19. A German company, Siemens, had begun constructing this plant before the Iranian Revolution but did not complete it because of promises made to the United States. See Charles Lane, "Germany's New Ostpolitik," *Foreign Affairs*, vol. 74 (November/December 1995), pp. 83–84.

20. See, for example, Neal Sher, "Comprehensive U.S. Sanctions against Iran: A Plan for Action," American Israel Public Affairs Committee, April 2, 1995; American Israel Public Affairs Committee, "Impeding Iran's Nuclearization; Deterring European and Japanese Investment: The Iran Foreign Oil Sanctions Act of 1995," Iran Report 3, November 20, 1995. For more on the intensive lobbying efforts of AIPAC, see Alikani, *Sanctioning Iran*, pp. 177–209.

21. In October 1994, Hamas claimed responsibility for a bus bombing that killed twenty-two people in Israel; in December 1994, a Hamas suicide bomber wounded thirteen people at a bus station in Jerusalem; in January 1995, Palestinian Islamic Jihad

(PIJ) claimed responsibility for two car bombs that killed ninteeen and wounded sixty-one; in April 1995, PIJ and Hamas claimed responsibility for separate car bomb attacks that killed a total of seven and wounded thirty-one. This violence—and explicit pleas from Israeli leaders for U.S. assistance in combating the threat from Iran—gave further impetus to those advancing more sanctions against Iran. See David Hoffman, "Israel Seeking to Convince U.S. That West Is Threatened by Iran; Jewish Leaders Say Only Washington Capable of Restraining Tehran," *Washington Post*, March 13, 1993, p. A14.

22. D'Amato first introduced the Comprehensive Iran Sanctions Act in October 1993; he reintroduced the bill in January 1995 after he had become chairman of the Senate Banking Committee. In addition, D'Amato introduced the Iran Foreign Sanctions Act of 1995 in March 1995.

23. At the time, Iran was just beginning to open its economy to foreign investment in its oil industry. The contract offered to Conoco was the first offered to a foreign company since the Iranian Revolution. It was a buy-back deal whereby Conoco was to be repaid for its investment in crude oil. See Jonathon Bearman, "White House Pans Conoco's 'Unhelpful' Agreement to Develop Iranian Oil Fields," *Oil Daily*, March 8, 1995.

24. For some examples of the criticism from the Clinton administration and members of Congress, see Department of State, Daily Press Briefing, Office of the Spokesman, March 7, 1995; The White House, Daily Briefing, Office of the Press Secretary, March 7, 1995; and Comprehensive Iran Sanctions Act of 1995, hearing before the Senate Banking, Housing and Urban Affairs Committee, 104 Cong. 1 sess., March 16, 1995.

25. See William J. Clinton, "Remarks at the World Jewish Congress Dinner in New York City," *Weekly Compilation of Presidential Documents*, May 8, 1995.

26. In January 1996, the Clinton administration did, in fact, allocate $20 million to encourage opposition movements in Iran. However, this fund was framed less as an instrument of regime change and more as an effort to put pressure on the regime to move away from extremist policies and toward democracy. See Kenneth Katzman, *Iran: Current Developments and U.S. Policy*, Congressional Research Service, Library of Congress, Issue Brief 93033, updated February 25, 1999, p. 15, and Economist Intelligence Unit, *Country Report: Iran* (First Quarter 1996), p. 9.

27. Sections 325 and 326 of the *Antiterrorism and Effective Death Penalty Act*, P.L. 104-132, 104 Cong. 2 sess. (GPO, 1996). In both cases, a national interest waiver is provided to the president.

28. This provision of the *Antiterrorism and Effective Death Penalty Act*, section 221, is commonly known as the Lautenberg amendment. It was specifically intended to facilitate the quest of victims of terrorism and their family members to sue state sponsors of terrorism.

29. See *Iran Foreign Oil Sanctions Act* (as introduced), S. 1228, 104 Cong. 1 sess. (GPO, September 1995), and *Iran Oil Sanctions Act* (as introduced), H.R. 3107, 104 Cong. 2 sess. (GPO, March 1996).

30. The menu of sanctions from which the president can select includes a ban on Export-Import Bank assistance, a ban on export licenses from the United States, a prohibition on any loan over $10 million from any U.S. financial institution, revocation of a bank's designation as a primary dealer of U.S. government securities or repository for U.S.

government funds, a prohibition on U.S. government procurement of goods from the sanctioned entity, and any additional sanctions that the president deems appropriate under the International Emergency Economic Powers Act. Initially, the threshold was $40 million dollars for Iran, but it was automatically reduced to $20 million after one year.

31. The national interest waiver is also provided for in the case of Libya; however, the second type of waiver is not. Kenneth Katzman, *The Iran-Libya Sanctions Act (ILSA)*, CRS Report RS20871, Congressional Research Service, updated July 3, 2001, p. 3.

32. Europe's response to ILSA was published in the European Commission's Council Regulation 2271/96 in November 1996. It protected European companies against "the effects of the extraterritorial application of" ILSA. The regulation also applied to the secondary sanctions in the Helms-Burton Act on Cuba, which also was passed in 1996. See Economist Intelligence Unit, *Country Report: Iran*, First Quarter 1997, p. 12; and *Bulletin of the European Union*, November 1996.

33. For more on the formulation of ILSA and European reaction to it, see Alikani, *Sanctioning Iran*, pp. 288–360.

34. See Jofi Joseph, "Pipeline Diplomacy: The Clinton Administration's Fight for Baku-Ceyhan," Woodrow Wilson School Case Study 1/99; and Fiona Hill, "A Not-So-Grand Strategy: United States Policy in the Caucasus and Central Asia since 1991," *Politique étrangère*, vol. 66 (January–March 2001), pp. 95–108.

35. A later policy decision sought to prevent any of the multiple pipelines from going through Iran in an effort to exclude Iran from the economic development of the region.

36. Technically, it is unclear whether ILSA is meant to consider such activity a "sanctionable" offense. However, in her announcement of the waiver for the Total deal in 1998, Secretary Albright made it clear that the United States would still consider applying sanctions to oil and gas pipelines that traverse Iran. See Madeleine K. Albright, "Statement on 'Iran and Libya Sanctions Act (ILSA): Decision in the South Pars Case,'" Department of State, Office of the Spokesman, May 18, 1998 (http://secretary.state.gov/www/statements/1998/980518.html [May 24, 2002]).

37. Khatami had earlier resigned from his ministerial position, citing pressure from conservative elements in the regime who wanted him to limit the freedom of Iranian intellectuals and artists. See Wilfried Buchta, *Who Rules Iran? The Structure of Power in the Islamic Republic* (Washington Institute for Near East Policy and Konrad Adenauer Stiftung, 2000), p. 30.

38. At the time of Khatami's election in 1997, 54 percent of Iran's approximately 60 million people were under the age of twenty. Buchta, *Who Rules Iran?* p. 38.

39. Some of the more important publications that sprouted were *Jame'e*, *Khordad*, *Sobh-e Emruz*, and *Neshat*, all of which have since been banned. See Ali M. Ansari, *Iran, Islam, and Democracy: The Politics of Managing Change* (London: Royal Institute of International Affairs, 2000), pp. 118–19.

40. "Interview with Iranian President Mohammad Khatami," *CNN*, January 7, 1998 (www.cnn.com/world/9801/07/iran/interview.html [May 24, 2002]).

41. The president vetoed the bill on the basis that it would threaten stability in Russia, the main target of the legislation. William J. Clinton, "Message to the House of Representatives Returning without Approval the 'Iran Missile Proliferation Sanctions Act of 1998,'" *Weekly Compilation of Presidential Documents*, June 29, 1998, pp. 1198–200.

42. In July 1998 and January 1999, President Clinton sanctioned ten Russian institutions for their alleged involvement in Iranian missile development. See David Stout, "U.S. Imposes Sanctions on Tech Labs In Russia," *New York Times,* January 13, 1999, p. A7.

43. The Iran Nonproliferation Act of 2000 has been used to sanction North Korean, Chinese, Armenian, and Moldovan entities.

44. In the State Department's annual *Report on International Religious Freedom,* Iran is criticized for infringing the rights of religious minorities, particularly those of the Baha'i faith. The 2000 report also criticized Iran for the highly publicized conviction of ten Jews and two Muslims for spying for Israel. See Department of State, *Report on International Religious Freedom,* various years. Despite congressional calls for further sanctions on Iran for its behavior, the Clinton administration refrained from imposing added measures, arguing that existing penalties against Iran and other countries met the requirements of the International Religious Freedom Act.

45. One exception to this general trend was the president's decision in August 1997 to close the remaining loopholes in U.S.-Iranian trade. William Clinton, *Executive Order No. 13059,* August 19, 1997.

46. The designation of the MKO as a terrorist organization was warranted by the group's activities, quite apart from its value as a gesture to Tehran. The designation also had the effect of denying the group's ability to raise funds in the United States.

47. Secretary Albright cited EU and Russian cooperation in achieving ILSA's objectives when issuing the national security waiver to France's Total and its Russian and Malaysian minority partners for their $2 billion deal to develop Iran's South Pars gas fields. Albright, "Statement on 'Iran and Libya Sanctions Act (ILSA).'"

48. See Miles A. Pomper, "Hill Applauds Clinton's Move to Ease Some Trade Sanctions against Iran, Libya and Sudan," *Congressional Quarterly Weekly,* May 1, 1999, p. 1040. Later that year, the Clinton administration approved the sale of spare parts of airplanes sold by Boeing to Iran before sanctions were in place. See John Lancaster, "Boeing Can Provide Parts to Iran Airline," *Washington Post,* December 4, 1999, p. A16.

49. See Madeleine K. Albright, *Remarks at 1998 Asia Society Dinner,* Department of State, Office of the Spokesman, June 17, 1998 (http://secretary.state.gov/www/statements/1998/980617a.html [May 24, 2002]). Also see Martin Indyk, *Iran and the United States: Prospects for a New Relationship,* Department of State, Office of the Spokesman, October 14, 1999, at the Asia Society (www.state.gov/www/policy_remarks/1999/991014_indyk_iran.html [May 24, 2002]).

50. Iranian officials did not make any response to Albright's June 1998 Asia Society speech for several weeks. Eventually, Supreme Leader Khamenei called it a "political gimmick" and a "hypocritical play." Jahangir Amuzegar, "Khatami's Iran, One Year Later," *Middle East Policy,* October 1998, pp. 76–94.

51. Madeleine Albright, *Remarks before the American-Iranian Council,* Department of State, Office of the Spokesman, March 17, 2000 (http://secretary.state.gov/www/statements/2000/000317.html [May 24, 2002]).

52. These concrete gestures were supplemented with more subtle measures, which included Albright's rearranging her schedule to attend President Khatami's speech promoting the "dialogue of civilizations" at the United Nations Millennium Summit on

September 6, 2000 and President Clinton's attending Khatami's speech to the United Nations Assembly the following day.

53. Two of the most prominent individuals targeted were Gholam-Hosein Karbaschi, the popular mayor of Tehran, who was sentenced to five years in jail in July 1998, and Abdullah Nouri, who was forced to resign as interior minister in June 1998 and then sentenced to five years in jail in November 1999. For more on this see Saïd Amir Arjomand, "Civil Society and the Rule of Law in the Constitutional Politics of Iran under Khatami," *Social Research*, vol. 67 (Summer 2000), pp. 283–302.

54. Economist Intelligence Unit, *Country Report: Iran*, Second Quarter 1999, p. 11. Also see Buchta, *Who Rules Iran?* pp. 178–82.

55. Ansari, *Iran, Islam, and Democracy*, p. 207.

56. The conference in Berlin was held in April 2000 in association with the German Green Party and was aimed at discussing the future of reform in Iran. It was interrupted by several exiled opposition groups opposed to the Islamic Republic of Iran. The footage of those demonstrations was used in the Iranian media by conservatives against reformers who attended the conference. See Ali M. Ansari, "Victims of Their Success," *The World Today*, vol. 57 (March 2001), pp. 10–12.

57. After Albright's speech, Iranian ambassador to the United Nations Hadi Nejad-Hosseinian indicated that Iran would be "prepared to adopt proportionate and positive measures in return." Nevertheless, few gestures that can be construed in this way followed. During a July 2000 trip to Germany, Khatami praised Albright's speech of March 2000 but said that the United States needed to take more concrete steps to improve relations with Iran. See William Drozdiak, "Iranian Leader Calls for Closer U.S. Relations," *Washington Post*, July 12, 2000, p. A17.

58. "Khamenei Says Only Strong Iran Can Deal with U.S.," *Reuters*, July 27, 2000.

59. See the Atlantic Council of the United States, *Thinking beyond the Stalemate in U.S.-Iranian Relations*, vol. 1, *Policy Review*, policy paper (May 2001), and vol. 2, *Issues and Analysis*, policy paper (July 2001); and Brent Scowcroft, "An Opening to Iran," *Washington Post*, May 11, 2001, p. A45.

60. For example, see Suzanne Maloney, "Elections in Iran: A New Majlis and a Mandate for Reform," *Middle East Policy*, vol. 7 (June 2000), pp. 59–66, and Andrew North, "Iran's Reformers Run into Trouble," *Middle East* (October 2000), pp. 10–11. Khatami won 77 percent of the 2001 vote.

61. Nineteen American servicemen were killed in the bombing in Saudi Arabia on June 25, 1996. On June 21, 2001, the Justice Department announced that it had indicted thirteen Saudis and a Lebanese who were members of the Saudi Hizbullah organization. U.S. officials admitted they did not have enough evidence to indict Iranian officials. The indictment said that the *groups* to which the indicted individuals belonged were "inspired, supported, and supervised" by elements of the Iranian government, rather than saying that the individuals were influenced directly by Iran. See Khobar Towers indictment (http://news.findlaw.com/cnn/docs/khobar/khobarindict61901.pdf [October 30, 2001]).

62. The extension of ILSA passed the House by a vote of 409-6 and the Senate 96-2. In both chambers, amendments supported by the Bush administration that would extend ILSA for only two years rather than five were voted down. The version as passed does include a clause that calls for the president to submit a report to Congress on the effectiveness of the act within two years. At that time the president could recommend

that ILSA be terminated. Initially, many expected the Bush administration to strongly oppose the continuation of ILSA—and possibly other sanctions on Iran—on numerous grounds, including the perceived urgent need to diversify U.S. energy supplies and boost global oil production. See Report of the National Energy Policy Development Group, *National Energy Report*, The White House (May 2001), chapter 8, p. 6.

63. Iran almost went to war with the Taliban in 1998 in reaction to the killing of nine Iranian diplomats and one journalist.

64. Even if these issues were addressed productively, pending lawsuits against Iran by American families that have suffered from Iranian-sponsored acts of terrorism will pose stumbling blocks in the path to better relations. The legal representatives of these families have sought to collect large punitive and compensatory damages awarded to the plaintiffs by seizing Iranian assets that are currently being examined under the Hague Tribunal process. The opposition of the Clinton administration to these efforts on the one hand and congressional support for them on the other resulted in a compromise registered in a section of the Victims of Trafficking and Violence Protection Act of 2000. See Section 2002 of *Victims of Trafficking and Violence Protection Act of 2000*, P.L. 106-386 (GPO, 2000); for more details, see the Atlantic Council of the United States, *Thinking beyond the Stalemate in U.S.-Iranian Relations*, vol. 1, pp. 18–20.

65. Iran's debt-servicing costs are entirely absent from the budget, as are the losses and debt obligations of state companies and profit-making institutions associated with the government. Economist Intelligence Unit, *Country Profile: Iran*, 1998–99, p. 13. It is important to note that the Iranian fiscal and calendar year runs from March 21 to March 20.

66. Economist Intelligence Unit, *Country Profile: Iran*, 2000, p. 20.

67. One study estimated that Iran suffered $500 billion in war damages from the Iran-Iraq war. Then-President Rafsanjani put the estimate between $600 million and $1 trillion. See Shireen T. Hunter, *Iran after Khomeini* (Center for Strategic and International Studies, 1992), pp. 72–73.

68. See Jahangir Amuzegar, "Iran's Post-Revolution Planning: The Second Try," *Middle East Policy*, vol. 8 (March 2001), pp. 25–42.

69. This was despite the favorable price of oil delivered by Iraq's invasion of Kuwait in 1990.

70. IMF, *Islamic Republic of Iran: Statistical Appendix* (October 1996), p. 56; IMF, *Islamic Republic of Iran: Recent Economic Developments* (December 1995), p. 104. Also see World Bank, *Global Development Finance 2001 CD-ROM*.

71. Germany reached an agreement with Iran to reschedule $2.6 billion in debt in February 1994. Under the agreement, Iran agreed to repay the short-term debt owed to Germany between 1996 and 2000 after a two-year grace period. After that, countries like France, Belgium, Japan, South Korea, and the Netherlands all reached similar agreements with Iran. By the end of 1994, Iran had rescheduled $9 billion in debt through bilateral arrangements. See "Iran Quarterly Country Profile," *Middle East Economic Digest* (March 1994). Also see Vahe Petrossian, "Iran: Hard Times Persist as the Isolation Eases," *Middle East Economic Digest*, December 23, 1994.

72. Imports fell to nearly $12 billion in 1995 from over $29 billion in 1992. IMF, *Direction of Trade Statistics*, various years.

73. See IMF, *Islamic Republic of Iran: Recent Economic Developments* (December 1995), appendix IV, p. 51, for the foreign exchange restrictions placed on Iranian non-oil exporters.

74. Only after the turn of the millennium did Iran's non-oil sector begin to revive, partially as a result of recent exchange rate reforms. In the year 2000, non-oil exports rose an estimated 23 percent over the previous year, reaching their highest level since 1994–95. Economist Intelligence Unit, *Country Report: Iran*, March 2001, p. 33.

75. Although Iran was technically in default on many of its loans in late 1998, none of its creditors declared it so. See Economist Intelligence Unit, *Country Report: Iran*, First Quarter 1999, pp. 25–26; Economist Intelligence Unit, *Country Report: Iran*, Fourth Quarter 1998, pp. 20–21; and Robert Corzine and Robin Allen, "The Wealth Dries Up," *Financial Times*, December 11, 1998, p. 19.

76. An additional factor in explaining Iran's difficulties with economic reform is the unfamiliarity of most of Khatami's advisers with the basic tenets of capitalism. Khatami and his team were heavily influenced by the socialist discourse of Islamism in the 1970s, and many retained a commitment to a state-run economy.

77. See Jahangir Amuzegar, "Iran's 'Virtual Democracy' at a Turning Point," *SAIS Review*, vol. 20 (Summer/Fall 2000), p. 108–09.

78. See Jahangir Amuzegar, "Khatami and the Iranian Economy at Mid-Term," *Middle East Journal*, vol. 53 (Autumn 1999), pp. 534–52; and Amuzegar, "Iran's Post-Revolutionary Planning."

79. This number is calculated based on the fact that Iranian oil exports averaged 2.6 million barrels a day from 1990 to 1997. Economist Intelligence Unit, *Country Profile: Iran*, various years.

80. Economist Intelligence Unit, *Country Report: Iran*, March 2001, pp. 34–35.

81. See Amuzegar, "Iran's Post-Revolution Planning." For more on efforts to create a "stabilization fund," see Economist Intelligence Unit, *Country Report: Iran*, December 2000, pp. 19–20.

82. It should be noted that Iran is included in the Middle East category.

83. Trading relations between the United States and Iran had already experienced a significant disruption in the aftermath of the 1979 revolution when the United States plummeted from being one of Iran's most important trading partners (accounting for almost one-fifth of imports in 1978) to supplying only 1.2 percent of Iran's imports in 1982. However, from that time until the sanctions were imposed, trade between the United States and Iran grew steadily, although on a much smaller trajectory than in previous times. IMF, *Direction of Trade Statistics Yearbook*, 1984.

84. Reportedly, many Iranian carpets made their way to the American market through Canada, although such activity was technically illegal under the *Code of Federal Regulations*, Title 31, part 560.407. See "US Sanctions," *Middle East Economic Digest*, April 6, 2001, p. 29.

85. The United States purchased 18.3 percent of Iran's non-oil exports in 1985. The methodology employed to calculate this number considers the fluctuations in Iranian non-oil exports throughout the period (their substantial rise in the early 1990s and their decline and stagnation in the later part of the 1990s). In addition to the reasons cited in the text for why this number overestimates the actual cost to Iran, a 300 percent tariff imposed on the import of Iranian pistachios in July 1986 would have all but eliminated the pistachio trade—even had sanctions not been in place—further minimizing the costs due to sanctions.

86. See appendix table 3A-1. Even recognizing these limitations on the direct costs of the import ban, diminished non-oil trade with the United States had a multiplier effect given that any net loss in sales further intensified Iran's acute foreign exchange constraints and frustrated its efforts to service its debt burden, import necessary inputs, and generate growth.

87. Together, American oil majors Exxon, Texaco, and Mobil bought $3.5 billion of this total, constituting 24 percent of Iranian crude exports. See the *Economist*, "A Convenient Marriage," p. 42.

88. The United States was responsible for approximately 600,000 barrels per day of Iranian oil at the time. See Fereidun Fesharaki and Shiva Pezeshki, "U.S. Ban on Iranian Oil Purchases Would Be Futile," *Oil & Gas Journal*, March 20, 1995, and "Clinton to Order Halt to All U.S. Trade with Iran," *Oil & Gas Journal*, May 8, 1995.

89. Patrick Clawson, "Iran," in Richard Haass, ed., *Economic Sanctions and American Diplomacy* (Brookings, 1998), p. 93.

90. Economist Intelligence Unit, *Country Report: Iran*, Third Quarter 1995, p. 15. The Economist Intelligence Unit reported that total Asian liftings increased from 790,000 barrels per day in 1995 to 1 million in 1996 while European liftings rose from 380,00 barrels per day to 495,000 over the same period. Economist Intelligence Unit, *Country Report: Iran*, First Quarter 1997, p. 15.

91. Iranian oil exports averaged 2.62 million barrels per day in 1995, down from 2.65 million in 1994. In 1996, exports averaged 2.63 million barrels per day. OPEC, *Annual Statistical Bulletin*, 1997, p. 79.

92. The regulations governing the implementation of President Clinton's May 1995 executive order exempted humanitarian donations to relieve human suffering: Title 31, Part 560.210, *United States Code of Federal Regulations*.

93. IMF, *Direction of Trade Statistics Yearbook*, 1999.

94. Hooman Estelami, "A Study of Iran's Responses to U.S. Economic Sanctions," *Middle East Review of International Affairs*, vol. 3 (September 1999).

95. Given that Iran's oil fields had been developed with American assistance and technology, much of the reparation of damage inflicted during the Iran-Iraq war as well as many of the spare parts required over time would ideally have been replaced with U.S. products.

96. A February 2001 article in the *Wall Street Journal* quoted a senior Iranian official as saying that the end of sanctions is in the interest of both the United States and Iran. He said, "We can buy anything we want via Europe. But they know we can't get it from America, so it's more expensive for us." See Hugh Pope and Neil King Jr., "Halliburton Connected to Office in Iran—Firm Cheney Headed Says It Doesn't Breach U.S. Sanctions Law," *Wall Street Journal*, February 1, 2001, p. A17.

97. Data compiled on request by U.S. Department of Commerce, Census Bureau, Foreign Trade Division, July 18, 2001.

98. According to the Commerce Department, 14 percent of U.S. exports to Iran before the sanctions were imposed were considered high-tech. Data compiled on request by U.S. Department of Commerce, Census Bureau, Foreign Trade Division, July 18, 2001.

99. The FY2001 Agriculture Appropriations bill included a provision that banned U.S. government export credits to Iran and other countries on the terrorism list. A presidential

waiver was provided for this provision. See Katzman, *Iran: Current Developments and U.S. Policy*, updated July 5, 2001, p. 10. Although trade in some commodities began to increase, the United States had not yet sold any wheat to Iran as of July 2001. This is surprising, given that the United States is the number-one exporter of wheat in the world and Iran is the second-largest importer of wheat in the world. Despite the liberalization of U.S. law, Iran continues to pay a premium on the wheat it imports from Canada.

100. The categorizations used are taken from the IMF, *Direction of Trade Statistics*, various years.

101. IMF, *Direction of Trade Statistics*, various years.

102. In 1987, 68 percent of Iran's exports went to industrialized countries; in 2000, this percentage had dropped to 54 percent. IMF, *Direction of Trade Statistics*, various years.

103. Of course, there were some direct losses associated with U.S. sanctions and American pressure. For instance, sanctions terminated all U.S. bilateral assistance to the Islamic Republic of Iran. Before the revolution, such U.S. flows consisted primarily of $63.2 million in loans from the U.S. Export-Import Bank to help finance sales of U.S. goods and services to Iran. This total is for the years from 1975 to 1978, which was the last year that any Export-Import Bank loans were extended to Iran. USAID, *U.S. Overseas Loans and Grants and Assistance from International Organizations*, various years. In the period 1953–79, the United States extended $1.13 billion in Export-Import loans to Iran. The total of all other nonmilitary assistance and loans in this more extended period was $893.9 million. USAID, *U.S. Overseas Loans and Grants and Assistance from International Organizations*, July 1, 1945–September 30, 1998, p. 11. Under American pressure, the Japanese government withheld the second disbursement (worth approximately $400 million) of a $1.4 billion loan to complete a hydroelectric dam in Iran before resuming its lending in 1999. Katzman, *Iran: Current Developments and U.S. Policy*, updated February 25, 1999, p. 14. Economist Intelligence Unit, *Country Report: Iran*, Fourth Quarter 1999, p. 27.

104. In 1974, Iran was judged to be too wealthy for World Bank lending, largely on account of the high oil prices of the early 1970s. However, in the wake of the devastation of the Iran-Iraq war, World Bank lending to Iran resumed until, in 1993, Congress protested a $460 million World Bank loan to Iran by cutting the Clinton administration's request for the U.S. contribution to the World Bank by the amount of the loan to Iran. Katzman, *Iran: Current Developments and U.S. Policy*, updated February 25, 1999, p. 14.

105. The Bank approved two loans totaling $232 million in 2000. One was for $87 million to finance the Second Primary Health Care and Nutrition Project and the other was for a $145 million loan for the Tehran Sewage Project. See "World Bank Approves Loans to Iran for Primary Health and Sewage," News Release No. 2000/352/S, World Bank, May 18, 2000. The bank approved nearly $700 million worth of loans for Iran in 2001.

106. One such case was Algeria, which received a $300 million CCFF in May 1999 because it was hurt by the drop in oil prices. See "IMF Approves CCFF Credit for Algeria," Press Release No. 99/19, IMF, May 26, 1999.

107. Domestic sensitivities to the economic programs that Iran would have been forced to adopt in exchange for CCFF assistance would have dampened Iranian enthusiasm for such a course, even if it were available.

108. Interview by author with H. Fetini of the World Bank, Washington, D.C., July 2001.

109. Of countries listed by the World Bank as "low income" or "lower middle income," only Belarus and Fiji had lower debt/GNP ratios than Iran's 9 percent in 1999. Iran is considered to be in the lower middle-income category: World Bank, *Global Development Finance 2001 CD-ROM.*

110. Italy agreed to extend a $1 billion credit line to Iran after Khatami visited in 1999; Japan has also agreed to provide $3 billion in finance and insurance cover for energy projects in Iran for a four-year period beginning in 2001. Spain, Germany, and Britain have also increased their export cover. See Economist Intelligence Unit, *Country Report: Iran*, September 2000, pp. 32–33; Economist Intelligence Unit, *Country Report: Iran*, December 2000, pp. 27, 30. Iran's launch of a Eurobond was one indication of Iran's ability to avoid the indirect effects of sanctions on the global financial market. See Economist Intelligence Unit, *Country Report: Iran*, June 2000, pp. 27–28. Economist Intelligence Unit, *Country Report: Iran*, March 2001, p. 35.

111. Reportedly, NIOC improved the terms of the buy-back deals in late 1995 in anticipation of more U.S. sanctions. The expected returns for foreign firms under the original buy-back terms could have been as low as 5 percent, but after the terms were revised, expected returns could be as high as 20 to 30 percent, although not all of that would necessarily go to the foreign firm. See Economist Intelligence Unit, *Country Report: Iran*, First Quarter 1996, p. 22.

112. For instance, it is reported that in the wake of Conoco's withdrawal from the Sirri deal, Total was able to negotiate a much more profitable contract than the one that Conoco had closed. Economist Intelligence Unit, *Country Report: Iran*, First Quarter 1999, p. 23.

113. The deputy director of NIOC's corporate planning, Ebrahim Bavarian, said that Iran needed to attract $50 billion in foreign investment by 2005 to meet its goal of producing 5.1 million barrels of oil a day by 2005. "Iran Nears the End of Buy-Backs," *Financial Times Energy Newsletters*, November 27, 2000.

114. See Economist Intelligence Unit, *Country Report: Iran*, December 2000, p. 25. Iran's limited spare capacity is also a result of the major subsidies Iran provides to its burgeoning population and the consequent high rates of domestic consumption of oil in Iran.

115. For charts of Iran's fluctuating oil production over the decades, see Manouchehr Takin, "Iran Seeks Large Volume of Capital Investment to Boost Upstream Action," *Oil & Gas Journal*, September 13, 1999, p. 27.

116. Iran once claimed foreign involvement in its energy sector was forbidden by the country's constitution.

117. Fereidun Fesharaki and Mehdi Varzi, "Investment Opportunities Starting to Open Up in Iran's Petroleum Sector," *Oil & Gas Journal*, February 14, 2000, pp. 44–52.

118. In 2000, the Majlis oil and energy commission alleged that foreigners had made "extraordinary profits" through the buy-back deals and demanded an investigation into existing contracts. There also have been efforts to penalize foreign firms developing oil fields that do not meet production expectations. See Guy Dinmore, "Oil Takeover Still Reverberates in Iran," *Financial Times*, March 20, 2001, p. 12; and Economist Intelligence Unit, *Country Report: Iran*, December 2000, p. 17.

119. See Economist Intelligence Unit, *Country Report: Iran,* September 2000, pp. 18–19; Amuzegar, "Iran's Post-Revolution Planning"; Robert Corzine, "Iran: The Buy-Back System, Unpopular with Many Foreign Oil Companies, Is Thought to be under Review," *Financial Times,* April 15, 1999, p. 6; and Fesharaki and Varzi, "Investment Opportunities Starting to Open Up in Iran's Petroleum Sector."

120. Senator D'Amato introduced the Iran Foreign Oil Sanctions Act of 1995—the bill that was later to become ILSA—on September 8, 1995. A modified version of the bill passed the Senate by voice vote at the end of the same year, with the House passing its version in June 1996 by unanimous consent.

121. Total had signed a contract for the Sirri deal before this flutter of negotiations and the passage of ILSA.

122. Closing a deal also required an Iranian commitment, which could not be automatically assumed in all circumstances, given residual trepidation in Iran about whether and how to involve foreign firms in the energy industry.

123. The Japanese firm JGC withdrew its consideration of several gas projects in 1996, citing financial reasons as well as "the political situation in Iran." Economist Intelligence Unit, *Country Report: Iran,* Second Quarter 1996, p. 20. Australia's BHP also withdrew from a $3 billion gas pipeline project from Iran to Pakistan and India. See Edward D. Porter, *U.S. Energy Policy, Economic Sanctions, and World Oil Supply,* American Petroleum Institute, June 2001, p. 8.

124. Total's minority partners were Gazprom (Russia) and Petronas (Malaysia). A letter from Senator Trent Lott (R-Miss.) urged the administration to reach a decision about the applicability of ILSA in this case. See Thomas W. Lippman, "Senators Ask Sanctions over Iranian Gas Deal," *Washington Post,* May 9, 1998, p. A20. As mentioned elsewhere, the promise of additional waivers was said to be contingent upon strong EU policies regarding Iran's support for terrorism and pursuit of weapons of mass destruction.

125. A number of investments were under review by the executive branch to determine whether they warrant the imposition of sanctions or the issuance of a waiver. As of August 2002, no determinations had been made and no foreign company had yet to bear the penalties mandated under ILSA. See Katzman, *The Iran-Libya Sanctions Act (ILSA).*

126. According to Mehdi Hosseini, Iran's deputy minister of petroleum for international affairs, as of late 2000, five buy-backs deals worth approximately $10 billion were almost completed, in addition to the $10 billion in agreements already signed since 1995. Economist Intelligence Unit, *Country Report: Iran,* September 2000, p. 27.

127. There is naturally an important connection between increased production and the price of oil. However, if Iran exported an additional 200,000 barrels a day and the additional oil brought down world oil prices by $1 a barrel, then Iran still would benefit more from the sale of those 200,000 barrels at somewhat lower prices than it would from the sale of 200,000 fewer barrels at the high prices that existed during the time. The U.S. Energy Information Administration believes that a loss of 1 million barrels a day from world markets results in a $3 to $5 price rise in world oil markets.

128. Total proven oil reserves in the Caspian are estimated to be between 18 and 35 billion barrels, of which Iran's share is approximately 100 million barrels. Possible oil reserves in the Caspian are estimated to be much as an additional 235 billion barrels, of which Iran's share may be as high as 15 billion barrels. Proven gas reserves in the Caspian are estimated to be close to 236 to 337 trillion cubic feet. Iran does not claim any proven

gas reserves in the Caspian at this time. However, possible total Caspian gas reserves may include an additional 326 trillion cubic feet, of which Iran's share would be 11 trillion cubic feet. Energy Information Administration, *Caspian Sea Region*, June 2000 (www. eia.doe.gov/emeu/cabs/caspgrph.html#tab1 [May 24, 2002]). Only as of May 2000 did the Majlis approve legislation allowing NIOC to offer buy-back projects in the Caspian Sea; in the past, Iran has refrained from such activity, arguing that surrounding states should first settle territorial disputes before huge efforts to develop the Caspian are under way. Economist Intelligence Unit, *Country Report: Iran*, June 2000, pp. 24–25.

129. Of course, U.S. policy is not the only factor accountable for the slow growth of the region. Political instability between countries, domestic turmoil within nations, and uncertainties over the magnitude of the energy reserves in the area also all played a role.

130. Iran already operates oil swap arrangements for Kazakh crude. Although the regulations governing U.S. sanctions allow American firms to apply for licenses to undertake oil swaps, as of July 2002, none had been approved. Katzman, *Iran: Current Developments and U.S. Policy,* updated June 11, 2001, p. 10. For a further consideration of the Caspian pipeline options, see Julia Nanay, "Whither the Oil Industry? The Fate of the Caspian Hangs in the Balance," *SAIS Review*, vol. 19 (Winter 1999), pp. 272–81.

131. As noted earlier, Europe and Japan continued and expanded their economic and political relations with Iran. Moreover, as discussed in more detail in the next section, since Khatami's election in 1997, Iran improved its relations with the six states of the Gulf Cooperation Council.

132. See Geoffrey Kemp, "Iran: Can the United States Do a Deal?" *Washington Quarterly,* vol. 24 (Winter 2001), pp. 109–24, and Stephen C. Fairbanks, "Iran: No Easy Answers," *Journal of International Affairs,* vol. 54 (Spring 2001), pp. 447–64.

133. During the June 2001 presidential election campaign, Khatami declared, "As long as American politicians act under the influence of certain lobbies, harming even the interests of American companies, and hindering the Iranian economy by sanctions and embargoes, there will be no change." "Khatami Says No Change in U.S. Ties until Sanctions Lifted," *Agence France-Presse*, June 5, 2001.

134. Bonyads are large state-run foundations that were created after the revolution to safeguard Iran's revolutionary principles and to look after the poor. They have become multibillion dollar conglomerates controlling large parts of the Iranian economy. The bazaaris are Iran's traditional import-export merchants, who wield considerable influence over economic policy. For more on bonyads see Suzanne Maloney, "Agents or Obstacles? Parastatal Foundations and Challenges for Iranian Development," in Parvin Alizadeh, ed., *The Economy of Iran: The Dilemmas of an Islamic State* (I. B. Taurus, 2000), pp. 145–76.

135. Although the Clinton administration did not respond to Khatami's CNN interview with a lifting of any sanctions, verbal acknowledgments were made of its significance. For instance, in President Clinton's 1998 Id al-Fitr message, the president declared, "Iran is an important country with a rich and ancient cultural heritage of which Iranians are justifiably proud. We have real differences with some Iranian policies, but these are not insurmountable. I hope that we have more exchanges between our peoples and that the day will soon come when we can enjoy once again good relations with Iran." See William J. Clinton, "Videotaped Remarks on Id al-Fitr," January 29, 1998, *Public Papers of the Presidents: William Jefferson Clinton*, 1998, vol. 1 (GPO, 1999), pp. 136–37.

136. For example, in October 2000, 228 members of the House of Representatives called for support to the Iranian opposition in a "statement of policy." The House members called on the United States to "align its goals" with the National Council of Resistance, which the State Department says is a front for the outlawed Mujahedin-e Khalq Organization. See David Briscoe, "House Issues Iran Policy Statement," *Associated Press*, October 11, 2000. For another example of congressional displeasure with the regime, see *Congressional Record*, daily edition, June 3, 1998, vol. 144, no. 70, pp. E1000-1001.

137. See Martin S. Indyk, "The Clinton Administration's Approach to the Middle East," speech to the Washington Institute for Near East Policy, May 18, 1993 (www.washingtoninstitute.org/pubs/indyk.htm [May 24, 2002]), and Lake, "Confronting Backlash States," pp. 45–55.

138. See Indyk, "The Clinton Administration's Approach to the Middle East."

139. See Shireen Hunter, "Is Iranian Perestroika Possible without Fundamental Change?" *Washington Quarterly*, vol. 21 (Autumn 1998), pp. 23–41.

140. Kenneth Katzman, *U.S.-Iranian Relations: An Analytic Compendium of U.S. Policies, Laws, and Regulations* (Atlantic Council, December 1999), p. 139.

141. As of January 26, 2001, no penalties under this law had been imposed. See Kenneth Katzman, *Iran: Arms and Technology Acquisitions,* updated January 26, 2001 (Congressional Research Service), p. 7.

142. The Gore-Chernomyrdin agreement was signed in June 1995. According to its terms, Russia agreed not to conclude any new arms agreements with Iran, although it could fulfill all past contracts it had concluded with Iran, as long as the goods were shipped by December 31, 1999. In exchange, the United States agreed not to impose sanctions on Russia under the Iran-Iraq Nonproliferation Act of 1992 for its earlier military sales. The United States also agreed to allow Russia membership in the Wassenaar Agreement, which was concluded in July 1996. See Katzman, *Iran: Arms and Technology Acquisitions*, pp. 5–7; and John M. Broder, "Despite a Secret Pact by Gore in '95, Russian Arms Sales to Iran Go On," *New York Times*, October 13, 2000, p. A1.

143. Anthony Cordesman, "The Gulf and Transition: US Policy Ten Years after the Gulf War: The Challenge of Iran," Center for Strategic and International Studies, October 2000 (www.csis.org/gulf/reports/subiran.pdf [May 6, 2002]).

144. Indyk, "The Clinton Administration's Approach to the Middle East."

145. Lake, "Confronting Backlash States." Similarly, Martin Indyk claimed that the United States was willing to listen to Iran, but "in the absence of dramatic changes in Iran's behavior, we will work energetically to persuade our European and Japanese allies, as well as Russia and China, that it is not in their interests to assist Iran to acquire nuclear weapons or the conventional means to pose a regional threat." Indyk, "The Clinton Administration's Approach to the Middle East."

146. See Bruce O. Riedel, "U.S. Policy in the Gulf: Five Years of Dual Containment," speech at the Washington Institute for Near East Policy, May 6, 1998 (www.washingtoninstitute.org/media/riedel.htm [May 24, 2002]).

147. While the rhetoric coming from the president was more moderate, other actors—such as Supreme Leader Ayatollah Ali Khamenei—continued to make extreme statements.

148. See President Rafsanjani, Interview with Cable News Network, cited in Associated Press, July 2, 1995. See Gary Sick, "Rethinking Dual Containment," *Survival*, vol. 40 (Spring 1998), p. 32, footnote 34.

149. "Interview with Iranian President Mohammad Khatami," *CNN*, January 7, 1998.

150. At the time, some analysts pointed to tentative signs that Iranian support to groups like Hizbullah was declining. See Economist Intelligence Unit, *Country Report: Iran* (First Quarter 1996), p. 10, and Sick, "Rethinking Dual Containment," p. 15.

151. On a May 1999 visit to Syria, Khatami met with the secretary general of Hizbullah and praised the group as an "ideological and humanitarian movement" trying to liberate Lebanon from Israeli occupation. See Zeina Karam, "Khatami Praises Hizbollah Fight against Israel in Lebanon," *Associated Press*, May 15, 1999

152. Notably, this conference was organized by a reformist parliamentarian leader, Ali Akbar Mohtashemi, who also is widely regarded as the godfather of Hizbullah.

153. See Department of State, *Patterns of Global Terrorism*, various years. Also see comments by Ambassador Michael Sheehan, *Speech at the Brookings Institution*, Washington, D.C., February 10, 2000 (www.state.gov/www/policy_remarks/2000/000210_sheehan_brookings.html [May 24, 2002]).

154. See Department of State, *Patterns of Global Terrorism*, 2001 and various years. According to a statement made by George Tenet, the director of the CIA, in February 1999, "hard-liners, such as Supreme Leader Khamenei, continue to view terrorism as a legitimate tool of Iranian policy and they still control the institutions that can implement it." George Tenet, testimony given at Current and Future Threats to National Security before the Senate Armed Services Committee, 106 Cong. 1 sess., February 2, 1999.

155. See Sick, "Rethinking Dual Containment." For examples see Economist Intelligence Unit, *Country Report: Iran*, Second Quarter 1996, p. 4; Economist Intelligence Unit, *Country Report: Iran*, Third Quarter 1996, p. 4; Economist Intelligence Unit, *Country Report: Iran*, Second Quarter 1997, p. 1; Economist Intelligence Unit, *Country Report: Iran*, Fourth Quarter 1997, p. 6; Economist Intelligence Unit, *Country Report: Iran*, Third Quarter 1997, p. 5.

156. However, Iranian claims of sovereignty over Abu Musa and the Greater and Lesser Tunbs Islands—contested by UAE—continue to be a point of controversy between Iran and the GCC countries. See Cordesman, "The Gulf and Transition: U.S. Policy Ten Years after the Gulf War: The Challenge of Iran," p. 8.

157. After meeting with Iran's foreign minister, Kamal Kharrazi, UK foreign secretary Robin Cook announced that Britain would restore formal relations with Iran. He received assurances that the Iranian government would not threaten the life of Salman Rushdie, although the fatwa issued by the Ayatollah Khomeini was not rescinded. Other EU nations had restored formal relations with Iran in November 1997 after the resolution of the Mykonos affair involving the shooting of Iranian Kurdish dissidents at a Berlin restaurant in 1992. See David Gardner, "UK and Iran Restore Diplomatic Ties after Pledge on Rushdie," *Financial Times*, September 25, 1998, p. 24; and Economist Intelligence Unit, *Country Report: Iran*, Fourth Quarter 1999, p. 12.

158. However, given the impossibility of proving a negative, one must acknowledge that sanctions and U.S. pressure more generally may have constrained the Iranian regime from supporting further terrorist attacks.

159. For more on the Mykonos trial and its impact, see Geoffrey Kemp, "The Challenge of Iran for U.S. and European Policy," in Richard N. Haass, ed., *Trans-Atlantic Tensions: The United States, Europe, and Problem Countries* (Brookings, 1999), pp. 54–55; and Peter Rudolf, "Critical Engagement: The European Union and Iran," in Haass, ed., *Trans-Atlantic Tensions*, pp. 72, 80–84.

160. See CIA Nonproliferation Center, *Unclassified Report to Congress on the Acquisition of Technology Relating to Weapons of Mass Destruction and Advanced Conventional Munitions, 1 January through 30 June 2000*, February 2001. For a detailed historical record of Iranian efforts in the nuclear realm, see Anthony Cordesman, "The Gulf and Transition: U.S. Policy Ten Years after the Gulf War: Iranian and Iraqi Weapons of Mass Destruction and the U.S. Response," Center for Strategic and International Studies, October 2000 (www.csis.org/gulf/reports/subproliferation.pdf [July 10, 2001]). It is, however, worth noting that a minority of observers hold that the Iranian nuclear program is much more limited than commonly asserted.

161. Iran signed the Chemical Weapons Convention in January 1993; the Majlis ratified the convention on June 8, 1997. Nevertheless, Iran reportedly has stockpiled large quantities of sulfur, mustard, phosgene, and cyanide agents. Some experts maintain that Iran already can deploy biological weapons and may possess some rudimentary means of disseminating them. See CIA, *Unclassified Report to Congress*; "Iran Has Vast Stockpiles of CW Agents, says CIA," *Jane's Defence Weekly*, August 14, 1996, p. 3.

162. See Walter Pincus, "Iran, Iraq Could Join Missile Threat to U.S.; Report May Bolster Calls for Defense System," *Washington Post*, September 10, 1999, p. A3.

163. These trends continued and possibly accelerated after President Khatami's election in 1997. See William J. Clinton, "Statement on Signing the Iran Nonproliferation Act of 2000," *Weekly Compilation of Presidential Documents*, March 20, 2000, vol. 36, no. 11, p. 550; Katzman, *Iran: Arms and Technology Acquisitions*, p. 2; and Michael Eisenstadt, "Living with a Nuclear Iran?" *Survival*, vol. 41 (Autumn 1999), pp. 124–48. Again, other analysts would argue otherwise. See Sick, "Rethinking Dual Containment," pp. 16-17.

164. U.S. officials remain concerned about Russia's involvement with Iran's Bushehr reactors, even though Bushehr is a light-water reactor and its development has been monitored by the International Atomic Energy Agency (IAEA). The Russian government made some notable efforts to increase its oversight of such activities; however, it was also lax in implementing the new measures. CIA, *Unclassified Report to Congress on the Acquisition of Technology Relating to Weapons of Mass Destruction and Advanced Conventional Munitions, 1 January through 30 June 2000*. Alleged Russian plans to construct additional nuclear reactors with Iran brought a torrent of opposition from Washington in 2002.

165. While Iran is moving toward self-sufficiency in its chemical efforts, it still vigorously pursues foreign material and expertise in the development of its biological warfare program. Although many of these inputs can be acquired under the guise of satisfying legitimate civilian needs, Iran also seeks the aid of foreign scientists, Russians in particular, to assist in its biological endeavors. Iran's latest missile endeavors—the Shahab-3, with a range of 800 to 950 miles, which was tested in the summer of 1998 and again in 2000, and the 1,250-mile-range Shahab-4—appear to be based extensively on the Iranian-funded North Korean Nodong missile and Soviet SS-4 technology. See "Biological Warfare: The Poor Man's Atomic Bomb—IRAN," *Jane's Intelligence Review*,

March 1, 1999, p. 44; Judith Miller with William Broad, "Iranians, Bioweapons in Mind, Lure Needy Ex-Soviet Scientists," *New York Times*, December 8, 1998, p. 1; and Katzman, *Iran: Current Developments and U.S. Policy*, updated February 25, 1999, p. 3.

166. See Department of State, *Country Report on Human Rights Practices: Iran*, various years; Commission of the European Communities, *Communication from the Commission to the European Parliament and the Council: EU Relations with the Islamic Republic of Iran*, February 7, 2001; and Human Rights Watch, "Iran: Human Rights Developments," in *World Report 2000* (www.hrw.org/wr2kl/mideast/iran.html [May 28, 2002]).

167. For example, in 2000 and 2001, former officials of the Intelligence Ministry were tried and convicted for the 1998 killings of dissidents. See Ed Blanche, "Rogue Agent Convictions Leave Many Questions Unanswered," *Middle East*, March 2000, pp. 13–15.

168. See John F. Burns, "Its Voters Have Spoken. Now Meet Iran's Gunmen," *New York Times*, March 19, 2000, p. A16; "Tehran Shuts Reformist Newspapers," *Financial Times*, April 24, 2000, p. A1; Susan Sachs, "Iran's Self-Fulfilling Prophecy," *New York Times*, February 27, 2000, p. 4.

169. According to the U.S. government and other sources, some religious minorities (the Baha'i in particular) are still subject to restrictions on the practice of their religion, while imprisonment and detention on the basis of religious beliefs is not uncommon. Apart from its treatment of religious minorities, torture, unlawful imprisonment, and extrajudicial executions continue to mar Iran's human rights record. See Department of State, *Annual Report on International Religious Freedom: 2000*, September 2000; and Human Rights Watch, "Iran: Human Rights Developments," in *World Report 2000*. On July 1, 2000, at the end of trials widely viewed as unfair, Iran convicted ten Iranian Jews of having illegal contacts with Israel and sentenced them to long jail sentences. See Susan Sachs, "10 Jews Convicted by Iranian Court in Espionage Case," *New York Times*, July 2, 2000, p. A1.

170. Although Iranian officials place population growth at 1.6 percent a year as of November 2000, the average remained somewhere between 3–5 percent throughout the 1980s and early part of the 1990s. See Economist Intelligence Unit, *Country Report: Iran*, December 2000, p. 23. Although the government reported that only one of every ten Iranians was unemployed, nonofficial sources estimate the true level of unemployment to be much higher, possibly in the range of 25 percent. Economist Intelligence Unit, *Country Profile: Iran*, 1998–99, p. 15; Economist Intelligence Unit, *Country Report: Iran*, December 2000, p. 23.

171. Economist Intelligence Unit, *Country Report: Iran*, December 2000, pp. 22–23.

172. Economist Intelligence Unit, *Country Profile: Iran*, 2000, p. 41.

173. The real value of the Iranian rial has been much more dependent on fluctuations in the price of oil over the decades than on the existence or imposition of sanctions. Moreover, as the health of Iran's economy has improved, the currency's worth has been much less vulnerable to external shocks from sanctions and other factors. As evident in the collapse of the rial after the arrest of Tehran's mayor, Gholam-Hosein Karbaschi, in 1998, U.S. sanctions have not been the only force exerting pressures on the currency.

174. See, for instance, Porter, *U.S. Energy Policy, Economic Sanctions, and World Oil Supply*; William F. Martin, testimony at The Iran-Libya Sanctions Act before the Senate Banking, Housing, and Urban Affairs Committee, 107 Cong. 1 sess., June 28, 2001.

175. Existent spare capacity not only has some relation to the price of oil, but it allows the world to absorb shocks or supply disruptions that may occur for any reason in an oil-producing country. See Amy Jaffe, *The Political, Economic, Social, Cultural, and Religious Trends in the Middle East and the Gulf and Their Impact on Energy Supply, Security, and Pricing* (James A. Baker Institute for Public Policy, Rice University, April 1997).

176. Technically, sanctions provided an economic benefit to the United States by allowing it to "save" any direct aid that would have been granted to Iran in the absence of sanctions. Moreover, a variety of legislation passed by Congress curtailed American contributions to a number of international institutions providing aid or loans to Iran. Most notable, in protest of a $470 million World Bank loan to Iran in 1993, Congress cut the Clinton administration's request for the U.S. contribution to the World Bank by the same amount. Similarly, the United States saved much smaller sums as the result of legislative provisions that forced the administration to withhold the proportionate share of American contributions to programs run by international organizations in Iran. Although these provisions do not bar international organizations that receive U.S. funding from operating in Iran (as well as other countries), they do ensure that U.S. funding to these institutions is diminished as a result of it. Rather than reporting a net savings, these funds would have likely been allocated elsewhere.

177. Boeing and BP America had to forgo deals collectively worth close to $1 billion in 1993 (even before the sanctions were in place) due to such fears. See R. Jeffrey Smith and Peter Behr, "Administration Bars Chemical Plant Sale to Iran; Two Other Controversial Export Proposals Are Left Unresolved by Meeting," *Washington Post*, January 6, 1993, p. A21, and Stuart Auerbach, "Iran Seeking Jets from Airbus Industries; Boeing, GE Unable to Win Administration Approval of Proposed Sale," *Washington Post*, August 19, 1993, p. D9.

178. Note that $2 billion of exports still only account for less than 0.05 percent of U.S. exports during that time. The low value of this figure reflects not only the insubstantial trade ties that existed between the United States and the Islamic Republic of Iran—particularly when compared with those under the shah's regime a decade or so earlier—but also Iran's harsh import compression in the last few years. The calculation relies on a counterfactual that estimates hypothetical U.S. exports to Iran by gauging actual non-U.S. industrial country exports to Iran. This allows the counterfactual to be more dynamic, by taking into account fluctuations that might have occurred due to global or other factors.

179. The assets of these American companies had already been nationalized right after the 1979 revolution.

180. U.S. firms were responsible for approximately 20 percent of Iranian crude before the sanctions were applied in 1995. Moreover, the Economist Intelligence Unit claims that in addition to these responsibilities, American companies were believed to be purchasing billions of dollars of Iranian crude on the spot market before sanctions were imposed. Economist Intelligence Unit, *Country Report: Iran,* First Quarter 1995, p. 7. This $2 billion figure is calculated by taking 10 percent (the estimated profit margin) of the 15–20 percent of Iran's export earnings from oil over March 1995–2000 (which represents the approximate value of the amount that would have been lifted by U.S. companies). See appendix table 3A-3.

181. See Jahangir Amuzegar, "Iranian Oil Buybacks: A Formula No One Likes," *Oil and Gas Journal*, August 27, 2001, pp. 20–22, and Guy Dinmore, "Parliament Probes Oil Deals," July 19, 2001.

182. Although the magnitude of this loss clearly depends on the investment opportunities offered by Iran, one relevant benchmark might be the percentage (30–50 percent) of the contracts won by U.S. firms in Azerbaijan. See Ernest H. Preeg, *Feeling Good or Doing Good with Sanctions: Unilateral Economic Sanctions and the U.S. National Interest* (Center for Strategic and International Studies, 1999), p. 69.

183. In the words of two scholars, "dual containment is a geopolitical dead end—at best a holding pattern for more auspicious times." Graham E. Fuller and Ian O. Lesser, "Persian Gulf Myths," *Foreign Affairs*, vol. 76 (May/June 1997), p. 47.

184. See Carnegie Endowment for International Peace, *An Agenda for Renewal: U.S.-Russian Relations*, December 2000, pp. 24–36.

185. Of course, support for the Baku-Ceyhan pipeline cannot be evaluated only in terms of the costs and benefits related to Iran. For instance, the significance of this support to Turkey, an important NATO ally, also must be considered.

186. See Hill, "A Not-So-Grand Strategy," and Fiona Hill, "The Caucasus and Central Asia," Brookings policy brief 80 (May 2001).

187. See Patrick Clawson, testimony at The Iran-Libya Sanctions Act before the Senate Banking, Housing, and Urban Affairs Committee, 107 Cong. 1 sess., June 28, 2001, and Stuart Eizenstat, testimony at The Role of Sanctions in U.S. National Security Policy before the Senate Foreign Relations Committee, 106 Cong. 1 sess., July 1, 1999.

188. Albright, "Statement on 'Iran and Libya Sanctions Act (ILSA)': Decision in the South Pars Case.'"

189. Interview of former senior U.S. official by author, Washington, D.C., 2001.

190. Interview of congressional aide by author, Washington, D.C., 2001.

191. See Barbara Crossette, "Americans of Two Minds on Sanctions, a Poll Finds," *New York Times*, April 23, 2000, p. 7, and Lawrence G. Potter, "The Middle East and the Millennium," *Great Decisions 2000* (Foreign Policy Association, January 2000).

192. In return for Russia's agreement to curtail arms sales, the Clinton administration promised not to impose sanctions mandated under the 1992 Iran-Iraq Nonproliferation Act.

193. Not only were European countries dependent on Iran to satisfy a large share of their energy needs, but trade between the European continent and Iran had blossomed in the early 1990s. See Reissner, "Europe and Iran: Critical Dialogue," p. 36; Kemp, "The Challenge of Iran for U.S. and European Policy," pp. 48–70; and Peter Rudolf, "Critical Engagement: The European Union and Iran," pp. 71–101.

194. See Robert S. Ross, "China," in Richard N. Haass, ed., *Economic Sanctions and American Diplomacy* (Brookings, 1998), pp. 10–34.

195. President Clinton signed the bill into law in the wake of the TWA 800 crash (which was subsequently determined to have been caused by mechanical failure). At the signing ceremony, he declared, "With this legislation we strike hard where it counts, against those who target innocent lives and our very way of life . . . I resolve to hunt down, prosecute, and punish terrorists and to put pressure on states that support them." *Public Papers of the Presidents: William Jefferson Clinton*, 1996, vol. 2 (GPO, 1997), p. 1254.

196. As it was, the State Department carried out intensive negotiations with Congress to moderate the terms of the bill.

197. Lake, "Confronting Backlash States," and Tarnoff, "Containing Iran" (www.state.gov/www/regions/nea/951109.html [May 28, 2002]).

198. See Robert S. Litwak, *Rogue States and U.S. Foreign Policy: Containment after the Cold War* (Woodrow Wilson Center Press, 2000), pp. 158–97, and Meghan L. O'Sullivan, "The Dilemma of U.S. Policy toward 'Rogue' States," *Politique étrangère* (Spring 2000).

199. See Stephen C. Fairbanks, "Iran: No Easy Answers," *Journal of International Affairs*, vol. 54 (Spring 2001), pp. 447–64.

200. If the United States had detailed information on the location of Iran's WMD research and development facilities, such strikes could have set back Iran's weapons programs, but not necessarily changed the country's ambitions to attain WMD.

201. This is particularly true given that in the 1981 Algiers Accord the United States pledges noninterference in Iranian domestic (or other) affairs.

202. As mentioned earlier, under the U.S. State Department's legal categorization, the MKO has been designated a foreign terrorist organization (FTO).

203. In his first interview in four years in April 2001, Reza Pahlavi, the son of the former shah, called for the creation of a secular constitutional monarchy or republic and the overthrow of the Islamic Republic. See Adel Darwish, "The Shah Speaks Out," *Middle East*, April 2001, pp. 16–18.

204. As discussed in earlier sections, domestic political struggles in Tehran are likely to have precluded Iranian leaders from responding to U.S. overtures. Some, however, argue that because the gestures made did not include the easing of restrictions on the Iranian energy sector, they were too insignificant to elicit a positive response from Iran. See, for example, "U.S. Sanctions," *Middle East Economic Digest*, April 6, 2001, p. 29.

205. This would be true in all cases unless the initial measures taken by the United States, such as rescinding ILSA, were much more significant.

206. See Reissner, "Europe and Iran: Critical Dialogue."

207. This conclusion is based on the assumption that the leverage Europe had with Tehran was heightened in the absence of American involvement in Iran at the time.

208. For other discussions of first steps, see the Atlantic Council of the United States, *Thinking beyond the Stalemate in U.S.-Iranian Relations*, vol. 1, *Policy Review*, and vol. 2, *Issues and Analysis*; Puneet Talwar, "Iran in the Balance," *Foreign Affairs*, vol. 80 (July/August 2001), pp. 58–71; and Suzanne Maloney, "America and Iran: From Containment to Coexistence," Brookings policy brief 87, August 2001.

209. Further down the road, security considerations permitting, the United States might be able to facilitate the visa approval process for Iranians wishing to visit America, with the hope that Iran will eventually allow the establishment of a U.S. office to handle visa requests in the American Interests Section in the Swiss Embassy in Tehran. Thus far, Iran has rejected this idea. See Kemp, "Iran: Can the United States Do a Deal?" p. 123.

210. Although the perception is that ILSA places limitations on the activities of foreign firms only, ILSA refers to "entities" without reference to whether they are U.S. or foreign companies. Therefore, even if the president lifted the executive orders mandating sanctions on Iran, under ILSA U.S. companies would still be effectively restricted from investing amounts over the $20 million limit in Iran's energy sector. See the

Atlantic Council of the United States, *Thinking beyond the Stalemate in U.S.-Iranian Relations*, vol. 1, p. 11.

211. A notable exception is Senator Chuck Hagel, who has spoken out often for rethinking ILSA. See *Remarks by Senator Chuck Hagel to the American Iranian Council*, June 27, 2001.

## Chapter Four

1. Over time, as discussed later in the chapter, Congress passed legislation that imposed additional sanctions on countries on the terrorism list.

2. See Erin Day, "Economic Sanctions Imposed by the United States against Specific Countries: 1979 through 1992" (Congressional Research Service, August 10, 1992), p. 594.

3. See Amatzia Baram, "U.S. Input into Iraqi Decisionmaking, 1988–1990," in David W. Lesch, ed., *The Middle East and the United States: A Historical and Political Reassessment* (Westview Press, 1996), pp. 325–27; Elaine Sciolino, *The Outlaw State: Saddam Hussein's Quest for Power and the Gulf Crisis* (John Wiley & Sons, 1991), pp. 140–42. Incidentally, Iran was placed on the terrorism list in 1984.

4. Some of this trade included dual-use items, the sales of which were approved with licenses by the Department of Commerce. See Sciolino, *The Outlaw State*, pp. 141–42.

5. See Farhang Rajee, ed., *The Iran-Iraq War: The Politics of Aggression* (University of Florida Press, 1993), p. 1.

6. This process produced National Security Directive (NSD) 26, entitled "U.S. Policy toward the Persian Gulf," which was signed by the president on October 2, 1989. See James A. Baker III, *The Politics of Diplomacy: Revolution, War, and Peace, 1989–1992* (G. P. Putnam's Sons, 1995), pp. 270–74.

7. See Kenneth Juster, "The United States and Iraq: Perils of Engagement," in Richard N. Haass and Meghan L. O'Sullivan, eds., *Honey and Vinegar: Incentives, Sanctions, and Foreign Policy* (Brookings, 2000), pp. 51–69.

8. The transition from engagement to confrontation did not happen overnight; in late 1989, the U.S. government had frozen loan guarantees to Iraq at the behest of the Treasury Department and the Department of Defense. See Baram, "U.S. Input into Iraqi Decision-Making," pp. 313–40.

9. George H. W. Bush, *Executive Order No. 12722*, August 3, 1990, and *Executive Order No. 12724*, August 13, 1990.

10. UN resolution 665, which authorized all appropriate measures to enforce UN resolution 661, was passed shortly after 661. United Nations Security Council, *Security Council Resolution 665 (1990)*, S/RES/665 (United Nations, August 25, 1990).

11. For a sample of the debate that occurred in Congress over the passage of the resolution supporting the use of force, see "Confrontation in the Gulf; Day 3: Remarks in Congress during the Last Hours of Debate," *New York Times*, January 13, 1991, p. 10. Also see William Webster, testimony given at *The Persian Gulf Crisis: Hearing before the House Armed Services Committee*, 101 Cong. 2 sess., December 5, 1990, and Richard Cheney and Colin Powell, testimony given at *The Persian Gulf Crisis*, December 14, 1990.

12. While more than forty countries joined in the military operations of *Desert Storm*, 122 of 159 members of the United Nations supported the UNSC resolutions against Iraq.

13. See George Bush and Brent Scowcroft, *A World Transformed* (Alfred A. Knopf, 1998), chapter 18, pp. 450–87.

14. United Nations Security Council, *Security Council Resolution 687*, S/RES/687 (1991) (United Nations, April 8, 1991).

15. UN resolutions 773 and 833 repeated the demand that Iraq recognize the UN-demarcated border in the face of Iraqi noncompliance.

16. On July 29, 1992, Edward J. Perkins, the U.S. permanent representative to the United Nations, told a subcommittee of the U.S. House Foreign Affairs Committee: "Iraqi performance in each of these (weapons-related) areas repeats a constant pattern: There is a period of non-cooperation and deceit; this is followed by defiance when confronted by UN officials; when defiance calls forth Security Council threats, it gives way to limited compliance; this is followed by new deceits and non-cooperation elsewhere." Edward J. Perkins, "Statement by the US Permanent Representative to the United Nations before the Subcommittee on Europe and the Middle East and on Human Rights and International Organizations of the House Foreign Affairs Committee," Washington, July 29, 1992. "Iraq's Non-Compliance with UN Security Council Resolutions," *U.S. Department of State Dispatch*; Washington; August 3, 1992, p. 602.

17. UN resolution 661 provided for the import of humanitarian goods into Iraq and UN resolution 666 clarified the provisions. United Nations Security Council, *Security Council Resolution 666 (1990)*, S/RES/666 (United Nations, September 13, 1990).

18. UN resolutions 706 (passed on August 15, 1991) and 712 (passed on September 19, 1991) permitted the Iraqi government to sell up to $1.6 billion of oil. UN resolution 986, which was passed in April 1995 and agreed to by Iraq in May 1996, allowed Iraq to export $2.14 billion worth of oil every six months to purchase humanitarian supplies under UN monitoring; in February 1998, the scheme was revised to allow exports worth $5.6 billion every six months (UN resolution 1153). As mentioned later in the chapter, the cap on oil sales was ultimately removed in December 1999 by UN resolution 1284.

19. The no-fly zone over northern Iraq (above the 36th parallel) was established in April 1991, while the no-fly zone over southern Iraq (below the 32d parallel) was established in August 1992. It was hoped that by denying Iraqi aircraft the right to fly over huge swathes of Iraq, the no-fly zones would both protect these regions from attack by Saddam's forces and frustrate Iraq's military, thereby helping to provoke a coup from within Saddam's inner circle. The U.S. view was, and remains, that UN resolution 688, which prohibits Saddam from repressing his own people, provides the necessary authorization for the no-fly zones. See Patrick E. Tyler, "After the War; Bush Sees Accord on 'Safe Havens' for Kurds in Iraq," *New York Times*, April 12, 1991, p. A1, and Michael R. Gordon, "British, French and U.S. Agree to Hit Iraqi Aircraft in the South," *New York Times*, August 19, 1992, p. A1.

20. See United Nations Security Council, *Sixth Report of the Executive Chairman of the Special Commission Established by the Secretary-General Pursuant to Paragraph 9(b)(i) of Security Council Resolution 687 (1991) on the Activities of the Special Commission*, S/26910 (United Nations, December 21, 1993), paragraph 19.

21. See United Nations Security Council, *Sixth Report of the Executive Chairman*. Also, see the interview with former UNSCOM executive chairman Rolf Ekeus in J. Peter Scoblic and Matthew Rice, "Shifting Priorities: UNMOVIC and the Future of Inspections in Iraq," *Arms Control Today*, vol. 30 (March 2000), pp. 3–6.

22. See "Iraq: Splits in U.N. Security Council Widen on Oil Embargo," *Inter Press Service*, July 17, 1994.

23. William Drozdiak, "France Hosts Iraqi Official, Moves to End Ostracism of Baghdad," *Washington Post*, January 7, 1995, p. A18.

24. See Economist Intelligence Unit, *Country Report: Iraq* (Fourth Quarter 1991), p. 16; Economist Intelligence Unit, *Country Report: Iraq* (Second Quarter 1992), p. 16. See Kenneth Timmerman, "West Is Poised to Rearm Saddam," *Wall Street Journal*, September 27, 1994, p. 14, for a discussion of some of the business links being forged between Iraq and European countries at the time.

25. The United States objected to the passage of UN resolutions containing any language favorable to Iraq. In fact, in November 1994, the United States objected to wording in a Security Council declaration regarding Iraq's recognition of Kuwait. The draft sponsored by Russia, China, and France said that Iraq's recognition of Kuwait was "an important step in the right direction toward implementation" of UN resolutions, whereas the United States favored the language "a step in the direction towards implementation." A compromise was reached with the declaration stating the recognition was "a significant step in the direction towards implementation." See Stanley Meisler, "U.N. Welcomes Iraq's Kuwait Stance, Is Split on Curbs," *Los Angeles Times*, November 17, 1994, p. A6, and United Nations Security Council, *Statement by the President of the Security Council*, S/PRST/1994/68 (United Nations, November 16, 1994).

26. The United States dispatched an aircraft carrier, warplanes, and more than 50,000 troops to Kuwait. See Michael Gordon, "At Least 36,000 U.S. Troops Going to Gulf in Response to Continued Iraqi Buildup," *New York Times*, October 10, 1994, p. A1. The UN passed resolution 949 on October 15, 1994, forbidding the redeployment of Iraqi troops along the Kuwaiti border. United Nations Security Council, *Security Council Resolution 949*, S/RES/949 (United Nations, October 15, 1994).

27. R. Jeffrey Smith, "Iraq Reveals Bid to Build an A-Bomb; New Data Show Wide Arms Effort," *Washington Post*, August 24, 1995, p. A1.

28. In an October 1995 report to the Security Council, UNSCOM executive chairman Rolf Ekeus wrote, "The Commission's preliminary analysis of this (new) information reveals that Iraq has been concealing proscribed activities and that, consequently, some of the assessments in the Commission's earlier reports have to be revised." United Nations Security Council, *Eighth Report Submitted under Paragraph 8 of Security Council Resolution 715 (1991)*, S/1995/864 (United Nations, October 11, 1995), paragraph 106.

29. Although Iraq agreed to negotiate the terms of an oil for food program as early as January 1996, it stalled the process, preventing rapid commencement of the scheme.

30. Revenues from Iraqi oil sales were to be placed out of Saddam's reach in a UN escrow account and drawn on to finance Iraqi purchase of humanitarian goods. Although Iraq could negotiate contracts with foreign firms as it pleased, these contracts were subject to the approval of the UN Security Council's sanctions committee. Contracts either deemed to fall outside of the program's humanitarian purpose or judged to have dual-use applications could be contested and put on hold by a member of the sanctions committee. The sanctions committee was composed of representatives of all fifteen members of the Security Council. For more on the logistics of the Oil for Food program, see United Nations Security Council, *Memorandum of Understanding between the Secretariat of the United Nations and the Government of Iraq on the*

*Implementation of Security Council Resolution 986 (1995)*, S/1996/356 (United Nations, May 20, 1996).

31. See, for instance, Mariam Shahin, "Ten Years on the War of Attrition Continues," *Middle East*, July/August 2000, pp. 8–10, and Karine Morin and Steven H. Miles, "The Health Effects of Economic Sanctions and Embargoes: The Role of Health Professionals," *Annals of Internal Medicine*, January 18, 2000, pp. 158–61.

32. Business links forged through this program and Iraq's negotiation of executory oil contracts created strong commercial incentives for state oil companies to use their political power to lobby for the lifting of the sanctions on Iraq. Substantial levels of debt owed by Iraq to China, France, Russia, and others since before the Gulf War also added to the push for resumption of normal economic relations. It is estimated that Iraq owes Russia $8 billion and France $7.5 billion. Ken Juster, "Iraq: An American Perspective," in Richard N. Haass, ed., *Transatlantic Tensions: The United States, Europe, and Problem Countries* (Brookings, 1999), p. 107, and "Russia Challenges Sanctions with Agreement on Cultural Centers in Iraq," *Associated Press*, September 26, 2000. Iraq is also estimated to owe Kuwait and Saudi Arabia $35 billion in debts from the Iran-Iraq war. Economist Intelligence Unit, *Country Profile: Iraq*, 2001, p. 33. Although earlier estimates placed Iraq's external debt in the realm of $150 billion, as of July 2001 the Economist Intelligence Unit estimated it to be $53 billion. Economist Intelligence Unit, *Country Profile: Iraq*, 2001, p. 33–34.

33. The northern no-fly zone was also extended from the 32d parallel to the 33d parallel. In opposition to this extension and to U.S. missile strikes on Iraq, France discontinued its involvement in patrolling the no-fly zones. See Thomas Lippman, "France Refuses Christopher Bid for Aid in Expanded Iraqi 'No-Fly' Zone," *Washington Post*, September 6, 1996; p. A32–41.

34. See, for instance, John Lancaster, "Saddam's Cover: A Veneer of Legitimacy; Argument That Iraqi Move Was a Justified Internal Act Has Found an Audience Abroad," *Washington Post*, September 5, 1996, p. A18.

35. For more on these crises, see Juster, "Iraq: An American Perspective," especially pp. 108–10.

36. Some contend that Primakov received substantial personal payoffs from Iraq. See Richard Butler, *The Greatest Threat: Iraq, Weapons of Mass Destruction, and the Crisis of Global Security* (New York: PublicAffairs, 2000), p. 106–07.

37. In return for its concessions, Iraq also secured some conciliatory language in the memorandum. For instance, paragraph 2 of the MOU said, "The United Nations reiterates the commitment of all Member States to respect the sovereignty and territorial integrity of Iraq." Also, paragraph 3 added, "UNSCOM undertakes to respect the legitimate concerns of Iraq relating to national security, sovereignty and dignity." The final paragraph of the MOU said, "The lifting of sanctions is obviously of paramount importance to the people and Government of Iraq and the Secretary-General undertook to bring this matter to the full attention of the members of the Security Council." United Nations Security Council, *Memorandum of Understanding between the United Nations and the Republic of Iraq*, S/1998/166 (United Nations, February 27, 1998).

38. United Nations Security Council, *Security Council Resolution 1154 (1998)*, S/RES/1154 (United Nations, March 2, 1998).

39. See Barbara Crosette, "Top U.N. Arms Inspector Tries to Quiet Ex-Iraq Team Member," *New York Times*, October 24, 1998, p. A4.

40. See United Nations Security Council, *Security Council Resolution 1194 (1998)*, S/RES/1194 (United Nations, September 9, 1998).

41. See Carla Anne Robbins, "U.S., Britain Seek Restraint in Iraq Standoff," *Wall Street Journal*, August 17, 1998, p. A16.

42. See Charles Trueheart, "U.S. Flanks Covered in Latest Showdown; France, Russia Drop Defense of Baghdad," *Washington Post*, November 13, 1998, p. A38.

43. See Barbara Crossette, "As Tension Grows, Few Voices at U.N. Speak Up for Iraq," *New York Times*, November 13, 1998, p. A1.

44. This course of events led President Clinton, in a news conference, to spell out conditions that Iraq had to meet to satisfy U.S. standards of "full cooperation." See "Remarks on the Situation in Iraq and an Exchange With Reporters, November 15, 1998," *Public Papers of the Presidents, William Jefferson Clinton: 1998*, vol. 2 (GPO, 1999), pp. 2035–038.

45. The IAEA did not make similar claims at the time.

46. Russia recalled its ambassador to the United States in protest of the air strikes. See Steven Erlanger, "U.S. Decision to Act Fast, and Then Search for Support, Angers Some Allies," *New York Times*, December 17, 1998, p. A14.

47. See Joel Greenberg, "Attack on Iraq: The Palestinians; Clinton's Ratings Take Dip in West Bank," *New York Times*, December 19, 1998, p. A9, and Serge Schmemann, "Attack on Iraq: The Reaction; Attacks Breed a Complex Unease about U.S. Goals," *New York Times*, December 20, 1998, p. A21.

48. For instances of such criticism, see Ronald Steel, "American Bombs Make Iraq Stronger," *New York Times*, December 20, 1998, p. A13; Rod Barton, "Iraq Is Down but Not Out," *New York Times*, December 23, 1998, p. A27; and Frank Smyth, "After the Shelling Stops: We Need More Than Missiles to Oust Saddam," *Washington Post*, December 20, 1998, p. C1.

49. General Anthony C. Zinni stated that it had "delayed Iraq's development of ballistic missiles by at least a year." Office of the Assistant Secretary of Defense for Public Affairs, "Defense Department News Briefing by Secretary of Defense William S. Cohen and General Anthony C. Zinni," December 21, 1998.

50. For a discussion of these two tensions in the development of U.S. policy toward Iraq, see Robert Litwak, *Rogue States and U.S. Foreign Policy* (Baltimore: Woodrow Wilson Center Press, 1999), pp. 123–57.

51. On May 21, 1991, just three months after the end of the Gulf war, President George H.W. Bush declared that the United States would use the threat of its veto on the UN Security Council to keep UN sanctions on Iraq until Saddam was out of power. His views were echoed later the same day by his press secretary, Marlin Fitzwater. Two weeks earlier, Bush's deputy national security adviser, Robert Gates, had also expressed this view in a speech. Such views, however, were rarely voiced in public after these early days. See Roland Dannreuther, "The Gulf Conflict: A Political and Strategic Analysis," Adelphi Papers 264 (Oxford, England: International Institute for Strategic Studies, Winter 1991/92) p. 66, and Patrick E. Tyler, "After the War: Bush Links End of Trading Ban to Hussein Exit," *New York Times*, May 21, 1991, p. A1.

52. See R. Jeffrey Smith and Julia Preston, "U.S. Drops Demand for Saddam's Ouster," *Washington Post*, March 30, 1993, p. A17.

53. See the White House, Office of the Press Secretary, "Press Briefing by Dee Dee Myers," March 28, 1993.

54. One significant element of the Annan-Aziz Memorandum of Understanding struck in February 1998 was that it explicitly linked the removal of sanctions to paragraph 22 of UN resolution 687 concerning disarmament. See Litwak, *Rogue States and U.S. Foreign Policy*, pp. 135–36.

55. Secretary of State Madeleine Albright, "Preserving Principle and Safeguarding Stability: United States Policy toward Iraq," U.S. Department of State, Office of the Spokesman, comments delivered at Georgetown University, March 26, 1997. The text of this speech can be found at http://secretary.state.gov.//www/statements/970326.html [June 6, 2002].

56. For example, see Thomas Pickering, "Remarks to the Washington Institute for Near East Policy," Department of State, Office of the Spokesman, September 19, 1997 (www.state.gov/www/policy_remarks/970919_pickering_mepolicy.html [June 6, 2002]), and Madeleine K. Albright, "The U.S. Will Stand Firm on Iraq, No Matter What," *New York Times*, August 17, 1998, p. A15.

57. For official articulations of the dual containment strategy, see Martin S. Indyk, "The Clinton Administration's Approach to the Middle East," speech to the Washington Institute for Near East Policy, May 18, 1993 (www.washingtoninstitute.org/pubs/indyk. htm [June 6, 2002]), and Anthony Lake, "Confronting Backlash States," *Foreign Affairs*, vol. 73 (March/April 1994), pp. 45–55.

58. The law makes the imposition of some sanctions mandatory (such as the barring of U.S. government procurement and U.S. export sanctions) as well as authorizes the imposition of discretionary sanctions (the suspension of U.S. aid, military sales, and other military and dual-use exchanges and the voicing of U.S. opposition to international loans).

59. See, for instance, H. Res. 322, which was adopted by the House on November 12, 1997, and S. J. Res. 54 (which became P.L. 105-235 on August 14, 1998). The Senate failed to pass an accompaniment to H. Res. 322, as some members of the body wanted the resolution to explicitly call for the United States to overthrow the Iraqi regime.

60. See Christopher Wren, "France Calls U.S. Callous for Allowing Iraq to Suffer," *New York Times*, September 25, 1999, p. A4.

61. A French proposal, which Russia and China backed as a first step toward the ultimate goal of removing sanctions, recommended that UNSCOM be replaced by a new agency whose focus would be primarily on monitoring Iraq to ensure that new weapons facilities were not built rather than on uncovering and destroying existing weapons. Once Iraq demonstrated cooperation with the new monitoring commission, most sanctions would be lifted. In contrast, a British/Dutch proposal, supported by the United States, advocated a "search and destroy" weapons inspection team to resume UNSCOM's work. Under the terms of this proposal, foreign involvement in Iraq's oil industry and easing of the sanctions on oil exports would follow once Iraqi cooperation with the weapons team was well-established. Sanctions would be fully lifted only when the UN weapons inspection body verified Iraq's complete disarmament. See "French Proposals

for Iraq (new)" found on the website of the French Embassy in the United Kingdom at www.ambafrance.org.uk/db.phtml?id=3092 [November 3, 1999], and see "Iraq: UK/ Netherlands Draft Resolution" (http://linux.clare.cam.ac.uk/~saw27/casi/info/uk-dutch.html [June 6, 2002]). Also see Economist Intelligence Unit, *Country Report: Iraq*, Third Quarter 1999, p. 15.

62. Those who voiced reservations over the resolution pointed out that its wording focuses on monitoring Iraq's ability to reconstitute weapons of mass destruction, not on destroying already existing ones. See the interview with Rolf Ekeus in J. Peter Scoblic and Matthew Rice, "Shifting Priorities: UNMOVIC and the Future of Inspections in Iraq."

63. United Nations Security Council, *Security Council Resolution 1284 (1999)*, S/RES/1284 (United Nations, December 17, 1999)

64. The final vote of the Security Council was 11-0, with Malaysia also abstaining. The American deputy permanent representative to the United Nations, Ambassador A. Peter Burleigh, commented after the vote that "no Council member would say that Iraq has met its obligations. . . . We expect all members of the Council, regardless of their vote on this resolution, to join in pressing Iraq for full and immediate implementation." A. Peter Burleigh, "Explanation of U.S. Vote on UN Security Council Omnibus Resolution on Iraq" (Department of State, December 17,1999) (www.state.gov/ www/regions/ nea/iraq_remarks.html [June 6, 2002]).

65. Moreover, few countries apart from the United States and some European nations supported efforts to establish Saddam and other top Iraqis as war criminals. The Clinton administration continued to back such efforts, largely through its support of INDICT, a private London-based initiative working to catalogue and publicize alleged Iraqi war crimes. In Europe, such efforts gained strength in the wake of a December 2000 resolution of the European Parliament supporting a tribunal and the June 2001 launch of an investigation of Saddam Hussein's war crimes by a Belgian court.

66. Although Syrian president Bashar Assad made a pledge to Secretary Powell that this trade would be brought within the UN program, the volume of oil flowing to Syria through this pipeline was estimated to be up to 180,000 barrels per day as of March 2002. Economist Intelligence Unit, *Country Report: Iraq*, March 2002, p. 19.

67. Saddam distributed $10,000 to each of the families of Palestinian "martyrs" killed in clashes with Israel once the al-Aqsa intifada began. Iraq also sought to donate $949 million from Iraq's Oil for Food fund to the Palestinians for humanitarian purposes, although the United Nations did not permit the transfer. See Molly Moore, "With Money for 'Martyrs,' Iraq Invests in Image," *Washington Post*, January 30, 2001, p. A1, and Nicole Winfield, "U.S., British Question Funds," *Associated Press*, January 8, 2001.

68. Although UN resolutions did not explicitly ban all flights to Iraq, for the first ten years that the sanctions were in place, a virtual air ban was upheld. Controversy around the meaning of the UN resolution regarding flights to Iraq arose in 2000. The United States claimed that only flights with explicit permission from the UN Sanctions Committee could travel to Iraq; other countries, including France and Russia, claimed that only planes carrying cargo to and from Iraq needed such authorization and that passenger flights were exempt. See "U.S. Disputes French View of Iraqi Air Embargo," *Reuters*, August 4, 2000; Waiel Faleh, "Russians in Iraq without U.N. OK," *Associated Press*, August 19, 2000; Mouna Naim, "Passenger Flights Are Being Organized in Order

to Break Air Embargo Imposed on Iraq," *LeMonde*, August 23, 2000; and "UN Sanctions on Iraq Do Not Forbid Passenger Flights: Russian Diplomat," *Agence France-Presse*, September 15, 2000.

69. See Hassan Hafidh, "Iraq Stops Oil Exports, Insists on Surcharge," *Reuters*, December 1, 2000.

70. For example, see Colin Powell, testimony at *U.S. Foreign Policy: Hearing before the House International Relations Committee* and at *The Fiscal Year 2002 Foreign Operations Budget: Hearing before the Senate Foreign Relations Committee*, 107 Cong. 1 sess., March 8, 2001.

71. In the domestic realm, Powell's plan met opposition from both those demanding a tougher approach toward Saddam Hussein and those pushing for a more lenient strategy on humanitarian grounds. In the international realm, regional leaders offered conditional support in the initial negotiation phases but remained concerned about their economic well-being under a new sanctions regime that would challenge well-established informal economic networks and possibly cause Iraq to retaliate by stopping all trade with its neighbors. For an example of congressional apprehension about Powell's plan, see the remarks of Rep. Benjamin Gilman at *U.S. Foreign Policy: Hearing before the House International Relations Committee*, 107 Cong. 1 sess., March 8, 2001. For criticisms from both the right and left, see A. M. Rosenthal, "Colin Powell's 2nd Iraq Blunder," *New York Daily News*, March 2, 2001; "Smarting over Iraq: It's Time to Get Serious about Toppling Saddam," *Wall Street Journal*, July 8, 2001; and Shibley Telhami, "Time for Realism on Handling Iraq," *Washington Post*, June 20, 2001, p. A27.

72. In 1990, Iraq boasted a GDP of approximately $60 billion. However, Iraqi GDP sank to $10 billion in following years, to rise only to $31.8 billion in 2000. Economist Intelligence Unit, *Country Profile: Iraq*, 1996/1997, p. 13; Economist Intelligence Unit, *Country Profile: Iraq*, 1999/2000, p. 20; Economist Intelligence Unit, *Country Profile: Iraq*, 2001, p. 21.

73. In these measures in 1999, Iraq ranked behind Qatar, Israel, Kuwait, UAE, Bahrain, Oman, Saudi Arabia, Lebanon, Tunisia, Libya, Algeria, Egypt, Morocco, Jordan, Syria, Iran, and Yemen. By these indicators, only war-torn, famine-stricken Sudan appeared to be in worse economic condition than Iraq in that year. See Economist Intelligence Unit, *Country Profile: Iraq*, 1999/2000, p. i.

74. Economist Intelligence Unit, *Country Profile: Iraq* (1999/2000), p. 5. The Economist Intelligence Unit roughly calculated the total cost of the Iran-Iraq war to Iraq to be between $115 and $137 billion, once arms purchases, forgone oil revenues and non-oil income, compensation to victims' families, and damaged pipelines are taken into account. See Economist Intelligence Unit, *Country Report: Iraq*, Fourth Quarter 1998, p. 12. One estimate suggests that Iraqi foreign debt at the close of the Iran-Iraq war stood at $60 to $80 billion, $35 billion of it to Kuwait and Saudi Arabia. Economist Intelligence Unit, *Country Report: Iraq*, Third Quarter 1990, p. 6.

75. Fadhil J. Chalabi, "The Opening of Iraq: Post-Sanctions Iraqi Oil, Its Effects on World Oil Prices," *Oil & Gas Journal*, February 14, 2000, pp. 41–43.

76. Because the state of the Iraqi economy is heavily dependent on the price of oil, these figures to some extent also represent the state of the international oil market at either end of the decade. Figures from Anthony H. Cordesman, "The Gulf in Transition: US Policy Ten Years after the Gulf War: The Challenge of Iraq" (Center for Strategic and

International Studies, October 2000), pp. 18–19 (www.csis.org/gulf/reports/subiraq.pdf [August 16, 2001]).

77. See Economist Intelligence Unit, *Country Report: Iraq*, Second Quarter 1990, p. 12. Also see Economist Intelligence Unit, *Country Report: Iraq*, First Quarter 1990, p. 5; Economist Intelligence Unit, *Country Report: Iraq*, Third Quarter 1990, p. 13.

78. Some analysts allege that the inability of the regime to meet the rising socioeconomic expectations of the population spurred Iraq to invade Kuwait in 1990. See Amatzia Baram, "The Iraqi Invasion of Kuwait: Decision-Making in Baghdad," in Baram and Barry Rubin, eds., *Iraq's Road to War* (New York, St. Martin's Press, 1993, 1996), pp. 6–9.

79. The Harvard Study Team, "The Effect of the Gulf War on the Children of Iraq," *New England Journal of Medicine*, vol. 325, no. 13 (1991).

80. Productive capacity was down from 3.5 million to 1.46 million barrels per day after the war; refining capacities initially plummeted, although Iraq was able to restore them to 460,000 barrels per day in 1991, yet they were still down from 550,000 before the war. By 1993 Iraq's refining capacity had reached 567,000 barrels per day. Economist Intelligence Unit, *Country Profile: Iraq*, 1999/2000, p. 26. Also see United Nations Secretariat, *Report to the Secretary-General on Humanitarian Needs in Iraq* (United Nations, July 15, 1991).

81. Organization of Petroleum Exporting Countries, *Annual Statistical Bulletin*, 1999 (Vienna, Austria: OPEC), p. 46.

82. According to a UN report, the production of potable water fell from 7 million cubic meters a day before the war to 1.5 million afterward. United Nations Secretariat, *Report to the Secretary-General on Humanitarian Needs in Iraq* (United Nations, July 15, 1991), p. 18.

83. Estimates vary widely on the number of Iraqi casualties from the Gulf war. For various estimates, see John G. Heidenrich, "The Gulf War: How Many Iraqis Died?" *Foreign Policy*, no. 90 (Spring 1993), pp. 108-125; Thomas A. Keany and Eliot A. Cohen, *Gulf War Air Power Survey, Summary Report* (Department of the Air Force, 1993), p. 249; and Richard Garfield, *Morbidity and Mortality among Iraqi Children from 1990 to 1998: Assessing the Impact of Economic Sanctions* (Goshen, Indiana: Institute for International Peace Studies, University of Notre Dame and the Fourth Freedom Forum, March 1999), pp. 10–11.

84. Economist Intelligence Unit, *Country Report: Iraq* (Fourth Quarter 1993), pp. 5, 15.

85. The *Middle East Economic Digest* estimated that Iraq owed western industrialized countries' export credit agencies a total of $13.7 billion at the time of the Gulf war. Simon Edge, "Iraq: Counting the Cost of Credit," *Middle East Economic Digest*, vol. 36 (November 27, 1992), p. 31. According to the OECD, Iraq had received approximately $73 million in direct overseas development assistance between 1988 and 1990, primarily from Arab countries and agencies. This number declined considerably throughout the 1990s, although some countries continued to grant Iraq bilateral humanitarian assistance outside UN programs. OECD, *Geographical Distribution of Financial Flows to Developing Countries*, 1992, p. 156.

86. UN resolution 1175, passed on June 19, 1998, was the first to approve $300 million for the purchase of oil industry spare parts, and UN resolution 1302, passed June 8, 2000, doubled that amount to $600 million. United Nations Security Council, *Security*

*Council Resolution 1175 (1998)*, S/RES/1175 (June 19, 1998), and *Security Council Resolution 1302 (2000)*, S/2000/1302 (June 8, 2000).

87. Many oil industry experts believe that, in lifting large volumes of oil, Iraq has endangered the long-term viability of some of its oil fields. For instance, see a Middle East Institute conference summary, "The Iraqi Oil Industry after Sanctions," *Middle East Institute Newsletter*, vol. 51, no. 3 (May 2000). Also see United Nations Security Council, *Report of the Group of Experts Established Pursuant to Paragraph 12 of Security Council Resolution 1153 (1998)*, S/1998/330 (April 15, 1998), and *Report of the Team of Experts Established Pursuant to Paragraph 15 of Security Council Resolution 1330 (2000)*, S/2001/566 (June 6, 2001), which reiterates the concerns of previous UN oil experts who visited Iraq.

88. Chalabi, "The Opening of Iraq."

89. Fadhil Chalabi estimates that with the assistance of foreign investors, Iraq could reach these levels (from 2000 levels) in five or six years. See "Iraq and the Future of World Oil," *Middle East Policy*, vol. 7 (October 2000), pp. 163–73.

90. As long as Iraq has been under sanctions, it has not been subject to OPEC quotas. According to Energy Information Administration estimates, an additional million barrels per day on the market can translate into as much as a $3 to $5 decrease in the price of oil. Even if this relationship is significantly overstated, Iraq's production of a few million more barrels of oil per day could bring down the price of oil considerably. Moreover, some analysts contend that the existence of spare capacity (even if not used) can also have a dampening effect on the price of oil; therefore, even if Iraq did not produce at these levels, but maintained the spare capacity to do so, the price of oil could be affected.

91. This judgment excludes permanent damages done to Iraq's oil fields as a result of damaging extraction practices currently occurring.

92. See Economist Intelligence Unit, *Country Report: Iraq*, Fourth Quarter 1990, pp. 11–13.

93. The rationing began in September 1990; as of early 1993, monthly rationing consisted of flour, rice, sugar, tea, and soap. The amount of food provided varied, as did the consistency with which a full ration was available over time. Initially, the average Iraqi could live off the ration alone for ten to fourteen days of the month, and many supplemented it with food bought on the black market with money they obtained by selling their possessions. Economist Intelligence Unit, *Country Report: Iraq*, First Quarter 1993, p. 15.

94. Economist Intelligence Unit, *Country Report: Iraq*, First Quarter 1993, p. 5; Economist Intelligence Unit, *Country Report: Iraq*, Fourth Quarter 1992, p. 15.

95. Economist Intelligence Unit, *Country Report: Iraq*, Second Quarter 1993, pp. 1–2; Economist Intelligence Unit, *Country Profile: Iraq*, 1996/97, p. 10.

96. According to the FAO, Iraq imported 3,439 tons of wheat and wheat flour in 1989 before the sanctions were imposed, slightly less than half of that amount in 1992 (1,619 tons), and less than a quarter of that amount in 1994 (799 tons). Food and Agriculture Organization of the United Nations, *Trade Yearbook*, 1990, 1993, 1996.

97. Economist Intelligence Unit, *Country Report: Iraq*, Third Quarter 1992, p. 19, and Fourth Quarter 1992, p. 15.

98. Economist Intelligence Unit, *Country Report: Iraq*, Third Quarter 1992, p. 19; Fourth Quarter 1993, p. 5; and Second Quarter 1993, p. 5.

99. See Paul Lewis, "U.N. Council Votes to Use Iraqi Assets Frozen Abroad," *New York Times*, October 3, 1992, p. A2. This was the first time ever that the UN seized a country's money. Iraq called the decision by the Security Council "an illegal act of confiscation, a modified form of bank robbery Texas-style." From "Furious Iraq Calls Seizure of Its Assets U.N. 'Robbery'," *Orlando Sentinel Tribune*, October 4, 1992, p. A23.

100. The Third River Project was launched by the Iraqi government in March 1992 and completed in October 1996. The project drained marshes in southern Iraq, officially to reduce salinity in farmland between the Tigris and Euphrates rivers.

101. Economist Intelligence Unit, *Country Report: Iraq*, Fourth Quarter 1991, p. 13, and First Quarter 1993, p. 14.

102. In May 1994, Iraq formed a new government with Saddam heading it directly for the first time in many years. This new government introduced draconian measures to curb profiteering and hoarding, but to little long-term effect.

103. Economist Intelligence Unit, *Country Report: Iraq*, First Quarter 1996, p. 17.

104. Economist Intelligence Unit, *Country Report: Iraq*, Third Quarter 1996, pp. 16–18.

105. Another factor prompting Saddam to take this action was the poor harvest occurring at this time.

106. Economist Intelligence Unit, *Country Profile: Iraq*, 1999/2000, p. 33, and May 2000, p. 5.

107. The agricultural sector in particular suffered as a result of the Oil for Food scheme, with the volume of crops declining since the onset of the program. This effect is understandable, given that Iraqi farmers could not compete with the larger amounts of food suddenly being imported into the country and distributed for free. UN resolution 1284 makes reference to the fact that some of the proceeds from Iraqi oil sales could be spent on "local goods." Although it is not entirely clear what this would entail, such a move could boost production within Iraq. See the conclusion to this chapter.

108. See OPEC, *Annual Statistical Bulletin*, 1998, pp. 47, 80.

109. In terms of dollar value, Iraqi production and export under the Oil for Food program exceeded 1989 levels in 2000. This reflects the high price of oil in the late 1990s and 2000, as well as increasing Iraqi capability.

110. The Economist Intelligence Unit estimated that before 1996, the regime spent approximately $100 million a month on food imports. Economist Intelligence Unit, *Country Report: Iraq*, Second Quarter 1997, p. 17.

111. Under the Foreign Operations Appropriations bills passed since 1994, the United States is obligated to impose sanctions against countries violating the sanctions against Iraq. However, this legislation grants the president the ability to waive the sanctions if it is in the U.S. national interest. Both Jordan and Turkey have been granted waivers for their trade with Iraq outside the Oil for Food program. The Kurds in northern Iraq also have benefited substantially from this illicit trade. Although estimates of the amount of money the Kurds earn from taxing the oil smuggling are not readily available, reports suggest it could be as high as $1 million per day. "Increased Level of Freedom and Prosperity for Kurds Living in Northern Iraq, despite Continued Hardships for Other Kurdish Factions," National Public Radio, *Morning Edition*, Quil Lawrence reporting, July 4, 2000; also see Howard Schneider, "The Squeeze on Iraq Allows Its Kurds to Flourish," *Washington Post*, January 30, 2000, p. A20, and Warren P.

Strobel, "Freed from Saddam's Grip," *U.S. News and World Report*, September 11, 2000, pp. 56–57.

112. Reports of Iraqi smuggling through Iran first surfaced in 1994. In December 1994, the United States formally lodged a complaint with the UN Sanctions Committee that Iran was helping sell Iraqi oil. However, complaints of this nature go back to March 1993, when the United States quietly lodged a protest with Tehran about one large shipment of Iraqi oil allegedly bought by Iran.

113. In the late 1990s, one of the most popular routes for illegal Iraqi oil was from the Iraqi ports of Abu Flus and Umm Qasr, through the Shatt al-Arab waterway into the Gulf with Iranian protection, and over to Fujaira and Dubai in the UAE. In 2000, Iran opened up Qeys Island to Iraqi oil smugglers for transfers of oil to ships that can better evade the interdiction force. The oil transfers at Qeys Island, a small tourist resort off Iran's southern coast, represent a substantial escalation in Iran's collusion in the smuggling trade, although U.S. officials are still uncertain of whether this operation is condoned by Iranian President Khatami. See Robin Wright, "Iran Opens Key Isle to Iraqi Oil Smugglers, U.S. Says," *Los Angeles Times*, July 3, 2000, p. A1; Robin Wright, "Iran Reportedly Allows Iraqi Oil in Its Sea Lanes," *Los Angeles Times*, June 6, 2000, p. A1.

114. More concrete estimates of the volume of smuggling were deduced in the late 1990s and 2000, based largely on the volumes of oil intercepted by the Multilateral Interdiction Force, which patrols the international waters of the gulf for illicit shipments of Iraqi oil.

115. From 1993 to 1995, Iraq produced approximately 600,000 barrels a day, although its *pre-war* consumption was only 350,000 barrels a day. Economist Intelligence Unit, *Country Report: Iraq*, First Quarter 1995, p. 18.

116. Department of State, *Saddam Hussein's Iraq*, September 1999 (updated 3/24/00), p. 39 (http://usinfo.state.gov/regional/nea/iraq/iraq99.htm [June 6, 2002]), and William Drozdiak, "Iraq Imperils OPEC Plan; With World Economy Shaky, Illegal Oil Shipments Go Unchallenged," *Washington Post*, February 10, 2001, p. E1.

117. An Iraqi company called Asia and run by Saddam's immediate family is reported to have control over much of the illegal trade with Turkey, Iraq, Iran, and Syria. See Matthew McAllester, "Fatter in Lean Times," *Newsday*, June 19, 2000, p. 8.

118. "Sources of Revenue for Saddam & Sons: A Primer on the Financial Underpinnings of the Regime in Baghdad," Coalition for International Justice (June 27, 2002). For estimates of the regime's profits, Department of Energy, Energy Information Administration, *Country Analysis Brief on Iraq*, May 2001 (www.eia.doe.gov/emeu/cabs/iraq2.html [June 6, 2002]).

119. For more information on proposed production-sharing agreements, see Economist Intelligence Unit, *Country Report: Iraq*, Second Quarter 1999, p. 23

120. In the 1990s, Iraq began to offer foreign companies production-sharing agreements for the first time since the Iraqi oil industry was nationalized in the 1970s. Economist Intelligence Unit, *Country Profile: Iraq*, 1999/2000, p. 26.

121. French understandings with the Iraqis were less formal than the signed contracts of the Russians and the Chinese. For an update of the agreements signed by Iraq with foreign oil companies to develop its resources, see Energy Information Administration, *Country Analysis Brief on Iraq* (Department of Energy, May 2001) (www.eia.doe.gov/emeu/cabs/iraq2.html [June 6, 2002]).

122. As mentioned, UN procedures mandate that Iraq negotiate deals with countries and companies from which it wishes to import goods permitted under the Oil for Food program and submit the contracts to the UN Sanctions Committee for approval. The export of Iraqi oil is also approved by the committee and the proceeds of the sales are directed to a UN escrow account.

123. There are several ways to analyze the trends discussed here. One could look at the final destination of the oil, as was done in the previous paragraph. The number of contracts awarded to companies in a particular country also could be examined. However, because this would obscure the size of each contract, this study analyzes the numbers of barrels (totaled from the amount awarded in each contract) that companies in each country were permitted to lift.

124. Economist Intelligence Unit, *Country Report: Iraq*, Fourth Quarter 1997, p. 17; "Iraq to Give Friendly Countries Priority on Crude Contracts," *Platt's Oilgram Price Report*, June 27, 1997, p. 1.

125. These figures were compiled from information in the weekly updates provided by the United Nations Office of the Iraq Program and numerous issues of the *Middle East Economic Survey* from 1996 to 2000.

126. The United States, Britain, Japan, and Switzerland were named as hostile. See Roula Khalaf, "Iraq Bans Food Imports from 'Hostile Countries,'" *Financial Times*, January 5, 1999, p. 5.

127. The creation of the United Nations Compensation Commission was authorized by UN resolution 687. The purpose of the commission is to administer the process through which Iraqi funds are used to satisfy claims made against Iraq for its invasion and occupation of Kuwait. Economist Intelligence Unit, *Country Report: Iraq*, Third Quarter 1999, p. 25; "Iraq Urges U.N. Not to Cut Any Oil Money for Compensation," *Associated Press*, May 18, 1999.

128. Algeria, Jordan, Tunisia, and Yemen also signed economic agreements with Iraq.

129. In January 2001, the UN approved the establishment of a border office between Iraq and Saudi Arabia to facilitate trade between the two countries. See Economist Intelligence Unit, *Country Report: Iraq*, February 2001, p. 29.

130. The GCC states of Qatar, Oman, Bahrain, and the UAE were the first to reestablish diplomatic ties with Iraq in early 2000. Since that time, numerous European and other countries have followed suit, including France, Russia, Austria, Switerland, Japan, Syria, and Egypt.

131. See Litwak, *Rogue States and U.S. Foreign Policy*, pp. 140–49.

132. See Amatzia Baram, "The Iraqi Armed Forces and Security Apparatus," *Conflict, Security, and Development*, no.1, vol. 2 (2001); Ofra Bengio, "How Does Saddam Hold On?" *Foreign Affairs*, vol. 79, (July/August 2000), pp. 90–103; Regis W. Matlak, "Inside Saddam's Grip," *National Security Studies Quarterly*, Spring 1999, pp. 1–28; and Kanan Makiya, "Dark Truth in Saddam's Iraq," *Dissent*, vol. 45, no. 3 (Summer 1998), pp. 52–60.

133. See Bush and Scowcroft, *A World Transformed*, especially chapters 15 through 17, on U.S. efforts to build both international and domestic consensus in the period between the Iraqi invasion and the start of the Gulf war.

134. Some opposed military force in 1990, arguing that sanctions needed more time to take effect and force Iraq to withdraw from Kuwait. See "Confrontation in the Gulf; Day 3: Remarks in Congress during the Last Hours of Debate," *New York Times*, January 13, 1991.

135. One notable exception was the amassing of Iraqi troops on the border with Kuwait in 1994.

136. See Anthony H. Cordesman, *Iraq and the War of Sanctions: Conventional Threats and Weapons of Mass Destruction* (Westport, Conn.: Praeger, 1999), and Cordesman, "US Policy Ten Years after the Gulf War." There are, however, allegations that Iraq has been able to reconstitute its conventional weaponry more than most analysts anticipated. Also see "Baghdad Resurgent," *Jane's Defence Weekly*, July 25, 2001, pp. 24–27.

137. Department of State, Bureau of Arms Control, *World Military Expenditures and Arms Transfers*, 1998, table 1.

138. Cordesman, "US Policy Ten Years after the Gulf War," pp. 40, 45.

139. See Rolf Ekeus, speech given at the Carnegie Endowment for International Peace Conference on Nuclear Nonproliferation and the Millennium: Prospects and Initiatives, Washington, D.C., February 13, 1996, quoted in David Cortright and George Lopez, *The Sanctions Decade: Assessing UN Strategies in the 1990s* (Boulder, Colo.: Lynne Rienner Publishers, 2000), p. 54.

140. See United Nations Security Council, *Letter Dated 9 April 1998 from the Secretary-General Addressed to the President of the Security Council, appendix: Fifth Consolidated Report of the Director General of the International Atomic Energy Agency under Paragraph 16 of Security Council Resolution 1051 (1996)*, S/1998/312 (1998), paragraph 34.

141. See United Nations Security Council, *Letter Dated 27 January 1999 from the Permanent Representatives of the Netherlands and Slovenia to the United Nations Addressed to the President of the Security Council, annex: Letter Dated 25 January 1999 from the Executive Chairman of the Special Commission established by the Secretary-General Pursuant to Paragraph 9(b)(i) of Security Council Resolution 687 (1991) addressed to the President of the Security Council*, S/1999/94 (January 29, 1999).

142. The international community has been unable to verify to what extent Iraq has reconstituted its weapons programs, yet the doggedness with which Iraq defended and pursued its WMD efforts suggests that Iraq has spent the last two years of the decade and beyond engaged in such pursuits. A minority, however, believes that Iraq has not sought to rearm itself; see Scott Ritter, "The Case for Iraq's Qualitative Disarmament," *Arms Control Today*, vol. 30 (June 2000), pp. 8–14.

143. Moreover, in 2000, the CIA reported that Iraq continued to work on aerial vehicles and missile systems it believes are intended for the delivery of chemical or biological agents. The June 2000 test of the Al-Samoud ballistic missile, although permitted under UN resolutions because of its short range, further heightens suspicions about Iraq's WMD activities. See Central Intelligence Agency, *Unclassified Report to Congress on the Acquisition of Technology Relating to Weapons of Mass Destruction and Advanced Conventional Munitions, 1 January through 30 June 2000* (www.gov/cia/publications/bian/bian_feb2001.htm [August 6, 2001]; also see Steven Lee Myers, "Flight Tests by Iraq Show Progress of Missile Program," *New York Times*, July 1, 2000, p. 1.

144. A study conducted by the Defense Intelligence Agency in March 1991, before UNSCOM was created, estimated that once sanctions were lifted, Iraq could produce a nuclear weapon within two to four years. In the absence of the Gulf war, the study estimated that Iraq could have attained a nuclear weapon by 1993. Furthermore, the DIA estimated that it would take Iraq three to five years to return its chemical weapons program to pre-war levels and five to eight years to fully resume its biological program. This

report is cited in Michael R. Gordon and General Bernard E. Trainor, *The Generals' War* (Boston: Little, Brown and Company, 1995), pp. 517–518, endnote no. 16.

145. In January 2001, Saddam's son, Uday, began to advocate changing the map on the Iraqi legislature's emblem to show Kuwait as part of Iraq, calling into question the significance of this achievement. See "Saddam's Son Uday Wants Iraq Map to Include Kuwait," *Reuters*, January 15, 2001.

146. For example, Iraq initially denied it had ever maintained a uranium enrichment project or a biological weapons program for offensive purposes, only to later admit to such activities once defectors made such denials unsustainable. See United Nations Security Council, *Report of the Ninth IAEA On-Site Inspection in Iraq under Security Council Resolution 687 (1991), 11–14 January 1992, S/23505 (January 28, 1992)*, pp. 3–13, and United Nations Security Council, *Report of the Secretary-General on the Status of the Implementation of the Special Commission's Plan for the Ongoing Monitoring and Verification of Iraq's Compliance with Relevant Parts of Security Council Resolution 687 (1991)*, S/1995/864 (October 11, 1995). Iraqi efforts to conceal information from inspectors or obstruct their access to suspicious sites are well documented in the latter United Nations Security Council report and in *Report of the Secretary-General on the Activities of the Special Commission Established by the Secretary-General Pursuant to Paragraph 9(b)(i) of Resolution 687 (1991)*, S1996/258 (April 11, 1996). Also see Richard Butler, *The Greatest Threat: Iraq, Weapons of Mass Destruction, and the Crisis of Global Security* (New York: Public Affairs, 2000), and Tim Trevan, *Saddam's Secrets: The Hunt for Iraq's Hidden Weapons* (London: HarperCollins, 1999).

147. UNSCOM reported that inspectors had found Russian gyroscopes at the bottom of the Tigris River in November 1995. See Vladimir Orlov and William C. Potter, "The Mystery of the Sunken Gyros," *Bulletin of the Atomic Scientists*, vol. 54 (November/December 1998), pp. 34–39. Allegations of illegal arms exports to Iraq through Jordan or the UAE have been frequent. See, for example, David Hoffman, "Iraq Sought Russian Arms Technology; Probe Details Moscow Deal for Missile Equipment in '94," *Washington Post*, October 18, 1998, p. A24, and David Albright and Khidhir Hamza, "Iraq's Reconstitution of Its Nuclear Weapons Program," *Arms Control Today*, vol. 28 (October 1998), pp. 9–15.

148. Department of State, Coordinator for Counterterrorism, *Patterns of Global Terrorism*, various years. Under provisions of the 1996 Antiterrorism and Effective Death Penalty Act, the State Department designated Mujahedin-e Khalq a foreign terrorist organization in October 1997.

149. See Freedom House, *Freedom in the World: The Annual Survey of Political Rights and Civil Liberties, 2000–2001* (Washington: 2001) (www.freedomhouse.org/research/freeworld/2001/countryratings/iraq.htm [June 7, 2002]; Department of State, Bureau for Democracy, Human Rights, and Labor, *Annual Report on International Religious Freedom for 2000: Iraq*, September 5, 2000 (www.state.gov/www/global/human_rights/irf/irf_rpt/irf_iraq.html [June 7, 2002]); Department of State, Bureau for Democracy, Human Rights, and Labor, *2000 Country Reports on Human Rights Practices: Iraq*, February 2001 (www.state.gov/g/drl/rls/hrrpt/2000/nea/index.cfm?docid=787 [June 7, 2002]); and Human Rights Watch, *World Report 2001* (www.hrw.org/wr2kl/mideast/iraq.html [June 7, 2002]).

150. See Department of State, US/UN Press Release, "Statement by Ambassador James Cunningham, United States Deputy Permanent Representative to the United

Nations, on the Kuwaiti POWs Issue," April 26, 2000, and Department of State, Bureau for Democracy, Human Rights, and Labor, *1999 Country Reports on Human Rights Practices: Iraq*, February 25, 2000.

151. The World Bank, *World Development Indicators, 2001 CD-ROM*.

152. According to household surveys conducted in November 2000, 16.2 percent of children under five years of age suffered from chronic malnutrition, 9.7 percent were underweight, and 3.1 percent were acutely malnourished. This was an improvement over rates from 1997, which were 30.3 percent, 15.9 percent, and 3.1 percent respectively. Economist Intelligence Unit, *Country Report: Iraq*, 2001, p. 16.

153. UN figures indicate that the enrollment ratio for primary and secondary education declined from 89 percent in 1980 to 66 percent in 1995. Adult literacy increased over time, although it remained fairly low at 58 percent in 1995. UNESCO (http://unescostat. unesco.org/en/stats/stats0.htm [June 7, 2002]).

154. Beyond pushing many Iraqis to the edge of existence, many analysts point out that widespread economic insecurity has also had significant consequences for the social fabric of Iraqi society, with dramatic increases in crime, corruption, and general lawlessness. Some posit that more subtle social changes—such as marked reductions in the numbers of Iraqis getting married and a rise in religious practice—are associated with the hardships endured in Iraq. Environmental hazards have also increased, with a growing number of oil spills occurring in the Gulf as a result of smuggling efforts. See Sarah Graham-Brown, *Sanctioning Saddam: The Politics of Intervention in Iraq* (New York: I. B. Taurus Publishers, 1999); Qais N. Al-Nouri, "The Impact of the Economic Embargo on Iraq Families: Re-Structuring of Tribes, Socioeconomic Classes and Households," *Journal of Comparative Family Studies*, vol. 28 (Summer 1997), pp. 99–112.

155. Despite the numerous claims about sanctions-induced deaths in Iraq, no field surveys of child mortality rates in Iraq were conducted between 1991 and July 1999. See Amatzia Baram, "The Effect of Iraqi Sanctions: Statistical Pitfalls and Responsibility," *Middle East Journal*, vol. 54 (Spring 2000), p. 202.

156. "Health Ministry Releases Figures on Deaths under Sanctions," Iraq News Agency, July 1, 2000, in Foreign Broadcast Information Service, *Daily Report, Near East/South Asia*, July 5, 2000.

157. For instance, UNICEF reported in 1995 that sanctions had resulted in the deaths of more than 1.2 million Iraqi children. UNICEF, *The Status of Children and Women in Iraq: A Situation Report* (United Nations, September 1995).

158. As persuasively argued by Amatzia Baram, in order for these figures to be correct, a number of assumptions about conditions in Iraq—all of them very difficult to sustain—would have to be true. See Baram, "The Effect of Iraqi Sanctions," especially pp. 195–99.

159. See Garfield, *Morbidity and Mortality among Iraqi Children from 1990 to 1998*, p. 35.

160. See UNICEF, *Child and Maternal Mortality Survey, 1999: Preliminary Rreport*, July 1999, especially pages 10–14.

161. The ability of every Iraqi to cope with the social and economic effect of sanctions has depended on a variety of factors, such as his initial level of income and assets, skills, and family network. For a much fuller treatment of these differential impacts, see Graham-Brown, *Sanctioning Saddam*, especially pp. 179–212.

162. These important differences have often been concealed by studies and reports that either extrapolate from small samples in Baghdad or average findings across Iraq's governorates. See Baram, "The Effect of Iraqi Sanctions," p. 195.

163. See UNICEF, *Child and Maternal Mortality Survey in Dohouk, Erbil and Al-Suleimaniyah Governorates, 1999* (United Nations, August 1999), p. 10.

164. Tikrit, Saddam's birthplace, and the area around it is one of the main sources of recruits for Saddam's security apparatus.

165. See Kevin Whitelaw and Warren P. Stobel, "Inside Saddam's Iraq," *U.S. News and World Report*, September 11, 2000, pp. 52–57; also see Amatzia Baram, "Between Impediment and Advantage: Saddam's Iraq," *USIP Special Report* (Washington, June 1998), especially p. 5, which contains a map indicating the uneven living conditions within Baghdad.

166. Prior to the Gulf war, the average daily caloric intake of the average Iraqi citizen was 3,189 kilo-calories. Before the inception of the Oil for Food program, the Iraqi government provided food rations that amounted to roughly 1,093 to 1,295 kilo-calories per day; by April 2001, the Oil for Food program enabled the government to provide 2,209 kilo-calories per day to the public. It should be noted that even while the calories may be sufficient, these rations still lacked in essential nutrients and vitamins. Moreover, since the scheme began, the price of food on the open market stabilized, although many goods remained too expensive for a majority of Iraqis. As explored in the previous section, the steady operation of the program was closely tied to relative stability of the exchange rate and therefore to the level of inflation and consumer prices for food on the open market. See Economist Intelligence Unit, *Country Report: Iraq*, May 2000, p. 21. For the statistics, see Baram, "The Effect of Iraqi Sanctions," p. 215, and United Nations Security Council, *Report of the Secretary-General Pursuant to Paragraph 5 of Resolution 1330 (2000)*, S/2001/505 (May 18, 2001), p. 9.

167. According to the Garfield study, the main causes of child death have been diarrhea and respiratory illnesses brought on by factors such as contaminated water, poor food, and insufficient health services. See Garfield, *Morbidity and Mortality among Iraqi Children from 1990 to 1998*, p. 36.

168. See United Nations Security Council, *Report of the Secretary-General Pursuant to Paragraphs 28 and 30 of Resolution 1284 (1999) and Paragraph 5 of Resolution 1281 (1999)* (March 10, 2000), p. 28.

169. A 1999 UN report concluded that only about half of schools examined in Iraq were "appropriate and safe" learning institutions for children, down from 65 percent just two years earlier. United Nations Security Council, *Report of the Secretary-General Pursuant to Paragraph 6 of Security Council Resolution 1210 (1998)* (May 18, 1999), paragraph 58.

170. UN resolution 986, which is the basis for the Oil for Food Program, is slightly more liberal than the original resolutions calling for such a program (resolutions 706 and 712). For instance, resolution 706 required Iraq to provide a statement each month to the Security Council of the gold and foreign currency reserves it holds and resolution 986 makes a specific affirmation that nothing in the resolution should be construed as infringing on the sovereignty or territorial integrity of Iraq.

171. See United Nations Security Council, *Report of the Secretary-General Pursuant to Paragraphs 28 and 30 of Resolution 1284 (1999) and Paragraph 5 of Resolution 1281*

*(1999), S/2000/208* (March 10, 2000), p. 25. Moreover, movements to increase Iraqi rations in the 1990s were always done at UN insistence, never in response to government initiatives. Baram, "The Effect of Iraqi Sanctions," p. 216.

172. For example, the Secretary-General reported that, as of April 2001, Iraq had not yet submitted one application for its health sector under phase IX of the program, which began in December 2000. See United Nations Security Council, *Report of the Secretary-General Pursuant to Paragraph 5 of Security Council Resolution 1330 (2000)*, S/2001/505 (May 18, 2001), pp. 10–11.

173. See United Nations Security Council, *Report of the Secretary-General Pursuant to Paragraph 5 of Security Council Resolution 1330 (2000)*, S/2001/505 (May 18, 2001), pp. 21–22.

174. As of April 30, 2000, $251.7 million in medical supplies remained in the central warehouses, up from $187.8 million on October 30, 1999. See United Nations Security Council, *Report of the Secretary-General Pursuant to Paragraph 5 of Security Council Resolution 1281 (1999)*, S/2000/520 (United Nations, June 1, 2000), p. 7, and United Nations Security Council, *Report of the Secretary-General Pursuant to Paragraph 6 of Security Council Resolution 1242 (1999)*, S/1999/1162 (November 12, 1999), paragraph 42.

175. United Nations Security Council, *Report of the Secretary-General Pursuant to Paragraph 6 of Security Council Resolution 1210 (1998)*, S/1998/187 (February 22, 1999), paragraphs 29 and 30.

176. Ibid.

177. For reports of smuggled medicine, see Economist Intelligence Unit, *Country Report: Iraq*, First Quarter 1998, p. 10, and Roland Watson, Richard Beeston, and Michael Theodoulou, "Saddam Sells Medicines and Aid for Life's Little Luxuries," *London Times*, October 4, 2000.

178. See United Nations Security Council, *Report of the Secretary-General Pursuant to Paragraph 5 of Security Council Resolution 1281 (1999)*, S/2000/520 (June 1, 2000), paragraphs 55, 70.

179. According to the U.S. State Department, in addition to providing luxury items to those in his inner circle, Saddam chose to spend vast amounts of money on constructing lavish presidential palaces. Department of State, *Saddam Hussein's Iraq*.

180. Economist Intelligence Unit, *Country Report: Iraq*, First Quarter 1997, p. 18.

181. Baram, "The Effect of Iraqi Sanctions," pp. 209–10.

182. Access was refused despite the perception of many that the report might serve Saddam's quest to get the United Nations to lift sanctions. The request for this report—initiated by France and cosponsored by Britain—was contained in UN resolution 1302, passed in June 2000. China and other members of the Security Council wanted sanctions mentioned as the cause of the hardships in Iraq, but the United States objected. See United Nations Security Council, *Security Council Resolution 1302 (2000)*, S/RES/1302 (2000) (June 8, 2000); Colum Lynch, "U.N. Council Seeks Study of Iraqi Situation," *Washington Post*, June 10, 2000, p. A20; and "UN-Iraq," *Platt's Oilgram News*, June 12, 2000.

183. For more on NGOs operating in Iraq since the Gulf war, see Graham-Brown, *Sanctioning Saddam*, pp. 261–94.

184. Although the UN does not officially reveal which country is responsible for a hold, press reports have stated that the majority of the holds on contracts have been ini-

tiated by the United States. A story from July 2001 said that the United States alone was responsible for $3 billion in holds and that the total was approximately $3.6 billion. See Colum Lynch, "Trade Deal Won Chinese Support of U.S. Policy on Iraq," *Washington Post*, July 6, 2001, p. A17.

185. United Nations Security Council, *Letter Dated 3 October 2000 from the Secretary-General to the President of the Security Council*, S/2000/950 (October 3, 2000).

186. UN resolution 1409 was not the first attempt to expedite the Oil for Food program. In 2000, the United Nations established a more modest expedited review process. By using a list of preapproved items, the process helped reduce the number of contracts on hold by more than $1 billion between March and August of 2000. Nevertheless, as of 30 June 2001, more than 1,300 contracts (worth almost $3.6 billion) were still on hold, out of nearly 17,000 applications (worth $25.1 billion) that had been approved by the United Nations since the inception of the program. See United Nations Office of the Iraq Program, "Accelerated Procedures for the Approval of Contracts for Specified Humanitarian Supplies for Iraq," August 29, 2000 (www.un.org/depts/oip/cps/ 000719acc.htm [November 2, 2000]); Department of State, "State Department Daily Press Briefing by Philip T. Reeker," August 2, 2000; and United Nations Office of the Iraq Program, "Basic Figures" (www.un.org/depts/oip/latest/basicfigures.html [August 8, 2001]).

187. See, for instance, United Nations Commission on Human Rights, Subcommission on the Promotion and Protection of Human Rights, *The Adverse Consequences of Economic Sanctions on the Enjoyment of Human Rights: Working Paper Prepared by Mr. Marc Bossuyt*, E/CN.4/Sub.2/2000/33 (United Nations, June 21, 2000).

188. For instance, the United States, Japan, Kuwait, Saudi Arabia, and the European Community contributed close to $20 billion to form the Economic Action Plan, a scheme devised to defray some of the economic hardship borne by the "frontline" states of Egypt, Jordan, and Turkey in order to sustain their support for the sanctions against Iraq. See Kimberly Elliott, Gary Hufbauer, and Jeffrey Schott, "The Big Squeeze: Why the Sanctions on Iraq Will Work," *Washington Post*, December 9, 1990, p. K1, and Eric D. K. Melby, "Iraq," in Richard N. Haass, ed., *Economic Sanctions and American Diplomacy* (Council on Foreign Relations, 1998) p. 115.

189. See John Ward Anderson, "Turkey Welcomes U.S. Change on Iraq Sanctions," *Washington Post*, March 4, 2001, p. A23, and Karen Thomas, "Jordan Faces Sanctions Dilemma," *Lloyd's List*, July 30, 2001, p. 16.

190. For a description of some of the costs borne by Jordan, Turkey, Egypt, and others, see Melby, "Iraq," pp. 113–15.

191. Because Iraq had nationalized its oil industry in the 1970s, U.S. companies did not face major losses of capital assets in Iraq (as they did in Libya) when sanctions were imposed in 1990.

192. In fact, Russian and Chinese firms have embarked on initial work that can be done outside Iraq. The Department of Energy reports that Russia's Lukoil has prepared a plan to install equipment at West Qurna. There are reports, however, that U.S. companies—along with Canadian and Vietnamese ones—have held discussions with Iraq about the development of the oil industry once sanctions are lifted. Energy Information Administration, *Country Analysis Brief on Iraq*, September 2000.

193. However, given the volatile situation in Iraq and recent pronouncements that the Iraqi regime will sign no more contracts with foreign companies unless they are willing

to start development immediately—it would be premature to conclude that all these contracts will stand. Speculation that sanctions will remain in place until a regime change occurs in Baghdad—which might require new rounds of negotiations for the development of oil fields—further decrease the prospect of all of these contracts being executed. Economist Intelligence Unit, *Country Report: Iraq*, First Quarter 2000, p. 23; Economist Intelligence Unit, *Country Report: Iraq*, May 2000, p. 25.

194. By the time Iraq invaded Kuwait in the summer of 1990, Iraq was the third-largest U.S. trading partner in the Middle East, after Saudi Arabia and Israel. The United States was importing about 9 percent of its oil from Iraq and, owing to U.S. agricultural credits extended to Saddam's regime, Iraq had become the ninth-largest market for American agricultural products. When sanctions terminated U.S. exports to Iraq, virtually no U.S. military sales had been made to Iraq in almost twenty years, with the exception of a small number of commercial military exports that were delivered to Iraq in the late 1980s. Rather, the majority of U.S. sales to Iraq in 1990 were cereal goods (28 percent), machinery (19 percent), and transport equipment (17 percent). Economist Intelligence Unit, *Country Report: Iraq*, Second Quarter 1996, p. 21; OPEC, *Annual Statistical Bulletin*, 1992, pp. 80, 95; Juster, "The United States and Iraq: Perils of Engagement," p. 62; Defense Security Cooperation Agency, *Facts Book*—Foreign Military Sales, Foreign Military Construction Sales, and Military Assistance, various years.

195. The Office of Foreign Assets Control encouraged these firms to file claims of their losses, which were to be later adjudicated and possibly settled with payments from the UN Compensation Fund. OFAC received claims equaling $5 billion, $2 billion of which were for Commodity Credit Corporation agricultural loan guarantees and $700 million for oil that had not yet met its destination. Melby, "Iraq," p. 114.

196. Although U.S. agricultural exports to Iraq resumed in 1997 under the UN program, actual sales fell far short of pre-invasion levels and were unlikely to reach substantial amounts as long as Iraq denied contracts to countries with "hostile" attitudes. Nevertheless, American firms benefited more from the Oil for Food program than straightforward trade data reflect, as these statistics do not take into account sales made to Iraq by U.S. subsidiaries abroad. Although the UN seeks to keep information concerning these sales confidential, reports suggest that Iraq has legitimately purchased sizable quantities of American spare parts for its oil industry through the Oil for Food program from these channels. The Washington Post reported that more than a dozen U.S. companies have signed contracts with Iraq worth millions of dollars for oil-related equipment since 1998. See Colum Lynch, "U.S. Firms Aiding Iraqi Oil Industry; Commerce with Baghdad Grows Quietly as Washington Urges Regime Change," *Washington Post*, February 20, 2000; p. A23.

197. OPEC countries, most notably Saudi Arabia, increased their production sufficiently to offset 75 percent of the Iraqi and Kuwaiti output. See Melby, "Iraq," p. 113. Also see "Peace Effort Seen Stalling Oil Price Rise," *New York Times*, August 15, 1990, p. D3.

198. In 1990, Iraq was exporting 514,500 barrels a day to the United States. Between 1990 and 1991, Saudi Arabia's exports to the United States increased from 1.24 million barrels a day to 1.745 million barrels, Venezuela's exports increased from 777,600 barrels a day to 860,700, Gabon's exports increased from 76,000 barrels a day to 106,100, and Iran's exports went from zero in 1990 to 39,800 barrels a day in 1991. OPEC, *Annual Statistic Bulletin*, 1992, pp. 78–85. U.S. domestic production increased from 7.355 mil-

lion barrels a day in 1990 to 7.417 million barrels in 1991. Department of Energy, Energy Information Administration, "World Oil Production: Persian Gulf Nations, Non-OPEC and World" (www.eia.doe.gov/pub/energy.overview/monthly.energy/txt/mer10-1b [November 2, 2000]).

199. OPEC, *Annual Statistical Bulletin*, 1999, p. 117.

200. Department of Energy, Energy Information Administration, "Petroleum Imports by Country of Origin, 1960–2000" (www.eia.doe.gov/pub/pdf/multi.fuel/aer2000/sec5_11.pdf [August 9, 2001]).

201. This conjecture is based on the assumptions that Iraq would have let in foreign investors in the 1990s and that it would have not experienced further major upheavals (such as another war or severe internal strife).

202. For instance, in early 1990, the resumption of Iraqi oil production and talk of raising the limit on Iraqi oil exports under the Oil for Food program sent oil prices tumbling to their lowest level in years. In contrast, Iraq sent international oil prices soaring to nearly $30—a decade high—at the end of 1999 when it announced that it would suspend oil exports as a result of a dispute with the United Nations over sanctions. Similarly, Iraqi provocations in 2000 aggravated an already extremely tense oil market. See Bhushan Bahree, "U.N. Clears Way for Limited Iraqi Oil Exports—Approval of Food Proposal Signals That Shipments Will Resume in Days," *Wall Street Journal*, January 7, 1998, p. A16; Terzah Ewing, "Oil Prices Slip amid Mixed Signals about Iraq," *Wall Street Journal*, February 3, 1998, p. C17. See Barbara Crossette, "Denouncing U.N., Iraq Cuts Oil Sales Used to Buy Food," *New York Times*, November 23, 1999, p. A1; Carlos Tejada, "Iraq Effect on Oil Prices Is Likely to Be Short-Lived," *Wall Street Journal*, November 29, 1999, p. C2.

203. Some analysts consider price instability to be more detrimental to the global economy than high oil prices themselves. See Richard N. Haass, "Economic and Security Implications of Oil Price Increases," *Statement before the Senate Committee on Governmental Affairs*, March 24, 2000. *Newsday* published an abbreviated version of this testimony on March 29, 2000.

204. This leverage has increased with the rising price of oil and the unrest that high prices have caused in Europe. See T. R. Reid, "Pickets Continue Gas Blockades across Britain; Blair's Angry Words Fail to Ease Crisis," *Washington Post*, September 14, 2000, p. A23, and Jim Hoagland, "Fueling Protest," *Washington Post*, September 17, 2000, p. B7.

205. Groups such as the Chicago-based Voices in the Wilderness have called sanctions "a violation of international law and a crime against the human family," while others have claimed that sanctions constitute genocide against the Iraqi people. See Voices in the Wilderness (www.nonviolence.org/vitw [June 7, 2002]); International Action Center (www.iacenter.org [June 7, 2002]); International Relief Association; Iraq Action Coalition (http://leb.net/IAC [August 20, 2002]); Committee in Support of the Iraqi People. Also see Ramsey Clark, *The Children Are Dying: The Impact of Sanctions on Iraq* (New York: International Action Center, 1998); Geoff Simons, *The Scourging of Iraq: Sanctions, Law, and Natural Justice* (New York: St. Martin's Press, 1998); Anthony Arnove, *Iraq under Siege: The Deadly Impact of Sanctions and War* (Cambridge, Mass.: South End Press, 2000).

206. Certain members of Congress fervently criticized the Clinton administration for failing to take full advantage of the resources provided under the Iraq Liberation Act

and denounced U.S. policy toward Iraq under the Clinton administration as a failure. See Congressional hearings The Liberation of Iraq: A Progress Report: Hearing before the Subcommittee on Near Eastern and South Asian Affairs of the Senate Committee on Foreign Relations, 106 Cong. 2 sess., June 28, 2000, and United States Policy toward Iraq: Hearing before the Senate Armed Services Committee, 106 Cong. 2 sess., September 19 and 29, 2000, and Bob Kerrey (U.S. senator from Nebraska), "To Liberate Iraq," *Washington Post*, October 4, 1999, p. A23. Such criticism also emanated from the press, former policymakers, and political pundits from across the political spectrum. See Stephen Zunes, "Confrontation with Iraq: A Bankrupt U.S. policy," *Middle East Policy*, June 1998, pp. 87–107; Adel Darwish, "U.S. Policy in Disarray," *Middle East*, November 1999, pp. 9–10; Laura Myers, "Foreign Policy Leaders Push for Ouster of Saddam," *Associated Press*, February 20, 1998, and Walter Pincus, "U.S. Cautious on Backing Saddam's Foes; Albright Points Out Rifts among Opposition; Berger Evokes Bay of Pigs," *Washington Post*, February 23, 1998, p. A14; Hoagland, "'Pretend' Iraq Policy," *Washington Post*, July 2, 2000, p. B07; Richard Perle, testimony given at The Liberation of Iraq: A Progress Report: Hearing before the Subcommittee on Near Eastern and South Asian Affairs of the Senate Committee on Foreign Relations, 106 Cong. 2 sess., June 28, 2000; Gerald F. Seib, "Campaign Query: Who Will Act to Oust Saddam?" *Wall Street Journal*, June 28, 2000, p. A24.

207. See Pia Christina Wood, "Chirac's 'New Arab Policy' and Middle East Challenges: The Arab-Israeli Conflict, Iraq and Iran," *Middle East Journal*, vol. 52 (Autumn 1998), pp. 562–580.

208. See Cameron W. Barr, "Gulf Legacy: US Quietly Guards Oil," *Christian Science Monitor*, February 27, 2001.

209. The United States even objected to wording of UN resolutions that sought to recognize Iraqi progress.

210. In all likelihood, such action would have also created a domestic backlash for the Clinton administration.

211. Cortright and Lopez have argued this at length in *The Sanctions Decade*.

212. See "Iraq Says It Can Prove No More Mass Destruction Arms," *Reuters*, February 6, 2001.

213. For a development of this argument, see Amatzia Baram, "An Analysis of Iraqi WMD Strategy," *Nonproliferation Review*, vol. 8, no. 2 (Summer 2001), pp. 25–39.

214. Turkey in particular was worried that if Iraqi Kurds established their independence, its own tensions with its Kurdish minority would be inflamed. See Cengiz Candar, "Some Turkish Perspectives on the United States and American Policy toward Turkey," pp. 117–152, and Morton Abramowitz, "The Complexities of American Policymaking on Turkey," pp. 153–184, in Morton Abramowitz, ed., *Turkey's Transformation and American Policy* (Century Foundation, 2000).

215. Members of the Bush administration foreign policy team were also reluctant to expand the goals of the war beyond the two laid out and subsequently achieved: the ejection of Iraq from Kuwait and a downgrading of Iraqi weaponry.

216. See Ellen Laipson and others, "Symposium: After Saddam, What Then for Iraq?" *Middle East Policy*, vol. 6 (February 1999), pp. 1–26; Daniel Byman, "Iraq after Saddam," *Washington Quarterly*, vol. 24, no. 2 (Autumn 2001), pp. 151–62.

217. See UN resolution 687.

# Chapter Five

1. In a message to President Jimmy Carter and Ronald Reagan in October 1980, Qadhafi protested American involvement in the Middle East by objecting to its "occupation" of Egypt, among other issues. See Richard Halloran, "Libyans Are Challenging U.S. Forces in War of Nerves," *New York Times*, October 24, 1980, p. A8.

2. The United States did not immediately condemn the new government, in part because it was known that the new leaders were not pro-Soviet. See Mahmoud G. El Warfally, *Imagery and Ideology in U.S. Policy toward Libya, 1969-1982* (University of Pittsburgh Press, 1988), pp. 59–62.

3. For an account of the making of U.S. policy during this time from a Reagan administration official, see Raymond Tanter, *Rogue Regimes: Terrorism and Proliferation* (St. Martin's Press, 1998), pp. 121–68.

4. After Reagan's December 1981 appeal for all Americans to leave Libya, U.S. oil companies agreed to remove American personnel, replacing them with foreign employees. See Brian L. Davis, *Qaddafi, Terrorism and the Origins of the U.S. Attack on Libya* (Praeger, 1990), p. 49; and John M. Goshko, "U.S. Asks Americans to Leave Libya Soon; Danger of Regime Cited," *Washington Post*, December 11, 1981, p. A1. Commonly referred to as a "travel ban," the U.S. Constitution only allows the U.S. government to curtail the right of its citizens to use American passports to travel to a country. See Jeffery P. Bialos and Kenneth I. Juster, "The Libyan Sanctions: A Rational Response to State-Sponsored Terrorism?" *Virginia Journal of International Law*, vol. 26 (Summer 1986), pp. 829–31.

5. See Davis, *Qaddafi, Terrorism and the Origins of the U.S. Attack on Libya*, pp. 41–51.

6. Bob Woodward, "CIA Anti-Qaddafi Plan Backed: Reagan Authorizes Covert Operation to Undermine Libyan Regime," *Washington Post*, November 3, 1985, p. A1.

7. Over time, more sanctions came to be associated with this designation, including a formalized ban on military sales and bans on credit guarantees from agencies like the Export-Import Bank and the Commodity Credit Corporation.

8. In 1973, the United States restricted the military items it would sell to Libya and withheld the release of aircraft that Libya had already paid for on the basis that such sales would add to Libya's military strength. See Tim Niblock, *Pariah States and Sanctions in the Middle East* (Lynne Rienner Publishers, 2001), p. 27.

9. Ronald Reagan, *Proclamation 4901—Imports of Petroleum*, March 10, 1982. At the time, international oil prices had fallen, leading analysts to speak of a "world oil glut" and to downplay any adverse impact the oil ban might have on the U.S. economy.

10. Senator Hart's July 1981 amendment to a foreign operations appropriations bill—which called for a ban on oil imports from Libya—was rejected by the Senate in favor of a substitute amendment. The successful amendment condemned Libya for its support of terrorism and its destabilizing influence in Africa, while calling on the president to conduct a review of steps the United States could take to put political and economic pressure on Libya, including the possibility of tariffs or an embargo on Libyan oil. This revised amendment passed by a vote of 47-44. See *Congressional Record*, October 21, 1981, pp. 24644–55.

11. Libyan extremism in its external affairs reflected growing radicalism within Libya's borders. From 1978 to 1988—a period one scholar referred to as "the revolutionary decade"—Qadhafi promoted the role of revolutionary committees within the

country in an effort to radicalize the population and sought to eliminate any form of private ownership of means of production.

12 . Ronald Reagan, *Executive Order 12543*, January 7, 1986; Ronald Reagan, *Executive Order 12544*, January 8, 1986.

13. Administration officials were anxious to avoid the tensions that the extension of U.S. sanctions to American subsidiaries in Europe had caused during the Siberian pipeline crisis just a few years earlier.

14. On February 7, 1986, the United States revised the sanctions to allow U.S. oil companies to continue operations in Libya temporarily to prevent a windfall to Libya. Special exemptions were arranged that allowed U.S. oil companies to continue operations until June 30 of that year, when they were forced to enter into standstill agreements with Libya. See General Accounting Office, *Libya Trade Sanctions*, NSIAD-87-132BR (May 1987), p. 16; and Gary Clyde Hufbauer, Jeffrey J. Schott, Kimberly Ann Elliot, *Economic Sanctions Reconsidered: History and Current Policy*, 2d ed. (Washington: Institute for International Economics, 1990), pp. 143–44.

15. Soon after the airport attacks occurred, the Abu Nidal organization, which was closely linked to Libya, claimed responsibility. Nevertheless, the United States was unable to determine which targets in Libya were connected to Abu Nidal. See Davis, *Qaddafi, Terrorism and the Origins of the U.S. Attack on Libya*, pp. 81–82.

16. See "The President's News Conference, January 7, 1986," *Public Papers of the Presidents: Ronald Reagan, 1986, vol. I* (Government Printing Office, 1988), p. 18. Another U.S. official at the time claimed that the sanctions were part of a "graduated curve," designed to convince Qadhafi that terrorism is not cost free. See David Hawley, "Libyan Sanctions: Reagan Goes It Alone," *Middle East Economic Digest*, January 11, 1986, p. 18.

17. On January 27, 1986, the foreign ministers of the countries of the European Common Market met and agreed to ban arms sales to countries that were "clearly implicated in supporting terrorism." Although Libya was not mentioned by name, the measures were intended to target the North African country. However, given that Britain, France, West Germany, and Italy had already banned arms sales to Libya, the move was not anticipated to have much additional effect.

18. Just three days after President Reagan announced the U.S. sanctions, Prime Minister Margaret Thatcher announced Britain would not impose such measures on Libya, saying that any goods they embargoed would be "supplied by other countries." See R.W. Apple Jr., "Libyan Issue Leaves Many Questioning Role of Allies," *New York Times*, January 19, 1986, p. 10.

19. The U.S. presence in the Gulf of Sidra was viewed by many as an American effort to provoke Libya, allowing the United States to justify further military actions against Qadhafi. See Edward Schumacher, "The United States and Libya," *Foreign Affairs*, vol. 65 (Winter 1986–87), p. 335; and Niblock, *Pariah States and Sanctions in the Middle East*, p. 31.

20. Some analysts claim that by undermining and demoralizing the Libyan military, these strikes eliminated the possibility of a military coup against Qadhafi. See Schumacher, "The United States and Libya," p. 338.

21. See David Hoffman, "The Summit in Tokyo: Summit Unites on Terrorism; 7 Nations Spell Out Countermeasures; Libya Cited By Name," *Washington Post*, May 6, 1986, p. A1; and "Terrorism Must Be Fought," *Washington Post*, May 6, 1986, p. A14 (copy of the statement issued).

22. See Elaine Sciolino, "U.S. Sees Qaddafi as Being Weaker," *New York Times*, January 10, 1988, p. A9. Gideon Rose claims that other important factors in this change of policy were "Qadhafi's persistence in power despite U.S. actions; his diminished momentum and external activities; and a change in Reagan administration personnel." Gideon Rose, "Libya," in Richard N. Haass, editor, *Economic Sanctions in American Foreign Policy* (Brookings, 1998), p. 134.

23. In 1991, the United States proscribed all transactions with forty-eight Libyan firms; the following year, forty-six companies were added to this list. See Economist Intelligence Unit, *Country Report: Libya*, Third Quarter 1991, p. 8. Concerns over Libya's pursuit of chemical weapons at a plant near Rabta briefly raised the prospects of a U.S. military attack. The U.S. decision not to attack Rabta followed a somewhat successful effort to get allies such as West Germany to clamp down on the cooperation of their own companies with Libya on Rabta; moreover, a major fire at the plant in March 1990 left it inoperable. For more on the Rabta case, see Edward M. Spiers, *Chemical and Biological Weapons: A Study in Proliferation* (St. Martin's Press, 1994), pp. 65–83.

24. Whereas previous terrorist incidents pointing to Libyan involvement had been unable to spur an international condemnation of Libya, the combined deaths of more than 400 people—many of them American, British, and French citizens—catalyzed an international coalition seeking justice for these acts.

25. Five of the fifteen members of the Security Council—China, Morocco, India, Cape Verde, and Zimbabwe—abstained from this vote.

26. Initially, Qadhafi declared that the two suspects, whom Libyan authorities were holding in Tripoli, could be tried by Libyan courts. Yet quickly, Qadhafi improved this offer, declaring Libya's willingness to extradite the two men to a third country if a panel of impartial judges found the claims against them to be of substance. For more on the development of Libyan compromises, see Niblock, *Pariah States and Sanctions in the Middle East*; and David Cortright and George Lopez, *Sanctions Decade: Assessing UN Strategies in the 1990s* (Lynne Rienner Publishers, 2000), pp. 107–21.

27. In July 1993, Senator Edward Kennedy and fifty-four of his Senate colleagues demanded tougher sanctions in a letter to President Clinton. See "Senators Urge Stronger Sanctions against Libya," *Associated Press*, July 27, 1993.

28. China, Pakistan, Morocco, and Djibouti abstained from this vote, while Russia reluctantly voted for it.

29. Most of the equipment subject to restrictions was needed for downstream operations. Exemptions were made for funds arising from the sale of hydrocarbon or agricultural products in order to ensure that Libya would still sell these items, thereby protecting trade important to much of Europe; however, the freeze of assets rendered Libya unable to pay its debts, causing Russia to suffer.

30. French demands were more easily met, as they did not require that Libya hand over suspects, only that it provide all information of potential use in the investigation surrounding the UTA bombing. United Nations Security Council, S/23306, December 20, 1991.

31. For more on the evolution of the positions of these organizations, see Niblock, *Pariah States and Sanctions in the Middle East*, pp. 46–48. The Non-Aligned Movement, China, and South Africa also eventually protested the Libyan sanctions.

32. In December 1995, the Clinton administration appealed to the United Nations to impose stricter sanctions on oil equipment sold to Libya. See Robert S. Greenberger and

Laurie Lande, "Europeans Are Irked by Senate Move to Punish Foreign Investments in Libya," *Wall Street Journal*, December 22, 1995, p. A4.

33. The menu of sanctions from which the president can chose includes a ban on U.S. Export-Import Bank assistance; a ban on U.S. export licenses to receive goods; restrictions on loans totaling more than $10 million a year from U.S. institutions; refusal of the right to be a primary dealer in U.S. government bonds; the refusal of the right to bid on U.S. government contracts; and a refusal of the right to export goods to the U.S. market.

34. In the case of Iran, the law also provided a "country waiver," which allowed the president to grant a blanket waiver to all companies from a particular country if it had imposed its own sanctions on Iran. This second type of waiver did not apply to Libya.

35. French Premier Lionel Jospin protested this legislation by saying that "no one accepts the idea that the United States can now impose their laws on the rest of the world." Quoted in Alan Cooperman, "Isolated by U.S., but Not by Europe," *U.S. News & World Report*, October 13, 1997, p. 42.

36. Part of the impetus for this law was an application by Louis Farrakhan to the U.S. Treasury Department requesting permission to accept $1 billion from Qadhafi. Treasury rejected this petition and the subsequent passage of the Antiterrorism and Effective Death Penalty Act ensured that no such transaction could occur in the future. See Dorothy J. Gaiter, "Treasury Rules Farrakhan Can't Take Gadhafi Gift," *Wall Street Journal*, August 29, 1996, p. B13.

37. Secretary of State Albright declared, "Granting waivers will prevent retaliation against U.S. firms, which the imposition of sanctions would probably engender, and avoid possible challenges based on claims related to treaties and other national obligations." Quoted in "U.S. Waives Sanctions on South Pars Field," *Oil and Gas Journal*, May 25, 1998, pp. 18–19.

38. Nevertheless, some statements of Clinton administration officials suggested otherwise. See Stuart Eizenstat, Testimony at Hearings on Sanctions in U.S. Policy, Hearing before the House International Relations Committee, 105 Cong. 2 sess., June 3, 1998 (www.state.gov/www/policy_remarks/1998/980603_eizen_sanctions.html [August 26, 2002]); Department of State, "Daily Press Briefing," Office of the Spokesman, December 2, 1999.

39. Besides trying to stem the erosion of international support for the UN sanctions, the United States viewed the compromise it offered with Britain as another means of building support for stricter penalties against Libya. The United States declared that if Libya did not accept the compromise strictly on the terms that it was offered, it would push for additional sanctions in the face of Libya obstreperousness.

40. South African president Nelson Mandela, on a visit to Tripoli in October 1997, presented Qadhafi with South Africa's Order of Good Hope, an award of the highest standing in South Africa. In addition, Turkish prime minister Necmettin Erbakan visited Libya in October 1996; Qadhafi met with the leaders of Burkina Faso, Chad, Mali, and Niger in August 1997.

41. See Douglas Jehl, "Arab Countries Vote to Defy U.N. Sanctions against Libya," *New York Times*, September 22, 1997, p. A12.

42. Libya had maintained that under the 1971 Montreal Convention (to which the United States, Britain, and Libya were all parties), it was not required to turn over the

suspects but could try them itself. See Niblock, *Pariah States and Sanctions in the Middle East*, pp. 45–46.

43. Libya held five main concerns: that the sanctions would not be suspended once the suspects were released; that the safety of the accused be ensured; that a different venue than a former U.S. air base be used for the trial; and that, if convicted, the accused be allowed to serve their sentences in Libya or the Netherlands. Finally, Qadhafi was concerned the trial would degenerate into an attack on the Libyan system overall. For more details on each of these concerns, see Niblock, *Pariah States and Sanctions in the Middle East*, chap. 7.

44. The differing attitudes of the United States and Britain were to a large extent reflective of the varying positions of the victims' families in each country. In Britain, the families were on the whole eager for a trial and for resolution of the affair. In contrast, the Families of Pan Am 103 in the United States preferred to continue to pressure Qadhafi until he acceded to U.S. and UN demands in full. As a result, the United States was more interested in using the time that Qadhafi was seeking "clarifications" to renew its campaign for tougher sanctions. See James Risen, "U.S. Planning to Seek Further Sanctions on Libya," *New York Times*, January 30, 1999, p. A3.

45. Even after the contents of the letter were made public on August 25, 2000, some accused the secretary general of appeasing or protecting Qadhafi; many of the families of the victims claimed that the letter reinforced their concerns that the trial would sidestep the key issue of involvement by top Libyan officials, including Qadhafi. See John R. Bolton, "Appeasing Gadhafi," *Washington Post*, August 29, 2000, p. A17; A. M. Rosenthal, "The Protecting of Killer Khadafy," *New York Daily News*, September 1, 2000, p. 53; and Barbara Slavin, "U.N. Letter Disturbs Flight 103 Relatives," *USA Today*, August 28, 2000, p. A11.

46. Libyan officials, including Qadhafi's brother-in-law, were found responsible for the UTA bombing in abstentia in an earlier French trial. Libya paid families of the UTA victims, insurance companies, and Air France a total of $31 million in compensation. Libya's compensation of the family of the British policewoman paved the way to the resumption of U.K.-Libyan relations in July 1999.

47. In November 1999, Libya placed eighty onshore and offshore contracts up for tender. In May 2000, Libya invited some fifty international oil and gas companies to a conference to discuss exploration and production sharing agreements. Several months later at a conference in Tripoli, Libya signaled its interest in foreign investment in areas other than the oil sector, particularly in infrastructure. See Economist Intelligence Unit, *Country Report: Libya*, First Quarter 2000, pp. 21–22; and Energy Information Administration, *Country Analysis Brief on Libya* (Department of Energy, July 2001); and "Libya Fishing for Foreign Investment," *Middle East Economic Digest*, December 1, 2000, p. 6.

48. The day the verdict was given, President George W. Bush declared that the United States would keep pressure on Libya until it accepted responsibility for the actions of its officials. See White House, "Remarks by the President before Meeting with Bipartisan Members of Congress," Office of the Press Secretary, January 31, 2001 (www. whitehouse. gov/news/releases/20010131.html [August 28, 2001]); and White House, "Remarks by the President before Cabinet Meeting," Office of the Press Secretary, January 31, 2001 (www.whitehouse.gov/news/releases/20010131-2 [August 28, 2001]).

49. See E. Anthony Wayne, Renewal of the Iran-Libya Sanctions Act, testimony before the Senate Committee on Banking, Housing, and Urban Affairs, 107 Cong. 1 sess., June 28, 2001(GPO, 2002).

50. On May 27, 1999, the Senate passed a nonbinding resolution by a vote of 98-0 which called on President Clinton to block the lifting of UN sanctions. Economist Intelligence Unit, *Country Report: Libya*, Third Quarter 1999, p. 14. The United States and Britain continued to state that they will veto any immediate attempts to remove the sanctions. See Economist Intelligence Unit, *Country Report: Libya*, February 2001, p. 12; April 2001, pp. 13–14.

51. Although U.S. sanctions were eased slightly in April 1999 to allow for the export of U.S. food and medicine to Libya, Congress approved these changes in an effort to ease the farm crisis in the United States, rather than as a gesture to Libya. In a minor development, U.S. oil executives from Amerada Hess, Conoco, Marathon, and Occidental were granted permission to travel to Libya in December 1999 to investigate the status of their investments there.

52. Some, including many of the families of the victims, felt the findings of the court definitively established a link between the bombing and the Libyan regime and called for an aggressive policy to hold Qadhafi accountable. See "Lockerbie Relatives in Sanctions Plea," *BBC News*, February 9, 2001.

53. All the while, the Families of Pan Am 103 continued to pursue their suits against the Libyan government in U.S. civil courts, a process that could stretch on well into the future and further complicate U.S.-Libyan relations.

54. Economist Intelligence Unit, *Country Report: Libya*, January 2002, p. 12.

55. Ibid., June 2002, p. 2.

56. Much of this retrenchment could have been avoided had Qadhafi been willing to pare back military procurement.

57. Libya also sought to renegotiate its existing obligations with countries like Turkey, the Soviet Union, and Yugoslavia, substituting oil for cash payments. The erratic price of oil in the 1980s increased uncertainty around barter transactions, making them even more unattractive than they would be in more stable times. See Teresa English, "Libya: The Opening Door," *Middle East Economic Digest*, August 11, 1989, p. 9.

58. Economist Intelligence Unit, *Country Report: Libya*, First Quarter 1979, p. 2.

59. See Mohammed E. Ahrari, *OPEC: The Failing Giant* (University Press of Kentucky, 1986), pp. 156–88.

60. See Muammar Qadhafi, *The Green Book* (Tripoli: Green Book World Center, 1980); and Muammar Qadhafi, *The Green Book Part II: The Social Base of the Third Universal Theory* (Tripoli: Green Book World Center, 1980).

61. The incompleteness and unreliability of the data on Libyan growth rates preclude the use of regression analysis from establishing more definitely the exact nature of the relationship between oil prices and Libyan growth.

62. Economic ties between Libya and the United States peaked in the late 1970s when the United States was importing almost 40 percent of Libyan crude oil exports. This relationship was already waning by the time the embargo was imposed, mostly as a result of weaker U.S. demand for crude oil.

63. See Economist Intelligence Unit, *Country Report: Libya*, Third Quarter 1983, p. 14. Imports from Libya's Ras Lanuf refinery were banned in late 1985, in large part

after intense lobbying from independent American oil refiners. See *Country Report: Libya*, Fourth Quarter 1985, p. 13.

64. Economist Intelligence Unit, *Country Report: Libya*, Third Quarter 1983, p. 15.

65. This figure does not take into account lost trade through U.S. subsidiaries. Although such trade was not prohibited by the U.S. sanctions, many subsidiaries scaled back their dealings with Libya as they were fearful of contravening the terms of the sanctions. The General Accounting Office reported a 73.6 percent drop in this trade from June 1986 to June 1987, indicating that U.S firms were not substantially redirecting their trade through their subsidiaries. See General Accounting Office, *Libya Trade Sanctions*, NSIAD-87-132BR (May 1987), p. 18.

66. See Judith Gurney, *Libya: The Political Economy of Oil* (Oxford: Oxford University Press, 1996), pp. 146–77.

67. At the time the oil embargo went into effect, American analysts predicted that, although the embargo would have no adverse effect on the United States, it could harm Libya by making it even harder to market its oil in the "oil surplus" of the time. Robert D. Hershey, "Little Impact Seen from Libyan Ban," *New York Times*, March 11, 1982, p. A11.

68. As of 1981, Libya relied on the United States for 6.3 percent of its imports, consisting mostly of machinery and transport equipment. IMF, *Direction of Trade Statistics Yearbook*, 1987, p. 260.

69. As mentioned in the previous section, aviation-related sales became subject to export controls in the 1970s; export controls on the supply of oil and gas equipment not available from non-U.S. sources came into effect in 1982. See Hufbauer, Schott, and Elliott, *Economic Sanctions Reconsidered*, pp. 140–41. See Economist Intelligence Unit, *Country Report: Libya*, Second Quarter 1978, p. 5; First Quarter 1982, p. 7; Fourth Quarter 1983, p. 10. In 1983 alone, the United States denied licenses to sell $597.5 million worth of large civil transport aircraft to Libya. See "Economic Sanctions to Combat International Terrorism," *Department of State Bulletin*, October 1986.

70. Economist Intelligence Unit, *Country Report: Libya*, First Quarter 1986, p. 13. As of March 2000, the U.S. Treasury calculated Libyan foreign assets in the United States were worth $992.4 million. The discrepancy between these two numbers reflects the fact that the U.S. Treasury invests frozen assets, allowing them to earn interest over the time that they are frozen. Office of Foreign Assets Control, *Terrorist Assets Report: 1999 Annual Report to the Congress on Assets in the United States Belonging to Terrorist Countries or International Terrorist Organizations* (Department of the Treasury, March 1, 2000), p. 9.

71. Libya, however, was allowed to purchase technical assistance from the World Bank if it wished.

72. OECD, *External Debt Statistics 1986–1987* (Paris, 1998).

73. In the late 1980s, shortages of foreign currency forced Libya to stop payments on many of its trade debts. This action led some western export credit agencies to refuse to extend further government medium- and long-term export credits for Libya. See Economist Intelligence Unit, *Country Profile: Libya*, 1996, p. 36.

74. European commercial interests were also fearful that Libya could retaliate for the 1986 bombing against Europe by terminating contracts or payments to suppliers. See David Hawley, "Libya: EEC Reaction Underlines Divisions," *Middle East Economic Digest*,

April 26, 1986, pp. 6–8; and Toby Odone, "Mixed Response from Shippers and Airlines," *Middle East Economic Digest,* April 26, 1986, p. 7.

75. In the estimation of the Economist Intelligence Unit, in the early 1990s, foreign contractors spent "as much time on getting their bills paid as on the work itself." Economist Intelligence Unit, *Country Report: Libya,* First Quarter 1992, p. 6.

76. See Judith Gurney, *Libya: The Political Economy of Oil* (Oxford: Oxford University Press, 1996), pp. 91–99.

77. According to the Energy Information Administration, U.S. companies were responsible for producing 400,000 barrels a day of Libya's oil in 1986; according to OPEC, Libya's average production for that year was 1.308 million barrels a day. Energy Information Administration, *Country Analysis Brief: Libya,* July 2001; and OPEC, *Annual Statistical Bulletin,* 1999. In August 1986, just two months after the withdrawal of five U.S. oil companies, Libya exported the highest volume of crude for the year. See "Libya Awaits Oil Price Rise," *Middle East Economic Digest,* September 20, 1986, p. 36; also see General Accounting Office, *Libyan Trade Sanctions,* pp. 14–15.

78. The sanctions deprived Libya of the U.S. technology, equipment, and know-how that had been critical in developing the industry through the 1950s, 1960s, and 1970s. Libya also lost some American technical expertise when U.S. firms were forced to terminate their consultancy work for Libyan development projects such as Libya's Great Man-Made River. However, the continued activity of U.S. subsidiaries in this field, as well as the fact that other international firms offered comparable expertise, limited these costs to Libya.

79. Some firms were fearful that they would fall "foul of US companies" if they assumed contracts American firms vacated. See Angus Hindley, "Libya Searches for Oil Prospects," *Middle East Economic Digest,* August 30, 1991, p. 5.

80. In large part, this was due to competing priorities held by the Libyan regime, most notably the continuation of the Great Man-Made River project.

81. International oil companies were leaving Libya even before sanctions were imposed. For instance, Exxon and Mobil left Libya in November 1981 and January 1983 respectively, before American sanctions would have forced them to withdraw. "High costs and a depressed oil market" were reasons cited for their actions. See Dirk Vandewalle, "The Libyan Jamahiriyya since 1969," in Dirk Vandewalle, ed., *Qadhafi's Libya: 1969–1994* (St. Martin's Press, 1995), p. 28.

82. See Angus Hindley, "Libya Searches for Oil Prospects," *Middle East Economic Digest,* August 30, 1991, p. 5.

83. Even with the inefficiencies in its industry, the estimated costs of production in Libya are among the lowest in the world, estimated by the Department of Energy to be in the range of $1 a barrel in some fields. See Energy Information Administration, *Country Analysis Brief: Libya* (Department of Energy, July 2001).

84. Since 1988, Libya has offered progressively more favorable terms to international investors. In some part, this trend is attributable to U.S. sanctions and the smaller number of firms that are able to compete for these contracts; however, the state of the international oil market, and the actions of Libya's regional competitors, are more important in explaining this trend.

85. Libya's per capita GDP fell from an estimated $7,311 in 1992 to an estimated $5,896 in 1999. Economist Intelligence Unit, *Country Profile: Libya,* 2001, p. 25.

86. In 1998, Libya's annual export earnings—at approximately $7 billion—were the lowest they had been since the oil price crash of 1986. IMF, *Direction of Trade Statistics*, various years.

87. Between June and September 1993, Libyan assets worth almost $3 billion were transferred out of banks reporting to the Bank for International Settlements. See Economist Intelligence Unit, *Country Report: Libya*, Second Quarter 1994, p. 20.

88. Reportedly, UN restrictions on parts and technology for the aviation sector were among the most poorly enforced. See David Cortright and George A. Lopez, *The Sanctions Decade: Assessing UN Strategies in the 1990s* (Lynne Rienner Publishers, 2000), p. 117.

89. The chairman of Libya Arab Airlines estimated the losses to the airline industry to be near $900 million, a figure deemed reasonable by outside sources. Economist Intelligence Unit, *Country Report: Libya*, Third Quarter 1997, p. 15, Second Quarter 1998, p. 14.

90. See Gurney, *Libya: The Political Economy of Oil*, pp. 221–22.

91. Economist Intelligence Unit, *Country Report: Libya*, Third Quarter 1995, p. 12.

92. For the attitudes of some of those working in Libya at the time, see Angus Hindley, "The Lockerbie Conundrum," *Middle East Economic Digest*, September 10, 1993, pp. 2–4.

93. The "parallel" account system allowed Libya to use its oil revenues for the purchases of goods from other countries. For more on the functioning of the parallel account system, see Angus Hindley, "Libya: Getting Paid under Sanctions," *Middle East Economic Digest*, December 17, 1993, p. 27; and Angus Hindley, "Contractors Face Hard Times in Libya," *Middle East Economic Digest*, January 28, 1994, pp. 2–3.

94. Due to the UN assets freeze, these pursuits occurred in secrecy, limiting the ability to estimate the value of reserves and assets stashed in banks and investments beyond UN control. See Niblock, *Pariah States and Economic Sanctions in the Middle East*, pp. 66–67.

95. The Great Man-Made River project was a plan to pipe millions of gallons of water from freshwater aquifers in the southeast of the country to major urban areas in the north and to the Sirte region in Libya to provide irrigation for agriculture. It was inaugurated in 1984 but ran into numerous problems.

96. Figures derived from IMF, *Tunisia: Statistical Appendix*, IMF Country Report No. 01/37, February 2001, p. 5.

97. The benefits of tourism would be even greater than these sums, as a tourist industry would be a source of growth for Libya's non-oil sector and bring in foreign exchange that could be usefully applied elsewhere.

98. Economist Intelligence Unit, *Country Report: Libya*, April 2002, p. 22.

99. Libya is eager to draw investment into its largely undeveloped gas industry. Not only does it see great potential in serving European gas needs, but it hopes to substitute the use of gas for that of oil domestically. There is growing international interest, signaled by a $5.5 billion joint venture between Italy's Agip-ENI and Libya's National Oil Company, which aims to export 8 billion cubic meters of gas from Libya to Italy and France over twenty-four years. See Energy Information Administration, *Country Analysis Brief: Libya*.

100. See Economist Intelligence Unit, *Country Report: Libya*, Second Quarter 1998, p. 16.

101. See United Nations Conference on Trade and Development, *World Investment Report,* various years.

102. For instance, at the time ILSA was being considered by the U.S. Congress, Agip-ENI was in negotiations with Libya over its massive Western Libyan Gas Project. The Italian company argued that any subsequent deal would be exempt from ILSA sanctions, because the original contract was signed in 1993. See Economist Intelligence Unit, *Country Report: Libya,* Third Quarter 1996, pp. 15–16; Fourth Quarter 1996, pp. 17–18.

103. OPEC, *Annual Statistical Bulletin,* 1999, p. 13.

104. In 2000, 2001, and 2002, international oil and gas executives ranked Libya as the top exploration spot in the world in a poll conducted by the U.K.-based firm Robertson International. See Economist Intelligence Unit, *Country Report: Libya,* April 2002, pp. 17–18.

105. Arab reluctance to contravene the sanctions stemmed from the realization that such action would weaken their calls for the fulfillment of UN resolution 242, which calls on Israel to swap land for peace with its neighbors.

106. For more on Qadhafi's relations with Africa and his United States of Africa ideas, see Asteris Huliaras, "Qadhafi's Comeback: Libya and Sub-Saharan Africa in the 1990s," *African Affairs,* vol. 100 (Jan. 2001), pp. 5–25.

107. See Ray Takeyh, "Qadhafi's Libya and the Prospect of Islamic Succession," *Middle East Policy,* vol. 7 (February 2000), pp. 154–64.

108. In addition to the UN sanctions, many European countries placed some visa restrictions on the travel of Libyan citizens.

109. See Mary-Jane Deeb, "Political and Economic Developments in Libya in the 1990s," in Yayha Zoubir, ed., *North Africa in Transition: State, Society, and Economic Transformation in the 1990s* (Gainesville: University Press of Florida, 1999), pp. 77–89; and Schumacher, "The United States and Libya," p. 337.

110. This opposition was responsible for a rising number of assassination attempts against Qadhafi in the late 1990s and growing unrest in Libya's east until Qadhafi's security forces crushed it in a 1998 operation.

111. International Institute for Strategic Studies, *The Military Balance* (Oxford University Press, various years).

112. According to the U.S. Arms Control and Disarmament Agency, almost half of this outlay was spent on Soviet arms. Economist Intelligence Unit, *Country Report: Libya,* Fourth Quarter 1987, p. 14; Fourth Quarter 1985, p. 6.

113. U.S. Arms Control and Disarmament Agency, *World Military Expenditures and Arms Transfers, 1995* (GPO, 1996), p. 133.

114. According to the U.S. government, Libya imported no arms in 1993 and 1995; its arms imports were valued at $10 million in 1994, $20 million in 1996, and $5 million in 1997. Bureau of Arms Control, *World Military Expenditures and Arms Transfers* (Department of State, 1998), p. 144.

115. During this period, the United States became concerned that Libya was disguising the construction of an underground chemical weapons plant at Tarhouna, some 40 kilometers outside of Tripoli. Although it was unable to prove these allegations, construction at Tarhouna stopped in 1997, a development that is possibly related to Libya's difficulty in obtaining vital chemicals and other related equipment. See "Libya

Hampered by Decade-Old U.N. Ban, Says CIA," *Jane's Defence Weekly*, August 12, 1998, p. 1.

116. Economist Intelligence Unit, *Country Report: Libya*, Fourth Quarter 1990, p. 4.

117. Bureau of Arms Control, *World Military Expenditures and Arms Transfers* (Department of State, various years).

118. Reportedly, Libya quickly renewed talks with Russia on military cooperation to upgrade Libya's aging Soviet-era weaponry. Russian press reports say that Russia and Libya signed $100 million worth of contracts for munitions and repair of armored vehicles and antiaircraft complexes. See Anton Chernik, "Russia Retains a Constant Partner," *Defense and Security*, May 8, 2001, p. 2; and "Russia to Modernize Libya's Military Hardware, No Fresh Arms Sales," *Agence France-Presse*, May 7, 2001.

119. Ronald Reagan, *Executive Order 12513*, January 7, 1986.

120. See Ronald Neumann, Testimony at U.S. Policy toward Libya, before the Subcommittee on Near Eastern and South Asian Affairs of the Senate Foreign Relations Committee, 106 Cong. 2 sess., May 4, 2000 (GPO, 2002).

121. During discussions about adding Libya to ILSA in December 1995, D'Amato also cited Libya's "long and documented history of obscene violations of human rights," as a reason why Libya should be included in the sanctions legislation.

122. See Ronald E. Neumann (then-deputy assistant secretary of state for near eastern affairs), "Libya: A U.S. Policy Perspective," *Middle East Policy*, vol. 7 (February 2000), pp. 142–45.

123. One U.S. official declared that Libya's actions "were not window dressing, but a serious, credible step to reduce its involvement with that terrorist organization (the ANO)." Neumann, "Libya: A U.S. Policy Perspective." For annual reports on Libya's involvement in terrorism, see Department of State, *Patterns of Global Terrorism*, various years.

124. Department of State, *Patterns of Global Terrorism*, 2001, p. 67.

125. See Ray Takeyh, "The Rogue Who Came in from the Cold," *Foreign Affairs*, vol. 80 (May–June 2001), pp. 62–72.

126. After a spate of suicide bombings in Israel in February 1996, Qadhafi praised the attacks, blamed Israeli policy for the violence, and called on Arab states to help the Palestinians combat "Israeli terrorism." See "Gadhafi Calls for Arab Aid to Support Anti-Israel Palestinians," *Associated Press*, March 23, 1996; and "France Warns Iran, Libya," *United Press International*, March 5, 1996.

127. In 1999, Qadhafi told Palestinian militants that Libya would deal only with Arafat's Palestinian Authority. See Howard Schneider, "Libya, Seeking Investors, Moves from Fringe toward Mainstream," *Washington Post*, July 20, 1999, p. A13.

128. Frank Anderson, "Qadhafi's Libya: The Limits of Optimism," *Middle East Policy*, vol. 6 (June 1999), pp. 68–79.

129. After Libyan armed forces withdrew from Chad, a new Chadian government convinced Libya to take the dispute over the Aouzou Strip to the International Court of Justice; in 1994, the court ruled in favor of Chad, a decision by which Libya has abided. See Economist Intelligence Unit, *Country Profile: Libya*, 1996, p. 9.

130. For more on Egyptian-Libyan relations see Clyde R. Mack, "Libya" (Congressional Research Service, August 28, 2001), p. 9. In the 1990s, Egypt and Libya not only pledged to integrate their economies, but to work together to resolve the conflict in

neighboring Sudan. See Asteris Huliaras, "Qadhafi's Comeback: Libya and Sub-Saharan Africa in the 1990s," *African Affairs*, 2001, 100, pp. 5–25, especially pp. 23–24.

131. See Huliaras, "Qadhafi's Comeback," pp. 5–25, especially pp. 16–18.

132. In April 1999, Qadhafi facilitated a peace accord between Uganda and the Congo as well as sent Libyan troops to Uganda to enforce it. In August 1999, the government of Sudan accepted a Libyan-Egyptian plan to end the civil war there, although the initiative had borne little fruit by 2001. See "Qaddafi Says Farewell, Arabia, and Sets His Sights on Africa," *Economist*, April 24, 1999, pp. 43–44; Economist Intelligence Unit, *Country Report: Libya*, Third Quarter 1999, p. 16; and Ed Blanche, "Sudan Accepts Peace Plan," *Jane's Defence Weekly*, September 1, 1999.

133. See Central Intelligence Agency, *Unclassified Report to Congress on the Acquisition of Technology Relating to Weapons of Mass Destruction and Advanced Conventional Munitions, 1 July through 31 December 2000*, September 7, 2001.

134. See Andrew Koch, "USA Rethinks Libya's Status," *Jane's Defence Weekly*, July 19, 2000, pp. 22–23.

135. The Department of Defense claimed that China was providing missile technology and training to Libya in April 2000. See Bill Gertz, "Beijing Delivered Missile Technology to Libya, U.S. Says," *Washington Times*, April 13, 2000, p. A1.

136. See Central Intelligence Agency, *Unclassified Report to Congress on the Acquisition of Technology Relating to Weapons of Mass Destruction and Advanced Conventional Munitions, 1 January through 30 June 2000*, February 2001.

137. See Federation of American Scientists, "Libya's Special Weapons" (www.fas. org.nuke/guide/libya [October 3, 2001]).

138. By the calculations of Freedom House, a nonprofit organization that monitors democracy and freedom around the world, restrictions on political and civil liberties in Libya increased throughout the 1980s and 1990s. See Freedom House, *Freedom in the World*, various issues.

139. Economist Intelligence Unit, *Country Report: Libya*, Fourth Quarter 1991, p. 8.

140. Qadhafi met these challenges to his rule by further consolidating his power in an inner circle and lashing out at opponents, domestically and abroad, with brutality. See Bureau of Democracy, Human Rights and Labor, *Country Report on Human Rights Practices: Libya, 2000* (Department of State, February 2001); and Amnesty International, *Annual Report on Libya, 2001* (http://web.amnesty.org/web/ar2001.nsf/ webmepcountries/LIBYA?OpenDocument [September 9, 2001]).

141. U.S. military aid to Libya's neighbors was also important in affecting this calculus. Such aid to Tunisia increased from $15 million in 1981 to $95 million in 1982; that to Sudan more than tripled to reach $100 million while military aid to Egypt rose from $550 million to $900 million during the same year. Economist Intelligence Unit, *Country Report: Libya*, Third Quarter 1981, p. 5.

142. See Ray Takeyh, "The Evolving Course of Qaddafi's Foreign Policy," *Journal of Libyan Studies*, vol. 1 (Winter 2000), pp. 41–53. In 2002, Libya announced its intention to withdraw from the Arab League only to decide to stay in one month later.

143. Although U.S. sanctions, like UN ones, did increase uncertainty and therefore prod inflation upward, the magnitude of this effect was much smaller under unilateral sanctions.

144. See Cortright and Lopez, *The Sanctions Decade*, p. 116.

145. See World Bank, *World Development Indicators*, CD-ROM, 2001. Although there are no statistics on income inequality in the 1990s, one can infer that the gulf between the rich and the poor widened during the decade from the frequency with which Qadhafi promised to redistribute the country's oil wealth in his addresses to the nation. See Economist Intelligence Unit, *Country Report: Libya*, First Quarter 1994, p. 7.

146. As discussed in the economic section, sanctions spurred inflation upward by undermining the Libyan dinar and by complicating the transport of goods to Libya.

147. Economist Intelligence Unit, *Country Report: Libya*, Second Quarter 1998, p. 14.

148. Libya has provided no official statistics concerning inflation, or any other macroeconomic indicators, since 1990.

149. Economist Intelligence Unit, *Country Report: Libya*, July 2002, p. 13. Niblock claims that salaries in the public sector "have remained static since 1982." See Niblock, *Pariah States and Sanctions in the Middle East*, p. 74.

150. The Libyan regime sought to minimize the discontent fomented by inflation by subsidizing basic food goods and prioritizing foreign exchange for the import of food and other consumer items. Moreover, in 1996, in an effort to curb inflation, Qadhafi unleashed "purification committees" or groups of vigilantes who patrolled the shops of private traders, threatening and inflicting violence if their prices were deemed exorbitant. Niblock estimates that the real value of wages fell by approximately 35 percent a year in the mid-1990s. Niblock, *Pariah States and Sanctions in the Middle East*, p. 75.

151. Libyan officials claimed that more than 17,000 people were denied urgent medical treatment abroad as a result of sanctions, leading to the deaths of most of them. See Economist Intelligence Unit, *Country Report: Libya*, Second Quarter 1998, p. 14.

152. Libya's average population growth in 1997 was estimated to be 3.4 percent a year—one of the highest rates in the world. Economist Intelligence Unit, *Country Profile: Libya*, 2001, pp. 14, 43.

153. Turkey also suffered as a result of Libyan difficulties in paying its debt. When Turkish prime minister Necmettin Erbakan came under fire both in the United States and in Turkey for visiting Tripoli in October 1996, he claimed that the main impetus for his trip was to find a way to collect some of Libya's debt to Turkey. See Kelly Couturier, "Erbakan Survives Criticism on Libya," *Financial Times*, October 17, 1996, p. 3; and Tyler Marshall, "U.S. Decries Turkish Chief's Trip to Libya," *Los Angeles Times*, October 9, 1996, p. A4.

154. During the period 1992–99, Tunisia averaged 4.89 percent GDP growth per year, up from an average of 3.51 percent growth in the years 1985–91. IMF, *World Development Indicators*, CD-ROM, 2001.

155. UN Secretary General Kofi Annan noted the success of sanctions in the Libyan case, declaring "that no country likes to be treated as an outcast and outside the society of nations." United Nations, "Transcript of Press Conference by Secretary-General Kofi Annan at Headquarters, 5 April," SG/SM/6944, April 5, 1999.

156. It would be incomplete to view the impact of Libyan sanctions on U.S. energy interests totally in isolation from sanctions policies on other oil exporters. This cumulative impact of sanctions is taken up in the conclusion of this book.

157. It is worth noting that U.S. oil giants Exxon and Mobil left Libya *before* American sanctions would have forced them to withdraw, citing Libya's "unilateral manipulation of price, taxes, and royalties." Economist Intelligence Unit, *Country Report: Libya*, First

Quarter 1983, p. 11. Occidental also sought to reduce its commitments in Libya in 1984, citing commercial reasons more than political ones. See Economist Intelligence Unit, *Country Report: Libya,* Second Quarter 1984.

158. There is a wide variety of opinion about the value of these assets. Commonly accepted estimates place their value in the neighborhood of $2 billion to $4 billion. See Economist Intelligence Unit, *Country Report: Libya,* Second Quarter 1989, pp. 11–12.

159. "Libya: U.S. Softens Sanctions Policy," *Middle East Economic Digest,* February 15, 1986, pp. 20–21.

160. Both the U.S. administration and Libyan authorities demonstrated some flexibility in allowing these firms to maintain the titles to their local assets for three years after the imposition of the sanctions while the Libyan National Oil Corporation assumed full operational responsibility. However, at the end of this period, efforts to enable the American companies to regain some control over their assets were unsuccessful in light of renewed U.S. sanctions in 1989. The United States was willing to let American oil companies resume control over some of their assets by allowing them to transfer the titles of their assets in Libya to their foreign subsidiaries. This move would enable the companies to continue lifting oil, sell it to non-U.S. destinations, and conduct operations through foreign subsidiaries. Despite this easing of the sanctions, the trade embargo, restrictions on Americans traveling to Libya, and other sanctions remained, leading the Libyan authorities to reject this compromise. Since that time, Libya maintained control over these assets, claiming that U.S. firms were still welcome to reclaim them if sanctions were lifted. See Economist Intelligence Unit, *Country Report: Libya,* Second Quarter 1989, p. 12; Third Quarter 1989, p. 12; and Fourth Quarter 1989, p. 11.

161. It may be no coincidence that several European companies expressed interest in taking over American assets in Libya shortly before the ILSA legislation was drafted. Moreover, after UN sanctions were lifted, the German firm Wintershall expressed interest in assuming operation of these fields. See Energy Information Administration, *Country Analysis Brief: Libya,* July 2001.

162. Overall trade losses diminished further with the 1999 decision to allow U.S. exports of food and medicine to Libya and subsequent Libyan purchases of corn and wheat. According to the U.S. Department of Agriculture, in 2000, Libya imported almost $18 million worth of American agricultural products, mostly wheat. In September 2000, Libya also bought 26,100 tons of U.S. corn, its first such purchase since 1985–86. See U.S. Department of Agriculture, Foreign Agricultural Service, "BICO Export Commodity Aggregations" (www.fas.usda.gov/ustrdscripts/USReport.exe [August 28, 2001]); and Economist Intelligence Unit, *Country Report: Libya,* November 2000, pp. 28–29.

163. UN sanctions—rather than adding to these losses—staunched them by prohibiting all sales of aviation spare parts and equipment to Libya, thereby limiting the opportunity costs of U.S. sanctions to American firms. However, the continued exclusion of the U.S. aviation sector from the Libyan market in the wake of the suspension of UN sanctions ensured that these costs were merely delayed, not averted. Since UN sanctions were suspended, Libya has vigorously sought to refurbish and refit its airline. After reaching an agreement with Airbus Industrie in 1999 for the purchase of twenty-four new planes, complications arose because a number of parts for the planes were manufactured in the United States and are subject to U.S. sanctions. These problems have led

Libya to threaten that it would purchase new airliners from Russia or Ukraine. See Economist Intelligence Unit, *Country Report: Libya,* July 2001, pp. 20–21.

164. While UN sanctions denied all countries the ability to sell certain types of oil equipment to Libya, their suspension—and Libya's accelerated efforts to revitalize its energy sector—has meant that opportunity costs for U.S. firms have begun again to mount.

165. The growing voice of American business against unilateral sanctions was the only major constituency arguing in Libya's favor.

166. The United States also believes that Libya had a role in a number of other terrorist attacks in the 1980s, such as a car bombing outside the U.S officer's club in Naples and several other bombings close to the second anniversary of the U.S. air raids in April 1988. See Department of State, *Patterns of Global Terrorism,* 1988, pp. 45–46.

167. See Terence Roth, "German Firm Tied to Libyan Facility Will Be Broken Up— Part of Imhausen-Chemie, Chemical-Plant Builder, to Be Acquired by Swiss," *Wall Street Journal,* June 21, 1991, p. A8.

168. For more on the constraints of a legalistic approach, see Gideon Rose, "Libya," in Richard N. Haass, ed., *Economic Sanctions in American Foreign Policy* (Brookings, 1998), pp. 129–56.

169. See Jane Rosen, "UN Demands Pan Am Suspects: Libya Told to Hand over Two Men for Trial," *Guardian,* January 22, 1992, p. 20.

170. It is no coincidence that calls to investigate the humanitarian effects of sanctions on Libya accompanied growing dissatisfaction with the sanctions. See "Libya-U.N.: Africa urges compromise in Libyan sanctions row," *Inter Press Service,* September 25, 1997. In mid-December 1997, in response to a specific Libyan request and mounting concern of the OAU, UN Secretary General Kofi Annan sent a UN team to Libya to investigate the humanitarian effects of the UN sanctions. See United Nations Security Council, *Report of the Fact-Finding Mission to the Libyan Arab Jamahiriya to the Secretary General,* S/1998/201 (United Nations, March 6, 1998).

171. Qadhafi quickly withdrew his support for Saddam Hussein during the Gulf crisis once military action in the Gulf appeared inevitable, demonstrating the ability of the Libyan leader to modify his behavior when presented with strong disincentives.

172. This concentration of power in one individual can inhibit the efficacy of sanctions when the person in charge is impervious to international pressure.

173. For more on the nature of the Libyan regime, see Moncef Djaziri, "Creating a New State: Libya's Political Institutions," in Dirk Vandewalle, editor, *Qaddafi's Libya, 1969-1994,* pp. 177–202.

174. Niblock, *Pariah States and Sanctions in the Middle East,* p. 39.

175. Qadhafi's relatively weaker domestic position in the mid-1990s may have prevented him from handing over the Lockerbie suspects at an earlier date. One of the Lockerbie suspects was a member of the powerful Megariha tribe in Libya, a group on which Qadhafi's regime depended for domestic support. See Mary-Jane Deeb, "Qadhafi's Changed Policy: Causes and Consequences," *Middle East Policy,* vol. 7 (February 2000), pp. 146–53.

176. Before the passage of UN resolution 1192 in August 1998, Libya had been concerned that the surrender of the suspects would not trigger the suspension of sanctions, but that the United States would continue to claim Libya's action fell short of full compliance.

177. David Cortright and George Lopez call this "a reverse bargaining dynamic." Cortright and Lopez, *The Sanctions Decade*, p. 109. Domestic factors, particularly in Britain, also played an important role in the extension of this offer. Whereas the Conservative government of John Major had been very reluctant to compromise on the Lockerbie issue, the Labour government of Tony Blair came to office in 1997 advocating a more flexible approach. See Adel Darwish, "Sanctions against Libya Lifted after Eight Years," *Middle East*, May 1999, pp. 14–16.

178. See John Bolton, Testimony at U.S. Policy toward Libya, Hearing before the Near Eastern and South Asian Affairs Subcommittee of the Senate Foreign Relations Committee, 106 Cong. 2 sess., May 4, 2000 (GPO, 2000).

179. See Deeb, "Political and Economic Developments in Libya in the 1990s," pp. 81–82.

180. In December 1994, the French publication *Marches Tropicaux* published a study estimating that within one year, a full oil embargo would lead to the collapse of the Libyan economy because Libya lacks an industrial and agricultural base. See Economist Intelligence Unit, *Country Report: Libya,* Second Quarter 1995, p. 16.

181. European countries did in fact reject such efforts. They admitted that they could have secured their oil from other sources, but complained that such a transition would be costly, as their refineries were equipped to process the low-sulfur crude Libya produced.

182. See Ronald Neumann, "U.S. Policy toward Libya" (Department of State, November 30, 1999).

183. The meeting was held at the UN on June 11, 1999, and was called by UN Secretary General Kofi Annan to discuss what the Security Council required to end the sanctions. It was attended by Annan, Libya's ambassador to the UN, and an American and British representative. The United States and Britain both said Libya had yet to live up to all the requirements of the UN Security Council resolutions. See Judith Miller, "In Rare Talks with Libyans, U.S. Airs Views on Sanctions," *New York Times*, June 12, 1999, p. A4.

184. The Libyan Fighting Group is not only an Islamist group opposing Qadhafi's rule, but it is also an organization blacklisted by the United States for connections with al-Qaida.

185. The Iran-Contra scandal also diminished the credibility of U.S. efforts to keep weapons away from countries deemed to be state sponsors of terrorism. More specifically, the credibility of U.S. policy toward Libya was undercut by what were viewed as minimal penalties levied on U.S. firms which violated the sanctions.

186. In a perversion of the effects of ILSA, in October 2000, all fifteen countries of the EU supported a Libyan-sponsored UN resolution condemning the use of unilateral sanctions. The EU spokesperson claimed that the EU was registering its objection to the application of national legislation to third parties. See "UN General Assembly Backs Libya Resolution Criticizing Sanctions," *Oil Daily*, October 30, 2000, p. 1434.

# Chapter Six

1. Only weeks after the coup, al-Bashir became a lieutenant general; in October 1993, he became president of Sudan.

2. Over the years since OLS was founded in 1989, the United States has played a central role in its works, providing more than $1 billion to it in the first decade of its existence.

3. See Madeleine K. Albright, "Remarks on the New Economic Sanctions against Sudan," U.S. Department of State, Office of the Spokesman, November 4, 1997 (http://secretary.state.gov/www/statements/971104.html [May 17, 2001]).

4. See *Condemning the National Islamic Front (NIF) Government for Its Genocidal War in Southern Sudan, Support for Terrorism, and Continued Human Rights Violations, and for Other Purposes*, H. Con. Res. 75, 106 Cong. 1 sess. (Government Printing Office, 1999) and *Relating to the Activities of the National Islamic Front Government in Sudan*, S. Res. 109, 106 Cong. 1 sess. (GPO, 1999), condemning the NIF and urging further pressure on it. Also see congressional statements such as those by Representative Edward Royce in which he declares the importance of "the U.S. and its allies (to) keep up the pressure on this repressive and dangerous regime." *Congressional Record*, September 30, 1999, p. H9029.

5. Although the assassins were sentenced to life imprisonment after a trial in Sudan, President Nimeiri later shortened their sentences, much to the chagrin of the United States. See Ted Dagne, "Sudan: Humanitarian Crisis, Peace Talks, Terrorism, and U.S. Policy," Congressional Research Service, Library of Congress, May 8, 2002; and Department of State, *Background Notes: Sudan* (June 1995).

6. U.S. military assistance to Sudan peaked in 1981–86 when it averaged nearly $100 million a year.

7. Although the Addis Ababa Agreement had been forged under Nimeiri years earlier in 1972, a failing economy and growing pressure to accommodate Islamic fundamentalist political forces led Nimeiri to breach it. See Francis Deng, *War of Visions: Conflict of Identities in the Sudan* (Brookings, 1995), pp. 12–13; Ann Mosely Lesch, *The Sudan: Contested National Identities* (Indiana University Press, 1998), esp. pp. 45–60.

8. The three years that al-Mahdi was in power were characterized by instability and indecision, as the rapid rise and fall of ruling coalitions between al-Mahdi's Umma Party, the Democratic Unionist Party (DUP), the National Islamic Front (NIF), and minor southern parties led to short-lived political initiatives that were quickly reversed. See Lesch, *The Sudan: Contested National Identities*, esp. pp. 76–87; and G. Norman Anderson, *Sudan in Crisis: The Failure of Democracy* (University of Florida Press, 1999).

9. Despite this action, Washington stayed on good terms with al-Mahdi until his overthrow a year later. Aid that had already been obligated in previous fiscal years was not affected by the Brooke amendment provisions. Erin Day, "Economic Sanctions Imposed by the United States against Specific Countries: 1979 through 1992" (Congressional Research Service, August 10, 1992), p. 93.

10. Section 513 (now called section 508) of the Foreign Operations Appropriations bill prohibits U.S. economic and military aid to countries where democratically elected governments have been overthrown. At the time of the coup in Sudan in 1989, these sanctions were redundant, as the Brooke amendment sanctions were still in force. Erin Day, "Economic Sanctions Imposed by the United States against Specific Countries: 1979 through 1992," pp. 93–94.

11. Sudan's decision cost it the support of its neighbor Egypt, which was a traditional ally, as well as Saudi Arabia and Kuwait, which both had provided aid to Sudan before the

Gulf war. The only country to openly embrace Sudan at this time was Libya. See William C. Mann, "Last 100 Days Have Been Rough for Sudanese Junta," *Associated Press*, November 17, 1990, and statement by Herman J. Cohen, assistant secretary of state for African affairs, before the Subcommittee on African Affairs of the Senate Foreign Relations Committee, 101 Cong. 2 sess., November 27, 1990.

12. Congress included in the Foreign Operations Appropriations bill a specific prohibition on International Military Education and Training (IMET) and Foreign Military Financing programs to Sudan. However, earlier sanctions imposed under the Brooke amendment and section 513 sanctions had already terminated such programs.

13. President George H. W. Bush, "Memorandum on Modifications of the Generalized System of Preferences," April 25, 1991.

14. In its 1991 *Patterns on Global Terrorism*, released in April 1992, the State Department noted that in the previous year Sudan had enhanced its relations with international terrorist groups, including the Abu Nidal organization. It also noted that Sudan "maintained ties" to state sponsors Libya and Iraq and was improving relations with Iran. The publication also noted reports that the NIF government allowed terrorist groups to train on its territory and had offered Sudan as a "sanctuary to terrorist organizations." See Department of State, *Patterns of Global Terrorism 1991*, April 1992, and Department of State, *Patterns of Global Terrorism 1992*, April 1993.

15. Herman Cohen, Situation on the Horn of Africa, testimony before the African Affairs Subcommittee of the Senate Foreign Relations Committee, 102 Cong. 2 sess., March 19, 1992; and Herman Cohen, South Africa, testimony before the African Affairs Subcommittee of the Senate Foreign Relations Committee, 102 Cong. 2 sess., September 23, 1992. Also see Economist Intelligence Unit, *Country Report: Sudan*, Fourth Quarter 1989, p. 16; Fourth Quarter 1992, p. 16.

16. See Cohen, Situation on the Horn of Africa, testimony, March 19, 1992.

17. Economist Intelligence Unit, *Country Report: Sudan*, Fourth Quarter, 1991, pp. 11–14.

18. Moreover, Osama bin Laden later entered Sudan in the early 1990s. For a more detailed description of Sudan's involvement in terrorism at the time, see Tim Niblock, *Pariah States and Sanctions in the Middle East* (Lynne Rienner Publishers, 2001), pp. 200–01.

19. See "Daily Press Briefing" (Department of State, Office of the Spokesman, August 18, 1993).

20. Other miscellaneous restrictions related to being designated a state sponsor of terrorism include the prohibition on U.S. firms claiming tax credits for their involvement in the country, the granting of executive authority to impose an import ban on trade with the country, as well as a provision for the imposition of secondary sanctions against countries or institutions that aid terrorist activities in the country.

21. See Niblock, *Pariah States and Sanctions*, pp. 201–02.

22. United Nations Security Council, *Security Council Resolution 1044 (1996)*, S/RES/1044 (United Nations, January 31, 1996).

23. United Nations Security Council, *Security Council Resolution 1054 (1996)*, S/RES/1054 (United Nations, April 26, 1996).

24. On November 22, 1996, the Clinton administration declared its intention to bar senior Sudanese officials from entering the United States. See President William Jefferson

Clinton, "Suspension of Entry as Immigrants and Nonimmigrants of Persons Who Are Members or Officials of the Sudanese Government or Armed Forces," White House, Office of the Press Secretary, November 22, 1996.

25. Economist Intelligence Unit, *Country Report: Sudan*, February 2001, p. 18.

26. United Nations Security Council, *Security Council Resolution 1070 (1996)* S/RES/1070 (United Nations, August 16, 1996).

27. See the section later in this chapter on the humanitarian costs of sanctions for more details on this episode.

28. See Francis M. Deng, "Egypt's Dilemmas on Sudan," *Middle East Policy*, vol. 4 (September 1995).

29. Niblock, *Pariah States and Sanctions*, p. 206.

30. Many U.S. nongovernmental activists sympathetic to the south, as well as President Isiaias Afewerki of Eritrea, enthusiastically advanced the idea that the NDA could be made into an effective military organization.

31. Sudan's relationships with its neighbors deteriorated sharply on account of Khartoum's reported support for their opposition groups, including the Eritrean Islamic Jihad, the Eritrean Liberation Front, the Islamic Front for the Liberation of Oromia (Ethiopia), and the Lord's Resistance Army (Uganda). See subsequent sections on Sudanese support for terrorism.

32. See A. M. Rosenthal, "On My Mind; Persecuting the Christians," *New York Times*, February 11, 1997, p. A21.

33. Compare *Expressing the Sense of the Senate with Respect to the Tragic Humanitarian Crisis in Sudan*, S. Res. 94, 103 Cong. 2 sess. (GPO, 1994); *Expressing the Sense of the Congress with Respect to the Situation in Sudan*, H. Con. Res. 131, 103 Cong. 1 sess. (GPO, 1993) to *Freedom from Religious Persecution Act of 1997*, S. 772, 105 Cong. 1 sess. (GPO, 1997); *Freedom from Religious Persecution Act of 1997*, H.R. 1685, 105 Cong. 1 sess. (GPO, 1997); and *To Prohibit Economic Assistance, Military Assistance, or Arms Transfers to the Government of Sudan until Appropriate Action Is Taken to Eliminate Chattel Slavery in Sudan, and for Other Purposes*, H.R. 3766, 104 Cong. 2 sess. (GPO, 1996).

34. Interview by author, Washington, 2001.

35. In August 1996, the Antiterrorism and Effective Death Penalty Act became law. Although it prohibited any financial transactions between U.S. companies and countries on the terrorism list, the regulations were originally written to exempt Sudan and Syria except when the transactions were known to be linked to terrorist activity. See Title 31, Part 596, *U.S. Code of Federal Regulations*, August 22, 1996. In addition, in February 2000, the Treasury Department issued a clarification of the 1997 executive order that confirmed that U.S. companies and individuals were prohibited from doing business with the Greater Nile Petroleum Operating Company in Sudan. Letter from R. Richard Newcomb, director, Office of Foreign Assets Control, Department of the Treasury, Washington, April 13, 2000.

36. As discussed in greater detail later in the chapter, efforts to create a stringent sanctions regime were undercut by a domestic move to limit the costs to U.S. businesses by exempting Sudanese exports of gum arabic from the trade embargo.

37. See John Shattuck, assistant secretary of state for democracy, human rights and labor, Testimony at *Religious Persecution* before the House International Relations Committee, 105 Cong. 1 sess. September 9, 1997, for executive concerns over the legislation. Also see

Donna Cassata, "Congress Enters Uncharted Territory with Bill on Religious Persecution," *Congressional Quarterly*, September 13, 1997.

38. See "Statement by the Press Secretary: Humanitarian Exemptions from Sanctions," White House, Office of the Press Secretary, April 28, 1999, and "Statement by the Press Secretary: Implementing Humanitarian Exemptions from Sanctions," White House, Office of the Press Secretary, July 26, 1999.

39. Burma (Myanmar), China, Iran, Iraq, and the Milosevic regime and the Taliban movement in Afghanistan were also named severe violators in 1999. Department of State, *Annual Report on International Religious Freedom for 1999*, September 9, 1999. In the following year, the U.S. Commission on International Religious Freedom (the independent body created by the International Religious Freedom Act) recommended that Laos, North Korea, Saudi Arabia, and Turkmenistan be added to this list, although the State Department chose not to designate them. See U.S. Commission on International Religious Freedom, "Report of the U.S. Commission on International Religious Freedom on the International Religious Freedom Act and the State Department's Annual Report on International Religious Freedom—2000," December 8, 2000. The commission reiterated these recommendations in August 2001 when it asked Secretary of State Colin Powell to designate Burma, China, Iran, Iraq, Laos, North Korea, Saudi Arabia, Sudan, and Turkmenistan as "countries of particular concern" for their restrictions on religious freedom. See "Letter to Colin Powell, Re: Recommended Designation of 'Countries of Particular Concern'" (U.S. Commission on International Religious Freedom, August 16, 2001), www.uscirf.gov/crptPages/cpcLetter.php3 (October 29, 2001).

40. Department of State, *Annual Report on International Religious Freedom for 1999*, September 9, 1999, and Department of State, *Annual Report on International Religious Freedom for 2000*, September 5, 2000. These reports also note that government security forces regularly harass citizens on the basis of their religious beliefs and mentions the role that religion plays in the practice of slavery in Sudan.

41. See "U.S. Won't Add to Sanctions on 5 Nations," *Washington Post*, December 24, 1999, p. A7.

42. David Ottaway, "Wielding Aid, U.S. Targets Sudan; $20 Million to Be Sent to Neighbors Who Are Backing Rebel Forces," *Washington Post*, November 10, 1996, p. A34. Tim Niblock reports that it was widely expected that some of the equipment provided to these states would end up in the hands of the armed Sudanese opposition. Niblock, *Pariah States and Sanctions*, p. 208.

43. See James Risen, "Question of Evidence: A Special Report: To Bomb Sudan Plant, or Not: A Year Later, Debates Rankle," *New York Times*, October 27, 1999, p. A1.

44. See "Press Availability with Secretary of State Madeleine K. Albright and Kenyan President Daniel Arap Moi," Department of State, Office of the Spokesman, October 22, 1999.

45. Niblock, *Pariah States and Sanctions*, p. 208.

46. See Economist Intelligence Unit, *Country Report: Sudan*, February 2001, p. 17.

47. Ibid.

48. "Appointment of Special Envoy for Sudan, Statement by the Press Secretary," White House, Office of the Press Secretary, August 27, 1999.

49. Chevron, however, had vacated the area in the 1980s after becoming the target of rebel attacks. Economist Intelligence Unit, *Country Profile*, 1990–91, p. 25.

50. The agreement formalizing the consortium was signed in March 1997. "Arakis, Partners Sign Accord with Sudan Oil Oil Production," *Wall Street Journal*, March 5, 1997, p. C20.

51. Occidental had expressed interest in joining Arakis in its development of the pipeline to transport oil from its fields and had entered into negotiations for a $930 million deal with the Sudanese government to build a pipeline. However, the passage of the Antiterrorism and Effective Death Penalty Act in April 1996, which prohibited investment in most countries on the terrorism list, created uncertainty as to whether Occidental could continue its involvement in Sudan. Although, when published several months later, the regulations provided a loophole for investment in Sudan and made the Occidental investments possible, Khartoum excluded Occidental from the pipeline deal, probably in the belief that further U.S. sanctions would follow. Some saw the move as retaliation for the Clinton administration's providing of military assistance to Uganda, Ethiopia, and Eritrea, countries that were providing support for the SPLA. See David Ottaway, "U.S. Eased Law on Terrorism to Aid Oil Firm; Exemption Let Occidental Seek Major Deal in Sudan," *Washington Post*, January 23, 1997, p. A1; and David Ottaway, "GOP Targets Sudan Loophole; Administration Approval of Transactions with Khartoum Prompts Scrutiny," *Washington Post*, February 7, 1997, p. A1

52. See Niblock, *Pariah States and Sanctions*, pp. 212–13. In late 2000, Sudanese officials met with ministers from Egypt and eight other African states under the auspices of the World Bank, the United Nations, several European countries, and the United States to discuss plans for the distribution of Nile resources. See "Nile River Politics: Who Receives Water?" Stratfor.com, August 10, 2000 (www.stratfor.com/MEAF/commentary/0008100107.htm [August 10, 2000]).

53. Like that regarding Iran, European foreign policy toward Sudan is coordinated under the Common Foreign and Security Policy.

54. *Making Appropriations for Foreign Operations, Export Financing, and Related Programs for the Fiscal Year Ending September 30, 2001, and for Other Purposes*, Conf. Rept. 4811, 106 Cong. 2 sess. (GPO, 2000). Concerns that such action would further encourage the use of aid as a weapon of war in an already highly politically charged humanitarian setting prevented President Clinton from using this authority.

55. See *Sudan Peace Act*, H.R. 2052, 107 Cong. 1 sess. (GPO, 2001). On June 13, 2001, the House voted 422-2 for the passage of this bill, which provided $10 million in funds for the SPLA and would mandate capital market sanctions on those foreign companies investing in the oil industry in Sudan. In late 2000, both Houses of Congress had passed the Sudan Peace Act. The version of the Sudan Peace Act passed by the House at the end of the legislative session in 2000 contained a provision imposing capital market sanctions on oil companies investing in Sudan's oil industry. The version passed by the Senate did not contain the sanctions. The end of the 2000 legislative calendar precluded these bills from being reconciled. As mentioned in the text, the version of the Sudan Peace Act that became law on October 15, 2002, did not include capital market sanctions, although some members of Congress continue to advocate their imposition.

56. See John Donnelly and Anthony Shadid, "U.S. Welcomes Sudan's Aggressive Response," *Boston Globe*, October 5, 2001, p. A25; and Robin Wright and James Gerstenzang, "Sudan, a Bin Laden Haven, Cracks Down on Extremists," *Los Angeles Times*, September 27, 2001, p. A1.

57. The Economist Intelligence Unit gauges that the Sudanese economy grew 23.5 percent from 1996 to 1999. Economist Intelligence Unit, *Country Report: Sudan*, August 2000, p. 22.

58. International Monetary Fund, *Sudan: Recent Economic Developments*, June 1999, p. 8; Economist Intelligence Unit, *Country Report: Sudan*, February 2001, p. 11.

59. IMF, *Direction of Trade Statistics*, various years.

60. The IMF reported that "Sudan has made considerable progress in stabilizing the macroeconomic situation and moving forward the structural reform agenda" in its *Sudan: Staff Report for the 2000 Article IV Consultation and Fourth Review of the First Annual Program under the Medium-Term Staff-Monitored Program,* June 2000, p. 34. See also IMF, *Sudan: Recent Economic Developments*, June 1999, pp. 7–8.

61. As discussed in greater depth later in the section, Sudan's relationship with the IMF went from bad to worse in the early 1990s, leading to the suspension of Sudan's voting rights in the organization in 1993.

62. Economist Intelligence Unit, *Country Profile: Sudan*, 1998–99, p. 42.

63. In 2001, Sudan exported an average of 230,000 barrels of oil a day. Economist Intelligence Unit, *Country Report: Sudan,* July 2002, p. 3.

64. Economist Intelligence Unit, *Country Report: Sudan,* February 2001, p. 22. The IMF reported that Sudan exported $1.37 billion worth of goods in 2000 (approximately 70 percent of which was oil). IMF, *Direction of Trade Statistics Quarterly*, September 2001, p. 238.

65. Under the current structure of investments, such as that underpinning GNPOC, foreign companies garner 20 percent of profits from oil and an additional 38 percent of the profits to recoup their initial investment, which is expected to take three to four years. After this time, this 38 percent will go to the government. See Economist Intelligence Unit, *Country Report: Sudan*, Fourth Quarter 1999, p. 25.

66. In 1996, the year before trade sanctions went into effect, exports to the United States only accounted for 3.7 percent of total overseas sales. IMF, *Direction of Trade Statistics*, various years.

67. In 1996, gum arabic accounted for 56 percent of all Sudanese exports to the United States; in 1997, this percentage was 49 percent. A large part of the remainder of these exports was sesame products. Derived from data from U.S. Census Bureau, "U.S. Trade with Sudan in 1996" (www.census.gov/foreign-trade/sitc1/1996/c7320.htm [October 31, 2001]); and U.S. Census Bureau, "U.S. Trade with Sudan in 1997" (www.census.gov/foreign-trade/sitc1/1997/c7320.htm [October 31, 2001]); U.S. Department of Commerce, Bureau of the Census, Foreign Trade Division, Report IM 145; and IMF, *Direction of Trade Statistics*, 1999.

68. After nearly a year of uncertainty, the regulations governing the sanctions on Sudan were written to allow American companies to apply for licenses to import gum arabic from Sudan. Initially, these procedures were believed to be a temporary effort to accommodate importers who would need to diversify their supply of gum arabic; in an effort to help U.S. consumers of gum arabic, the U.S. Agency for International Development even began programs in other African countries to encourage them to cultivate gum arabic. However, over time, this exemption became institutionalized.

69. See Economist Intelligence Unit, *Country Report: Sudan,* August 2000, p. 29.

70. However, the value of Sudanese gum arabic exports declined as a result of the weakening of gum arabic prices. See IMF, *Sudan: Statistical Appendix*, July 2000, p. 30.

71. This is true both as a percentage of total Sudanese imports and in absolute terms. See Economist Intelligence Unit, *Country Report: Sudan*, Fourth Quarter 1996, p. 23; and IMF, *Direction of Trade Statistics*, various years. The patterns begin to change in the late 1990s and early 2000s—as demonstrated in figure 6-4—as Sudan focuses on importing equipment for its oil industry.

72. For instance, shortly after the imposition of U.S. sanctions, a Japanese firm assumed the business that an American company, Caterpillar, had been forced to terminate. See Michael S. Lelyveld, "U.S. Exporters Caught in Sanctions Cross-Fire," *Journal of Commerce*, March 30, 1998, p. 18.

73. See Office of Foreign Assets Control, *Terrorist Assets Report: 2000 Annual Report to the Congress on Assets in the United States Belonging to Terrorist Countries or International Terrorist Organizations* (Department of the Treasury, January 2001), p. 8.

74. However, some U.S. firms—such as Occidental and Mobil—had to relinquish small investments or operations.

75. As of 2002, no lending is possible pending full settlement of the country's arrears, although the Bank has been working with Sudan in conjunction with other regional countries in its Nile Basin Initiative. See www.nilebasin.org.

76. In its 1990 announcement, the IMF noted that Sudan ignored the IMF's preferred creditor status and paid off other creditors while not repaying the IMF. IMF, "Press Release No. 90/49," External Relations Department, September 14, 1990; and World Bank, "Country Brief: Sudan," September 2000.

77. IMF, *Sudan: Statistical Appendix*, July 2000, p. 35.

78. Ibid., pp. 35–36.

79. Aid from Arab countries peaked in 1983 at $450.2 million, yet dropped to $7.7 million in 1990, $1.8 million in 1993, and to a mere $200,000 in 1994. Economist Intelligence Unit, *Country Profile: Sudan*, 1997–98, p. 32.

80. By the end of 1999, Sudan had re-established working relations with the Saudi Fund for Development, the Abu Dhabi Fund, and the OPEC fund as well as solidified its relations with the International Fund for Agricultural Development and the Islamic Development Fund. See IMF, *Sudan: Statistical Appendix*, June 2000, p. 33. In January 2002, the EU announced it would resume aid to Sudan through the Cotonou Agreement. Yet, as of mid-2002, the EU had not disbursed any such aid, keeping it pending improvements in governance and the human rights situation. Economist Intelligence Unit, *Country Report: Sudan*, June 2002, p. 14.

81. Libya, however, did agree to forgive $300 million of Sudan's debt. Economist Intelligence Unit, *Country Report: Sudan*, Fourth Quarter 1999, p. 30.

82. Canada has declared that Sudan will be considered for HIPC initiatives "once they demonstrate they are fully committed to the principles of peaceful development and good governance, including the protection of human rights." Ken Warn, "Canada Agrees to Debt Moratorium," *Financial Times*, December 20, 2000, p. 4.

83. Economist Intelligence Unit, *Country Profile: Sudan*, 1997–98, p. 44.

84. Concern about the widely fluctuating exchange rate forced the government to suspend the operations of nonbank currency dealers in July 1996. Some were allowed

to reopen two weeks later, but under new guidelines. A government committee then set the exchange rate. Economist Intelligence Unit, *Country Profile: Sudan*, 1997–98, p. 33.

85. For an exception to calls for additional punitive measures on Sudan, see a 2001 Center for Strategic and International Studies (CSIS) task force report that advocates the adoption of more flexible measures in order to gear U.S. policy toward the goal of ending the war. Francis M. Deng and J. Stephen Morrison, "U.S. Policy to Bend Sudan's Ear: Report of the CSIS Task Force on U.S.-Sudan Policy," Center for Strategic and International Studies, February 2001.

86. As mentioned in an earlier note, the EU decided in principle to resume aid to Sudan through the Cotonou Agreement in January 2002. Cotonou joins the EU with African, Caribbean, and Pacific countries; EU aid through the organization is conditional on respect for human rights and good governance.

87. In the past, the National Democratic Alliance not only supported sanctions but called for more stringent multilateral measures. Economist Intelligence Unit, *Country Report: Sudan*, Second Quarter 1997, p. 17.

88. See Madeleine Albright, "Remarks on New Economic Sanctions against Sudan," Department of State, Office of the Spokesman, November 4, 1997, May 17, 2001.

89. As mentioned earlier, these sanctions first came into effect in 1988 as a result of Sudan's inability to pay its arrears in 1988 and were later reinforced in February 1990 as a result of the coup.

90. See "Report of an Investigation into Oil Development, Conflict and Displacement in Western Upper Nile, Sudan," October 2001, p. 35.

91. In fact, official arms transfers from the Middle East—the most significant supplier of weaponry to Sudan—actually declined over the 1990s. See U.S. Department of State, Bureau of Arms Control, *World Military Expenditures and Arms Transfers*, various years.

92. See Economist Intelligence Unit, *Country Report: Sudan*, Second Quarter 1995, p. 13; Second Quarter 1997, p. 13.

93. See William Jefferson Clinton, Executive Order 13067, November 3, 1997, and Susan Rice, testimony given at Crisis in Sudan and Northern Uganda before the Subcommittees on Africa and on International Operations and Human Rights of the House International Relations Committee, 105 Cong. 2 sess., July 29, 1998 (commdocs.house. gov/committees/intrel/hfa51667.000/hfa51667_0.htm [August 26, 2002]).

94. See Niblock, *Pariah States and Sanctions*, pp. 211–14.

95. In its 2002 counterterrorism report, the U.S. Department of State stated, "Sudan and Libya seem closest to understanding what they must do to get out of the terrorism business, and each has taken measures pointing it in the right direction." Department of State, *Patterns of Global Terrorism*, 2001, May 2002, p. 63.

96. Department of State, *Patterns of Global Terrorism*, 2001, May 2002.

97. A September 2001 congressional report said that, of the Middle Eastern countries on the terrorism list, Sudan was the closest one to qualifying for removal. See John Donnelly and Anthony Shadid, "U.S. Welcomes Sudan's Aggressive Response," *Boston Globe*, October 5, 2001, p. A25.

98. In 2002, bilateral relations between Sudan and Uganda appeared to be improving after Khartoum allowed Ugandan forces into southern Sudan to pursue the Lord's

Resistance Army—a recent addition to the U.S. list of foreign terrorist organizations. Economist Intelligence Unit, *Country Report: Sudan*, June 2002, p. 15.

99. Technically, legislation had to be passed the following year to legalize the formation of political associations provided for in the constitution.

100. Former prime minister and Umma Party leader Sadiq al-Mahdi returned from exile in November 2000 and embarked on discussions with the government about the possibility of his involvement. A year later, Ahmed al-Mirghani, deputy head of the Democratic Unionist Party (a small splinter opposition group), returned to Sudan.

101. Both the government of Sudan and the southern opposition forces have been accused of severe human right violations. See "Country Reports on Human Rights Practices, 2000: Sudan," Department of State, Bureau of Democracy, Human Rights and Labor, February 2001; and *Civilian Devastation: Abuses by All Parties in the War in Southern Sudan*, Human Rights Watch/Africa, 1994.

102. See "Country Reports on Human Rights Practices, 2000: Sudan," Department of State, Bureau of Democracy, Human Rights and Labor, February 2001; "Report of the United States Commission on International Religious Freedom on Sudan," United States Commission on International Religious Freedom, March 21, 2001 (www.uscirf.gov/reports/21Mar01/sudan_21Mar01.php3 [June 11, 2001]).

103. Although the government denies that slavery exists in Sudan, it created a Committee for the Eradication of the Abduction of Women and Children in May 1999. This body, while claiming some results, was largely seen as an insufficient response to the problem. The U.S. State Department reported in February 2001 that 10,000–15,000 Sudanese, primarily from the Dinka tribe, remained in conditions of slavery at the close of 2000. "Country Reports on Human Rights Practices, 2000: Sudan," Department of State, Bureau of Democracy, Human Rights and Labor, February 2001.

104. See "Sudan: The Human Price of Oil," Amnesty International, March 5, 2000 (web.amnesty.org/ai.nsf/Index/AFR540012000?OpenDocument&of=COUNTRIES\SUDAN [June 11, 2001]); and John Harker, "Human Security in Sudan: The Report of a Canadian Assessment Mission," Canadian Ministry of Foreign Affairs, Ottawa, January 2000.

105. Despite a May 25, 2001 pledge by the Sudanese government to halt bombings of civilian targets, four Sudanese civilians were reportedly killed in a bombing as the World Food Program was distributing food on June 6, 2001. This renewed bombing was condemned by the State Department, see "Daily Press Briefing," Department of State, Office of the Spokesman, June 8, 2001.

106. See "Famine in Sudan, 1998: The Human Rights Causes," Human Rights Watch, February 8, 1999 (www.hrw.org/reports/1999/sudan/SUDAWEB2.htm#P374_19682 [June 11, 2001]).

107. See Francis M. Deng and J. Stephen Morrison, "U.S. Policy to End Sudan's War: Report of the CSIS Task Force on U.S.-Sudan Policy," Center for Strategic and International Studies, February 2001, pp. 7–8.

108. See "Sudan: 600,000 People at Immediate Risk of Starvation," United Nations Office for the Coordination of Humanitarian Affairs, February 27, 2001; "UN-OCHA Sudan Situation Report," United Nations Office for the Coordination of Humanitarian Affairs, April 2001; see "News Release: Major Food Crisis Looms in Sudan," World Food Program, March 29, 2001.

109. Harsh weather conditions, government interference in the distribution of aid and other security problems, as well as underfunding by international donors, hampered the effectiveness of humanitarian relief efforts to alleviate the hardship. Besides the government's abuses, the southern rebels have also at times hindered the distribution of food. In early 2000, the SPLA insisted that all NGOs operating in areas it controlled sign a Memorandum of Understanding (MOU), which imposed certain conditions on them. Eleven of the forty NGOs operating in the area refused to sign the MOU, fearful that it would compromise their neutrality. They were forced to withdraw from the area, although some later returned. In the meantime, the EU withheld aid to NGOs that did sign the MOU. See "World Report 2001: Sudan," Human Rights Watch (www.hrw.org/wr2k1/africa/sudan.html [June 11, 2001]).

110. See Dagne, "Sudan: Humanitarian Crisis, Peace Talks, Terrorism, and U.S. Policy," p. 8. This money was largely channeled through OLS, which operates primarily in the south of the country where the population has been most at risk. Although the Sudanese government has been able to impede these humanitarian operations in a variety of ways, it does not *directly* benefit from any of the funds flowing to OLS. Nevertheless, Khartoum reportedly benefits from some diversion of relief assets in government-controlled areas of the south.

111. "Remarks by Secretary of State Colin L. Powell and USAID Administrator Andrew Natsios following their meeting with UN and NGO representatives," Department of State, Office of the Spokesman, Kampala, Uganda, May 27, 2001.

112. Riots have troubled northern cities as people have protested, in part, because of the lack of basic services. See Economist Intelligence Unit, *Country Report: Sudan*, November 2000, p. 12.

113. Sudan once had some of the best educational and health facilities in the region. See Economist Intelligence Unit, *Country Profile: Sudan*, 1997–98, p. 17.

114. Some expatriates seeking to remit earnings to Sudan in U.S. dollars may have experienced initial difficulties, although they could have been overcome by sending them in other currencies. Economist Intelligence Unit, *Country Report: Sudan*, Fourth Quarter, 1997, p. 7.

115. Economist Intelligence Unit, *Country Report: Sudan*, Fourth Quarter 1996, p. 15.

116. Ibid., Second Quarter 1997, pp. 16–17.

117. Although a small sum, these costs were fairly concentrated. Caterpillar, for instance, lost a $35 million contract to sell machinery to Sudan as a consequence of the sanctions. See William Lane, testimony given at *Economic Sanctions Reform* before the Subcommittee on International Economic Policy, Export and Trade Promotion, of the Senate Foreign Relations Committee, 105 Cong. 2 sess., March 25, 1998 (www.usaengage.org/legislative/lane.html [August, 26, 2002])).

118. Although the lack of financing for these sales has continued to hinder them, some agricultural exports to Sudan have resumed. The $14 million figure is derived from IMF, *Direction of Trade Statistics*, and figures available at U.S. Census Bureau, "U.S. Trade with Sudan in 1996" (www.census.gov/foreign-trade/sitc1/1996/c7320.htm); and U.S. Census Bureau, "U.S. Trade with Sudan in 1997" (www.census.gov/foreign-trade/sitc1/1997/c7320.htm).

119. See Economist Intelligence Unit, *Country Report: Sudan*, Second Quarter 1998, p. 27; First Quarter 1996, p. 22.

120. The U.S. Department of Energy's Information Agency estimated that as of January 2001 Sudan's total *proven* reserves were 262.1 million barrels (www.eia.doe. gov/emeu/cabs/sudan.html [October 2002]).

121. In 2002, Talisman was widely rumored to be interested in selling its assets in Sudan, largely on account of pressure from human rights activists in Canada and elsewhere. See Economist Intelligence Unit, *Country Report: Sudan,* June 2002, p. 23.

122. For instance, see H. Con. Res. 75, 106 Cong. 1 sess. (GPO, 1999) and S. Res. 109, 106 Cong. 1 sess. (GPO, 1999) passed 416 to 1 and by unanimous consent respectively.

123. See "Policy Creep," *Financial Times,* May 14, 2001, p. 10; and Matthias Muindi, "Christian Right Might Inflame War," *Africanews,* May 2001.

124. See Barbara Crossette, "To-the-Wire Fighting for U.N. Seats; U.S. Tries to Block Sudan," *New York Times,* October 6, 2000, p. A13; and Karen DeYoung, "An Uncharitable Dispute; Relief Organizations Want U.S. Government to Moderate Hard-Line Stance on Sudan," *Washington Post,* January 5, 2000, p. A15.

125. Interviews of European diplomats by author, Washington, 2001. Some also interpret the crafting of regulations for Sudan under the Antiterrorism and Effective Death Penalty Act as an attempt to allow Occidental to explore the construction of an oil pipeline in Sudan.

126. One European diplomat in the face of the NDA's successful excursion into Kassala in 2002 claimed, "It was obvious to foreign observers that these kinds of successes could not be achieved by the opposition without serious foreign assistance, assistance beyond the type that neighboring countries might provde." The Kassala offensive was launched by the NDA but used mainly SPLA troops. Quote from interview by author, Washington, 2001.

127. Interview by author, Washington, 2001.

128. Amnesty International, *Annual Report 2001*, May 2001.

129. Other countries placed on the U.S. terrorism list will take note if the United States "moves the goalposts" once Sudan has adequately addressed U.S. concerns related to terrorism.

130. The embassy was closed in 1996 for security reasons, not diplomatic ones.

131. Currently, the most sensitive area is foreign investment in Sudan's oil industry, although investment in other areas of infrastructure—particularly water power and electricity—are rapidly assuming importance. In the medium term, as Sudan's economic convalescence continues, debt restructuring and access to lending from the international financial institutions will be of the highest priority.

132. The United Nations is already involved in similar initiatives, not necessarily related to Sudan. See the Global Compact initiative (http://unglobalcompact.org).

133. The Sullivan Principles were mandatory for U.S. firms after the passage of the Comprehensive Anti-Apartheid Act of 1986, although non-U.S. firms were also encouraged to adhere to them.

134. Foreign corporations—and the companies that handle their entry into global capital markets—have already revealed themselves to be vulnerable to public pressure from human rights groups and other activists. Although not the only factor causing the initial public offering of PetroChina to fall short of its expected $10 billion earnings on the New York Stock Exchange, the steady erosion of public image resulting from a prolonged activist movement publicizing the involvement of PetroChina's parent company,

CNPC, in Sudan was certainly an important factor. Other companies involved in Sudan, such as Fosters of Canada, have also cited NGO activism as an impediment to greater success in their fund-raising efforts. See Michael M. Phillips, "PetroChina's IPO Roadshow Opens, While Opposition Forces Rally Nearby," *Wall Street Journal*, March 23, 2000, p. A14; and Murray Hiebert, "Market Morality," *Far Eastern Economic Review*, April 6, 2000, pp. 56–58; Economist Intelligence Unit, *Country Report: Sudan*, June 2000, p. 22.

135. See the chapters on Iran and Libya in this book concerning tensions over the secondary sanctions mandated by the Iran-Libya Sanctions Act.

136. In April 2002, Talisman decided to issue a $365 million corporate bond in the United Kingdom, rather than in the United States as it had done on every previous occasion. Economist Intelligence Unit, *Country Report: Sudan,* June 2002, p. 24.

137. The May 2001 decision of the U.S. Securities and Exchange Commission to press companies to provide full disclosure of their activities in countries such as Sudan before they list themselves on stock exchanges will help NGOs publicize to potential shareholders the involvement of companies in conflict settings. See letter from Laura S. Unger, acting director of the Securities and Exchange Commission to Congressman Frank P. Wolf, Washington, May 8, 2001.

## Chapter Seven

1. More specifically, President George W. Bush declared, "Either you are with us, or you are with the terrorists." George W. Bush, "Address to a Joint Session of Congress and the American People," White House, September 20, 2001.

2. Colin L. Powell, "Interview on CNN's Late Edition," Department of State, September 16, 2001 (www.state.gov/secretary/rm/2001/index.cfm?docid=4924 [October 25, 2001]).

3. The State Department added the Islamic Movement of Uzbekistan to its list of Foreign Terrorist Organizations in September 2000. President Bush's Executive Order 13224 of September 23, 2001, named the Libyan Islamic Fighting Group as a terrorist group whose financial assets would be targeted. The United States added Jaish-I-Mohammed to the list of groups subject to financial sanctions on October 12, 2001, shortly before Secretary of State Powell's trip to India.

4. See David Cortright and George A. Lopez, *The Sanctions Decade: Assessing UN Strategies in the 1990s* (Lynne Rienner Publishers, 2000), pp. 27–29.

5. For more on the crafting of road maps, see Richard N. Haass and Meghan L. O'Sullivan, "Conclusion," in Richard N. Haass and Meghan L. O'Sullivan, eds., *Honey and Vinegar: Incentives, Sanctions, and Foreign Policy* (Brookings, 2000), pp. 168–72.

6. See Frederick Z. Brown, "The United States and Vietnam: Road to Normalization," in Haass and O'Sullivan, *Honey and Vinegar*, pp. 137–58.

7. See Robert S. Suettinger, "Sanctions That Worked? The United States, China and Intellectual Property Rights," paper prepared for *Terms of Engagement: Policy Alternatives to Sanctions*, conference of the Brookings Institution and the McCormick Tribune Foundation, Chicago, 1999.

8. For a variety of opinions on the effectiveness of the Yugoslav sanctions in the mid-1990s, see Susan L. Woodward, *Balkan Tragedy: Chaos and Dissolution after the*

*Cold War* (Brookings, 1995), esp. pp. 289–94; Stephen John Stedman, "The Former Yugoslavia," in Richard N. Haass, ed., *Economic Sanctions and American Diplomacy* (Council on Foreign Relations, 1998), pp. 177–96; and Cortright and Lopez, *The Sanctions Decade*, pp. 63–86.

9. According to several scholars, the economic devastation of Yugoslavia—which was partially attributable to sanctions—directly impinged on the subsidies provided to the Republika Srpska by the Milosevic regime. See Milica Delevic, "Economic Sanctions as a Foreign Policy Tool: The Case of Yugoslavia," *International Journal of Peace Studies*, vol. 3 (January 1998), p. 79.

10. See Cortright and Lopez, *The Sanctions Decade*, pp. 68–70.

11. See Ivo H. Daalder, *Getting to Dayton: The Making of American's Bosnia Policy*, (Brookings, 2000), p. 19.

12. Terminating economic activity with state-owned institutions is critical not only to place pressure on the regime but to minimize vested interests in the United States and other sender countries that would resist a change in regime given the economic losses it would cause them. As seen in chapter 4, the signing of executory contracts between foreign oil companies and the Iraqi state-run National Oil Company (NOC) created yet another reason why certain countries were unlikely to favor regime change in Iraq.

13. In actuality, the Comprehensive Anti-Apartheid Act (CAAA) did not demand that a new government take power before sanctions were lifted. Instead, the goals specified were more modest—such as releasing Nelson Mandela from prison, repealing the state of emergency and apartheid laws, legalizing banned political parties, and initiating talks with the black opposition—yet they inevitably set the stage for a domestic shift in power.

14. However, in December 1963, the United Nations did pass a resolution urging countries to impose a voluntary arms embargo.

15. For example, Britain banned arms exports to South Africa as early as 1964 and banned imports of South African weapons in 1985. Japan prohibited direct investment in South Africa in 1964 and restricted the import of iron and steel from South Africa in 1986. The International Olympic Committee expelled South Africa in 1970, and many countries—in Europe, Canada, Japan, and the United States—developed investment codes for South Africa. See Neta C. Crawford and Audie Klotz, eds., *How Sanctions Work: Lessons from South Africa* (St. Martin's Press, 1999), pp. 283–87.

16. For more specifics about what U.S. sanctions prohibited and allowed, see Pauline Baker, "The United States and South Africa: Persuasion and Coercion," in Haass and O'Sullivan, eds., *Honey and Vinegar*, pp. 106–07.

17. See Baker, "The United States and South Africa: Persuasion and Coercion."

18. The third section of every case chapter—"Explaining the Record of Sanctions"— contains a detailed analysis of what is briefly summarized here.

19. The United States was involved in conflict resolution efforts of the Intergovernmental Authority on Development (IGAD), which began in 1993 at the initiative of Sudan's neighbors, Djibouti, Eritrea, Ethiopia, Kenya, Somalia, and Uganda.

20. As discussed in chapter 6, the United States also played a large role in international humanitarian relief work in Sudan. However, these efforts were also not well coordinated with the more political objectives of U.S. Sudan policy. See *Interagency Review of*

*U.S. Government Civilian, Humanitarian and Transition Programs* (Department of State, January 2000), annex 3.

21. The goals outlined by President Clinton when he announced the sanctions were to "encourage democratization and human rights in Burma." He "urged" the junta to lift all restrictions on Suu Kyi, respect rights of free expression, assembly, and association, and embark on a dialogue with democratic leaders and ethnic minorities about Burma's political future. See William Jefferson Clinton, "Statement on Investment Sanctions against Burma," *Public Papers of the Presidents: William Jefferson Clinton, 1997,* vol. 2 (GPO, 1998), p. 476. Positive steps—such as meetings between the junta and Suu Kyi in October 2000 and Suu Kyi's release from house arrest in May 2002—have not yet led to any substantive changes.

22. Although this strategy may not be very effective in achieving U.S. goals, it may have the highest utility of the options open to policymakers not wishing to expend much political capital to further U.S. goals in Burma or Myanmar, given that few regard the country as central to U.S. interests.

23. At one point, Pakistan was subject to sanctions under both the Pressler and Glenn amendments owing to its nuclear activities and section 508 sanctions because of the October 1999 coup. Aid to Sudan is restricted because of its designation as a state sponsor of terrorism, its June 1989 coup, which evoked section 508 sanctions, and a general provision in the annual foreign operations appropriations bill that bans direct aid to Sudan and several other countries (section 507).

24. The threshold for investment in Libya's oil industry was lowered from $40 million to $20 million in 2001.

25. Although the president did not technically need congressional support for easing the trade sanctions that had been imposed under the Trading with the Enemy Act, he did need Congress to approve money for the shipment of heavy fuel oil to North Korea until the reactors are built. See Larry A. Niksch, "North Korea's Nuclear Weapons Program," (Congressional Research Service, September 21, 2001), pp. 7–9.

26. Ideally, as discussed subsequently, restrictions on U.S. travel to a country should not be used as a political stick or carrot but should be imposed and repealed strictly in relation to the security situation.

27. "Most-favored-nation" trading status was later changed to "normal trade relations" to reflect the fact that the vast majority of countries trade with the United States under these conditions.

28. At the time, the president could reissue a waiver of the Jackson-Vanik amendment for China, which would allow China's MFN status to be renewed. Congress, however, could successfully block this renewal, either by issuing a joint resolution of Congress or, if need be, by overriding the president's veto of the congressional resolution by a two-thirds vote. For a fuller discussion of these dynamics, and how they contrasted with dynamics previous and subsequent to 1991–92, see Robert S. Ross, "China," in Haass, *Economic Sanctions and American Diplomacy,* pp. 10–34.

29. However, as discussed throughout this book, particularly in the chapter on Iraq, UN-U.S. tension is much more likely to undermine the effectiveness of sanctions than to increase it.

30. See Dennis Kux, *The United States and Pakistan, 1947–2000: Disenchanted Allies,* (Washington: Woodrow Wilson Center Press, 2001), pp. 256–94.

31. In 1986, only 1.4 percent of U.S. exports went to China. By 2000, this proportion had risen to 4 percent, including exports to Hong Kong (which were not included in the 1986 number). IMF, *Direction of Trade Statistics*, various years.

32. As discussed in chapter 3, U.S. objectives toward Iran often defy clear classification, given the multitude of groups holding quite different goals at various times.

33. Although multilateral sanctions are the desired form of international cooperation in most circumstances, smaller acts of collaboration, such as when other countries joined the United States in keeping Sudan off the UN Security Council in 2000, are also important to note.

34. See, for example, Elliott Abrams, "Words or War: Why Sanctions Are Necessary," *Weekly Standard*, July 27, 1998, p. 17.

35. One might point to international sanctions against South Africa as an example that defies this generalization. However, while it is true that U.S. sanctions against South Africa were entirely a product of Congress, the extent to which these sanctions—rather than intense pressure from civil society groups in other countries—deserve credit for the widening of the campaign against South Africa is open to debate.

36. As discussed in chapter 6, Egypt argued for a very limited set of measures to be put in place against Khartoum, even though the United States was interested in more wide-ranging sanctions.

37. See, for instance, Dick Kirschten, "Chicken Soup Diplomacy," *National Journal*, January 4, 1997, pp. 13–17.

38. In fact, much more threatening to Sudanese exports were Khartoum's efforts to bolster the price of gum arabic artificially.

39. Both Iran's ineligibility for a Contingency and Compensatory Financing Facility from the IMF and Sudan's need to be included in HIPC initiatives are discussed in detail in the respective chapters.

40. In some cases, the impact of sanctions on planning can have effects that are positive for the target. As discussed in chapter 5, the U.S. ban on Libyan oil imports in 1982 encouraged Libya to invest in refineries and downstream operations abroad in order to better secure markets for its oil. These investments furthered the integration of Libya and Europe, providing another point of European resistance to economic sanctions against Tripoli.

41. See Meghan L. O'Sullivan, "The Dilemma of U.S. Policy toward 'Rogue' States," *Politique Etrangère*, Spring 2000.

42. Having multilateral support for such an endeavor is of course preferable, although not necessary.

43. This influence will be tempered by the fact that the United States is not the only arbiter between countries and the international system. Often, U.S. sanctions alone cannot block a country from joining an international organization or reaping benefits from it. For instance, the United States holds no veto over lending decisions by the World Bank and the International Monetary Fund. However, the United States can couple its own restrictions on lending to a country with intense diplomatic efforts to get other countries to support it.

44. After more than a decade of multilateral economic pressure, Iraq remained defiant, with the Baghdad regime resisting UN demands for its disarmament.

45. Although not immediately apparent, this statement also holds true when applied to secondary sanctions; friendly countries—while on the whole reluctant to comply with

U.S. laws threatening secondary sanctions—were more likely to comply with them than countries with poor relations with the United States. This is particularly true concerning the threat of secondary sanctions on countries that make military sales to states on the U.S. terrorism list.

46. Peru's rapid compliance with U.S. demands in 1992 is one example of how targeted sanctions can produce results with countries having friendly relations with the United States. In April 1992, President Alberto Fujimori suspended the constitution and dissolved the congress and judiciary, causing the United States to suspend all but humanitarian aid. By June, Fujimori had agreed to hold elections and draft a new constitution, prompting the United States to resume aid to Peru. "External economic pressures" were seen as a critical factor compelling Fujimori to reverse his actions. See Sally Bowen, "Fujimori's Promise Leaves Many Questions: Skeptics Home in on a Lack of Detail," *Financial Times*, June 3, 1992, p. 6; and Barbara Crossette, "Ire in Congress Delays Nicaragua Aid as U.S. Resumes Help for Peru," *New York Times*, June 4, 1992, p. A9.

47. By definition, the risks of threatening or employing sanctions in such circumstances can also be greater to the United States.

48. After the first UN sanctions went into effect in November 1999, "tens of thousands" of protestors marched on UN offices in Kabul in protest. See Sayed Salahuddin, "Afghans Attack U.N. Sites as Sanctions Take Effect," *Washington Post*, November 15, 1999, p. A17.

49. Immigration issues, for instance, have been a constant point of friction, as have confrontations over mail and telephone service between Cuba and the United States.

50. Where the leadership of a country is cohesive and consolidated within one person, party, or organization, the response to sanctions will be more straightforward. In such cases, the regime will be able to determine its response to sanctions—either negatively or positively—and stand by it with fewer domestic machinations. Saddam Hussein's decision to resist the full disarmament of Iraq is an extreme example of how the tenacity of one person or a highly consolidated and personalized regime can dramatically determine the course of a country's future.

51. Even President Khatami's interview with CNN in January 1998, during which he called for a "dialogue among civilizations," was seen by some in Iran as a risky move.

52. In the thirty-day window between the passage of UN Resolution 1267 (which threatened limited sanctions if the Taliban did not turn over Osama bin Laden) and the implementation of sanctions, the Taliban offered to place bin Laden under house arrest and try him before a court of Islamic scholars. This compromise was rejected by the United Nations.

53. Two of the most obvious signs of this hardening of opinion by the Taliban were the destruction of the ancient Buddhas at Bamiyan in February 2001 and the Taliban policy of forcing Hindus to wear special badges in the summer of 2001. Although it is difficult to conclude what role, if any, sanctions played in this shift in the Taliban, what is certain is that sanctions were not the only impetus in this direction. For instance, the death of Mullah Mohammed Rabbani (from cancer) in April 2001 removed an alternative, more moderate locus of power within the movement.

54. In general, modest goals are perceived to pertain to "low" politics (which is commonly associated with issues such as human rights, the environment, and the eradication

of poverty); ambitious goals are generally viewed as relating to "high" politics (which is commonly associated with geostrategic issues such as war and security).

55. As noted, the demands placed on Libya had also changed slightly; in 1999, Libya was allowed to surrender the suspects to a temporary Scottish court in the Netherlands, whereas earlier in the decade, the United Nations had called for Libya to hand over the suspects to the United States or Britain.

56. As described in chapter 2, utility is the ability of sanctions to achieve their goals at reasonable costs.

57. For specific recommendations on further improving the ability of humanitarian exemptions and programs to alleviate suffering, see Cortright and Lopez, *The Sanctions Decade*, pp. 227–28.

58. Just as globalization diminishes the impact of certain unilateral sanctions on the target country, it also eases the costs paid by American businesses when the United States imposes sanctions.

59. These channels do not necessarily have to be at the ambassador-rank level.

60. Only two countries have ever been removed from the terrorist list, both in extraordinary circumstances. South Yemen was removed when it ceased to exist after its merger with North Yemen in 1990; Iraq was taken off the list in 1982, more in response to the U.S. desire not to handicap Iraq in its war against Iran than as an acknowledgment of its improved behavior in the realm of terrorism.

61. As of October 2001, the designation of "not fully cooperating with U.S. antiterrorism efforts" had only been used in one instance. The State Department chose to designate the Taliban as a supporter of terrorism in this fashion to avoid the appearance that the United States recognized it as the proper government of Afghanistan. See National Commission on Terrorism, *Countering the Changing Threat of International Terrorism*, June 2000.

62. Such an approach would not be unprecedented. During the cold war, Congress was less active in legislating sanctions apart from cutoffs in foreign aid. Instead, it played somewhat more of a consultative role. For instance, in the 1980s, rather than passing its own sanctions, Congress passed legislation urging the president to consider a U.S. ban on imports of Libyan oil.

# Index